PORTUGAL

Executive Editorial Director   David Brabis
Chief Editor   Cynthia Clayton Ochterbeck

THE GREEN GUIDE PORTUGAL

Editor   Gwen Cannon
Principal Writer   Peter D. Smith
Production Coordinator Allison M. Simpson
Cartography   Alain Baldet, Peter Wrenn
Photo Editor   Cecile Koroleff, Lydia Strong
Proofreader   Gaven R. Watkins
Layout & Design   Ute Weber
Cover Design   Ute Weber, Laurent Muller

Contact Us: The Green Guide
                            Michelin Maps and Guides
                            One Parkway South
                            Greenville, SC 29615
                            USA
                            ☎ 1-800-423-0485
                            www.michelintravel.com
                            michelin.guides@us.michelin.com

                            Michelin Maps and Guides
                            Hannay House
                            39 Clarendon Road
                            Watford, Herts WD17 1JA
                            UK
                            ☎ (01923) 205 240
                            www.ViaMichelin.com
                            travelpubsales@uk.michelin.com

Special Sales: For information regarding bulk sales,
                            customized editions and premium sales,
                            please contact our Customer Service
                            Departments:
                            USA   1-800-423-0485
                            UK   (01923) 205 240
                            Canada 1-800-361-8236

Note to the reader
While every effort is made to ensure that all information printed in this guide is correct and up-to-date, Michelin Maps and Guides (Michelin Tyre PLC; Michelin North America, Inc.) accepts no liability for any direct, indirect or consequential losses howsoever caused so far as such can be excluded by law.

One Team …
A Commitment to Quality

There's just one reason our team is dedicated to producing quality travel publications—you, our reader. We want you to get the maximum benefit from your trip—and from your money. In today's multiple-choice world of travel, the options are many, perhaps overwhelming.

In our guidebooks, we try to minimize the guesswork involved with travel. We scout out the attractions, prioritize them with star ratings, and describe what you'll discover when you visit them.

To help you orient yourself, we provide colorful and detailed, but easy-to-follow maps. Floor plans of some of the cathedrals and museums help you plan your tour.

Throughout the guides, we offer practical information, touring tips and suggestions for finding the best views, good places for a break and the most interesting shops.

Lodging and dining are always a big part of travel, so we compile a selection of hotels and restaurants that we think convey the feel of the destination, and organize them by geographic area and price. We also highlight shopping, recreational and entertainment venues, especially the popular spots.

If you're short on time, driving tours are included so you can hit the highlights and quickly absorb the best of the region.

For those who love to experience a destination on foot, we add walking tours, often with a map. And we list other companies who offer boat, bus or guided walking tours of the area, some with culinary, historical or other themes.

In short, we test and retest, check and recheck to make sure that our guidebooks are truly just that: a personalized guide to help you make the most of your visit. After all, we want you to enjoy traveling as much as we do.

The Michelin Green Guide Team

PLANNING YOUR TRIP

WHEN AND WHERE TO GO   14

Driving Tours.................... 14
When to Go 14

KNOW BEFORE YOU GO   15

Useful Web Sites 15
Tourist Offices................... 15
International Visitors 15

GETTING THERE   17

By Air........................... 17
By Sea 17
By Rail 17
By Coach........................ 17
Driving in Portugal 18

GETTING AROUND   19

By Air........................... 19
By Train......................... 19
By Coach........................ 19

WHERE TO STAY AND EAT   20

Where to Stay 20
Where to Eat 21

WHAT TO DO AND SEE   22

Outdoor Fun 22
Activities for Children........... 24
Calendar of Events.............. 24
Shopping 27
Sightseeing 27
Books........................... 28

USEFUL WORDS & PHRASES 30

BASIC INFORMATION   32

INTRODUCTION TO PORTUGAL

NATURE   36

Geological Formation............ 36
Relief 37
Regions and Landscape.......... 37
Parks and Reserves 40
Vegetation...................... 40

HISTORY   41

Time Line 41
The Great Discoveries........... 47

ART AND CULTURE   50

Architecture 50
Art.............................. 58
Azulejos 64
Literature 66
Cinema 68

THE COUNTRY TODAY   70

Economy 70
Government 70
Architectural Traditions 71
Handicrafts 73
Festive Portugal................. 75
Food............................ 77
Wine............................ 79

SYMBOLS

- Tips to help improve your experience
- Details to consider
- Entry Fees
- Walking tours
- Closed to the public
- Hours of operation
- Periods of closure

CONTENTS

DISCOVERING PORTUGAL

Abrantes............ 86
Albufeira............ 87
Alcobaça............ 88
Algarve............. 90
Almansil............ 95
Castelo de Almourol.. 96
Amarante............ 97
Arouca.............. 97
Serra de Arrábida..... 98
Arraiolos............ 100
Aveiro.............. 100
Avis................ 105
Quinta da Bacalhoa.. 105
Barcelos 106
Mosteiro de Batalha . 108
Beja 111
Belmonte........... 112
Ilha da Berlenga..... 113
Braga.............. 113
Bragança 118
Bravães............ 120
Mata do Buçaco..... 120
Caminha............ 123
Caramulo 124
Carvoeiro 125
Cascais 125
Castelo Branco 126
Castelo de Vide 129
Castro Marim 129
Alto Vale do
   Rio Cávado....... 130
Chaves.............. 132
Coimbra 134
Conímbriga 142
Costa da Caparica ... 144
Carato 144
Vale de Douro....... 145
Elvas............... 148
Ericeira 149
Cabo Espichel 149
Estoril 150
Serra da Estrela 150
Estremoz 153
Évora 155
Évoramonte......... 162
Faro 163
Fátima 166
Figueira da Foz...... 168

Guarda 168
Guimãres 171
Lagos.............. 175
Lamego............ 178
Leça do Bailio 179
Leiria 179
Lindoso............ 180
Lisboa 182
Plácido and Convento
   de Mafra......... 230
Serro do Marão...... 233
Marvão 234
Mértola............ 235
Miranda do Douro... 235
Mirandela.......... 236
Monsanto.......... 237
Monsaraz 238
Montemor-o-Velho.. 239
Moura 240
Nazaré............. 240
Óbidos............. 243
Olhão.............. 245
Oliveira do Hospital . 246
Ourém............. 246
Paco de Sousa....... 247
Palmela............ 248
Parque Nacional da
   Penda-Gerês..... 248
Peniche............ 251
Pinhel 252
Pombal 253
Ponte de Lima....... 254
Portalegre 254
Portimão 256
Porto 256
Póvoa de Varzim 269
Palácio nacional
   de Queluz........ 270
Ponta de Sagres and
Cabo de São Vicente. 272
Santa Maria de Feira. 273
Santarém 274
São João de Tarouca. 276
Serra de
   São Mamede..... 277
Sernanchelhe 277
Serpa 278
Sesimbra........... 278

Setúbal 279
Silves 282
Sintra.............. 283
Serra de Sintra 286
Tavira.............. 288
Tomar 289
Parque Arquelógico
   do Vale do Côa ... 291
Valença do Minho ... 294
Viana do Alentejo ... 295
Viana do Castelo 296
Vila do Conde 299
Vila Franca de Xira... 300
Vila Real 301
Vila Real de
   santo António.... 304
Vila Viçosa 304
Vilamoura 307
Viseu 308

Madeira and the Azores   314

The Madeira Archipelago   314

Madeira............ 315
Porto Santo 337

The Azores Archipelago   339

São Miguel.......... 346
Santa Maria 353
Terceira............ 355
Graciosa 361
Faial 363
Pico 366
São Jorge 370
Flores.............. 372
Corvo.............. 375

Index............376
Maps and Plans ..385
Legend..........386

HOW TO USE THIS GUIDE

Orientation

To help you grasp the "lay of the land" quickly and easily, so you'll feel confident and comfortable finding your way around the region, we offer the following tools in this guide:

- Detailed table of contents for an overview of what you'll find in the guide, and how it is organized.
- Map of Portugal at the front to the guide, with the Principal Sights highlighted for easy reference.
- Detailed maps for major cities and villages, including driving tour maps and larger-scale maps for walking tours.
- Map of Driving Tours, each one numbered and color coded.
- Principal Sights ordered alphabetically for quick reference.

Practicalities

At the front of the guide, you'll see a section called "Planning Your Trip" that contains information about planning your trip, the best time to go, different ways of getting to the region and getting around, basic facts and tips for making the most of your visit. You'll find driving and themed tours, and suggestions for outdoor fun. There's also a calendar of popular annual events. Information on shopping, sightseeing, kids' activities and sports and recreational opportunities is also included.

LODGINGS

We've made a selection of hotels and arranged them within the cities, categorized by price to fit all budgets (see the Legend at the back of the guide for an explanation of the price categories). For the most part, we selected accommodations based on their unique regional quality, their Portuguese feel, as it were. So, unless the individual hotel embodies local ambience, it's rare that we include chain properties, which typically have their own imprint. If you want a more comprehensive selection of accommodations, see the red-cover *Michelin Guide Spain and Portugal*.

RESTAURANTS

We thought you'd like to know the popular eating spots in Portugal. So we selected restaurants that capture regional flavor and local atmosphere. We're not rating the quality of the food per se. As we did with the hotels, we selected restaurants for many towns and villages, categorized by price to appeal to all wallets. If you want a more comprehensive selection of dining recommendations in the country, see the red-cover *Michelin Guide Spain and Portugal*.

Attractions

Principal Sights are arranged alphabetically. Within each Principal Sight, attractions for each town, village, or geographical area are divided into local Sights or Walking Tours, nearby Excursions to sights outside the town, or detailed Driving Tours—suggested itineraries for seeing several attractions around a major town. Contact information, admission charges and hours of operation are given for the majority of attractions. Unless otherwise noted, admission prices shown are for a single adult only. Discounts for seniors, students, teachers, etc. may be available; be sure to ask. If no admission charge is shown, entrance to the attraction is free.
If you're pressed for time, we recommend you visit the three- and two-star sights first: the stars are your guide.

STAR RATINGS

Michelin has used stars as a rating tool for more than 100 years:

★★★	Highly recommended
★★	Recommended
★	Interesting

SYMBOLS IN THE TEXT

Besides the stars, other symbols in the text indicate tourist information 🖪; wheelchair access ♿; on-site eating facilities ✕; camping facilities ⚠; on-site parking 🅿; sights of interest to children 🄺🄸🄳; and beaches ⌓.
See the box appearing on the Contents page for other symbols used in the text.
See the Maps explanation below for symbols appearing on the maps.
Throughout the guide you will find peach-coloured text boxes or sidebars containing anecdotal or background information. Green-coloured boxes contain information to help you save time or money.

Maps

All maps in this guide are oriented north, unless otherwise indicated by a directional arrow. See the map Legend at the back of the guide for an explanation of other map symbols. A complete list of the maps found in the guide appears at the back of this book.

Addresses, phone numbers, opening hours and prices published in this guide are accurate at press time. We welcome corrections and suggestions that may assist us in preparing the next edition. Please send your comments to:

Michelin Maps and Guides
Hannay House
39 Clarendon Road
Watford, Herts WD17 1JA
UK
travelpubsales@uk.michelin.com
www.michelin.co.uk

Michelin Maps and Guides
Editorial Department
P.O. Box 19001
Greenville, SC 29602-9001
USA
michelin.guides@us.michelin.com
www.michelintravel.com

Principal sights

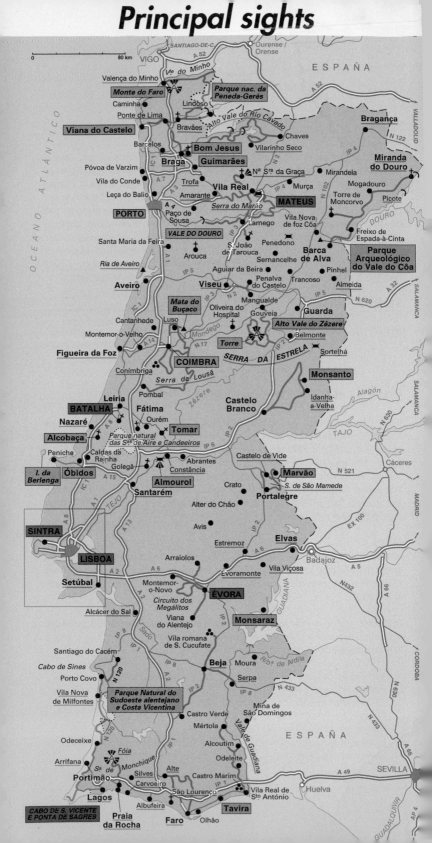

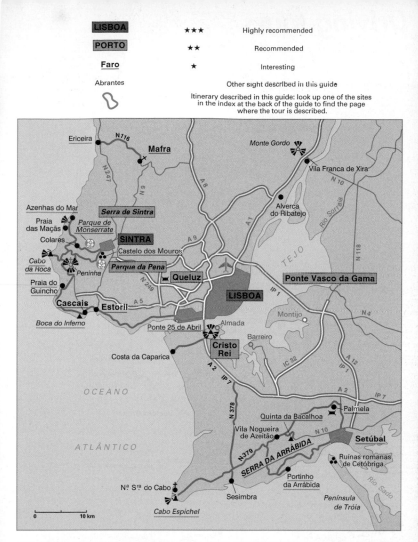

Driving tours

- **1** Le Minho : 250 km (7 days)
- **2** Trás-os-Montes et Vale do Douro : 600 km (7 days without hikes)
- **3** Centre and Baira Litoral : 350 km (5 days)
- **4** Serra da Estrela and Baira Baixa : 350 km (5 days)
- **5** Historic West : 450 km (5 days)
- **6** Tagus Basin and Alto Alentejo : 450 km (5 days)
- **7** Alentejo : 400 km (5 days)
- **8** Algarve : 450 km (4 days)

★★ **VALE DO DOURO** Name under which a route is described. See the Index for the page number.

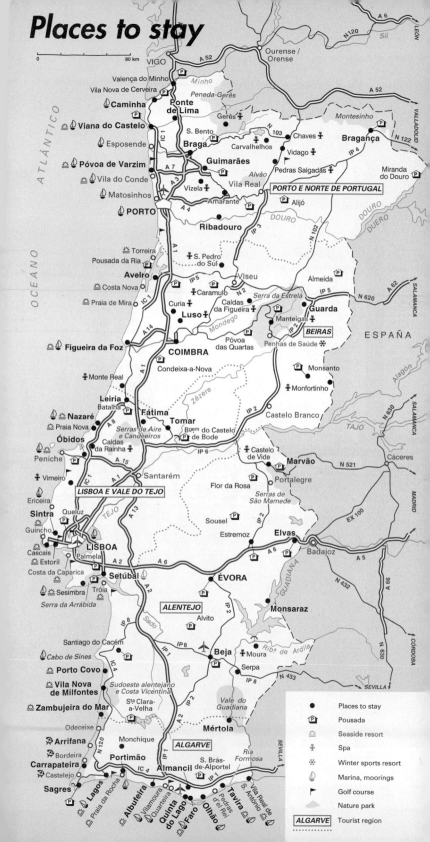

Places to stay

0   80 km

A window in the Alfama, Lisbon
B.Brillion

WHEN AND WHERE TO GO

Driving Tours

See the Driving Tours map on p 10.

When to Go

Portugal has a relatively mild climate. However, the best time to visit the country depends on the region you wish to visit. The north is cooler than the south, particularly in the mountains, where winter can be especially harsh. In mid-summer the temperatures can rise pretty high making it uncomfortable to those unaccustomed to such heat. For a tour of the whole country, spring or autumn are the best seasons.

SPRING

Spring is the best time to visit the south of the country if you wish to avoid the heat of summer and the masses who flock to the beaches in the Algarve. It is also the season when the flowers which adorn so many houses come into full bloom and the countryside is green.

Late March and April (depending on the date of Easter) offer the added attractions of Holy Week festivities.

SUMMER

Inland, the summer months are hot and dry, but in the coastal areas the heat is tempered by sea breezes. Many *romarias*, festivals, feast days and sporting events take place during the summer months (*see Calendar of Events*) and of course it's the best time to head for the beaches. Average sea temperatures are as follows: 16-19°C/61-66°F on the west coast; 21-23°C/70-73°F on the Algarve coast. Average summer temperatures for the major towns and cities are: Oporto – 20°C; Lisbon – 26°C; Évora – 29°C; Faro – 28°C.

AUTUMN

In the north with the chestnut trees and the vineyards, the countryside takes on some lovely tints. The Douro valley with its many vineyards becomes a hive of activity during the grape harvest (mid-September to mid-October). Autumn is also the ideal time to visit the Minho and Trás-os-Montes regions. Average temperatures in these two regions are 13°C/55°F and 8°C/45°F respectively (between October and December).

WINTER

Winter is a pleasant season to visit the Algarve coast, where bathing is possible from March to November (sea temperature: 17°C; air temperature: 18°C), the Costa de Estoril (sea temperature: 16°C; air temperature: 17°C), and, above all, Madeira and the Azores (sea and air temperature: 21°C), where winters are mild and sunny. The Algarve is transformed at the end of January when the almond trees are in blossom.

In winter, skiers flock to the winter sports centres in the Serra da Estrela. Golfers can visit Portugal at almost any time of the year, particularly in the south where the winters are warm and often sunny. Around Lisbon, too, virtually the whole year is good for golf though around Porto winters can be a little chilly. Best time for golf overall is September-December, then March-June.

KNOW BEFORE YOU GO

Useful Web Sites

www.visitportugal.pt
The official Portugese Tourism Web site with a wealth of well-presented information on everything from themed itineraries to upcoming events to where to stay and eat.

www.portugal.org/tourism
An excellent source of basic information and details are handily laid out on a region-by-region basis.

www.portugal-live.net
A good Web site for those looking for hotels in particular, plus lots of information on tourist sights.

www.portugal.com
A commerical site through which you can make reservations for restaurants and hotels; good suggestions for holiday programmes.

Tourist Offices

PORTUGUESE NATIONAL TOURIST OFFICES

London:
4th Floor, 22-25A Sackville Street, London WIX 1DE, ☏ (020) 7494 14 41; fax (020) 7494 18 68; iceplond@dircon.co.uk

New York:
590 Fifth Avenue, 4th floor, New York NY 10036-4704, ☏ (212) 354 44 03/4; fax (212) 764 61 37; Tourism@Portugal.org

Toronto:
60 Bloor Street West, Suite 1005, Toronto, Ontario M4W 3B8, ☏ (416) 921 73 76; iceptor@idirect.com

Dublin:
54 Dawson Street, Dublin 2, ☏ (01) 670 91 33; (01) 670 91 34; fax (01) 670 9141; icepdub@dub.icep.ie

LOCAL TOURIST OFFICES

- **ICEP** (Investimentos, Comércio e Turismo de Portugal). Posto de Turismo – Praça dos Restauradores, Palácio Foz, Lisboa. ☏ 213 46 33 14/213 46 36 43
- **Direcção Geral de Turismo**, Avenida António Augosto de Aguiar, 86, 1050 Lisboa – ☏ 213 57 50 86; Praça Dom João I, 25-4°, 4000 Porto. ☏ 222 00 58 05.

Tourist Information Centres – All Portuguese towns have a Tourist Information Centre, known as Posto or Comissão de Turismo or simply Turismo, marked on Michelin town plans with an ⓘ. The addresses of individual Tourist Offices are listed in the introductions to the Principal Sights.

International Visitors

PORTUGUESE EMBASSIES AND CONSULATES

- **Portuguese Embassy, London:** ☏ (020) 7235 5331.
- **Portuguese Consulate, London:** ☏ (020) 7581 8722.
- **Honorary Consulate, Manchester:** ☏ (0161) 228 3116.
- **Portuguese Consulate, Washington DC:** ☏ (202) 332 3007.

Consulates in Boston, Chicago, Houston, Los Angeles, Miami, New Orleans, New York and San Francisco

FOREIGN EMBASSIES AND CONSULATES IN PORTUGAL

- **British Embassy:** Rua São Bernardo, 33, 1249-082 Lisboa, ☏ 213 96 11 91.
- **British Consulates:** Rua São Bernardo, 33, 1249-082 Lisboa, ☏ 213 92 41 59.

Avenida da Boa Vista, 4100-120
Porto, ☎ 226 18 47 89
Quinta do Bom Jesus, Rua
das Almas 23, Pico da Pedra,
9600 Ribeira, Grande, Açores,
☎ 296 49 81 15.
Apartado 417, 9000 Funchal,
Madeira, ☎ 291 22 01 61.

- **American Embassy:**
  Avenida das Forças Armadas,
  1600-081 Lisboa, ☎ 217 27 33 00.
- **American Consulates:**
  Honorary Consul in Madeira and
  the Azores.
- **Canadian Embassy:** Avenida da
  Liberdade, 200-3, 1269-121 Lisboa,
  ☎ 213 47 48 92.
- **Canadian Consulate:**
  Honorary Consul in Faro and the
  Azores.
- **Embassy of Ireland:** Rua da
  Imprensa à Estrela 1-4°, 1200-684
  Lisboa, ☎ 213 92 94 40.

DOCUMENTS

Because Portugal is part of the
European Union, holders of any EU
passport do not need **visas** to enter
Portugal, although visas may be
necessary for some Commonwealth
visitors and for those planning a stay
of more than three months. For anyone travelling by air or sea some form
of photo identification is nowadays
necessary. The most widely accepted
form of identification is a **passport**.
US citizens should obtain the booklet
Your Trip Abroad which provides useful
information on visa requirements, customs regulations, medical care, etc for
international travellers. Apply to the
Superintendent of Documents, PO Box
371954. Pittsburgh, PA 15250-7954.
☎ 202-512-1800.

CUSTOMS

Sales of duty-free goods no longer
exist as such within the EU, though
visitors from other countries can
purchase items without tax, according
to the limits set by their home country
(or other country to which they are
next travelling).
The US Customs Service (PO Box 7407,
Washington, DC 20044. ☎ 202-927-
6724; www.customs.gov) offers a
publication *Know Before You Go* for US
citizens.

PETS

For cats and dogs, a general health
certificate and proof of rabies vaccina-
tion should be obtained from your
local vet before departure. UK citizens
taking animals to Portugal may need
to obtain a "pet passport" but may run
into quarantine restrictions if they try
to bring the pet back to the UK. Ask
your vet.

HEALTH

The old **Form E111**, which entitled
the holder to urgent treatment in case
of an accident or unexpected illness
in EU countries, has been replaced
by the **European Health Insurance
Card** (EHIC). Valid for between three
and five years this card should be
presented to the relevant medical
services before treatment, as not
all treatments are available without
charge. The card can be obtained
from the NHS, Newcastle-upon-Tyne,
either by post (forms available at Post
Offices), by phone ☎ 0845 606 2030,
or on-line at: www.ehic.org.uk.
Other **medical insurance** is advisable.
Since medical insurance is not always
valid outside of the United States,
American travellers are advised to take
out supplementary medical insurance
with specific overseas coverage.
Chemists *(farmácias)* or pharmacists
are open weekdays 9am to 1pm and
3pm to 7pm, Saturdays 9am to 1pm.

Accessibility

Many of the sights and places listed
in this guide are accessible to people
with special needs and their helpers.
Sights marked with the ♿ symbol
have wheelchair access but it is advisable to telephone prior to your visit
to re-check. A very useful Web site for
details of accessibility in Portugal (and
elsewhere) is:
www.disabledholidaydirectory.co.uk

GETTING THERE

By Air

Various airlines operate regular services to the international airports in Portugal (Lisbon, Oporto and Faro). Contact airlines and travel agents for information and timetables.
British Airways and **TAP Air Portugal** operate daily flights from London to Lisbon (2hr), Oporto (1hr 45min) and Faro (2hr 30min). There are also many budget flights between the UK and Portugal, including services by **Monarch, easyJet** and **Ryanair**. Flights to the Azores operate via Lisbon. There are several direct flights between London and Funchal (Madeira).

- **TAP Portugal**: ☎ 0845 601 0932; www.flytap.com
- **British Airways:** ☎ 0870 55 111 55; www.britishairways.com
- **Monarch**: www.flymonarch.com
- **easyJet**: www.easyjet.com
- **Ryaniar**: www.ryanair.com

TAP Air Portugal, United and Continental operate daily flights from New York to Lisbon (6hr 30min). There are numerous connecting flights from many other major American cities.

TAP ticket office – 3rd floor, 608 Fifth Avenue, New York 10020, ☎ (212) 969 5775 or toll-free for information and reservations, ☎ 800 221 7370.

By Sea

There are no direct ferry services between Great Britain and Portugal. However, Brittany Ferries operates a car-ferry service between Plymouth and Santander in northern Spain two to three times a week; journey time: 24hr. Distances from Santander are 960km/600mi to Lisbon, 800km/500mi to Oporto and 1 280km/800mi to the Algarve. For reservations, contact:

Brittany Ferries, ☎ 08709 076 103 – www.brittanyferries.com.

Across the Channel then on through France and Spain
Although a long journey by road it is possible to use the Channel Tunnel or cross-Channel services and then drive. The distance to Lisbon by road when you have landed from the car ferry or taken the Channel Tunnel is about 2 100km/1 300mi. The most direct route is via Paris, Bordeaux, Irun and then either San Sebastián or Valladolid or Burgos, Salamanca, Vilar Formoso and Coimbra to Lisbon.

By Rail

It is possible to travel to Portugal from the UK by train (through France and Spain) although it is a long trip and possibly more expensive than flying, albeit a most pleasant way to travel. Details from:

- **Rail Europe**: ☎ 0870 584 8848; www.raileurope.com
- **Eurostar**: ☎ 0875 186 186, www.eurostar.com.
- **Eurotunnel**: ☎ 08705 353 353; www.eurotunnel.com
- **European Rail**: ☎ (020) 7387 0444; www.europeanrail.com

By Coach

Fairly regular coach services to Portugal are operated from London (Victoria Coach Station) by **Eurolines**, a consortium of coach operators in conjunction with National Express. To the main destinations they operate year-round but other cities are served only on a seasonal basis. The journey takes a couple of days. For details contact your nearest National Express Office or Agent.

Driving in Portugal

DOCUMENTS

Nationals of EU countries require a national **driving licence**; nationals of non-EU countries require an **international driving licence**.

For the vehicle it is necessary to have the registration papers (log-book) and a national identification plate of the approved size.

An International Insurance Certificate (Green Card) is compulsory. Third party insurance is also compulsory in Portugal. Special breakdown and get-you-home packages are a good idea (AA, Five Star RAC, National Breakdown, Europ-Assistance). Members of the American Automobile Association should obtain the brochure "Offices to Serve You Abroad."

If the driver of the vehicle is not accompanied by the owner, he or she should have written permission from the owner to drive in Portugal.

DRIVING REGULATIONS

- The minimum driving age is 17.
- Traffic drives on the right.
- It is compulsory for the front-seat passengers to wear seat belts.

The rules of the road are the same in Portugal as in other continental countries and Portugal uses the international road sign system.

The Portuguese road network includes over 300km/186mi of motorways. Tolls are payable on some motorways and bridges.

Maximum speed limits are:
- 120kph/75mph on motorways (*auto-estrada*);
- 90kph/56mph on dual carriageways (*estrada com faixas de rodagem separadas);*
- 90kph/56mph on other roads;
- 50kph/31mph in built-up areas.

BREAKDOWN SERVICE

The Portuguese Automobile Club (Automóvel Club de Portugal), Rua Rosa Araújo 24, Lisboa 1200, ☎ 213 18 01 00, offers members of equivalent foreign organisations medical, legal and breakdown assistance.

PETROL/GASOLINE

Diesel and unleaded petrol (*gasolina sem chumbo*) are generally available throughout the country. Credit cards are accepted in most petrol stations but visitors are strongly advised to have other means of payment with them. Petrol stations are generally open from 7am-midnight, although some open 24hr a day.

CAR RENTAL

The major car rental firms have offices in all large towns. Cars may be hired from branches at airports, main stations and large hotels. The minimum age to qualify for car rental is 21.

The Department of State publishes a pamphlet *A Safe Trip Abroad* which is available from the Superintendent of Documents, PO Box 371954, Pittsburgh, PA 15250-7954. ☎ 202-512-1800. Fly-drive schemes are operated by major airlines. Major car hire companies include:

Avis	☎ 213 46 26 76	www.avis.com
Hertz	☎ 213 81 24 30/ 36	www.hertz. com
Europcar	☎ 219 40 77 90	www.europcar. com

ROUTE PLANNING

Available on the Internet, this service offers various routes to drivers, distances between towns and cities, as well as details of restaurants and bars at **www.ViaMichelin.com**.

Maps and plans – Michelin map 733 at a 1:1 000 000 scale covers the whole of the Iberian Peninsula, as does the Michelin Atlas Spain & Portugal (scale: 1:400 000). Map 733 at a 1:400 000 scale covers Portugal and includes an index and an enlarged inset map of Lisbon. Michelin plan 39 with a scale of 1:10 000 covers the city of Lisbon, with details on one-way streets, main car parks and public buildings.

GETTING AROUND

By Air

TAP Air Portugal operates flights from Lisbon and Oporto to Madeira (Funchal) and from Lisbon to the Azores (Ponta Delgado on São Miguel). Local airlines operate inter-island flights in the Azores. Internal flights are the most practical way of travelling from the north to south.

Major airports – Lisbon, Oporto, Faro, Funchal and Porto Santo (on Madeira); Ponta Delgada, Santa Maria and Terceira (in the Azores).
Journey times: Lisbon – Oporto: 45min; Lisbon – Faro: 40min; Lisbon – Funchal: 1hr 40min; Lisbon – Ponta Delgada: 1hr 50min.
◆ **TAP Air Portugal**: Praça do Marquês do Pombal, 3A, Lisboa; ☎ 213 17 91 60; www.flytap.com.
◆ **Portugália**: Aeroporto de Lisboa; ☎ 218 40 89 99; www.flypga.com.
◆ **SATA**: Air Açores; ☎ 296 28 23 11 www.sata.pt.

By Train

Portuguese Railways – Caminhos de Ferro Portugueses (CP) has a rail network linking major cities and an inter-city service. The *rápidos* or express trains are fast. The *directos* or inter-city trains are slower, make more stops and have both first and second class compartments.
There is a tourist pass which is valid on the entire rail network for a period of 7, 14 or 21 days. For further information ☎ 218 88 40 25; www.cp.pt

By Coach

Portugal's national coach network (Rodoviária Nacional) is extensive and covers all parts of the country. For information, contact: Rodoviária Nacional, Avenida Duque d'Avila 12 – 1000-140 Lisboa; ☎ 213 57 77 15. www.rede-expressas.pt (but only in Portuguese).

Railway station, Aveiro

G. Sioën/RAPHO

WHERE TO STAY AND EAT

Hotels and Restaurants are described in the Address Books within the *Discovering Portugal* section. *For coin categories, see the cover flap.*

Where to Stay

HOTELS

The **Michelin Guide Spain & Portugal** guide is revised annually and is an indispensable complement to this guide, with information on hotels and restaurants including category, price, degree of comfort and setting. Towns underlined in red on the Michelin map 733 are listed in the current edition of the *Michelin Guide Spain & Portugal* with a choice of hotels and restaurants.

The Portuguese Tourist Board also publishes a list with hotel categories ranging from one-star to five-star establishments. In Portugal hotel prices are inclusive of VAT (12% or 21%) and the price of breakfast is almost always included in the cost of the room.

POUSADAS

The state-owned *pousadas* are marked by a "g" sign on the Map of Places to Stay on p11 and on the Michelin map 733. Special mention should be made of around thirty Portuguese *pousadas*, most of which are extremely comfortable, restored historic monuments (castles, palaces and monasteries) in beautiful sites or excursion centres. The *pousadas* are very popular and usually full so it is always wise to book in advance. For further information, contact ENATUR, Avenida Santa Joana Princesa 10, 1749-090 Lisboa, ☎ 218 48 12 21, or the Portuguese National Tourist Office, or check the Web sites: www.pousadasportugal. com or www.pousadasofportugal. com.

ESTALAGEMS

These are similar types of establishments, often refurbished historic buildings, but they are privately owned.

RESIDENCIAS

These comfortable guest houses are almost on a par with some hotels but they do not serve meals.

PENSÕES

A *pensão* is a more modest guest house.

BED AND BREAKFAST

Again the type of accommodation on offer is varied, although the term **Turismo de Habitação (TH)** usually covers historic houses and manors. There are numerous establishments in northern Portugal but again it is necessary to book in advance. In the north, contact Associação do Turismo de Habitação, Praça da Répública, 4990 Ponte de Lima, ☎ 258 74 16 72 or 258 74 28 27.

For accommodation in rural houses apply to ANTER (Associação de Turismo no Espaço Rural), Rua 24 de Julho, 1-1° – 7000-673 Évora, ☎ 266 74 45 55.

CAMPING

See △ sign on Michelin map 733. In Portugal independent camping outside of official sites is not allowed. The local tourist information centres can provide a list of official campsites. The official classification awards stars (1 to 4) to state-owned sites and lists private ones. The *Roteiro Campista* guide, containing details of all campsites and their location, is available from Roteiro Campista, Rua do Giestal 5, 1300-274 Lisboa, at a cost of €10.

Federação Portuguesa de Campismo, Av Coronel Eduardo Galhardo, 24D, 1170-105 Lisboa ☎ 218 12 68 90/1 or 218 12 69 00.
Go to: www.roteirocampista.pt. There is an English part of this Web site. When you arrive at a campsite you will be asked for your passport and for an international camping carnet, which is obligatory. You can get details on these carnets from the Fédération Internationale de Camping et Caravanning (F.I.C.C) – www.ficc.be. It is advisable to book in advance for popular resorts during summer.

YOUTH HOSTELS (POUSADAS DE JUVENTUDE)

Portugal's 22 youth hostels (including two in the Azores) are open to travellers with an International Card. For further information, contact MOVIJOVEM, Pousadas de Juventude, Av. Duque de Ávila, 137, 1069-017 Lisboa, ☎ 213 13 88 20 or 213 52 86 21. Hostelling International/American Youth Hostel Association (☎ 202 783 6161) publishes the *International Hostel Guide for Europe* listing properties throughout Europe. You can get good information on youth hostels and other budget accommodation (as well as flights) from: www.studentflights.co.uk/hostels/portugal.

Where to Eat

RESTAURANTS

The Portuguese keep fairly similar dining hours to the British and Americans. As a general rule, restaurants serve lunch from noon to 2.30pm and dinner from 7pm onwards.
A wide selection of gourmet restaurants can be found in the **Michelin Guide Spain & Portugal**. All towns with a restaurant listed in the *Michelin Guide Spain & Portugal* are underlined in red on the Michelin map 733.
A further selection of restaurants can be found in the Address Books in the *Discovering Portugal* section of this guide. *For coin categories shown for the restaurants, see the cover flap.*
In some of the more popular restaurants, particularly in the north, two prices are written by the same item. The first price denotes a full portion *(dose)* and the second is for the half-portion *(meia dose)*. Hors-d'œuvres are often served prior to the meal (cheese, cured ham, spicy sausage, olives, tuna and croquettes) and are added to the bill. It is customary to leave a tip of about 10% of the total bill. For further information on Portuguese food and wine, please consult the Introduction to this guide.

Azulejo, Palácio dos Marqueses de Fronteira - Lisbon

J.P. Lescouret / EXPLORER

WHAT TO DO AND SEE

Outdoor Fun

SAILING

There are ample opportunities for sailing in Portugal with its long coastline, the Tagus estuary and inland stretches of water. Many northern European yachtsmen stop at a Portuguese port as they sail round to the Mediterranean. In season it is possible to hire boats with or without crew. Apply to the Federação Portuguesa de Vela, Doca de Belém, 1300-082 Lisboa, ☏ 213 64 11 52 or 213 62 02 15; www.fpvela.pt – though a better Web site (in English) is: www.manorhouses.com/ports.

Coastlines where sailing is possible are marked by the symbol ⚓ on the Map of Places to Stay and on Michelin map 733. Marinas marked on Michelin map 733 have been selected for their facilities and infrastructure. Check weather bulletins before heading out to sea.

WINDSURFING

Although this sport can be enjoyed all around the coast, the most important areas are around Estoril (Praia do Guincho) and Lisbon, the Algarve coast and the islands of the Madeira archipelago. In these areas you are sure to be able to hire boards and find a school. There are strict rules concerning windsurfing and it is best to enquire at the local surfing school or club.

SCUBA DIVING

The more rugged coastlines (Ilha da Berlenga, Peniche and the Sesimbra coast) offer ideal conditions for this sport. The sea caves along the Algarve coast between Albufeira and Sagres are popular with scuba divers.

WATERPARKS

These are mainly located around Lisbon and in the Algarve (& see ALGARVE). Further information can be obtained from Tourist Offices.

BEACHES

The symbol ⚑ on Michelin map 733 and on the Map of Places to Stay at the front of the guide highlights the best beaches. The Portuguese coastline is a series of beaches from north to south. The best known are the great sandy stretches of the **Algarve,** where both the climate and temperature of the sea (17°C in winter, 23°C in summer) are pleasant.

The **Costa Dourada** between Cabo São Vicente and Setúbal is a more rugged coastline with tiny curves of sand at the foot of imposing cliffs and a colder and rougher sea (15°C in winter and 19°C in summer).

The **Costa de Lisboa** from Setúbal to Cabo da Roca includes the pleasant, well sheltered beaches of the Serra de Arrábida, the great expanse of dunes of the Costa da Caparica south of the

Seaside resort, Costa Nova

G. Dumour

Tagus and the very crowded beaches of Cascais and Estoril which are popular with Lisbonites.

The **Costa de Prato,** extending from Cabo da Roca to Aveiro, has flat sandy beaches. North of Nazaré the fishermen's boats can be seen high on the beaches. The **Costa Verde** from the Douro northwards to the Spanish border has fine sandy beaches backed inland with a pleasantly green countryside.

Many of Portugal's beaches are supervised and it is important to heed the flags: red – it is forbidden to enter the sea even to paddle; yellow – no swimming; green – it is safe to paddle and swim; blue and white chequered – beach temporarily unsupervised.

FISHING

Freshwater angling

This is done mostly in the north for trout, salmon, barbel and shad (Rio Minho and the Douro) and in the numerous mountain torrents of the Serra de Estrela (carp, barbel and trout).

A fishing permit can be obtained from the Federação Portuguesa da Pesca Desportiva, Rua Sociedade Farmacêutica 56-2°, 1150-341 Lisboa, ☎ 213 56 31 47. Enquire at the local Tourist Information Centres for the opening dates of the fishing season.

Sea angling

In the north the catch usually includes skate, cod, dogfish and sea perch while in the south Mediterranean species are more common.

GOLF

Portugal's mild climate enables golfers to play year-round. The country has a wide selection of courses to choose from, most of which are of championship standard. Details can be found on: www.portugalvirtual/pt_golf and www.portugalgolf.pt.

Golf courses with the number of holes and their telephone numbers are listed in the current edition of the *Michelin Guide Spain & Portugal* under the nearest town and are indicated on the Michelin Map 733 by the 🚩 symbol.

OTHER SPORTS

Football

The Portuguese are great football (soccer) fans. The teams with the greatest following are Oporto's FC Porto (European Champions League Winners in 2004) and Lisbon's Benfica and Sporting. Tickets for matches involving the big three are difficult to obtain as there are so many season-ticket holders. Games are generally played on Sunday afternoons.

Alvor golf course

B. Barbier

Bullfights

The season begins at Easter and ends in October. For further information, contact local Tourist Offices.

Spas

Portugal's tradition of elegant spas dates from the late 19C. The country's 40 or so spas cater to people with a wide variety of ailments. The ‡ symbol on the Map of Places to Stay in the Introduction and Michelin map 733 indicates some of the more important ones.

For further information, contact the Associação das Termas de Portugal, Avenida Miguel Bombarda, 110-2°, Dt°, 1050-167 Lisboa – ☏ 217 94 05 74; www.supra.pt/termas-portugal.

Bird-watching

Bird-watching is becoming increasingly popular, especially in the south of the country where many migratory birds can be observed at certain times of the year. A very comprehensive Web site that lists when and where various species are likely to be encountered is: www.birding-in-portugal.com. You can also visit (and book holidays on-line with) www.limosaholidays.co.uk.

Activities for Children

In this guide, sights of particular interest to children are indicated with a **Kids** symbol. Some attractions may offer discount fees for children. ☞ *For specific activities in Lisbon, see the chapter in Discovering Portugal.*

Calendar of Events

Detailed calendars of events are published by the local Tourist Information Centres. The following list is a selection of the most well-known events. *Map references in parentheses (U5) are given for places not featured in this guide but referred to on Michelin map 733.*

WEEK PRECEDING SHROVE TUESDAY

Ovar (J4) — Carnival: procession of floats.
Torres Vedras (O2) — Carnival: procession of floats.
Loulé — Carnival and Almond Gatherers' Fair.

HOLY WEEK

Braga — Holy Week ceremonies and processions.

EASTER SUNDAY

Loulé — Pilgrimage in honour of Our Lady of Pity. Repeated on the following two Sundays.

29 APRIL TO 3 MAY

Barcelos — Festival of Crosses, Pottery Fair and folk dancing.

3 TO 5 MAY

Sesimbra — Festival in honour of Our Lord Jesus of the Wounds: fishermen's festival dating from the 16C. Procession on 4 May.

FIRST SUNDAY AFTER 3 MAY

Monsanto — Castle Festival.

SECOND WEEKEND IN MAY

Vila Franca do Lima — Rose Festival: Mordomias procession in which the mistress of the house bears on her head a tray of flowers arranged to represent one of the many provincial coats of arms.

12 AND 13 MAY

Fátima — First great pilgrimage. Candlelight procession at 9.30pm on the 12th and International Mass on the 13th. These take place every evening on the 12th and 13th of every month until October.

SECOND HALF OF MAY

Leiria — Fair and agricultural machinery exhibition with town festival on 22 May (processions, celebrations etc).

THIRD TUESDAY AFTER WHITSUN

Matosinhos — Pilgrimage in honour of the Senhor of Matosinhos: folk dancing.

6, 7, 8 JUNE

Amarante — St Gonsalo Festival.

FIRST FORTNIGHT IN JUNE

Santarém — National Agricultural Show: folklore.

12 TO 29 JUNE

Lisboa — Popular saints' festival: marchas.

13 JUNE

Vila Real — St Anthony's Festival: procession, fireworks. St Anthony's Festival from 6 to 17 June.

23 TO 24 JUNE (ST JOHN)

Braga — St John's Midsummer Festival.
Oporto — Popular saints' festival.
Vila do Conde — Lacemakers' procession.

LAST WEEK IN JUNE TO FIRST WEEK IN JULY

Póvoa de Varzim — St Peter's Festival.

28 TO 29 JUNE

Sintra — St Peter's Fair.
Vila Real — St Peter's Fair.

FIRST WEEK IN JULY (EVERY 2 YEARS)

Tomar — Tabuleiros Festival.

Mordomas procession during the Rose Festival at Vila do Lima

JULY AND AUGUST

Estoril — Handcrafts fair: the Portuguese regions are all represented.

FIRST WEEKEND IN JULY (EVEN YEARS)

Coimbra — Festival of the Queen, Saint Isabel of Portugal.

FIRST WEEKEND IN JULY

Vila Franca de Xira — Festival of the Red Waistcoats.

26 JULY TO 17 AUGUST

Setúbal — St James' Fair: bullfights and folk groups.

IN JULY AND PART OF AUGUST

Aveiro — The Ria Festival with a competition for the best decorated prow.

FIRST WEEKEND IN AUGUST

Guimarães — St Walter's Festival: fair, decorated streets, giants procession.
Peniche — Festival in honour of Our Lady of Safe Travel.

25

The Days of the Week

While Monday in Portuguese is the second day of the week *(segunda-feira)*, Tuesday the third *(terça-feira)*, Wednesday the fourth *(quarta-feira)*, Thursday the fifth *(quinta-feira)* and Friday the sixth *(sexta-feira)*, Sunday, the first day of the week, remains that of the Lord *(domingo)* and Saturday, the seventh, the sabbath *(sábado)*.

This denomination is believed to have originated in the 6C when São Martinho, Bishop of Braga, took the Christians to task for using the traditional calendar dating from the time of the Chaldeans and thereby dedicating each day to a pagan divinity: the Sun, the Moon, Mars, Mercury, Jupiter, Venus and Saturn.

THIRD WEEK IN AUGUST

Viana do Castelo — Pilgrimage in honour of Our Lady of Sorrow.

THIRD SUNDAY IN AUGUST

Miranda do Douro — St Barbara's Festival: dance of the Pauliteiros.

END OF AUGUST TO BEGINNING OF SEPTEMBER

Lamego — Romaria of Our Lady of Remedies.

FIRST WEEK IN SEPTEMBER

Palmela — Grape Harvest Festival: benediction of the grapes, running of the bulls through the streets, fireworks.

8 SEPTEMBER

Mirando do Douro — Pilgrimage in honour of Our Lady of Nazo at Póva *(11km/7mi north)*: a fair precedes the pilgrimage and a festival ends the celebrations.

BEGINNING 8 SEPTEMBER

Nazaré — Romaria of Our Lady of Nazareth.

4 TO 12 OCTOBER

Vila Franca de Xira — Handicrafts Fair, running of the bulls through the streets, touradas.

SECOND SUNDAY IN OCTOBER

Nazaré — National Gastronomy Fair: food, handicrafts, folklore.

12 AND 13 OCTOBER

Fátima — Last annual pilgrimage.

THIRD SUNDAY IN OCTOBER

Castro Verde — October Fair which goes back to the 17C: agricultural show and handcrafts.

FIRST FORTNIGHT IN NOVEMBER

Golegã — National Horse Show and the Feast of St Martin: benediction of the horses, a tradition dating back to the 17C.

World Heritage List

In 1972, the United Nations Educational, Scientific and Cultural Organisation (UNESCO) adopted a Convention for the preservation of cultural and natural sites. To date, more than 150 countries have signed this international agreement, which has listed over 500 sites "of outstanding universal value" on the World Heritage List. Each year, a committee of representatives from 21 countries, assisted by technical organisations (ICOMOS – International Council on Monuments and Sites; IUCN-International Union for Conservation of Nature and Natural Resources; ICCROM – International Centre for the Study of the Preservation and Restoration of Cultural Property, the Rome Centre),

In Portugal, the following have been designated as World Heritage sites:

♦ **Central Zone of the town of Angra do Heroísmo, Azores**
♦ **Mosteiro dos Jerónimos and Torre de Belém, Lisbon**
♦ **Mosteiro da Batalha**
♦ **Convento de Cristo, Tomar**
♦ **Historical centre of Evora**
♦ **Mosteiro de Santa Maria, Alcobaça**
♦ **Cultural landscape of Sintra**
♦ **Historical centre of Oporto**
♦ **Parque Arqueológico do Vale do Côa**

evaluates the proposals for new sites to be included on the list, which grows longer as new nominations are accepted and more countries sign the Convention. To be considered, a site must be nominated by the country in which it is located.

The protected cultural heritage may be monuments (buildings, sculptures, archeological structures etc) with unique historical, artistic or scientific features, groups of buildings (such as religious communities, ancient cities), or sites of exceptional beauty (human settlements, magnificent landscapes, places of cultural interest) which are the combined works of man and nature. Natural sites may be a testimony to the stages of the earth's geological history or to the development of human cultures and creative genius or represent significant ongoing ecological processes, contain superlative natural phenomena or provide a habitat for threatened species.

Signatories of the Convention pledge to co-operate to preserve and protect these sites around the world as a common heritage to be shared by all humanity.

Some of the most well-known places which the World Heritage Committee has inscribed include: Australia's Great Barrier Reef (1981), the Canadian Rocky Mountain Parks (1984), The Great Wall of China (1987), the Statue of Liberty (1984), the Kremlin (1990), Mont-Saint-Michel and its bay (France – 1979), Durham Castle and Cathedral (1986).

Shopping

Traditional Portuguese crafts will catch your eye, and the prices are attractive, too. From the north to the south, variety is found in the choice of colours and natural materials. In Viana do Castelo, look for hand-embroidered linen and cotton (tablecloths and napkins, shirts, aprons etc) and the classic filigree jewellery in both silver and gold. Embroidered bedspreads are a good buy in Castelo Branco, as are the hand-made rugs from Arrailos, while many places offer ceramics (Caldas da Rainha, Coimbra etc) and pottery (Barcelos, Alentejo, Algarve). Woodworkers make decorative objects, kitchen utensils and toys, tinsmiths are famous for *almutelias*, the traditional recipients for olive oil, while glass-makers still continue their activity in Marinha Grande. *Azulejos* tiles are found everywhere, as are objects and kitchenware made of copper (including the typical *cataplana* from the Algarve). ♨ *For more information, see Architectural Traditions in the Introduction.*

Sightseeing

TIMES AND CHARGES

As admission times and charges are liable to alteration, the information below is given only as a general guideline.

Kid Kervella/HOA QUI

Traditional embroidery

Opening times and other relevant information concerning all sights in the descriptive part of this guide accompanied by the symbol ◷. Prices quoted are shown by the symbol ⬭ and apply to individual adults with no reduction; if no price is shown admission is free. Special conditions for both times and charges are generally granted to groups if arranged beforehand.

Opening and closing times are given, but remember that some places do not admit visitors during the last hour or half hour.

Most tours are conducted by Portuguese-speaking guides but in some cases the term "guided tours" may cover groups visiting with recorded commentaries. Some of the larger and more popular sights may offer guided tours in other languages.

For most towns the address and/or telephone number of the local Tourist Information Centre, indicated by the symbol ▤, is given below. These centres are able to help tourists find accommodation and provide information on exhibitions, performances, guided tours, market days and other items of local interest.

City tours are given regularly during the tourist season in Coimbra, Faro, Lisbon, Oporto and Viana do Castelo.

Apply to the Tourist Information Centre.

Books

CONTEMPORARY PORTUGAL

Karen Brown's Portugal: Exceptional Places to Stay 2007 – Karen Brown (Karen Brown Guides 2006)

Fado Portugues: Songs from the Soul of Portugal (with audio CD) – Donald Cohen/David Martins (Music Sales Corp. 2004)

Working and Living in Portugal – Harvey Holton (Cadogan Guides 2005)

Buying a Property in Portugal – Harvey Holton/John Howell (Cadogan Guides 2003)

Complete Guide to Buying Property in Portugal – Colin Barrow (Kogan Page 2002)

Walking in Portugal – Bethen Davies/ Bn Cole (Pila Pala Press 2000)

HISTORY

Portuguese Seaborne Empire – CR Boxer (Carcanet Press 1991)

Christopher Columbus and the Portuguese, 1476-1498 – Rebecca Catz (Greenwood Press 1993)

Wellington's Peninsular Victories – Michael Glover (The Windrush Press 1996)

A Soldier of the Seventy-first – Christopher Hibbert (ed) (The Windrush Press 1996)

Portugal 1715-1808 – David Francis (Tamesis Books 1976)

The Pope's Elephant – Silvio A Bedini (Carcanet Press 1997)

A Concise History of Portugal – David Birmingham (Cambridge University Press 1993)

A Companion History of Portugal – Jose Hermano Saraiva, Ian Robertson, Ursula Fonss (Carcanet Press 1997)

The Portuguese – Marion Kaplan (Penguin Books 1998)

In Search of Modern Portugal, the Revolution and its Consequences – Lawrence S Graham, Douglas Wheeler (University of Wisconsin Press 1983)

The Making of Portuguese Democracy – Kenneth Maxwell (CUP 1997)

Hamilton's Campaign with Moore and Wellington During the Peninsular War – Anthony Hamilton, James Colquhoun (Howell Press 1998)

The Journal of a Voyage to Lisbon – Henry Fielding, T Keymer (ed) (Penguin Books 1989)

They Went to Portugal Too – Rose Macaulay (Carcanet Press 1990)

Journey to Portugal: In Pursuit of Portugal's History and Culture – Jose Saramago (Harvest Books 2002)

Portugal: A Traveller's History – Harold Livermore (Boydell Press 2004)

ART AND ARCHITECTURE

Architectural Practice in Europe: Portugal – (RIBA Publications 1991)

The Age of the Baroque in Portugal – Jay A Levenson (ed) (National Gallery of Art 1993)

The Fires of Excellence – Miles Danby, Matthew Weinreb (Garnet Publishing 1996)

Portuguese Gardens – Helder Carita, Homem Cardoso (Antique Collectors' Club 1991)

Houses and Gardens of Portugal – Marcus Binney, Patrick Bowe, Nicolas Sapieha, Francesco Venturi (Rizzoli Publications 1998)

Gardens of Spain and Portugal – Barbara Segall (Mitchell Beazley 1999)

Landscapes of Algarve – Brian Anderson, Eileen Anderson (Sunflower Books 1996)

Landscapes of the Azores – Andreas Stieglitz (Sunflower Books 1992)

WINE

Some useful Web sites for those interested in Portuguese wines.

- *www.portugal-info.net/wines*
- *www.portuguesewine.com*
- *www.wine-searcher.com/regions/portugal/1*
- *www.gastronomias.com/wines*
- *www.wineanorak.com/portugals_wineregions.htm*
- *www.wineonline.ie/library/portugal.htm*

A SELECTION OF PORTUGUESE AUTHORS

The Lusiads – Luiz de Camões, trans WC Atkinson (Penguin Books 1952)

A Centenary Pessoa – Fernando Pessoa, E Lisboa (ed), H Macedo (trans) (Carcanet Press 1995)

Selected Poems – Fernando Pessoa, J Griffin (trans) (Penguin Books 1996)

Always Astonished: Selected Prose – Fernando Pessoa, E Honig (trans) (City Lights Books 1988)

Esau and Jacob – Machado de Assis (Peter Owen 1966)

Travels in My Homeland – Almeida Garrett (Peter Owen 1986)

USEFUL WORDS & PHRASES

Common Words

bank; exchange	**banco; câmbio**
boat	**barco**
bus; tram	**autocarro; eléctrico**
car	**carro**
car park	**parque de estacionamento**
chemist	**farmácia**
customs	**alfândega**
district	**bairro**
doctor	**mêdico**
entrance; exit	**entrada; saída**
expensive	**caro**
good afternoon	**boa tarde**
good morning	**bom dia**
goodbye	**adeus**
guide	**guia**
halt	**paragem**
I beg your pardon	**desculpe**
information	**informações**
large; small	**grande; pequeno**
letter; postcard	**carta; postal**
letter-box	**caixa de correio**
light	**luz**
madam	**minha senhora**
miss	**menina**
at what time ...?	**a que hora ...?**
much; little	**muito; pouco**
how much ...?	**quanto custa ...?**
noon	**meio-dia**
road works	**obras**
petrol; oil	**gasolina; óleo**
danger	**perigo**
please	**(se) faz favor**
prohibited	**prohibido**
post office; stamp	**correio; selo**
river; stream	**rio; ribeira**
ruins	**ruínas**
sir	**senhor**
square	**largo; praça**
station; train	**estação; comboio**
street; avenue	**rue; avenida**
thank you	(said by a man) **obrigado**
	(said by a woman) **obrigada**

today	**hoje**
toll	**portagem**
tomorrow morning	**amanhã de manhã**
tomorrow evening	**amanhã à tarde**
to the left	**à esquerda**
to the right	**à direita**
town; quarter	**cidade**
where; when	**onde? quando?**
yes; no	**sim; não**
where is?	**onde é...?**
the road to ...?	**a estrada para ...?**
at what time ...?	**a que hora ...?**
how much ...?	**quanto custa..?**
road works	**obras**
danger	**perigo**
prohibited	**prohibido**

Sightseeing

abadia	abbey
albufeira	reservoir
andar	storey
baixa	town centre
barragem	dam
câmara municipal	town hall
capela	chapel
casa	house
castelo	castle, citadel
centro urbano	town centre
chafariz	fountain
chave	key
citânia	prehistoric city
convento	convent,
mosteiro	monastery
cruz; cruzeiro	cross; calvary
escada	stairs, steps
excavações	excavations
fechado, aberto	closed, open
igreja	church
ilha	island
local	site
mata	wood
mercado, feira	market, fair
miradouro	belvedere
paço, palácio	palace, castle
parque	park
porto	harbour, port
praia	beach
quinta	country property

sé	cathedral	**açucar**	sugar
século	century	**água; copo**	water; glass
solar	manor-house	**(pequeno)**	(small)
tapete; tapeçaria	tapestry	**almoço**	breakfast
tesouro	treasure; treasury	**azeite**	olive oil
		café com leite	coffee with milk
torre	tower	**carne**	meat
torre de menagem	keep	**cerveja**	beer
túmulo	tomb	**conta**	bill
vista	view, panorama	**ementa, carta**	menu
dirigir-se a...	apply to...	**fresco**	cold, chilled
pode-se visitar?	may one visit?	**gelo**	ice-cream; ice cube
		jantar, ceia	dinner
		lista	menu (à la carte)
		óleo	peanut oil
		pão	bread
		peixe	fish
		pimenta, sal	pepper, salt
		prato do dia	dish of the day
		sumo de fruta	fruit juice
		vinho branco	white wine
		vinho tinto	red wine

Dining

Note: for more detailed restaurant terminology consult the *Michelin Guide Spain & Portugal*.

Typical Dishes

Açorda de Mariscos	Bread soup with clams and prawns, mixed with garlic, eggs, coriander and spices
Amêijoas à Bulhão Pato	Small clams cooked in olive oil, garlic and coriander
Arroz de Marisco	Rice with clams, shrimp, mussels and coriander
Bacalhau	Cod
Cabrito	Roast goat
Caldeirada	Spicy fish and seafood stew
Caldo verde	Potato and cabbage stew
Canja de Galinha	Chicken bouillon with rice and hard egg yolks
Carne de porco à Alentajana	Diced pork in olive oil, garlic and coriander sauce, served with potatoes and small clams
Cataplana	Steamed seafood with pieces of ham
Chouriço	Smoked sausage
Cozido	Pot roast with meat, sausage and vegetables
Feijoada	Beans prepared with pork, cabbage and sausage
Gaspacho	Cold vegetable soup
Leitão assado	Grilled suckling pig, served hot or cold
Presunto	Smoked ham
Salpicão	Spicy smoked ham
Sopa à Alentajana	Garlic and bread soup, served with a poached egg and coriander
Sopa de Feijão verde	Green bean soup
Sopa de Grão	Chickpea soup
Sopa de Legumes	Vegetable soup
Sopa de Marisco	Seafood soup
Sopa de Peixe	Fish soup

BASIC INFORMATION

Business Hours

MONUMENTS, MUSEUMS AND CHURCHES

Monuments and museums are generally open 10am to 12.30pm and 2pm to 6pm. Some churches are only open during service early in the morning or in the evening. For more detailed information, please consult the admission times and charges in the *Discovering Portugal* section.

SHOPS

Generally open weekdays 9am to 1pm and 3pm to 7pm (some department stores stay open during the lunch hour). Most shops are closed on Saturday afternoons and most all day Sunday. Shopping centres are the exception as they are open every day of the week from 10am to 11pm.

ENTERTAINMENT

Evening performances begin about 9.30pm and *fados* at about 10.30pm.

Electricity

Electric current – 220 volts. Plugs are two-pin.

Major Holidays

1 January
Shrove Tuesday
Good Friday
25 April (Liberation Day)
1 May (Labour Day)
10 June (Death of Camões national holiday)
15 August
5 October (Republic Day)
1 November (All Saints' Day)
1 December (Independence Day)
8 December
25 December

In addition to the list below each town or locality celebrates the feast day of its patron saint (St Anthony in Lisbon – 13 June; St John in Oporto – 24 June). For local holidays contact the Tourist Information Centres.

Mail

POST OFFICES (CORREIOS)

Post Offices are open weekdays from 9am to 6pm; the smaller branches may close for lunch from 12.30pm to 2.30pm. The main post offices in large towns and those in international airports have a 24-hour service.
Stamps *(selos)* are sold in post offices and shops displaying the sign CTT Selos.
The **Michelin Guide, Spain & Portugal** gives the post code for every town covered. Letter boxes and phone booths are red.

Money

Portugal is part of the Euro zone. There are no restrictions on the amount of euro currency that you may bring into the country. At the start of 2007 exchange rates were: €1= US$1.32; £1 = €1.49. Euro notes come in denominations of €5, €10, €20, €50, €100, €200 and €500. Beware of accepting notes of high value (€200 and €500) as these are a favourite of counterfeiters. Most shops and all taxis wil refuse any note larger than €100.

CURRENCY EXCHANGE AND CREDIT CARDS

Banks, airports and some stations have exchange offices. Commissions vary so check before cashing.
All major credit cards (American Express, Diners Club, Visa and MasterCard) are accepted but always

check in advance. MULTIBANCO is a national network of automatic cash dispensers which accept international credit and debit cards and enable cash withdrawal 24 hours a day.

Banks are generally open Mondays to Fridays 8.30am to 3pm. These times are subject to change, especially in summer. Most banks have cash dispensers which accept international credit cards *(see above)*.

Newspapers

The main Portuguese newspapers are the following: *O Diário de Notícias, O Correio da Manhã,* and *O Público*. Oporto has its own daily newspaper, *O Jornal de Notícias*. Weekly publications include *O Expresso*, which has the widest readership, *O Seminário, O Independente* and *O Jornal*.

Taxes and Tipping

The bill is usually inclusive of service charges and VAT (12-21%). An extra tip can be left for special service. 10% of the fare is the usual amount given to taxi drivers , about €2 per bag for hotel porters.

Telephone

Phonecards are widely used and can be purchased at Telecom Portugal shops, post offices and some kiosks and *tabacarias*. You can also use, and will find less expensive, the type of

phonecards you can buy at home for use overseas. Some phone boxes also accept credit card payments. Cellphones work almost everywhere and your normal cellphone operator will have details. International calls may be made from modern phone boxes or from post offices; in bars and hotels be prepared to pay more than the going rate. For **international calls** dial: 00 + 44 for the United Kingdom; 00 + 353 for Ireland; 00 + 1 for the United States and Canada followed by the area code (deleting the first zero where appropriate) and the number.

To call Portugal from the United Kingdom or Ireland dial 00 + 351, followed by the nine-digit number.

Internet cafés can be found in most large towns and you'll find Wi-Fi hotspots at many places.

Temperature and Measurement

Portugal uses the metric system, distances in kilometres (km), temperatures in Celsius. Roughly speaking 85°F = 30°C and in speed 48kph = 30mph; 80kph = 50mph and 112kph = 70mph.

Time

Mainland Portugal is the same as Greenwich Mean Time, although summer time is used so the time is always the same as the UK. Madeira is 1hr behind mainland Portugal and the Azores are 2hr behind.

Ponta da Piedade – Algarve

G. Simeone/PHOTONONSTOP

NATURE

Portugal has a wide variety of landscapes, from the mountainous north-east to the flatter areas near the coast and in the south. The continental part of the country in the southwest of the Iberian Peninsula occupies a relatively small area of 88 944km²/34 341sq mi (560km/350mi from north to south and 220km/137mi from west to east). Generally speaking, the altitude decreases from the Spanish border towards the Atlantic and from north to south; the Tagus (Tejo) divides a mountainous region in the north from an area of plateaux and plains in the south. The archipelagos of Madeira and the Azores have a surface area of 782km²/302sq mi and 2 335km²/902sq mi respectively (see Madeira and the Azores).

Geological Formation

In the Primary Era the north of Portugal was affected by Hercynian folding which

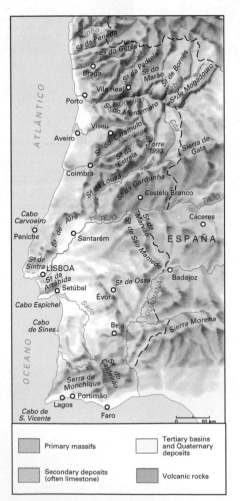

resulted in the emergence of hard granite and shale mountain ranges. These were worn down in the Secondary Era to form a vast plateau out of which rose erosion resistant heights such as the Serra de São Mamede. In the Tertiary Era, the raising of the Alps and Pyrenean folding led to a brutal upheaval of the plateau, dislocating it into a series of small massifs such as the Serra do Marão and Serra da Estrela. The massifs were separated by fissures near which emerged thermal and mineral springs and, especially in the north, metal deposits. The upheavals were accompanied in some cases by eruptions of a volcanic nature which formed ranges such as the Serra de Sintra and Serra de Monchique. It was at this point that the Tagus and Sado basins were formed and the coastal plains folded into the low ranges of the Serra de Aire, Serra do Caldeirão and Serra da Arrábida. This zone of faults in the earth's crust is still subject to geological disturbance as shown in the earthquake which destroyed Lisbon in 1755 and even more recent tremors.

The coastline became less indented in the Quaternary Era through erosion of the Estremadura and Alentejo cliffs and alluvial accumulation in the Aveiro and Sines areas.

Relief

The Cantabrian Cordillera extends westwards into Portugal, north of the Douro, where it takes the form of massive mountain ranges separated by heavily eroded valleys.

Between the Douro and the Tagus, the Castilian sierras extend into Portugal as particularly high relief. Monte da Torre in the Serra da Estrela is Portugal's highest mainland peak (1 993m/6 539ft). The Mondego and Zêzere valleys surround the ridge. South of the Tagus lies a plateau which drops towards the sea. Its vast horizons are barely interrupted by the minor rises of the Serra de Monchique and Serra do Caldeirão.

The 837km/520mi of coast offer incredible variety, with beaches of fine sand sheltered by rock cliffs, creeks, and promontories such as Cabo Carvoeiro, Cabo Espichel and Cabo de São Vicente. Wide estuaries are occupied by the country's main ports: Oporto on the Douro, Lisbon on the Tagus and Setúbal on the Sado. Fishing harbours like Portimão have developed in bays, or, as with Peniche and Lagos, in the protection of headlands. However, most of the coast consists of flat sandy areas sometimes lined by offshore bars as in the eastern offshore Algarve and along Ria de Aveiro.

Regions and Landscape

The areas described below correspond to the old historical provinces which closely reflected the country's natural regions. Portugal's present administrative divisions, known as districts, are also given. 👁 *See Provinces and Districts map in The Country Today in Introduction.*

THE NORTH

The old provinces of the Minho and Douro are green and heavily cultivated while the inland regions of Trás-os-Montes, Beira Alta and Beira Baixa are bleaker and drier.

Douro vineyards

G. Sioën/RAPHO

The Minho (Districts: Braga and Viana do Castelo) and the Douro (District: Porto)

The region is part of the tourist area around Oporto and Northern Portugal. The greater part of the Minho and Douro provinces consists of granite hills covered with dense vegetation. The exceptions to these are the bare summits of the Serra do Gerês, Serra do Soajo and Serra do Marão, which make up the Parque Nacional da Peneda-Gerês, and are strewn with rocky scree. The fields, enclosed by hedges and climbing vines, sometimes produce two crops a year. Vineyards, orchards and meadows contribute to the rural economy. Olive, apple and sometimes orange trees grow on the sunniest slopes. Main roads tend to follow lush river valleys like those of the Lima and the Vez. The region, with Porto (in Portuguese, Oporto) as capital, is an active one which has more than a quarter of Portugal's population.

Trás-os-Montes (Districts: Bragança and Vila Real)

Trás-os-Montes means "beyond the mountains". True to its name, this province of high plateaux relieved by rocky crests and deeply cut valleys, stretches out beyond the Serra da Marão and Serra do Gerês. The moorland plateaux, dominated by bare summits and covered with stunted vegetation, are used for sheep grazing. Remote villages merge into the landscape. The more populous river basins around Chaves, Mirandela and Bragança, with their flourishing fruit trees, vines, maize and vegetables, seem like oases in the bleak countryside.

The Alto Douro region in the south contrasts with the rest of the province by its relative fertility. The edges of the plateaux and the slopes down to the Douro and the Tua have been terraced so that olive, fig and almond trees can be grown, and particularly the famous vine which produces the grapes for port wine and *vinho verde*.

The Beira Alta (Districts: Guarda and Viseu) and Beira Baixa (District: Castelo Branco)

This region, the most mountainous in Portugal, is geographically a westward extension of the Spanish Cordillera Central. The landscape consists of a succession of raised rock masses and downfaulted basins. The mountains, of which the principal ranges are the Serra da Estrela and Serra da Lousã, have thickly wooded slopes crowned with rocky summits. Occasional reservoirs fill the sites of ancient glaciary corries or gorges hollowed out of the quartz.

The greater part of the population lives in the Mondego and Zêzere valleys. The Mondego valley, a vast eroded corridor and a main communications route, is rich arable land; on sunny hillsides vines may often be seen extending the vineyards of the Dão region. The Upper Zêzere valley, known as the Cova da Beira, specialises more in livestock, wheras the main town, Covilhã, has an important wool industry.

THE CENTRE

The Beira Littoral (Districts: Coimbra and Aveiro)

This low lying region cut by many water courses corresponds approximately to the lower valleys of the Vouga, the Mondego and the Lis. There are rice fields in the irrigated areas around Soure and Aveiro. The coast consists of long straight beaches and sand dunes anchored by vast pinewoods such as Pinhal de Leiria and Pinhal do Urso, while at Aveiro, the *ria* or lagoon provides an original touch to the scenery. Inland, the cottage gardens of wheat and maize are bordered by orchards and vines. There are also some beautiful forests, including Mata do Buçaco. The region's two main centres are Coimbra with its famous university and Aveiro with its *ria* and salt-pans.

Estremadura (Districts: Leiria, Lisboa and Setúbal)

In the past, this was the southern limit of the lands reconquered from the Moors, hence the name Estremadura which means extremity. Today, the region, which includes the Lisbon area, contains a third of the country's population.

Between Nazaré and Setúbal the countryside is gently undulating. Villages of single storey houses are surrounded by fields of wheat and maize. Olives, vines and fruit trees grow between clumps of pine and eucalyptus.

Along the coast, where tall cliffs and sandy beaches alternate, there are many fishing villages. The Serra de Sintra is a pleasant wooded range near Lisbon, while the Serra da Arrábida, south of the Tagus, provides shelter for small seaside resorts.

The region's activities are centred on Lisbon, the political, administrative, financial and commercial capital.

The Ribatejo (District: Santarém) –

The Riba do Tejo, or banks of the Tagus, is an alluvial plain formed in the Tertiary and Quaternary Eras. On the hills along the north bank, farmers cultivate olives, vines and vegetables. The terraces along the south bank grow wheat and olives. The plain is covered with rice fields, market gardens and above all acres of grassland on which horses and fighting bulls are reared. The region, with its main centre in Santarém, is renowned for its Portuguese-style bullfights known as *touradas*.

THE SOUTH

The Alentejo (Districts: Beja, Évora and Portalegre)

The Alentejo, meaning beyond the Tagus (*Além Tejo*), covers nearly a third

B. Knal/PIX

Alentejo countryside

of the total land area of Portugal. It is a vast flat plain practically without relief, except for the Serra de São Mamede. There is almost no natural vegetation; as a proverb says, "there's no shade in the Alentejo". However, in spite of the difficulties of irrigation, the land is seldom left fallow. The Alentejo, Portugal's granary, is also the region of the cork oak, the ilex (holm oak) and the olive tree; in addition plums are grown around Vendas Novas and Elvas, while sheep and herds of black pigs are still reared on the poorer land. The vast stretches of open countryside dotted with old villages make the region one of Portugal's most attractive.

Traditionally, the region has been one of huge estates centred on a *monte* or large remote whitewashed farmhouse, built on a rise. The other local inhabitants live in villages of low houses with big chimneys. The situation changed after the Carnation Revolution when the land reform of July 1975 split up the estates into smaller **co-operatives**. As this has not been very successful, there has been a return to medium and large scale properties.

The coast is generally uninviting although several seaside resorts are beginning to develop. There are few harbours apart from Sines which is well-equipped.

There are no large towns; Evora with its 35 000 inhabitants acts as the regional capital but lives mainly from tourism.

The Algarve (District: Faro)

Portugal's southernmost province takes its name from the Arabic *El Gharb* meaning "west" for this was in fact the most westerly region conquered by the Moors. The Algarve, separated from the Alentejo by shale hills, is like a garden: flowers grow alongside crops and beneath fruit trees allowing one to see geraniums, camellias and oleanders, cotton, rice and sugar cane as well as carobs, figs and almonds. Many cottage gardens are surrounded by hedges of aloes *(agaves)*. The villages have brightly whitewashed houses with decorative chimneys. To the west rises a mountain range of volcanic rock, the Serra de Monchique, covered in lush vegetation. The coast is very sandy. The *Sotavento* stretch east of Faro is protected by offshore sandbanks, while the *Barlavento* section to the west consists of beaches backed by high cliffs which form an impressive promontory at Cabo de São Vicente.

Over the last few years the Algarve has undergone extensive tourist development, sometimes to the detriment of traditional activities such as fishing, canning, horticulture and the cork industry. Most of the small fishing villages have become vast seaside resorts.

The main towns are Faro, Lagos and Portimão.

Parks and Reserves

There are several conservation areas in Portugal to protect the beauty of the landscape and local flora and fauna.

NATIONAL PARK

Portugal's only national park is that of **Peneda-Gerês** (72 000ha/177 919 acres) in the north *(see Parque Nacional da PENEDA-GERÊS)*.

NATURE RESERVES

Among Portugal's specially protected areas are the nature reserves of **Montesinho** (75 000ha/185 333 acres) near Bragança, **Douro Internacional** (86 500ha/213 741 acres) in a grandiose setting of natural beauty, **Alvão** (7 220ha/17 841 acres) near Vila Real, and **Serra da Estrela** (100 000ha/247 110 acres). Near Fátima are the nature reserves of **Serra de Aire** and **Serra dos Candeeiros** (34 000ha/84 017 acres), which form a beautiful limestone landscape with many caves, **Sintra-Cascais** (23 280ha/57 527 acres), nestled between the ocean and surrounding forest, **Serra da Arrábida** (10 820ha/26 737 acres), **Serra de São Mamede** (3 1750ha/78 457 acres), the **Guadiana valley** (69 600ha/ 171 981 acres) alongside the river of the same name, **Sudoeste Alentejano and Costa Vicentina** (74 7 88ha/184 801 acres), and **Ria Formosa** (18 400ha/45 468 acres), an ecosystem which is home to a variety of rare sea birds. All these nature reserves are in mountainous regions with the exception of the last two, situated in the Algarve, where the aim is to protect coastal areas from the harm caused by mass tourism and the rapid erosion of this coastline.

CONSERVATION AREAS

Many areas have been singled out for the protection of their flora and fauna. Among them are mountainous regions like **Serra de Malcata** (21 760ha/53 771 acres), swamps such as **Paúl de Arzila** (535ha/1 322 acres) and **Paúl do Boquilobo** (530ha/1 310 acres) and river estuaries which have a particularly rich birdlife, including the **Tagus estuary** (14 560ha/35 979 acres), the **Sado estuary** (22 700ha/56 094 acres) and **Sapal de Castro Marim-Vila Real de Santo António** (2 089ha/5 162 acres) in the Guadiana estuary. Dune areas including the **São Jacinto dunes** (666ha/1 646 acres) in Ria de Aveiro and those on the **Berlenga islands** (1 063ha/2 627 acres) off the coast of Peniche have also been designated as conservation areas. Most of the beauty spots in Madeira and the Azores are now classified as conservation areas *(see MADEIRA and the AZORES)*.

PROTECTED LANDSCAPES

Some of Portugal's coastal areas have been declared protected landscapes to prevent uncontrolled building development. They include **Esposende** (440ha/1 087 acres) and the **Costa da Caparica** (1 570ha/3 879 acres), as well as a number of other listed sites around the country.

Vegetation

The diversity of plants in Portugal is a visual reminder of the contrasts in climate and types of soil to be found.

The **robur** and **tauzin oak**, together with **chestnuts**, birches and maples, grow on the wet peaks over 500m/1 500ft.

South of the Tagus and in the Upper Douro valley where summers are very dry, there are dense woods of **ilex** (holm oak) and **cork oak** which grow beside heaths and moorlands sparsely covered with cistus, lavender, rosemary and thyme. Cork oaks are particularly abundant in the Alentejo. Portugal is the world's leading cork producer.

Eucalyptus mainly grows along the coast together with **maritime pines** and umbrella pines which form vast forests beside the beaches near Leiria, Coimbra and Aveiro. Aleppo pines dominate in the Serra da Estrela. Eucalyptus and pines are being planted on ever-increasing areas of land.

Mediterranean plant species acclimatise well in the Algarve where one may see **aloes** *(agaves)* as well as **carob**, **almond**, **fig**, **orange** and **olive** trees.

HISTORY

Until the 11C, Portugal was part of the Iberian Peninsula. The earliest people were of Celtic orgin, but were overrun, in succession, by the Greeks, Carthaginians, Romans, Visigoths and, in 711, the Moors, who remained in control for several centuries. Portugal's first attempt at independence came in 1065, though Spain regained control. In 1143, the country finally emerged as an independent kingdom.

Time Line.

9C-7C BC — The Greeks and the Phoenicians establish trading posts on the coasts of the Iberian Peninsula, inhabited in the west by Lusitanian tribes, originally a Celtiberian population.

3C-2C BC — The Carthaginians master the country; the Romans intervene (Second Punic War) and take over the administration of Lusitania, so named by Augustus. Viriate, chief of the Lusitanians, organises resistance and is assassinated in 139.

5C AD — The Suevi (Swabians) and Visigoths occupy most of the Iberian Peninsula.

MOORISH OCCUPATION

711 — The Moorish invasion from North Africa.

8C-9C — The Christian war of **Reconquest** of the Iberian Peninsula begins at Covadonga in Asturias, led by Pelayo in 718. By the 9C, the region of Portucale, north of the Mondego, has been liberated.

THE KINGDOM FOUNDED

In 1087, Alfonso VI, King of Castile and León, undertakes the reconquest of present-day Castilla-La Mancha. He calls upon several French knights, including Henry of Burgundy, descendant of the French king Hugues Capet, and his cousin Raymond of Burgundy.

When the Moors are vanquished, Alfonso offers his daughters in marriage to the princes. Urraca, heir to the throne, marries Raymond; Tareja (Teresa) brings the county of Portucale, which stretches between the Minho and Douro rivers, as her dowry to **Henry of Burgundy** in 1095. Henry thus becomes Count of Portugal.

Henry dies in 1114; Queen Tareja becomes regent pending the coming

Battle of Aljubarrota, 15C miniature

British Library, London /BRIDGEMAN-GIRAUDON

Sebastião I, the "Regretted"1554-1578

Dom Sebastião came to the throne in 1557 at the age of three. He was educated by a Jesuit priest who instilled in him the old-fashioned values of chivalry which his romantic, proud nature was prone to exacerbate. He believed that a mission had been conferred upon him: namely, to conquer Africa from the Moorish infidels. In 1578, having made the decision to fulfil his destiny, he set sail for Morocco along with 17 000 men and the finest of Portuguese nobility. However, with his soldiers poorly prepared and encumbered by their stately armour under a ruthless sun, his dream was to end in brutal fashion in the muddy reaches of the Malhazin river at Alcácer Quibir, where half of his armada was to die and the other half to be taken prisoner. His body was never found. The Spanish domination which followed encouraged the development of **Sebastianism**, which transformed the young king into a long-awaited Messiah to save Portugal, thus enriching the Portuguese soul with yet another type of nostalgic longing (*saudade*).

Dom Sebastião by Cristóvão Morais, 16C

Museu Nacional de Arte Antiga

of age of her son **Afonso Henriques**. But in 1128 the latter forces his mother to relinquish her power (☞ *see GUIMARÃES*); in 1139 he breaks the bonds of vassalage imposed upon him by Alfonso VII of Castile and proclaims himself King of Portugal under the name Afonso I; Castile finally agrees in 1143.

Afonso Henriques continues the reconquest and after the victory at Ourique (1139) takes Santarém and then Lisbon (1147) with the aid of the Second Crusade's fleet.

The capture of Faro in 1249 marks the end of Moorish occupation.

BURGUNDIAN DYNASTY (1128-1383) – WARS WITH CASTILE

1279-1325 — King Dinis I founds the University of Coimbra and establishes Portuguese, a dialect of the Oporto region, as the official language.

1369-83 — Taking advantage of the trouble in Castile, Fernando I attempts to enlarge his kingdom; in failing he proposes the marriage of his only daughter, Beatriz, to the King of Castile, Juan I.

13 June 1373 — First Treaty of Alliance with England (signed in London).

AVIS DYNASTY (1385-1578) – THE GREAT DISCOVERIES

(☞ *see The Great Discoveries section*)

1385 — Upon Fernando I's death in 1383, his son-in-law Juan of Castile claims the succession; but João, bastard brother of the late king and Grand Master of the Order of Avis is acclaimed to rule; the **Cortes** in Coimbra proclaims him King of Portugal under the name **João I**.

Seven days later, on 14 August, Juan of Castile confronts João of Avis at the **Battle of Aljubarrota** but fails. To celebrate his victory, João builds the monastery at Batalha. He marries Philippa of Lancaster, thus sealing the alliance with England which is to last throughout Portugal's history.

1386 — Treaty of Windsor with England.

1415 — The **capture of Ceuta** in Morocco by João I and his sons, including **Prince Henry**, puts an end to attacks on the Portuguese coast by Barbary pirates and marks the beginning of Portuguese expansion.

1420-44 — Settlement of the Madeira archipelago begins in 1420 and that of the Azores in 1444.

1481-95 — **João II**, known as the Perfect Prince, promotes maritime exploration; however, he mistakenly rejects Christopher Columbus' project. During his reign Bartolomeu Dias rounds the Cape of Good Hope (1488) and the **Treaty of Tordesillas** is signed (1494), dividing the New World into two spheres of influence, the Portuguese and the Castilian.

1492 — Christopher Columbus discovers America.

1495-1521 — Reign of **Manuel I**. In order to marry Isabel, daughter of the Catholic Monarchs of Spain, he has to fulfil the condition of expelling the Jews from Portugal. This he orders in 1497 and Portugal loses a great many traders, bankers and learned men. **Vasco da Gama** discovers the sea route to India in 1498 and **Pedro Álvares Cabral** lands in Brazil in 1500. **Magellan**'s expedition from 1519-22 is the first to circumnavigate the world.

August 1578 — The young king **Sebastião I** is killed and succeeded by his great uncle, Henrique I, whose death marked the beginning of the end of Portugal's supremacy. To ensure Portuguese succession, three of his cousins lay claim to the crown: Dom António, Prior of Crato, the Duchess of Bragança and the King of Spain, Philip II, son of the Infante, Isabel. Philip II, who has won over the rich, gets the upper hand and arrives in Lisbon in 1580. The Prior of Crato seeks support in the Azores (🖰 *see The AZORES*).

SPANISH DOMINATION (1580-1640)

1580 — **Philip II** of Spain invades Portugal and has himself proclaimed king under the name Felipe I. Spanish domination lasts 60 years.

1 Dec 1640 — Uprising against the Spanish; the war of restoration of Portuguese supremacy ensues. Duke João of Bragança takes the title João IV of Portugal; the **Bragança family** remain as the ruling dynasty until 1910.

1668 — Spain recognises Portugal's independence.

THE 18C

1683-1706 — **Pedro II** on the throne.

1703 — Britain and Portugal sign the Methuen Treaty and a trade treaty facilitating the shipping of port to England.

1706-50 — The reign of **João V**, the Magnanimous, is one of untold magnificence – sustained by riches from Brazil – in keeping with the luxurious tastes of a king of the Baroque period. The finest testimony to the period is the monastery at Mafra (🖰 *see MAFRA*).

1 Nov 1755 — An earthquake destroys Lisbon.

1750-77 — **José I** reigns assisted by his minister, the **Marquis of Pombal**. Through the latter's policies, Portugal becomes a model of enlightened despotism. Pombal expels the Jesuits in 1759.

The Napoleonic Wars

Portugal joins the first continental coalition against Revolutionary France in 1793. In 1796 Spain leaves the Convention and allies itself to France. When Portugal refuses to renounce its alliance with England, Spain invades in 1801 and the resulting war is known as the **War of the Oranges**. To ensure a strict application of the blockade on Britain, Napoleon invades Portugal but his commanders have little success in a country supported by English troops under the command of Wellesley.

The future Duke of Wellington prefers guerrilla tactics and finally forces the French from the Peninsula.

Portugal suffers violence and depredations by both armies; and the political and moral effects are tragic along with material poverty. King João VI and his family spend a long exile in Brazil (1807-21).

THE DOWNFALL OF THE MONARCHY

1828-34 — **Civil War between liberals and absolutists**. In 1822 Brazil is proclaimed independent and Pedro IV, older son of João VI, becomes Emperor Pedro I of Brazil. In 1826, on the death of João VI, Pedro I retains the Brazilian throne and leaves the throne of Portugal to his daughter **Maria II**. A charter for a liberal constitution is adopted. Dom Pedro's brother Miguel, who has been appointed regent, champions the cause for an absolute monarchy and lays claim to the crown which he eventually obtains in 1828. A bitter struggle ensues between the absolutists and the liberal supporters of Dom Pedro. Aided by the English, Dom Pedro returns to Portugal to reinstate his daughter on the throne in 1834; the Evoramonte Convention puts an end to the Civil War. In 1836 Maria II marries Prince Ferdinand of Saxe-Coburg-Gotha who becomes king-consort the following year.

1855-90 — In spite of political restlessness during the reigns of **Pedro V** (1855-61), **Luís I** (1861-89) and **Carlos I** (1889-1908), a third Portuguese empire is reconstituted in Angola and Mozambique. The British Ultimatum ends endeavours by the Governor, **Serpa Pinto**, to set up a territorial belt linking Angola and Mozambique.

1899 — Treaty of Windsor.

1 Feb 1908 — Assassination in Lisbon of King Carlos I and the Crown Prince. Queen Amélia manages to save her youngest son who succeeds to the throne as **Manuel II**.

5 Oct 1910 — Abdication of Manuel II and Proclamation of the Republic.

THE REPUBLIC

1910-33 — The Republic cannot restore order. Entering the war against Germany in 1916 and sending troops to France only aggravates the domestic situation. General Carmona calls upon Oliveira Salazar, professor of economics at Coimbra University. **Dr Salazar** is appointed Minister of Finance, then in 1932, Prime Minister: he restores economic and political stability but in 1933 promulgates the Constitution of the New State instituting a corporative and dictatorial regime.

1939-45 — Portugal remains neutral during World War II.

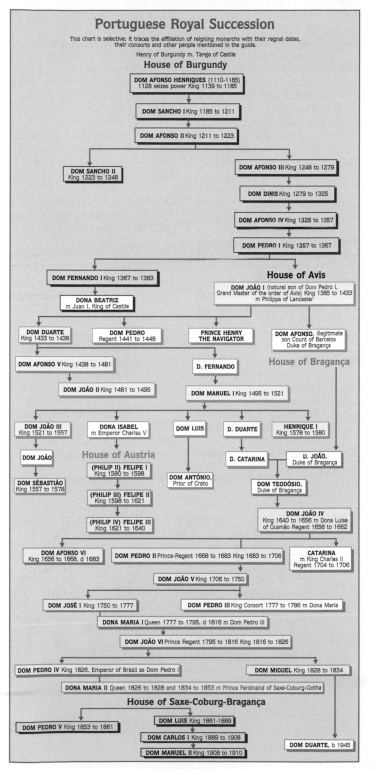

Portuguese Royal Succession

This chart is selective; it traces the affiliation of reigning monarchs with their regnal dates, their consorts and other people mentioned in the guide.

Henry of Burgundy m. Tareja of Castile

House of Burgundy

DOM AFONSO HENRIQUES (1110-1185)
1128 seizes power King 1139 to 1185

DOM SANCHO I King 1185 to 1211

DOM AFONSO II King 1211 to 1223

DOM SANCHO II King 1223 to 1248

DOM AFONSO III King 1248 to 1279

DOM DINIS King 1279 to 1325

DOM AFONSO IV King 1325 to 1357

DOM PEDRO I King 1357 to 1367

DOM FERNANDO I King 1367 to 1383

DONA BEATRIZ m Juan I, King of Castile

House of Avis

DOM JOÃO I (natural son of Dom Pedro I, Grand Master of the order of Avis) King 1385 to 1433 m Philippa of Lancaster

DOM DUARTE King 1433 to 1438

DOM PEDRO Regent 1441 to 1448

PRINCE HENRY THE NAVIGATOR

DOM AFONSO, illegitimate son Count of Barcelos Duke of Bragança

DOM AFONSO V King 1438 to 1481

D. FERNANDO

House of Bragança

DOM JOÃO II King 1481 to 1495

DOM MANUEL I King 1495 to 1521

DOM JOÃO III King 1521 to 1557

DONA ISABEL m Emperor Charles V

DOM LUIS

D. DUARTE

HENRIQUE I King 1578 to 1580

House of Austria

DOM JOÃO

(PHILIP II) FELIPE I King 1580 to 1598

DOM ANTÓNIO, Prior of Crato

D. CATARINA

D. JOÃO, Duke of Bragança

DOM SÉBASTIÃO King 1557 to 1578

(PHILIP III) FELIPE II King 1598 to 1621

DOM TEODÓSIO, Duke of Bragança

(PHILIP IV) FELIPE III King 1621 to 1640

DOM JOÃO IV King 1640 to 1656 m Dona Luisa of Gusmão Regent 1656 to 1662

DOM AFONSO VI King 1656 to 1668, d 1683

DOM PEDRO II Prince-Regent 1668 to 1683 King 1683 to 1706

CATARINA m King Charles II Regent 1704 to 1706

DOM JOÃO V King 1706 to 1750

DOM JOSÉ I King 1750 to 1777

DOM PEDRO III King Consort 1777 to 1786 m Dona Maria

DONA MARIA I Queen 1777 to 1795, d 1816 m Dom Pedro III

DOM JOÃO VI Prince Regent 1795 to 1816 King 1816 to 1826

DOM PEDRO IV King 1826, Emperor of Brazil as Dom Pedro I

DOM MIGUEL King 1828 to 1834

DONA MARIA II Queen 1826 to 1828 and 1834 to 1853 m Prince Ferdinand of Saxe-Coburg-Gotha

House of Saxe-Coburg-Bragança

DOM PEDRO V King 1853 to 1861

DOM LUIS King 1861-1889

DOM CARLOS I King 1889 to 1908

DOM MANUEL II King 1908 to 1910

DOM DUARTE, b 1945

1949 — Portugal is one of the founding members of NATO.

1961 — India annexes Goa, a Portuguese territory since 1515.

1968-70 — Salazar, whose accident near the end of 1968 prevents him from taking part in affairs of state, dies in July 1970. His successor, Caetano, continues a ruinous and unpopular anti-guerrilla war in Africa.

1974 — **Carnation Revolution** (Revolução dos Cravos): the Armed Forces Movement, led by General Spínola, seizes power on April 25. Independence of Guinea-Bissau.

1975 — Independence of Cape Verde Islands, Mozambique, Angola and São Tomé.

1976 — General António Ramalho Eanes is elected President of the Republic. Independence of East Timor. Autonomy is granted to Macau, Madeira and the Azores.

1980 — The conservative party wins the general election. Sá Carneiro forms a government, but dies in a plane crash on 4 December. General Eanes's presidential mandate is renewed.

1986 — Portugal becomes a member of the EEC on 1 January. Mário Soares is elected President on 16 February.

March 1986 — 600 years of friendship between Britain and Portugal celebrated with Queen Elizabeth and Prince Philip's state visit.

1991 — Mário Soares is re-elected president.

1994 — Lisbon chosen as European Capital of Culture.

1996 — Jorge Sampaio elected President of the Republic.

1998 — Lisbon hosts **Expo'98**.

1999 — Portugal converts its currency to the Euro.

2001 — Socialists win elections and Sampaio becomes Premier.

2002 — Another change as Social Democrats take over with José Barroso becoming the leader.

2004 — Barosso resigns to become President of the European Commission. Social Democrat Pedro de Santana Lopes becomes Premier. Portugal hosts the very successful Euro "04 football championships, won by Greece.

2005 — Socialists win over 50% of the parliamentary seats and José Pinto de Sousa becomes Premier.

2006 — Anibál Cavaçao Silva elected President of the Republic.

The Carnation Revolution (1974)

C.Costa Madeira/Arquivo Nacional de Fotografia, Lisboa

The Great Discoveries

On 25 July 1415, some 200 ships under the command of Dom João I and his three sons, including Prince Henry, set sail from Lisbon. The **capture of Ceuta** in Morocco put the Portuguese in control of the Straits of Gibraltar. They hoped the expedition would reward them with gold and slaves from the Sudan.

At the end of the Middle Ages, wealth lay in the hands of the Moors and Venetians, who monopolised the spice and perfume trade from the Orient. To bypass these intermediaries, a sea route had to be found, and Henry the Navigator was to devote his life to this dream.

Prince Henry the Navigator (from a 15C polyptych of the Adoration of St Vincent)

THE SAGRES SCHOOL

Prince Henry the Navigator (1394-1460) retired to the Sagres promontory together with cosmographers, cartographers and navigators to try and work out a sea route from Europe to India. **Madeira** was discovered in 1419 by João Gonçalves Zarco and Tristão Vaz Teixeira, the **Azores** in 1427 (supposedly by Diogo de Silves), and in 1434 **Gil Eanes** rounded **Cape Bojador**, then the farthest point known to western man. Each time they discovered new land the mariners erected a **padrão**, a cairn surmounted by a cross and the arms of Portugal, to mark their presence. Prince Henry inspired new methods of colonisation by setting up **trading posts** *(feitoras)*, exchanges and banks. These offices, set up and run by private individuals, sometimes fostered the development of towns independent of the local powers, such as Goa. Companies were created to control trade in a particular commodity, for which the monopoly rights were often acquired. There were also **deeds of gift**, usually of land, to ships' captains with the proviso that the area be developed. Henry died in 1460, but the stage was set.

THE GREAT DISCOVERIES

The major discoveries were made during the reigns of João II and Manuel I who were both grand nephews of Henry the Navigator. **Diogo Cão** reached the mouth of the Congo in 1482 and the whole coast of Angola then came under Portuguese control. In 1488 **Bartolomeu Dias** rounded the Cape of Storms, which was immediately rechristened the Cape of Good Hope by Dom João II. A few years earlier **Christopher Columbus**, the Genoese navigator mar-

Evanescent Riches

Portugal, however, had overspent its strength; the population had halved from two to one million, many having gone overseas; riches encouraged idlers and adventurers; land was not tilled and wheat and rye had to be imported; crafts and skills were lost; the cost of living rose steeply. Gold was exchanged for goods from the Low Countries and France until Portugal's riches were dissipated and virtually nothing remained. The final blow came on 4 August 1578, when the young King Sebastião I was killed at El-Ksar El-Kebir in Morocco (see History). Two years after his death Portugal came under Spanish control.

ried to a Portuguese, had had the idea of sailing to India by a westerly route. His proposals, rebuffed in Lisbon, found favour with the Catholic Monarchs and in 1492 he discovered the New World. In 1494, under the **Treaty of Tordesillas** and with the Pope's approval, the Kings of Portugal and Castile divided the newly discovered and as yet undiscovered territories of the world between them: all lands west of a meridian 370 sea leagues west of the Cape Verde Islands were to belong to Castile, all east to Portugal. The position of the dividing meridian has led some historians to speculate as to whether Portugal knew of the existence of Brazil even before its official discovery by **Pedro Álvares Cabral** in 1500.

The exploration of the African coast by the Portuguese continued. On 8 July 1497 a fleet of four ships commanded by Admiral **Vasco da Gama** sailed from Lisbon with the commission to reach India by way of the sea route round the Cape. By March 1498 Vasco da Gama had reached Mozambique and on 20 May he landed in Calicut (Kozhicode, southern India): the sea route to India had been discovered. This epic voyage was later

Vasco da Gama, 15C painting

sung in **The Lusiads** *(Os Lusíadas)* by the poet Camões.

In 1501 **Gaspar Corte Real** discovered Newfoundland, but King Manuel was interested primarily in Asia. Within a few years the Portuguese had explored the coastlines of Asia. By 1515 they were in control of the Indian Ocean, thanks to fortified outposts like Goa which had

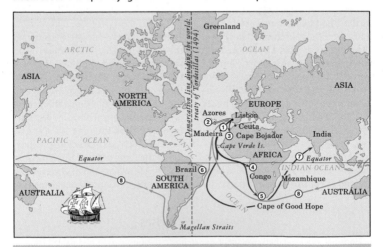

PRINCIPAL PORTUGUESE EXPEDITIONS (1419–1522)

1 Madeira (João Gonçalves Zarco and Tristão Vaz Teixaira, 1419)
2 The Azores (1427)
3 Cape Bojador (Gil Eanes, 1434)
4 Mouth of the Congo River (Diogo), Cão, 1482)
5 Cape of Good Hope (Bartolomeu Dias, 1488)
6 Brazil (Pedro Álvares Cabral, 1500)
7 Mozambique and India (Vasco da Gama, 1498)
8 Circumnavigation of the globe (Magellan's expedition, 1522)

been established by **Afonso de Albuquerque** in 1510.

It was, however, on behalf of the King of Spain that the Portuguese **Fernão de Magalhães** (Magellan) set out in 1519 and landed in India in 1521. Though he was assassinated by the natives of the Philippines, one of his vessels continued the journey to become the first to circumnavigate the world in 1522.

In 1517 King Manuel I sent an ambassador to **China** but this proved a failure and it was not until 1554 that the Portuguese were able to trade with Canton and make contact with Macau. In 1542 the Portuguese arrived in Japan where they caused political upheaval by introducing firearms. The Jesuits, whose Society of Jesus had been founded in 1540, became very active there and by 1581 there were almost 150 000 Christians.The Discoveries had a huge impact on western civilization. New products – the sweet potato, maize, tobacco, cocoa and indigo – were introduced to Europe; gold from Africa and America flooded in through the Tagus. Portugal and Spain became great powers.

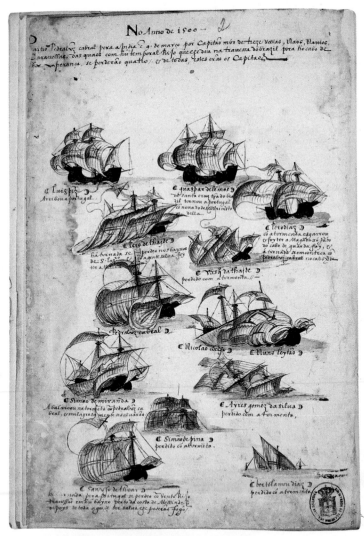

Pedro Álvarez Cabral's armada – Book of the Armadas, 16C

ART AND CULTURE

Architecture

RELIGIOUS ARCHITECTURE

Cross-section of a church

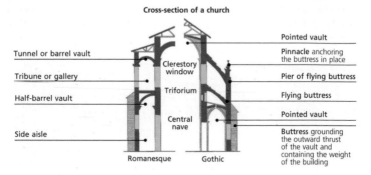

Tunnel or barrel vault

Tribune or gallery

Half-barrel vault

Side aisle

Clerestory window

Triforium

Central nave

Pointed vault

Pinnacle anchoring the buttress in place

Pier of flying buttress

Flying buttress

Pointed vault

Buttress grounding the outward thrust of the vault and containing the weight of the building

Romanesque   Gothic

LISBON – Ground plan of Igreja de Santa Maria (Mosteiro dos Jerónimos), Belém

This church is a **hall-church** (the nave is the same height as the aisles; when these have different heights a distinction is made between the central nave and the aisles).

Coro alto: tribune or gallery (situated here above the entrance) containing the stalls reserved for the clergy

Nave with three aisles: divided lengthways into a **central or main nave** and **side aisles,**

and transversely into **bays**

Transept: transversal aisle separating the chancel from the nave

Porch

Chancel, known as the *capela mor* in Portugal

West portal, or main portal, here situated under the porch

Pillar

South portal

Transept arm

FREIXO DE ESPADA-À-CINTA – South porch of the church

The small parish church is attributed to Boytac and displays the main characteristics of the **Manueline style:** twisted columns interspersed with rings, vegetal decoration and spiral pinnacles. This decoration, an extension of the Mudéjar style, is not unlike the Plateresque style found in Spain. In this church, the style is only evident on the portals, but it later became more popular and could also be found inside buildings and on façades.

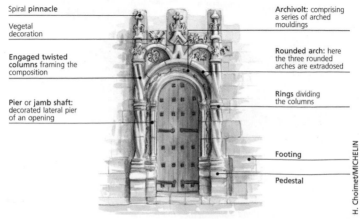

Spiral **pinnacle**

Vegetal decoration

Engaged twisted columns framing the composition

Pier or **jamb shaft:** decorated lateral pier of an opening

Archivolt: comprising a series of arched mouldings

Rounded arch: here the three rounded arches are extradosed

Rings dividing the columns

Footing

Pedestal

H. Choimet/MICHELIN

RATES – Chevet of Igreja de São Pedro (12C–13C)

This church is typical of the Portuguese Romanesque style and is part of the remains of a monastery founded by Henry of Burgundy for the monks of Cluny.

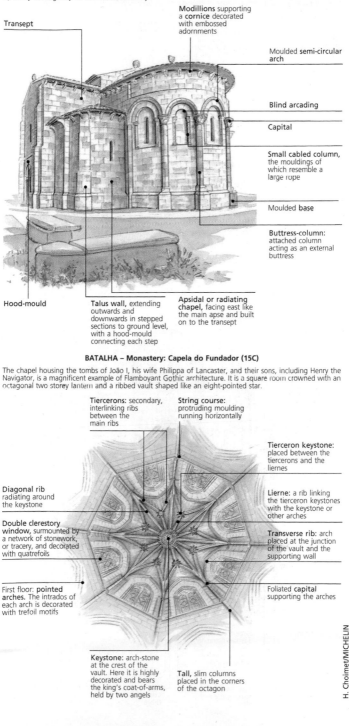

Modillions supporting a **cornice** decorated with embossed adornments

Transept

Moulded **semi-circular arch**

Blind arcading

Capital

Small cabled column, the mouldings of which resemble a large rope

Moulded **base**

Buttress-column: attached column acting as an external buttress

Hood-mould

Talus wall, extending outwards and downwards in stepped sections to ground level, with a hood-mould connecting each step

Apsidal or radiating chapel, facing east like the main apse and built on to the transept

BATALHA – Monastery: Capela do Fundador (15C)

The chapel housing the tombs of João I, his wife Philippa of Lancaster, and their sons, including Henry the Navigator, is a magnificent example of Flamboyant Gothic architecture. It is a square room crowned with an octagonal two storey lantern and a ribbed vault shaped like an eight-pointed star.

Tiercerons: secondary, interlinking ribs between the main ribs

String course: protruding moulding running horizontally

Tierceron keystone: placed between the tiercerons and the liernes

Diagonal rib radiating around the keystone

Lierne: a rib linking the tierceron keystones with the keystone or other arches

Double clerestory window, surmounted by a network of stonework, or tracery, and decorated with quatrefoils

Transverse rib: arch placed at the junction of the vault and the supporting wall

First floor: pointed arches. The intrados of each arch is decorated with trefoil motifs

Foliated capital supporting the arches

Keystone: arch-stone at the crest of the vault. Here it is highly decorated and bears the king's coat-of-arms, held by two angels

Tall, slim columns placed in the corners of the octagon

H. Choimet/MICHELIN

MAFRA – Basilica (18C)

This basilica is a masterpiece of 18C Portuguese architecture, which is heavily influenced by Italian neo-Classicism and German Baroque. It took its inspiration from Saint Peter's in the Vatican and the Gesù Church in Rome.

Twinned transverse arch which supports the barrel vault, decorated with caissons

Cornice with a hood-mould underlined by dentils between two moulded strips

Triangular pediment decorated with a group of sculptures (Christ crucified, the Glory and two angels in adoration)

Rounded arch decorated with flowerets

Pendentive: a concave triangle connecting the surface of the dome and the walls

Lunette: part of a barrel vault which does not extend as far as the keystone and which opens out the upper sections of a bay

Corner piece

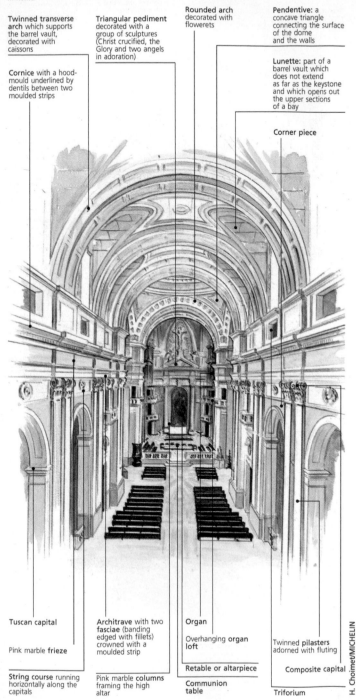

Tuscan capital

Pink marble **frieze**

String course running horizontally along the capitals

Architrave with two **fasciae** (banding edged with fillets) crowned with a moulded strip

Pink marble **columns** framing the high altar

Organ

Overhanging **organ loft**

Retable or altarpiece

Communion table

Twinned **pilasters** adorned with fluting

Composite capital

Triforium

H. Choimet/MICHELIN

CIVIL AND MILITARY ARCHITECTURE

ÓBIDOS – Castle (13C-14C)

The fortress built by the Moors on the site of a Luso-Roman hillfort was considerably modified after the reconquest of Óbidos. However, Arab influence is still evident, particularly in the pyramidal shape of the merlons on the Dom Ferdinand Tower and in the absence of architectural features such as machicolations on the 42ft/13m-high walls.

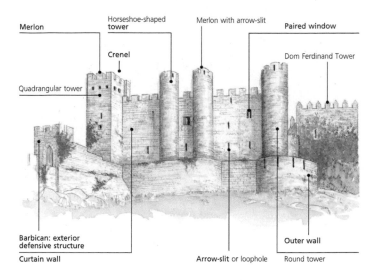

Merlon

Horseshoe-shaped tower

Merlon with arrow-slit

Paired window

Crenel

Dom Ferdinand Tower

Quadrangular tower

Barbican: exterior defensive structure

Outer wall

Curtain wall

Arrow-slit or loophole

Round tower

Mudéjar influence (13C-16C)

After the Christian Reconquest an artistic style developed in the Iberian peninsula which borrowed certain decorative features from Islamic art and which became known as Mudéjar, the name given to Muslims who had remained under Christian rule. In Portugal this influence is particularly noticeable in the **Évora** region, where King Manuel I had a palace built, of which only one pavilion remains.

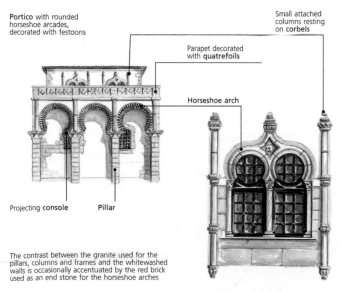

Portico with rounded horseshoe arcades, decorated with festoons

Small attached columns resting on **corbels**

Parapet decorated with **quatrefoils**

Horseshoe arch

Projecting **console**

Pillar

The contrast between the granite used for the pillars, columns and frames and the whitewashed walls is occasionally accentuated by the red brick used as an end stone for the horseshoe arches

Paired windows under rounded horseshoe arches with a curved moulded frame

H. Choimet/MICHELIN

53

GUIMARÃES – Paço dos Duques de Bragança (15C)

Built by the first Duke of Bragança, the palace has been restored to its original appearance and bears traces of both Norman and Burgundian influence. Its defensive character can be seen in the huge corner towers, crenels and covered machicolations. It prefigures the buildings dating from the Renaissance period with their sloping roofs, numerous chimney pots and large windows.

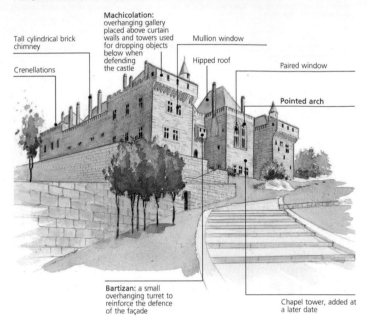

Tall cylindrical brick chimney

Crenellations

Machicolation: overhanging gallery placed above curtain walls and towers used for dropping objects below when defending the castle

Mullion window

Hipped roof

Paired window

Pointed arch

Bartizan: a small overhanging turret to reinforce the defence of the façade

Chapel tower, added at a later date

ÉVORA – Cloisters of the old university (16C)

The former Jesuit university (Antiga Universidade dos Jesuitas) was inspired by the Italian Renaissance. The central triple-bayed avant-corps, flanked by attached pilasters topped by statues, leads to the Sala das Actas (Hall of Acts). Above the central bay a crowned attic ornamented with an escutcheon bears a broken pediment decorated with a group of sculptures. Note the rounded arcades supported by slender columns and a pedestal in the upper gallery and by columns in the portico.

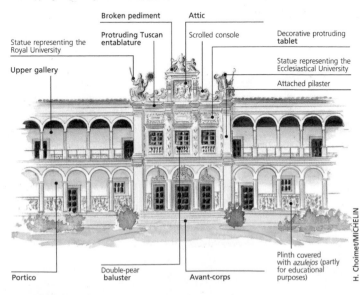

Broken pediment

Attic

Protruding Tuscan entablature

Scrolled console

Decorative protruding tablet

Statue representing the Royal University

Upper gallery

Statue representing the Ecclesiastical University

Attached pilaster

Portico

Double-pear baluster

Avant-corps

Plinth covered with *azulejos* (partly for educational purposes)

H. Choimet/MICHELIN

LISBON – Praça do Comércio (18C)

After the earthquake on 1 November 1755, the Marquis of Pombal decided to demolish and rebuild the Baixa district. Between Terreiro do Paço, renamed Praça do Comércio, and the Rossio, he created a district built on a grid plan, with streets intersecting at right angles where all the buildings had three floors and where just a few decorative features distinguished one street from the next. This new style, partly inspired by the city's architectural past, became known as the **Pombaline style**.

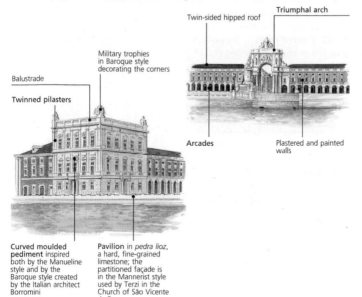

Triumphal arch

Twin-sided hipped roof

Military trophies in Baroque style decorating the corners

Balustrade

Twinned pilasters

Arcades

Plastered and painted walls

Curved moulded pediment inspired both by the Manueline style and by the Baroque style created by the Italian architect Borromini

Pavilion in *pedra lioz*, a hard, fine-grained limestone; the partitioned façade is in the Mannerist style used by Terzi in the Church of São Vicente de Fora

LISBON – Main railway station, Praça do Rossio (19C)

Built in 1886-87 by José Luis Monteiro, the façade of this building, a beautiful example of the neo-Manueline style, conceals an iron structure. The harmony of the three sections on the first floor is achieved through slender polygonal columns which rest on the sloping retaining walls of the ground floor. The crowning aedicule above houses a clock. The decorative elements used (cabling, rings and spiral pinnacles) are typical of the Manueline style.

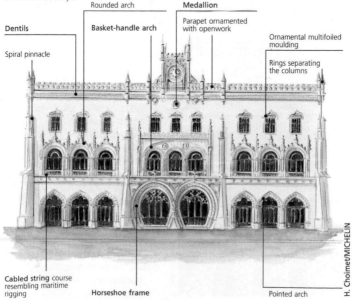

Rounded arch

Medallion

Dentils

Basket-handle arch

Parapet ornamented with openwork

Ornamental multifoiled moulding

Spiral pinnacle

Rings separating the columns

Cabled string course resembling maritime rigging

Horseshoe frame

Pointed arch

H. Choimet/MICHELIN

ARCHITECTURAL TERMS

(**Cadeiral**: *words in bold italics are in Portuguese or Spanish*)

Adufa: A protective lattice screen made of small strips of wood arranged on the outside of windows.

Ajimez: a paired window or opening.

Apse: the generally rounded end of a church behind the altar. The exterior is called the east end.

Altar Mor: the high altar.

Armillary sphere: a globe made up of hoops to show the motions of the heavenly bodies. As the emblem of King Manuel I, it is often portrayed in Manueline art.

Artesonado: a marquetry ceiling in which raised fillets outline honeycomb-like cells in the shape of stars. This particular decoration, which first appeared under the Almohads, was popular throughout the Iberian Peninsula in the 15C and 16C.

Atlas (or **telamon**): support in the form of a carved male figure.

Atrium: a forecourt or open central courtyard in a Roman house.

Azulejos: glazed, patterned, ceramic tiles *(see p 53)*.

Bastion: a projecting part of a fortification built at the angle of, or against the line of, a wall.

Cadeiral: the choir stalls in a church.

M. Chaput/MICHELIN

Campanile: a bell-tower, often detached from the church.

Chicane: a zig-zag passageway.

Chrisma: the monogram of Christ, formed by the Greek capital letters *khi* (X) and *rhô* (P), the first two letters of the word Christos.

Churrigueresque: in the style of the Churrigueras, an 18C family of Spanish architects. Richly ornate Baroque decoration.

Citânia: a term used to describe the ruins of former Roman or pre-Roman settlements on the Iberian Peninsula.

Coro: the part of a chancel containing the stalls and used by canons and other members of the clergy.

Cupola (or **dome**): curved roof, most often hemispherical, crowning the top of a building.

Empedrado: a typical surface covering for Portuguese pavements and streets made from stones of various types and colours to create attractive designs.

Entablature: beam member made up of the architrave, frieze and cornice.

Foliage (or **foliated scrolls**): sculptural or painted ornamentation depicting foliage, often in the form of a frieze.

Gable: the decorative, triangular upper portion of a wall which supports a pitched roof.

M. Chaput/MICHELIN

M. Chaput/MICHELIN

Glacis: an embankment sloping gently down from a fort.

Grotesque: (from *grotta* or *grotto* in Italian); a fantastic or incongruous ornament used in the Renaissance.

Hypocaust: a space under a floor in a Roman house where hot air or furnace gases were used for heating.

Impluvium: a square basin in the atrium of a Roman house for collecting rain water.

Jacente: a funerary statue.

Judiaria: an old Jewish quarter.

Lantern: the part of a dome which opens laterally.

Lavabo: a fountain basin in cloisters used by monks for their ablutions.

Levada: Irrigation channels used to provide water.

Lombard arches: a decorative device in Romanesque architecture consisting of small slightly projecting blind arcades linking vertical bands.

Modillion: a small console supporting a cornice.

Moucharaby: a wooden lattice-work screen placed in front of a window.

Mouraria: a former Moorish district.

Mozarabic: the work of Christians living under Moorish rule after 711. On being persecuted in the 9C, they sought refuge in Christian areas bringing with them Moorish artistic traditions.

Mudéjar: the work of Muslims who remained under Christian rule following the Reconquest. It is used to describe work reminiscent of Moorish characteristics which was undertaken between the 13C and 16C.

Padrão: a stone monument erected by the Portuguese to denote possession of lands they discovered.

Peristyle: a row of columns surrounding a court, garden or façade.

Plateresque: a style that originated in Spain in the 16C and is derived from the word *plata* (silver); it is used to describe finely carved decoration inspired by the work of silversmiths.

Predella: the lower part of a retable.

Púlpito: a pulpit.

Retable: an altarpiece; marble, stone or wood decoration for an altar.

Rinceau: used in painting and sculpture. An ornamental motif of scrolling foliage, usually vine. Often part of a frieze.

Rococo: a late-Baroque style of decoration with asymmetrical patterns involving scroll-work, shell motifs etc.

Sé: a cathedral or episcopal seat; from the Latin *sedes* meaning seat.

Stucco: a type of moulding mix consisting mainly of plaster, used for coating surfaces.

Tree of Jesse: a genealogical tree showing Christ's descent from Jesse through his son David.

Talha dourada: carved, gilded woodwork typical of Portuguese Baroque.

Tracery: intersecting stone ribwork in the upper part of a window, a bay or rose window.

Triptych: a painting or sculpture comprising three hinged panels which can be folded over.

OM PREHISTORY TO THE LATE MIDDLE AGES

Prehistoric sites such as the megaliths around Évora, the rock engravings in the Vale do Côa, as well as Iron Age ruins in Citânia de Briteiros, and the Roman remains at Conímbriga, Tróia and Évora will interest the lover of Antiquity. There are also small pre-Romanesque churches which recall the different architectural influences that swept across the Iberian Peninsula from the north and the east. These influences include Visigothic (Igreja de São Pedro de Balsemão near Lamego and Igreja de Santo Amaro in Beja), Mozarabic (Capela de São Pedro de Lourosa in Oliveira do Hospital) and Byzantine (Capela de São Frutuoso near Braga).

THE MIDDLE AGES (11C-15C)

Romanesque Art

The Romanesque influence arrived in Portugal in the 11C. Brought from France by Burgundian knights and monks, it retained many French traits. Nevertheless, the influence of Santiago de Compostela, particularly in northern Portugal, produced a style more Galician than French which was further enhanced through the use of granite. Monuments have a massive and rough appearance with capitals that show the granite's resistance to the mason's chisel. Cathedrals were rebuilt at the same time as local fortified castles and often resemble them. The cathedrals in Coimbra, Lisbon, Évora, Oporto and Braga are good examples. Country churches, built at a later date, sometimes have richly carved main doorways. The interior design, frequently including pointed arches and even groined vaulting, was often transformed by Manueline or Baroque additions.

Gothic Art

While the Romanesque style blossomed in chapels and cathedrals in the north, Gothic architecture developed most vigorously at the end of the 13C in Coimbra and Lisbon in the form of large monasteries. The churches, designed with a nave and two corresponding aisles with polygonal apses and apsidal chapels, retain the proportions and simplicity of the Romanesque style. The *Mosteiro de Alcobaça* served as a model for the 14C cloisters of the cathedrals in Coimbra, Lisbon and Évora. Flamboyant Gothic found its most perfect expression in the **Mosteiro da Batalha** even though this was only completed in the Manueline period.

Mosteiro da Batalha

Sculpture

Gothic sculpture developed in the 14C for the adornment of tombs, but barely featured as decoration on tympana and doorways. Capitals and cornices were ornamented only with geometric or plant motifs with the exception of a few stylised animals or occasional human forms (capitals in the Mosteiro de Celas in Coimbra). Funerary art flowered in three centres, Lisbon, Évora and Coimbra from where, under the influence of **Master Pero**, it spread into northern Portugal, principally to Oporto, Lamego, Oliveira do Hospital and São João de Tarouca. The most beautiful tombs, those of Inês de Castro and Dom Pedro in the Mosteiro de Alcobaça, were carved from limestone. Coimbra's influence continued into the 15C under **João Afonso** and **Diogo Pires the Elder**. A second centre developed at Batalha inspired by **Master Huguet** (tombs of Dom João I and Philippa of Lancaster).

Military Architecture

The Portuguese, in the wars first against the Moors and then the Spanish, built castles. The first examples mark the successive stages of the **Reconquest**, the second, dating from the 13C to the 17C, guard the major routes of communication. Most of these castles, built in the Middle Ages, are similar in style, double perimeter walls circling a keep or *Torre de Menagem*, crowned with pyramid capped merlons, a trace of the Moorish influence.

THE MANUELINE PERIOD (1490-1520)

The Manueline style marks the transition from Gothic to Renaissance in Portugal. Its name recalls that it flowered during the reign of Manuel I. Despite the brevity of the period in which it developed, the Manueline style's undeniable originality has given it major importance in all aspects of Portuguese art.

It reflects the passion, which inspired all of Portugal at the time, for the sea and of faraway territories which had just been discovered, and manifests the strength and riches accumulating on the banks of the Tagus.

Architecture

Churches remained Gothic in their general plan, in the height of their columns and network vaulting – but novelty and movement appeared in the way columns were twisted to form spirals; triumphal arches were adorned with mouldings in the form of nautical cables; ribs of plain pointed arched vaulting were given heavy liernes in round or square relief; these, in their turn, were transformed by further ornamentation into four-pointed stars or were supplemented by decorative cables occasionally intertwined into mariners' knots. The contour of the vaulting itself evolved, flattening out and resting on arches supported on consoles. The height of the aisles was increased, so giving rise to true hall-churches.

Sculpture

The Manueline style shows its character in the form of decoration. Windows, doorways, rose windows and balustrades are covered with sprigs of laurel leaves, poppy heads, roses, corn cobs, acorns, oak leaves, artichokes, cardoons, pearls, scales, ropes, anchors, terrestrial globes, armillary spheres and lastly the Cross of the Order of Christ which forms a part of every decorative scheme.

Artists

Diogo de Boytac was responsible for the first Manueline buildings, the Igreja do Convento de Jesus at Setúbal, and the cathedral *(sé)* at Guarda. He also contributed to the construction of the Mosteiro dos Jerónimos in Belém, Lisbon, the Igreja do Mosteiro da Santa Cruz in Coimbra and the Mosteiro da Batalha. His artistry lay in magnificent complication: twisted columns, of which he was the master, were covered with overlapping laurel leaves, scales and rings; doorways, which were a major element in Manueline art, stood in a rectangular setting bordered by turned columns crowned with spiralled pinnacles; in the centre of the whole or above it stood the Manueline emblems of the shield, the Cross of the Order of Christ and the armillary sphere.

Mateus Fernandes, whose art was distinctly influenced by the elegance of Flamboyant Gothic, brought a Manueline touch to Batalha. Decoration, which he usually designed as an infinitely repeating plant, geometric or calligraphic motif, takes precedence over volume – the doorway to the Capelas Imperfeitas (Unfinished Chapels) at Batalha is outstanding for the exuberance of its decoration.

Diogo de Arruda was the most original Manueline artist. He designed the famous and marvellously inventive Tomar window. Nautical themes were a positive obsession with this artist.

Francisco de Arruda was the architect of Lisbon's Torre de Belém. He rejected the decorative excesses of his brother, preferring the simplicity of Gothic design embellished with Moorish motifs.

The Arruda brothers were recognised equally as the "master architects of the Alentejo", where they displayed their skill in combining the Manueline style with Moorish themes which gave rise to an entirely new style, the **Luso-Moorish**. This is characterised by the horseshoe arch adorned with delicate mouldings. Most of the seigneurial mansions and castles in the Alentejo, as well as the royal palaces in Sintra and Lisbon, bear the stamp of this style.

Simultaneously, as Manueline architecture was reaching its peak at the end of the 15C, Portuguese sculpture came under Flemish influence due to **Olivier de Gand** and **Jean d'Ypres** – their masterpiece is the carved wooden altarpiece in Coimbra's Sé Velha. **Diogo Pires the Younger** followed, adopting Manueline themes in his work, the best example of which is the font in the Mosteiro de Leça do Bailio (1515).

In the early 16C artists came from Galicia and Biscay to work in northern Portugal. There they helped build the churches at Caminha, Braga, Vila do Conde and Viana do Castelo. The obvious influences in their work are Flamboyant and Spanish Plateresque. From 1517 onwards, two Biscayan artists, **João** and **Diogo de Castilho** worked successively in Lisbon, Tomar and Coimbra. Their art, which had much of the Plateresque style in it, became integrated in the Manueline style (Mosteiro dos Jerónimos).

Window in the Convento de Cristo, Tomar

Y. Travert/DIAF

PAINTING FROM 1450 TO 1550

The Primitives (1450-1505)

The early painters were influenced by Flemish art which was introduced into Portugal partly through the close commercial ties between Lisbon and the Low Countries.

Only **Nuno Gonçalves**, author of the famous **São Vicente polyptych** *(see Museu de Arte Antiga, Lisbon)* remained truly original, not least in the way the picture's composition evoked a tapestry more than a painting. Unfortunately none of his other works are known except for the cartouches for the Arzila and Tangier tapestries which hang in the Collegiate Church of Pastrana in Spain. A group of "masters", including the **Master of Sardoal**, left a good many works which may be seen throughout the country's museums in the sections on Portuguese Primitives. Among the Flemish painters who came to Portugal, **Francisco Henriques** and **Carlos Frei** stand out for their rich use of colour.

The Manueline Painters (1505-50)

The Manueline painters created a true Portuguese School of painting which was characterised by delicacy of design, beauty and accuracy of colour, realism in the composition of the backgrounds, life-size human figures and an expressive naturalism in the portrayal of people's faces tempered, however, with a certain idealism. The major artists in the school worked in either Viseu or Lisbon.

The **Viseu School** was headed by **Vasco Fernandes**, known as Grão Vasco (Great Vasco), whose early works, including the altarpiece at Lamego, reveal Flemish influence. His later work showed more originality, a richness of colour as well as a sense of the dramatic and of composition (as in his paintings from Viseu cathedral which may now be seen in the town's Museu Grão Vasco). **Gaspar Vaz**, whose works can be seen in the Igreja São João de Tarouca, began painting at the Lisbon School, but painted his best pictures while at Viseu.

The **Lisbon School** – established around **Jorge Afonso**, painter for King Manuel I – saw the development of several very talented artists:

♦ **Cristóvão de Figueiredo** evolved a technique which recalls the later impressionists and the use of black and grey in portraiture. His style was imitated by several artists including the Master of Santa Auta in his altarpiece for the original Igreja da Madre de Deus in Lisbon.

♦ **Garcia Fernandes**, archaic in style, showed a preciosity in his portraits.

♦ **Gregório Lopes**, whose line and modelling were harsher, painted

The Annunciation by Frei Carlos

Court life. He excelled in backgrounds which present contemporary Portuguese life in exact detail (altarpiece in the Igreja de São João Baptista in Tomar).

THE RENAISSANCE

The Renaissance style, which retained its essential Italian and French characteristics in Portugal, spread – particularly in sculpture – from Coimbra, where several French artists had settled.

Nicolas Chanterene, whose style remained entirely faithful to the principles of the Italian Renaissance, undertook the decoration of the north door of the Mosteiro dos Jerónimos in Belém before becoming the master sculptor of the Coimbra School. The pulpit in the Igreja da Santa Cruz in Coimbra is his masterpiece. **Jean de Rouen** excelled in altarpieces and low reliefs, as may be seen in the Mosteiro de Celas in Coimbra. **Houdart** succeeded Nicolas Chanterene in 1530 at Coimbra as grand master of statuary. His sculptures are easily recognisable for their realism.

The advance in architecture, which came later than in the other arts, was brought about by native Portuguese: **Miguel de Arruda** introduced a classical note to Batalha after 1533; **Diogo de Torralva** completed the Convento de Cristo in Tomar; **Afonso Álvares** began the transition to classical design by giving buildings a monumental simplicity.

CLASSICAL ART

The classical period saw the triumph of the Jesuit style with **Filippo Terzi**, an Italian architect who arrived in Portugal in 1576, and **Baltazar Álvares** (1550-1624); churches became rectangular in plan and were built without transepts, ambulatories or apses.

Painting came under Spanish influence and produced only two major artists: **Domingos Vieira** (1600-78), whose portraits are vividly alive, and Josefa de Ayala, known as **Josefa de Óbidos** (1634-84). A feeling for classical composition is apparent in the work of the gold and silversmiths of the period. The 17C was marked by the Indo-Portuguese

Museu Nacional de Arte Antiga – L. Pavão/ANF-IPM

style of furniture, typified by marquetry secretaries, rare woods and ivory.

BAROQUE ART (LATE 17C-18C)

The Baroque style, which owes its name to the Portuguese word *barroco* – a rough pearl – corresponds to the spirit of the Counter Reformation.

Architecture

Baroque architecture abandoned the symmetry of the classical style and sought movement, volume, a sense of depth through the use of curved lines and an impression of grandeur. The beginning of Baroque architecture coincided with the end of Spanish domination. In the 17C, architecture took on an austere and simple appearance under **João Nunes Tinoco** and **João Turiano**, but from the end of the century onwards façades became alive with angels, garlands and the interplay of curving lines, particularly at Braga. The architect **João Antunes** advocated an octagonal plan for religious buildings (Igreja da Santa Engrácia in Lisbon). In the 18C King João V invited foreign artists to Portugal. The German **Friedrich Ludwig** and the Hungarian **Mardel**, both trained in the Italian School, brought a monumental style, best be seen in the Mosteiro de Mafra. True Baroque architecture developed in the north and can be seen in both religious and civic buildings (Igreja de Bom Jesus near Braga and Solar de Mateus near Vila Real), where the whitewashed façades contrast with the pilasters and cornices which frame them. In Oporto, **Nicolau Nasoni**, of Italian origin, adorned façades with floral motifs, palm leaves and swags, while in Braga, architecture bordered on Rococo in style (Palácio do Raio in Braga, Igreja de Santa Maria Madalena in Falperra).

Decoration

Azulejos and *Talha Dourada* were popular forms of decoration, the latter being the Portuguese name for the heavily gilded wood used in the adornment of church interiors, including, from 1650 onwards, high altarpieces which were first carved before being gilded. In the 17C altarpieces resembled doorways; on

Baroque detail – Évora Cathedral

either side of the altar, surrounded by a stepped throne, twisted columns rose up while the screen itself was covered in decorative motifs in high relief including vines, bunches of grapes, birds and cherubim. Altarpieces in the 18C were often out of proportion, invading the ceiling and the chancel walls. Entablatures with broken pediments crowned columns against which stood atlantes or other statues. Altarpieces were also surmounted by baldaquins.

Statuary

Many statues, generally in wood, were to be found on the altarpieces which decorated the churches. In the 18C statuary largely followed foreign schools: at Mafra, the Italian **Giusti** and his colleagues instructed many Portuguese sculptors, among them **Machado de Castro**; in Braga, Coimbra and Oporto, **Laprade** represented the French School; at Arouca, the Portuguese **Jacinto Vieira** gave his carvings a very personal, lively style. The idea of the Baroque cribs *(presépios)*, that can be seen in many churches, originate from southern Italy. In Portugal they are more naive but not without artistic merit. The figures in terracotta are often by **Machado de Castro, Manuel Teixeira** or **António Ferreira**. The talent of the Baroque sculptors is also evident in the many fountains found throughout Portugal especially in the Minho region. The monumental staircase of Bom Jesus near Braga is made up of a series of fountains in the Rococo style.

Painting

Painting is represented by **Vieira Lusitano** (1699-1783) and **Domingos António de Sequeira** (1768-1837), the latter a remarkable portraitist.

LATE 18C-19C

Architecture

The second half of the 18C saw a return to the classical style, seen in the work of **Mateus Vicente** (1747-86 – Palácio Real in Queluz), **Carlos da Cruz Amarante** (Igreja de Bom Jesus), and the Lisbon architects, particularly **Eugénio dos Santos** who created the Pombal style. In the late 19C when the Romantic movement favoured a revival of former styles, Portugal developed the neo-Manueline, an evocation of the period of the Great Discoveries exemplified by the Castelo da Pena in Sintra, the Palace-Hotel in Buçaco and the Estação do Rossio in Lisbon. At the time *azulejos* were being used to decorate entire house façades.

Sculpture

Soares dos Reis (1847-89) tried to portray the Portuguese *saudade* or nostalgia in sculpture; his pupil, **Teixeira Lopes** (1866-1918), revealed an elegant technique, particularly when portraying children's heads.

Painting

Portuguese painters discovered the naturalistic approach from the Barbizon school in France. Two painters, **Silva Porto** (1850-93) and **Marquês de Oliveira** (1853-1927) followed the Naturalist movement, while **Malhoa** (1855-1933), the painter of popular festivals, and **Henrique Pousão** (1859-84) were closer to Impressionism; **Sousa Pinto** (1856-1939) excelled as a pastel artist and **Columbano Bordalo Pinheiro** (1857-1929) achieved distinction with his portraits and still-life paintings.

20C

Architecture

The influence of Art Nouveau may be seen in buildings in Lisbon, Coimbra and Leira, while one of the finest examples of Art Deco in Portugal is the Casa de Serralves in Oporto. In the 1930s, the architect **Raúl Lino** built the Casa dos Patudos in Alpiarça, near Santarém. However, it was only in the 1950s that

Musée d'Art moderne, Paris/GIRAUDON © ADAGP 1998

The Game of Chess by Vieira da Silva

a noticeable development in housing came about which may be seen in council houses, garden cities and buildings like the Museu Gulbenkian in Lisbon. The Oporto School of architecture stands out for the modernism it advocates with internationally known architects such as **Fernando Távora** (b 1923) and **Álvaro Siza** (b 1933) who was commissioned to restore the Chiado quarter in Lisbon after it was partly destroyed by fire in 1988. The main architectural event in Lisbon in the 1980s was the construction of the post-modern Torres das Amoreiras designed by **Tomás Taveira**.

Sculpture

Francisco Franco (1885-1955) held great sway over the official sculpture of the period, including the commemorative monuments so popular under Salazar. More recently, **João Cutileiro** has come to prominence with his original collection of statues (Dom Sebastião in Lagos, and Camões in Cascais), while **José Pedro Croft** (stonework), **Rui Sanches** (woodwork) and **Rui Chafes** (metal) are all contemporary artists who adhere to a more conceptual style of sculpture (installations).

Painting

In the early 20C Portuguese painting mainly stuck to Naturalism; only a few artists diverged to follow the general trend; **Amadeo de Souza Cardoso** (1887-1918), a friend of Modigliani, worked in Paris assimilating the lessons of Cézanne and found his true expression first in Cubism then in a highly coloured variant of Expressionism; his friend **Santa Rita** (1889-1918), who died unexpectedly, made a great contribution to the Portuguese Futurist movement but destroyed much of his work. **Almada Negreiros** (1889-1970) was influenced by Cubism while at the same time remaining a classical draughtsman. He was also a poet and playwright. He painted the large frescoes in Lisbon's harbour stations in 1945 and 1948. **Maria Helena Vieira da Silva** (1908-92), who moved to Paris in 1928, derived her art from the Paris School, although in her space paintings the azulejo influence may be seen.

Among the best known contemporary painters are **Paula Rego** (b 1935), who draws upon Op-Art, **Júlio Pomar**, Lourdes Castro, **José de Guimarães** and, more recently, Julião Sarmento, Pedro Cabrita Reis, Alberto Carneiro (installations), Pedro Calapez (abstraction and volumetric forms), Álvaro Lapa, Pedro Portugal, Pedro Casquiero (abstraction), Graça Morais and Pedro Proença (allegorical images).

Azulejos

Ever since the 15C the *azulejo* has been a component of the different styles of Portuguese architecture that have followed one another through the centuries.

There is some controversy as to the etymological origin of the word *azulejo*; some say it comes from *azul* meaning blue, others that it in fact derives from the Arabic *az-zulay* or *al zuleich* which means a smooth piece of terracotta.

Origin

The first *azulejos* came from Andalucía in Spain where they were used as decoration in *alcázars* and palaces. They were introduced into Portugal by King Manuel I who, having been dazzled by the Alhambra in Granada, decided to have his Sintra palace decorated with these rich ceramic tiles. *Azulejos* at that time took the form of **alicatados**, pieces of monochrome glazed earthenware cut and assembled into geometric patterns. The process was superseded by that of the **corda seca** in which a fine oil and manganese strip were used to separate

15C Armillary Sphere

Museu Nacional do Azulejo – F. Matias/ANF-IPM

Nossa Senhora da Vida (detail), 16C

17C tapete style

the different enamels, and when fired, blackened to form an outline for the various motifs. Another method for separating the motifs was known as **aresta** and consisted of drawing ridges in the clay itself. In the 16C the Italian Francesco Nicoloso introduced the Italian **majolica** technique, in which the terracotta was covered with a layer of white enamel which could then be coloured. *Azulejos* thus developed into another type of artistic medium with a wide range of decorative possibilities. The Portuguese created a standard square with 14cm/5.5in sides and opened their own workshops in Lisbon.

Renaissance and Mannerist styles

Towards the middle of the 16C Flemish influence took precedence over Spanish, and more complex *azulejo* panels were used to decorate churches; the transept in the Igreja São Roque in Lisbon is a good example. *Azulejos* were in great demand for decorating summer houses and gardens. The finest examples may be seen at Quinta da Bacalhoa and date from 1565. They consist of wonderful multicoloured panels with an Italian majolica-ware quality, which illustrate allegories of great rivers. The panel of Nossa Senhora da Vida, in the Museu do Azulejo in Lisbon, dates from the same period.

17C

Portugal entered a period of austerity under Spanish domination. In order to decorate church walls without incurring great expense, simple monochrome tiles were used and placed in geometric patterns. The Igreja de Marvila in Santarém is a fine example. A style known as *tapete*, a sort of tile-carpet or tapestry, was developed, repeated in blocks of four, 16 or 36 tiles, which resembled oriental hangings on account of their geometric or floral patterns.

The restoration of the monarchy was followed by a period of great creative development. There was a return to figurative motifs on panels with illustrations of mythological scenes or caricatures of contemporary society life. Traditional blues and yellows were enhanced by greens and purples; there are fine examples at the Palácio dos Marqueses da Fronteira in Lisbon. Little by little, multicoloured tiles gave way to cobalt blue motifs on a white enamel background as may be seen in the Victory Room of the Palácio dos Marqueses da Fronteira.

18C

Tiles in the 18C were almost exclusively blue and white. This fashion developed from Chinese porcelain, popular at the time of the Great Discoveries. *Azulejos* were decorated by true artists and mas-

18C panel

ters including **António Pereira**, **Manuel dos Santos** and especially **António de Oliveira Bernardes** and his son **Policarpo**. Their works include the Capela dos Remédios in Peniche, the Igreja de São Lourenço in Almansil and the Forte de São Filipe in Setúbal.

The reign of João V (1706-50) was characterised by magnificence, with gold from Brazil funding all manner of extravagance. The taste of the day was for dramatic effect which expressed itself particularly well in *azulejos*. Panels became veritable pictures, with surrounds of intermingling festoons, tassels, fluttering angels and pilasters – the **Baroque style** in full bloom. The main artists at the time were **Bartolomeu Antunes** and **Nicolau de Freitas**. The second half of the 18C was marked by the **Rocaille style** (rock and shell motifs). There was also a return to polychromy with yellow, brown and purple being the dominant colours; painting became more delicate; smaller motifs were popular and frames were decorated with scrolls, plant motifs and shells as may be seen at the Palácio de Queluz, particularly along the Grand Canal. The opening of the Fábrica Real de Cerâmica in Rato in 1767 meant that *azulejos* could be manufactured in great quantity. The **neo-Classical style** during the reign of Maria I is notable for the refreshing subject matter of its tiles which were framed by garlands, pilasters, urns and foliage.

Literature

While remaining open to outside influences which are quickly and successfully assimilated, Portuguese literature is nonetheless original and reflects the lyrical and nostalgic spirit – the famous *saudade* of the people, as in the *fado*. Poetry has always held a privileged position with, as a figurehead, the monumental work of Camões.

The Middle Ages
The earliest known Portuguese literature dates from the late 12C with the poetry of the troubadours, influenced by Provençal lyricism. There were **Cantigas de Amor** for male voices, the more popular **Cantigas de Amigo** and the satirical **Cantigas de Escárnio e Maldizer** which were collected in anthologies or *cancioneiros*. The most famous of these, the *Cancioneiro Geral,* compiled by the Spaniard Garcia de Resende in the 16C, covered all the poetry written in Portuguese and Castilian over more than a century. King Dinis I, a poet himself, imposed the official use of Portuguese in the 13C. Dom Pedro was the major literary figure of the 14C. However, **Fernão Lopes** (born c 1380-1390), the chronicler of Portuguese kings and queens *(Chronicles of Dom Pedro, Dom Fernando, Dom João I and Dom Dinis)*, is considered *the* great name in medieval literature.

The Renaissance
The 16C introduced humanism and a revival of poetry and dramatic art which can be seen at its best in works by **Francisco Sá de Miranda** (1485-1558), **Bernardim Ribeiro** (1500-52), author of the

BOYER-VIOLLET

So we ploughed our way through waters
where none save Portuguese had ever sailed before.
To our left were the hills and towns of Morocco,
the abode once of the giant Antaeus;
land to our right there was none for certain,
though report spoke of it.
And now our course took us into regions and past
islands already discovered by the great Prince Henrique.

Luís de Camões
The Lusiads, Canto V

famous novel *Child and Damsel (Menina et Moça)*, **António Ferreira** (1528-69) in his *Lusitanian Poems (Poemas Lusitanos)* and *Castro*, and especially **Gil Vicente** (1470-1536), a great dramatist whose 44 plays painted a satirical picture of Portuguese society in the early 16C.

The greatest figure of the period, however, remains **Luís de Camões** or Camoens (1524-80) who, having demonstrated his virtuosity of verse in *The Lyric (A Lírica)*, shows himself to be the poet of the Great Discoveries in his vast portrait of *The Lusiads (Os Lusíadas*, 1572), which relates the epic voyage of Vasco da Gama in a similar way to the *Odyssey*. He led an adventurous life, which took him to Morocco (where he lost an eye) and to Goa.

Classicism

During the 60 years of Spanish domination, Portuguese literature was confined to the Academies in Lisbon and the provinces; Baroque affectation prevailed, but at the same time "Sebastianism" developed, a belief in the return of King Sebastião and the restoration of the country's independence. Much of the literary output consisted of chronicles and travel narratives including work by **Fernão Mendes Pinto** (1509-83) who wrote *Peregrination (Peregrinação)*. The Jesuit **António Vieira** (1608-97) revealed the growing personality of the immense colony of Brazil in his sermons and letters as a missionary.

18C

The Age of Enlightenment was represented in Portugal by scholars, historians and philosophers. Theatre and poetry came under French influence. **Manuel MB do Bocage** (1765-1805), of French descent, was the great lyric and satirical poet of this century.

19C

Romanticism took a firm hold thanks to **Almeida Garrett** (1799-1854), who was not only a poet (*Fallen Leaves – Fôlhas Caídas* and *Flores Sem Fructo*) and master of a whole generation of poets, but also a theatre reformer, playwright *(Frei Luís de Sousa)* and novelist *(Travels in My Homeland – Viagens na Minha Terra)*.

The century's other outstanding poets included **António F de Castilho** *(Amor e Melancolia)* and **João de Deus**. **Alexandre Herculano** (1810-77) introduced the historical novel and his *História de Portugal* was a great success. Among fellow historians, mention should be made of **Oliveira Martins**. The transition to realism came about with work by **Camilo Castelo Branco** (1825-90) whose best-known novel *Fatal Love (Amor de Perdição)* gives an account of society at the time. The end of Romanticism was signalled by the work of the Azorian **Antero de Quental** (1842-91), whose *Odes Modernas* were an instrument of social unrest. **Eça de Queirós** (1845-1900), a diplomat and a novelist, made a critique of the morals of his day through his works *(Cousin Bazilis, The Maias, Barbaric Prose, The Sin of Father Amaro (O Primo Basílio, Os Maias, Prosas Bárbaras, O Crime do Padre Amaro)*. **Guerra Junqueiro** (1850-1923) wrote satirical and controversial poems.

Contemporary authors

Fernando Pessoa (1888-1935), a complex and precursory genius, revived Portuguese poetry by using different names and personae, among them Ricardo Reis, Álvaro de Campos, Alberto Caeiro and Bernardo Soares, which enabled him to express himself in different styles. His *Book of Disquietude (Livro do Desassossego)* was published forty years after his death. Among his con-

Fernando Pessoa by Almada Negreiros (1964)

Fondation Gulbenkian, Paris

temporaries and successors mention should be made of his friend **Mario de Sá Carneiro**, who committed suicide at the age of 26 leaving some very fine poems, **José Régio** (*Poems of God and the Devil – Poesias de Deus e do Diabo*), **Natália Correia, António Ramos Rosa** and **Herberto Helder**. Among the main novelists are **Fernando Namora** (*The Wheat and the Chaff – O Trigo e O Joio*), **Ferreira de Castro** (1898-1974), who drew upon his experiences during a long stay in Brazil (*The Jungle* and *The Mission – A Selva, A Missão*), **Carlos de Oliveira** (1921-81), who wrote about life in small villages (*Uma Abelha na Chuva*), **Manuel Texeira Gomes** (*Letters with No Moral – Cartas sem nenhuma moral*), **Urbano T. Rodrigues** (*Bastards of the Sun – Bastardos do Sol*), **Agustina Bessa Luís** (*The Sibyl – A Sibila* and *Fanny Owen*), as well as regionalist authors like **Aquilino Ribeiro** and **Miguel Torga**. **Vergílio Ferreira** first wrote neo-realistic novels before adopting a very personal style in which he tackles existential problems (*Aparição*).

Over the last few decades Portuguese literature has undergone a veritable revival with writers such as **José Cardoso Pires** (*Ballad of Dog's Beach – Balada da Praia dos Cães*), **Lídia Jorge** (*A Costa dos murmúrios, Notícia da Cidade Silvestre*), **Vitorino Nemésio** and his beautiful novel *Mau Tempo no Canal* which takes place in the Azores, **António Lobo Antunes** (*South of Nowhere* and *An Explanation of the Birds – O Cús de Judas, Explicação dos Pássaros*), **Sofia de Melo Breyner**, whose work is mainly poetical and in a similar vein to **Nuno Júdice** (*Theory of Sentiment, A Field in the Depths of Time*), and Nobel Prize-winner **José Saramago**, who mixes all the great legends and figures of Portuguese history, including João V and Fernando Pessoa in his novels (*Memorial do Convento, The Year of the Death of Ricardo Reis, The Gospel According to Jesus Christ*).

Mention should also be made of the philosopher **Eduardo Lourenço** (*O Labirinto da Saudade*), **Eugénio de Andrade**, a major, prolific post-war poet, **Almeida Faria** who writes about memory, exile and nostalgia, and **Maria Judite de Carvalho** who is continuing her demanding work (*Os Armários Vazios*).

The former Portuguese colonies, particularly Brazil, contribute greatly to Lusitanian literature with authors such as **Jorge Amado**, José Lins do Rego etc. Angola also has a tradition of great storytellers and poets such as Luandino Vieira (*Velhas Estórias, Nós os de Makuiusu*), Pepetela (*As Aventuras de Ngunga*) and José Eduardo Águalusa (*A Nação Crioula, A Estação da Chuva*), as has Mozambique, with Mia Couto (*A Varanda do Frangipani, Contos do Nascer da Terra*) and Luís Carlos Patraquim (*Litemburgo Blues*). In Cape Verde the philologist Baltazar Lopes (*Chiquinho*) and the storyteller Manuel Lopes (*Os Flagelados do Vento Leste*) bear witness to the literary wealth of these West African islands.

Cinema

During the 1930s and 1940s the development of Portuguese cinema was marked by popular-based themes, rural films and moralistic comedies with leading actors

---

José Saramago, Winner of the 1998 Nobel Prize for Literature

Born in 1922 in Azinhaga, near Santarém, José Saramago lived in Lisbon from the age of three. He worked in a number of jobs (mechanic, draughtsman, social security employee, editor, translator and journalist) before publishing his first novel (*Terra do Pecado*) in 1947. He then worked for a publishing house and was the literary critic for the *Seara Nova* magazine. His second book, *Os Poemas Possíveis*, was not published until 1966, although his great literary success came in the 1980s with *Memorial do Convento* (1982), which retraces the construction of the Mafra monastery, *The Year of the Death of Ricardo Reis* (1984), *The Stone Raft* (1986), *History of the Siege of Lisbon* (1989) and *The Gospel According to Jesus Christ* (1991).

such as Beatriz Costa and António Silva. The ideology of the Salazar regime then began to dominate with the almost-official producer António Lopes Ribeiro. From the 1950s onwards, directors became a fundamental part of Portuguese cinema, which became known for its creativity and independence, while the 1960s were marked by the exodus of young Portuguese to France and Great Britain to study cinema. The best known directors of the time were **Paulo Rocha**, who was Jean Renoir's assistant, **Fernando Lopes** (Belarmino) and **António de Macedo** (Domingo à tarde). Paulo Rocha distinguished himself in 1963 with The Green Years (Verdes Anos) which made a break with films under the dictatorship and was the precursor for the "Cinema Novo" (New Cinema) movement, the equivalent of "New Wave" in France. He then went on to film in Japan (The Island of Loves – A Ilha dos Amores and The Mountains of the Moon – As Montanhas da Lua). Many directors returned to Portugal after the Carnation Revolution to make films with a militant, political bent, such as O Recado, which was produced during the dictatorship by **José Fonseca e Costa**. Other important directors of the period include **António Reis** (Jaime), **António Pedro de Vasconcelos** (O lugar do Morto) and **Lauro António** (A manhã Submersa).

The new generation of directors in the 1980s and 1990s imparted a certain artistic quality to Portuguese cinema. These directors set themselves apart by their great originality and include names such as **Joaquim Pinto**, **João Mário Grilo** (O Processo do Rei, Longe da Vista), **João Botelho** (A Portuguese

Farewell – Um Adeus Portugûes, Three Palm Trees – Três Palmeiras and Tráfico), **João César Monteiro** (Recollections of the Yellow House – Recordações da Casa Amarela and God's Comedy – A Comédia de Deus), **Pedro Costa** (O Sangue, A Casa da Lava and Ossos) and **Teresa Vilaverde** (Os Mutantes).

Portuguese cinema is dominated abroad by the extraordinary personality of **Manoel de Oliveira**, born in 1908. His early films were dedicated to his home town, Oporto, where he filmed from 1931 onwards. Later he turned to more imaginary themes and mainly drew upon Portuguese literature with works by Camilo Castelo Branco (Fatal Love – Amor de Perdição and The Day of Despair – O Dia do Desespero), and Agustina Bessa Luís (Francisca, adapted from Fanny Owen, which he co-wrote), as well as a number of Italian works such as Dante's Divine Comedy. French literature also provided him with inspiration, including Le Soulier de Satin by Paul Claudel, Valley of Abraham (Vale Abraão), inspired by Flaubert's Madame Bovary, and La Lettre, an adaptation of La Princesse de Clèves by Madame de Lafayette, and winner of the Prix du Jury at the 1999 Cannes Film Festival. Luís Miguel Cintra and Leonor Silva are actors who have frequently figured in his films, as have international stars such as Catherine Deneuve and John Malkovitch (The Convent), Michel Piccoli and Irène Papas (Party), and Chiara Mastroianni (La Lettre).

THE PORTUGUESE LANGUAGE

Portuguese is a Romantic language originating from Latin. Although the syntax and etymology are similar to Castilian, the pronunciation is totally different, being closer to French for letters such as j, c, z, ç and ch, but dissimilar with regard to its palato-alveolar fricatives (the pronunciation of s as sh), its nasals and its sibilants. With a very rich and expressive vocabulary, Portuguese lends itself very well to poetry and fado. More than 180 million people worldwide speak Portuguese; it is the seventh most widely spoken language.

Cinemateca Portuguesa

Valley of Abraham – film by Manoel de Oliveira

THE COUNTRY TODAY

Portugal today has a thriving economy, as seen from the vast amount of construction work in progress. It has become a vital part of the European Union and continues to play its part in the world economy. Tourism is of great importance, and the infrastructure within the country, so crucial to tourism, continues to be developed and modernised.

Economy

At the time of the 1974 Carnation Revolution, Portugal had fallen behind many of its European neighbours. Lack of investment in the country's industry and infrastructure under the Salazar regime was the cause, even though Portugal had significant gold reserves originating mainly from its mining concerns in its former colonies. Traditional activities, such as agriculture and fishing still formed the basis of the country's economy until its membership of the European Economic Community in 1986, which marked a transitional point in Portugal's development, thanks in part to EEC aid. Today Portugal remains one of the world's largest producers of wine and is the leading producer of cork – while leading industries in the industrial and transformation fields include shoe, textile and paper production, car manufacturing, metallurgy and mechanical engineering. Tourism is still very important.

Government

The **Constitution** promulgated on 2 April 1976 brought in a semi-presidential form of government. **Executive power** is held by the **President of the Republic** who is elected by universal suffrage for a five-year term (renewable once). The president appoints the **Prime Minister**, who represents the Parliamentary majority,

and, on his suggestion, the rest of the government. The revised Constitution of 1982 has limited the president's powers although he retains the right to veto laws approved by straight majority vote in the Assembly. **Legislative power** is held by a single Chamber of between 240 and 250 members who are elected for four years. The archipelagos of Madeira and the Azores are Autonomous Regions with their own Regional

PROVINCES AND DISTRICTS

○ Braga   District boundaries and capitals

MINHO   The old provinces

The Portuguese Flag

The green vertical stripe at the hoist and red stripe in the fly are divided by an armillary sphere bearing the Portuguese coat of arms. The sphere supports a white shield with five blue shields, each with five white disks symbolising Christ's wounds. The seven yellow castles represent the strongholds retaken from the Moors.

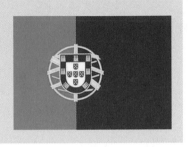

Government and Regional Assembly. The Assembly is elected by universal suffrage. The President of the Republic appoints a **Minister of the Republic** for each of the autonomous regions, who then appoints a **Regional Government President**.

ADMINISTRATIVE ORGANISATION

The old historical provinces of the Minho, Trás-os-Montes, Douro, Beiras (Alta, Baixa and Litoral), Ribatejo, Estremadura, Alentejo and Algarve no longer fulfil an administrative role but still denote the main regions of the country.

Portugal's present administrative organisation is as follows:

- **Distritos**: There are 18 districts in mainland Portugal, three in the Azores and one in Madeira. Health, education and finance are managed at district level.

- **Concelhos**: These councils represent municipal authority. There are 305 in all. A *concelho* is similar to a district borough or a canton. Each one has a town hall or *Paço do Concelho* and an executive committee or *Câmara Municipal* led by a president who acts as mayor. Both the president and the municipal assembly are elected by universal suffrage every four years.

- Lastly, each *concelho* consists of several **freguesias**, the smallest administrative unit, some of which represent a village, and others a district. There are approximately 4 200 *freguesias* in Portugal, responsible for keeping public records, civil status, the upkeep of natural heritage, and organising festivals and other local events.

Architectural Traditions

DOMESTIC ARCHITECTURE

Portugal has preserved different styles of traditional housing; these styles are most apparent in the Alentejo and the Algarve.

The North

The most popular building material is granite. Houses are massive with tiled roofs. As chimneys are very small or even non-existent, the smoke has to escape through gaps in the roof, the doorway or the windows. The outside stairway leads to a stone balcony or verandah large enough to be used as a living room.

On country estates in the Douro valley, simple cottages stand alongside elegant manor-houses *(solares)*, which are often whitewashed.

The Centre: Estremadura and Beira Litoral

The limestone used in the region's houses adds a pleasant touch to their appearance. The façades are often ornamented with cornices and stucco; outside staircases have disappeared.

Alentejo

The houses, built to shelter the inhabitants from the summer glare and heat, are low-lying single storey structures with whitewashed walls and small doors and windows. Nevertheless, the winters

Alentejo

R. Corbel

Algarve

R. Corbel

are so harsh that huge square or cylindrical chimneys are a local feature. Building materials vary according to the region: usually *taipa* (dried clay), or adobe (mud mixed with cut straw and dried in the sun), which was used in Moorish times. Bricks are used for decorative features, for chimneys, crenellations and verandahs, while around Estremoz marble is common.

The Algarve

The white houses squat low, several juxtaposed cubes making up each dwelling. The white flat-roofed houses in Olhão and Fuseta resemble the villages of North Africa. Very occasionally the terrace is replaced by a four-sided peaked roof, *telhado de tesoura*, which some attribute to a Chinese influence. Peaked roofs are mostly to be seen in Faro, Tavira and Santa Luzia. Chimneys are slender and elegant, gracefully pierced, painted white or built of brick laid in decorative patterns, crowned

with a ball, a finial, a vase, or an ornament of some kind.

Madeira and the Azores

In Madeira, traditional mountain dwellings have a thatched roof with two eaves which descend right down to the ground, thus covering the whole house. The main door on the front of the house is flanked by two small windows, with an occasional third one above it. All these openings are set into the wall with colourful surrounds. Houses in the Azores are similar to those in the Algarve, offering a reminder of the islands' first inhabitants. The Empires *(Impérios)* of the Holy Ghost are brightly-coloured original buildings, similar in style to chapels, which have large windows and are used to house objects for the worship of the Holy Ghost.

R. Corbel/MICHELIN

Minho

Madeira

R. Corbel

TRADITIONAL URBAN FEATURES

Pavements

Throughout the country and even in Madeira and the Azores, pavements and squares are paved with beautifully patterned compositions of alternating blocks of black basalt, golden sandstone, white limestone and grey granite. These are known as **empedrados**.

Windmills (Moinhos)

There were about 2 000 windmills in Portugal several years ago but most have now been abandoned and are in ruins. They may still be seen on hilltops around Nazaré, Óbidos and Viana do Castelo. Those most common today are the Mediterranean type in which a cylindrical tower built of stone or hard-packed clay supports a turning conical roof bearing a mast. The mast carries four triangular sails.

Stone monuments (Padrões)

These public monuments, memorials bearing the cross and the arms of Portugal, were erected by Portuguese explorers when they reached new lands. They may be seen in former colonies and in Madeira and the Azores.

Handicrafts

Portugal's arts and crafts are remarkably varied and unpretentious. The weekly markets held in most towns give a good idea of the skill of Portuguese craftsmanship.

Ceramics and pottery

There are many village potters *(olarios)* producing domestic and decorative earthenware which varies in shape and colour according to the region. In Barcelos, pots are glazed, colours bright with ornamentation consisting of leaves, stems and flowers; handsome multicoloured cocks are also made locally. Around Coimbra, the colour used is green with brown and yellow overtones and the decoration is more geometric. The potters of Caldas da Rainha use bright green and produce items with surprising shapes. Continuing the tradition set up by Rafael Bordalo Pinheiro (☞ *see LISBOA, Museu Rafael Bordalo Pinheiro*), water jugs, salad bowls and plates are all heavily adorned with leaves, flowers and animals. In Alcobaça and Cruz da Légua the potters work with more classical designs, distinguishing

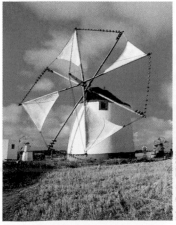

Windmills

Y. Cavaille - Ag. : EXPLORER

Caldas da Rainha pottery

Museu de Cerâmica – F. Matias - Ag.: ANF-IPM

Best-Known Handicraft Markets and Fairs

Barcelos: Pottery fair on Thursday mornings.
São Pedro de Sintra: Antiques fair on the second and fourth Sunday of the month.
Estremoz: Pottery market on Saturdays.
Estoril: Handicraft fair (Feira do Artesonato) in July and August.
Santarém: Agricultural fair in October.
Golega: Horse fair in November.

their ware by the variety of blues they use in its decoration.

In the Upper Alentejo (in Redondo, Estremoz and Nisa) the clay is encrusted with shining quartz particles or marble chips; in the Algarve amphorae are still made based on Greek and Roman models, while in Tras-os-Montes the potters damp down their ovens at the end of the firing to give the ware a black colour.

Lace

Lace is made virtually only along the coast. The decorative motifs used are fir cones and flowers, trefoils at Viano do Castelo where the lace looks more like tulle, and seaweed, shells and fish at Vila do Conde.

Embroidery

Madeira's embroidery is particularly well-known, although mainland Portugal also produces wonderful shawls, tablecloths and bedspreads. The best-known bedspreads *(colchas)* are from Castelo Branco and are embroidered with silk on linen. The tradition is a long-standing one, the work painstaking.

Filigree work

The working by hand of gold or silver wire which reached its height in the reign of King João V (1706-50) is still held in high regard in Portugal. The chief centre is the small town of Gondomar not far from Oporto. Delicate, intricate jewellery in the shape of hearts, crosses, guitars and above all caravels is fashioned from this extremely pliable wire. In the Minho, filigree earrings and brooches are worn to set off the regional costume.

Weaving and carpet-making

Hand weaving still flourishes in some mountain villages. Lengths of heavy frieze are woven on old looms to make capes and tippets. Guimarães specialises in bedspreads and curtains in rough cloth bordered with classical motifs in bright colours. The hemp or linen-based carpets embroidered in wool at Arraio-

Carved yoke from Minho

L.Y. Loirat / EXPLORER

los are the best known of their type and have simpler designs.

Woodwork

In the Alentejo many items made of wood, including trays, chairs and cupboards, are painted with brightly-coloured, naive motifs.

Painted whitewood is an important feature of traditional Portuguese handicraft and may be seen all over the country. Examples include ox yokes (the most famous being in the Barcelos region), painted carts (in the Alentejo and the Algarve) and carved and painted fishing boats (in the Ria de Aveiro and on many of the country's beaches).

Basketwork

Rushes, willows and rye straw are all used to make decorative and utilitarian wickerwork baskets. Pack saddles may be seen in Trás-os-Montes with twin pairs of deep cylindrical baskets on either side.

Cork

Wherever the cork oak grows (particularly in the Alentejo and the Algarve), a local craft has developed, making cork boxes, key rings, belts, bags, etc.

Festive Portugal

FADO

Historical outline

There are many theories about the origin of the *fado*: a monotonous chant that derived from the troubadour songs of the Middle Ages, or, a song with Moorish or Afro-Brazilian roots.

The *fado* first appeared in Portugal in the late 18C in the form of sentimental sailors' songs. It developed in the early 19C during the troubled times of the Napoleonic Wars, English domination and the independence of Brazil. These circumstances explain the popular response to the song, with its serious subject matter, usually the forces of destiny (the name *fado* is said to come from the Latin *fatum:* destiny) or human passions. It became popular in Lisbon in 1820 with the singer **Maria Severa**. In 1833 the first *fado* houses *(casas de fado)* opened and the song took on its present form. By the end of the century it had become a literary genre and the great poets and writers of the day tried their hand at it. A *fastida* figure began to appear in novels, wandering from *fado* house to *fado* house, sitting in a cloud of smoke, drinking and, eyes half-closed, listening to nostalgic tunes. At the beginning of the 20C the fado served

Festa dos Tabuleiros, Tomar

J.P. Garcin/DIAF

as a means for critics to voice their ideological quarrels.

The singer **Amália Rodriguez**, who died in 1999, brought the *fado* international fame, so much so that it has become the symbol of Portugal and its *saudade*.

Singing and playing the fado

The singer *(fadista)*, often a woman, is accompanied by one or two instrumentalists. The Portuguese guitar *(guitarra)* differs from the Spanish *(viola)* in having twelve strings as opposed to six, and is thus a more subtle instrument. The *fadista*, who is often dressed in black, stands straight, head thrown back, eyes half closed, and sings out in a strong, often deep, voice. The effect is very beautiful, moving and captivating.

The Lisbon *fado*, which can be heard in restaurants in the city's old quarters, more closely resembles the original *fado* form than the Coimbra version. This latter, which is gradually dying out, is sung only by men, dressed in large black student capes. The subject matter is generally about students' love affairs with working-class women.

ROMARIAS

Romarias are religious festivals held in honour of a saint. The most important are in northern Portugal, particularly in the Minho. Small *romarias* in mountain chapels last one day, but the larger ones in towns can last several days. Some groups, such as the fishermen of Póvoa de Varzim, hold their own *romarias*.

Collections

A few days prior to the festival the organisers make a collection. Gifts in kind are collected in baskets decked with flowers and garlands and are then auctioned. The collections, which mark the start of the festivities, are enlivened by players such as the *gaitero* or bagpiper, the *fogueteiro* or firework lighter and, in the Alentejo, the *tamborileiro* or tambourine player. Streets are carpeted with flowers.

The candle (Círio)

The most important part of the religious ceremony is the solemn bearing of a candle, from which the name *círio* has evolved to describe the focal point of the *romaria*. The candle is borne on a flower-decked cart; behind, led by the *gaitero*, follows a procession accompanying the statue of a saint or the Virgin covered in garlands, lace and flowers.

The procession circles the sanctuary two or three times accompanied by musical instruments and fire-crackers. The candle is then set down near the altar and the faithful advance to kiss the feet of the saint.

The "Saints of Intercession"

To win special favour from certain saints, believers perform acts of pen-

L. Gibert/RAPHO

Tourada

ance such as going round the sanctuary on their knees.

The traditional worship of the **Holy Ghost** is particularly deep-rooted in the Azores and Brazil. The famous *Tabuleiros* festival *(Festa dos Tabuleiros)* in Tomar, organised in bygone days by Holy Ghost brotherhoods, founded in the 14C, continues to this day.

Popular rejoicings

Once the religious ceremonies are over, the festivities, usually a meal, dancing and fireworks, begin. Local crafts are always on sale at a *romaria*.

TOURADAS: BULLFIGHTING

Unlike the Spanish *corrida*, part of the Portuguese *tourada* is performed on horseback, and the bull is not killed. The fight to the death was banned in the 18C. *Touradas* were originally created by the nobility to train for the battlefield, using Lusitanian horses which are renowned for their agility and intelligence (**** *see VILA FRANCA DE XIRA)*.

The bullfighting season in Portugal lasts from Easter to October; contests are usually held twice a week, on Thursdays and Sundays. The best known fights take place in the Praça de Touros in Lisbon, Santarém and Vila Franca de Xira, near the areas in the Ribatejo where the bulls are bred.

Food

Traditional Portuguese meals are copious and wholesome. The menu can consist of several dishes, usually prepared with olive oil and flavoured with aromatic herbs such as rosemary and bay leaves. Eggs play an important part in Portuguese food, being used in soups and often to accompany fish and meat dishes. Rice, for which the Portuguese developed a liking following their voyages to Asia, is the most favoured vegetable. Fried potatoes are also commonly served.

Soups

Soup is served at most meals. Among the many varieties are *canja de galinha*,

Caldeirada

chicken soup with rice, *sopa de peixe*, fish soup, *sopa de marisco*, seafood soup, *sopa de coelho*, rabbit soup, and *sopa de grão*, chickpea soup.

The most famous is the Minho **caldo verde** which is served north of the Mondego. This dish consists of a mashed potato base to which finely shredded green Galician cabbage is added; lastly olive oil and slices of black pudding, *tora*, are mixed in.

Bread soups or **açordas** are to be found in all regions, those of the Alentejo having many variations such as the *sopa de coentros* made with coriander leaves, olive oil, garlic and bread, with a poached egg on top.

In the south, **gaspacho**, a soup of tomatoes, onions, cucumbers and chillies seasoned with garlic and vinegar, is served cold with croutons.

Fish and seafood

Fish is a basic element of Portuguese cuisine. Cod, **bacalhau**, is the most common fish, particularly in the north, though there are issues involved with the dwindling stocks of cod in the Atlantic and surrounding areas. There are, it is said, 365 ways of preparing it (**** *see recipe for Bacalhau à Brás below)*.

Many other fish, however, are to be found in some part or other of the country: the aroma of grilled sardines wafts the streets of every coastal town; many types of fish are put into the **caldeirada** or stew made by fishermen on the beach.

You will get tunny fillets in the Algarve, river lampreys and salmon beside the Minho and shad beside the Tagus. Seafood *(mariscos)* including octopus is plentiful. Shellfish are delicious and varied especially in the Algarve where a special copper vessel, a *cataplana,* is used to cook clams and sausages spiced with herbs.

Crayfish *(lagosta)* prepared in the Peniche way, or steamed, are rightly famous.

Meat and game

Apart from pork and game, Portuguese meat is often very ordinary. Pork is cooked and served in a variety of ways. The **leitão assado**, or roast suckling-pig, of Mealhada (north of Coimbra) is delicious. Meat from various parts of the pig can also be found in stews, in linguiça or smoked pigs' tongue sausages, in smoked pork fillets, *paio,* and in smoked ham, *presunto,* at Chaves and Lamego. Ham and sausages are added to the **cozido à Portuguesa**, a hotpot of beef, vegetables, potatoes and rice, also to the local tripe prepared in the Oporto way, *dobrada,* a dish of pig or beef tripe cooked with haricot beans.

Pork in the Alentejo way, or **carne de porco à Alentejana**, is pork marinated in wine, garnished with clams. Other meat is mostly minced and consumed as meat balls, although lamb and kid are sometimes roasted or served on skewers.

Cheeses

Cheeses are made all over Portugal with several special varieties being made in the Azores. It is possible to visit several

A "faithful friend"

Cod *(bacalhau)* has played an important role in Portugal's maritime history, and is such a standby in family dining that it is commonly known as the "faithful friend". Fished in the cold, far-off waters of Newfoundland, it had to be salted to preserve it until the fishing fleet returned home. Emblematic of Portuguese cooking, a traditional dish for Christmas, a delicacy enjoyed by fishermen and peasants alike, cod is enjoyed throughout the country, particularly served as fish balls. **Bacalhau à Brás**, a cod recipe which originates from Lisbon, is now served the length and breadth of Portugal.

Ingredients for 4 people:

500g (about 1lb) of cod
500g of potatoes, fried
3 medium-sized onions
5 eggs, beaten
2 cloves of garlic
4 tablespoons of oil

Chopped parsley, black olives, salt and pepper

Soak the cod overnight, changing the water several times.

Shred the cod, taking care to remove the skin and any bones, and rinse through a cloth.

Peel the potatoes and cut into strips.

Slice the onions into thin rings.

F. Vasseur / VISA

Heat the oil in a frying pan with the garlic and remove when golden. Fry the onions until golden and add the cod. Leave on the heat for 5min, add the potatoes and garlic. Season with salt and pepper and add the beaten eggs and mix well. Sprinkle with parsley and decorate with the black olives.

cheese producers, many of which are small-scale cottage industries where you will get a personal tour as well as the opportunity to try (and hopefully buy) some off the often hand-made product. Ewes' milk cheese should be tried between October and May, notably the *Queijo da Serra da Estrela*, the *Queijo de Castelo Branco* and the creamy *Queijo de Azeitão* as well as goats' milk cheeses such as the *cabreiro*, the *rabaçal* from the Pombal region and the small soft white cheeses or *quejinhos* from Tomar, often served as an hors d'œuvre as is the fresh goat's cheese, *Queijo fresco*.

Desserts
Portugal has an infinite variety of cakes and pastries. Nearly all recipes include eggs and come in most instances from old specialities prepared in convents such as the **Toucinho-do-Céu**, **Barriga-de-Freira** and **Queijadas de Sintra**, with almonds and fresh sheep's milk. The dessert most frequently seen on menus, however, is the **pudim flan**, a sort of cream caramel, while the **leite-creme** is a creamier pudding made with the same ingredients. Rice pudding, **arroz doce**, sprinkled with cinnamon is often served at festive meals.

In the Algarve, the local figs *(figos)* and almonds *(amêndoas)* are made into the most appetising sweetmeats and tidbits.

A particularly delicious pastry is the **pasteis de nata**, a small custard tart sprinkled with cinnamon.

Wine

Portugal is the seventh largest wine-producer in the world and has a rich variety of wines, including the world famous **Port** and, although not quite as popular as it once was but still important, **Madeira**. The reasonably-priced wines bought locally or enjoyed in a restaurant are of good quality, suitable for all occasions and deserve to be better known.

Queijadas de Sintra

F. Vasseur/VISA

PORT

The vines of the Upper Douro and its tributaries produce a generous wine which is shipped from the city that gave it its name (Oporto) only after it has matured.

The English and Port
In the 14C some of the wines produced in the Lamego region were already being exported to England. In the 17C the Portuguese granted the English trading rights in exchange for their help against the Spanish. By the end of the 17C, once the port process had been developed, some Englishmen acquired country estates *(quintas)* in the Douro valley and began making wine. Through the **Methuen Treaty** (1703) the English crown obtained the monopoly of the Portuguese wine trade. However in 1756, to combat this English invasion, King Dom José I and the Marquis of Pombal founded the **Company of the Wines of the Upper Douro** *(Companhia Geral da Agricultura dos Vinhos do Alto Douro)* which fixed the price for all exported port. The following year the company defined the area in which port vines could be grown. Various English companies were set up, among them Cockburn, Campbell, Offley, Harris, Sandeman, Dow, Graham etc. The Portuguese followed suit in 1830 with their own companies with names like Ferreira and Ramos Pinto. In 1868 phylloxera raged throughout the

region but the vineyards were rapidly rehabilitated – many of the vineyards were grafted from phylloxera-resistant American stocks – and "vintage" port was being produced by the end of the 19C.

The vineyards

The area defined by law in 1757 for the cultivation of vines covers 240 000ha/593 000 acres of which a tenth consists of vineyards that stretch for about sixty miles along the Douro to the Spanish border. The approximate centre is situated at Pinhão. There are 25 000 vineyard owners. Port's inestimable quality is due to the exceptional conditions – hot summers, cold winters, and schist soil – under which the grapes are grown and ripened, and the processing of the fruit when harvested. The vines grow on steep terraces overlooking the Douro, a striking picture not only from an aesthetic point of view but also in terms of the extraordinary amount of work involved.

The making of port

The grape harvest takes place in late September. Men carry the bunches of grapes in wickerwork baskets on their backs. The cut grapes go into the press where mechanical crushing has taken the place of human treading which, with its songs and rhythmic tunes, was so highly picturesque. The must is sealed off during fermentation which reduces the sugar content to the right amount, then brandy – from Douro grapes – is added to stop the fermentation and to stabilise the sugar. In the spring the wine is taken by lorry and train to Vila Nova de Gaia. Up until a few years ago it was transported 150km/90mi along the Douro to Oporto in picturesque sailing craft known as *barcelos rebelos*. Some of these boats may be seen at Pinhão and Vila Nova da Gaia.

The wine is stored with the 58 port wine companies that have set up in Vila Nova da Gaia and matures in huge casks or, more commonly, in vats containing up to 1 000hl/26 400 imperial gallons. It is then decanted into 535l/118 gallon barrels *(pipes)* in which the porous nature of the wood augments the ageing process. The Wine Institute (Instituto do Vinho do Porto) sets the rules and controls the quality.

Types of port

Port, which is red or white according to the colour of the grapes from which it is made, has many subtleties – it can be dry, medium or sweet. The variety of port also depends upon the way it is made. Port aged in casks matures through oxidation and turns a beautiful amber

WINES AND REGIONAL SPECIALITIES

Wine-producing regions

Bucelas Major vineyards

colour; port aged in the bottle matures by reduction and is a dark red colour. The alcohol content is about 20%.

Vintage ports are selected from the best wines of a particularly fine year and are bottled after two years in casks. They then mature in the bottle for at least ten years or more before being served. Since 1974 all Vintage Port must be bottled in Portugal.

White port or **Branco** is less well known than the reds. It is a fortified wine made from white grapes. Dry or extra dry, it makes a good apéritif.

Blended ports are red ports made from different vintages from different years. The blending and ageing differ according to the quality required. They include:

♦ **Tinto**, the most common, which is young, vigorous, distinctly coloured and fruity.

♦ **Tinto-Alourado** or **Ruby**, which is older, yet rich in colour, fruity and sweet and is the result of the blending of different vintages from different years.

♦ **Alourado** or **Tawny** is blended with different vintages from different years and ages in wooden cakes. Its colour turns to a brownish gold as it ages. It should be drunk soon after it is bottled.

♦ **Alourado-Claro** or **Light Tawny** is the culmination of the former.

CHOOSING AND SERVING PORT

White port, which should be drunk chilled and is best served as an aperitif, is the least expensive followed by the reds (**Ruby** and **Tawny**). Very good quality Tawny ports will provide an indication of their age on the label (10, 20, 30 or more years spent in the barrel). Next come the ports which bear their vintage date *(colheita)*; they have been made with wines from the same year. The best and most expensive are **Vintage ports** and **Late Bottled Vintage Ports (L.B.V.)**. The former are made with wine from an exceptionally good year and are bottled after two to three years; likewise, the latter are made with wine from the same vineyard and are bottled after four to six years. These can be kept for many years provided that they are laid down horizontally and are stored at a suitable temperature. Vintage port should be served in a carafe and drunk quickly, preferably on the day the bottle is opened. All ports, with the exception of the whites, are a perfect accompaniment to game, hams, foie gras, cheeses, dried fruit etc.

For additional information on port, contact the Instituto do Vinho in Oporto (web site: http://www.ivp.pt) which, in association with other official organisations, particularly the Port Wine Route association in Peso da Régua and the region's tourist offices, has created a Port Wine Route within the official Douro region. The itinerary passes through 54 sites, including estates, **co-operatives** and wine information centres, providing visitors with an ideal opportunity to discover the beautiful landscapes of the region and to taste its most famous product.

Since 1963 the French have replaced the English as the largest importers of port.

MADEIRA

Madeira wine, which deserves to be better known, has always been particularly popular with the English. ♨ *See MADEIRA.*

OTHER WINES

Several regions in Portugal produce perfectly respectable wines which can be enjoyed in restaurants. One can ask for the *vinho da casa*, usually the local wine.

Vinho Verde

Vinho Verde from the Minho and the Lower Douro valleys can be white (tendency to gold) or deep red. Its name, "green wine" comes from its early grape harvest and short fermentation period which gives the wine a low alcohol content (8% to 11%) and makes it light and sparkling with a distinct bouquet and what might be described as a very slightly bitter flavour. It is best enjoyed young and chilled. It is an ideal aperitif and is a perfect accompaniment to both fish and seafood. The most renowned *vinho verde* is produced from the Alvarinho grape which enables the wine to be kept longer than wine produced from other grape varieties.

Dão

Vines growing on the granite slopes of the Dão valley produce a fresh white wine as well as a sweet red wine with a velvety texture and a heady bouquet which most closely resembles Bordeaux *crus*. *Quinta* wines are the equivalent of French *château* wines.

Bairrada

This very old vine-growing region produces a robust, fragrant red, as well as a natural sparkling wine which goes wonderfully well with roast suckling pig.

Colares

The vines grow in a sandy topsoil over a bed of clay in the Serra de Sintra. The robust, velvety, dark red wine has been famous since the 13C.

Bucelas

Bucelas is a dry, somewhat acidic straw-coloured white wine produced from vineyards on the banks of the Trancão, a tributary of the Tagus.

Other table wines

The Ribatejo vineyards produce good everyday wines; full bodied reds from the Cartaxo region and whites from Chamusca, Almeirim and Alpiarça on the far bank of the Tagus.

Also worth trying are the wines of Torres Vedras, Alcobaça, Lafões and Agueda, and the Pinhel and Mateus rosés.

In the Alentejo, full-bodied reds such as Reguengos, Borba and Redondo predominate. The one exception to this is the white Vidigueira wine.

In the Algarve, a small amount of wine is still produced in Lagoa, home to the country's oldest **co-operative**.

Dessert wines

Setúbal moscatel from the chalky clay slopes of the Serra da Arrábida is a generous fruity wine which acquires a particularly pleasant taste with age.

Fruity amber-coloured Carcavelos is drunk as an apéritif as well as a dessert wine.

Spirits

The wide variety of Portuguese brandies includes *ginginha*, cherry brandy from Alcobaça, *medronho*, arbutus berry brandy and *brandimel*, honey brandy from the Algarve. *Bagaço* or *bagaceira*, a grape marc, served chilled, is the most widely drunk.

Mineral water

Portugal produces fine mineral waters, such as the Água de Luso and the sparkling waters of Castelo, Carvalhelhos, Vidago and Pedras Salgadas. The most common beer served is light and similar to lager. The country's fruit juices, both still *(sem gás)* and sparkling *(com gás)*, are also excellent and refreshing.

G. Sioën/RAPHO

Innovation has good prospects whenever it is cleaner, safer and more efficient.

 The MICHELIN Energy green tyre offers
a shorter braking distance and lasts 25% longer*.
It also provides fuel savings of 2 to 3%
while reducing CO_2 emissions.

*on average compared to competing tyres in the same category.

MICHELIN
A better way forward

Palácio Nacional da Pena, Sintra
Raja/ZEFA-HOA QUI

ABRANTES

SANTARÉM

POPULATION 42 436– MICHELIN MAP 733

Abrantes occupies an open site★ on a hillside overlooking the right bank of the Tagus. The commanding fortress had fallen into decay more than two hundred years before the Peninsular War, when the town was entered first by French troops in 1807 and later by Wellesley who briefly made it his headquarters in 1809. The town is also known for its delicious confections, "Abrantes straw" or *palha de Abrantes*, so-called because the eggs from which it is made leave yellow straw-like streaks. 🛈 *Largo 1° de Maio – 2200-320 –* ☎ *241 36 25 55*

▶ **Orient Yourself:** North-east of Santarém, 140km/100mi from Lisbon.
☺ **Don't Miss:** The castle and the church.
🕓 **Organizing Your Time:** About a day to see eveything worthwhile.
🖉 **Also See:** Constância, the home to Portugal's great poet, Camões.

Sights

Castle

🕓*Open 10am-5pm.* 🕓*Closed Mondays.*
The keep has been converted into a **belvedere** from which there are views of the middle valley of the Tagus, the Serra do Moradal and the foothills of the Serra da Estrela.
The **Igreja de Santa Maria** (🕓*Church open 9am-6pm (5pm in winter). No charge.* ☎ *241 37 17 24)*, rebuilt in the 15C, includes a small **museum** with a 16C carving of the Trinity in polychrome stone and, on the high altar, a beautiful statue of the Virgin and Child dating from the 15C. The tombs of the Counts of Abrantes date from the 15C and 16C. Also worthy of note on one of the walls are the 16C Hispano-Moorish *corda seca azulejos*.

Igreja e Hospital da Misericórdia

🕓*To visit, contact Santa Casa da Misericórdia, up the street on the right -* ☎ *241 36 00 20.*
The church (1584) contains six 16C oil paintings on wood. Attributed to Gregório Lopes, they evoke the life of Christ. Also note the 18C gilded wood altar and an organ from the same period. The Sala do Definitório in the former hospital is decorated with attractive 18C *azulejo* panels beneath a coffered wood ceiling. The room also contains seven paintings representing the seven works of the Misericord. The collection of furniture includes a 16C *burra* (literally a she-ass) and an iron chest used to transport precious objects by ship.

Igreja de São João Baptista

Located left of Igreja da Misericórdia, this church was founded in 1300 by Queen Saint Isabel and rebuilt at the end of the 16C. The interior contains gilded wood Renaissance altars.

Constância

The poet Camões lived in this village, 12km/8mi west of Abrantes. His house is now a centre for the study of his many works. Attractive with flower-bedecked cobbled streets, the village itself has an interesting parish church.

ALBUFEIRA★

FARO

POPULATION 30 913 – MICHELIN MAP 733
LOCAL MAP SEE ALGARVE

Albufeira is a former Moorish stronghold that has kept its Arab name meaning "castle on the sea". Midway between Faro and Lagos it has, over the past few decades, become the most famous seaside resort in the Algarve with its international visitors and fashionable nightlife. Tourism has diminished the charm of the old fishing village in the centre. The beach is packed all summer and unless you are staying in one of the numerous hotels, which are fine for family holidays or for the younger crowd, it is not the sort of place to go if you are seeking peace and quiet. 🖪 *Ruta de Outubro,* ☎ *289 58 52 79*

Praia dos Barcos, Albufeira

Night-Life

Bars

The **Rua dos Bares** is a name that needs no further explanation! Here, the entertainment is out on the street itself, where the only problem is deciding which bar to go to first. One of the most popular, **Capítulo V,** is a bar/club with a pleasant terrace.

In Areias de São João, the Rua de Santa Eulália contains the largest number of bars, most of which have a dance floor, such as **Alabastro Café, 5° Elemento** and **Crazy Joe. Amnésia** is at nº19 Rua Alexandre Herculano, in the same part of town, while one of the major attractions of Albufeira's nightlife, Liberto's Bar, with its terrace, swimming pool, several bars and a dance floor, can be found a little farther along.

Night-clubs

Kiss, in Areias de São João, is one of Albufeira's oldest night-clubs, attracting a varied crowd all year round, as does **IRS,** another favourite haunt. The **Locomia,** overlooking Santa Eulália beach, has several outdoor areas, with appearances by guest DJs during the summer months. The **Palácio Latino** on the Praça de Touros organises concerts where clubbers can enjoy lively Latin rhythms.

ALCOBAÇA★★

LEIRIA

POPULATION 56 823 – MICHELIN MAP 733

One of the most beautiful Cistercian abbeys dating from the Middle Ages stands in the heart of this small town. Alcobaça is set in an agricultural region at the confluence of the Alcoa and Baça rivers which gave the town its name. Its main activities are fruit growing, wine-making and the production of a cherry liqueur called *ginginha*. Alcobaça is also an active commercial centre for the local pottery which is predominantly blue. ▯ *Praça 25 de Abril – 2460-018 – ☎ 262 58 23 77*

▶ **Orient Yourself:** North of Lisbon just inland from Nazaré.
🕭 **Don't Miss:** The Monastery of Santa Maria.
🕐 **Organizing Your Time:** Spend a morning in the monastery and wander around in the afternoon.
🕭 **Also See:** Nazaré, Obidos and the monastery at Batalha.

Mosteiro de Santa Maria ★★ *45min*

🕐*Open Apr-Sept 9am-7pm; Oct-Mar 9am-5pm.* 🕐*Closed 1 Jan, Good Fri, Easter Sun and 25 Dec.. ☎ 262 50 51 20. ⊚€3.*
The external appearance of the 18C Santa Maria Monastery belies the splendid Cistercian architecture within. Of the original façade, altered by successive 17C and 18C reconstructions in the Baroque style, only the main doorway and the rose window remain.

Church ★★

The church *(igreja)* has been restored to the nobility and clean lines of its original Cistercian architecture. It is one of the largest churches of its kind. The **Nave** is very spacious; the quadripartite vaulting is supported on transverse arches which, in turn, rest on mighty pillars and engaged columns. By terminating the latter 3m/10ft above the ground, the architect considerably increased the space available for the congregation and gave the church a unique perspective. The aisles have striking vertical lines; they are almost as tall as the nave is long.

B. Barbier

Dom Pedro's tomb

Inês de Castro's tomb (Túmulo de Inês de Castro) ★★
In the north transept (1).
The beautiful reclining figure of Inês de Castro lies upon a tomb on which the four panels are surmounted by a frieze bearing the Portuguese and Castro coats of arms. Depicted on the sides are scenes from the Life of Christ. The Last Judgement which adorns the panel at the statue's feet is particularly realistic; at the bottom on the left, the dead are standing before God in Judgement, and on the right, the damned are being hurled into the jaws of a monster symbolising hell.

Dom Pedro's tomb (Túmulo de Dom Pedro) ★★
In the south transept (2).
Beneath a severe reclining figure, Dom Pedro's tomb depicts, on its sides, the life of St Bartholomew, the King's patron saint. The panel at the foot depicts Dom Pedro's last moments. The **Transit of St Bernard** (3), a damaged terracotta depicting the death of the saint, stands in a chapel off the south transept. It was modelled by monks in the 17C. The **Chancel**, which is based on the design of Clairvaux, is surrounded by a vast ambulatory off which open two beautiful **Manueline doors** (4) dating from the 16C, and nine chapels adorned with polychrome wooden statues from the 17C and 18C.

Abbey buildings ★★

Claustro do Silêncio
The cloisters, which were built in the early 14C, have an attractive simplicity of line; between buttresses slender twin columns support with great elegance three rounded arches which are surmounted by a rose. The upper storey was added by Diogo and João Castilho in the 16C.
A staircase (5) leads to the **Monks' Dormitory**, a vast Gothic hall over 60m/195ft long. Two rows of columns with capitals divide the room into three sections. The **Kitchens** (6), which were enlarged in the 18C, are flanked to the east by the storeroom. The white tiled chamber is of monumental proportions, 18m/58ft high and with enormous open fireplaces; water is provided by a tributary of the Alcoa river. The **Refectory** is a large hall with ribbed vaulting. A stairway, built into the thickness of the wall and surmounted by a fine colonnade, leads to the reader's pulpit (7). Opposite the door, a **lavabo** and 17C fountain (8) jut out into the close.
In the 18C **Sala dos Reis** (Kings' Hall) a frieze of *azulejos* illustrates the foundation of the monastery; the statues carved by monks represent the Portuguese kings up to Dom José I. Note also a beautiful Gothic Virgin and Child.

Additional Sight

Museu da Junta Nacional do Vinho
1km/0.5mi along the N 8 in the direction of Leiria, on the right. ◷Open Mon-Fri 9am-12.30pm; 2pm-5.30pm; Sat-Sun, 9am-12.30pm; 2pm-5.30pm. ◷Closed holidays. €1.50. ☎ 262 58 22 22.
A wine **co-operative**'s warehouses are the setting for this wine museum with its collections of bottles (old Port and Madeira), wine vats, wine presses and stills.

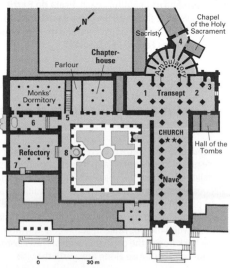

ALGARVE★★

MICHELIN MAP 733

The Algarve stretches across the whole of southern Portugal. Its name derives from the Arabic *El-Gharb* meaning "west". The landscape and climate, which is mild all year round, resemble that of North Africa, with figs, carobs, bougainvillaeas, geraniums and oleanders. The fine beaches, which have been extremely popular since the 1970s, have attracted extensive tourist development which has unfortunately disfigured parts of the coast. The far west is more natural.

The East Coast and Offshore

1 From Vila Real de Santa António to Faro
65km/40mi – allow a day

East of Faro the coast is known as the leeward shore or *Sotavento*. The area stretching westwards from Manta Rota near Cacela Velha forms an unusual lagoon landscape closed in by sandy islets. There are boat links between the mainland and the beaches on the offshore sand bars as well as footbridges over the lagoon. The entire coast from Manta Rota to Ançao near Quinta do Lago is a protected area, the **Parque Natural da Ria Formosa**, is 60km/37mi long, and covers 18 400ha/45 468 acres of dunes, channels and islands of great ornithological interest. The reserve is also rich in molluscs and crustaceans and is an important spawning area for fish.

Vila Real de Santo António and Monte Gordo
See VILA REAL DE SANTO ANTÓNIO.

Cacela Velha★
This pleasant hamlet is built around the ruins of a medieval fortress and a small church with an attractive doorway. From its rocky bluff it affords a fine **view** over the lagoon and fishing boats below. During the summer, the main lake, with its two small restaurants, is a popular place to savour local Algarve delicacies.
You next come into **Tavira**★ – *See TAVIRA*, before reaching **Pedras de El Rei,** a holiday village of villas and attractive gardens with a rail link *(10min)* to the offshore sandbank and its beautiful beach, **Praia do Barril**.
The Renaissance church on the outskirts of **Luz de Tavira** has an attractive Manueline doorway and flame ornaments around the roof. Continue to **Olhão** – *See OLHÃO* and on towards **Faro**★ – *See FARO*.

The Interior

2 Circuit around Faro via the Serra do Caldeirão
107km/67mi – allow a day

This tour takes you into a relatively unknown area of the Algarve, between the limestone hills of the "barrocal" and the schist mountains of the Serra do Caldeirão just a few kilometres from the coast yet far from its madding crowds. The flower-decked villages have managed to preserve their traditional appearance; handicrafts are still an important industry. In January and February the flowering almond trees carpet the mountains in a mass of white; spring heralds the appearance of the rock-rose with its white bloom, while in summer and winter oranges stand out against the green backdrop of the cottage gardens. The year-round scents of eucalyptus, pine, lavender and rock-rose alone are worth the visit.

Estói

▶ *Leave Faro on the N 2 heading north-east. After 10km/6mi, turn right along the Estói road (towards Tavira).*

Roman Ruins of Milreu
🕙*Open 9.30am-12.30pm and 2-6pm.* 🕙*Closed Mon.* ⊚€2. ☎ 289 99 78 23.
A square-shaped apse and two marble columns are all that remain of a 1C Roman settlement which was built around a temple. The brick foundations of the houses and baths surround the living quarters and pools, some of which still retain their polychrome mosaic designs. Particularly worthy of note is the **mosaico dos peixes grandes**, a mosaic of large fish on the wall of one of the pools.

Azulejo, Estói gardens

Gardens, Palácio de Estói
From Estói head 1km/0.5mi beyond Milreu.
The gardens are bordered with orange trees leading up to the Baroque façade of this small 18C palace. The balustered verandas, decorated with pools, statues, busts, marble and earthenware vases, blue and multi-coloured *azulejos* with mythological and fantastic figures, give an overall atmosphere of romantic charm.

▶ *Return to the N 2 and head north.*

São Brás de Alportel
This peaceful small town, originally named Xanabus by its Moorish founders, is built on elevated ground dotted with white houses. The town used to be the country's main centre for cork extraction and still retains a few cork-related industries.

Casa da Cultura António Bentes (Museu Etnográfico do Trajo Algarvio)
🕙*Open 10am-1pm and 2-5pm.* 🕙*Closed mornings on Sat, Sun and holidays.* ⊚€1.50. ☎ 289 84 26 18.

The coast near Praia da Rocha

This ethnographic museum, housed in an attractive 19C bourgeois mansion, contains an interesting collection of old carts and carriages, dolls and typical local dress. It also houses temporary exhibitions. The beautiful garden of the bishops of the Algarve's former residence can be seen in front of the museum.

▶ *Continue along the N 2 for 14km/9mi. The road winds its way through groves of eucalyptus and pine before reaching Barranco Velho. Here, head towards Querença along the N 396.*

Querença

The village nestles on the slope of a hill at an altitude of 276m/905ft. The foundation of the **Igreja de Nossa Senhora da Assunção** on the summit is attributed to the Knights Templar. Although the church was completely remodelled in 1745, it has retained its Manueline door. The interior contains some fine gilded carvings. Arbutuses abound in the surrounding fields, producing strawberry-like berries used to make the well-known **aguardente de medronho**, a local brandy.

▶ *Retrace your route, then take the road to Aldeia da Tôr, close to where you will see a Roman bridge. Head towards Salir.*

Salir

There is a fine view of the mountains from the ruined Moorish castle. To the northeast of the village, the Rocha da Pena sits atop a steep, rugged hill at an altitude of 479m/1571ft with its two walls dating from the Neolithic period.

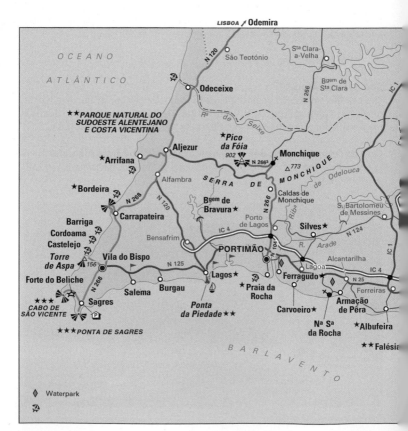

▶ *Take the N124 toward Alte.*

Alte★

The white houses of this attractive village of narrow, winding streets cling to the sides of a hill in the *serra*. In the lower part of the town, two rustic fountains, the Fonte Pequena and the Fonte Grande, provide a picnic spot.

▶ *Rejoin the N 124. At Benafim Grande, turn right on to a small road leading to the N 270, which you join at the village of Gilvrazino. Then head towards Loulé.*

Loulé

The town, which was inhabited by the Romans, has preserved a few remnants from the walls of its Moorish castle. Loulé is also famous for its Carnival, reputed to be the predecessor of the carnival in Rio de Janeiro. The Senhora da Piedade *romaria* held on the second Sunday after Easter originates from pre-Christian times.

▶ *Return to Faro on the N 125-4.*

The Rocky Coast

③ **From Faro to Portimão** *100km/62mi – allow a day*

The windward shore or *Barlaventa* is the Algarve's most famous stretch of coast. Ochre-coloured cliffs plunge down to the beach as far as Vilamoura, where the

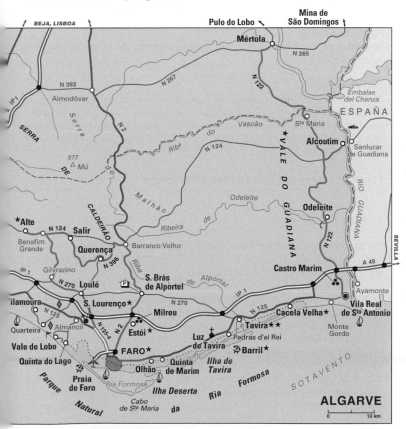

turquoise sea surges into coves and grottoes, some of which may be explored by boat. Unfortunately, the natural beauty has been marred in many places by intensive tourist development. Small harbours look lost among tall white apartment blocks, and in summer fishing boats are crowded out by beach umbrellas.

You arrive first in the hamlet of **São Lourenço**★ – & *See Almansil* – before getting on towards **Quinta do Lago and Vale do Lobo**, two holiday villages with golf courses, country clubs and smart hotels around which are dotted villas nestling among umbrella pines. There are footbridges across the lagoon to the beaches.You next pass **Quarteira and Vilamoura** – & *See Vilamoura* – before reaching **Albufeira**★ – & *See Albufeira* – **Carvoeiro**★ – & *See Carvoeiro* –and **Portimão** – & *See Portimão*.

Lagos and the West Coast

5 **From Portimão to Odeceixe** *140km/87mi – about one day*

The south coast around Lagos attracts fewer tourists and its small fishing villages have managed to keep their character. The west coast beyond Cabo de São Vicente is still very wild with tall, grey cliffs. The hinterland is undulating, with eucalyptus, pine trees and aloes, while the bright white villages have remained unspoiled. The region is ideal for anyone seeking a quiet spot and is particularly popular with campers.

Lagos★ – & *See LAGOS.*

Several roads lead southwards between Lagos and Vila do Bispo to beaches and fishing villages such as **Burgau** and **Salema**

Ponta da Piedade★★
The **setting**★★ of this seaside resort, its **sea caves** and clear green sea make it especially attractive.

Vila do Bispo
The bright white village is a junction for roads to the north, the Algarve and Sagres. The Baroque **church** – ○*Open every morning except Wed* –has a chancel in gilded wood and its walls are decorated with *azulejos* (1715). A door to the left of the chancel opens into a small museum of art which contains a beautiful crucifix. You then reach the very end of the Algarve,

Ponta de Sagres and Cabo de São Vicente★★★
& *See Ponta de SAGRES and Cabo de SÃO VICENTE.*

▶ *Return to Vila do Bispa.*

The **Torre de Aspa** belvedere *(6km/4mi west. Take the Sagres road, then bear right and follow the signs)*, which stands at an altitude of 156m/512ft, has a beautiful **view**★ of Cabo de São Vicente and Ponta de Sagres.

Castelejo, Cordoama, Barriga and **Mouranitos beaches** may be reached by car from Vila do Bispo. The scenery is wild with tall, grey cliffs. At **Carrapateira** a road runs around the headland west of the village. There are fine views of the steep rock-face and Bordeira's long sandy beach, before you approach **Aljezur** which consists of white-walled houses with brightly painted borders. A road from here leads west *(9km/5.5mi)* to **Arrifana**★ with its beach and fishing harbour nestling at the foot of a tall cliff. Finally you come into **Odeceixe** through eucalyptus trees. A road runs for 4km/2.5mi alongside the Seixe, a small coastal river and estuary with a **beach** at its mouth.

ALMANSIL

FARO

POPULATION 5 945 – MICHELIN MAP 733
LOCAL MAP SEE ALGARVE

This small village just off the main road has a lovely church that it is worth stopping to see.

▶ **Orient Yourself:** The village lies along the N125 that links Portimão to Faro.
ⓐ **Don't Miss:** The Church of São Lourenço - see below.
ⓢ **Organizing Your Time:** Make sure you have about two hours here.

Capela de São Lourenço ★

ⓞ*Open 10am-1pm and 2.30-5.30pm (6pm July to Sept).* ⓞ*Closed Sun.* ⊛*€2.* ☎ *289 39 54 51. – 2km/1mi east of Almansil, to the north of the road, in the hamlet of São Lourenço.*
The Romanesque chapel of St Lawrence, which was remodelled in the Baroque period, is decorated inside with **azulejos**★★ dating from 1730, the work of Bernardo, an artist known as Policarpo de Oliviera Bernardes. The walls and vaulting are covered with tiles depicting the life and martyrdom of St Lawrence: on either side of the chancel there are scenes depicting the blind and the distribution of money gained from the sale of sacred vessels. In the nave, on the south side, there is a meeting between the saint and the Pope, the saint in prison, and on the north side, preparation for the martyr's torture and St Lawrence on the grid being comforted by an angel. Outside, on the church's flat east end, a vast panel of *azulejos* shows St Lawrence and his gridiron beneath a baroque scallop shell.

Centro Cultural de São Lourenço

ⓞ*Open 10am-7pm.* ⓞ*Closed Mon.* ☎ *289 39 54 75.*
The centre, located directly below the church in a typical Algarve house, organises a year-round music and arts programme which includes Portuguese as well as performers from other countries.

B. Barbier/DIAF

Capela de São Lourenço

CASTELO DE **ALMOUROL**★★

SANTARÉM

MICHELIN MAP 733 – MICHELIN ATLAS SPAIN & PORTUGAL P 47 (N 4)

The fortress of Almourol, which stands with towers and crenellations on a small rocky island covered in greenery in the centre of the Tagus, was constructed by Gualdim Pais, Master of the Order of the Templars, in 1171 on the site of an earlier Roman fort.

▶ **Orient Yourself:** In the centre of a triangle formed by Santarém, Tomar and Abrantes.

🕐 **Organizing Your Time:** Two hours will suffice for this interesting castle.

👶 **Also See:** Fátima and Alcobaça.

The outstandingly romantic setting has given rise to many legends relating to the castle. In Francisco de Morais' long prose romance of chivalry, *Palmeirim de Inglaterra (Palmeirim of England)*, duels and fights follow in quick succession at the foot of the ramparts. Many other legends involve knights in shining armour and princesses locked in the tower. Nowadays, the proximity of a railway line and a military camp on the north bank of the Tagus provide a somewhat noisy background to this historical setting.

Visit

The castle can be reached directly by boat (operates from 9am until sunset ◉€0.50). Contact the Tourist Office in Vila Nova da Barquinha. ☎ 249 72 03 58.

▶ *Access from the N 3, north of the Tagus (2km/1mi east of Tancos). Leave the car along the river bank opposite the castle.*

From the landing stage, there is a good view of the castle in its attractive **setting**★★. The double perimeter wall, flanked by ten round towers, is dominated by a square keep *(access to the top by 85 steps and a low door)* commanding a panoramic **view**★ of the river and its banks.

Castelo de Almourol

G. Hallo/PIX

AMARANTE ★

PORTO

POPULATION 4 757 – MICHELIN MAP 733

LOCAL MAP SEE VALE DO DOURO

Amarante is a picturesque small town, with its 16C, 17C and 18C houses, complete with wooden balconies and wrought iron grilles, on a hillside overlooking the Tâmega. The town, well known for its pastries (*lérias, foguetes, papos de anjo*) and its *vinho verde* wine, comes alive each year on the first Saturday in June when it celebrates the feast day of its patron saint, Gonçalo. Gonçalo lived as a hermit in the 13C. He was also the patron saint of marriage and fertility. *Rua Cândido dos Reis – 4600-055 – ☎ 255 43 22 59 or 255 43 29 80*

▶ **Orient Yourself:** Inland from Porto, halfway to Vila Real.

☺ **Don't Miss:** All the churches in this village.

Sights

Igreja e Convento de São Gonçalo

The church, erected in 1540, and modified in the 18C, has some lovely gilded wooden Baroque furnishings: an altarpiece in the chancel, two pulpits and the superb **organ case**★ (early 17C) supported by three Tritons. St Gonçalo's tomb (d 1259) lies in the chapel on the left of the chancel.

Igreja de São Pedro

This 18C church has a Baroque façade decorated with statues of St Peter and St Paul. The unique nave, beneath a stucco-work barrel vault, is decorated with 17C bands of blue and yellow *azulejos*; the chancel, beneath a stone vault with sunken sculpted panels, has a gilded wooden altar. There is a coffered chestnut wood **ceiling**★, with elegant carving in the sacristy.

AROUCA

AVEIRO

POPULATION 4 374 – MICHELIN MAP 733

Arouca Monastery and a few houses on its perimeter lie deep in the hollow of a small green valley surrounded by wooded heights. Founded in 716 but rebuilt in the 18C after a fire, the monastery forms a baroque but unadorned group. *Praça Brandão Vasconcelos – 4540-110 – ☎ 256 94 35 75*

▶ **Orient Yourself:** 65km/42ml north-east of Aveiro on the N224.

Sights

Igreja do Mosteiro

🕒 *Open 9am-7pm.*

The single nave of the abbey church contains numerous gilded Baroque altars and several statues in Ançã stone carved by Jacinto Vieira. The 18C tomb worked in silver, ebony and quartz in the second chapel on the south side of the church contains the mummy of Queen Mafalda (1203-52), daughter of King Sancho I; she retired here in 1217.

Lower Chancel

The lower chancel *(coro baixo)* is ornamented with an 18C gilded organ loft, stalls with richly-carved backs and graceful statues of religious figures by Jacinto Vieira.

Museu de Arte Sacra de Arouca

Ⓞ*Open 10am-noon and 2-5.30pm.* Ⓞ*Closed Mons, Tues am, 1 Jan, Good Fri, Easter Sun, 1 May and 25 Dec.* ⸙*€2.50.*
This museum on the first floor of the cloisters contains Portuguese Primitive **paintings**★ dating from the late 15C to early 16C from the Viseu School, and works, including an *Ascension*, by the 17C artist Diogo Teixeira. There is also a statue of St Peter dating from the 15C.

SERRA DA ARRÁBIDA★

SETÚBAL
MICHELIN MAP 733

The Serra da Arrábida rises and falls over the southern part of the Setúbal peninsula, covering 35km/22mi between Cabo Espichel and Palmela. The line of hills is made up of the ends of Secondary Era limestone deposits, pushed back, broken and buried beneath more recent deposits, and which reappear on the north side of the Tagus abutting the Sintra Massif. The Parque Natural da Arrábida, which covers 10 800ha/26 688 acres between Sesimbra and Setúbal, was created to protect the local scenery and architecture.

▸ **Orient Yourself:** Cross the Vasca da Gama bridge from Lisbon and just keep going towards Setúbal.
🖝 **Don't Miss:** Sesimbra, the coast road and the views at Cabo Espichel.
Ⓞ **Organizing Your Time:** You'll need an entire day to do the full tour.
🔢 **Especially for Kids:** The Oceanographic Museum in Portinho da Arrábida.
🖝 **Also See:** Lisbon, of course, and nearby Setúbal.

Round trip from Sesimbra *77km/48mi – about 4hr*

The itinerary described below takes in the two very different sides of this small range of mountains, which is a mere 6km/4mi wide. The **southern side** slopes down to the ocean, ending in cliffs 500m/1 600ft high. The indented coastline, with its wonderful array of colours, is more reminiscent of the Mediterranean than the Atlantic. The **northern side**, with a more rounded relief, has a landscape of vineyards, orchards and olive groves and, on poorer ground, its original brush and pine woods.

Sesimbra –🖝 *See SESIMBRA.*

After Santana, the N 379 to the right winds between hills enlivened by orange trees and windmills.

▸ *2.5km/1.5mi before Vila Nogueira de Azeitão, turn right on N 379-1 towards Arrábida.*

After a brief run through olive groves and vineyards, the road begins a winding climb through dense vegetation. The sea appears far below.

▸ *Follow the signs to Portinho.*

Portinho da Arrábida★

The bay of Portinho da Arrábida, at the foot of the *serra*, forms an even curve, edged by a semicircular beach of fine white sand that is very popular at weekends. At the entrance to the village, the **Forte de Nossa Senhora da Arrábida**, built in the 17C as a protection against pirates, now houses a small **Museu Oceanográfico** (Kids ⊙Open Tue-Fri 10am-4pm; Sat 3pm-6pm; ⊙closed Sun, Mon and holidays; ⊛€1.50. ☎ 212 18 97 91 - www.icm.pt) with fine displays of sponges and various marine species. Steps lead from the left of the fort entrance down to a cave.

▷ *Continue along the N 379-1, leaving the lower corniche road on the right.*

Corniche road ★★

The corniche road *(estrada de escarpa)* follows a section of the mountain crestline with views of both the northern and southern slopes. On the left there is a view of Monte Formosinho (alt 499m/1 637ft) the *serra's* highest peak, and on the right of Portinho and the Sado estuary. Below, in the foreground, abutting on a cliff overlooking the sea stands the **Convento da Arrábida**, founded by Franciscans in 1542.

Setúbal★ – 👣 *See SETÚBAL.*

▷ *Leave Setúbal heading north on the N 252 and, before the motorway, take the N 379 to the left. You then reach* **Palmela**★ *(👣 See PALMELA). The N 379 runs near Bacalhoa (on the N 10 opposite the Rodoviária Nacional bus station) which can be reached from Vendas on the left, before you reach* **Quinta da Bacalhoa**★ *(👣 see Quinta da Bacalhoa). The N 10 passes through vineyards and orchards to Vila Nogueira de Azeitão.*

Vila Nogueira de Azeitão

Set amidst beautiful *quintas,* this town is famous for its moscatel. The main street is bordered with lovely Baroque fountains and the graceful buildings and gardens of the **Casa Vitícola José Maria de Fonseca**, a firm which has been making moscatel wine since 1834.

▷ *Return to Sesimbra on the N 379 via Santana.*

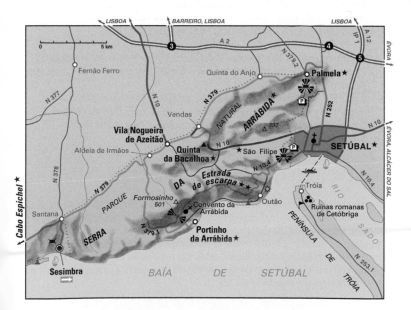

ARRAIOLOS

ÉVORA
POPULATION 7 567 – MICHELIN MAP 733

This charming village, perched on a hill in the great Alentejo plain about 22km/14ml north of Évora, has long been famous for its wool carpets. The 14C castle dominates the narrow streets of white-walled houses.

Arraiolos carpets

In the second half of the 17C, a small industry was established in the Arraiolos region, manufacturing hemp and linen carpets which were then embroidered with wool and used as chest and wall coverings. The carpets first followed Indian and Persian designs with animal figures and plant motifs but later the Oriental patterns and colourings were abandoned in favour of more popular, regional themes. They can be found on sale in the village in several shops.

Castle

The castle *(partially restored)* has a fine view of the village and olive groves beyond. The **Convento dos Lóios** has been converted into a *pousada*.

AVEIRO★

AVEIRO
POPULATION 73 136 – MICHELIN MAP 733
PLAN OF THE BUILT-UP AREA IN THE RED GUIDE PORTUGAL

Canals, small bridges, colorful barges that evoke the gondolas in Venice, and a fine museum give Aveiro the feel of a city of culture. The centre has many fine buildings, some in an Art Nouveau style, but the surrounding areas are impressive as well, canals and marches to the north, dunes and the beaches to the west.
🛈 *Rua João Mendonça 8 – 3800-200* ☎ *234 42 36 80 or 243 42 07 60*

▸ **Orient Yourself:** 70km/45ml south of Porto, 60km/38ml north of Coimbra.
🅿 **Parking:** There is free parking between the IP5 and the Canal de São Roque, just north of the old town.
😊 **Don't Miss:** The museum, but walk the old town to really see all the sights.
🕐 **Organizing Your Time:** You should be able to see the town in one day.
🧒 **Especially for Kids:** Take them for an adventure cruise on the lagoon.
👣 **Also See:** Coimbra and Viseu.

A Bit of History

Aveiro was once a busy fishing port, with boats returning from cod fishing off Newfoundland. However, in 1575 disaster struck. A violent storm closed the lagoon; the harbour silted up and the city, deprived of its industries, fell into decline.
An effort by the Marquis of Pombal to rehabilitate it in the 18C came to nothing as did several plans to breach the strand to the sea. Finally in 1808, with the aid of breakwaters built from stones taken from the old town walls, a passage was opened once more from the lagoon to the sea.

Ceramic and chinaware industries developed locally (Ílhavo and Vista Alegre), bringing prosperity, and with it came expansion and artistic renown: Aveiro became a
centre of Baroque art with a famous school of sculpture.

Aveiro today

Saltpans, grazing, rice paddies and land made fertile with seaweed gathered from the
sea floor are important but Aveiro remains primarily a fishing town: lamprey and sea
perch are caught in the lagoon, sardines and skate on the coast. Aveiro is Portugal's
third largest industrial centre after Lisbon and Oporto. Gourmets visiting the town
should try the *ovos moles*, a type of egg dessert, usually served in miniature painted
wooden barrels. In July or August, during the Ria Festival, a competition takes place
on the central canal to find the best painted prow from the fleet of wide-bottomed
moliceiros used for harvesting the seaweed in the estuary *(see Ria de Aveiro below)*.

A distinctive feature

Canals crisscross the town spanned by several small bridges; the graceful *moliceiros*
as well as their mooring posts inevitably bring to mind Venetian gondolas and their
palli. The immediate proximity of the river and its labyrinth of waterways gives
Aveiro its originality. In addition, the town centre has several lovely buildings, a

AVEIRO

14 de Julho Pr.	Y		Comb. da Grande		
5 de Outubro Av.	Y	44	Guerra R.	Z	13
Antónia Rodrigues R.	Y	3	Dr Lourenço Peixinho Av.	Y	
Apresentação Largo da	Y	4	Eça de Queiroz R.	Z	15
Belém do Pará	Y	6	Eng. Pereira da Silva R.	Y	17
Capitão Sousa Pizarro R.	Z	9	Gustavo F. P.-Basto R.	Z	18
Clube dos Galitos R.	Y	10	Humberto Delgado Pr.	Y	21
Coimbra R.	Y	12	Jorge de Lencastre R.	Y	22
			José Estevão R.	Y	24
José Rabumba R.	Y	27			
Luis de Magalhães R. do C.	Y	28			
Marquês de Pombal Pr.	Z	31			
República Pr. da	Y	34			
Santa Joana R.	Z	37			
Santo António Largo de	Z	39			
Viana do Castelo R.	Y	42			

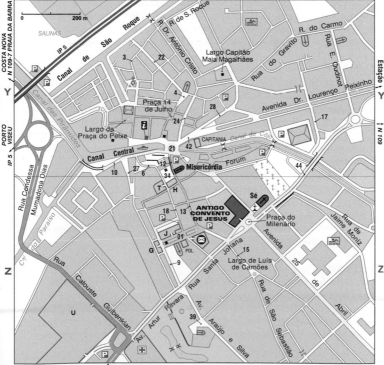

fine museum, a pleasant park and a main avenue with plenty of shade *(Avenida Dr Lourenço Peixinho)*. However, the jewel in Aveiro's crown is without doubt its magnificent museum, highlighting the exuberance and richness of the Baroque period and exhibiting a superb collection of sacred art. It is Portugal's second largest museum after the Museu Nacional de Arte Antiga in Lisbon.

Sights

Antigo Convento de Jesus★★
Open 10am-5.30pm. Closed Mon, 1 Jan, Good Fri, Easter Sun, 1 May and 25 Dec. €2 (no charge on Sun and mornings of holidays). ☎ 234 42 32 97 or 234 38 31 88. – Rua Santa Joana.

Museum★★
The Convent of Jesus was erected from the 15C to the 17C. Princess Joana, daughter of King Afonso V, retired here in 1472 and remained for the last 18 years of her life. In the 18C a Baroque façade was superimposed on the older front.

The museum exhibits various collections including sculptures of the Coimbra School (16C) and Portuguese Primitive paintings on wood. One is a lovely **portrait**★ of Princess Joana (late 15C), attributed to Nuno Gonçalves, remarkable for the severe sculptural features of the young girl dressed in court finery.

In the rooms devoted to Baroque art, there are statues in polychrome wood of the Aveiro angels, a strange Holy Family in earthenware from the workshop of Machado de Castro, and a lacquered wooden writing desk. The room where Saint Joana died in 1490 is now an oratory decorated with altarpieces and gilded wood.

Church★★
The church dates from the 15C, but the interior decoration was completed in the early 18C. The interior has some sumptuously carved and gilded wood, particularly in the **chancel**★★, a masterpiece of Baroque exuberance with its columns; scenes from the life of Saint Joana can be seen on *azulejos* panels. The **lower chancel**★*(coro baixo)*, with its painted wood ceiling, holds **St Joana's tomb**★★ (early 18C). This masterpiece by the architect João Antunes, a mosaic in polychrome marble, is supported by sitting angels, also in marble.

The Renaissance-style **cloisters** are surrounded by chapels, one of which contains the beautiful 15C **tomb of João de Albuquerque**. The refectory is totally covered with 17C *azulejos* decorated with floral motifs.

A tour of the Museum includes a visit to the church gallery or **coro alto** which is decorated with paintings and a 14C Crucifixion in which Christ's expression changes according to the angle.

Cathedral
This cathedral *(sé)* is the only remaining vestige of the former Convento de São Domingos, founded in 1423, but it has been greatly modified since it was first built. It has a Baroque façade and inside, a strange mixture of styles, including 17C and 18C polychrome *azulejos* on the walls of the nave and a 17C organ in the north arm of the transept. To the left of the entrance, there is an early Renaissance *Entombment*.

Cruzeiro de São Domingos
This Gothic-Manueline style calvary in front of the cathedral is an exact reproduction of the original, which is now housed inside the church.

Igreja da Misericórdia
The Church of the Misericord has an imposing finely-worked 17C doorway. Inside, the height of the nave and the 17C *azulejos* should be noted, as well as the church-wardens' pew opposite the pulpit.

Canal Quarter★ *2hr*

Some canals of the Ria de Aveiro continue right into the town; they are shored up by embankments which the water laps over at high tide.

Canal Central
Part of the canal is bordered by noble dwellings, their classical façades reflected in the water. The canal features a continuous spectacle of small boats, *moliceiros* or launches moving about and tying up. The best viewpoint is from the wide bridge-tunnel with balusters which divides it at the halfway point; this bridge is the main crossroads in the town *(Praça Humberto Delgado)*.

Canal de São Roque
This canal borders the built-up area to the north, and is spanned (in front of Rua Dr. António Cristo) by an elegant stone humpback footbridge. It divides the salt marshes from the salt warehouses which line the embankment among the low-roofed houses of the fishing quarter.

Ria de Aveiro★

The Ria de Aveiro appears as a vast lagoon marked by tides, dotted with islands and crisscrossed with channels. It is bordered by salt marshes and pine forests, behind an offshore bar some 45km/28mi long and not more than 2.5km/1.5mi wide, with a narrow bottleneck *(Estreito da Barra)* linking it to the ocean. The lagoon takes the shape of a triangle, and at high tide covers about 6 000ha/23sq mi, with an average depth of 2m/6.5ft. Rich in fish and fertile in the parts above sea level, the *ria* is particularly famous for its seaweed which is used as a fertiliser. The seaweed is traditionally collected in **moliceiros**, flat-bottomed boats with prows curved like swans' necks and painted with naive motifs in vivid colours. The boats either have a sail or are propelled with a pole. The rakes' prongs *(ancinhos)* for scraping or gathering up seaweed are hung around the tip of the prow. Unfortunately, the number of these boats is decreasing (some can be seen in front of the Tourist Office) although there is still an annual competition in July and August for the best decorated vessel.

Boat trips
⏱Allow a whole day for the complete tour including 3hr of relaxation on shore. Departures daily from Aveiro's Central Canal from 15 June to 15 Sept at 10am (return at about 5pm). For information and reservations apply to the Tourist Information Centre in Aveiro (Região de Turismo de Rota da Luz, Rua João Mendonça 8, 3800-200 Aveiro). Prices vary but are about €12 (€8 for children). ☎ 234 42 36 80 or 234 42 07 60.

Northern arm of the Ria

Bico
The interest of this small port, which is reached after crossing Murtosa, lies in the moliceiros that gather here on certain days.

Torreira
This is a small port on the *ria* where beautiful *moliceiros* may still be seen.
The Pousada da Ria, located between the two ports, is on the water's edge. The Reserva Natural das Dunas de São Jacinto is situated 2km/1mi before São Jacinto.

Reserva Natural das Dunas de São Jacinto
This nature reserve, which covers 666ha/1 645 acres of some of the best preserved dunes in Europe, is particularly interesting for its scenery, flora and fauna. A **visitor centre** contains exhibits about the rescue. *Guided tours (2hr 30min) at 9am and 1.30pm.* ○*Closed Thur, Sun and holidays.* ☏ *234 33 12 82 or 234 83 10 63.*

São Jacinto
The small resort in the pine woods at the end of the northern offshore bar on the Estreito da Barra is also a military camp and port. Oxen can be seen hauling up the fishing boats onto the beach.

Southern arm of the Ria

Ílhavo
This small former fishing port has become developed with some attractive turn-of-the-century villas such as the "Villa Africana", covered with *azulejos* in varying shades of yellow. Its fascinating **museum**★, devoted to fishing and the sea, has a comprehensive section on cod fishing, while a documentary dating from the 1970s shows the harsh reality of the fishing expeditions, some of which would last six months in the fishing grounds off Newfoundland.

Moliceiros on the Ria de Aveiro

Vista Alegre

This town has been a manufacturing centre of fine chinaware and glass since 1824. A small **museum** (🕐*Open 9am-12.30pm and 2-4.30pm (5pm Sat-Sun and holidays).* 🕐*Closed Mon, 1 Jan, Good Fri, Easter Sun, 1 May and 25 Dec. No charge.* ☎ *234 32 50 40/46)* on the factory premises recounts the developments in production since its earliest days through displays of machines, tools and examples of most of the pieces produced since its foundation.

AVIS

PORTALEGRE

POPULATION 4 893 – MICHELIN MAP 733

The first glimpse of Avis comes as a welcome sight as you cross the Alentejo plateau, covered mostly with cork oaks and olive trees. The town, about midway between Évora and Portalegre, has kept traces of its early fortifications and overlooks the confluence of the Seda and Avis rivers, now submerged below the waters of the reservoir serving the Maranhão power station, 15km/9mi downstream.

The N 243 from the south gives the best **view**★ of the town. Ramparts, a few medieval towers and the church of the Convento de São Bento, rebuilt in the 17C, stand witness today of the city's brilliant past. It was here, at the beginning of the 13C, that the military order founded in 1147 by Afonso Henriques to fight the Moors became geographically established. The oldest order of chivalry in Europe bore several names and followed the rules of several other orders before finally becoming the Order of St Benedict of Avis. It prospered in the Tagus region until 1789.

Avis was also the cradle of the dynasty which was to reign over Portugal from 1385 to 1580. On 7 August 1385 João (bastard son of Pedro I), Grand Master of the Order of Avis, was proclaimed king under the name **João I**. In February 1387 he married Philippa of Lancaster.

QUINTA DA **BACALHOA**★

SETÚBAL

MICHELIN MAP 733

This seigneurial residence, built at the end of the 15C and remodelled in the early 16C by the son of Afonso de Albuquerque, Viceroy of India, has both Renaissance and Moorish styles and rich **azulejo**★ decoration.

▶ **Orient Yourself:** The Quinta da Bacalhoa is on the N 10 as you leave Vila Fresca de Azitão heading towards Setúbal, opposite the bus station.

Visit

In the manor house a graceful loggia giving onto the gardens is adorned with polychrome *azulejo* panels depicting allegories of great rivers, including the Douro, Nile, Danube and Euphrates. The **Gardens** (👣 *Guided visit 9am-5pm;* 🕐*closed Sunday* *and holidays; €5; 212 18 00 11 - www.bacalhoa.com – advance reservations essential)* have a harmonious presentation and a pleasing freshness. In the formal garden, inspired by the style current in 16C France, clipped box trees alternate with fountains with mythological figures. An ornamental kitchen garden, where mandarin orange and walnut trees, bamboo and cinerarias grow, ends at an attractive pavilion and ornamental pool. The walls inside the pavilion are decorated with Spanish *azulejos* with geometrical patterns, but the most impressive panel is the Florentine-style depiction of **Susannah and the Elders**★, the oldest figurative panel in Portugal (1565). The tour ends in a walk beside a 15C gallery decorated with busts.

BARCELOS

BRAGA
POPULATION 125 000 – MICHELIN MAP 733

Barcelos is an attractive town on the north bank of the Cávado. It was the capital of the first county of Portugal and residence of the first Duke of Bragança, who was also the Count of Barcelos (see BRAGANÇA). It is now a busy agricultural centre and is well known for the production of pottery, ornamental crib figures, carved wood yokes and decorated cocks. *Largo da Porta Nova (Torre de Menagem) – 4750-329 253 81 18 82 or 253 81 21 35*

▶ **Orient Yourself:** 57km.43ml north-east of Porto.
Don't Miss: The market on Thursdays.
Organizing Your Time: 2 hours,10 minutes. That includes time for a coffee.
Also See: Braga, Viana do Costelo, Ponte de Lima.

The lively **market**, held on Thursday mornings, is one of Portugal's oldest and largest with agricultural products (hens, cockerels, vegetables, flowers) on one side and arts and crafts from the region and farther afield (pottery, baskets, hand-embroidered household linen, leather goods, harnesses and the famous cocks) on the other.

The Barcelos Cock
A pilgrim on his way to Santiago de Compostela was accused of theft as he was about to leave Barcelos. In spite of his honesty he found himself unable to offer a satisfactory defence and was condemned to die by hanging. He made one last plea. But the judge refused to be swayed in his condemnation of the stranger. The pilgrim therefore sought the protection of St James and, noticing the judge's repast of roast cock, declared that in proof of his innocence the cock would stand up and crow. The miracle occurred. The judge, in recognition of the pilgrim's innocence, set him free, and he erected a monument in memory of the miracle; it may now be seen in the museum in the former palace of the Ducal Counts of Barcelos.

Old Quarter

The main sights are centred on the **medieval bridge** over the Cávado in the southern part of the town.

Parish church
This 13C church, which was modified in the 16C and 18C, has a plain façade, flanked on the right by a square belfry, and a Romanesque doorway. The **interior**★ is glittering with gold and bordered with Baroque chapels. The walls are decorated with 18C **azulejos**. Some of the capitals are historiated.

Pillory

This pillory (*pelourinho*), which was erected in the Gothic period, has a hexagonal column upon which stands a graceful granite lantern.

Solar dos Pinheiros

This beautiful 15C Gothic manor house built of granite is adorned with three-storey corner towers.

Ruínas do Paço dos Duques de Bragança ou Condes de Barcelos

Barcelos cocks

These 15C palace ruins are the setting for a small open air **Museu Arqueológico** (*Open 9.30am-6pm; closed 1 Jan, Good Fri, Easter Sun, 1 May and 25 Dec; no charge; 253 82 12 51*).
Of particular interest are the steles and coats-of-arms of the House of Bragança, as well as the 14C monument set up in honour of the Barcelos cock *(see above)*.

Museu da Olaria

Open 10am-5.30pm; Sat-Sun and holidays, 10am-12.30pm and 2-5.30pm. Closed Mon, 1 Jan, Good Fri, Easter Sun, 15 Aug, 1 Nov and 24-25 Dec. €1.40. 253 82 47 41.
The ceramics museum in the basement of the palace contains one of the largest collections of its kind in Portugal, with pride of place given to the town's colourful emblem. An entire section is also devoted to the black tableware from the village of Prado, with illustrations of this age-old technique which is no longer used today. The museum is an ideal place in which to purchase the work of modern-day ceramists at reasonable prices. The best known include Mistério, who is continuing his family's traditions, and Júlia Ramalho, the grand-daughter of the already famous Rosa Ramalho.

Additional Sights

Campo da República

This vast esplanade in the centre of the town is the scene of the famous terracotta ware **market** held on Thursday mornings.

Igreja de Nossa Senhora do Terço★

On the northern side of Campo da República.
The Church of Our Lady of Terço was formerly part of a Benedictine monastery which was founded in 1707. The walls of the nave are covered with beautiful 18C **azulejos**★ depicting events in the life of St Benedict. The coffered ceiling is painted with 40 scenes of monastic life. The pulpit of gilded wood is richly ornamented.

Torre de Menagem

This tower, part of the remains of the 15C ramparts, now houses the Tourist Information Centre, where visitors can also purchase a range of arts and crafts.

Igreja do Bom Jesus da Cruz

The Church of Jesus, which is built in the Northern Baroque style, has an interesting plan in the shape of a Greek cross. According to legend, on 20 December 1504 a cross appeared on this very spot, following which a church was built to commemorate this miracle.

MOSTEIRO DA **BATALHA**★★★

LEIRIA

MICHELIN MAP 733

The Monastery of Batalha (Battle) is a mass of gables, pinnacles, buttresses, turrets and small columns standing majestically in a green valley. Although its setting is somewhat marred by the proximity of the N1 road, the rose gold effusion of its architecture remains one of the masterpieces of Portuguese Gothic and Manueline art. ▮ *Praça Mouzinho de Albuquerque– 2440-109* ☎ *244 76 51 80*

▶ **Orient Yourself:** On the N1 road, 118km/84ml south of Porto.
◷ **Organizing Your Time:** A couple of hours should allow you time to see it all.
☝ **Also See:** Alcobaça, Leiria, Nazaré.

A Bit of History

On 14 August 1385 on the plateau of Aljubarrota, 15km/9mi south of Batalha, two pretenders to the throne of Portugal faced each other, prepared to do battle: Juan I of Castile, nephew of the late king, and João I, Grand Master of the Order of Avis, who had been crowned king only seven days previously.

The opposing forces were of very different strengths: against the organised forces and 16 cannon of the Castilians, the Constable **Nuno Álvares Pereira** could only muster a squad of knights and foot soldiers. João I of Avis, knowing that defeat would mean Portugal passing under Spanish domination, made a vow to build a superb church in honour of the Virgin if she were to grant him victory. The Portuguese troops resisted and were victorious. Three years later the Mosteiro de Santa Maria da Vitória, subsequently known as the Mosteiro da Batalha, began taking shape.

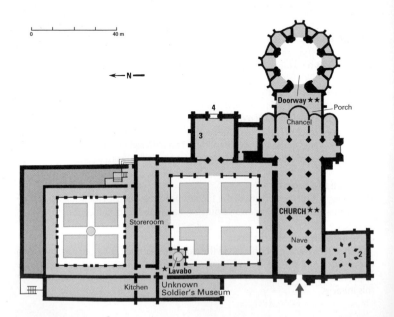

Visit *1hr*

○Open 9am-6pm (5pm Oct to Mar). ○Closed 1 Jan, Good Fri, Easter Sun, 1 May and 25 Dec. €3 (no charge Sun and holidays until 2pm). ☎ 244 76 54 97.

The **exterior** of the monastery, which in accordance with the Dominican rule has no belfry, possesses innumerable pinnacles, buttresses and openwork balustrades above Gothic and Flamboyant windows. The building is in fine-textured limestone, which has taken on a lovely ochre colour with time. The complicated structure at the east end of the church demonstrates the architectural problems arising from joining onto an earlier apse an octagonal rotunda which, by means of pillars, was to bear a vaulted ceiling.

The **Capela do Fundador**★ (Founder's Chapel), off the south aisle, is surmounted by an octagonal lantern supported by flying buttresses. The main façade is divided into three: the central part, decorated with a network of lancet-shaped blind arcades, is pierced by a beautiful Flamboyant window; the main doorway is richly carved,

Claustro Real, Mosteiro da Batalha

J.P. Lescouret/EXPLORER

bearing statues of Christ in Majesty, surrounded by the Evangelists, the twelve Apostles on the sides, and angels, prophets, kings and saints on the covings. The doorway's proportions appeared to better advantage when the church stood, as it did originally, below the level of the terrace outside.

Church★★

The church's vast **interior** is very plain, the outstanding element being the upward sweep of the vaulting. The chancel is lit by **stained-glass windows**★ which date from the 16C and depict scenes from the Life of the Virgin and Jesus Christ.

Capela do Fundador★

This square chamber, known as the Founder's Chapel, lit by Flamboyant windows, is covered with an octagonal lantern topped by a star-shaped cupola.

In the centre are the tombs (1) of King João I and his queen Philippa of Lancaster, the two figures reclining beneath delicately carved canopies. The Avis and Lancaster coats of arms appear on the tomb. Bays on the south and west sides contain the tombs of the founder's four younger sons (Duarte, the eldest was buried in the sanctuary), Fernando, João, Pedro and Prince Henry the Navigator, whose tomb (2) is covered with a canopy.

Claustro Real★★★

The Gothic and Manueline styles mix most successfully in the Royal Cloisters, the simplicity of the original Gothic design not being obscured by Manueline detail. The fleur-de-lis balustrade and the flowered pinnacles provide a motif which harmonises well with the Manueline tracery backing the carved marble arcades.

Chapter-House★★

The chapter-house *(sala do capitulo)* contains the tomb (3) of the Unknown Soldier where, in fact, the bodies of two Portuguese soldiers lie. Both died in the First World War, one in France, the other in Africa. The **vaulting**★★★ is an outstandingly bold feat; after two unsuccessful attempts the master architect Huguet managed to launch a square vault of some 20m/60ft without intermediary supports. The chamber is lit by a window containing early 16C **stained glass**★ (4) representing scenes of the Passion.

Lavabo★

The lavabo in the northwest corner of the cloisters consists of a basin with a festooned curbstone surmounted by two smaller basins. The light, filtering through the stone tracery between the arches, gives a golden glow to the stone and the water. The old refectory, which has a fine Gothic ceiling, houses the Museum of the Unknown Soldier.

Claustro de D Afonso V★

The coats of arms on the keystones to the vaulting in these fine Gothic cloisters are those of King Duarte I and King Afonso V.

▶ *Go round the outside of the chapter-house and through the porch to the Unfinished Chapels.*

Capelas Imperfeitas★★

Dom Duarte commissioned a vast mausoleum for himself and his descendents but he and his queen alone lie buried in the unfinished building open to the sky. A vast transitional Gothic Renaissance porch connecting the east end of the church with the doorway of the octagonal chamber was added later by Dom Manuel. This **doorway**★★, initially Gothic in style, was ornamented in the 16C with Manueline decoration; it opens towards the church with a curved arch beneath a powerful multilobed arch. The cut-away ornament of the festoons as well as the detailed decoration on the covings and the columns are particularly worthy of note.

BEJA★

BEJA
POPULATION 35 659 – MICHELIN MAP 733

Having been a brilliant Roman colony *(Pax Julia)*, the town became the seat of a Visigothic bishopric and then fell under Muslim control for four centuries. Today the capital of the Baixo Alentejo, it is a town of white houses and straight streets that is a flourishing agricultural market town. *Rua Capitão Francisco de Sousa 25 – 7800-451 – ☎ 284 31 19 91*

▶ **Orient Yourself:** Beja is 78km/57ml south of Évora.
⚘ **Don't Miss:** The cloisters in the old convent.
🕐 **Organizing Your Time:** You should see all you need within one day.
Kids **Especially for Kids:** The botanical gardens.
👁 **Also See:** The Guadiana valley.

Sights

Antigo Convento da Conceição ★
🕐*Open 9.30am-12.30pm and 2-5.15pm.* 🕐*Closed Mon, Sat and holidays.*
The Poor Clares Convent was founded by Dom Fernando, father of King Manuel, in 1459. The graceful Gothic balustrade crowning the church and the cloisters recalls that of the Mosteiro da Batalha.
Today the convent houses the regional museum, also known as the **Museu da Rainha Dona Leonor.** 🕐*Open 9.30am-12.30pm and 2-5.15pm.* 🕐*Closed Mon, Sat and holidays.* ⊛€2 (no charge Sun am.). ☎ 284 32 33 51.
The Baroque **church** was profusely decorated with gilded and carved woodwork in the 17C and 18C. The walls of the cloisters on the right are covered with *azulejos*. The chapter-house is richly decorated with beautiful 16C Hispano-Moorish *azulejos* from Seville and the vaulting is adorned with 18C floral motifs. A collection of Crucifixes is also on display. The rooms beyond contain paintings including a *St Jerome* by Ribera (17C) and a 15C *Ecce Homo*.
The first floor contains the Fernando Nunes Ribeiro archeological collection of engraved flagstones from the Bronze Age and Iron Age epigraphic stelae.
There is also a reconstruction of the cell window through which Sister Mariana Alcoforada is said to have talked to Count Chamilly.

Castle
🕐*Open in summer, 10am-1pm and 2-6pm; in winter, 9am-noon and 1-4pm.* 🕐*Closed Mon, 1 Jan, 25 Dec and local holidays.* ⊛€1.35 (no charge on Sun and holidays). ☎ 284 31 19 12.
The 13C castle's crenellated perimeter wall (housing a military museum), flanked by square towers, is overlooked at one corner by a high **keep**★ topped by pyramid-shaped merlons. The first floor, reached by a spiral staircase, has fine star vaulting resting on Moorish-style veined corner squinches.

Igreja de Santo Amaro★
This small Visigothic church, parts of which date back to the 6C, now houses the Visigothic art section 🕐*Same opening times as the Museu da Rainha Dona Leonor in the Convent (above).*

BELMONTE ★

CASTELO BRANCO
POPULATION 7 591 – MICHELIN MAP 733

This isolated town, perched high on a line of hills near the Serra da Estrela, has many churches that help create a vision of architectural harmony. The great navigator **Pedro Álvares Cabral,** who discovered Brazil in 1500, was born here. His statue stands on the main street which is named after him. ▯ *Praça da República, 18 – 6250-034 – ☎ 275 91 14 88*

▶ **Orient Yourself:** 25km.17ml south of Guarda.
 Don't Miss: The castle and as many churches as you wish to visit.
 Organizing Your Time: A couple of hours is enough to see it all.
 Also See: Guarda and the Serra da Estrela.

Sights

Castle
Open Oct-Apr, 9am-12,30pm; 2pm-5.30pm; May-Sept, 10am-1,30pm; 3pm-6.30pm. Closed 1 Jan, Good Fri, Easter Sun, 1 May and 25 Dec. No charge.
The castle was built in the 13C-14C by King Dom Dinis I; only the keep, the corner tower on the right with 17C balconies, and the section of the wall adjoining it on the left remain. A walk round the perimeter wall offers a fine **view** ★ of the countryside below.

Igreja de São Tiago
Open Oct-Apr, 9.30am-12.30pm; 2pm-6pm; May-Sept, 10am-12noon; 2.30pm-7pm. No charge.
Next to the castle and of an earlier period but modified in the 16C, the church still has some interesting elements inside dating from the Romanesque and Renaissance periods; a baptismal font, 16C frescoes in the chancel and 12C examples on the wall to the right. The Nossa Senhora da Piedade chapel, built in the 14C, contains a strange pulpit with a sounding-board and a polychrome Pietà carved from a single block of stone, as well as capitals which refer to the exploits of Fernão Cabral I, the father of Pedro Álvares Cabral.

Panteão dos Cabrais
Open summer,10am-12.30pm; 2pm-7pm. Winter 9.30am-12.30pm; 2pm-6pm. Closed Mon. Guided tours available. No charge. ☎ 275 91 14 88.
The pantheon containing the tombs of Pedro Álvares Cabral and his parents is in the late-15C chapel adjoining the Igreja de São Tiago.

Parish church
Open 9am-9pm.
The church, built in 1940, contains the picture of Our Lady of Hope, which, according to tradition, accompanied Pedro Álvares Cabral on his voyage of discovery to Brazil, as well as a replica of the cross used in the first mass celebrated there. The original can be seen in Braga Cathedral.

Torre Romana de Centum Cellas ★
4km/2.5mi to the north. Take the N 18 towards Guarda then, on the right, the road to Comeal (sign marked Monumento) where there is a road leading to the foot of the tower.
According to recent excavations, this impressive ruin is part of a 1C Roman villa which was connected to the tin trade along the road linking Mérida and Braga. Its square mass, made of pink granite blocks laid with dry joints, still stands with rectangular openings on three levels.

ILHA DA **BERLENGA**★★

LEIRIA
MICHELIN MAP 733

The Ilha de Berlenga, a reddish-coloured mass, which protrudes 12km/7mi out to sea from Cabo Carvoeiro, (Peniche, close to Óbidos), is the main island in an archipelago consisting of a number of rocky islets, the Estelas, the Forcadas and the Farilhões. Berlenga, 1 500m/4 921ft long and 800m/2 625ft at its widest point, reaches a height of 85m/279ft. The major attractions of this block of bare granite lie in its numerous indentations and headlands and in its marine caves.

Visit

Access
There is a regular boat service to the island from Peniche between 15 May and 20 Sept. Return (round trip) ticket: €17 per person; crossing time: 45min. For bookings, contact Contact Berlenga Turpesca de Tiago & Bernardo ☎ 262 78 99 60 , or contact the Tourist Office in Peniche. ☎ 262 78 21 53.

Boat trip★★★
Contact Berlenga Turpesca de Tiago & Bernardo, Largo da Ribeira, 2520 Peniche. ☎ 262 78 99 60.
Among the most striking sights of the trip are, south of the inn, the Furado Grande, a marine tunnel 70m/230ft long which ends in a small creek (Cova do Sonho) walled by towering cliffs of red granite; beneath the fortress itself is a cave known locally as the "Gruta Azul" or "Blue Grotto", where light refracts on the sea within, producing an unusual and most attractive emerald green pool.

Walk ★★
1hr 30min.
Take the stairway from the inn to the lighthouse. Halfway up turn to look at the fortress in its **setting**★; on reaching the plateau take a path on the left which goes to the west coast or Wild Coast. There is a good **view**★ from the top, of the rocks. Return to the lighthouse and descend a path leading to a small bay bordered by a beach and a few fishermen's cottages. Halfway down, to the left, the view of a creek where the sea roars and pounds in bad weather is particularly impressive.

BRAGA★

BRAGA
POPULATION 163 981 – MICHELIN MAP 733

Marked by its long clerical history, Braga is bristling with churches and monasteries and has a reputation for being rooted in the past. Nonetheless, as the capital of the Minho, it is an active industrial centre. A yoke fair is still held on Tuesdays on the fairground *(largo da feira).*  *Av. da Liberdade 1 – 4710-305 – ☎ 253 26 25 50*

▶ **Orient Yourself:** At the confluence of the rivers Este and Ávado, 54km/38ml north-east of Porto.
🅿 **Parking:** Use the underground parking in the town as surface parking is limited to two hours.

- 🏵 **Don't Miss:** Holy Week.
- 🕐 **Organizing Your Time:** Allow a complete day.
- 🕯 **Also See:** The upper Cávado valley, Porto and Guimarães.

A Bit of History

A very religious city

Bracara Augusta, an important Roman town, was made into their capital by the Suevi when they advanced upon the area in the 5C. The town was subsequently captured first by the Visigoths (who built the Igreja de São Frutuoso) and then the Moors and only regained prosperity after the Reconquest when it became the seat of an archbishopric.

BRAGA							
Abade Loureira R.	Y	3	Chãos R. dos	Y	12	General Norton de	
Biscainhos R. dos	Y	4	Conde de Agrolongo Pr.	Y	13	Matos Av.	Y	24
Caetano Brandão R.	Z	6	Dom Afonso Henriques R.	Z	15	Nespereira Av.	Y	25
Capelistas R. dos	Y	7	Dom Diogo de Sousa R.	YZ	16	São João do Souto Pr.	Z	27
Carmo R. do	Y	9	Dom Gonç. Pereira R.	Z	18	São Marcos R.	YZ	28
Central Av.	Y	10	Dom Paio Mendes R.	Z	19	São Martinho R. de	Y	30
			Dr Gonçalo Sampaio R.	Z	21	São Tiago Largo de	Z	31
			Franc. Sanches R.	Z	22	Souto R. do	YZ	33

Antigo Paço Episcopal	Y	A	Casa das Gelosias	Z	E	Igreja de Santa Cruz	Z	L
Capela da Nossa Senhora			Casa do Raio / casa do			Museu dos Biscaínhos	Y	M¹
da Penha de França	Y	B	Mexicano	Z	F		
Capela dos Coimbras	YZ	C	Fonte do Pelicano	Y	K		

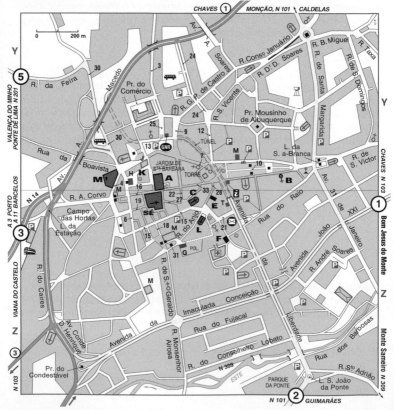

From this time onwards the influence of the Church became paramount, a feature now particularly apparent in the richness of the architecture; in the 16C the archbishop and patron Dom Diogo de Sousa presented the town with a palace, churches and calvaries in the Renaissance style; in the 18C the two prelates, Dom Rodrigo of Moura Teles and Dom Gaspar of Bragança, made Braga the centre of Portuguese Baroque art. Braga, once the seat of the Primate of All Spain, is still strongly ecclesiastical in character. Holy Week is observed with devotion and is the occasion for spectacular processions. The Feast of St John the Baptist on 23 and 24 June attracts crowds of local people and even many from as far as Galicia; they attend the processions, folk dancing and firework displays in the highly decorated town.

Cathedral★ *1hr 30min*

Guided tours (1hr), 8.30am-6.30pm. ☎ 253 26 33 17.
Only the south doorway and the arching over the main doorway remain from the original Romanesque cathedral. The portico with festooned Gothic arches is by Biscayan artists brought to Braga in the 16C by Diogo de Sousa. The moulded window frames date from the 17C. This same archbishop is responsible for the cathedral's east end bristling with pinnacles and balusters. The graceful **statue**★ of the Nursing Madonna (Nossa Senhora do Leite) beneath a Flamboyant canopy which adorns the east end exterior is said to be by Nicolas Chanterene.

Interior ★
The interior, which was transformed during the 18C, is striking in its contrast between the richness of the Baroque woodwork and the simplicity of the nave. The font (1) is Manueline: to the right, in a chapel closed by a 16C grille, lies the bronze tomb (*túmulo*, 15C) of the Infante Dom Afonso. The Chapel of the Holy Sacrament (Capela

Address Book

WHERE TO STAY
Albergaria Bracara Augusta – *Avenida Central, 134 – ☎ 253 20 62 60 - www.bracaraaugusta.com- 19 rooms.* A new hotel (2005) in a beautiful building. The rooms are very comfortable and well decorated in a contemporary style. A small garden at the rear is ideal for breakfast in good weather.

Hotel Residencial Dona Sofia – *Largo São João do Souto, 131, ☎ 253 26 31 60 – 34 rooms .* This comfortable hotel close to the cathedral is housed in a fully renovated old mansion with comfortable rooms, yet lacking in style.

EATING OUT
Anjou Verde - *Largo da Praça Velha, ☎ 21 253 26 40 10 - closed Sunday.* Lovely décor, lively and fresh; a very good vegetarian restaurant where the portions and flavours wil leave you delighted. A warm welcome.

Inácio - *Campo das Hortas, 4, ☎ 253 61 32 35 - closed Christmas, Easter, 2 weeks in Mar and Sept.* A restaurant where typical menus are served with exquisite care. The restaurant enjoys a high reputation and it is well deserved.

INTERNET
Biblioteca Pública da Universidade do Minho - *Antigo Paço Episcopal, Largo do Paço (2 places). Free.*
Café-Bar James Dean - *Rua Santo André, 85. 253 61 76 02. Daily 8am-10pm, Sun 1pm-7pm. 30min €1; 60min €1.75.*

TRANSPORT
Railway station - *Largo da Estação ☎ 253 27 82 52 -* Trains for Porto (journey 1hr) every 30min during the day.
Buses - *Praça da Estação Rodoviária ☎ 253 20 94 00.* There are extensive services with connections to many towns, particularly in the region. A comfortable and inexpensive way to travel.

do Sacramento) contains a fine 17C polychrome wooden altar (2) representing the Church Triumphant after a picture by Rubens.

The chancel, covered with intricate ribbed **vaulting**★, contains a Flamboyant **altar**★ (3) of Ançã stone carved on the front with scenes of the Ascension and of the Apostles. Above the altar is a 14C statue of St Mary of Braga. To the left of the chancel is a chapel (4) decorated with 18C *azulejos* by António de Oliveira Bernardes depicting the life of St Pedro de Rates, first bishop of Braga. A harmonious Baroque group is formed by the two 18C **cases**★ on either side of the balustraded organ loft.

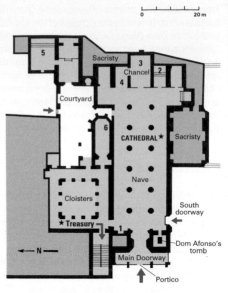

Treasury ★

The cathedral treasury *(tesouro)* €2 has a fine collection of 16C-18C vestments as well as a Manueline chalice, a 14C cross in rock crystal, a 17C silver-gilt reliquary cross, a 10C Mozarabic chest made of ivory, a 16C chalice, a 17C monstrance, Dom Gaspar of Bragança's 18C silver-gilt monstrance adorned with diamonds, and several statues including a 13C Christ and St Crispin and St Crispinian. A tour of the treasury includes the **Capela de São Geraldo** and the **Capela da Glória**★, the walls of the former decorated with 18C *azulejos* illustrating the life of St Gerald who was the first archbishop of Braga. The Gothic Chapel of Glory is decorated with 14C mural paintings in the Mudéjar style. The sides of the Gothic **tomb**★ (5) of the founder, Dom Gonçalo Pereira, in the centre of the chapel, bear reliefs of the Crucifixion and the figures of the Apostles, the Virgin and Child and clerics at prayer.

Capela dos Reis

The Kings' Chapel, with Gothic vaulting resting on beautiful brackets sculpted with human heads, contains the 16C tombs (6) of Henry of Burgundy and his wife Teresa, parents of Afonso Henriques, the first king of Portugal, and the mummy of Dom Lourenço Vicente (14C), archbishop of Braga, who fought at Aljubarrota.

Additional Sights

Antigo Paço Episcopal

The former Episcopal Palace is made up of three edifices dating from the 14C, 17C and 18C. The library, whose reading room has a beautiful gilt coffered ceiling, shelves 9C documents. The medieval north wing looks out over the pleasant Santa Bárbara Gardens, including the 17C fountain of St Barbara.

Capela dos Coimbras

Visits of the interior only on Thurdays from 9am-7pm.

The 16C Coimbras Chapel, next to an 18C church, has a crenellated and statue-ornamented tower built in the Manueline style. The Casa dos Coimbras, adjoining the chapel, dates from the same period and has an attractive portal and Manueline-style windows.

Museu dos Biscainhos

Open 10am-12.15pm; 2-5.30pm. Closed Mon, 1 Jan, Good Fri, Easter Sun, 1 May and 25 Dec. €2 (no charge on Sun and mornings of holidays). ☎ 253 20 46 50.

This 17C and 18C palace with its painted ceilings adorned with stuccowork and its walls decorated with panels of *azulejos* has been arranged with Portuguese and foreign furniture dating from the same period. There are carpets from Arraiolos, Portuguese silverware, porcelain and glassware. The graceful suite of rooms leads onto beautiful gardens with an ornamental pool and 18C-style statues.

Fonte do Pelicano

In front of the town hall there is a lovely Baroque fountain where the water spouts from a pelican and bronze cupids.

Capela da Nossa Senhora da Penha de França

Open 7.30am-noon. Closed during Aug. If closed during these times, please contact the gate of Lar D.Pedro V or ☎ 253 20 06 80.

The chapel is embellished with fine *azulejos* by Policarpo de Oliveira Bernardes and a 17C Baroque pulpit.

Stairway of the Five Senses, Santuário do Bom Jesus do Monte

Y. Travert/DIAF

Excursion

Santuário do Bom Jesus do Monte★★

6km/4mi east. Leave Braga by ① on the town plan.

The Baroque flight of steps to the Bom Jesus sanctuary is one of Portugal's most famous monuments. It is carved out of austere grey granite set off by whitewashed walls, an example of the Northern Baroque style. The Stairway of the Three Virtues is Rococo, while the church, which was built by Carlos Amarante between 1784 and 1811, is neo-Classical.

Escadaria dos Cinco Sentidos

Funicular to the top, 8am-8pm daily; departures every 30min. One-way journey: €2 free Sun and holiday mornings.

The Stairway of the Five Senses is a double staircase with crossed balustrades; the base consists of two columns entwined by a serpent; water pours from the serpent's jaws, flowing back over the length of its body. Above the Fountain of the Five Wounds (where water falls from the five bezants of the Portuguese coat of arms), each level is embellished by a fountain designed allegorically as one of the five senses. Water springs from the eyes representing sight, from the ears for hearing, from the nose for the sense of smell and from the mouth for taste. The sense of touch is shown by a person holding a pitcher in both hands and pouring water.

BRAGANÇA★

BRAGANÇA

POPULATION 14 662 – MICHELIN MAP 733

The medieval city within Brangança's ramparts stands on high overlooking the modern town. The best view★ is from the São Bartolomeu *pousada* or from the chapel look-out point beside it *(2km/1mi southeast).* 🛈 *Av Cidade de Zamora – 5300-111 – ☎ 273 38 12 73*

▶ **Orient Yourself:** 90km/60ml east of Chaves, close to the border with Spain.
👁 **Don't Miss:** The park at Montesinho and the border villages.
🕐 **Organizing Your Time:** Allow a day for the park and the town.
🕐 **Also See:** Chaves and Mirandela.

Medieval City★

Castle

Open 9am-noon and 2-5pm (5.30pm in summer). Closed holidays. €1.50(no charge Sun morning). ☎ 273 32 23 78.

The castle, which was built in 1187, comprises a tall square keep 33m/108ft high, flanked by battlemented turrets, and several towers, which house a small **military museum** *(Open 9am-12.30pm and 2-5.30pm. Closed Thur and holidays. No charge. ☎ 273 32 21 81)*; two halls are lit by paired Gothic windows. The panorama from the keep platform extends over the old town, the lower town and the surrounding hills.

Igreja de Santa Maria

The origins of the church date from the Romanesque period, although it was totally remodelled in the 18C. It has an elegant façade with a door which is framed by two

City walls, Bragança

J.P. Lesco.urret/EXPLORER

twisted columns decorated with vine plants; inside a fine ceiling painted in *trompe-l'œil* depicts the Assumption.

Domus Municipalis

🕐*Open 9am-12.30pm and 2-5pm.* 🕐*Closed Thur and holidays. No charge.* ☎ *273 32 21 81.*

This pentagonal-shaped building, erected in the 12C, is the oldest town hall in Portugal. It is pierced on every side by small rounded arches. A frieze of carved modillions runs beneath the roof. The interior consists of a vast chamber and, below, a basement with a former cistern.

Additional Sights

These may be seen in the lower town that was built in the 17C and 18C.

Largo da Sé

The square is adorned with a large Baroque cross which was originally a pillory. The cross is in front of the city's cathedral, which is adorned with *azulejos* and features Baroque carved and gilded altars inside.

Igreja de São Bento

This single-nave 16C church has a Renaissance-style painted wooden ceiling. The chancel, with its attractive **Mudéjar ceiling**, contains a valuable 18C gilded wooden altar screen.

Igreja de São Vicente

St Vincent's church is Romanesque in origin, but was totally reconstructed in the 18C. The interior contains a profusion of *talha dourada* work from the 17C, and the chancel is topped by a gilded vault. According to tradition, it was in this church that the secret wedding between Dom Pedro and Dona Inês de Castro took place (👣 *see ALCOBAÇA*).

Museu do Abade de Baçal ★

Open 10am-5pm (6pm Sat-Sun and holidays). Closed Mon, 1 Jan, Good Fri, Easter Sun, 1 May and 25 Dec. €2 (no charge on Sun and holidays until 2pm). ☎ 273 33 15 95.
The museum is housed in the former Episcopal Palace. The collections include archeological displays, paintings, items of local ethnological interest, coins and religious art. At the entrance, a video provides an insight into Trás-os-Montes costumes, and an interactive computer provides information on the museum, the region and its monuments. The ground floor contains a fine collection of funerary steles and milestones. On the second floor, the chapel of the former palace, with its painted ceiling, displays a set of 16C and 17C ecclesiastical vestments and polychrome pictures of saints. In Room 7, a 15C Virgin with Child in gilded and polychrome wood is worthy of particular note. The museum also contains an interesting collection of goldsmiths' art.

BRAVÃES ★

VIANA DO CASTELO
POPULATION 653 – MICHELIN MAP 733

Bravães is a tiny village in a secluded spot along the road between Ponte da Barca and Ponte de Lima. Its church is one of the finest Romanesque buildings in Portugal and is worth a visit.

Igreja de São Salvador★

Open 8am-7pm. ☎ 258 45 21 97.
The façade of this small Romanesque church (12C) has a remarkable **doorway**★ whose arching is covered in an intricate decoration representing doves, monkeys, human figures and geometrical motifs; richly historiated capitals crown naively carved statue columns. The tympanum, resting on the stylised heads of a pair of bulls, is ornamented with two angels in adoration of Christ in Majesty. A low relief of the Holy Lamb is carved into the tympanum of the south doorway, which is supported by two griffins.
Inside, the triumphal arch is embellished by a frieze influenced by Arabic design.

MATA DO BUÇACO ★★

BUÇACO FOREST – AVEIRO
MICHELIN MAP 733

The forest of Buçaco lies to the north of Coimbra near the Luso spa, crowning the northernmost peak of the Serra do Buçaco. It is enclosed by a stone wall pierced by several gates. The forest can be explored on foot and by car. ▯ Rua Emidio Navarro –3050-201– ☎ 231 93 91 33.

▸ **Orient Yourself:** Due north of Coimbra, about 25km/17ml.
⊚ **Don't Miss:** Explore the hidden forest. See the itineraries below.
⊙ **Organizing Your Time:** An hour or so by car but it's better to get out for the day.
Kids **Especially for Kids:** a picnic in the heart of the forest.
⚲ **Also See:** Aveiro and Coimbra.

The Forest

In the 6C Benedictine monks from Lorvão built a hermitage i
In 1628 the Barefoot Carmelites built a community and surrou
a wall. They continued to preserve and develop the forest by pl
and obtained a papal bull from Urban VIII threatening anyone c
with excommunication. In 1834 all religious orders in Portugal w
the Carmelite friars had to leave Buçaco. The forest was taken in ...uyal care and
then came under the Water and Forest Department of the government.

Visit
€2.50/car; 5 people or more €5.
The 105ha/250 acres of forest in Buçaco harbour 400 native varieties of tree and
about 300 exotic species, including ginkgos, monkey-puzzles, cedars, Himalayan
pines, thuyas, Oriental spruces, palms, arbutus, sequoias and Japanese camphor
trees as well as tree ferns, hydrangeas, mimosas, camellias, magnolias, philarias
and even lilies of the valley.

Palace-Hotel★
The hunting lodge, more like a stage set than a hotel, was commissioned by King
Carlos and built by the Italian architect Luigi Manini between 1888 and 1907. It is
flanked by a small tower surmounted by an armillary sphere. The decoration inside
is exuberant, its walls covered with huge *azulejos* panels depicting episodes from
Camões' **The Lusiads**, and battle scenes from the history of Portugal.

Convento dos Carmelitas Descalços
*Below the hotel . ⏰Open 9am-12.30pm and 2-5.20pm. ⏰Closed Sun, Mon and holidays. *€0.60.*
The remains of the Barefoot Carmelite Convent built, completed by 1630, comprise
a chapel, cloisters and monks' cells lined with cork to keep out the cold.

1 Fonte Fria and Vale dos Fetos★★
1hr 15min round trip on foot.

Palace-Hotel

B. Barbier/DIAF

Ermida Nossa Senhora de Assunção

The Hermitage of Our Lady of the Assumption is one of ten hermitages in the forest to which the monks used to retire. After seeing this you can move on to the **Fonte Fria.** The water of the Cold Fountain rises in a cave and spills out to form a cascade down a flight of 144 stone steps; at the bottom, hydrangeas and magnolias surround the pool into which the water flows and which also mirrors some majestic conifers nearby. There is a gate from the forest, the **Porta de Coimbra**, (Coimbra Gate) which was built at the same time as the 17C wall and has Rococo decoration.

▶ *Return by way of Avenida do Mosteiro, an avenue of superb cedars.*

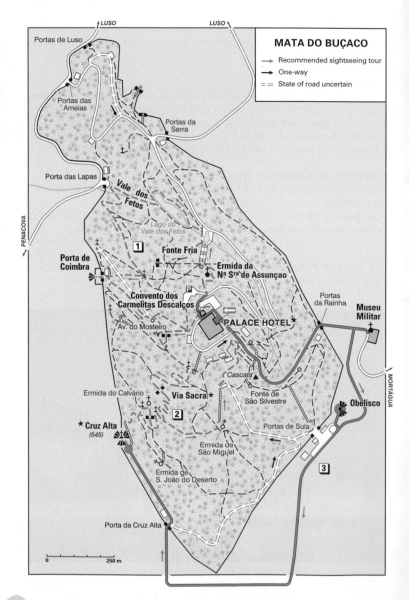

② Via Sacra and Cruz Alta★★ *1hr round trip on foot*

▸ *Take Avenida do Mosteiro below the convent, then turn left for the Via Sacra.*

The **Via Sacra**★ (Way of the Cross) was built in the Baroque style in the late 17C. The chapels along the way contain life-size terracotta figures enacting the road to Calvary. You then reach the **Cruz Alta**★★ at an altitude of 545m/1 788ft.

▸ *Return by the woodland paths which lead past various hermitages.*

③ The Cruz Alta by Car *6km/4mi*

A few hundred yards from the hotel is the waterfall (cascata), fed by the **Fonte de São Silvestro** nestling among ferns and hydrangeas.

Museu Militar
🕙 *Open 10am-12.30pm; 2pm-5pm.* 🚫 *Closed Mon, 1 Jan, Good Fri, Easter Sun and 25 Dec.* ✎€1. ☎ 231 93 93 10.
The military museum features the Battle of Buçaco and the campaigns of 1810, in which the Duke of Wellington faced the French.

CAMINHA

VIANA DO CASTELO
POPULATION 1 878 – MICHELIN MAP 733

The fortified town of Caminha was part of Portugal's northern frontier defences against Galician aspirations. It occupied a key position at the confluence of the Coura and the Minho and also controlled the Minho estuary, overlooked on the Spanish side by Monte Santa Tecla. Caminha is now a fishing village and craft centre for coppersmiths. 🗐 *Rua Ricardo Joaquim de Sousa – 4910-155 – ☎ 258 92 19 52*

▸ **Orient Yourself:** On the northern border, on the main road towards Vigo (Spain).
🕙 **Organizing Your Time:** About an hour will allow you time to see everything.
🐾 **Also See:** Valença do Minho, Viana do Castelo.

Praça do Conselheiro Silva Torres
The square is still largely medieval in character with ancient buildings grouped round a 16C granite fountain. The 15C **Casa dos Pitas** is Gothic and its emblazoned façade is elegant with curved windows. The town hall **(Paços do Concelho)** has a lovely coffered ceiling in the council chamber. The clock tower (Torre do Relógio) was once part of the 14C fortifications.

▸ *Go through this gate to Rua Ricardo Joaquim de Sousa which leads to the church.*

Parish church
⚯ *Closed until mid-2007.*
Inside is a magnificent *artesonado* **ceiling**★ of maplewood. Each octagonal panel, framed in stylised cabling, bears a rose at its centre. On the right, stands a statue of St Christopher, patron saint of boatmen. The Chapel of the Holy Sacrament, to the right of the chancel, contains a 17C gilded wood tabernacle illustrated with scenes from the Passion by Francisco Fernandes.

CARAMULO

VISEU

POPULATION 1 546 – MICHELIN MAP 733

Caramulo, a little to the south-west of Viseu, is a spa at an altitude of 800m/2 625ft on a wooded hillside in the Serra de Caramulo. Parks and gardens enhance this town on the schist and granite massif which is wooded with pines, oaks and chestnuts and also has crops such as maize, vines and olives. The western slope, which descends gently towards the Aveiro coastal plain, is completely different from the eastern slope where the sharper relief is cut away by tributaries of the Mondego ⏃ *Estrada Principal do Caramulo – 3475-031 – ☎ 232 86 14 37*

Sight

Museu do Caramulo★
🕐*Open 10am-1pm and 2-5pm (6pm Mar-Sept).* 🕐*Closed Jan 1, Good Friday, Easter Sunday, 24-25 Dec.* ⊚€6. ☎ *232 86 12 70 - www.muse-caramulo.net.*
The museum, which is also called the Fundacão Abel Lacerda after its founder, comprises two sections. An **Ancient and Modern Art Exhibition** contains statues from the 15C Portuguese School including a Virgin and Child, a series of tapestries from Tournai representing the arrival of the Portugueuse in India and a large number of paintings by contemporary artists: Picasso (still-life), Fernand Léger, Dufy, Dalí and Braque. The other part contains an interesting **Automobile Exhibition** ★ with some 50 vehicles, all beautifully maintained in working order, on display. Among the oldest are an 1899 Peugeot and a 1902 Darraco; the most prestigious include Hispano-Suizas, Lamborghinis and Ferraris. There are also some bicycles and motorbikes.

Excursions

Pinoucas★ *3km/2mi.*

▶ *Leave Caramulo heading north on the N 230; after 2km/1.5mi bear left on a dirt track which ends at the watchtower 1km/0.5mi farther on.*

From the top (alt 1 062m/3 481ft) there is an impressive **panorama** over the Serra de Caramulo.

Serra de Caramulo *7.5km/4.5mi.*

▶ *Leave Caramulo heading west on Avenida Abel Lacerda which becomes the N 230-3; 3km/2mi farther on you pass on your left the road leading to Cabeço da Neve.*

Caramulinho★★
30min round trip on foot, by a rocky path which has 130 steps cut into its face.
The tip of the Serra do Caramulo (alt 1 075m/3 527ft) makes an excellent **viewpoint** over the Serra da Lapa in the northeast, the Serra da Estrela in the southeast, the Serra da Lousã and Serra do Buçaco to the south, over the coastal plain to the west, and over the Serra da Gralheira to the north.

▶ *Return to the intersection with the Cabeço da Neve road, which you then take to the viewpoint.*

Cabeço da Neve
Alt 995m/3 264ft. This balcony summit has plunging **views** to the south and towards the east, over the lower wooded mountain dotted with villages, the Mondego basin and the Serra da Estrela.

CARVOEIRO★

FARO
MICHELIN MAP 733 – LOCAL MAP SEE ALGARVE

Built into a narrow indentation in the cliff, this fishing village has become a pleasant seaside resort that has not yet been spoilt by modern buildings. ⊠ *Praia do Carvoeiro – 8400-517 Lagoa – ☎ 282 35 77 28*

▶ **Orient Yourself:** On the Algarve coast between Faro and Albufeira.

Algar Seco★★
500m/1/3mi beyond the Miradouro de Nossa Senhora da Encarnação, plus 30min round trip on foot. Leave the car in the car park.
Below Cabo Carvoeiro, the **marine site** of Algar Seco is reached through a maze (including 134 steps) of reddish rocks sculpted by the sea in the shape of peaks and arches. On the right *(sign "A Boneca")*, a short tunnel leads under a conically formed ceiling into a cavern (converted into a refreshment room in summer) which has two natural "windows" from which there is a view encompassing the western cliffs. On the left, a path leads to a headland from which one can see the entrance to a deep underwater cave.
The **sea caves** of Cabo Carvoeiro can be visited by boat during the season. ⓒ*To visit the sea caves, ask the fishermen in Algar Seco or on Praia do Carvoeiro.*

CASCAIS★

LISBOA
POPULATION 29 882 – MICHELIN MAP 733

Cascais is both a traditional fishing port of age old tradition and a bustling holiday resort. It is progressively expanding into a smart suburb of Lisbon with its developed centre and pleasant pedestrian streets lined with shops and restaurants. It is also a pleasant place to visit. ⊠ *Rua Visconde da Luz – 2750-415 – ☎ 214 86 82 04 or 214 86 70 44*

▶ **Orient Yourself:** West along the coast from Lisbon.
🅿 **Parking:** Not too difficult, apart from Fri/Sat evenings.
🐾 **Don't Miss:** The old town hall square which is lively; Boca de Inferno.
ⓒ **Organizing Your Time:** It's the place to stay for a weekend.
🐾 **Also See:** Estoril, with its lovely casino.

A Bit of History

Tourism came to Cascais in 1870 when the court moved here for the summer to escape the heat of Lisbon. With the court came a tradition of elegance and a group of architects. The royal palace or former citadel on the promontory which protects the bay on the southwest is now a residence of the Head of State.

Sight

Museu-Biblioteca dos Condes de Castro Guimarães

Museum: 🔊 *Guided tours (30min), 10am-5pm.* ⏰*Closed Mon and holidays.* ⊜€1.50 *(no charge on Sun).* ☎ *214 82 54 07. Library:* ⏰*Open 9am-5pm (1pm Sat).* ⏰*Closed Sun, holidays and Sat in July, Aug and Sept.* ☎ *214 82 54 07/01.*

On the coast road, this 19C noble residence, with a central patio, has a collection of 17C Portuguese and Indo-Portuguese furniture and *azulejos*, 18C and 19C Portuguese gold and silversmith work and pottery, 18C bronzes, carpets and Chinese vases and many valuable books (one of which is a 16C *Chronicles of D. Afonso Henriques*).

Excursion

From Cascais to Praia do Guincho★

8km/5mi heading west on the coast road – about 30min.
On leaving Cascais, pass the former royal palace on the left.

Boca do Inferno★

A restaurant with a few pines standing on the left marks the site of this **abyss**★ formed by marine erosion. The sea, entering under a rock arch, booms and crashes particularly in stormy weather. The power of the ocean is spectacular to watch.

The road continues as a *corniche* above the sea, offering some fine views of the wild coast. Beyond Cabo Raso (small fort), where the road turns off towards the Serra de Sintra, stretches of sand pounded by rough seas can be glimpsed between the rocky points.

Praia do Guincho★

This immense beach is backed by windswept dunes and a small fort; the imposing headland, Cabo da Roca, can be seen. This is a popular spot for windsurfing.

CASTELO BRANCO

CASTELO BRANCO
POPULATION 55 909 – MICHELIN MAP 733

The town was well fortified as it lay strategically close to the Spanish border, but it nevertheless suffered a number of invasions and occupations – events which have left few historic monuments. The maraudings of the Napoleonic troops in 1807 were among the most devastating. The scant ruins of a Templars' stronghold dominate the town. Today the capital of Beira Baixa is a peaceful, flower-decked city living on its trade in cork, cheese, honey and olive oil. It is particularly known for the fine bedspreads (**colchas**) embroidered in different colours in a tradition going back to the 17C. 🗺 *Alameda da Liberdade – 6000-074 – ☎ 272 33 03 39.*

▸ **Orient Yourself:** The southern edge of the Serra da Estrela, a little north of the Tagus as it spills into Portugal from Spain.
🔎 **Don't Miss:** The new Cargaleiro museum and the village of Monsanto.
🕐 **Organizing Your Time:** Give yourself a half day here.
🔥 **Also See:** The southern slopes of the Serra da Estrela.

Sights

Museu Francisco Tavares Proença Júnior

○*Open 10am-12.30pm; 2pm-5.30pm.* ○*Closed Mon, 1 Jan, Good Fri, Easter Sun, 1 May and 25 Dec.* ●*€2 (no charge Sun and holidays 10am-12.30pm).* ☎ *272 34 42 77.*
This museum is housed in the old episcopal palace and contains an interesting collection of coins, earthenware, ancient weapons and Roman pottery on the ground floor, and 16C Flemish tapestries *(Story of Lot)* on the staircase. Exhibits upstairs include more tapestries, paintings of the 16C Portuguese School (a **Santo António** attributed to Francisco Henriques) and antique Portuguese furniture.

Gardens, Antigo Paço Episcopal★★

○*Open 9am-5pm (7pm in summer).* ○*Closed 1 Jan and 25 Dec.* ●*€2.*
The 17C gardens belonged to the Episcopal Palace and now form an unusual ensemble of topiary, banks of flowers, ornamental pools, fountains and Baroque statues. An alley, which runs beside the Crown Lake and ends in two flights of steps, is lined by balustrades peopled with statues: the Apostles and the Evangelists on the right, the Kings of Portugal on the left.

Convento da Graça e Museu de Arte Sacra da Misericórdia

►*Guided tours (20min), 9am-noon; 2pm-5pm.* ○*Closed Sat-Sun and holidays.* ●*€0.50.* ☎ *272 34 44 54, ext 57.*
Opposite the palace is the Convento da Graça, which has retained a Manueline door from its primitive early-16C construction. Inside the Santa Casa da Misericórdia, a small sacred art museum contains the statues of Queen Saint Isabel and St John of God with a pauper, a Virgin and Child, a 16C St Matthew and two marble statues of Christ on the cross.

Medieval town

The medieval town **(cidade medieval)**, with its traditional stone-paved narrow streets and clothes and cages hanging from the windows, has preserved a few interesting buildings such as the former Paços do Conselho (Town Hall) on the Praça Velha, dating from the 1600s but significantly remodelled since, the 17C Arco do Bispo on the attractive Praça Camões, as well as several other delightful palaces.

Gardens, Antigo Paço Episcopal

Museu Cargaleiro ★

🕐 *Open 10am-1pm; 2pm-6pm.* 🚫*Closed Mon.* ∞€2. ☎ *272 33 73 94.*
This is a museum of contemporary works by the Portuguese artist Manual Cargaleiro (who was responsible for the decoration of the Champs-Élysées-Clémenceau metro station in Paris). Works by his friends are also here, including a Picasso. Engravings, ceramics and paintings fill this interesting gallery.

Excursions

Tour via Monsanto *150km/94mi.*

▶ *Leave Castelo Branco by ② on map and follow the N 233 northeast to Penamacor.*

Penamacor

Situated at an altitude of 600m/1 968ft, the village, which dates from Roman times, is crowned by a castle, the construction of which was ordered by Dom Sancho I in 1209; parts of the wall and the keep can still be seen today. The panoramic view over the plain and surrounding hills is impressive, and the walk through the old part of Penamacor is particularly pleasant.

The **Igreja da Misericórdia** (🕐*Open 9am-5pm.* 🚫*Closed Sun and holidays.* ☎ *272 39 41 33)* has a fine Manueline door and a high gilded wood altar.

The **Convento de Santo António** (🕐*Open 9am-5pm.* 🚫*Closed Sun and holidays.* ☎ *272 39 41 33),* founded in the 16C, contains a chapel with a roof and pulpit in lavish **talha dourada** style.

▶ *Take the N 332 south as far as Medelim, and then the N 239 east.*

Monsanto★★ 👣 *See MONSANTO.*

▶ *Return to Medelim and take the N 332 south.*

Idanha-a-Velha★

This tiny village was a prosperous Roman settlement. At first sight it seems more like an open-air museum with excavations everywhere, evoking a sense of the past. By following the signposted path you will pass the 13C Torre dos Templários, a Templars' tower built on top of a Roman temple; the cathedral **(sé)**, rebuilt five times on a site with paleo-Christian origins; a Roman bridge rebuilt during the Middle Ages; and many other historical remains.

▶ *Rejoin the N 332 south to Alcafozes, then follow the N 354 towards Ladoeiro. From here, return to Castelo Branco on the N 240.*

CASTELO DE VIDE★

PORTALEGRE
POPULATION 2 558 – MICHELIN MAP 733
LOCAL MAP SEE SERRA DE SÃO MAMEDE

Castelo de Vide lies at the foot of its castle, which stands perched on an elongated foothill of the Serra de São Mamede just to the north of Portalegre, very close to the Spanish border . It owes its attraction to old whitewashed houses stepped high up the hillside along winding alleys brilliant with flowers. The town is also a spa; its waters are beneficial for various ailments. *Rua Bartolomeu Álvares da Santa, 81-83 – 7320-117 ☎ 245 90 13 61 or 245 90 13 50*

Sights

Praça de Dom Pedro V
On this square the Igreja de Santa Maria stands opposite two 17C buildings, the Baroque Palácio da Torre and the Santo Amaro Hospital. Also overlooking the square are a fine 18C mansion and the late-17C town hall.

▶ *Behind the Igreja de Santa Maria, take the street leading to the Fonte da Vila and the Judiaria, the old Jewish quarter of the town.*

Castle
The castle is always open. The keep is open from 9am-12.30pm and 2-5.30pm (10am-7pm in summer). No charge. Go through the outer walls.
A stairway at the foot of a round 12C tower leads to the **keep**. From the room with a Gothic cupola and a cistern, there is a picturesque **view**★ of the town.

CASTRO MARIM

FARO
POPULATION 4 549 – MICHELIN MAP 733
LOCAL MAP SEE ALGARVE

Castro Marim abuts a high point overlooking the ochre-coloured and marshy Lower Guadiana plain near its outflow into the Gulf of Cádiz. Facing the Portuguese town across the estuary – and the border – is the Spanish town of Ayamonte. Castro Marim, which was already in existence in Roman times, became the seat of the Knights of Christ on the dissolution of the Order of Templars in Portugal in 1321, until it was transferred to Tomar in 1334. *Praça 1° de Maio, 2-4 – 8950-150 – ☎ 281 53 12 32*

Visit

The ruins of Castro Marim's fortified **castle**, (*Open daily 9am-7pm (6pm Oct to Apr). No charge),* which was built of red sandstone and demolished by the earthquake of 1755, stand to the north of the village, while the remains crowning a hill to the south are of the 17C Forte de São Sebastião. Within the partly restored walls is another castle dating back to the 12C. The parapet walk affords a view over the small city with the 17C Forte de São Sebastião in the foreground, the salt marshes, the Guadiana, the bridge between Portugal and Spain, and the Spanish town of Ayamonte to the east and Vila Real de Santo António and the coast to the south.

ALTO VALE DO RIO CÁVADO ★

UPPER CÁVADO VALLEY – BRAGA AND VILA REAL
MICHELIN MAP 733

The course of the Cávado river above Braga is steeply enclosed between the Serra do Gerês and the Serras de Cabreira and do Barroso. In this rocky upper valley, as in its tributary, the Rabagão, a series of dams control reservoir lakes of a deep blue colour which are surrounded by wooded mountain slopes crested by bare peaks – altogether a highly picturesque landscape.

▸ **Orient Yourself:** In the very north of Portugal – the lakes form part of the frontier with Spain.

☺ **Don't Miss:** Montalegre, Braga or Chaves.

🕐 **Organizing Your Time:** You could spend a couple of days enjoying the scenery in this part of Portugal.

👟 **Also See:** Parque Nacional da Peneda-Gerês.

A Bit of History

The Cávado, which is 118km/73mi long, rises to an altitude of 1 500m/4 859ft in the Serra do Larouco not far from the Spanish frontier; after crossing the Montalegre plateau, the river course drops sharply as it follows a series of rock faults running northeast-southwest. The hydro-electric development of this upper valley began in 1946. There are dams at Alto Cávado, Paradela, Salamonde and Caniçada on the Cávado, at Alto Rabagão and Venda Nova on the Rabagão and at Vilarinho des Funas on the Homen.

From Braga to Chaves *235km/141mi*

Allow about half a day (not including visit to Braga). 👟 *For local map see Parque Nacional da PENEDA-GERÊS.*

Braga★ 👟 *See BRAGA.*

▸ *Leave Braga by ① in the direction of Chaves.*

Immediately upon leaving Braga, the Cávado valley on the left becomes deep and wild; the road climbs along the south slopes which are covered with pine trees and eucalyptus. 11km/7mi farther, the castle of Póvoa de Lanhoso can be seen. After this village, the Cávado valley is hidden, while on the right the parallel valley of the Rio Ave appears. Then the road climbs up through a landscape of bare and rocky crests.
A little before Cerdeirinhas, the N 103 turns and descends overlooking the Cávado river which it follows, running along the edge of the Parque Nacional da Peneda-Gerês. The road then begins to wind and turn, affording precipitous **views**★ of two reservoirs: the 15km/9mi-long **Represa de Caniçada**★ and the Salamonde. Both lie below pine scattered slopes, dominated by the bare summits of the Serra do Gerês.

▸ *Bear left off the N 103 on the Paradela road over the crest of the Vanda Nova dam; at the next crossroads bear right.*

As the road rises rapidly, the **views**★★ of the Serra do Gerês become even more beautiful. A little before Paradela, on the left, there is a village built on a rocky projection at the foot of a shale hillock, which has been strangely slashed and hollowed out at the back by a gigantic quarry.

▷ *The road crosses Paradela and arrives at the dam of the same name.*

At Paradela you enter the eastern part of the **Parque Nacional da Peneda-Gerês**, known as the Barroso region, where local traditions have been kept very much alive, before reaching **Represa da Paradela**★. This reservoir lake, sitting at an altitude of 112m/367ft above the Cávado river, has a lovely mountain **setting**★.

Pitões das Júnias, a village 15km/9mi north of Paradela, has some Romanesque ruins belonging to a Benedictine monastery which dates back to the Visigothic period. Several arches indicate where the cloisters once stood.

▷ *Return to the N 103. The road runs alongside the* **Venda Nova reservoir**.

Vila da Ponte
This village perches upon a rock spur.

▷ *After Pisões, a path to the right leads to the Alto Rabagão dam.*

Barragem do Alto Rabagão★
The dam stands as a massive concrete wall. Go to the crest of the dam at the end of the road, where there is a good **view** over the reservoir-lake.

▷ *Return to the N 103. The road skirts the north edge of the lake before turning left to Montalegre.*

Montalegre
Montalegre was built in a beautiful **setting**★ at an altitude of 966m/3 170ft. Old red-roofed houses encircle the walls of the ruined 14C castle, the keep of which commands the wild and mountainous plateau.
The pine and heather-lined N 308 on the plateau returns to the N 103. Then the road crosses arid rock-strewn moors covered with heather and cut by streams. The plateau suddenly disappears as the **view**★★ extends dramatically to take in a vast green and cultivated basin at the far end of which can be seen the low-lying old villages of **Sapiãos** and **Boticas**.

B. Brillion/MICHELIN

Upper Cávado Valley

Serra do Barroso★

Continuing along the N 311, pass through **Carvalhelhos**, famous for its waters. On the next summit, with access via a dirt road, observe the **Castro de Carvalhelhos**, a settlement dating from the Iron Age, with its foundations, doors and walls still clearly visible. A road leads from Carvalhelhos to **Alturas do Barroso**, a traditional village in these harsh, isolated mountains. From there, head to **Vilarinho Seco**★, the most traditional mountain village in this area. It has no modern buildings, and the rural two-storey dwellings (with the animals and straw below) of loose, dark stone with wooden veranda and staircase and thatch roof appear not to have changed in centuries. Hens and goats run loose, with the most frequent traffic on the street the pairs of the impressive breed of Barroso oxen.

▶ *Rejoin the N 311 at Viveiro towards Sapiãos, then follow the N 103 to Chaves.*

CHAVES

VILA REAL
POPULATION 43 558 – MICHELIN MAP 733

Trás-os-Montes is an arid province, but Chaves is well favoured as it was built on the banks of the Tâmega, in the centre of a particularly fertile sunken basin. The small town of Aquae Flaviae, known to the Romans for its thermal springs, was transformed into an important stopping point on the Astorga-Braga road when Trajan built a bridge over the Tâmega, within its bounds. In 1160, after being recaptured from the Moors, Chaves was fortified to ensure its command of the valley facing the Spanish fortress of Verín. In the 17C ramparts were added, after the style of the French military architect Vauban. Even now the old castle huddled close by picturesque white houses with corbelled wooden verandas gives the town considerable style. It is now a quiet spa town (🕭 *see below*), equally known for its excellent smoked ham *(presunto)*. 🛈 *Terreiro de Cavalaria – 5400-193 –* ☎ *276 34 06 61*

▶ **Orient Yourself:** 63km/44ml north-east of Vila Real, very close to the Spanish border.
🕓 **Organizing Your Time:** Half a day should be just enough.
🕭 **Also See:** Bragança and Vila Real.

Sights

Ponte Romana
You get a general view of the Roman bridge from the gardens which run down to the river. With the passing of the years it has lost its stone parapets and even some arches, but nevertheless adds considerably to the charm of the town.

Praça de Camões
Overlooking this graceful square right in the heart of old Chaves are several interesting monuments, including the statue of Dom Afonso, first Duke of Bragança.

Igreja da Misericórdia★
The façade of this small 17C Baroque church is embellished with verandas and twisted columns. The inside walls are covered with *azulejos* showing scenes from the Life of Christ and the Bible, attributed to Oliveira Bernardes. There is a large gilded

wooden altarpiece; the ceiling is decorated with 18C paintings, one of which, in the centre, is a Visitation.

Museu da Região Flaviense

Open 9am-12.30pm and 2-5.30pm; Sat/Sun 2pm-5.30pm. Closed Mon and holidays. €1 (includes visit to Museu Militar). ☎ 276 34 05 00

This museum, which is housed in a fine 17C building, contains archeological and ethnological collections. A room on the ground floor contains prehistoric stone relics – the main piece in the display is a megalithic **figure in human form** (about 2000 BC) – and Roman remains including sculptures and milliary columns. Exhibits upstairs include ancient coins, a banknote plate, a magic lantern and radio receivers dating from the early wireless days.

Torre de Menagem

This massive square tower with battlements at the corners is all that remains of the castle. Built by King Dinis in the 14C, the castle was the residence of the first Duke of Bragança, illegitimate son of Dom João I.

The Waters and Spas

Chaves is situated in an area rich in thermal springs which originate from the North/South fault line in the Alto Tâmega region. All these springs have their own curative virtues and are part of a general network known as the "Alto Tâmega thermal system".

Caldas de Chaves – *Guided tours (30min - but you must reserve 15 days in advance), 9am-noon; 5-7pm; Sun and holidays, 8-11am. Closed during Holy Week and on 25 Dec. No charge. ☎ 276 33 24 45.* These hot water springs (73°C/163°F) were already popular with the Romans, who gave the town the name of Aquae Flaviae. The waters are alkaline, warm and rich in sodium bicarbonate, and are recommended for digestive disorders, rheumatism and hypertension. The modern spa buildings are situated in a thermal park by the river.

Termas de Vidago – *Open 8am-noon and 4-7pm. Closed Sun and 1 Oct to 31 May. ☎ 259 43 71 60. – 11km/7mi from Chaves.* This estate, in an attractive leafy park, has been totally restored and is now one of the best-equipped spas in the area. At its entrance, the majestic rose-coloured façade of the Art Deco-style **Palace-Hotel** transports the visitor back to the beginning of the century. This elegant ambience continues inside, with the exquisite decoration of the same period in keeping with the peacefulness of the setting. The bicarbonated water from Vidago is sold all over the country. The Vidago spa receives visitors with disorders of the digestive, respiratory and nervous systems.

Termas de Pedras Salgadas – *Closed until late 2007. ☎ 259 43 71 60. 31km/19mi from Chaves.* This magnificent 40ha/100-acre park, which is home to the spa buildings, is well worth a visit in its own right. The pervading atmosphere in the estate, which was created in 1904, and where the marks of time have been progressively repaired, is nonetheless one of abandon and nostalgia. The buildings and decoration include beautiful fountains, bathhouses and a casino, all dating from the beginning of the century. The sodium bicarbonated waters at Pedras Salgadas are recommended in the treatment of bone and digestive system disorders.

Caldas Santas de Carvalhelhos – *Open 1 July to 30 Sept. 8am-12 noon; 3pm-6pm. ☎ 276 41 51 50 – 30km/19mi from Chaves.* This spa resort is in a pleasant park crisscrossed by small streams and surrounded by the Barroso mountains. It is situated next to the bottling plant for this famous sparkling water, known for the treatment of digestive system and circulatory problems.

COIMBRA★★

COIMBRA
POPULATION 148 122 – MICHELIN MAP 733

Overlooked by the tall tower of its old university, Coimbra stands on a hillside at the foot of which flows the Mondego. Many poets, inspired by the romantic setting★, have immortalised the charm of the city, an old capital of Portugal, and have helped to make it a centre of fine arts and letters. Although the town has spread substantially over recent decades, and has been surrounded by modern districts, the centre is still distinctly divided into the upper town *(A Cidade Alta)*, which is traditionally the university and episcopal quarter, and the lower town *(A Cidade Baixa)* or shopping area. ▯ *Largo D. Dinis – 3020-123 – ☎ 239 83 25 91 Praça da República – 3000-343 – ☎ 239 83 32 02*

- ▶ **Orient Yourself:** Midway between Porto and Lisbon, inland a little.
- ▣ **Parking:** There is a large parking area *(free)* on the other side of the Santa Clara bridge, along the banks of the Mondego river. In town parking is hard to find.
- ⊚ **Don't Miss:** The University library in particular.
- ◐ **Organizing Your Time:** At least a full day to fully explore.
- 𝗞𝗶𝗱𝘀 **Especially for Kids:** Portugal dos Pequeninos.
- ◔ **Also See:** The ruins at Conimbriga; Figueira da Foz.

The University
The University was originally established in Lisbon by King Dinis in 1290 and only transferred to Coimbra in 1308. Teachers from Oxford, Paris, Salamanca and Italy were drawn to the new university, making the town one of the most important humanist centres of the period.

The Coimbra School of Sculpture
In the early 16C several French sculptors formed a group of artists under the protection of their patron, Cardinal Georges d'Amboise. Nicolas Chanterene, Jean de Rouen, Jacques Buxe and Philippe Houdart joined with the Portuguese João and Diogo de Castilho in about 1530 to create a school of sculpture in the town. Their art was inspired by Italian decorative forms: doorways, pulpits, altarpieces and the low reliefs surrounding altars were delicately carved out of the fine Ança stone.

General view of Coimbra

Student life

The city, peaceful throughout the summer, reawakens with a start at the beginning of the academic year and the return of the 20 000 students, many of whom live in groups known as "republics" in an ancient tradition (👁 *see opposite*). They adorn their briefcases with different coloured ribbons to denote their faculty.

Old Town and University★

The old town lies on the Alcáçova hill, reached by a tangle of narrow alleys cut by steps with expressive names such as Escadas de Quebra-Costas (Broken Ribs Steps).

Porta de Almedina

This gateway with an Arab name (*medina* means city in Arabic) is one of the last remaining sections of the medieval wall. It is surmounted by a tower and adorned with a statue of the Virgin and Child which stands between two coats of arms.

Sé Velha★★

🕐*Open Mon-Thurs and Sat: 10am-1pm; 2pm-6pm; Fri 10am-1pm; May-Sept 1pm-2pm except Fri; Sundays open from 11am for Mass.* 🚫*Closed holidays.*

The **old cathedral**, Portugal's earliest, was built between 1140 and 1175 by two French master craftsmen, Bernard and Robert. In the **Interior** a wide gallery above the aisles opens onto the nave by means of a graceful triforium with Byzantine capitals, which, like the lantern over the transept crossing, show Oriental influence. The Flamboyant Gothic **altarpiece**★ in gilded wood at the high altar is by the Flemish masters Olivier de Gand (Ghent) and Jean d'Ypres. At the base, the four Evangelists support the Nativity and the Resurrection; above, surrounded by four saints, an attractive group celebrates the Assumption of the Virgin. In the **Capela do Sacramento**★ there is a good Renaissance composition by Tomé Velho, one of Jean de Rouen's disciples. Below a figure of Christ in Benediction surrounded by ten Apostles, the four Evangelists face the Virgin and Child and St Joseph across the tabernacle.

The late-13C **cloisters** (🎫€1) are an example of transitional Gothic architecture; they were restored in the 18C. Blind arcades are surmounted by round bays filled with a variety of tracery. In the chapter-house, on the south side, lies the tomb of Dom Sesnando, first Christian governor of Coimbra, who died in 1091.

The Republics

Republics were created at the end of the 18C by students who wanted to introduce the French revolutionary ideas of the time into their communities. Although they were residences in which debate and protest flourished, as time passed they were also to become a cheap and practical form of accommodation. They generally number between 12 and 20 students, usually from the same region, who live together, renting vast apartments and managing the group budget in turn. Traditionally, they employ the services of a maid *(tricana)* to prepare meals, which are eaten communally. As you wander around the city you will probably come across some of these republics, which are recognisable by flags or paintings on the façades of their buildings. The **República dos Kágados** *(Rua do Correio, 98)*, which was founded in 1933, is currently the oldest republic in the city, while the **Real República Corsário das Ilhas** *(Couraça dos Apóstolos, 112)* is distinguishable by the pirates on its flag. Most of the republics have humourous names, often based on plays on words.

Sé Nova

🕐Open 9am-12.30pm; 2pm-6pm. 🚫Closed Sun, Mon and holidays.

The **new cathedral**, the construction of which started in 1598, was part of the Jesuit's college of the "Eleven Thousand Virgins" until the order was disbanded in 1759. The façade comprises two superimposed sections; the four niches in the lower part house statues of saints from the Society of Jesus. The vast, single-nave interior is covered by a barrel vault topped by a high lantern. The Baroque-style predominates in the side chapels and high altar, where an imposing gilded wood altarpiece and a magnificent silver throne are of particular note. The baptismal font to the left of the entrance is Manueline in style and was originally part of the old cathedral.

Address Book

WHERE TO STAY

Astória – Av. Emídio Navarro 21, ☎ (239) 85 30 20 - www.almeida-hotels.com - 🖾– 64 rooms ⌂. The Astória is magnificently situated overlooking the Mondego river in an elegant, Parisian-style turn-of-the-century building. The hotel, which in the past was popular with artists and writers, has still managed to retain a certain charm, particularly in its dining and reading rooms.

Pensão Santa Cruz - Praça 8 de Maio, 21 (reception on 2nd floor), ☎ 239 82 61 97 - www.pensaosantacruz.com 14 rooms. The main charm of this little pensão is its location, close to the University and in the heart of things. The rooms, which are showing their age, are with or without shower. There staff are welcoming, but remember that this is the heart of the night-life area so it's not exactly calm at night.

Residencial Vitória – R. da Sota, 11-19, ☎ 239 82 40 49 or 239 84 28 96 20 rooms ⌂. Recently renovated, the rooms at this small hotel are comfortable if somewhat basic. Good location and some rooms are air-conditioned.

Residencial Domus – R. Adelion Veiga, 62 (reception on 1st floor) – ☎ 239 83 85 84 - residencialdomus@sapo.pt – 20 rooms ⌂. A good welcome at this quiet and comfortable hotel set back from the road. Room are furnished in rustic style and most have an en-suite bathroom.

Residencial Coimbra – R. das Azeiteiraas, 55-61 – ☎239 83 79 96/7 – 15 rooms⌂. In a small side street in the city centre this quiet hotel has very comfortable rooms. A great mix of budget and class which comes as a nice surprise.

EATING OUT

Shmoo Café – R. Corpo de Deus, 68 – ☎ 965 21 45 75 (mobile) - www.shmoocafe.blogspot.com – open Mon-Fri noon-3pm; 8pm-2am; Sat 8pm-2am. Close to the Santa Clara church, this tiny café painted bright red has vivid colours in its dishes as well. A wonderful mix of ideas, from beautiful salads to exotic fruit and vegetables; meat and cheese dishes served on wooden platters. A very contemporary place at the heart of the town.

Snack-Bar Daniel Sun – R. da Lousa, 50-52 ☎ 934 83 09 76 (mobile) - closed Sun. This little bar close to praça 8 de Maio is very traditional and well-frequented by the locals, who will sit at the bar and order octopus salad, mussels, grilled cod and other tasty dishes of meat as well as fish. If you want to feel like a local this is the place.

Adega Paço do Conde - R. Paço do Conde, 1 - ☎ 239 82 56 05 - closed Sun. A traditional Portuguese restaurant offering quality fish and meat dishes. You can eat in one of two small salons or in a larger dining room, the latter obviously not quite as intimate and quiet as the others. Very good service.

Feb – R. do Corvo, 8-16 b 239 8 81 48 - closed Sun. In a road off praça 8 de Maio, this restaurant is highly prized by the locals for the quality of its cuisine. Ignore the ground-floor bar as the restaurant is on the first floor.

Universidade Velha★★

Open Apr-Oct 9.30am-7pm; Nov-Mar 9.30am-5pm. Closed Jan 1 and Dec 25. €5 (library only €3.50; Ceremonial Hall only €3.50; chapel, free). ☎ 239 85 98 00.

The old university is housed in buildings that once belonged to the royal palace and were restored and modified to become the Paço dos Estudos in 1540.

The **courtyard** *(pátio)* is dominated by an 18C tower. To the left, the courtyard extends to a terrace which provides a fine panorama of the Mondego and the plain beyond. Opposite are the library and chapel and, on the right, the graceful **Paços da Universidade.** This Manueline building was endowed with a colonnaded gallery called the Via Latina in the late 18C. The central body of the building is surmounted by a triangular pediment *(tickets should be purchased at the entrance to this building).*

A staircase leads to the first floor and the loggia, formerly for women only, which gives on to the **Sala dos Capelos** (Ceremonial Hall) where formal events such as the inauguration of rectors, the defence of theses and the conferring of degrees take place. The name derives from the cap *(capelo)* given to students on graduating. The vast hall, once the palace assembly-room, has a fine 17C painted ceiling and is adorned with a series of portraits of the kings of Portugal. Beside it is the private examination room which was remodelled in 1701. It has a painted ceiling and is hung with portraits of former rectors.

An exterior balcony provides a beautiful **view**★ of the city, the old cathedral and the more recent districts near the Mondego.

The burning of the ribbons

The ribbons which fringe the students' black capes indicate the academic subject of the wearer: blue for the arts, yellow for medicine, and red for law. At the beginning of May, the old cathedral square is the setting for a festival marking the end of the university year, during which the ribbons are burned in large cauldrons. This ceremony is followed by a serenade, balls and, to close the festivities, a tea dance!

Library, Universidade Velha

J.D.Sudres/DIAF

Chapel★

This Manueline chapel *(capela)*, with an elegant door, is by Marcos Pires. It is decorated with 17C *azulejos* and a painted ceiling and also possesses a fine 18C **organ loft**★★. A small **Museum of Sacred Art** adjoins the chapel.

Library★★

The library was built during the reign of João V in 1724 and consists of three large rooms, where precious wood furnishings are highlighted by Baroque decorations of gilded wood. Gilded Chinese-style patterns have been painted on green, red or gold lacquer work. The ceilings painted in false perspective are by Lisbon artists influenced

Door of Universidade Velha chapel, Coimbra

M. Dusart

COIMBRA

8 de Maio Pr.	Y	56	Brasil R. do	X	Dom Dinis Largo	ZDr A.
Adelino Veiga R.	YZ		Carmo R. do	Z	J. de Almeida R.	V
Afrânio Peixoto R.	V		Colégio Novo R. do	Y 12	Dr Dias da Silva Av.	VX
Ameias Largo	Z	2	Combatentes de Gde		Dr João Jacinto R.	Y 18
Antero de Quental R.	V	3	Guerra R. dos	X 13	Dr Júlio	
António Augusto			Comércio Pr. do	Z	Henriques Alameda	X 21
Gonçalves R.	X	4	Cónego Urbano		Elísio de Moura Av.	VX
Augusta R.	V	5	Duarte Av.	X	Emídio Navarro Av.	Z
Augusto Rocha R.	V	6	Couraça dos		Erva Terreiro da	Z
Aveiro R. de	V	8	Apóstolos R.	YZ	Fernandes Tomás R.	Z 25
Bernardo de			Coutinhos R.	Y 15	Fernando Namora Av.	X
Albuquerque R.	V	9	Direita R.	Z	Fernão de Magalhães Av.	Y
Borges Carneiro R.	Z	10	Dom Afonso		Ferreira Borges R.	Z 27
			Henriques Av.	V 17	Figueira da Foz R. da	V 28

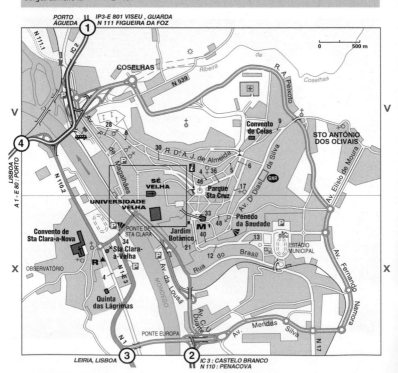

by Italian art. Ladders have been fitted into the shelving itself for easy access. The 30 000 books and 5 000 manuscripts are classified according to subject matter.

▶ *On leaving the university, take Rua Guilherme Moreira to the Almedina gate.*

Additional Sights

Casa Museu Bissaya-Barreto

⤷ *Guided visit (45min) Tues-Sun, 3pm-5pm.* ◷*Closed Mon, weekends in Oct and holidays.* ⊛*€2.50.* ☎ *239 85 38 00.*

The former residence of Bissaya-Barreto (1886-1974), professor, surgeon, member of parliament and friend of Salazar, has preserved its original decoration. Built in 1925 in neo-Baroque style, it is surrounded by a small, delightful garden decorated with statues and *azulejos*. The interior reveals the aesthetic tastes of its former owner: a 19C French lounge, *azulejos* from different periods, ceilings painted with frescoes,

Guerra Junqueiro R.	V	30	Lousã Av. da	X		República Pr. da	V	46
Guilherme Moreira R.	Z	31	Manutenção Militar R.	Y	37	Sá da Bandeira Av.	Y	
Ilha R. da	Z		Marnoco e Sousa Av.	X	40	Santa Teresa R. de	X	48
Jardim Arcos do	X	33	Mendes Silva Av.	X		Saragoça R. de	Y	50
João das Regras Av.	X	34	Moeda R. da	Z		Sè Nova Largo da	Z	
José Falcão R.	Z	35	Olímpio Nicolau Rui			Sobre Ribas R. de	Z	52
Lisboa Couraça de	Z		Fernandes R.	Y		Sofia R. de	Z	
Louça R. da	Z		Padeiras R. das	Z		Sota R. da	Z	
Loureiro R. do	Z		Padre António Vieira R.	Z		Visconde da Luz R.	Y	54
Lourenço de Almeida			Portagem Largo da	Z	42			
Azevedo Av.	V	36	Quebra-Costas Escadas do	Z	44			

Casa Museu			Mosteiro de Santa Cruz	Y		Parque de Santa Cruz /		
Bissaya-Barreto	X	M¹	Museu da Cidade	Z	M³	Jardim da Sereia	V	
Casa do Arco	Y	A	Museu da Santa Casa			Penedo da Saudade	X	
Convento de Celas	V		da Misericórdia	Y	M⁴	Porta de Almedina	Z	P
Convento de Santa			Museu Nacional			Portugal dos Pequeninos	X	R
Clara-a-Velha	X		Machado de Castro	Z	M²	Quinta das Lágrimas	X	
Convento Santa			Núcleo da Cidade			Sé Nova	Y	
Clara-a-Nova	X		Muralhada	Z	E	Sé Velha	Z	
Igreja de São Tiago	Y		Paço de Sub-Ripas	Y	N	Torre do Anto	Y	
Jardim Botânico	X					Universidade Velha	Z	

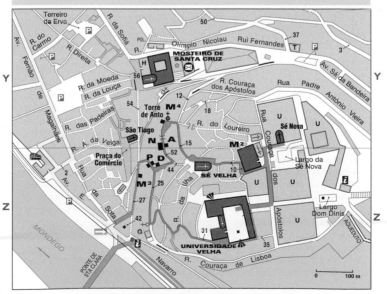

porcelain from the Indies company and from Saxony, silverware, Italian marble, an interesting library with books dating from the 16C and 17C, a collection of paintings based on the theme of the mother and child (including a *Virgin and Child* by Josefa de Óbidos), and several canvases by José Malhoa, Sousa Pinto and António Vitorino.

Jardim da Sereia or Parque de Santa Cruz

The entrance to this delightful 18C garden is through two towers adorned with arches. A staircase leads to a grotto-like fountain decorated with statues. Picnic tables, a lake surrounded by sculpted boxwood creating a maze effect and exotic trees provide welcome cool and a haven of peace and quiet.

Mosteiro de Santa Cruz★

🕐*Church open Mon-Sat, 7.30am-noon; 2pm-6pm; Sacristry and cloisters Mon-Sat 9am-noon; 2pm-5pm; Sun 4pm-5pm* ⌨*€2.50.*

The Manueline ceiling of the **Church**★ is supported by twisted columns and brackets. The walls are adorned with *azulejos* depicting the life of St Augustine. The Renaissance **pulpit**★ by Nicolas Chanterene is a masterpiece. Two bays on either side of the high altar contain the tombs of the first two kings of Portugal, Afonso Henriques and Sancho I, surrounded by a late Gothic-early Renaissance decoration. A door at the back of the chancel leads to the **Sacristia** (sacristy) in which hang four early 16C Portuguese paintings. The visit continues with the **Sala do Capitulo** (chapter-house) which has a fine Manueline ceiling and 17C *azulejos*.The **Claustro do Silêncio**★ were designed by Marcos Pires in 1524. The galleries are decorated with *azulejos* of parables from the Gospel. Three low-relief sculptures illustrate scenes of the Passion after Dürer engravings. In the **gallery** *(coro alto – access through the sacristy)* at the entrance to the church are beautiful 16C wooden **stalls**★ carved and gilded by Flemish artists and the Frenchman, François Lorete.

Botanical Gardens

🕐*Open 9am-5.30pm (8pm Apr to Sept).* ☎ *239 82 28 97.*

These terraced botanical gardens *(jardim botânico)*, which were laid out in the 18C in accordance with reforms introduced by Pombal, have a wide variety of rare trees including many tropical species.

Holy Queen Festival

At the beginning of July in even-numbered years, the city pays homage to its patron saint. On the Thursday evening, the statue of the saint is removed from the Convento de Santa-Clara-a-Nova and carried in procession across the bridge and through the city's streets to the Igreja da Graça, where it remains until the following Sunday, when it is returned to the convent. The streets are crowded with people, some of whom make the journey barefoot or on their knees, and the statue often takes several hours to travel just a few metres. The youngest members of the procession dress up as cherubs, King Dinis or Queen Isabel in memory of the miracle of the roses: when the queen, who was hiding bread in her lap to give to the poor, was asked by the king what she was carrying, she was said to have replied: "these are roses, my lord..."; when she went to remove the bread from the folds of her dress, a quantity of rose petals miraculously fell out. This is why Coimbra's inhabitants throw rose petals onto the statue from their windows, which are draped with brightly coloured bedspreads and large flags for the occasion. At midnight, a huge firework display illuminates the Mondego.

South Bank of the Mondego

Convento de Santa Clara-a-Nova

🕒 *Open Tues, 8.30am-6.30pm; Thur, Fri, Sat 8.30am-6pm; Weds 8.30am-noon; 2pm-6pm; Sun 8.30am-noon; 3pm-6pm. Free for the church but Cloisters ⊚€1.50 ☎ 239 44 16 74.*

The chancel in this vast convent contains the 17C silver tomb of Queen St Isabel by Teixeira Lopes.

At the end of the lower chancel *(coro baixo)*, behind the wrought-iron screen, is the queen's original **tomb**★ (14C) of painted Ança stone made during her lifetime.

Portugal dos Pequeninos

Kids 🕒 *Open Mar-May 10am-7pm; Jun-15 Sept, 9am-8pm; 16 Sept-Feb 10am-5pm. ⊚€7 (€3.50 under 14yrs and over 65s; reduced prices for gardens only and only in low season. ☎ 239 80 11 70.*

An attraction for children where scale models of Portuguese monuments including those of former overseas colonies may be seen. One of the houses contains a children's museum, the **Museu da Criança**.

Portugal dos Pequeninos

B. Brillion/MICHELIN

Quinta das Lágrimas

🕒 *Open 9am-5pm. ⊚€0.75. ☎ 239 80 23 80.*

The name of this wooded park, the Villa of Tears, recalls the legend described in verse by Camões of Inês de Castro's murder here on 7 January 1355 by King Afonso's Chief Justice and two of his henchmen.

Miradouro do Vale do Inferno

4km/2mi. Leave by ③ and take a narrow road on the right towards the Vale do Inferno (steep climb); at a fork bear right.

The belvedere provides a good **view**★ of Coimbra.

Address Book

NIGHTLIFE

The town, very quiet in the summer, bursts into life once the academic year starts. The students start the evening by meeting at the outdoor cafés in the Praça da República for an apéritif. They then move on to one of the bars around the cathedral (**Boémia Bar, Piano Negro, Bigorna Bar or Salão Brasil**), some of which have live music, or to night-clubs such as **Via Latina** (with its outdoor terrace), **Scotch Club** (which stays open latest) or **OK Bar**. Also currently in fashion are the bars and clubs on the other side of the river. The **Galeria de Santa Clara** bar and art gallery with its pleasant garden (in front of one of the side gates of Portugal dos Pequeninos) and the **Bar de São Francisco**, a little farther along, are also very popular, as are **le Calhabar** (*R. do Brasil)* and **Noites Longas** (*R. Almeida Garret).*

In the foyer of the **Teatro Academica Gil Vicente (TAGV)** there is a bar that is at the centre of Coimbra's night life. It's brightly and colourfully designed, is great fun and is a great place to mix and meet.

Quebra Costas (*Escadas do Quebra Costas 45-49 ☎239 82 16 61 - www.quebracostas.com*) is another hot spot at night, but not in the praça da República area – this one is near the old Cathedral and has a charming terrace to escape the heat inside. Finally, **A Capela** (*Capela de Nossa Senhora da Vítoria, b239 83 39 85*) has a nightly fado show at 9pm. €5. Not to be missed. Very good value and nice surroundings.

CONÍMBRIGA★

COIMBRA
MICHELIN MAP 733

The Roman ruins of Conímbriga are among the finest in the Iberian Peninsula. A Celtic city stood on this spot as long ago as the Iron Age. The present ruins, however, are those of a Roman town situated on either side of an important road which connected Lisbon and Braga. In the 3C, threatened by Barbarian invasion, the inhabitants were compelled to build ramparts, leaving some of the houses outside the wall. Material from these houses was used in the construction of the fortifications. In spite of these measures, Conímbriga fell to the Suevi in 468 and the town declined.

▶ **Orient Yourself:** Just 14km/9ml south of Coimbra.
⊛ **Don't Miss:** Particularly the mosaics in the House of Fountains.
◷ **Organizing Your Time:** About two to three hours.
Especially for Kids: A great place for them to begin to understand how people (including children) live in a bygone age.
⛃ **Also See:** Coimbra and Figuera da Foz.

Visit

◷*Open Jun-Sept 9am-8pm; Oct-May 10am-6pm.* ◷*Closed holidays; museum closed Mon.* ⊛*€3, no charge Sundays (includes the ruins and museum).* ☎ *239 94 11 77; www. conimbriga,pt. Leave the car in front of the museum and take the path towards the ruins, following the route marked on the plan.*

Cross the **Casa da Cruz Suástica** (House of the Swastika) and the **Casa dos Esqueletos** (House of the Skeletons), paved with fine mosaics, before reaching the baths and the interesting *laconicum* (a type of sauna) (1). You then come to the **Casa de Cantaber**★, which is one of the largest in the western Roman world and is said to have belonged to Cantaber, whose wife and children were captured by the Suevi during an attack on the town in 465. The tour begins with the private baths: the *frigidarium* (2) with its cold baths, the *tepidarium* (warm baths) and the *caldarium* (hot baths) (3) over the *hypocaust* (heated space connected with the furnace). The hypocaust's layout gives an idea of the plan for the fireplaces and the underground system of warm air circulation; a few lead pipes remain.

You then arrive at the northern entrance to the house: a colonnade (4) preceded the *atrium* (entrance vestibule) (5). As you pass from the *atrium* to the central peristyle (6), note an unusual stone (7) in the pavement, cut away to a rose tracery through which the drain can be seen. The *impluvium* (a basin for collecting rain water) (8) is to the left of the peristyle. Leading off from the *impluvium* were the bedrooms.

Mosaics, Casa dos Repuxos

From the *triclinium* (sitting and dining room) (9) you can see three pools. The most interesting of these pools (10) is encircled by columns of which one has retained its original stucco painted in red. A suite of three rooms (11) adjoining the wall has a lovely pool and flower beds in the shape of a cross.

Excavations northwest of the Casa de Cantaber have uncovered the centre of the **ancient town** *(cidade antiga)*, in particular the **forum**, a hostelry and baths. To the southwest the craftsmen's quarter and the monumental baths have also been discovered. The **aqueduct** *(aqueduto)*, which was some 3.5km/2mi long, brought water from Alcabideque to the supply tower by the reconstructed arch abutting on the wall.

Casa dos Repuxos (House of the Fountains)★★
Access by footbridge to the north.

The villa, which belonged to a Roman named Rufus, dates from the early 2C although it was built on the site of a 1C building. The layout of the rooms is easy to follow on account of the column bases and the paving which consists largely of wonderful mosaics. Inside are the *atrium* (12), the peristyle (13) and the *triclinium* (14), which was bordered by a pool.

Around these rooms were the living quarters and communal rooms. The **mosaics**★★ covering the floors show extraordinary variety.

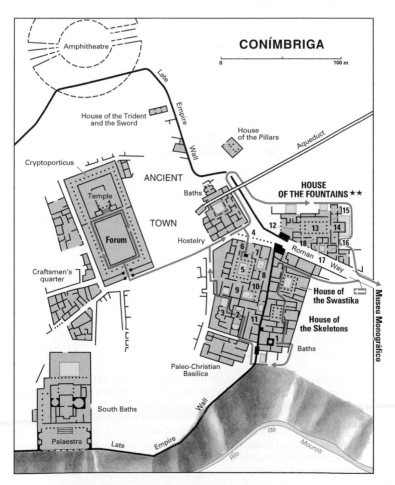

In a room to the left of the *triclinium*, a fine polychrome composition (15) shows hunting scenes, the Four Seasons and a quadriga.

Another room (16) giving onto the *impluvium* presents some elegant figures at a deer hunt. A *cubiculum* (bedroom) (17) has ornamental tiling with geometrical designs and plant motifs surrounding Silenus astride an ass being pulled forward by its halter. Next door, a sitting room (18), opening on to the peristyle, is decorated with an outstanding mosaic: in the centre of an ornament representing wading birds, dolphins and sting rays, a marine centaur surrounded by dolphins brandishes a standard and a fish. Lastly, in the southwest corner of the peristyle, Perseus stands, holding in his right hand Medusa's head which he appears to be offering to a monster from the deep.

COSTA DA CAPARICA

SETÚBAL
MICHELIN MAP 733 LOCAL MAP P9

The Costa da Caparica is the nearest seaside resort to Lisbon on the southern shore of the Tagus. With its vast beaches, which are less polluted than those on the northern shore, it is one of the most popular weekend spots with Lisbonites *(Lisboetas)*. The resort is constantly being developed parallel to the ocean and the ridge of sand dunes which protects it from the wind. In season, a **small train** runs along the coast for 11km/7mi, giving access to the immensely long beach. Fishing boats, their prows adorned with a painted star or eye, may still be seen bringing in their nets helped by holiday-makers.

CRATO

PORTALEGRE
MICHELIN MAP 733

As early as 1350, Crato (about 20km/12ml due west of Portalegre) became the seat of a priory for the Order of the Knights Hospitallers of St John of Jerusalem, which later became the Order of the Knights of Malta. The title of Grand Prior of Crato was bestowed up until the late 16C. In 1356 the command of the knights' residence was transferred to the monastery-fortress in the neighbouring village of Flor da Rosa; Crato, however, retained its role as a priory. While Crato's castle was burnt in 1662 by Don Juan of Austria, several old houses may still be seen.
🛈 *Largo do Município – 7430-130 – ☎ 245 9 71 61*

Mosteiro de Flor da Rosa ★
Entrance to the museum is free. Ask for the key at the reception desk of the nearby pousada.
The monastery-fortress of the Order of the Knights of Malta was built in 1356 by Prior Álvaro Gonçalves Pereira, father of Nuno Álvares Pereira who defeated the Castilians at the Battle of Aljubarrota. It forms a compact group of fortified buildings within a crenellated perimeter wall.
The **church**★ on the right has been extremely well restored; the simplicity of its lines and the height of its nave are outstanding. The small flower-decked cloisters in the centre are robust in design but are given an overall elegance by their graceful late Gothic network vaulting.

VALE DO **DOURO**★★

MICHELIN MAP 733

The Douro, which rises in Spain, flows in an erratic course through northern Portugal before reaching the Atlantic near Porto. Its valley is fertile, with vineyards, orchards and olives growing in abundance as they have done for centuries. The landscape has been enhanced by beautifully built quintas. Port is the main wine produced here but the valley is also the centre for the famous *vinho verde*.

▶ **Orient Yourself:** The valley runs across the northern part of Portugal
🖼 **Don't Miss:** The wine route!
🕐 **Organizing Your Time:** Two or three days of peace and quiet are ideal.
Kids **Especially for Kids:** A cruise on the Douro is fun.
🖼 **Also See:** The Vale Do Cõa achaeological park.

The Vinho Verde Region★

1 **From the Barragem do Carrapatelo to Lamego**
62km/38.5mi – about 2hr 30min – 🖼 *See map.*

The lower valley of the river, near Oporto, is not the domain of the great wine of that name but that of the well-known **vinho verde** (green wine), so-called because the local climate is such that the grapes cannot fully ripen here. The real port is made much farther east, from Régua to the Spanish border. The Douro, widened by successive dams, runs hemmed in by steep hills and winds round in great twists and turns. The shale and granite slopes, more wooded on the north bank and more cultivated on the south bank, where little white villages seem to hang between the vines, terraced olive groves and corn fields, with the river below, have created a delightful landscape, despite the reminders of industrial civilization evidenced by the railway line, the Carrapatelo dam *(barragem)*, a few factories, and the installations for transporting coal from the Pejão mines on the south bank.

Grape picking

L.Y. Loirat/EXPLORER

Barragem do Carrapatelo

This dead-weight dam is 170m/558ft long. A hydro-electric station and a fish ladder occupy its south bank. On the north bank, a lock with the greatest displacement in Europe drops 43m/141ft.

Cinfães

Cinfães is the commercial centre for *vinho verde*.

▶ *Continue along N 222 to Anreade; turn right on the road towards Ovadas, heading south; 5.5km/ 3mi on, bear left.*

Priorado de Santa Maria de Cárquere

Only the church and the funeral chapel of the Lords of Resende remain, linked by a monumental arch. The church, restored in the 13C, 14C, 16C and 17C (the square crenellated tower and chancel are Gothic, the façade and nave Manueline) still has a Romanesque doorway decorated with small columns and capitals with interlacing. The chancel, under diagonal ribbed vaulting, has a door on the left with a high pediment and a double string course of billets. The chapel, which has a remarkable Romanesque window with capitals of sculpted pelicans, contains four stone sarcophagi carved with animals and inscriptions.

▶ *Return to N 222 and turn right.*

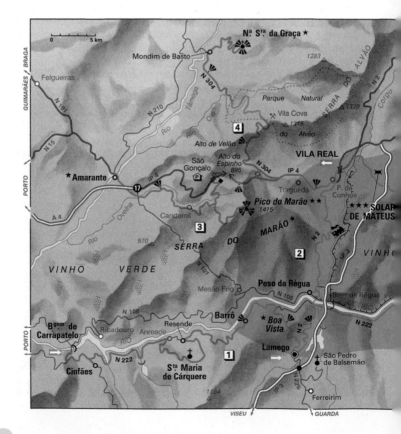

Resende is an important wine production centre. From the village of Barrô, there is a good view of the valley's wooded slopes; the 12C Romanesque church has a richly carved tympanum and a beautiful rose window.

▷ *After 6km/3.5mi turn right on N 226.*

Miradouro da Boa Vista★

There is a magnificient view from this belvedere of the Douro valley. High up, cut out against the sky, are the whitish summits of the Serra do Marão.

▷ *Continue until you arrive at* **Lamego** *(See LAMEGO).*

The Port Region★★

② Round trip from Lamego

112km/70mi – about 3hr – local map below

As the local saying goes: "God created the Earth and man the Douro". One has to see the way the steep banks of the Douro have been shaped meticulously into terraces, each one comprising several rows of vines, to understand the enormous amount of work man has put into these hillsides for more than 20 centuries. The sight is particularly fascinating between mid-September and mid-October when the terraces are invaded by thousands of grape-pickers. The vineyards cover an area of 42 500ha/105 000 acres and it is their grapes, which ripen in the shelter of the valley where the temperature in summer can easily reach 40°C/106°F, that produce port. The road then leads to **Lamego** (*See LAMEGO).*

The picturesque N 2 runs above the Corgo valley to **Vila Real**. *See VILA REAL.*

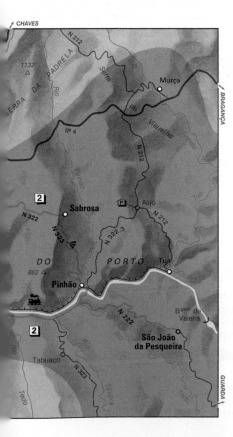

▷ *Leave Vila Real on N 322 and continue east towards* **Sabrosa** (the town is Magellan's birthplace), passing, on the way **Solar de Mateus** ★★. *See VILA REAL.*

Road from Sabrosa to Pinhão ★★

After Sabrosa, the N 323 descends towards the Douro and overlooks the deep valley of the Pinhão. 7km/4mi before Pinhão there is a fine **view**★ of a bend in the Douro and its confluence with the Pinhão river.

Pinhão

Pinhão, which stands at the junction of the Douro and Pinhão rivers, is an important port production centre. The **railway station** is decorated with *azulejos* illustrating the sites and the traditional costumes of the valley. Nowadays, all the wine is transported by road.

By making an excursion eastwards to **São João da Pesqueira** *(18km/11mi of hairpin bends on N 222)* you will see the terraced hillsides of vineyards in the Torto valley. São João da Pesqueira is a large village on the plateau with an arcaded main square around which stand a chapel and white balconied houses. After Pinhão, N 222 follows the valley westwards between shale slopes which have been terraced and contained by small drystone walls. The land is exclusively given over to vines.

Serra do Marão★   ♿   *see Serra do MARÃO*

③ **From Vila Real to Amarante**

④ **From Vila Real to Mondim de Basto**

ELVAS★

PORTALEGRE
POPULATION 23 504 – MICHELIN MAP 733

Elvas, only a few miles from the Spanish citadel of Badajoz, is an impressive for-tification still surrounded by ramparts. The town was not freed by the Christians from the Moorish occupation until 1226, although Lisbon had been liberated almost a hundred years earlier. Elvas subsequently resisted many assaults by the Spanish until 1580 when it was attacked by Philip II's troops. Today Elvas is an important agricultural centre, famous for its sugar plums, and is a textile manufacturing centre (cotton). 🚩 *Praça da República – 7350-126 –* ☎ *268 62 22 36*

Sights

City walls (Muralhas)★★

The Elvas fortifications are the most accomplished example of 17C military architecture in Portugal. Fortified gates, moats, curtain walls, bastions and gla-cis form a remarkable defensive group completed to the south and north by the 17C Santa Luzia and the 18C Graça forts, each perched on a hill.

Aqueduto da Amoreira★

The aqueduct was constructed between 1498 and 1622 to the plans of Francisco de Arruda. It begins 7.5km/5mi south-west of the town to which it still brings water.

Cathedral

The cathedral *(sé)*, originally Gothic, was rebuilt in the 16C by Francisco de Arruda in the Manueline style. The inte-

G. Biollay /DIAF

Pillory, Elvas

rior, whose pillars were decorated in the Manueline period, contains an 18C chancel entirely faced with marble.

Igreja Nossa Senhora da Consolação ★

The Church of Our Lady of Consolation on the south side of Largo de Santa Clara was built in the 16C in the Renaissance style. It is an octagonal building the interior of which, covered by a cupola resting on eight painted columns, is entirely decorated with fine 17C multi-coloured **azulejos**★. The pulpit, supported by a marble column, has a 16C wrought-iron balustrade.

Castle

⏱Open 9.30am-1pm; 2.30pm-5.30pm; Sun and holidays 9.30am-1pm. ⏱Closed Jan 1, Easter Sunday, May 1 and Dec 25. ☞€1.50, free on Sundays and holidays.
The castle was constructed originally by the Moors and reinforced in the 14C and 16C. From the top of the ramparts there is a panorama of the town and its fortifications and the surrounding countryside scattered with olive trees and isolated farmsteads.

ERICEIRA★

LISBOA

POPULATION 8 780 – MICHELIN MAP 733

The village, a lively seaside resort perched on a cliff facing the Atlantic, has preserved its old quarter around the church, its maze of alleyways and its picturesque fishing harbour. Ericeira was the scene of an historic event on 5 October 1910: King Manuel II sailed from its harbour into exile, while the Republic was being proclaimed in Lisbon. It has a picturesque harbour and the area around the Parish Church is also worth a visit. The Church is decorated with azulejos.

CABO ESPICHEL★

SETÚBAL

MICHELIN MAP 733

Cape Espichel, at the southern tip of the Serra da Arrábida, is a true World's End, beaten continuously by violent winds. The cliff drops a sheer 100m/350ft to the sea. It was off this cape that Dom Fuas Roupinho vanquished the enemy in 1180 in a brilliant victory at sea, when Portuguese sailors succeeded in capturing several enemy ships. The remains of the Santuário de Nossa Senhora do Cabo have been a popular pilgrimage centre ever since the 13C, though these buildings were erected during the 18C by pilgrims.

Sight

Santuário de Nossa Senhora do Cabo

⏱Open 9.30am-6pm. ☎ 212 68 10 31.
This church, built in the classical style at the end of the 17C, has a Baroque interior.

ESTORIL★

LISBOA
POPULATION 25 230 – MICHELIN MAP 733
PLAN IN THE MICHELIN GUIDE SPAIN AND PORTUGAL

Estoril has developed into a refined and attractive beach and winter resort, favoured by a mild climate and a temperature which averages 12°C/54°F in winter. It lies on the corniche road linking Lisbon and Cascais, a point on the Costa de Estoril which is famous for its luminous skies. Formerly a small village known to a few for the healing properties of its waters, Estoril now attracts an elegant international circle who come for the resort's entertainments (golf, casino and sea fishing), its sporting events (motor and horse-racing, regattas), its pleasant location facing Cascais bay, its park of tropical and exotic plants and trees, palm-lined avenues, beaches of fine sand and its highly successful festivals (Festival of the Sea in July).

SERRA DA ESTRELA★

GUARDA AND CASTELO BRANCO
MICHELIN MAP 733
MICHELIN ATLAS SPAIN & PORTUGAL PP 35 (K 6,7) AND 48 (L 6,7)

The Serra da Estrela, a great mountain barrier 60km/40mi long by 30km/20mi wide is the highest massif in Portugal. Above the cultivated and wooded slopes appear the arid and boulder strewn summits, the tallest of which is Torre with an altitude of 1 993m/6 539ft. Tourism is developing in this formerly isolated area: Penhas da Saúde has become a winter sports resort; Covilhã, Seia, Gouveia and Manteigas, small towns within reach of the plain, have become starting points for mountain excursions.

▶ **Orient Yourself:** In the triangle formed by Coimbra, Viseu and Guarda.
⊗ **Don't Miss:** The Zézere glacial valley and the view from the summit of Torre.
⊙ **Organizing Your Time:** A couple of days to look around the region.
⦿ **Also See:** Coimbra and Guarda.

The Monte da Torre Road★★

1 From Covilhã to Seia *49km/30mi – about 2hr.*
This itinerary includes the highest road in Portugal.

On leaving **Covilhã**, the road rises rapidly before you arrive at **Penhas da Saúde,** a popular winter and summer resort.

▶ *Leave the Manteigas road on the right.*

After a bend bringing the road parallel with the upper valley of the Zêzere, the **landscape**★ takes on a desolate appearance. There is an interesting **view**★ from a belvedere on the left, a short distance from the summit, of the glacial upper valley of the Zêzere. The river's source is hidden by a 300m/900ft-high granite cone, known locally as the "slender pitcher" (Cântaro Magro).

▶ *Bear left to Torre.*

Torre★★
From the summit the **panorama** includes the Mondego valley, the Serra da Lousã and the Zêzere valley. The "long lake", Lagoa Comprida is the largest single expanse of water in the *serra*. The descent into the Mondego valley is swift and the **views**★★ are magnificent.

After **Sabugueiro**, a village of granite-walled houses, the road drops steeply into **Seia**, a small town pleasantly situated at the foot of the *serra*.

Upper Valley of The Zêzere★★

② From Gouveia to Covilhã via Manteigas
77km/48mi – about 2hr 30min. This route crosses the massif by way of the upper valley of the Zêzere.

Gouveia is a small, attractive town built halfway up the side of the Mondego valley. The upper plateaux are soon reached; some of the granite boulders have been worn into astonishing forms, such as the Old Man's Head, **Cabeça do Velho**, which rises from a mass of rocks on the left of the road. The source of the Mondego (Nascente

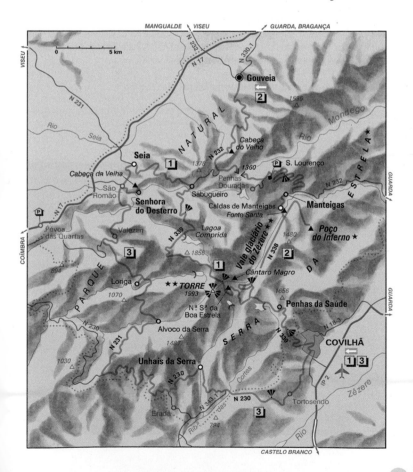

do Mondego – *signposted*), the longest river flowing solely in Portugal, rises to an altitude of 1 360m/4 462ft just before Penhas Douradas. The road runs past the Pousada de São Lourenço with a fine view of Manteigas and the Zêzere valley opposite. The descent becomes brutal as hairpin bends twist down to the Zêzere valley; a belvedere, not far from the *pousada*, affords an upstream **view**★ of the valley which is commanded by **Manteigas** with its 17C houses with wooden balconies.

▶ *At Manteigas leave the N 232 and turn right.*

A short distance beyond the small spa of **Caldas de Manteigas**, the mountain solitude takes over. However, cultivated terraces can be seen on the lower slopes. After the bridge over the Zêzere, the road (in poor condition) continues upstream until it reaches the rock face of the glacial valley (*see below*); it then climbs to the top.

▶ *Turn left into a narrow unsurfaced road to Poço do Inferno (6km/4mi).*

Poço do Inferno ★
The Well of Hell is a wild, wooded defile with a beautiful **waterfall**★.

Vale Glaciário do Zêzere★★
This valley is a perfect example of glacial relief with U-shaped contours with consequent steep slopes, hanging tributary valleys and connecting gorges, a cirque at the highest point, cascades, enormous erratic boulders strewn on the bottom, and scraggy vegetation on the slopes. The road bears westward and passes near the source of the Zêzere – signposted "Cântaros" (the source is not visible from the road but it can be reached on foot through huge boulders). A little farther, at a fountain, there is a lovely extensive **view**★ across the glacial valley.

▶ *At the final pass, take the N 339 on the left towards Covilhã.*

C. Pinheira/DIAF

Upper Zêzere Valley

Covilhã

Covilhã, spread over the wooded foothills of the Serra da Estrela, is both a health resort and an excursion centre, as well as the dormitory town for the Penhas da Saúde winter sports resort.

The Western Side of the Serra★

③ From Covilhã to Seia via Unhais da Serra

81km/50mi – about 2hr

This route goes round the *serra* by the west along a road that runs almost constantly at an altitude of between 600m-700m/2 000ft-2 300ft.

▶ *Leave Covilhã by the N 230 going south. The Serra da Estrela's high peaks come into sight beyond Tortosendo.*

Unhais da Serra

This small spa and health resort claims a lovely **setting**★ at the mouth of a torrent-filled valley. Villages such as **Alvoco da Serra**, situated half way up the hillside, and **Loriga**, perched upon a spur in the valley, now come into view.

▶ *At São Romão turn right in the direction of Senhora do Desterro.*

Senhora do Desterro

The road climbs the Alva valley to Senhora do Desterro where you leave the car. Take the path on the left which will bring you *(15min round trip on foot)* to the Cabeça da Velha (Old Woman's Head), a granite rock worn by erosion.

▶ *Return to the road which leads to **Seia** and to the itinerary described.*

ESTREMOZ★

ÉVORA

POPULATION 16 657 – MICHELIN MAP 733

Approached from the south, the old town appears perched on a hill overlooking the bright whitewashed houses of the modern town below. Estremoz, standing in a region of marble quarries, is a pleasant city, still possessing its 17C ramparts and dominated by its medieval castle. It is, and has been since the 16C, a well-known centre for Alentejo pottery which can be seen attractively displayed on the Rossio (main square) at the Saturday market. 🛈 *Rossio do Marquês de Pombal –7100-505– ☎ 268 33 35 41*

▶ **Orient Yourself:** Halfway between Elvas and Évora.
🖄 **Don't Miss:** The Saturday morning market.
🕐 **Organizing Your Time:** Two or three hours allows you to see all you need.
Kids Especially for Kids: The Centro Ciência Viva (Living Science Centre)
👶 **Also See:** Vila Viçosa, Elvas and Évora.

Sights

Torre de Menagem

The keep has now been converted into one of the most famous *pousadas* in Portugal. It was built in the 13C and is crowned with small pyramid-shaped merlons and flanked in its upper part by galleries supported on consoles.

Capela da Rainha Santa Isabel

Open 9.30am-11.30pm; 2pm-5pm. Closed Mon and holidays.For the key ask at the Galeria de Desenho, Largo Dinis.

The chapel walls are covered with beautiful *azulejos* depicting scenes from the life of **Queen Saint Isabel of Aragon**, wife of King Dinis. The Miracle of the Roses scene is the most delightful: in it, the queen, surprised by the king as she is carrying bread to distribute to the poor, opens the pleats of her skirt to banish her husband's suspicions, revealing only roses within the folds.

Sala de Audiência de Dom Dinis

A beautiful **Gothic colonnade**★ is the outstanding feature of King Dinis's Audience Chamber whose stellar vaulting dates from the Manueline period. Queen Saint Isabel and King Pedro I both died in this room, in 1336 and 1367 respectively.

Museu Municipal

Open Apr to Sept, 9am-12.30pm and 3-7pm; Oct to Mar, 9am-12.30pm and 2-5pm. Closed Mon and holidays. €1.50 . ☎ 268 33 92 00 (ext 246).

The museum is housed in a fine building opposite the keep. Among its collections are Estremoz pottery and crib figures, religious works of art etc.

Centro Ciëncia Viva

Open daily except Monday and holidays, 10am-6pm €5 (concessions €2.50) 268 33 32 46.

Located in a 16C convent this interesting interactive centre is part of the University of Évora. There is a geology museum and other exhibits which are of interest to both adults and children.

Igreja de Nossa Senhora dos Mártires

2km/1mi south on the road to Bencatel.

The church dates from 1744 and has a monumental Gothic east end. The nave, which is preceded by a triumphal Manueline arch, contains beautiful *azulejos (Flight into Egypt, The Last Supper, The Annunciation)* as does the chancel *(Nativity, Presentation in the Temple)*.

ÉVORA★★★

ÉVORA

POPULATION 56 359 – MICHELIN MAP 733

Évora, a walled town since Roman times, is now most attractively Moorish in character with alleys cut by arches, brilliant white houses, flower-decked terraces, openwork balconies and tiled patios. From its rich past Évora retains several medieval and Renaissance palaces and mansions which in themselves provide a panoply of Portuguese architecture. They are at their most impressive at night (floodlit during the summer from 9pm to midnight) standing out against a starry sky. The Alentejo capital is today an important agricultural market and the base for several dependent crafts and industries (cork, woollen carpets, leather and painted furniture). *Praça do Giraldo – 7000-508 – ☎ 266 70 26 71 or 266 70 24 01.*

▶ **Orient Yourself:** Along the A6 east of Lisbon, about 150km/110ml.
P **Parking:** Park outside the town where it is free and unrestricted.
☺ **Don't Miss:** The university, the Roman temple and the cathedral.
◔ **Organizing Your Time:** You could see it in half a day though it merits more.
Kids Especially for Kids: The Vasco da Gama palace with its history of the Great Discoveries.
ᴓ **Also See:** Elvas, Estremoz and Monsaraz.

Address Book

WHERE TO STAY

◠◠◠◠ **Hotel da Cartuxa** – *Tv. da Palmeira, 4,* ☎ *266 73 93 00 - www.hoteldacartuxa.com –* ⚒ ᴓ ▤ *91 rooms.* A modern hotel close to the city walls west of the old town. Very well furnished, the rooms are ideal and at the rear, have balconies. Lovely pool and gardens that look out over the city walls.

◠◠◠◠ **Pousada dos Lóios** – *Largo Conde de Vila Flor,* ☎ *266 70 40 51 - www.pousadas.pt–* ⚒ ▤ *36 rooms.* This elegant, luxurious *pousada* is situated in the buildings of the 16C Lóios convent. White-covered tables in the restaurant surround a patio on which orange trees grow. The chef has chosen to produce traditional cuisine which is delicious. There is a pool and solarium.

◠◠◠ **Albergaria Solar de Monfalim** - *Largo da Misericórdia, 1,* ☎ *266 75 00 00 - www.monfalimtur.pt -* ▤

P *26 rooms* ▭. All the rooms in this peaceful hotel, set in a 16C mansion, are different, though the comfort level remains the same. A very nice place to stay for this price level.

◠◠◠ **Casa de São Tiago** – *Largo Alexandre Herculano, 2,* ☎ *266 70 26 86 - www.casa-stiago.com – 7 rooms.* A delightful 16C house with its own inner garden and small orchard in the historical centre of the town. All the rooms are decorated with antique furniture. Don't miss the breakfast, which includes home-made jams and other delicacies.

◠◠ **Residencial Policarpo** – *R. da Freiria de Baixo, 16,* ☎ *266 70 24 24 - www.pensaopolicarpo.com -* ✉ P *20 rooms.* An old house beautifully restored is now a small hotel. The rooms are not all large but are comfortable and breakfast on the terrace is a nice change. Good quality for this price.

ÉVORA

1° de Maio Pr.	BZ
5 de Outubro R.	BYZ 37
Acaçarias R. das	BY
Alcouchel Portas de	AZ
Álvaro Velho Largo	BZ 3
António José de Almeida R.	CZ
Aviz R. de	BY 4
Aviz Porta de	AY
Avíz Largo de	BY
Bombeiros Voluntários de Évora Av.	CZ 6
Calvário R. do	AY
Cândido dos Reis R.	AY
Cano R.a do	AY
Caraça Trav. da	BZ 7
Cardéal Rei R. do	CY
Casoa Portas de	AY
Castelos Largo dos	CZ
Cenáculo R. do	BY 9
Chafariz d'El-Rei R. do	CZ
Cháo das Covas Largo de	AY
Cicioso R. de	BZ
Colegiais Largo dos	BY
Colégio Largo do	CY
Combatentes da Grande Guerra Av. dos	BZ 10
Conceição Santos R. D. M. Da	CZ
Conde de Vila-Flor Largo	BY 12
Cordovil R.	BY
Dinis Miranda Av.	ABZ
Diogo Cão R.	BZ 13
Dom A. E. Nunes R.	BCZ
Dr da Fonseca R.	CZ
Dr Ev. Cutileiro Largo	BY
Florbela Espanca Praceta	CY
Fontes R. das	BY
Freiria de Baixo R. da	BY 15
General Humberto Delgado Av.	ABZ
Germano Vidigal Av.	CZ
Giraldo Pr. do	BY
Gulbenkian Av. da	BZ
Infante D. Henrique Av.	CZ
João de Deus R.	AY 16
Joaquim-António de Aguiar Pr.	AY
José Elias Garcia R.	AY 18
Lagar dos Dizimos R. do	BZ 19
Lisboa Av. de	AY
Luís de Camões Largo	AY 21
Machede R. de	BZCY
Machede Portas de	CY
Machede Largo de	CY
Manuel Trindale Salgueiro Av. D.	BY
Marquês de Marialva Largo	BY 22
Mendo Estevens R.	CZ
Menino Jesus R. do	BY 24
Mercadores R. dos	AZ
Miguel Bombarda R.	BZ
Misericórdia Largo	BZ 25
Moeda R. da	AZ
Mouraria R.	BY
Muro R. do	AY
N. S. da Conceição Azinhaga	CY
Nova R.	BY
Penedos R. dos	AY
Penedos Largo dos	AY 28
Raimundo R. do	AZ
Raimundo Portas de	AZ
República R. da	BZ
Romão Ramalho R.	ABZ
Santa Clara R. de	AZ 30
São João de Deus Av. de	CYZ
São Manços R. de	BZ 31

São Miguel Largo de	BY	32
Senhor da Pobreza Largo	CZ	33
Serpa Pinto R.	AZ	
Serra da Tourega R. de	BCY	
Torta Trav.	AZ	34
Universidade Av. da	CY	
Valasco R. do	CZ	
Valdevinos R.	BZ	
Vasco da Gama R.	BY	36

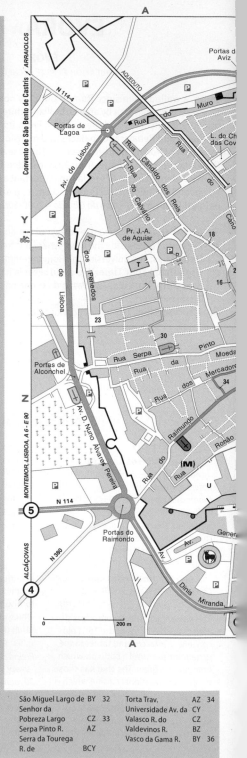

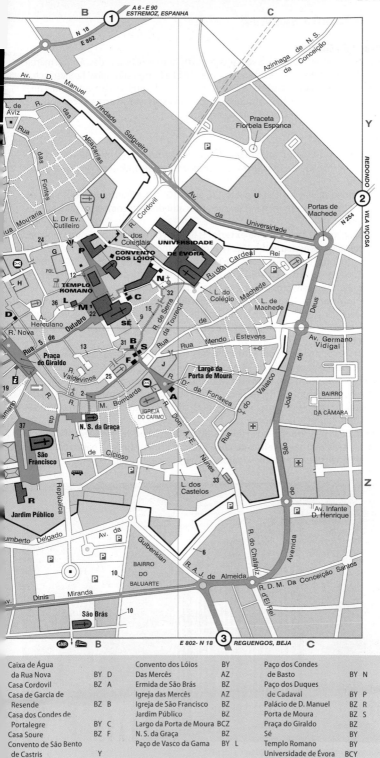

Caixa de Água da Rua Nova	BY D	Convento dos Lóios	BY
Casa Cordovil	BZ A	Das Mercês	AZ
Casa de Garcia de Resende	BZ B	Ermida de São Brás	BZ
Casa dos Condes de Portalegre	BY C	Igreja das Mercês	AZ
Casa Soure	BZ F	Igreja de São Francisco	BZ
Convento de São Bento de Castris	Y	Jardim Público	BZ
		Largo da Porta de Moura	BCZ
		N. S. da Graça	BZ
		Paço de Vasco da Gama	BY L

Paço dos Condes de Basto	BY N
Paço dos Duques de Cadaval	BY P
Palácio de D. Manuel	BZ R
Porta de Moura	BZ S
Praça do Giraldo	BZ
Sé	BY
Templo Romano	BY
Universidade de Évora	BCY

Old Town (Cidade Velha)

Praça do Giraldo

The bustling town centre is a vast square partly bordered by arcades. An 18C marble fountain by Afonso Álvares stands on the site of a former triumphal Roman arch. It leads into **Rua 5 de Outubro**, a narrow street which climbs to the cathedral and is lined with houses bearing wrought-iron balconies, as well as arts and crafts shops; no 28 has a niche decorated with *azulejos*.

Cathedral★★

Open 9am-12.30am and 2pm-5pm. Closed Mon and 25 Dec; museum closed Mon. €1 (Church only) €1.50 (church and cloisters) €3 (church, cloisters, museum). 266 75 93 30.

The cathedral was built in the late 12C and 13C in the Transitional Gothic style. While it has Romanesque characteristics, the cathedral was completed under Gothic influence.

The plain granite façade of the **exterior** is flanked by two massive towers crowned by conical spires added in the 16C. The tower on the right consists of several turrets similar to those on the Romanesque lantern-tower over the transept.

The main doorway is decorated with figures of the Apostles supported by consoles. The sculptures were probably carved in the late 13C by French artists.

In the **interior**★ the large nave, with broken barrel vaulting, has an elegant triforium. To the left, on a Baroque altar, is a 15C multicoloured stone statue of the Virgin with Child; opposite is a 16C statue, in gilded wood, of the Angel Gabriel attributed to Olivier of Ghent.

A very fine octagonal **dome**★ on squinches, from which hangs a chandelier, stands above the transept crossing. The arms of the transept are lit by two Gothic rose windows: the north one shows the Morning Star and the south the Mystic Rose.

In the north transept the Renaissance archway to a chapel is decorated with a marble sculpture by Nicolas Chanterene. The south transept contains the tomb of the 16C humanist André de Resende.

The chancel was remodelled in the 18C by Friederich Ludwig, architect of the monastery at Mafra. The **Cadeiras do coro**★ **(Choir stalls)**, made of oak, were carved in the Renaissance period by Flemish artists. They are decorated with sacred and

Roman temple and cathedral tower

Y. Travert/DIAF

secular motifs; note in particular the scenes on the lower panels showing peasants at their everyday tasks (grape-picking, pig-sticking and sheep-shearing). The large Renaissance organ is thought to be the oldest in Europe.

Museu de Arte Sacra★

This museum contains vestments, a collection of ecclesiastical plate, including an ivory 13C French figure-triptych of the **Virgin**★★, and a 17C reliquary cross of St Lenho in silver gilt and multicoloured enamel decorated with 1426 precious stones.

The **Gothic cloisters**★, which were built between 1322 and 1340, have a massive appearance which is further accentuated by their granite composition, despite the elegance of rounded bays with radiating tracery. Statues of the Evangelists stand in each of the four corners. The southwest corner provides a good view of the Romanesque belfry. An adjoining chapel contains the 14C tomb of the founder-bishop and 14C statues of the Angel Gabriel and a polychrome Virgin whose posture shows French influence.

Paço de Vasco da Gama

Open 9am-5pm Mon-Sat. Ring the ball for entry. ☎ 266 70 33 27.
This 15C mansion was built by the famous navigator and contains many items relating to the Great Discoveries, among them many paintings (which detail some of the fantastic animals encountered around the world) and frescoes. The building itself is impressive with cloisters, arcades and a chapel. Part of it is still used as lodging for Jesuit priests.

Templo Romano★

This Corinthian-style Roman temple erected in the 2C was probably dedicated to Diana. The capitals and bases of the columns are of Estremoz marble, the column shafts of granite. The temple owes its relative preservation to its conversion into a fortress in the Middle Ages and its excavation only a century ago.

Convento dos Lóios★

The Dos Lóios or St Eligius monastery, dedicated to St John the Evangelist, was founded in the 15C. It is now home to the city's *pousada*, as well as a **church**★ (*Open 10am-12.30pm; 2pm-6pm (5pm winter); closed Mon; €3 (€5 combined with the halls in the Palace of the Dukes of Cadaval); ☎ 266 70 47 14).*
The church façade was remodelled after the earthquake of 1755 with the exception of the porch which protects a Flamboyant Gothic doorway.

The nave, with lierne and tierceron vaulting, is lined with beautiful *azulejos* (1711) by António de Oliveira Bernardes, depicting the life of St Laurence Justinian, patriarch of Venice, whose writings influenced the Lóios monks. Two grilles in the pavement enable the castle's cistern, on the left, and an ossuary, on the right, to be seen.

Conventual buildings

The conventual buildings have been converted into a *pousada*. The chapter-house **door**★ has outstanding architectural elegance and is a good example of the composite Luso-Moorish style; the crowning piece over the doorway and the piers topped by pinnacles which serve as a framework to the door are Gothic inspired; the columns are twisted and Manueline in style and the twin bays with horseshoe arches are, like the capitals, reminiscent of Moorish design.

Paço dos Duques de Cadaval

Open 10am-12.30pm; 2pm-6pm (winter 5pm). Closed Mondays and holidays. €2.50 (combined ticket with the church of the Couvent dos Loios). ☎266 70 47 14.
The **Palace of the Dukes of Cadaval** (presently occupied by the Direcção de Estradas de Évora – Évora Road Network Dept) is protected by two crenellated towers and has a façade that was remodelled in the 17C. It was given by King João I to his councillor,

Martim Afonso de Melo, *alcalde* of Évora, in 1390. Kings João III and João V also lived within its walls at different periods.

The Dukes of Cadaval's **art gallery** contains a collection of historic documents on the Cadaval family and two fine Flemish commemorative plaques in bronze, dating from the late 15C.

▶ *Retrace your steps to the street between the Convento dos Lóios and the Museu Regional. Turn left into the street running perpendicular to the east end of the cathedral.*

Paço dos Condes de Basto

The Palace of the Counts of Basto was built over the remains of the Roman wall including the Sertório Tower. The Gothic palace's main front has several paired Mudéjar windows.

▶ *Return to the east end of the cathedral and continue round.*

Casa dos Condes de Portalegre is a delightful Gothic and 16C Manueline-style mansion with a patio surrounded by a hanging garden and an openwork balcony.

The **Casa de Garcia de Resende** is a 16C house in which the humanist Garcia de Resende (1470-1536) is said to have lived. Manueline decoration adorns the three sets of paired windows on the first floor.

The **Porta de Moura** gateway with its two towers formed part of the medieval town fortifications. A niche at the foot of the left tower contains a crucifix.

The picturesque **Largo da Porta de Moura** square is divided into two parts. On the larger of the two, in the centre, stands a beautiful Renaissance **fountain**★ which consists of a column surmounted by a white marble sphere.

Several lovely houses border the square: the 16C **Casa Cordovil** on the south side has an elegant loggia with twin arcades, festooned horseshoe arches and Moorish capitals, and a crenellated roof surmounted by a conical spire. On the west side, steps descend to the church of the former Carmelite Convent which has a Baroque **doorway**. On the east side are the Law Courts, housed in a modern building.

The 15C **Casa Soure** was formerly a part of the palace of the Infante Dom Luis. The Manueline façade has a gallery of rounded arches crowned by a conical spire.

▶ *Head toward Largo da Graça by way of Travessa da Caraça.*

Igreja de São Francisco

This early 16C church, which is preceded by a portico pierced by rounded, pointed and horseshoe arches, is crowned with battlements and conical pinnacles. The Manueline doorway is surmounted by a pelican and an armillary sphere, the respective emblems of João II and King Manuel.

The **interior**★, with ribbed vaulting, is surprisingly wide. The chancel contains two galleries, on the right, Renaissance, on the left, Baroque. The former chapter-house is furnished with a balustrade of fluted marble and turned ebony columns and, as a covering to the walls, *azulejos* depicting scenes from the Passion.

▶ *Take the door to the left of the balustrade in the former chapter-house.*

Capela dos Ossos★

◷ *Open 9am-12.30pm; 2.30pm-5.45pm (5.15pm in winter).* ₰€1. ☎ 266 70 45 21.

This macabre ossuary chapel was built in the 16C by a Franciscan to induce meditation in his fellow men. The bones and skulls of 5 000 people have been used to face the walls and pillars.

Capela dos Ossos

Public Gardens (Jardim Público)

The public gardens are just south of the Igreja de São Francisco. Part of the 16C **Palácio de Dom Manuel** – which has unfortunately been thoroughly remodelled – and the ruins of another 16C palace still stand in the gardens. Note the paired windows with horseshoe arches in the Luso-Moorish style. The itinerary continues past the market (pottery stalls) which is held every morning.

Additional Sights

Fortifications★

Traces of the 1C Roman wall, reinforced by the Visigoths in the 7C, can be seen between the Paços dos Duques de Cadaval and dos Condes de Basto (Largo dos Colegiais). The 14C medieval wall marks the town limits to the north and west. The 17C fortifications now form the boundary of the public gardens to the south.

Universidade de Évora (Antiga Universidade dos Jesuitas)

◷*Open Mon-Fri, 8am-6pm (8pm in Aug); Sat-Sun and holidays, 8am-1pm and 3-6pm.* ◷*Closed holidays.*

The university occupies the former Jesuit University; the building's inner courtyard is of particular interest.

Buildings in the 16C Italian Renaissance style surround what is known as the main **Students' Cloisters**★ *(Claustro Geral dos Estudos)* with its arched gallery – the whole forming a graceful inner court. Facing the entrance, the pediment over the portico to the Sala das Actas (Hall of Acts) is decorated with statues personalising the royal and the ecclesiastical universities.

The classrooms opening onto the gallery are adorned with 18C *azulejos* representing the subjects taught in the different rooms – physics, history, philosophy and mathematics.

ÉVORAMONTE★

ÉVORA
POPULATION 1 835 – MICHELIN MAP 733

The small fortified town of Évoramonte, along the A6 about 25km/17ml east of Évora, has a remarkable **setting**★ at the top of a high hill in the Alentejo. It was at Évoramonte on 26 May 1834 that the **Convention** was signed which ended the civil war and under which the son of João VI, Pedro IV, Emperor of Brazil, compelled his brother Miguel I, an extremist whom he had vanquished at the Battle of Asseiceira, to abdicate in favour of his niece Maria and to go into exile.

Access
1.5km/1mi from the modern village. Follow the signs to "Castelo de Évoramonte". After skirting the base of the 14C-17C ramparts, go through the entrance gate.

Sights

Castle★
⊙*Open Jun-Sept 10am-1pm; 2pm - 6pm; Oct-May 10am-1pm; 2pm-5pm.* ⊙*Closed Jan 1, Easter Sunday, May 1 and Dec 25.* ⊛*€1.50 (free Sunday and holidays 10am-1pm).* ☎ *268 95 00 25.*

The castle which was first Roman, then Moorish, then radically remodelled in the 14C, emerges as a Gothic-style military monument in spite of further reconstruction in the 16C. The medieval keep is girdled by rope motifs which knot in the middle of each façade. Inside, the central part of the castle consists of three superimposed storeys; each storey is covered with nine Gothic arches resting on sturdy central pillars, those on the ground floor being massive and twisted.

From the top, there is a **panorama**★ of the surrounding countryside speckled with olive trees and small white villages, and to the northeast, Estremoz.

Casa da Convenção
The house where the Convention was signed bears a commemorative plaque.

Parish church
The parish church, with its original transverse bell gable, has a distinctive outline as it stands at the end of the main street.

Castle, Évoramonte

B.Brillion/MICHELIN

FARO★

FARO

POPULATION 57 151 – MICHELIN MAP 733
LOCAL MAP SEE ALGARVE

The capital of the Algarve is sited on Portugal's most southerly headland. Faro lives on salt collected from the salt marshes, fishing (tunny and sardine), cork factories and marble works, food processing (beans) and canning, and its plastics and building industries. The building of the airport nearby has turned Faro into the main arrival point for year-round visitors attracted to the seaside resorts along the Algarve coast. Faro's vast sandy beach, on an island, also attracts a great many tourists. ▯ *Rua da Misericórdia 8-12 – 8000-269 –* ☎ *289 80 36 04*

Address Book

WHERE TO STAY

◉ **Pensão Residencial Central** – *Largo Terreiro do Bispo, 12,* ☎*289 80 72 91 (closed 1st week in May)* 🍴 *8 rooms.* A small, recently refurbished hotel with lovely light and comfortable rooms, several with a nice-sized bath. The best address in town at this price.

◉ **Pensão Residencial Oceano** - *Trv. Ivens, 21-1°* ☎*289 80 55 91, closed Christmas 22 rooms.* Ideal location in the pedestrianised area close to the marina. The rooms have been recently redecorated with lovely white wood furniture and bed covers in pink. Bathrooms come with a bath. The staircase leading to reception is a little narrow so don't take really big bags!

◉ **Pensão Residencial Adelaide** – *R. Cruz das Mestras, 9,* ☎*289 80 23 83* 🍴 ▤ *19 rooms* ⌑. A small hotel with big rooms and pleasant furnishings. The rooms overlook the street, which can be busy, particularly at weekends.

◉◉◉◉ **Faro** – *R. D Francisco Gomes, 2 289 83 08 30 - www.hotelfaro.pt; 90 rooms* ⌑. Simplicity and light are the two words that come to mind in describing the rooms at this newly refurbished hotel near the port. Breakfast is served on the top floor terrace, shaped like a boat and with a magnificent view over the marina and old town.

EATING OUT

◉ **Chalavar** - *R. Infante D Enrique, 120* -☎ *289 82 24 45,* 🍴 *closed Sunday.* A lively and friendly restaurant owned by a fisherman - so you'll not be surprised that the menu has lots of fish!. Big portions and very tasty.

◉ **Pontinha** – *R. Pé da Cruz, 5 289 82 06 49 - closed Sundays.* At the back of the pedestrian zone on the praça da Liberdade, a simple restaurant which has a large choice, among them many local specialities, so if you want to eat like a local, this could be the place.

◉◉◉ **Mesa dos Mouros** - *Largo da Sé, 10 - 289 87 88 73 open noon-3pm; 7.30pm-11pm, closed Sunday.* If you are passing the cathedral on your evening stroll do not hesitate to stop here for a refined and elegant dinner, often accompanied by a concert from the local family of storks. Very reasonably priced for this quality of food.

◉◉◉ **O Aldeão** - *Largo de S. Pedro, 54-57* ☎*289 82 33 39, closed Sunday.* On the square where S Pedro's church is located, this restaurant has charm andd style. Once inside you will delight in discovering the regional dishes from the Algarve nd the Alentejo regions. Most enjoyable.

◉◉◉ **Camané** – *Praia de Faro 9km/6mi to the west of Faro – Av. Nascente –* ☎ *289 81 75 39. Closed Mondays and two weeks in May.* This restaurant has a pleasant outdoor terrace overlooking the Formosa river. Seafood specialities are served.

FESTIVALS

Festa do Morisco à Ohlão – roundabout the 10th August each year – seafood, dancing and traditional music.

FARO

1° de Maio R.	Y	
1°de Dezembro R.	YZ	56
5 de Outubro Av.	Y	57
Arco R. do	Z	32
Baptista Lopes R.	Y	33
Carmo Largo de	Y	7
Conselheiro Bivar R.	Y	9
Conselheiro Tomas Ribeiro R.	Y	34
Cunha Matos R.	Y	35
D. F. Gomes Pr.	Y	12
D. F. Gomes R.	Y	36
Dr Teixeira Guedes R.	Y	14
Ferreira de Almeida Pr.	Y	16
Filipe Alistão R.	Y	18
Francisco Barreto R.	Y	19
Gil Fanes R.	Y	38
Gomes Freire R.	Y	39
Horta Machado R.	Y	40
Ivens R.	Y	21
José Estevão R.	Y	37
Monsenhor Boto R.	Z	41
Mouras Velhas Largo das	Y	24
Mouzhinho de Albuquerque R.	Y	42
Município R. do	Z	43
Norberto Silva R.	Z	44
Nova do Castelo R.	Z	45
Pé da Cruz Largo do	YZ	25
Rasquinho R.	Z	46
Rebelo da Silva R.	Y	47
Repouso R. do	Z	48
Sacadura Cabral R.	Y	49
Santo António R. de	Y	
São Pedro Largo de	Y	26
São Sebastião Largo de	Y	28
São Sebastião R.	Y	50
Senhora da Saúde Estrada da	Y	51
T. Valadim R.	Y	52
Teófilo Braga R.	Y	53
Trem R. do	Z	54
Vasco de Gama R.	Y	55

Museu de Etnografia Regional	Y	M³	Museu Municipal	Z	M²

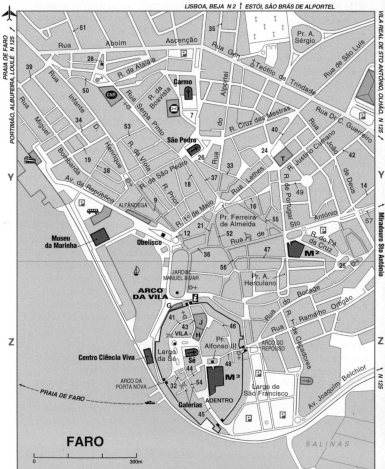

▶ **Orient Yourself:** On the Algarve coast, midway between east and west.
▣ **Parking:** Very difficult – stay outside the town at the Largo de São Francisco.
☺ **Don't Miss:** The old town, the promenade and the beach. And the storks!
◷ **Organizing Your Time:** About one day to enjoy it and soak up some sun.
☖ **Also See:** Portimão, Silves and Tavira.

Old Town★

The old town lies south of the Jardim Manuel Bivar, a peaceful quarter resting in the shadow of the circle of houses which stand like ramparts around it.

Arco da Vila

The Arco da Vila is the finest of the gateways in the old Alfonso wall. It has Italian-style pilasters and, in a niche, a white marble statue of St Thomas Aquinas. The top of the bell-tower above the arch has long been a nesting spot for a family of storks.

Cathedral

◔*Open Mon-Sat 10am-6pm (Sat 10am-1pm).* ◔*Closed holidays.* ☞*€2.50.*
Only the entrance's imposing tower-portico remains from the original church built on the site of an old mosque following the Reconquest in 1251. Today, the edifice combines a mix of styles, including a panelled ceiling covered with 17C *azulejos* and a Renaissance altarpiece in the choir. It also preserves a medieval **bell tower** which has beautiful views of the town and the coast.

Museu Municipal

◔*Open Jun-Sept, Tue-Fri 10am-8pm; Sat-Sun 1.30pm-8pm; Oct-May, Tue-Fri 9am-6pm; Sat-Sun 11.30am-6pm.* ◔*Closed holidays.* ☞*€2.* ☎ *289 89 74 00.*
The municipal museum is in the former Convent of Nossa Senhora de Assunção which dates from the 16C.
The archeological collection **(Museu Arqueológico Lapilar do Infante Dom Henrique)** is housed in the cloister galleries built by Afonso Pires and contains various remains found at Milreu, capitals, mosaics, a Roman tomb from the 1C, a 15C sarcophagus, a 16C bishop's throne and ancient weapons and coins. Moorish earthenware jars and Mudéjar *azulejos* evoke the Muslim and post-Muslim periods of local art. The **Ferreira de Almeida collection** on the first floor includes sculptures, 18C paintings and Spanish and Chinese furniture.
During the summer months, concerts (classical, jazz, *fado* etc) are held in the chapel. A programme of events is available at the Tourist Office.

Museu Marítimo

◔*Open Mon-Fri 9am-11am; 2pm-4.30pm.* ◔*Closed holidays.* ☞*€1.* ☎ *289 89 49 90.*
The Maritime Museum is housed in the harbour-master's office. The most noteworthy exhibits are the many model ships and the displays of different types of fishing, for tunny (tuna), sardines, octopus and so on.

FÁTIMA

SANTARÉM

POPULATION 10 337 – MICHELIN MAP 733

The sanctuary at Fátima is one of the most famous in the world. Great pilgrimages numbering thousands of believers visit the shrine on the 13th of every month, especially in May and October, the dates of the first and final apparitions. Many travel to the shrine on foot and, along every road that crosses the plateau, an impressive number of pilgrims may be seen. Despite the myriad souvenir shops around the sanctuary, the site has retained its atmosphere of spirituality. It is also a very cosmopolitan place, with members of religious orders and visitors from around the world. *Av. José Alves Correia da Silva – 2495-402 – ☎ 249 53 11 39*

- ▶ **Orient Yourself:** Inland from Nazaré, halfway between Lisbon and Coimbra.
- **Don't Miss:** The feeling of this place of pilgrimage.
- **Organizing Your Time:** If you arrive at the time of a pilgrimage, visiting the sights will take longer. At other times one day will be sufficient.
- **Also See:** the monastery at Batalha, Tomar.

The apparitions

On 13 May 1917, three young shepherds, **Francisco**, **Jacinta** and **Lúcia**, were minding their sheep at Cova da Iria when suddenly the sky lit up: the Virgin appeared before them standing in an oak tree, and spoke. Her message, repeated at each apparition on the 13th of every subsequent month, was a call for peace. It was particularly apt since Europe had then been at war for three years, Portugal fighting with the Allies. It was only in 1930 that the Bishop of Leiria authorised the celebration of belief in Our Lady of Fátima (Nossa Senhora de Fátima). In May 2000 Pope John Paul II travelled to Fàtima to beatify two of the young shepherds, Jacinta and Francisco.

The Pilgrimage

Basílica

Closing the end of the huge esplanade (540m x 160m/1 772ft x 525ft) is the neo-Cassical basilica (capacity: more than 300 000 pilgrims) which is extended on either

Our Lady of Fátima pilgrimage

G. Durand/DIAF

side by a semicircular peristyle and dominated by a 65m/200ft tower. Inside are the tombs of Francisco and Jacinta who died in 1919 and 1920. The oldest of the three, Lúcia, is now a nun in a convent near Coimbra.

Capela das Aparições

An evergreen oak grows on the esplanade, replacing the one in which the Virgin appeared. Nearby, on the spot where the Virgin appeared, the Chapel of the Apparitions contains a statue to Our Lady of Fátima.

The great pilgrimages

The great pilgrimages include processions with burning torches, nocturnal vigils, the celebration of solemn masses on the esplanade, the benediction of the sick and finally "farewell" processions. The fervour of the thousands of pilgrims at prayer, many of whom cover the approaches to the basilica on their knees, is deeply moving.

Visit

Museu de Cera

Open Apr to Oct, 9.30am-6.30pm; Nov to Mar, 10am-5pm; Sundays open at 9am. Closed 25 Dec. €4.50 *249 53 93 00 - www.mucefa.pt.*
This wax museum contains a beautifully rendered pageant of 28 tableaux recounting the story of the apparitions.

The Parque National das Serras de Aire and de Candeeiros★

Grutas de Mira de Aire★

In the village, to the right of the N 243 going towards Porto de Mós. Guided tours (40min), Oct to Mar, 9.30am-5pm (6pm Apr and May; 7pm June and Sept; 8.30pm July and Aug). €4.80. *244 44 03 22 - www.grutasmiradaire.com.*
These caves, the biggest in Portugal, which are also called the Old Windmill Caves **(Grutas dos Moinhos Velhos)**, discovered in 1947 and then linked together by artificial tunnels, total a length of more than 4km/2.5mi and reach a depth of 110m/360ft.
From chamber to gallery the sight is impressive, especially in the two biggest caves, the "Grand Salon" and the "Red Chamber". The reddish-tinted walls, due to iron oxide, the opalescence of the rock deposits with their evocative shapes ("jewels" from the Pearl Chapel; the Medusa, the Martian, the Organ etc), the sound of subterranean water, all exert their fascination. In the vast end gallery you can marvel at the "Great Lake" which collects all the water from the streams and the "Black River" which rises several days a year and floods the lower part of the caves.

Grutas de São Mamede

Guided tours (25min), Jul-Sept 9am-7pm; Apr-Jun 9am-6pm; Oct-Mar 9am-5pm. 244 70 38 38 - www.grutasmoeda.com. €5 *– From Cova da Iria (Fátima), 7.5km/4.5mi on the N 356 towards Batalha; take the road to Mira de Aire on the left, then the access lane to the caves on the left upon leaving the village of São Mamede.*
A legend whereby bandits were said to have hurled down the body of a traveller along with his purse, in their excessive haste, has led them to be called the Money Caves, **Grutas da Moeda**. One can count up to nine "chambers", and the variety of colours and folds therein, a waterfall, strange multi-coloured calcarious deposits in the Shepherd's Chamber, are worth seeing.

Grutas de Alvados

Access by the N 361 between Alvados and Serra de San António. Guided tours (35min), Jun-Aug, 10am-8pm; Sept-May 10am-5pm. €4.60 (€3 for children). www. grutasalvadas.com. These caves were discovered in 1964 on the northwest flank of the Pedra de Altar hill. They extend for 450m/1 476ft across about 10 chambers linked artificially by long tunnels, each having its own small limpid lake and colourful rock deposits. They have an additional attraction due to the golden colour of the walls, the number of stalactites and stalagmites joined together forming pillars, and the zigzag cracks in the ground.

Grutas de Santo António

Access by the N 361 to the north of Serra de Santo António. Guided tours (35min), Jun-Aug, 10am-8pm; Sept-May 10am-5pm. €4.80 (children €3) - ticket also covers Alvados – www.grutassantoantonio.com.
An access tunnel had to be constructed for visitors. The three chambers (the main one with an area of 4 000m²/4 784sq yd is 43m/141ft high) and a short gallery all have delicate rose-coloured concretions. In one of the secondary chambers there is a small lake.

FIGUEIRA DA FOZ★

COIMBRA
POPULATION 62 224 – MICHELIN MAP 733
PLAN IN THE MICHELIN GUIDE SPAIN AND PORTUGAL

Figueira da Foz, which commands the mouth of the Mondego river, due west of Coimbra, is overlooked from behind by the Serra da Boa Viagem. Tourists congregate on the west side of the town, attracted by the vast beach of fine sand which lines the wide curve of Figueira bay. This bay, previously known as Mondego bay, is overlooked by a fort of golden stone which was captured from the French by students of Coimbra University. Shortly before this momentous event Wellington landed the first British troops here in August 1808. From Figueira began the advance south which was to bring the first battles of the Peninsular War not far from Óbidos at Roliça and Vimeiro. Figueira, which was built in the last century, lives primarily from its fishing industry (sardines and cod) and its shipyards. *Av. 25 Abril – 3080-086 – ☎ 233 40 28 27 or 42 26 10*

GUARDA

GUARDA
POPULATION 43 759 – MICHELIN MAP 733

Guarda, a pleasant health resort and the highest town in Portugal, stands at an altitude of 1 000m/3 281ft in the eastern foothills of the Serra da Estrela. Its name "protector" recalls that at one time it was the main stronghold of the province of Beira Alta near Spain. Medieval castles and fortresses are dotted throughout the region guarding the border. Over the last few years the town has sprouted modern quarters around its medieval centre which is enclosed within the remains of ancient fortifications. *Praça Luis de Camões – 6300-725 – ☎ 271 22 18 17*

▶ **Orient Yourself:** East of Viseu, not too far from the border with Spain.
☺ **Don't Miss:** The Eastern fortified towns.
🕐 **Organizing Your Time:** A couple of days would allow you to make several excursions.
👍 **Also See:** Belmonte and Viseu.

Sights

Fortifications
The best preserved remains of the fortifications are the Torre dos Ferreiros (Blacksmiths' Tower), the 12C and 13C keep (Torre de Menagem) and the Porta d'El Rei and Porta da Estrela (King's and Star Gates).

Cathedral ★
🕐*Open 10am-12.30pm; 2pm-5pm.* ☎ *271 32 03 12.* 🕐*Closed Mon and the last weekend of each month, Jan 1, Easter Sunday, May 1 and Dec 25. Free.*
The cathedral *(sé)* was begun in 1390 in the Gothic style, but as it was only completed in 1540, Renaissance and Manueline elements are clearly visible in its decoration. The granite edifice is crowned with pinnacles and trefoils which give it a certain resemblance to the monastery at Batalha.
The northern façade is embellished with an ornate Gothic doorway surmounted by a Manueline window. In the main façade, a Manueline doorway is framed by two octagonal towers emblazoned at their bases with the coat of arms of Bishop Dom Pedro Vaz Gavião, who played a part in getting the cathedral completed.

Interior ★
The lierne and tierceron vaulting over the transept crossing has a key-stone in the form of a cross of the Order of Christ. In the chancel is a Renaissance altarpiece made of Ançã stone in the 16C and gilded in the 18C. Attributed to Jean de Rouen, the high relief, which includes over one hundred figures, depicts scenes in the Lives of the

Remains of the fortifications, Guarda

Virgin and Christ on four levels from the base to the top. A 16C altarpiece in the south apsidal chapel, also attributed to Jean de Rouen, represents the Last Supper.

Museu da Guarda
⊘Open 10am-12.30pm; 2pm-5.30pm. ⊘Closed Mon, 1 Jan, Good Fri, Easter Mon, 1 May and 25 Dec. ∞€2 (no charge Sun or holiday mornings). ☎ 271 21 34 60.
The regional museum, which is housed at the foot of the ramparts in the former bishop's palace, dates from the early 17C and has preserved its Renaissance cloisters. The collections include displays of regional archeology as well as painting and sculpture.

The Eastern Fortified Towns
Distances indicated are from Guarda.

Medieval strongholds, built in the 17C-18C to protect the border, and numerous fortified small towns or villages still seem to mount guard at the top of a hillock or a steep headland, in the heart of the Beira Alta.

Almeida★
49km/30mi to the northeast. Less than 10km/6mi from the border, the peaceful little town of Almeida crowns a hill 729m/2 491ft high with its ramparts. Taken by the Spanish in 1762, then by the French under Massena in 1810, it has, nevertheless, kept intact its double **fortifications**★, in the form of a six-pointed star in pure Vauban style, which were completed in the 18C. Three arched gateways with monumental porches preceded by bridges, give access to the interior. A medieval fortress dating from the time of King Dinis, this village clustered round a hill has only one ruined tower remaining, next to a Gothic gate

Castelo Melhor★
77km/ 47.5mi to the northeast.
Visible from the N 222, the village clings to the flanks of a rocky peak dotted with olive trees. A medieval **wall**★ reinforced with round towers encircles the grassy and bare summit.

Castelo Mendo
35km/ 21.5mi to the east.
Cobbled alleys crisscross on a rocky hillock among the remains of a Gothic wall, where the main gate is wedged between two towers. The village still has the marks of a flourishing past with a few Renaissance buildings, including a 17C church.

Celorico da Beira
28km/17.5mi to the northwest.

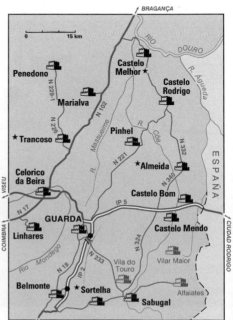

This busy small town is on the extreme north of a wooded ridge at the end of the Serra da Estrela. The square keep of the ancient castle rises up at the top, surrounded by a small wall.

Linhares
49km/30mi to the west (the last 6km/3.5mi after Carrapichana follow a winding road).
The beautiful outer wall of the castle, built at the time of Dinis I, with its two square crenellated towers, runs round the top of a granite spur dominating the upper valley of the Mondego. The village has a 16C pillory with an armillary sphere.

Marialva
69km/43mi to the north.
The remains of a castle built in 1200 cover a rocky ridge which has extensive views over the Bevesa plain. Between the ruins of the outer wall, a crenellated keep and another tower still set in its wall, there are scattered ruins of the old village and a church with a Manueline doorway.

Penedono
74km/46mi to the north.
The town of Penedono is perched on a rocky crest 947m/3 106ft high in the Beira Alta. It is overlooked on its northern side by a graceful and triangular fortified **castle** (*Open all day. Closed Good Fri and Easter Sun. No charge. If closed, ask for the key from Sr. Luís Martins in the building next to the castle. ☎ 254 50 41 50 or 254 60 57 70*), crowned with pyramidal merlons. A 16C **pillory** stands before the steps leading up to the castle. Pass through the ramparts and turn left towards the simple entrance gate which is flanked by two battlemented turrets.

Sabugal
33km/20mi to the southeast.
The small city of Sabugal, on a hillock round its fortified castle, dominates the Côa valley. Founded by Alfonso X of León at the beginning of the 13C, it became Portuguese in 1282 on the marriage of Isabel of Aragon and King Dom Dinis of Portugal. The present appearance of the **castle** dates from the late 13C.

Sortelha★
45km/28mi to the south.
This 12C **stronghold**★, hemming in the old village with its picturesque granite houses, stands on a spur dominating the upper Zêzere valley. You enter it through one of the Gothic gates of the fortified wall, where the two existing square towers have their own surrounding wall with machicolated gateways.

GUIMARÃES★★

BRAGA
POPULATION 158 897 – MICHELIN MAP 733

In the 10C, soon after it was founded by the Countess Mumadona, Guimarães consisted of a monastery with a defensive tower and a few neighbouring houses. In the Middle Ages new quarters were added. Nowadays Guimarães is a prosperous commercial city with cutlery, tanning and kitchenware industries and crafts such as gold and silversmith work, pottery, embroidery, linen damask and the carving of wooden yokes. ▯ *Praça de Santiago – 4800-421 – ☎ 253 51 87 90*

▶ **Orient Yourself:** North-east of Porto about 22km/15ml south-east of Braga.

🅿 **Parking:** To visit the old town, leave your car in the underground car-park in the República do Brasil, south-east of the town. There is also a large parking area at the rear of the castle.

🔊 **Don't Miss:** Make sure you stop for a glass of wine at one of the terrace cafés on the Largo da Oliveira or the praça da São Tiago.

🕐 **Organizing Your Time:** A good half day, though a full day would be better.

🗝 **Also See:** Braga and Porto.

A Bit of History

The cradle of Portugal

In 1095 Alfonso VI, King of León and Castile, bestowed the County of Portucale on his son-in-law, Henry of Burgundy. Henry had the tower at Guimarães converted into a castle and installed his wife the Princess Teresa (Tareja) there. In about 1110 Teresa bore Henry a son, **Afonso Henriques**, who succeeded his father in 1112. The young prince revolted against his mother, and on 24 June 1128 seized power following the Battle of São Mamede. Then he succeeded in vanquishing the Moors at Ourique on 25 July 1139 and was proclaimed King of Portugal by his troops.

Gil Vicente (1470-1536)

The poet and goldsmith, Gil Vicente, born in Guimarães in 1470, lived at the courts of King João II and King Manuel I. He wrote plays to entertain the king and the court, and mysteries *(autos)* to be performed in the churches. His forty-four plays provide a precise if satirical panorama of Portuguese society at the beginning of the 16C, while the variety of his inspiration allied to the lightness of his touch and finesse of his style make him the virtual creator of the Portuguese theatre.

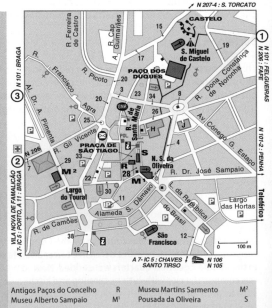

GUIMARÃES

Agostinho Barbosa R.	3
Alberto Sampaio Av.	4
Conde Margaride Av.	7
Condessa do Juncal Largo da	11
Condessa Mumadona Largo da	8
D. João IV Av.	12
Dom Alfonso Henriques Av.	16
Dona Teresa R. de	15
Doutor Joaquim de Meira R.	17
Duques de Bragança R.a	19
Gen. Humberto Delgado Av.	20
João Franco Largo de	22
Martins Sarmento Largo	23
Navarros de Andrade Largo	25
Nuno Alvares R.	26
Oliveira Largo da	28
Paio Galvão R.	29
Rainha R. da	30
Santo António R.a de	33
Serpa Pinto R.	34
Toural Largo do	
Valentin Moreina de Sá Largo	38

Antigos Paços do Concelho	R	Museu Martins Sarmento	M²
Museu Alberto Sampaio	M¹	Pousada da Oliveira	S

Castle Hill

Castle★

⏱ *Open 9.30am-12.30pm; 2pm-5.30pm.* ⏱ *Closed Mon; 1 Jan, Good Fri, Easter Mon, 1 May and 25 Dec.* ⬡ *€1.50 (keep).* ☎ *253 41 22 73.*

In the 10C Countess Mumadona had the 28m/92ft keep built to protect the monastery and small town in its midst. The castle was later built under Henry of Burgundy and reinforced in the 15C. Seven square towers surround the keep.

Igreja de São Miguel do Castelo

⏱ *Open 9.30am-12.30pm; 2pm-5.30pm.* ⏱ *Closed Mon, 1 Jan, Easter Sunday, May 1, Dec 25. Free.* ☎ *253 41 22 73.*

This small 12C Romanesque church contains a font in which Afonso Henriques was baptised, in addition to a great many funerary slabs.

Paço dos Duques de Bragança★

⬤ *Guided tours (30min), 9.30am 5.30pm.* ⏱ *Closed Mon, 1 Jan, Good Fri, Easter Mon, 1 May and 25 Dec.* ⬡ *€3 (no charge on Sun and holiday mornings).* ☎ *253 41 22 73.*

The palace was built in the early 15C by the first Duke of Bragança, Afonso I, natural son of King Dom João I. The architecture shows a strong Burgundian influence, particularly in the roof and the unusual 39 brick chimneys. The palace was one of the most sumptuous dwellings in the Iberian Peninsula until the 16C when the court moved to Vila Viçosa after which it was seldom visited.

The vast rooms were heated by huge fireplaces. On the first floor the eye is caught by the **ceilings**★ of oak and chestnut in the Dining and Banqueting Halls and the 16C and 18C **tapestries**★. The Tournai tapestries depicting the capture of Arzila and Tangiers are in fact copies of the series woven after cartoons by Nuno Gonçalves. Other decoration includes Persian carpets, 17C Portuguese furniture, Chinese porcelain, weapons and armour, as well as Dutch and Italian paintings.

The Historical Centre★★

Wide avenues mark the limits of the harmonious, well-preserved historical quarter which makes a pleasant stroll with its maze of streets, squares and old houses.

Address Book

WHERE TO STAY

◯ **Residencial das Trinas** - *R. das Trinas, 29,* ☎*253 51 73 58* ▦*11 rooms.* A small pensão in the old town which is both central and welcoming. The rooms are furnished in a traditional style with TV and air-conditioning, and look aout over the street, though the view from the rear is better. The quality is very good for this price range.

◯ **Residencial Mestre d'Avis** - *R. D João I, 40 -* ☎*253 42 27 70. 16 rooms.* Near the historic centre of town, this imposing building hides behind it very well appointed rooms, though some are a little on the small side. The proprietor

is very knowledgeable about the town and is a very good guide.

◯◯◯ **Paço de São Cipriano** - *Tabuadelo (6km/4ml south of Guimarães)* ☎*253 56 53 37 - www.pacoscipriano.com* ▣⬛ *7 rooms* ▭. Set within a huge estate, this beautiful hotel will appeal to lovers of antiquity. The gardens are stunning, the aromas from flowers scintillating. All in all, a beautiful place to stay.

◯◯◯◯ **Pousada de Nossa Senhora da Oliveira** – *Rua de Santa Maria, –* ☎ *253 51 41 57 - www.pousada.pt* ▦ *16 rooms* ▭. This welcoming inn at the heart of the city's historical centre has a good restaurant serving regional specialities.

Convento de Nossa Senhora da Oliveira

The monastery dedicated to Our Lady of the Olive Tree was founded by Countess Mumadona in the 10C. Only the Gothic collegiate church with its Romanesque cloisters and chapter-house (now the museum) remains.

Colegiada de Nossa Senhora da Oliveira

The main doorway of this collegiate church is surmounted by a 14C Gothic pediment. Inside, note the silver altar in the Chapel of the Holy Sacrament (Capela do Santíssimo Sacramento). A Gothic **shrine** in front of the church contains a *padrão* commemorating the victory over the Moors at the Battle of the Salado in 1340. Legend has it that

Colegiada de Nossa Senhora da Oliveira, Guimarães

during the completion of the porch in 1342 the trunk of the olive tree, which stood in front of the church, suddenly sprouted leaves: thus, the church's name.

Museu Alberto Sampaio★

Open 10am-6pm. Closed Mon, 1 Jan, Good Fri, Easter Sun, 1 May and 25 Dec. €2 (no charge Sun morning). ☎ 253 42 39 10.

The museum is housed in the conventual buildings. The 13C Romanesque cloisters have interesting historiated capitals. In the east corner of the cloisters is a door from the former 10C Monastery of Mumadona.

In a Gothic chapel to the right on entering is the fine **recumbent figure**★ in granite of Dona Constança de Noronha, wife of Dom Afonso, first Duke of Bragança. Rooms off the cloisters contain paintings of the Portuguese School, especially some by António Vaz, who was born at Guimarães, and Baroque altarpieces.

On the first floor are several statues including the 15C alabaster statue of Our Lady of Pity and a large wooden altarpiece from the 16C. The galleries that follow contain **church plate**★. Much of the collegiate church treasure was donated by Dom João I. In addition to the tunic worn by João I at the Battle of Aljubarrota, the room of the same name also contains the silver-gilt **triptych**★ said to have been taken by the king from the Castilians at the battle. It shows the Nativity, Annunciation, Purification and Presentation at the Temple on the left and, on the right, the shepherds and the Magi. Among other pieces of the treasure, note a silver-gilt Gothic chalice with enamel embossing, a Manueline monstrance attributed to Gil Vicente and a finely engraved 16C Manueline **cross**★ depicting scenes from the Passion.

Additional Sights

Museu Martins Sarmento

Guided tours (30min), 9.30am-noon; 2-5pm. Closed Mon, holidays and 24 June (local holiday). €1.50. ☎ 253 41 59 69.

The museum, which is housed partly in the Gothic cloisters of the Church of São Domingos, includes a large collection of archeological exhibits from the pre-Roman cities of Sabroso and Briteiros (*see BRAGA*).

Altarpiece, Igreja de São Francisco

Igreja de São Francisco

The church was built early in the 15C but was remodelled in the 17C so that only the main door and the east end have retained their original Gothic character. The capitals in the main doorway represent the legend of St Francis. The interior suffered some unfortunate remodellings in the 17C and 18C. The chancel, which contains a Baroque altar carved in wood and gilded, is decorated with 18C **azulejos**★ depicting the life of St Anthony. In the **sacristy**★(○*Open 9.30am-noon; 3pm-5pm. Suday 9.30am-1pm.* ○*Closed Mon; access through the south transept)* one can see a fine coffered ceiling ornamented with grotesques and an Arrábida marble table standing against an elegant Carrara marble column. The chapter-house, which gives onto 16C Renaissance cloisters, is closed by a fine Gothic grille. Note, to the right of the church, a beautiful façade adorned with *azulejos*.

LAGOS★

FARO

POPULATION 25 264 – MICHELIN MAP 733
LOCAL MAP SEE ALGARVE

Lagos was the capital of the Algarve from 1576 to 1756. Today, in spite of great popularity with tourists, it has managed to preserve both character and charm with its fort, walls and old quarter. The most attractive approaches to Lagos are from Aljezur in the north along the N 120 or from Vila do Bispo in the west along the N 125. From both of these roads there are **views**★ of the town and the large marina which now lines the bay. Apart from being a seaside resort and a fishing port well sheltered by the Ponta da Piedade promontory, Lagos is also an important yachting centre organising international regattas. ⊞ *Rua Vasco da Gama (São João) – 8600-753 –* ☎ *282 76 30 31*

▶ **Orient Yourself:** On the Algarve coast, quite a long way west.

🅿 **Parking:** A large parking area in the Avda. dos Desocobrimentos.

🚫 **Don't Miss:** The church of S. Antonio.

🕐 **Organizing Your Time:** Visit the sights in the morning and the beach in the afternoon..

🐾 **Also See:** Faro,Cabo S Vicente, Sagres.

The harbour in the past

Lagos was an important harbour at the time of the Great Discoveries and it was from here that most of the African expeditions put to sea. It served as Prince Henry the Navigator's principal maritime base and as the port of registry to Gil Eanes who, in 1434, rounded for the first time in history Cape Bojador, a point on the west coast of the Sahara which until then had been the last outpost of the habitable world. On Prince Henry's orders, one expedition followed another down the coast of Africa, each time adding to the knowledge of ocean currents and improving navigational techniques.

Sights

Praça da República

A **statue of Prince Henry the Navigator**, erected in 1960 to commemorate the 500th anniversary of his death, stands in the middle of the square. Its presence explains why the square is better known as the Praça Infante Dom Henrique. The house with arcades on the right side of the square is the former slave market, **Mercado de Escravos**. The present building was reconstructed after the earthquake in 1755.

▸ *Take Rua Henrique Correia da Silva leading straight off the square.*

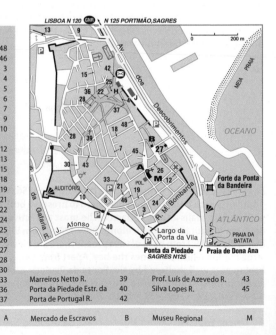

LAGOS	
25 de Abril R.	48
5 de Outubro R.	46
Adro R. do	3
Alfonso de Almeida R.	4
Armas Pr.a de	5
Atalaia R. da	6
Cândido dos Reis R.	7
Capelinha R. da	9
Cardeal Netto R.	10
Castelo dos Governadores R. do	12
Cemitério R. do	13
Conselheiro J. Machado R.	15
Dr. Joaquim Tello R.	18
Dr. Mendonça R.a	19
Forno Traverssa do	21
Garrett R.	22
Gen. Alberto Silveira R.	24
Gil Eanes Pr.	25
Henrique C. Silva R.	26
Infante D. Henrique Pr.	27
Infante de Sagres R.	28
João Bonança R.	30
Lançarote de Freitas R.	33
Luís de Camões Pr.	36
Marquês de Pombal R.	37

Marreiros Netto R.	39	Prof. Luís de Azevedo R.	43
Porta da Piedade Estr. da	40	Silva Lopes R.	45
Porta de Portugal R.	42		

Igreja de Santo António	A	Mercado de Escravos	B	Museu Regional	M

Forte da Ponta da Bandeira

Igreja de Santo António★

🕐*Open 9.30am-12.30pm; 2pm-5pm.* 🕐*Closed Mon and hols.* ⊛*€2.20 (combined ticket with Museu Municipal - below).* ☎ *282 76 23 01.*

The plain façade gives no inkling of the exuberance and virtuosity of the **Baroque decoration**★ which reigns inside. Outstanding are the ceiling painted in false relief, the Eucharistic symbols and statues of gilded wood in the chancel, the walls and the gallery ceiling.

Museu Municipal

🕐*Open 10am-1pm and 2-6pm.* 🕐*Closed Sun afternoon, Mon and hols.* ⊛*See above.* ☎ *282 76 14 10.*

The regional museum adjoining the Igreja de Santo António contains an interesting archeological collection (coins and fragments of mosaics) and an ethnographical section devoted to the Algarve (note the cork work).

Forte da Ponta da Bandeira

🕐*Open 9.30am-12.30pm; 2pm-5pm.* 🕐*Closed, Mon and hols.* ⊛*€2* ☎ *282 76 14 10.*

The 17C fort juts out into the sea guarding a small harbour. There are boat trips from the harbour to Ponta da Piedade. Cross the drawbridge to enter the inner courtyard. The halls contain displays on the Great Discoveries. The chapel is decorated with 17C **azulejos**. There is a **view** from the terrace of the town and the coast.

LAMEGO

VISEU

POPULATION 28 085 – MICHELIN MAP 733
LOCAL MAP SEE VALE DO DOURO

Lamego is an attractive small episcopal and commercial town known for its sparkling wine and its smoked ham. It lies near the Douro valley in a landscape of green hills covered with vines and maize. The town, which is rich in 16C and 18C bourgeois houses, is overlooked by two hills on which stand respectively the ruins of a 12C fortified castle and the Baroque Santuário de Nossa Senhora dos Remédios, famous for the annual pilgrimages held in late August-early September. *Av. Visconde Guedes Teixeira – 5100-074 – ☎ 254 61 20 05*

▶ **Orient Yourself:** South of Vila Real by about 40km/31mi.
⊘ **Don't Miss:** Santuário Nossa Senhora dos Remédios.
◷ **Organizing Your Time:** Allow two hours.
◔ **Also See:** Amarante, the Douro Valley and Vila Real.

Sights

Museu de Lamego ★

◷*Open 10am-12.30pm; 2pm-5pm.* ◷*Closed Mon, 1 Jan, Good Fri, Easter Sun, 1 May, 8 Sept and 25 Dec.*⊜€2 *(no charge Sun morning).*

The museum is housed in the former episcopal palace, a majestic 18C building.
The right-hand section of the ground floor contains mainly religious sculpture from the Middle Ages to the Baroque period and a fine collection of coats of arms which adorned the façades of mansions belonging to the nobility.
On the first floor two series of works – paintings and tapestries – are particularly noteworthy. The **five paintings on wood**★ (early-16C) by Vasco Fernandes were part of the altarpiece in Lamego's cathedral (◔ *see Viseu School of Painting, p 310*). From left to right they show the Creation, Annunciation, Visitation (the most outstanding in the series), the Presentation at the Temple and Circumcision. The six **16C Brussels tapestries**★ are of mythological scenes (note the myth of Oedipus and the rich composition of the Temple of Latone). On the first floor are two Baroque chapels of carved and gilded wood, one of which, São João Evangelista from the Convento das Chagas, has statues and niches. There is also a Chinese room, gold and silver plate and ceramics.
The second ground-floor section contains another Baroque chapel and some fine 16C and 18C *azulejos*, in particular polychromed ones from the Palácio Valmor in Lisbon.

Capela do Desterro

◷*Apply to Senhora Aurora Rodrigues, Rua Cardoso Avelino, no 11-2 or ☎ 254 61 37 88.*
This chapel, built in 1640, is decorated inside with 18C carved and gilded woodwork and 17C *azulejos*; the coffered **ceiling**★ is outstanding with painted scenes from the Life of Our Lord.

Santuário de Nossa Senhora dos Remédios

The 18C façade, on which stucco serves to highlight the elegant granite curves, overlooks the crossed ramps of the **staircase** ornamented with *azulejos* and bristling with a multitude of pinnacles which recalls that of Bom Jesus near Braga.
The view from the church parvis *(access by car possible: 4km/2.5mi)* extends over Lamego to the heights on the horizon which border the Douro.

LEÇA DO BAILIO

PORTO
POPULATION 19 659 – MICHELIN MAP 733

It is said that after the First Crusade, the domain of Leça do Bailio was given to brothers of the Order of the Hospital of St John of Jerusalem who had come from Palestine probably in the company of Count Henry of Burgundy, father of the first King of Portugal. Leça was the mother house of this Order (now the Order of Malta) until 1312 when this was transferred to Flor da Rosa. **The town is just 8km/5ml north of Porto.**

Igreja do Mosteiro★

This fortress church, built in granite in the Gothic period, is characterised outside by pyramid-shaped merlons emphasising the entablature by the tall battlemented tower surrounded with balconies and machicolated watchtowers, and by the very plain main façade adorned only with a door with carved capitals below and a rose window above.

The bare interior is well proportioned. The historiated capitals portray scenes from Genesis and the Gospels – of particular note are Adam and Eve with the serpent and the angel. Several of the Hospitallers are buried here. The chancel, which has stellar vaulting, contains the 16C tomb of the bailiff Frei Cristóvão de Cernache, which is surmounted by a painted statue (16C) while the north apsidal chapel houses the tomb of the prior Frei João Coelho, with a reclining figure by Diogo Pires the Younger (1515).

The Manueline-style **font**★, carved in Ança stone (👆 *see The Coimbra School of Sculpture, p 126)* by the same artist, is octagonal and rests on a pedestal adorned with acanthus leaves and fantastic animals.

LEIRIA

LEIRIA
POPULATION 119 319 – MICHELIN MAP 733

Leiria is pleasantly situated at the confluence of two rivers, the Liz and the Lena, and at the foot of a hill crowned by a medieval castle. Its role as a crossroads near well-known beaches – notably Nazaré – the sanctuary of Fátima and the magnificent architecture of Batalha and Alcobaça, makes it a favoured stop off place for the holidaymaker, the pilgrim and the art-loving tourist. *Jardim Luís de Camões – 2400-172 – ☎ 244 82 37 73*

- ▶ **Orient Yourself:** Midway between Lisbon and Coimbra on the N8 coast road.
- **Don't Miss:** The castle.
- **Organizing Your Time:** A full day is fine, with time to relax.
- **Especially for Kids:** A walk in the pine forest.
- **Also See:** Alcobaça, the monastery at Batalha and Fátima.

Craftsmanship and Folklore

The Leiria region has kept alive its old tradition of popular art and folklore. The glazed and multi-coloured pottery of Cruz da Légua and Milagres, the decorated glassware of Marinha Grande, the willow baskets and ornaments and the woven coverlets of Mira de Aire are among the best known crafts of the district.

The traditional festivals and customs have lost none of their spontaneity. The folklore of the Leiria region is closely associated with that of its neighbour, the Ribatejo. The women's costumes consist of a small black felt hat with feathers, a coloured blouse edged with lace, a short skirt and shoes with wide low heels. It differs from that of the Ribatejo only by the addition of a gold necklace and earrings. Folk dancing displays are held every year at the time of the Leiria exhibition-fair (first to last Sunday in May) and in particular on 22 May, the town's local holiday.

Pinhal de Leiria

This vast pine forest extending to the west of the town has resulted in the growth of lucrative wood and paper industries in the area.

Castle ★

◷ *Open Apr-Sept 10am-6pm; Oct-Mar, 9.30am-5pm. Closed Mon; 1 Jan and 25 Dec.* ◉ *€2.24.*

In an exceptional **site**★, inhabited even before the arrival of the Romans, Afonso Henriques, first King of Portugal, had a fortified castle built in 1135. This castle formed part of the defence of the southern border of the kingdom of Portugal at the time, Santarém and Lisbon still being under Moorish domination. After the fall of these two cities in 1147, the castle lost its significance and fell into ruin. In the 14C, King Dinis, who undertook first the preservation and then the extension of the pine forest at Leiria, rebuilt the castle in order that he might live in it with his queen, Saint Isabel.

Visit

About 30min.

The present buildings, modified in the 16C, have been restored. After entering the first perimeter of castle walls through a door flanked by two square crenellated towers, you reach a pleasantly shaded garden courtyard. A stairway to the left leads to the centre of the castle. The royal palace is then on the left, the keep is straight ahead, and on the right the remains of the 15C chapel of Nossa Senhora da Pena with a graceful lanceolate Gothic chancel and an arcade decorated with Manueline motifs.

Paço Real (Royal Palace)

A staircase leads to a vast rectangular hall with a gallery adorned with depressed, three-centred arches resting on slender twin columns. The gallery, once the royal balcony, affords a good **view** of Leiria lying below.

The narrow streets in the working class district of the town beneath the castle are a pleasant place for a stroll.

LINDOSO ★

VIANA DO CASTELO
MICHELIN MAP 733
LOCAL MAP SEE PARQUE NACIONAL DA PENEDA-GERÊS

Built like an amphitheatre against the southern flanks of one of the last mountains in the Serra do Soajo, Lindoso, in the far north of Portugal on the border with Spain, sets out its austere granite houses in tiered rows up to a height of 462m/1 516ft, perfectly integrated into the rocky landscape – despite the presence of a few recent constructions – and surrounded by cultivated terraces (maize, vines). The castle stands on a hillock where there is also an unusual group of *espigueiros* (◔ *see below*).

B. Brillion/MICHELIN

Granaries

From Ponte da Barca to Lindoso *31km/20mi.*

The road, bordered with pine trees, tangerine trees and oleanders, winds around the wooded slope of the Serra do Soajo, with a view of the arid and rocky Serra da Peneda which rises on the other side of the Lima valley. At the crossroads with the road leading to Entre-Ambos-os-Rios, continue on the N 203 which starts a steep climb into the Parque Nacional da Peneda-Gerês and has views overlooking the meandering river, which is enlarged by a dam upstream. It ends up as a corniche road, and stops when it reaches the castle of Lindoso.

Granaries★
Covering a rocky platform at the foot of the castle, the 60 or more *espigueiros* are grouped together, resembling a cemetery. They are small granite buildings, perched on piles, and most of them have one or two crosses on the roof. Their very careful construction dates back to the 18C and 19C. They are still used today for drying maize.

Castle
Guided tours (20min), 9.30am-12.30pm and 2-5.30pm. ◯*Closed Mon.* ⊚€1.50. ☎ 258 51 53 38.
Facing the border, the castle was attacked several times by the army of Philip IV of Spain during the War of Independence in the 17C.
Restored, it appears again as a crenellated feudal keep in the middle of a small 17C square with a surrounding wall with bastions and watch turrets. From the watchpath there are views over the Lima valley and the surrounding Portuguese and Galician mountains.

LISBOA★★★

LISBON – LISBOA
POPULATION 681 000 – GREATER LISBON 4.8 MILLION
MICHELIN MAP 733

The capital of Portugal stands midway between north and south. At the time of the Great Discoveries, Lisbon, according to the Portuguese poet Camões, was the "princess of the world... before whom even the ocean bows."

The old town was built on the northern shore of the "Straw Sea", as the bulge in the Tagus River ("Tejo" on map) was called on account of the golden reflections of the sun at this spot. Lisbon has a jumbled skyline, its buildings dotted over seven hills offering wonderfully varied views. The attraction of the city lies in its light, its pastel ochres, pinks, blues and greens, and the mosaic paving of its streets and squares – the small black and white paving-stones made of limestone and basalt known as *empedrados*. With its maze of narrow streets in the old quarters, its magnificent vistas along wide avenues, its lively harbour and exotic gardens, Lisbon is a delightful patchwork to explore on foot or see from ancient trams.

The capital is at its most light-hearted when celebrating the feasts of the popular saints in June. St Anthony's is a particularly joyful occasion when young men and women *(marchas populares)* parade down Avenida da Liberdade in traditional costume.

While Lisbon bears the stamp of its past, it has set its sights firmly on the future ever since Portugal became a member of the European Community in 1986. New business districts have been developed, particularly around **Campo Pequeno** and **Campo Grande**, while the Centro Cultural de Belém, which was completed in 1992, was built to further the historical and cultural importance of this part of the city. The famous post-modern towers of **Amoreiras**, adventurous pink, blue and grey constructions by the architect Tomás Taveira, caused a sensation when they first went up, while other towers, such as the headquarters of the BNU (also by Tomás Taveira) and the Caixa Geral de Depósitos savings bank, have sprung up around Campo Grande to become landmarks within the city.

The choice of Lisbon as the site for Expo'98 resulted in a large-scale rebuilding programme along the Tagus, particularly at the Olivais docks, near to the site where the exhibition was based, and the Santo Amaro, Santos and Alcântara docks, with their leisure facilities, which include bars, restaurants and discos.
🗊 *Restauradores (Palácio Foz) – 1250-187 – ☎ 213 46 33 14 or 213 46 36 43*

▶ **Orient Yourself:** A little more than halfway down the coast from north to south, on the Atlantic at the mouth of the Tagus.

🅿 **Parking:** Best forget a car in the city and use public transport.

😀 **Don't Miss:** The castle, the port area, the Gulbenkian Museum, and the restaurants!

🕑 **Organizing Your Time:** Four days might be enough to soak up the atmosphere without cultural overload.

👶 **Especially for Kids:** The Oceanarium with its wonderful marine life, the Calouste Gulbenkian Planetarium, the Museum of the Marionettes (puppets) and the Zoo.

🖐 **Also See:** Spend a day out along the coast (take the railway that runs right along the sea-wall) to Cascais. Or go the other way, across the Vasco da Gama bridge to Setúbal. And don't forget to go to Sintra with its wonderful palace and cosy town centre.

A Bit of History

The Beginning

Lisbon was, according to legend, founded by Ulysses but exactly where that comes from nobody really knows. It was, though, founded by Phoenicians in 1200 BC who landed here on their seaborne travels and named it "serene harbour" – obviously a haven of peace and calm water after the rough water of the Atlantic after they had passed through what is now the Straits of Gibraltar.

The town soon became a regular stop on the route to northern Europe for traders from the Mediterranean: Greeks, Carthaginians and eventually Romans, who conquered the city in AD 138. Subsequently, it was under Barbarian rule and then Arab in 714 when it was given the name Lissabona. Not until 1147 did King Dom Alfonso retake the city for the Portuguese, though it did not become the capital of Portugal – that honour was given to Coimbra until 1255 when Dom Afonso III chose Lisbon as the seat of government.

The Age of the Great Discoveries

Lisbon benefited from the riches that accumulated after the voyage of Vasco da Gama to the Indies in 1497-9 and the discovery of Brazil by Pedro Álvares Cabral in 1500. New trade routes developed; merchants flocked to Lisbon which was packed with small traders buying and selling gold, silver, spices, ivory, silks, precious stones and rare woods. Monuments, including the Mosteiro dos Jerónimos and Torre de Belém, were built. The decoration of these buildings, which was always inspired by the sea, became known as the Manueline style after King Manuel.

General view of the Alfama

Museu Nacional do Azulejo -

Azulejos panel showing Lisbon before the 1755 earthquake

The earthquake

On 1 November 1755 the town was shaken by an exceptionally violent earth tremor: churches, palaces and houses collapsed; fire spread; survivors rushed to take refuge in the Tagus, but a huge wave came upstream, breaking over and destroying the lower town. Lisbon's riches were engulfed. The King, Dom José I, escaped as did his minister, Sebastião de Carvalho e Melo, the future **Marquis of Pombal**. The minister immediately began the rebuilding of Lisbon to plans and in a style utterly revolutionary for the period. The straight wide avenues and the plain and stylised houses to be seen in the Baixa today are Pombal's legacy.

The Lines of Tôrres Vedres

The Lines of Tôrres Vedras was the name given to a system of defence lines conceived by the Duke of Wellington in 1810 to protect Lisbon from attach by French troops. These lines were an assemblage of fortifications, embrasures and roads rather than a continuous line; they stretched from Tôrres Vedras, 70km/43mi north of the city to Alhandra. The plan paid off, for the French, under Masséna, decided the city was too well protected and withdrew. Lisbon was saved.

The Carnation Revolution

At 4.30am on 25 April 1974, Portuguese radio broadcast a message from the command of the Movement of the Armed Forces (Movimento das Forças Armadas) calling upon the population to keep calm and remain indoors. This was the beginning of the *coup d'état* led by General António de Spínola against the regime instituted by Salazar and maintained by his successor Caetano. Spínola's take-over was virtually bloodless and his soldiers, with a red carnation stuck in the barrel of their rifles, were acclaimed by the citizens of Lisbon, who, ignoring the orders, surged out of their homes onto Praça do Comércio.

Lisbon Today

Lisbon is a delightful city with numerous focal points which can all be admired from the Tagus. Modern though the city is, its 18C layout and many buildings add to its considerable charm. The Praça do Comércio encompasses a maze-like network of streets in the Baixa district, which is the lower part of town extending towards Rossio: the Praça dos Restauradores and the Avenida da Liberdade, the city's main boulevard, are lined with trees. On the hill to the right stands the imposing Castelo São Jorge surrounded by the ancient districts of Alfama and Mouraria, while the hill to the left houses the city's commercial area of Chiado, with the working-class residential areas of Bairro Alto and Madragoa beyond. Then you reach the slightly more refined areas of Lapa, Alcântara and Belém. The areas along the Tagus have been taken over by nightclubs, restaurants and bars, turning this old industrial area into a thriving, lively community.

Beyond the city many new housing developments continue to appear on the landscape, as you see when you fly into Lisbon airport. Yet despite the rush and bustle, Lisbon remains perhaps the friendliest capital city in Europe.

Address Book

USEFUL INFORMATION

TOURISM OFFICES

Palácio Foz - *Praça dos Restauradores, 1250-187.* ☎ *213 46 33 14 or 213 46 63 07 9am-8pm.*

Lisbon Welcome Centre - *Entrance Rua do Arsenal. Open daily 9am-8pm.* Tourist information office, a fashion boutique, an auditorium, art-gallery, café and a food shop. Internet access. *www.visitlisboa.com*

Information Bureau - *At the exit of the Vasco da Gama shopping centre (parc des nations).* Maps and plans, free baggage storage. Cartão do Parque sold here

Lisbon Tourism Bureau - *Kiosk next to the Portuguese pavilion.* Information about the Parque das Nacoes *(Park of Nations)*: information is also available on the Web site: www.parquedasnacoes.pt

Lisboa Card - A great idea to help visitors enjoy their stay so much more, the card gives free,unlimited travel on public transport (bus, tram, métro and funicular) together with free or reduced entry to most of the museums and cultural sites in Lisbon (including the Monastery of Belém and the Palace at Sintra). **Price:** ⊛€13.50 (24hr); €23 (48hr); €28 (72hr) - children's prices are lower. ⊟ For more information ☎ 213 46 33 14 or 210 31 28 10. You can also buy this card at the airport, tourism offices, and elsewhere.

Cartão do Parque - *⊛€16.50; 4-12 year-olds and over 65 €8.50.* This card gives visitors reduced prices on many attractions, including the Oceanário, the Pavilhaô do Conhecimento, rail journeys and the téléphérique, amongst others. It is valid for one month from the first time you use it.

EMERGENCY PHONE NUMBERS

✚ **Emergency Services – 112**
✚ **Emergency Pharmacy – 118**
✚ **Police** – 213 46 61 41 or 213 47 47 30

OTHER USEFUL PHONE NUMBERS

Special telephone for assistance for international visitors – 800 296 296
Telephone enquiries – 118

Railways – 218 88 40 25 (intercity trains – 217 90 10 04)

Taxis –
 Radio Taxis de Lisboa 218 11 90 00;
 Teletaxi – 218 11 11 00

International telegrams – 182

Main Post Office – Praça dos Restauradores. Open Mon-Fri 8am-10pm; Sat/Sun 9am-6pm 213 21 14 50 or 213 23 89 71

Lisbon Airport – 218 41 37 00

TAP Air Portugal –
 (Airport) 218 41 35 00
 or Reservations 707 205 700

Portugaália – (Airport) 218 93 80 70

USEFUL INTERNET ADDRESSES

www.cm-lisboa.pt
www.atl-turismolisboa.pt
www.setecolinas.pt

TRANSPORTATION

BY AIR

The airport is about 6km/4ml from the city centre (Rossio). A bus (Aerobus no. 91 ⊛€3) runs from downtown to the airport with service from 7.45am-9pm, departures every 30mn. Taxis to the airport from downtown cost around ⊛€10 with a surcharge for luggage of €1.50. There is a surcharge after midnight as well. Allow 30-40min for the trip, more at peak periods.

BY RAIL

Estação de Santa Apolónia – services to the north of Portugal and international

Estação do Cais do Sodré – services about every 15min to Estoril and Cascais Journey takes about 40min to Cascais. Last train 1.30am.

Estação do Rossio – suburban trains to the north-west and Sintra. Trains for Sintra leave every 10min or so. Journey takes about 35min. Last train 11pm.

Estação Sul e Suesta – for services to Alentejo and the Algarve via the ferry that gives accesto the station at Barreiro.

Estação do Oriente – superb intermodal station (metro, bus, train) with serviceto the north, connecting with trains for Santa Apolónia and Sintra.

BY BOAT

The *cacilheiros*, which serve the towns on the opposite banks of the Tagus, give you a wonderful chance to cruise on the river. Throughout the day departures are about every 15min. Tickets are on sale from machines at the stations and cost €0.70 for Cachilhas.

- **Estação Fluvial do Terreiro do Paço** – for Montio, Seixal, Barreiro and trains to Alentejo and the Algarve. Also the departure point for Tagus river cruises.
- **Estação do Cais do Sodré** – serves Cacilhas and Almada.
- **Estação de Belém** – services to Brandão and Trafaria.
- **Estação Fluvial do Parque das Nações** – services to Barreiro.

GETTING AROUND LISBON

With Lisbon being a busy and compact city it is normally better to use public transport. Driving and, particularly, parking, can be a problem.

ON FOOT

The best way to discover Lisbon and its various neighbourhoods – Baixa, av de Liberdade, Chiado/Bairro Alta and Alfama – is on foot, using the lift where possible . As parts of the city are quite hilly it helps to be in reasonably good physical shape.

BY CAR

In Lisbon a car is more of an hindrance than a help. In the day the traffic is very heavy, particularly in the older quarters in the centre where the streets are narrow and very congested. Parking spaces are scarce, partly because parking meters have not invaded Lisbon as they have other cities, most cars, once parked, stay there all day.

Baixa now has several underground car parks (Praça dos Restauradores, Rossio, Praça do Comércio, the Armazéns do Chiado shopping gallery); but in the northern sectors of the city parking is virtually impossible, particularly in the Alfama and Bairro Alto areas where many streets are pedestrianised anyway. Of the hotels only the large hotels have parking spaces available.

Car Rental – Most care rental companies have offices at the airport. You can get the same rates through your hotel or at the tousim office in Lisbon (Palácio Foz), which can show you the best rates on offer.

Taxis – A good way of getting round Lisbon, taxis are plentiful and less expensive than you might imagine – certainly less than in any comparable city in Europe. Most of them are beige and the price is shown on meters, at least within Lisbon. Outside the city centre fares are calculated on a per kilometre rate, though if you go farther afield you can negotiate a price.

PUBLIC TRANSPORT

See the map on the inside back cover.

In a city as hilly as Lisbon there are some interesting and novel means of transport, including funiculars, elevators and tramways – the older trams in Lisbon were actually built in Sheffield. And using public transport enables you to mingle with the locals. The metro is run by a company separate to that which operates the buses and trams, so tickets are not interchangeable.

Times of Transport – Bus and trams operate to a regular timetable between 7am and 1am with a frequency of between 11 and 15mn until arounf 9.30pm. The last bus, no 45 (Cais do Sodré, Baixa, Av. de Liberdade) leaves at 1.55am. The funiculars stop at 11pm. You can buy individual tickets on the bus or tram, but if you are staying a few days in Lisbon, it makes sense to buy a passe turístico available for four days at a cost of €12.10, or seven days for €19.20 and can be used on buses, trains and funiculars. You can also buy bus tickets for €1.20 that are good for two journeys. Particularly good value is the Pass 7 Colinas, available for the metro and the local train network. This costs €3 for one day, €13.25 for five days and can be topped up.

These tickets can be purchased at the kiosks at bus and metro stations and will have the sign "Venda de Passes" on the front.

You can also buy bus and tram maps (€5) at the same kiosks or from the tourism office in praça dos Restauradores.

An urban guide, *le Guia Urbano*, or more detailed local guides can be bought at tourist offices, bookshops and newsagents. Information on bus, trams and funiculars can be obtained by calling ☏ 213 63 20 21.

Accessibility – Buses and trams in Lisbon are not really very user-friendly for disabled travellers, but there is a door-to-door minibus service (available for the same price as regular public transport) for those with special needs. It is, however, essential to make a reservation not less than two days in advance. ☏ 217 58 56 76 (lines open from 7am-midnight).

Funiculars – Elevador da Bica: R. de S. Paulo/Largo do Calhariz; Elevador da Glória : Restauradores/São Pedro de Alcântara; Elevador do Lavra: Largo da Anunciação/R. da Câmara Pestana; Elevador de S. Justa: . de Santa Justa (to viewpoint).

One of Lisbon's trams (eléctricos)

M. Chapt.t/MICHELIN

Bus – Principal routes: no 45 (Prior Velho/Cais do Sodré); no 83 (Portela/Cais de Sodré); no 46 (Est. Sta. Apolónia/Damaia); no 15 (Cais do Sodré/Sete Rios); no 43 (Praça Figuira/Buraca).

Metro – Metro stations are shown on the plan on the inside back cover. The network comprises four lines:
- ◆ Blue (Baixa-Chiado/Amadora Este)
- ◆ Red (Odivelas/Rato)
- ◆ Green (Cais do Sodré/Telheiras)
  Yellow (Oriente/Alameda).

The metro operates from 6.30am until 1am. Most metro stations are user-friendly for those with disabilities - www.metrolisboa.pt
Several stations are decorated with azulejos by well-known Portuguese artists. Worth a special mention are Cidade Universitária (Vieira da Silva), Alto dos Moinhos (Júlio Pomar), Campo Grande (Eduardo Nery) Marqués de Pombal (Menez) and Baixa-Chiado (Álvaro Sizo Vieira).

Tranways (Eléctricos) – The old tramways are one of the charms of Lisbon as well as being one of the best ways to see the city and avoid climbing its hills! Little by little they are being replaced by newer models. Two lines in particular serve a number of monuments and museums: no 15 (Praça da Figuiera/Algés: praça do Comércio – Mosteiro

dos Jerónimos–Museu Nacionl de Arqueologia–Museu da Marinha--Discoveries Monument–Tower of Belém. The no 28 (Martim Moniz/Prazeres) serves São Vicente de Fora church–Museum of Decorative Arts–São Jorge castle–cathedral–Baixa–Chiado museum–largo do Chiado–São Bento–Basilica d'Estrela.

Téléphérique – This runs for just over a kilometre in the Parque das Nações just above the banks of the Tagus, with a fine view over the park, over the Vasco da Gama bridge and, in the evening, of the sunset over the river. It's a good way to get around in this area without getting tired, particularly on hot days. *Operates Jun-Sept 11am-8pm; weekend and holidays 10am-9pm; Oct-May 11am-7pm; weekend and holidays 10am-8pm. Parque das Nações* ☏€5.50 (return), €3.50 one-way. ☏ 218 95 61 43.

Electric train – An electric train makes a circuit of the Parque das Nações every 30mn from 10am-6pm with a stop at the Centro Vasca da Gama. ☏€1.50.

Cycle Rental – Rental points in front of the Centro Vasca da Gama; the Oceanário; near the Parque Adrenalina. midday-8pm. From about Parque das Nações ☏€2 for 30min.

CITY TOURS

By bus or tram –*Praça do Comércio* ☏ 213 58 23 34. Two bus circuits:

towards the North, the Park of Nations and return along the banks of the Tagus; Belém.

Two circuits on red tramway: Alfama, Mouraria, Graça; Chiado and the western neighbourhoods.

There is also another tramway that is practical for visitors, the Collinas de Lisboa, which runs all year in the areas of Lapa, Alfama and Chiado. *June-Sept 10am-7pm; Oct-May 10am-6pm. €17 return trip.* 213 63 20 21.

Cityline – *Praça de Pombal (terminal and information)* 213 19 10 90. *Daily 9am-6pm. €15.* A full city tour from the port area to Belém, Estrela and the north of Lisbon.

Tagus cruises – *Estação Fluvial do Terreira do Paço (Estação do Sul e Sueste – opposite the praça do Comércio)* 218 85 56 30 - www.transtejo.pt *daily 11am and 5pm €20 (children 6-12yrs and seniors €8).*

INTERNET ACCESS

For laptops with a Wi-fi card there are hotspots all over the city, especially at the airport, in shopping centres and in many larger hotels. For regular internet access (without a laptop) try the following:

Portugal Telecom – *Praça D. Peddro IV, 68 (Rossio)* *Open 8am-11pm €1 for 30min.* One of the cheapest in Lisbon, very friendly and efficient but normally very busy during the day.

Lisbon Welcome Centre – *Praçca do Comércio . Open 9am-8pm. €3 per hr.* Central location.

Correios de Portugal (Post Office) – *Praça dos Restauradores. Open Mon-Fri 8am-10pm; Sat/Sun 9am-6pm.* The main post office in Lisbon and use of the internet is free.

NetCenter Café – *Rua Didrio de Noticias, 157-159 (Bairro Alto)* *Open 4pm-2am. www.netcentercafe.com* – A warm and friendly welcome in the heart of Bairro Alto. Free internet use – but only when you buy something to eat or drink!

Pavilhão do Conhecimento – *Parque das Nações, Alameda dos Oceanos* – *Open Tue-Fri 10am-6pm; Sat/Sun 11am-5pm.* 218 91 71 71 €3/hr. The museum's cyber-café has 36 computers.

Lojas Inlisboa.com – *R. da Atalaia, 153.* 213 43 19 11 – *www.inlisboa. com* – *Open 11am-midnight. €1 for 15min.* If you need to surf the net choose this small boutique in Bairro Alto. Students from the art school have created Web space where you can surf the Web while viewing their work as postcards, lithographs or in other forms. The same group has a second location as below.

Lojas Inlisboa.com – *Av de Liberdade, 1 e 7.* 213 43 19 11. *Open 11am-1am.*

WHERE TO STAY

BAIXA

Pensão Imperial – *Praça dos Restauradores, 78-4°-* 213 42 01 66 *17 rooms.* A small and friendly pensão whose façade is covered in blue azulejos. The rooms are well furnished and have flower-filled balconies. Try to get a room overlooking either the square or the hill looking towards the castle. You'll find the lift a little compact!

Pensão Pérola da Baixa – *R. da Glória, 10-2°-* 213 46 28 75 - 11 *rooms.* A small, central pensão, neat and tidy where you will find the bed-linen has been beautifully made. There are also some pious statuettes. A very nice place.

Portugal – *R. João das Regras, 4 -* 218 87 75 81 - *www.hotelportugal. com* - *59 rooms* . Centrally located, this hotel has spacious and comfortable rooms decorated with antique furniture. Internet access for guests. Without doubt a hotel of quality offering good service.

Lisboa Tejo – *Rua dos Condes de Monsanto, 2 -* 218 86 61 82 - *www.evidenciahoteis.com;* 51 *rooms* . Next to the Praça da Figueira this hotel, entirely renovated by Portuguese designers has comfortable and beautifully decorated rooms. Despite the double-glazing, some of the rooms overlooking the main road can be a little noisy. Very good breakfast.

CHIADO

Pensão Estrela do Mondego – *Calçada do Carmo, 25 2°* 213 24 08 40 *10 rooms.* The rooms of this small pensão, next to the Rossio station, are comfortable and clean, and have air-conditioning. Tiny bathrooms with just a shower cubicle. Some rooms overlook the station.Budget-friendly!

🛏 **Residencial Iris** – *Rua da Glória, 2-A, 1°* ☎ *213 42 31 57 - 10 rooms*. Set back from the Ave de Liberdade, this lodging is an ideal location for those on a budget. Most of the rooms are reasonably sized and have showers that are not fully enclosed.

🛏🛏 **Residência Roma** – *Tv. da Glória, 22-A,* ☎ *213 46 05 57 - www. residenciaroma.com* 🖿 *– 28 rooms*. This simple hotel close to the Praça dos Restauradores is a good place to stay In the centre of Lisbon. The refurbished rooms are light and spacious.

🛏🛏🛏🛏 **Metropole** – *Praça do Rossio, 30 -* ☎ *213 21 90 30 - www. metropolealmeidahotles.com* 🖿 *36 roooms* 🛏. Very well located in the busy Rossio square, the Metropole has classic and comfortable rooms in a turn-of-the-century building. Some rooms have a magnificent view over the castle.

🛏🛏🛏🛏 **Lisboa Regency Chiado** – *R. Nova do Almada, 114* ☎ *213 25 61 00 - reservations.chiado@madeiraregency. pt -* 🖿 🅿 *40 rooms* 🛏. Located above the Armazéns do Chiado retail gallery, this hotel designed by the celebrated architect Álvaro Siza is decorated with great taste in a Portuguese-Asian style; the rooms have every modern comfort and magnificent views over the Tagus, the castle and the city.

🛏🛏🛏🛏 **Bairro Alto Hotel** – *Praça Luis de Camões, 8 -* ☎ *213 40 82 88 - info@bairroaltohotel.com -* 🖿 🅿 *55 rooms* 🛏. Located in the Luis de Camões square, this luxury hotel occupies the former Grand Hotel of Europe, one of whose regular guests was Sarah Bernhardt. Completely renovated in 2005, the rooms have every conceivable luxury and are decorated with refined taste. On the sixth floor is a terrace with great views over the city. There is a fitness studio.

BAIRRO ALTO

🛏🛏 **Pensão Londres** – *Rua Dom Pedro V. 53, 1* ☎ *213 46 87 39 – www. pensaolondres.com.pt – 40 rooms* 🛏. This *pensão* occupies four floors of a handsome building on the edge of the Bairro Alto, Lisbon's pulsating night-life district. Certain rooms have original ceilings and good views of the Castelo São Jorge. A clean and well-maintained establishment offering reasonable rates in a good location.

🛏🛏 **Residencial Alegria** - *Praça da Alegria, 12* ☎ *213 22 06 70 - mail@ alegrianet.com -* 🖿 *35 rooms* 🛏. A lovely hotel with its façade painted bright yellow and its balconies, filled with flowers, overlooking the Praça da Alegria. Ask for the rooms on the upper floors as they are quieter.

🛏🛏🛏 **Casa de S. Mamede** - *R. da Escola Politécnica, 159 -* ☎ *213 96 31 66 - casadesaomamede@hotmail.com -* 🖿 *28 rooms* 🛏. This charming hotel sits in an 18C mansion and still has a family feel to it, with azulejos and turn-of-the-century furniture. It really is in an ideal location, among the antique shops, close to the Principe Real and the botanical gardens.

ALFAMA

🛏 **Pensão Ninho das Aguias** – *Costa do Castelo, 74* ☎ *218 85 40 70 -* 🖿 *16 rooms*. Near the castle, this pretty villa has rooms with or without a bathroom, but all the balconies overlook the cathedral. On the top floor is a terrace with a good view over the city. This ideal location gives immediate access to the castle or to Afama.

🛏🛏🛏🛏 **Palácio Belmonte** – *Páteo D. Fradique, 14* ☎ *218 81 66 00 - office-palaciobelmonte.com -* 🛏 *11 suites* 🛏. A hotel that evokes memories of a 17C palace, perched on the highest point of the hill by the castle and renovated in a Franco-Portuguese style. Private terraces with all suites and a black-marble pool. If you really need to celebrate try the Himalaya Suite with a 360° bird's-eye view over the city. This is definitely a prized address.

GRAÇA

🛏🛏🛏🛏 **Albergaria Senhora do Monte** – *Calçada do Monte 39,* ☎ *218 86 60 02 - senhoradomonte@ hotmail.com –* 🖿 *28 rooms* 🛏. The principal attraction of this modern hotel located off the beaten track in the residential Graca district is the

York House

outstanding view of Lisbon from all but five of the rooms. For those who really want to splurge, request one of the three rooms with terrace (higher rate). Even if you choose not to stay here, you can enjoy the view from the top floor bar. Access is not very practical on foot, so plan on using taxis or the no 28 tram. Internet access for guests.

BELÉM

Pensão Residencial Setubalense – *R. de Belém, 28* ☎ *213 63 66 39* 📠 *30 rooms* 🛏. For those who prefer to stay in a quiet, calm and elegant part of the city, away from the bustle of the city cenre, this little pensão is ideal, close to the Mosteiro dos Jerónimos. A beautiful pink-coloured façade and with rooms that are simple and comfortable – some even have a circular bed!

NORTH OF THE CITY

As Janelas Verdes – *R. das Janelas Verdes, 47, Lapa* ☎ *213 96 81 43 - www.heritage.pt.* 📠 *29 rooms* 🛏. Located just a few steps from the Museum of Antique Art, this beautiful 18C mansion has been transformed into an hotel welcoming and comfortable, decorated with the personal touch. The rooms are not large and do look out over the busy street, so are not always quiet. At the back of the hotel a lovely terrace/patio is the ideal place for breakfast in the open in the summer months. Internet access.

Britânia – *R. Rodrigues Sampaio, 17, Estrela* ☎ *213 15 50 16 - www.heritage.pt* 📠 *32 rooms* 🛏. Restored to its elegant 1940s appearance, this landmark hotel designed by Cassiano Branco (architect of the Éden Teatro on the nearby Praça dos Restauradores) is both charming and comfortable. Spacious, well-appointed and quiet rooms, a good location and an understated "retro" ambience make the Britânia a good find.

NH Liberdade – *Av de Liberdade, 180B* ☎ *213 51 40 60 - www.nh-hotels.com* 🛁 🅿 *83 rooms* 🛏. Lovers of refinement cannot afford to miss this elegant, ultra-modern hotel just off Lisbon's main street, in the small Tivoli Forum. On the roof is a pool and a terrace with wonderful panoramic views over the city and the Tagus. The rooms ade decorated in minimalist style. Very chic!

York House – *R. das Janelas Verdes, 32, Lapa* ☎ *213 96 25 44; www.yorkhouselisboa.com -* 📠 *34 rooms* 🛏. Lisbon's best known historic inn has every modern comfort, yet with an atmosphere of relaxed calm as befits the 17C convent in which it is housed. The rooms overlooking the street are best avoided, as this is the heart of the night-life district. The handsome dining room looks onto a cobblestone courtyard. The inn's location near the Museu de Arte Antiga is not ideal for visiting Lisbon on foot.

M.Borgese/TOP

WHERE TO EAT

CHIADO

Adega das Cegonhas – *Traversa Conde de Soure, 7* ☎ *213 46 45 55 - closed for two weeks in August and every Sunday*. A tiny restaurant whose tables are mounted on the bases of old sewing machines – you can also eat outside on the pavement. It's a very popular local restaurant serving excellent grilled sardines and other fish and a great favourite with the locals. Not too easy to find, it is just off the rua da Rosa.

Doce Real – *R. D. Pedro V, 119-121* ☎ *213 46 59 23 - closed Sunday*. A tiny but friendly café situated on the border of Bairro Alto between Príncipe Real and R. da Rosa. There's just enough space to enjoy a snack of shrimp or cod fritters. Whether at a table or standing at the counter, you'll find the food delicious.

Heróis- Café Lounge – *Calçada do Sacramento, 18* ☎ *213 42 00 77 Tues-Sun 10am-2am*. Frequented by lovers and designers of fashion, this café lounge is close the the Carmelite church. A wonderful buffet at lunchtime will satisfy any appetite whilst in the evening the culinary inspiration is Mediterranean.

Bota Alta – *Tv. da Queimada 35* – ☎ *213 42 79 59*. Pleasant local restaurant with a lively atmosphere. Good cuisine with fish featuring heavily on the menu.

Pap' Açorda – *Rua Atalaia 57* – ☎ *213 46 48 11 –reservations recommended – Closed Sundays and Monday lunchtimes*. One of the highlights of the Bairro Alto. Excellent cuisine in a theatrical decor, with performances by some of Lisbon's celebrities.

Tavares – *R. do Misericórdia, 37, closed Sunday lunchtime and all day Saturday*. ☎ *213 42 11 12*. Classic international cuisine served with flair in a rich turn-of-the-century setting. A salon-de-thé is at the side.

ALFAMA

Pateo 13 – *Calçadinha de Sto Estêvão, 13* ☎ *218 88 23 25*. In the warren of tiny streets in Alfama you will come across this lively and very typically Portuguese restaurant where grilled fish and meat form the basis of the menu.

Chapitô/Restô – *R. Costa de Sto Estêvão, 13* ☎ *218 86 73 74 - www.chapito.org - open Tue-Sun 7.30pm-2am; Sat/Sun also 10am-2pm - reservations recommended*. Unique for its view over Lisbon and the Tagus, and with a lively atmosphere, this is really two restaurants: one in the open air with a good but simple cuisine; the other inside with more elaborate cuisine and higher prices. Try to get there to watch the sunset over the Tagus.

Mesa de Frades – *R. dos Remédlos, 139A* ☎ *218 88 45 99 - closed Monday*. An old chapel is the setting for this restaurant with a typically Brazilian and Portuguese cuisine. The terrace is the ideal place to sit on a warm day and watch the world go by.

Santo António de Alfama – *Beco São Miguel, 7* ☎ *218 88 13 28 - open Wed-Sun evenings, reservation recommended*. Founded by two friends, one a pianist the other an actor, this restaurant is a meeting place for artists of all kinds. Three rooms on three floors give it an elegant bistrot feel. A cocktail to start, croquettes with a dip, *magret de canard* and then an irresistible chocolate *gâteau* to finish. Delicious!

Viagem de Sabores – *R. S. João de Praça, 103* ☎ *218 87 01 89 - open evenings*. In the heart of Alfama a warm welcome awaits you in this elegant restaurant made up of several

Fish marinated in white wine

F. Vasseur/VISA

arched rooms overseen by its French chef. Everything matches the name – a voyage of flavours – tuna steak Thailandaise, veal *marocaine* (Moroccan), grapefruit with crab.

Divina Comida – *Largo de S. Martinho, 6-7 218 87 55 99 - closed Sundays*. A nice play on words for the name of this elegant restaurant (*comida* means food). For a small place close to the Santa Luzia mirador it has a nice raised terrace under the trees, beautiful rooms filled with soft light and and a carefully prepared internationally inspired menu with a good choice – prawns in ginger, fettucine with curry.

Café Taborda – *R. Costa do Castelo, 75 218 87 94 84 - reservations recommended, closed Monday*. With an arty atmosphere this is a restaurant with an exceptional view over the city. A pleasant garden is the perfect place for an *apéritif*. Internet access.

GRAÇA

Via Graça – *Rua Damesceno Monteiro 9b – 218 87 08 30 – www. viagracaclix.pt – - Closed Saturday and Sunday lunchtimes*. Situated below the Miradouro de Nossa Senhora do Monte, this sophisticated restaurant decorated in contemporary style offers superb views of Castelo São Jorge and the centre of the city. An ideal location for a romantic dinner for two.

BY THE TAGUS

Alcântara Café – *Rua Maria Luisa Holstein 15 – 213 63 71 76*. This brasserie-style café-restaurant is situated in an old factory, and adjoins the Alcântara-Mar night-club. A young, elegant and fashionable ambience in amazing industrial-baroque decor. The entrance is slightly hidden down a dark side-street in the port area but it's worth searching for it.

Café Malaca – *Cais dos Gas (back of the Cais do Sodré station) - 967 10 41 42*. On the first floor is the Naval Club of Lisbon, a small restaurant whose cuisine is inspired by the voyages of the Portuguese adventurers, with a particular Asian influence. Especially good are the Vietnamese dishes and you are guaranteed a very warm welcome.

BELÉM

Caseiro – *Rua Belém 35 – 213 63 88 03. Closed Sundays and throughout August*. An eclectic décor in which onions, garlic and banknotes from around the world hang from the walls. Typical Portuguese cuisine.

O Funil – *Av. Elias Garcia 82A – 217 96 60 07. Closed Mondays and Sunday evenings*. Bacalhau à Funil (cod) is one of the main specialities of this restaurant. Excellent wine list.

WEST OF THE CITY

Os Tibetanos – *Rua do Salitre, 117 – 213 14 20 38 - reservations recommended. Closed weekends and holidays*.
This small restaurant, slightly tucked away, is near the botanical garden and has tasty vegetarian cuisine with Tibetan inspiration at very reasonable prices. Nice feeling inside.

Pão de Canela – *Praça das Flores, 27/28 213 97 22 20 - open 7am-10pm*. Breakfast or lunch on the terrace, dinner inside where the décor is of light wood, and a menu based around fruit, light pastry or quiches: everything is possible in this restaurant ideally located in the shadow of the Praça das Flores on the edge of Bairro Alto.

Comida de Santo – *Calçada Engenheiro Miquel Pais, 39 – 213 96 33 39 *. On the side of the Principe Real this restaurant has a wonderful menu direct from north-eastern Brazil. You certainly won't go hungry here and the clientele are both elegant and relaxed.

Picanha – *R. das Janelas Verdes, 96, Lapa 213 97 55 40 - closed Sat/Sun lunchtimes. *. Very close to the Museum of Antique Art this is the place for meat-eaters with an appetite! Brazilian cuisine is again the theme and includes *pincanha (roast meat cut from large skewers carried by the waiters)*, served with rice and black beans.

Porco Preto – *R. Marcos Portugal, 5 213 96 48 95 - reservasporco-preto.com - open mon-Sat 12.30-3pm and 8pm-midnight, reservations recommended*. On the beautiful Praça das Flores this beautifully designed restaurant has a concept unique to Lisbon: a menu exclusively devoted to the black pork of Alentejo (similar to pata negra in Spain). Exceptional value for food this good and a very intimate atmosphere.

◎◎◎◎ **Casa da Comida** – *Tv. das Amoreiras 1 – ☎ 213 88 53 76 - reservascasadacomida.pt – closed Saturday lunchtimes and Sundays*. This immaculate, elegant restaurant in a verdant courtyard with an azulejo-covered fountain serves sophisticated, imaginative cuisine. One of the best tables in the city.

ALMADA

◎◎◎ **Ponto Final** – *Cais do Ginjal, 72, Cacilhas - From the landing stage turn to right immediately and go along to the end of the quays (15mn walk) 212 76 07 43 closed Tuesdays*. 🍴. You have the feeling that you are at the end of the world here with the whole of Lisbon laid out before you. Come here in the evening to look at Lisbon by night. You dine on a jetty out over the Tagus itself. Excellent traditional cuisine – grilled meat, fish and simmered rice *(carapauzinhos con arroz de tomate, pataniscas com arroz de feijão)*. Very good wine list in a friendly and magical ambience.

TAKE A BREAK

BAIXA

Confeitaria Nacional – *Praça Figueira 18B. ☎213 42 44 70 - open Mon-Sat 8am-8pm*. This old pastry shop (1829) is one of the best in Lisbon and should be on your list of places to visit. A huge choice of pastries and traditional sweets.

Pastelaria Suiça – *Praça. D. Pedro IV, 100, Rossio. ☎213 21 40 90 - open 7am-9pm*. One of the busiest places in the Baixa and a good meeting place. Outdoor terraces in the Rossio and Praça da Figueira, with views of the Castelo de São Jorge. Snacks, excellent cakes and fruit juices.

BAIRRO ALTO

Panificação Reunida de S. Roque
- Rua Dom Pedro V, 57B ☎213 22 43 56. Ceramic tiles with 1920s floral motifs add a particular charm to this boulangerie-pâtisserie in which you can enjoy good coffee with sweet pastries. Buy some of the bread that is presented in large panniers behind the counter.

Antiga Confeitaria de Belém – **Fábrica dos Pastéis de Belém** – *Rua Belém 84/8 – Open daily from 8am to 11.30pm*. The small Belém cakes, known as *pastéis de nata*, attract great numbers of Lisbonites and tourists alike to this pastry shop. The famous mini-tarts (their recipe is a closely-guarded secret) are still made here in the old ovens which give them their highly-distinct taste. They can be bought in boxes of six to take away or eat heated in one of the pastry shop's *azulejo*-decorated rooms. A Lisbon institution.

B. Brillion/MICHELIN

Café Nicola, Rossio

NIGHTLIFE

BAIXA

Café Nicola – *Praça Dom Pedro IV, 25, open every day 10am-7pm* ☎ *213 46 05 79* A Lisbon landmark steeped in history. It was here that the first Portuguese woman dared to put an end to the exclusively-male character of the city's cafés. There are jazz concerts between May and July.

Ginginha do Rossio – *Largo de São Domingos, 8. Open 9am-11pm.* After wandering through the Baixa, try a glass of the famous *ginginha* (cherry brandy) either at the bar or sitting at the pavement tables outside. A unique café with a unique atmosphere!

CHIADO

A Brasileira – *Rua Garrett 120 –* ☎*213 46 95 41. Open daily 8am-2am.* A well-known café with a literary tradition. Artists, fashion designers, tourists and residents all meet in this legendary establishment.

Café No Chiado – Largo do Picadeiro, 10-12 ☎ 213 46 05 01 - open 11am-2am. Next to the San Carlos theatre you can taste the best mango mousse in the world here. Well, in Lisbon! Lovely shaded terrace in the summer months.

BAIRRO ALTO

Frágil – *Rua Atalaia 126-8 –* ☎*213 46 95 78. Open from 11pm to 4am – Closed Sundays.* One of the classics of Lisbon night-life. The décor in this bar-disco-theque is always original and changes every three months or so. A trendy and eclectic clientele of night-time regulars.

Hot Clube – *Praça da Alegria, 39 213 46 73 69. Open Tues-Sat 10pm-2am; shows at 11pm and 12.30am.* The oldest jazz club in Lisbon. Many internationally renowned acts perform here on Fridays and Saturdays.

Pavilhão Chinês – *Rua D. Pedro V 89 – Open 6pm-2am; Sunday 9pm-2am.* Originally a grocer's shop that was transformed into a bar in 1986. The walls are covered with glass cases containing a varied collection of objects, including lead soldiers, contemporary engravings, humorous ceramics and models of war planes. Billiard table at the back of the bar.

ALFAMA

Bar das Imagens/Costa Do Castelo – *Calçada Marqués de Tancos, 1-1B* ☎*218 88 46 36 - bardasimagensmail.telepac.pt - closed Jan and Feb.* Halfway up the hill towards the castle this bar has a wonderful view out over the city and the 25 de Abril bridge. It combines two bars in one. Without having to go outside you can pass from a traditional bar to a terrace bar with DJ.

Kapital – *Av. 24 de Julho 68 – Open from 10.30pm to 4am – Closed Mondays and*

A typical Portuguese bar

J.N. de Soye/RAPHO

Wednesdays. This night-club is very popular with Lisbonites. Elegant, airy decor on three floors, each with a bar. Terrace on the top floor.

Lux – *Av. Infante D. Henrique, Armazém A – Cais da Pedra in Santa Apolónia – Open Tues-Fri 6pm-4am; Fri/Sat 6pm-7am.* Created by the former owner of the legendary Frágil, Lux is currently one of the hottest venues in the city, housed in an old warehouse opposite Santa Apolònia railway station. The first floor is open for afternoon tea at 4pm, while the club takes on a "cocktail lounge" feel in the evening with its decor of 1960s chairs and tables (which can even be purchased by customers). The disco above the lounge is open from Thursday to Saturday from midnight onwards. Another attractive feature is the terrace overlooking the Tagus.

ENTERTAINMENTS AND SHOWS

Publications – *L'Agenda Cultural* is a monthly publication with a schedule of all cultural events in Lisbon. It's available free from main tourist offices, hotels and on kiosks throughout the capital. You can find details on: www.lisboacultural.pt
Another publication, in English and Portuguese, is called *"Follow Me Lisboa"* with lists of shows, events and details of all the museums in Lisbon. Available free from most tourist attractions. Other publications, such as **Público** (daily paper) and **Expresso** (weekly paper) provide details of cultural events both in Lisbon and elsewhere in Portugal.

ABEP– *Praça dos Restauradores - ☏ 213 42 53 60 – A* kiosk hat sells tickets for different eventstheatres, sports, concerts and so on.

Quiosque Cultural de S. Mamede – *R. de São Mamede, 30 - Principe Real.* This kiosk, set up by the city of Lisbon, has information on all the cultural activities in Lisbon.

BAIXA

Coliseu dos Recreios – *R. das Portas de Sto. Antão, 96.* ☏ *213 24 05 80 - www.coliseulisboa.com* A huge auditorium, restored in 1994, which holds operas, concerts and shows of all kinds.

Teatro Nacional D. Maria II – *Praça D. Pedro IV 213 25 08 35 - www.teatrodmaria.pt* A varied and classical programme.

CHIADO

Teatro da Trinidade – *Largo da Trinidade, 7 213 42 00 00 - www.teatrotrinidade.inatel.pt.* Popular theatre.

Teatro Nacional de S. Carlos – *Largo de S. Carlos 213 25 30 45 - www.saocarlos.pt.* Opera, ballet and classical concerts.

BAIRRO ALTO

Adega do Machado – *Rua do Norte 91 –* ☏ *213 22 46 60– Open Tuesdays to Sundays from 8pm-3am.* An excellent folklore show early in the evening, followed by traditional *fado*.

Adega do Ribatejo – *Rua Diário Notícias 23 –* ☏ *213 46 83 43 – Open 9pm-midnight.* One of the venues with the most authentic *fado* and a lively, friendly atmosphere.

O Faia – *Rua Barroca 54/56* ☏ *213 42 67 42 – Open -8pm -2am; Closed Sundays.* Authentic Lisbon *fado* in a district where *fado* is the traditional form of expression.

Café Luso – *Tv. Queimada 10 –* ☏ *213 42 22 81 – www.cafeluso.pt -Open 8pm-2am – Closed Sundays.* Very popular with tourists. Evening entertainment begins with a folklore show, followed by *fado*.

Teatro Municipal São Luís – *Rua António Maria Cardoso 38 – Bairro Alto –* ☏ *213 25 76 40.* Traditional programme.

Teatro Maria Vitória – *Parque Mayer – Av. da Liberdade –* ☏ *213 46 17 40 – Closed Mondays.* Plays by both foreign and Portuguese playwrights.

ALFAMA

O Cabacinha – *Lg. Limoeiro 9/10 –* ☏ *218 87 22 040 – Fado on Fri/Sat at 8.30pm.* A venue for true *fado* lovers.

Parreirinha de Alfama – *Beco Espírito Santo 1 –* ☏ *218 86 82 09 – Open 8pm-2am – Closed Sundays.* Traditional *fado* house popular with tourists.

Taverna del Rei – *Largo do Chafariz de Dentro 15 (corner of Rua São Pedro) –* ☏ *218 87 67 54 – www.tavernadelrey.com - Open 6pm-3am – Closed Sundays.*

Portuguese cuisine on offer to diners while they listen to authentic *fado*.

BELÉM

Centro Cultural de Belém – *Praça do Império* – ☎ *213 61 24 00* – *www.fdesccb. pt* – The cultural centre organises a large number of events, including concerts and temporary exhibitions. The monthly programme is available throughout the city.

OTHER DISTRICTS

Culturgest – Caixa Geral de Depósitos – *Rua Arco do Cego* – ☎ *217 90 51 55* – *www.cultgest.pt - booking office open 11am-7pm*. This enormous building in neo-Classical style is the headquarters of the Caixa Geral de Depósitos savings bank. It houses a cultural centre with two auditoriums and two exhibition galleries. The programme of musical events is of extremely high quality, while art exhibitions on show here often include works by contemporary international artists. Information on events is listed in the *Agenda Cultural* magazine.

Praça de Touros do Campo Pequeno – *Av. da República, Campo Pequeno* – ☎ *217 93 24 42* . Bullfights *(touradas)* every Thursday *(though these days vary – more information from Tourist Office)* at 5pm and 10pm from May to September in this remarkable neo-Moorish red-brick building.

Grande Auditório Gulbenkian – *Av de Berna, 45A (next to the Museum)* ☎*217 82 30 41 - www.musica-gulbenkian.pt* Various concerts from time to time.

Cinemateca Portuguesa – *Rua Barata Salgueiro 39 – Av. da Liberdade* – ☎ *213 59 62 00 - www.cinematica. pt*. Convivial cinema showing old films in various languages. Avant-garde Portuguese films for real cinema-buffs. Snacks (quiches and cakes) are on sale in the foyer. Shows at 3.30pm, 7pm, 9.30pm and 10pm daily except Sundays. The Cinemateca also houses a Cinema Museum displaying documents and equipment.

Teatro da Comuna – *Praça de Espanha* – ☎ *217 22 17 70*. A traditional programme of theatre, plus a bistro-style café-theatre for contemporary music

Campo Pequeno bullring

T. Perrin/HOAQUI

concerts (rock, jazz, music from around the world) every Sunday at 10pm.

Teatro Municipal Maria Matos – *Rua Frei Miguel Contreiras 52 – Campo de Ourique* – ☎ *218 43 88 00 - www.egeac. pt*. Comedy and plays for children.

Timpanas – *Rua Gilberto Rola 24 Alcântara* – ☎ *213 90 66 55* – *www.timpanas. pt - Open from 8.30pm to 2am - show at 9.30pm – Closed Tuesdays*. A good place to hear some excellent *fado*.

Senhor Vinho – *Rua Meio Lapa 18 – Lapa* – ☎ *213 97 26 81 - www. restsrvinho.com – Open daily 8pm-2am – Closed Sundays – Fado at 9.30pm*. Elegant, traditional *fado* venue with performances by some famous artists. Traditional Portuguese cuisine and a remarkable wine list.

The Lisbon Players – *R da Estrela 10 – Estrela* – ☎ *213 96 19 46 - www. lisbonplayers.com.pt*. A group of amateur playwrights organising plays and operas in English with audience participation.

Escola Portuguesa de Arte Equestre – *Palácio Nacional de QUELUZ* (👣 *see QUELUZ*) – ☎ *214 35 89 15 - www.cavalonet.com – shows every Wednesday at 11am from May-October (except August)*. The school, which keeps alive the tradition of Portuguese equestrian art, particularly with Lusitanian thoroughbreds, was founded by King João V at the end of the 18C.

BEACHES

Lisbonites have a wide choice of beaches close at hand for holidays, weekends or an hour or two after work.
& *See map of Principal Sights.*

BEACHES TO THE NORTH OF LISBON

Although closer to the centre of the city, the beaches along the fast highway between Lisbon and Cascais are not as pleasant as those specified below.

Praia do Guincho – & *See CASCAIS.*

Praia das Maçãs – An attractive beach with fine sand near the Azenhas do Mar.

Azenhas do Mar – A small beach (covered at high tide) with a natural swimming pool at the foot of this whitewashed village perched on the cliff.

Ericeira – A family beach next to the small town of the same name.

ON THE OTHER SIDE OF THE TAGUS

To get to these beaches you will either need to cross the Ponte 25 de Abril (☺heavily congested on weekends), take a train to Fogueteiro station, or perhaps catch a boat.

Costa da Caparica – *Access by car via the Ponte 25 de Abril, by bus (departures from Praça de Espanha) or boat (to Cacilhas from the Terreiro do Paço river station). From Cacilhas, take a bus south to Costa da Caparica.* & *See COSTA DA CAPARICA .*

Sesimbra – An attractive beach near the road, lined with restaurants specialising in grilled fish and seafood.

Portinho da Arrábida – Delightful, small sandy beach nestled in a bay.

SHOPPING CENTRES

There are several situated outside the historical heart of the city. The following two shopping centres are the largest of these and the most interesting to visit. They are normally open every day from around 9am until late, often 10pm or midnight.

Amoreiras Shopping Centre – *Av. Eng. Duarte Pacheco.* 300 shops, a supermarket, 55 restaurants and 10 cinema screens.

Colombo – *Avenida do Colégio Militar – Metro: Colégio Militar.* One of the largest shopping centres in Europe with 421 shops, 10 cinema screens, 55 restaurants and a leisure area.

MARKETS

Markets are ideal places for bargain-hunters with a multitude of inexpensive items on sale, including clothes, cotton piqué quilts, earthenware crockery, basketwork, arts and crafts, and antiques. Lively local markets are also extremely entertaining, although arrive early if you want to avoid the crowds, and ☺watch out for pickpockets.

M. Chaput/MICHELIN

Feira da Ladra

S. Grandadam/ EXPLORER

Torres das Amoreiras

Feira da Ladra – *Campo Sta Clara – Alfama – Tuesdays from 7am to 1pm and Saturdays from 7am to 6pm.* Lisbon's "Feira da Ladra" flea market literally means "The Thieves' Fair". However, most vendors sell their own goods. The market is a good place to hunt for second-hand clothes, silverware, furniture, old books and so on.

Mercado da Ribeira Nova – *Av. 24 de Julho – Mondays to Saturdays from 6am to 2pm.* Wonderful food market where colours, smells and the sales pitch of its vendors all blend together.

Feira de Carcavelos – *In the centre of Carcavelos 21km/13mi west of Lisbon on the Estoril road. Every Thursday morning.* Inexpensive clothes market selling seconds with minor – and often barely discernable – defects. A number of well-known French and British brand names are often on sale here, particularly cotton goods.

Feira de Sintra – *Largo de São Pedro à Sintra – The second and fourth Sunday of the month, all day.* This large market in one of Sintra's delighful squares sells the same goods as most other markets, plus plants and animals. Around the square you will also find small craft and antique stalls.

ART GALLERIES

Art galleries are usually closed on Sundays.

Associação José Afonso – *Rua Voz Operário 62 – Graça.* This traditional shop also contains an art gallery which makes a point of exhibiting the work of young artists.

Galeria 111 – *Campo Grande 114 – Campo Grande.*

Galeria 1991 – *Rua Marcos Portugal 28/30 – Príncipe Real.*

Galeria Arte Periférica – *Centro Cultural de Belém (Shops 5 and 6).*

Galeria Graça Fonseca – *Rua da Emenda 26C/V – Chiado.* A gallery which often hosts photographic exhibitions.

Galeria Luís Serpa – *Rua Ten. Raul Cascais 1B – Príncipe Real.* Exhibitions of paintings and sculpture by contemporary artists.

Galeria Módulo – *Cç. Mestres 34 A/B – Campolide.* Contemporary artists.

Galeria Palmira Suso – *Rua das Flores 109 – Bairro Alto.* Contemporary Portuguese artists.

Galeria de S. Francisco – *Rua Ivens 40 – Chiado.* Modern painting.

Novo Século – *Rua Século 23 A/B – Bairro Alto.* Contemporary art.

INDEX OF STREETS IN LISBON

Street	Grid	No.
5 de Outubro Av.	CN	
Achada L. da	PY	
Adelino Amaro da Costa L.	PY	
Adiça R. da	RY	
Afonso de Albuquerque Pr.	T	
Afonso III Av.	DP	4
Agulheiros Beco dos	RV	
Ajuda Calç. da T	AQ	
Alcaçarías L. das	SY	
Alecrim R. do	JZ	
Alegria R. da	JX	
Alexandre Herculano R.	CR	7
Alfândega R. da	PZ,LZ	10
Aliança Operária R.	AQ	12
Almada Trav. do	PY	
Almirante Gago Coutinho Av.	DN	
Amoreiras R. das	CP	13
Angelina Vidal R.	LV	
António Augusto de Aguiar Av.	CP	15
António José de Almeida Av.	DP	18
António Maria Cardoso R.	JZ	21
António Pereira Carrilho R.	DP	22
Arco do Dona Rosa Esc.	SV	
Arco Grande da Cima	SV	
Arsenal R. do	KZ	
Atafona L. da	PX	
Atalaia R. da	JY	28
Augusta R.	KY	
Augusto Rosa R.	QY,LY	31
Avelino Texeira da Mota Av.	DN	32
Barão R. do	LY	33
Barbadinhos Calç. dos	DQ	35
Barrelas R. das	SZ	
Bartolomeu de Gusmão R.	QX,LY	36
Bartolomeu Dias R.	T,AQ	37
Belém R. de	T,AQ	39
Benfica Estr. de	AN	
Berlim Av. de	DN	
Berna Av. de	CP	42
Bica do Marquês R. da	AQ	45
Boavista R. da	JZ	
Bombarda R.	LV	
Brasil Av. do	DN	
Brasilia Av. de	T,AQ	
Cais de Santarém R. do	RZ,LZ	49
Calhariz de Benfica Estr. do	AP	51
Calvário L. do	BQ	54
Campo das Cebolas	QZ,LZ	
Campo de Santa Clara	MX	
Campo dos Mártires da Pátria	KV	
Campo Grande	CN	
Campolide R. de	BP	60
Cardosa R. da	RX	
Carlos Pinhão Av.	DNP	62
Carmo R. do	KY	63
Carneiro Beco do	SX	
Carolina M. de Vasconcelos R.	AN	64
Casal Ribeiro Av.	CP	66
Cascais R.	BQ	67
Caselas Estr. de	AQ	68
Castelo Costa do	PQV	
Castelo Espl. do	QX	
Castelo Vila do	PV	
Cavaleiros R. dos	LX	
Cegos R. dos	RVX	
Ceuta Av. de	BQ	69
Chafariz de Dentro L. do	SY,MY	71
Chão da Feira R. do	QX,LY	70
Chão do Loureiro Trav.	PX	
Chelas Estr. de	DP	
Chiado L. do	KY	72
Cidade do Porto Av.	DN	
Columbano Bordalo Pinheiro Av.	BP	73
Combatentes Av. dos	BN	74
Combro Calç. do	JY	
Comércio Pr. do	KZ	
Conceição R. do	PY	
Conceição da Glória R.	JX	75
Conde de Penafiel Calç. do	PX	
Conselheiro F. de Sousa Av.	BP	79
Contador-Mor L. do	RX	
Correeiros R. dos	KY	82
Correia Estr. da	AN	84
Correio Velho Calç	PY	
Corvos R. dos	SX,MX	85
Costa do Castelo	LX	
Cruz da Pedra Calç. da	DP	87
Cruzeiro R. do	AQ	88
Cruzes Beco das	SX	
Cruzes da Sé R.	LZ	90
Damas R. das	QX	
Damasceno Monteiro R.	LV	
Descobertas Av. das	AQ	
Diário de Notícias R. do	JY	91
Dom Carlos I Av.	CQ	94
Dom João da Câmara Pr.	KX	97
Dom João V R.	CQ	99
Dom Luís I R.	JZ	
Dom Pedro IV Pr.	KX	
Dom Pedro V R.	JX	
Dom Vasco R. de	AQ	103
Dom Vasco da Gama Av.	AQ	105
Domingos Sequeira R.	BQ	106
Doutor Alfredo Bensaúde Av.	DN	
Duque de Saldanha Pr.	CP	112
Duque de Terceira Pr.	JZ	
Elias Garcia R.	AN	
Engenheiro Duarte Pacheco Av.	BP	115
Engenheiro Ferreira Dias R.	DN	116
Escadinhas de Santo Estêvão	SX	
Escola Politécnica R. da	CQ	120
Escolas Gerais R. das	SX,LY	118
Espanha Pr. de	CP	124
Espírito Santo B. do	SX	
Espírito Santo R. do	QX	
Estados Unidos da América Av.	DN	
Estrela Calç. da	CQ	125
Fanqueiros R. dos	PYZ,KY	127
Farinhas R. das	PV	
Ferreira Borges R.	BQ	132
Figueira Pr. da	KX	
Flores de Santa Cruz R. das	QV	
Fonte R. da	AN	138
Fontes Pereira de Melo Av.	CP	139
Forças Armadas Av. das	CN	142
Formosa Beco da	SX	
Funil Trav. do	QX,LY	148
Galhardas Az. das	BN	
Galvão Calç. do	T,AQ	149
Garrett R.	KY	
General Norton de Matos Av.	BN	
Glória R. da	JX	
Glória Calç. da	JX	151
Graça L. da	LX	
Graça R. da	LV	
Graça Calç. da	RV,LX	152
Gualdim Pais R.	DP	153
Guilherme Braga R.	SX,LY	154
Ilha da Madeira Av.	AQ	155
Império Pr. do	T,AQ	156
India Av. da	T AQ	
Infante D. Henrique Av.	QSZ,MY	
Instituto Bacteriológico R. do	KV	160
Ivens R.	KY	
Jardim do Tabaco R. do	SX,MY	165
Jerónimos R. dos	T	
João de Barros R.	AQ	168
João de Freitas Branco R.	BN	169
Joaquim António de Aguiar R.	CP	171
Judaria R. da	RY	
Junqueira R. da	AQ	
Lagares R. dos	LX	
Laranjeiras Estr. das	BNP	172
Leite de Vasconcelos R.	MX	
Liberdade Av. da	JV	
Limoeiro R. do	RXY,LY	175
Linhas de Torres Alam. das	CN	
Lóios L. dos	QY	
Lóios Beco dos	RV	
Londres Pr. de	DP	177
Luís de Camões Pr.	JY	
Lusíada Av.	ABN	
Luz Estr. da	BN	
Madalena R. da	PYZ	
Marcos Estr. dos	AQ	
Marechal Craveiro Lopes Av.	CN	
Marechal Gomes da Costa Av.	DN	
Marechal Teixeira Rebelo Av.	AN	179
Maria da Fonte R.	LV	
Marquês da Fronteira R.	CP	181
Marquês de Ponte de Lima R.	PV	
Marquês de Tancos Calç. do	PX	

Martim Moniz L.   KX 184
Mata Trav. da   PQY
Mayer Parque   JV
Menino Deus L. do   RV
Mexias Beco do   SX
Miguel Bombarda Av.   CP 186
Milagre de São António
Beco do   QX
Mirante R. do   MX
Mirante Calç. do   AQ 189
Misericórdia R. da   JY 190
Mónicas Trav. RV
Monte Trav. do   LV
Mouzinho de
Albuquerque Av.   DP 192
Norberto de Araújo R.   RY,LY 193
Norte R. do   JY 194
Nova do Almada R.   KY
Oliveirinha R. da   RV
Ouro R. do   KY
Outeirinho da
Amendoeira L.   SV
Paço do Lumiar Estr. do   AN
Padaria R. da   PYZ
Padre Cruz Av.   BN
Palma R. da   KV
Paraíso R. do   MX
Pascoal de Melo R.   DP 196
Pedras Negras Trav. das   PY
Pedras Negras R. das   PY
Pedro Álvares Cabral Av.   CQ 199
Pedrouços R. de   AQ 202
Pontinha Estr. da   AN 208
Portas de Santo Antão
R. das   KX
Portas do Sol L. das   RX,LY 210
Prata R. da   KY
Príncipe Real Pr. do   JX
Queluz Estr. de   AQ
Recolhimento R. do   QX
Recolhimento Beco do   QX
Regedor R. do   PX
Regueira R. da   SX,LY 214
Relógio Rot. do   DN 215

Remédios R. dos   SX
República Av. da   CP 216
Restauradores Pr. dos   KX
Restelo Av. do   T,AQ 217
Ribeira das Naus Av. da   KZ
Rio de Janeiro Av.   CN
Rodrigues de
Freitas L.   RV,LX 220
Roma Av. da   CN
Rosa R. da   JY
Rosa L. da   PV
Rovisco Pais Av.   DP 222
S. Bartolomeu Trav. de   QX
S. Bento R. de   CQ 237
S. Crispim Esc. de   QXY
S. Cristóvão R. de   PX
S. Domingos L. de   KX 240
S. Filipe Neri R. de   CP 241
S. Francisco Calç. de   KZ 243
S. Francisco Xavier R. de   T
S. João da Praça
R. de   QRY,LY 246
S. José R. de   JV
S. Julião R. de   PY
S. Lázaro R. de   KX
S. Lourenço R. de   PV
S. Mamede R. de   PQY
S. Miguel L. de   RSY
S. Miguel R. de   SX,LY 249
S. Paulo R. de   JZ
S. Pedro R. de   SY,LY 250
S. Pedro de Alcântara
R. de   JX 252
S. Pedro Mártir R. de   PV
S. Rafael L. de   RY
S. Tiago R. de   RX,LY 253
S. Tomé R. de   RV,LX 255
S. Vicente L. de   SV
S. Vicente R. de   RSV
S. Vicente Calç. de   SX,LX 256
Saco R. do   KV
Sacramento Calç. do   KY 225
Salitre R. do   JV
Salvador R. do   RX,LY 226

Salvador L. do   RX
Santa Catarina R. de   JY 228
Santa Cruz do Castelo R.   QX
Santa Helena Beco de   RX
Santa Justa R. de   KY 229
Santa Luzia Trav. de   RX,LY 231
Santa Marinha Trav. de   RV
Santa Marinha R. de   RV
Santa Marinha L. de   RV
Santana Calç. de   KX
Santo André Calç. de   QV,LX
Santo António da Sé L.   LY 233
Santo António dos
Capuchos R.   KV 234
Santo Condestável
Av. do   DN 235
Santo Estêvão L. de   SX
Santo Estêvão
Escadinhas de   MY 236
Sapadores R. dos   MV
Sapateiros R. dos   KY 258
Saraiva de Carvalho R.   BQ 259
Saudade R. da   QY LY
Sé L. da   QY
Sé Cruzes da   QY
Século R. do   JX
Seminário R. do   AN 261
Senhora da Glória R.   MV
Serpa Pinto R.   KZ 262
Sodré Cais do   JZ
Tapada Calç. da   AQ
Telhal R. do   KV
Telheiras Estr. de   BN 265
Terreiro do Trigo R. do   SX,LY 267
Terreiro do Trigo L. do   RSY
Tijolo Calç.   SV
Torre de Belém Av.   T,AQ 268
Vale de Sto António
R. do   MV
Verónica R. da   MX
Vigário R. do   SX,MY 270
Vítor Cordon R.   KZ
Voz do Operário R.   LX
Xabregas R. de   DP 271

INDEX OF SIGHTS IN LISBON

Áera Int. Norte   DN
Alto de Santa Catarina   JZ   A[1]
Antiga Faculdade de
Ciências   CQ
Aqueduto das Águas
Livres   ABP
Bairro Alto   JY
Baixa   KY
Basílica da Estrela   BQ   A[2]
Belém   AQ
Biblioteca Municipal   CP   B[1]
Caixa Geral de Depósitos   CP   B[2]
Casa de Janelas
geminadas   RY
Casa do Alentejo   KX   C[4]
Casa do Fado e da Guitarra
Portuguesa   SY
Casa dos Bicos   LZ,QZ C[1]
Casa Fernando Pessoa   BQ   C[2]
Casa-Museu Anastácio
Gonçalves   CP   M[1]
Casa-Museu de Amália
Rodrigues   CQ
Castelo de São Jorge   PQV

Centro Científico e
Cultural de Macau   AQ   C[3]
Centro Cultural de Belém   AQ   T
Centro de Arte Moderna   CP   M[2]
Chiado   KY
Éden Teatro   KX   T[1]
Elevador da Bica   JY
Elevador de Santa Justa   KY
Escadinhas de Santo
Estêvão   SY
Estação do Oriente   DN
Estação do Rossio   KX
Estação do Sul e Sueste   LZ
Fundação Arpad
Szenes - Vieira da Silva   CP   M[3]
Igreja da Conceição
Velha   LZ,PZ D[1]
Igreja de Santa Engrácia   MX
Igreja de Santa Maria   T
Igreja de São Miguel   RYZ
Igreja de São Roque   JX
Igreja de São Vicente
de Fora   SV
Igreja do Carmo-
Museu Arqueológico   KY   M[4]
Igreja e convento N. S.
da Graça   LX

Igreja Santo António
da Sé   LY,PQY
Jardim Botânico   CQ,JV
Jardim Botânico (Ajuda)   AQ
Jardim Boto Machado   MX
Jardim da Estrela   BQ
Jardim do Ultramar   T
Jardim Zoológico   BN
Madre de Deus   DP
Mãe d'Água das
Amoreiras   CQ   K[1]
Miradouro de Monsanto   AP
Miradouro de
Santa Luzia   RX,LY L[1]
Miradouro de São
Pedro de Alcântara   JX   L[2]
Mosteiro dos Jerónimos   AQ   T
Museu da Carris   ACQ   M[26]
Museu da Cidade   CN   M[6]
Museu da Marinha   T,AQ M[7]
Museu da Música   BN   M[9]
Museu de Água da EPAL   DQ   M[5]
Museu de Arte Popular   T   AQ
Museu de Arte Sacra de
São Roque   JKX   M[11]
Museu de Artes
Decorativas   RX,LY M[13]

Museu de Design	CQ	M14
Museu de Etnologia	AQ	M25
Museu Gulbenkian	CP	
Museu Militar	MY	M15
Museu Nacional de Arqueologia	T	
Museu Nacional de Arte Antiga	BQ	M16
Museu Nacional do Azulejo	DP	M17
Museu Nacional do Chiado	KZ	M18
Museu Nacional do Teatro	BN	M19
Museu Nacional do Traje	BN	M21
Museu Nacional dos Coches	AQ, T	
Museu Rafael Bordalo Pinheiro	CN	M23
Núcleo Arqueológico da Rua dos Correeiros	KY, P	
Oceanário	DN	
Paço Real	PX, LY	
Padrão dos Descobrimentos	AQ, T	
Palacio da Ajuda	AQ	
Palácio da Assembleia da República	CQ	
Palácio das Necesidades	BQ, R	
Palácio de Fronteira	ABP	
Palácio Foz	JKX	
Palácio Lavradio	MX	
Parque das Nações	DN	
Parque Eduardo VII	CP	
Parque Florestal de Monsanto	APQ	
Pavilhão Atlântico	DN	
Pavilhão da Realidade Virtual	DN	M30
Pavilhão do Conhecimento	DN	M32
Planetário Calouste Gulbenkian	T	
Ponte 25 de Abril	ABQ	
Ponte Vaco de Gama	DN	
Rossio	KX	
Santo Estêvão	SX, MY	
Sé	QY, LY	
Teatro da Trindade	JKY	T2
Teatro Nacional D. Maria II	KX	T3
Teatro Nacional de São Carlos	KZ	T4
Teatro Romano	QY	
Teatro São Luís	KZ	T5
Torre (Alfama)	RY	
Torre de Belém	AQ	T
Torre Vasco de Gama	DN	
Torres das Amoreiras	BP	

LISBOA

5 de Outubro Av.	CNP	273
Afonso III Av.	DP	4
Alexandre Herculano R.	CPQ	7
Aliança Operária R.	AQ12	
Amoreiras R. das	CPQ	13
António Augusto de Aguiar Av.	CP	15
António José de Almeida Av.	DP	18
António Pereira Carrilho R.	DP	22
Avelino Texeira da Mota Av.	DN	32
Barbadinhos Calç. dos	DQ	35
Bartolomeu Dias R.	AQ	37
Belém R. de	AQ	39
Berna Av. de	CP	42
Bica do Marquês R. da	AQ	45
Calhariz de Benfica Estr. do	AP	51
Calvário L. do	BQ	54
Campolide R. de	BP	60
Carlos Pinhão Av.	DNP	62
Carolina M. de Vasconcelos R.	AN	64
Casal Ribeiro Av.	CP	66
Cascais R.	BQ	67
Caselas Estr. de	AQ	68
Ceuta Av. de	BPQ	69
Columbano Bordalo Pinheiro Av.	BP	73
Combatentes Av. dos	BN	74
Conselheiro F. de Sousa Av.	BP	79
Correia Estr. da	AN	84
Cruz da Pedra Calç. da	DP	87
Cruzeiro R. do	AQ	88
Dom Carlos I Av.	CQ	94
Dom João V R.	CQ	99
Dom Vasco R. de	AQ	103
Dom Vasco da Gama Av.	AQ	105
Domingos Sequeira R.	BQ	106
Duque de Saldanha Pr.	CP	112
Engenheiro Duarte Pacheco Av.	BP	115
Engenheiro Ferreira Dias R.	DN	116
Escola Politécnica R. da	CQ	120
Estrela Calç. da	CQ	125
Ferreira Borges R.	BQ	132
Fonte R. da	AN	138
Fontes Pereira de Melo Av.	CP	139
Forças Armadas Av. das	CN	142
Galvão Calç. do	AQ	149
Ilha da Madeira Av.	AQ	155
Império Pr. do	AQ	156
João de Barros R.	AQ	168
João de Freitas Branco R.	BN	169
Joaquim António de Aguiar R.	CP	171
Laranjeiras Estr. das	BNP	172
Londres Pr. de	DP	177
Marechal Teixeira Rebelo Av.	AN	179
Marquês da Fronteira R.	CP	181
Miguel Bombarda Av.	CP	186
Mirante Calç. do	AQ	189
Mouzinho de Albuquerque Av.	DP	192
Pascoal de Melo R.	DP	196
Pedro Álvares Cabral Av.	CQ	199
Pedrouços R. de	AQ	202
Pontinha Estr. da	AN	208
Relógio Rot. do	DN	215
República Av. da	CP	216
Restelo Av. do	AQ	217
Rovisco Pais Av.	CDP	222
S. Bento R. de	CQ	237
S. Filipe Neri R. de	CP	241
Santo Condestável Av. do	DN	235
Saraiva de Carvalho R.	BQ	259
Seminário R. do	AN	261
Telheiras Estr. de	BN	265
Torre de Belém Av.	AQ	268
Xabregas R. de	DP	271

Alto de Santa Catarina	JZ	A1
Casa do Alentejo	KX	C4
Casa dos Bicos	LZ	C1
Éden Teatro	KX	T1
Igreja da Conceição Velha	LZ	D1
Igreja do Carmo-Museu Arqueológico	KY	M4
Igreja Santo António da Sé	LY	E
Jardim Boto Machado	MX	F
Miradouro de Santa Luzia	LY	L1
Miradouro de São Pedro de Alcântara	JX	L2
Museu de Arte Sacra de São Roque	JKX	M11
Museu de Artes Decorativas	LY	M13
Museu Nacional do Chiado	KZ	M18
Núcleo Arqueológico da Rua dos Correeiros	KY	P
Paço Real	LY	Q
Palácio Lavradio	MX	S
Teatro da Trindade	JKY	T2
Teatro Nacional D. Maria II	KX	T3
Teatro Nacional de São Carlos	KZ	T4
Teatro São Luís	KZ	T5

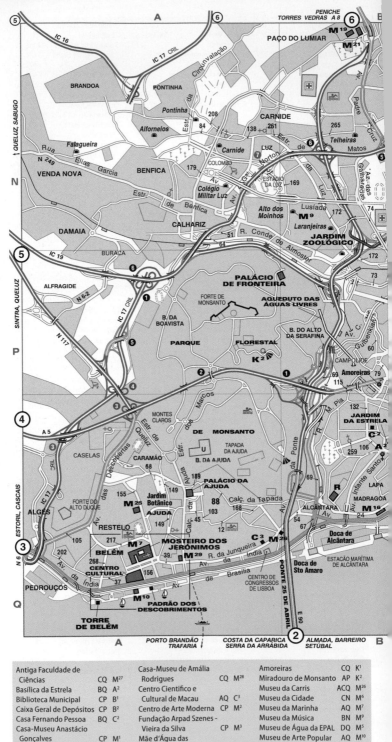

Antiga Faculdade de Ciências	CQ	M²⁷
Basílica da Estrela	BQ	A²
Biblioteca Municipal	CP	B¹
Caixa Geral de Depósitos	CP	B²
Casa Fernando Pessoa	BQ	C²
Casa-Museu Anastácio Gonçalves	CP	M¹
Casa-Museu de Amália Rodrigues	CQ	M²⁸
Centro Científico e Cultural de Macau	AQ	C³
Centro de Arte Moderna	CP	M²
Fundação Arpad Szenes - Vieira da Silva	CP	M³
Mãe d'Água das		
Amoreiras	CQ	K¹
Miradouro de Monsanto	AP	K²
Museu da Carris	ACQ	M²⁶
Museu da Cidade	CN	M⁶
Museu da Marinha	AQ	M⁷
Museu da Música	BN	M⁹
Museu de Água da EPAL	DQ	M⁵
Museu de Arte Popular	AQ	M¹⁰

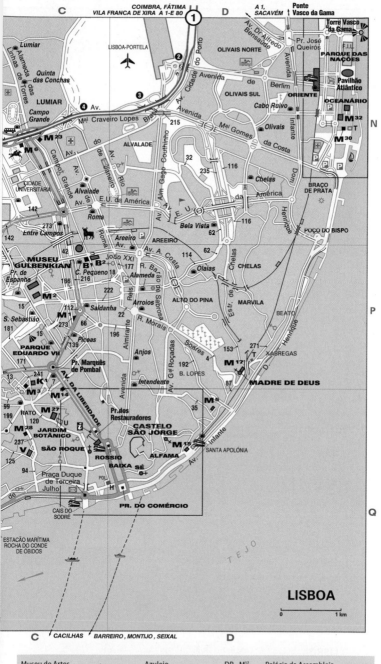

Museu de Artes Decorativas	LY	M¹³	Azulejo	DP	M¹⁷	Palácio da Assembleia da República	CQ	V
Museu de Etnologia	AQ	M²⁵	Museu Nacional do Teatro	BN	M¹⁹	Palácio das Necesidades	BQ	R
Museu do Design	CQ	M¹⁴	Museu Nacional do Traje	BN	M²¹	Pavilhão da Realidade Virtual	DN	M³⁰
Museu Militar	DQ	M¹⁵	Museu Nacional dos Coches	AQ	M²⁹	Pavilhão do Conhecimento	DN	M³²
Museu Nacional de Arte Antiga	BQ	M¹⁶	Museu Rafael Bordalo Pinheiro	CN	M²³			
Museu Nacional do								

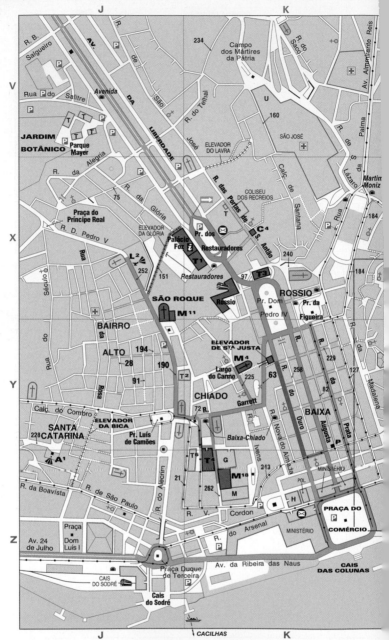

LISBOA

Alfândega R. da	LZ	10
António Maria Cardoso R.	JZ	21
Atalaia R. da	JY	28
Augusta R.	KY	
Augusto Rosa R.	LY	31
Barão R. do	LY	33
Bartolomeu de Gusmão R.	LY	36
Cais de Santarém R. do	LZ	49
Carmo R. do	KY	63
Chafariz de Dentro L. do	MY	71
Chão da Feira R. do	LY	70
Chiado L. do	KY	72
Conceição da Glória R.	JX	75
Correeiros R. dos	KY	82
Corvos R. dos	MX	85
Cruzes da Sé R.	LZ	90
Diário de Notícias R. do	JY	91
Dom João da Câmara Pr.	KX	97
Escolas Gerais R. das	LY	118
Fanqueiros R. dos	KY	127
Funil Trav. do	LY	148
Garrett R.	KY	
Glória Calç. da	JX	151
Graça Calç. da	LX	152
Guilherme Braga R.	LY	154
Instituto Bacteriológico R. do	KV	160
Jardim do Tabaco R. do	MY	165
Limoeiro R. do	LY	175
Martim Moniz L.	KX	184
Misericórdia R. da	JY	190
Norberto de Araújo R.	LY	193

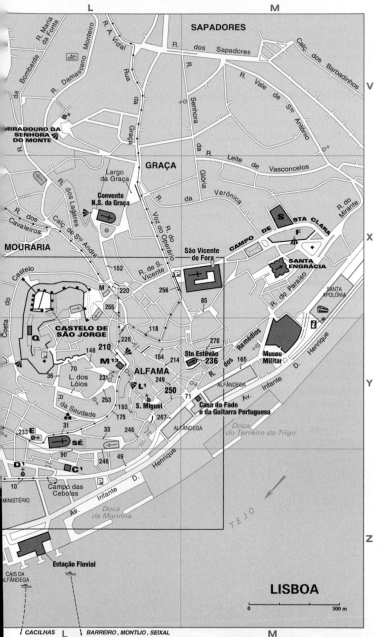

Norte R. do	JY 194	S. Pedro de Alcântara		Santo António dos	
Ouro R. do	KY	R. de	JX 252	Capuchos R.	KV 234
Portas do Sol L. das	JX 210	S. Tiago R. de	LY 253	Santo Estêvão	
Prata R. da	KY	S. Tomé R. de	LX 255	Escadinhas de	MY 236
Regueira R. da	LY 214	S. Vicente Calç. de	LX 256	Sapateiros R. dos	KY 258
Rodrigues de Freitas L.	LX 220	Sacramento Calç. do	KY 225	Serpa Pinto R.	KZ 262
S. Domingos L. de	KX 240	Salvador R. do	LY 226	Terreiro do Trigo R. do	LY 267
S. Francisco Calç. de	KZ 243	Santa Catarina R. de	JY 228	Vigário R. do	MY 270
S. João da Praça R. de	LY 246	Santa Justa R. de	KY 229		
S. Miguel R. de	LY 249	Santa Luzia Trav. de	LY 231		
S. Pedro R. de	LY 250	Santo António da Sé L.	LY 233		

To get to know the city's various neighbourhoods you might find it best to walk round rather than drive (which, in Lisbon like any big city, can be frustrating to say the least). We suggest the following as a good way to improve your knowledge of Lisbon and to see the main sights.

The Baixa★★ *2hr – Follow the itinerary suggested on the plan.*

This part of the city, which was completely devastated by the earthquake and tidal wave in 1755, was rebuilt to plans laid down by the Marquis of Pombal.

Praça dos Restauradores
The square owes its name to the men who in 1640 led the revolt against the Spanish and proclaimed the independence of Portugal. The fine red roughcast façade on the west of the square belongs to the **Palácio Foz** built by an Italian architect in the early 19C. Today it houses Lisbon's Tourist Information Centre *(Posto de Turismo)*.

Next door is the **Éden Teatro**, designed by Cassiano Branco in 1937. Part of its Art Deco façade and its monumental staircase remain from the original building which is now occupied by the Virgin Megastore. Avenida da Liberdade runs northeast off the square to the Parque Eduardo VII. Parallel to the avenue is **Rua Portas de Santo Antão**, a pedestrian street with cinemas, cafés and shops. The **Casa do Alentejo** at no 58 has an unusual Moorish courtyard and a restaurant with abundant *azulejo* decoration. **Estação do Rossio**, the station, has a 19C neo-Manueline **façade**★ with wide horseshoe-shaped openings, and serves the town of Sintra, among others.

Rossio★
Praça Dom Pedro IV, the lively main square of the Baixa, dates from the 13C. Its present appearance is due to Pombal: 18C and 19C buildings line it on three sides, the ground floors being given over to cafés such as the famous Nicola with its Art Deco façade, and small shops that have kept their decoration from the beginning of

Rua Augusta

Pedro IV or Maximilian of Austria?

The statue atop the column in the centre of the Rossio is in fact believed to have originally been cast as Maximilian of Austria, Emperor of Mexico. The boat transporting the statue to Mexico called at Lisbon when news of the emperor's assassination was heard. The captain, faced with the dilemma of what to do with the statue, left it in Lisbon, and a decision was finally made to use it to replace the existing one of Pedro IV which was rather rudimentary.

the century. Among these are the tobacconist's near Nicola with *azulejos* by Rafael Bordalo Pinheiro, and the corner shop which serves *ginginha*, the well-known cherry liqueur, off Largo de São Domingos, next to a milliner's dating from the last century. The north side of the square is bordered by the **Teatro Nacional Dona Maria II**, built in 1840 on the site of the former Palace of the Inquisition. The façade is adorned with a statue of Gil Vicente, the father of Portuguese theatre. In the middle of the square, between the Baroque fountains, is the bronze statue of Dom Pedro IV, after whom the square is named and who was crowned Pedro I, Emperor of Brazil.

Parallel to the Rossio to the east is the **Praça da Figueira**, a square of classical buildings with an equestrian statue of Dom João I in the centre.

South of the square is the grid of Baixa streets, some pedestrian, which forms Lisbon's main shopping district. The streets running south between the Rossio and Praça do Comércio are named after guilds. Among them are Rua dos Correeiros (Saddlers' Street) and Rua dos Sapateiros (Cobblers's Street). The three main ones are Rua do Ouro (Goldsmiths' Street), **Rua Augusta** and Rua da Prata (Silversmith's Street).

Rua do Ouro (or Rua Áurea)

In the 15C and 16C, this street was the gold trading area of Lisbon; today it is lined with banks, jewellers and goldsmiths.

Praça do Comércio (or Terreiro do Paço)★★

The finest square in Lisbon is the site where the Royal Palace once stood, facing the Straw Sea *(Mar da Palha)*. The palace was destroyed by the earthquake. The square was designed as a whole and is an excellent example of the Pombaline style. It is 192m/630ft long by 177m/581ft wide and lined on three sides by classical buildings with tall arcades supporting two upper storeys with red façades.

A 19C Baroque triumphal arch forms a backdrop to the equestrian statue of King José I. This statue by the late 18C sculptor Machado de Castro is cast in bronze and is the reason for the square also being known as Black Horse Square.

On 1 February, 1908, King Carlos I and his heir, Prince Luís Felipe, were assassinated on the square.

Southeast of the square is Lisbon's South Station, the **Estação do Sul e Sueste** *(estação fluvial on plan)*, which is decorated with *azulejo* panels of towns in the Alentejo and the Algarve. Passengers embark from here by ferry to the railway station on the opposite shore of the Tagus for destinations south and southeast.

Elevador de Santa Justa★

○*Open daily 7am-11pm.* ☞€1.50. ☎ 218 91 98 98.

The lift was built in 1901 by Raúl Mesnier de Ponsard, a Portuguese engineer of French origin who was influenced by Gustave Eiffel. Before the fire it gave direct access to Chiado. From the upper platform there is a good **view**★ of the Rossio and the Baixa, 32 metres above the street.

Chiado★ *1hr 30mn*

The name Chiado applies not only to Largo do Chiado but also to a whole district of which the main streets, Rua Garrett and Rua do Carmo, link the Rossio to Praça Luís de Camões. The lift ascends to the area struck by fire on 25 August 1988. The four blocks of buildings damaged were mainly shops including the *Grandella* department store (since replaced by the *Printemps* store) and the famous *Ferrari* tearoom. Over 2 000 people lost their jobs as a result of this tragedy, though no lives were lost. Immediately after the event, the mayor of Lisbon entrusted the rehabilitation of the area to the well-known Portuguese architect Álvaro Siza who put forward a resolutely classical plan to rebuild and safeguard the façades of the buildings, and to transform their interiors into pleasant patios, elegant shops and café terraces.

P. Ancenay/PIX

Igreja do Carmo and Museu Arqueológico★

○*Open 10am-6pm (5pm in winter).* ○*Closed Sundays, Jan 1, May 1 and Dec 25.* €*2.50* 213 46 04 73 *or* 213 47 86 29.
Once through the doorway of the Carmelite Church, the visitor is struck by the atmospheric aura of the ruins and the silence. The church was devastated by the earthquake on 1 November 1755.
Today, the ruins of the late 14C Gothic church, built by Constable Nuno Álvares Pereira, house an archeological museum. Among the collections are Bronze Age pottery, marble low reliefs, Romanesque and Gothic tombs (including the recumbent statue of Fernão Sanchez, illegitimate son of Dom Dinis) and Spanish Arabic *azulejos*.

Ruins of the Igreja do Carmo

Rua do Carmo and Rua Garrett★

These elegant streets with their old-fashioned shop fronts are renowned for their bookshops, patisseries and cafés. The most famous of the latter is the **Brasileira**, once frequented by the poet Fernando Pessoa whose centenary was celebrated in 1988. A bronze statue of the poet stands at one of the tables on the terrace.

Museu Nacional do Chiado ★

R Serpa Pinto, 4 ○*Open Tues-Sun, 10am-6pm.* €*3 (free Sun and holidays until 2pm).* 213 43 21 48 - www.museudochiado-ipmuseus.pt.
The building, originally a 13C abbey, was transformed into a contemporary arts museum in 1911. Following the 1988 fire, it was refurbished by the French architect, Jean-Michel Wilmotte. The museum displays an exhibition of predominantly Portuguese paintings, drawings and sculpture from the period between 1850 and 1950. The first floor is devoted to French sculpture, including Rodin's *Bronze Age* and Canto da Maia's *Adam and Eve*. Soares dos Reis' sculpture *O Desterrado (The Exile)* stands out among the works on the second floor. Various periods are represented: the **Romantic**, **Naturalist** (*A Charneca de Belas* by Silva Porto, *Concerto de Amadores* by Columbano, and *A Beira-Mar* by José Malhoa) and **Modernist** (*Tristezas* by Amadeo de Souza-Cardoso, *O Bailarico no Bairro* by Mário Eloy, *Nú* by Eduardo Viana, and the drawing *A Sesta* by Almada Negreiros), and a small collection of **Symbolist** and **neo-Realist** works.

Teatro Nacional de São Carlos

Rua Serpa Pinto, 9 - ☎ 213 25 30 45. www.saocarlos.pt.
This lavish theatre, situated in a calm area overlooking the Tagus, was built in 1793 in neo-Classical style with a façade inspired by the San Carlo theatre in Naples and is the venue for regular concerts, ballet and operas.

Praça Luís de Camões

The square, with a statue of the great poet at its centre, was one of the stages for the revolution on 25 April 1974. The square is the transition zone between the Chiado and the Bairro Alto. To the south, at the foot of Rua do Alecrim, the Tagus comes into view.

Rua da Misericórdia

The street is part of the Praça Camões and borders the Bairro Alto quarter to the west of Chiado.

Museu da Farmacia (Pharmacy Museum)

Rua Marechal Saldanha, 1 ⏱Open 0am-6pm ☞€2 ☎ 213 40 06 80.
This museum, little known to tourists, is in a palace dating from 1870 and contains over 14 000 objects from all over the world; pharmacies dating from the 15C to 19C are represented including a Chinese pharmacy from Macao that was functioning until 1996.

Bairro Alto★*3hr*

This picturesque working-class quarter dating from the 16C has kept its character in spite of it becoming the centre for trendy fashion houses, designers, restaurants and *fado* houses over the past few years. The main shopping streets are **Rua do Diário de Notícias** and **Rua de Atalaia**. Sunsets over the Tagus are wonderful when viewed from the **Alto de Santa Catarina**★ belvedere with its statue of Adamostor, the giant who was transformed into the Cape of Storms (Cape of Good Hope).

Igreja de São Roque★

⏱*Open 8.30am-5.30pm.*
The Church of St Rock was built in the late 16C by the Italian architect Filippo Terzi. The original façade collapsed in the great earthquake of 1755.The **interior**★ decoration is striking. The wooden ceiling, painted with scenes of the Apocalypse above the nave, is by artists of the Italian School. The third chapel on the right has 16C **azulejos** and a painting on wood of the Vision of St Rock by the 16C artist Gaspar Vaz.
The **Capela de São João Baptista**★★ *(4th on the left),* a masterpiece of Italian Baroque, was built in Rome by Salvi and Vanvitelli with the help of 130 artists. After being blessed by the Pope, it was transported to Lisbon in three ships and re-erected in this church in about 1750. The columns are of lapis lazuli, the altar front of amethyst, the steps of porphyry, the angels of white Carrara marble and ivory, the pilasters of alabaster; the flooring and the wall pictures are coloured mosaics, and the friezes, capitals and ceiling are highlighted with gold, silver and bronze. The first chapel on the left contains two paintings attributed to the school of Zurbarán *(Nativity* and *Adoration of the Magi),* and the **sacristy** has a 17C coffered ceiling and paintings of St Francis by Vieira Lusitano and André Gonçalves.

Museu de Arte Sacra de São Roque ★

⌖ *Currently closed for renovation.*
The museum abuts on the church and contains 16C Portuguese paintings and part of the treasure from the Capela do São João Baptista. The furnishings and ecclesiastical

plate by 18C Italian artists are outstanding for their Baroque decoration. There is also a collection of **vestments**★ in silk or lamé embroidered in gold.

Miradouro de São Pedro de Alcântara★

The belvedere takes the form of a pleasant garden suspended like a balcony over the lower town with a wide **view**★★ of the Baixa, the Tagus and Castelo de São Jorge on the hill opposite *(viewing table)*.

▶ *The Calçada da Gloria funicular descends to Praça dos Restauradores.*

Jardim Botânico (Botanical Gardens)

Entry via the old Faculty of Science, Rua Escola Politécnica, 56-58, or via Rua da Algeria ○*Open summer 9am-8pm; Sat, Sun and holidays 10am-8pm; rest of the year 9am-6pm, weekends and holidays 10am-6pm.* ○*Closed Jan 1, Dec 25.* ✆€1.50 ☎ 213 92 18 30. This beautiful garden, established in 1873 to further the study of plants and part of the Academy of Sciences, is one of the most respected in Europe for its collection of subtropical flora. There are ideal spots for picnics and a majestic avenue of palms.

Alfama★★ *4hr*

The most pleasant way to see the Alfama quarter, which may be approached from above, Largo das Portas do Sol, or from below, alongside the Tagus, is simply to spend time wandering through the district, preferably in the morning when the market is open. Give yourself a half day in this neighbourhood.

The Alfama, a district demarcated by the castle to the north, Graça and Mouraria to the northeast and the Tagus to the south, is a maze of narrow streets and alleys *(becos)*, steps and archways, and is one of the oldest in the city. It was largely spared in the earthquake, a symbol of hope to Lisbonites. Today it is a bustling, lively area, houses fronted by wrought-iron balconies bursting with flowers, and decorated with *azulejos* representing The Virgin and St Anthony (patron saint of Lisbon).

Cathedral★★

○*Open 9am-7pm (cloisters open 2pm-7pm Jun-Sept; Oct-May Sat 10am-6pm; Sunday 2pm-6pm.* ○*Closed public holidays.* ✆€2.50. ☎ 218 87 66 28.
Lisbon's cathedral *(sé)*, like those of Oporto, Coimbra and Évora, was once a fortress, as can be observed from the two towers flanking the façade and its battlements. It was built in the Romanesque style in the late 12C, shortly after Afonso Henriques had captured the town with the aid of the Crusaders. The architects, it is believed, were the Frenchmen Robert and Bernard who designed Coimbra Cathedral. Remodelling followed the earthquake of 1755 when the chancel collapsed. Much of its former Romanesque appeal can be seen on the façade and in the nave, although Gothic features and the remodelling of the 17C and 18C are still apparent.

In the **interior**, the nave, supported by wide arches and graceful groined vaulting, is in plain Romanesque style. An elegant triforium runs above the aisles and the transept. The Bartolomeu Joanes Chapel, off the north aisle, containing a lovely terracotta crib by Machado de Castro, is Gothic in style.

The chancel, with its groined vaulting, was rebuilt in the 18C, but the ambulatory, pierced with lancet windows, kept the earlier Gothic style of the 14C when it was remodelled. The third chapel on the south side contains the 14C **Gothic tombs**★ of Lopo Fernandes Pacheco, companion in arms to King Afonso IV, and his wife. Note an elegant Romanesque wrought iron **grille**★ enclosing a chapel near the entrance to the cloisters.

The rather damaged **cloisters** are in the late-13C style of Cistercian Gothic: the lower gallery is supported alternately by massive buttresses and Gothic arches, above which are star-shaped oculi. The chapter-house contains the tomb of Lisbon's first bishop. Excavations in the garden of the cloisters have led to the discovery of vestiges from the Phoenician (8C BC) and Roman periods, as well as the ruins of a former mosque (9C and 10C).

Treasury★
Access to the treasury on the right, near the entrance to the cathedral. ⓒOpen 10am-5pm. ⓒClosed Sun and holidays. ⬭€2.50.
A staircase leads to a series of rooms displaying magnificent vestments, reliquaries and gold and silver plate. The impressive 18C chapter room contains the **King Dom José I monstrance**, richly decorated with 4 120 precious stones.

Not far from the cathedral stands the **Igreja de Santo António da Sé** which was built in 1812 on the site of the house in which St Anthony of Padua (1195-1231), known to the city's inhabitants as Saint Anthony of Lisbon, was born. He is Lisbon's patron saint and a small museum, the **Museu Antoniano**, *(ⓒOpen 10am-1pm and 2-6pm. ⓒClosed Mon and holidays. ⬭€1.25 ☎ 218 86 04 47)*, testifies to his popularity.

Miradouro de Santa Luzia★
A small terrace near the Igreja de Santa Luzia has been laid out as a lookout point on the remains of the old Arab fortifications. It affords an excellent **view**★★ of the Tagus, the harbour and, just below, the Alfama quarter, a maze of alleys from which rise the belfries of São Miguel and São Estêvão. The outer walls of the Igreja de Santa Luzia are covered with small panels of *azulejos*, one of which shows Praça do Comércio and another Lisbon's capture by the Crusaders and the death of Martim Moniz in the Castelo de São Jorge. *Azulejos* covering a wall marking the south edge of the square show a general view of Lisbon.

Largo das Portas do Sol★
The Sun Gateway was one of the seven gates into the Arab city. The square, situated on the other side of the Church of Santa Luzia, has a pleasant small esplanade which offers a wonderful **view**★★ over the rooftops, São Vicente de Fora and the river.

Museu de Artes Decorativas – Fundação Ricardo Espírito Santo da Silva★★
Largo das Portas do Sol, 2. ⓒOpen 10am-5pm. ⓒClosed Mon, 1 Jan, Good Fri, 1 May and 25 Dec. ⬭€5. ☎ 218 88 46 00 www.fress.pt.
The former palace of the Counts of Azurara (17C) and the wonderful collections it contains were bequeathed to the city of Lisbon by Ricardo Espírito Santo Silva. The museum brings to life the Lisbon of the 17C and 18C through a series of small, intimate rooms decorated with *azulejos* and frescoes on three floors. Level 4 (second floor) is quite elegant, while Level 3 displays interiors with a plainer, yet no less handsome, decorative touch. The Portuguese and Indo-Portuguese furniture is particularly interesting; there are also collections of silver, Chinese porcelain and several tapestries from the 16C and 18C.
Starting from Largo das Portas do Sol, take the steps down from **Rua Norberto de Araújo**, which are supported on one side by the Moorish town wall.

Igreja de São Miguel
Although the church is medieval in origin, it was rebuilt after the earthquake. It contains some fine Baroque woodwork.

Largo de São Rafael
On the west side of this small square surrounded by 17C houses, there still stands the remains of a **tower** which formed part of the Arab wall and later the defences of Christian Lisbon until the 14C when King Fernando had a new wall built.

Rua da Judiaria (Jewish Quarter)

In this street stands a 16C **house** with paired windows, above the fortification of the old Arab wall.

Rua de São Pedro and Rua dos Remédios

These are the busiest trading streets in the Alfama, lined with small shops and taverns. Rua de São Pedro is at its liveliest in the morning when its fish market is held. At the top of Rua dos Remédios, note on the left-hand side the Manueline door on the Igreja do Santo Espírito. Farther along, at number 2 Calçadinha de Santo Estêvão, another doorway from the same period can be seen.

Fish market, Rua de São Pedro

Escadinhas de Santo Estêvão★

The harmonious interplay of stairs, terrace and architecture make this one of the Alfama's most picturesque spots. As you head behind the Igreja de Santo Estêvão, note a balcony and a panel of *azulejos*. Climb the stairs which skirt alongside the church. At the top you have a fine **view**★ over the rooftops to the harbour and Tagus.

Beco de Carneiro

An extremely narrow street with very steep steps. At the bottom of the street to the right you will see a **public washing-place**. Look behind you for a fine view of the façade of the Igreja de Santo Estêvão.

Beco das Cruzes

At the corner of this street and Rua de Regueira stands an 18C house where the overhanging upper floors are supported by carved corbels. Above one of the doors a panel of *azulejos* shows the Virgin of Conception; from the same spot there is a view up the alley to where it is crossed by an arch surmounted by a cross.

▶ *Take Beco de Santa Helena back up to Largo das Portas do Sol.*

▶ *Take Travessa de Santa Luzia, which leads to the castle.*

Castelo de São Jorge★★

🕒*Open 9am-9pm (Nov-Feb until 6pm)* €3 ☎ *218 80 06 20.*

The castle stands high above the city in a remarkable position. Built by the Visigoths in the 5C, enlarged by the Moors in the 9C and then modified during the reign of Afonso Henriques, it has since been turned into a shaded flower garden. After passing through the outer wall you reach the former parade ground from where there is a magnificent **view**★★★ of the Tagus.

The castle's ten towers are linked by huge battlemented walls. Once through the barbican at the castle entrance, steps lead to the parapet walk and the towers which provide **viewpoints** over the town. In the north wall there is a door where the Portuguese knight **Martim Moniz** lost his life as he prevented the Moors from shutting the gate while Afonso Henriques was making his attack.

The Royal Palace, **Paço Real**, built on the site of a former Arab palace, was used as the royal residence by the kings of Portugal from the 14 to 16C.

Around the Alfama

The following sights can all be reached on tram no 28.

Mosteiro de São Vicente de Fora

○*Open 9am-6pm.* ○*Closed Mon, 1 Jan, Easter Sun and 25 Dec.* ⊘€4. ☏ *218 88 56 52.*

This monastery church was built by the Italian architect Phillippe Terzi between 1582 and 1627. Its name Fora, meaning beyond the wall, derives from the fact that, when it was built, it was outside the city walls.

The interior, covered with a fine coffered vault, is outstanding for the simplicity of its lines. On the south side of the church, the **cloisters** have walls covered in 18C **azulejos**★ illustrating the *Fables* of La Fontaine. Galleries lead to the former monks' refectory which, after the reign of Dom João IV, was transformed into a pantheon for the House of Bragança.

Campo de Santa Clara★

The attractive square between the churches of São Vicente and Santa Engrácia is the setting on Tuesdays and Saturdays for the **Feira da Ladra**, a colourful flea-market. On the northern side of the square stands the graceful 18C **Palácio Lavradio**. The small **Jardim Boto Machado** offers a haven of peace and tranquillity amid its exotic plants.

Igreja de Santa Engrácia ★

○*National pantheon open 10am-5pm.* ○*Closed Mon, 1 Jan, Easter Sun, 1 May and 25 Dec.* ⊘€2 *(no charge on Sun and holidays until 2pm).* ☏ *218 88 15 29.*

Begun in the 17C the church was never completed. In the form of a Greek cross, it is now surmounted by a cupola inaugurated in 1966 which completes the Baroque façade. The church houses the cenotaphs of six great Portuguese men: Luís de Camões, Prince Henry the Navigator, Pedro Álvares Cabral, Vasco da Gama, Afonso de Albuquerque and Nuno Álvares Pereira.

Graça

This popular residential district, where several villas from the last century can still be seen, is situated on the hill to the north of the city, overlooking the Alfama.

Igreja and Convento de Nossa Senhora da Graça

This imposing religious complex on the Graça hill dominates the city. The church and convent were founded in the 13C, but have been rebuilt on a number of occasions, particularly after the earthquake in 1755. Note the bell-tower from 1738 next to the convent doorway. The interior is Baroque and contains fine 17C and 18C *azulejos*. Opposite the church there is a belvedere with an extensive **view**★ over the city.

Miradouro da Senhora do Monte

This vantage point offers an extensive **view**★★★ over Lisbon and in particular over the Castelo de São Jorge and the Mouraria quarter. The chapel next to the belvedere dates from 1796, although its origins can be traced back to 1147, the year of Lisbon's reconquest.

Igreja da Conceição Velha

The **south side**★ of the transept, the only remains of the original church which collapsed in the earthquake of 1755, is a fine example of the Manueline style. The carving on the tympanum shows Our Lady of Compassion sheltering with her cloak Pope Leo X, Dom Manuel, Dona Leonor, bishops and others.

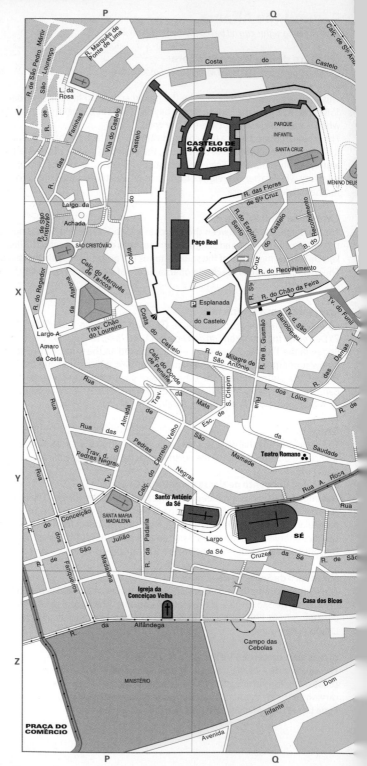

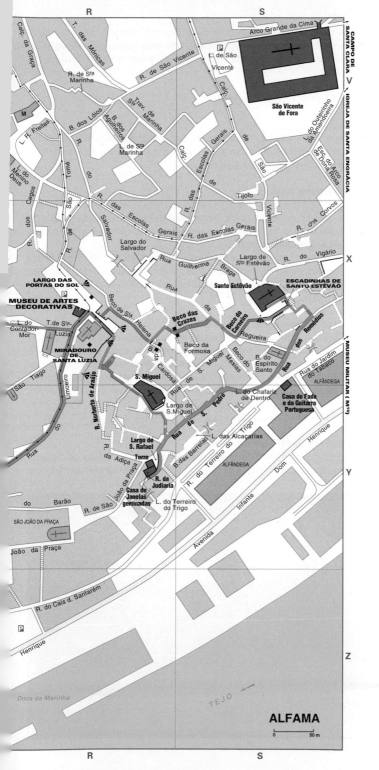

ALFAMA

0   50 m

Casa dos Bicos

This **House of Facets**, faced with diamond-shaped bosses, once formed part of a 16C palace, damaged in the 1755 earthquake. It belonged to the son of Afonso de Albuquerque, the viceroy of India. It lost its entire top floor, but it was rebuilt in 1982.

The Port and the Tagus

Porto de Lisboa

The port is one of the busiest in Europe extending over some 20km/12mi along the bank of the Tagus from Algés to Sacavém. Agricultural products, essentially wine and cork, are shipped abroad through the port.

Boat trips on the Tagus★

The trips give a good view of Lisbon and its surroundings and the harbour where, in addition to the commercial traffic, Venetian style barges with large triangular sails may sometimes be seen. In the summer, some boats offer excursions along the coast between Lisbon and Cascais.

The crossing of the estuary in one of the regular ferries makes a pleasant trip as well as giving fine **views**★★ of the city. Approaching Lisbon by boat at Terreiro do Paço is a wonderful experience, providing the visitor with the feeling of having entered the very heart of the city.

Ponte Vasco da Gama ★★

This magnificent road bridge was built across the Tagus between 1995 and 1998, to alleviate traffic congestion on the 25 de Abril bridge. The gently curving bridge is 18km/11mi long, 10km/6mi of which passes over water. At its lowest point, the bridge has the illusion of balancing directly on the Tagus. This superb feat of engineering is made up of several sections supported on pillars, some of which rise to 150m/490ft and are buried to a depth of 95m/310ft. The height of the superstructure varies from 14m/46ft to 30m/94ft to enable shipping to pass beneath it.

Parque das Nações (Expo'98 site)

The site which hosted Expo'98 is spread out along the Tagus in front of the Doca dos Olivais to the east of the city. It has a plethora of bars, restaurants, gardens and

Estação do Oriente

shops. There are twenty or so works by contemporary Portuguese and foreign artists including João Cutileiro in the Passeio das Tágides, an immense iron oxide-coated steel sculpture by Jorge Vieira; stone paving by Fernando Conduto, works by Pedro Cabrita Reis and Pedro Calapez, and stone-paving by Pedro Proença.

Estação do Oriente ★
This work by the Spanish architect Santiago Calatrava is covered by a strong yet delicate arborescent steel and glass structure which provides the building with an abundance of natural light. This intermodal complex houses a railway station, a metro and a suburban and regional bus terminal.

The Wellington Plate
The Portuguese government offered a sumptuous 1 000-piece service of banquet silver to the Duke of Wellington in gratitude for his delivery of the nation from French invaders. The service was made in the Lisbon Arsenal to designs by the court painter Domingos António Sequeira. It took 142 craftsmen the better part of five years to complete. Pieces from the service, including the 26ft-long centrepiece, are on display in Apsley House in London and were regularly used by the duke for the Waterloo banquets. The Museu Nacional de Arte Antiga has some of the drawings.

Oceanário de Lisboa ★★
Kids ⏱Open daily, 10am-6pm (7pm in summer). €10 (children under 12 €5). ☎ 218 91 70 02; www.oceanario.pt.
Designed by the American architect Peter Chermayeff, Europe's largest aquarium has five main tanks providing an introduction to the natural habitats of the Arctic, Indian, Pacific and Atlantic Oceans. In total over 15 000 marine animals and 250 species of plants are exhibited here. Visitors are plunged deep into the marine world with its sounds and smells on a tour around the enormous 5 000m^3/176 570cu ft main tank, representing the high seas, as grouper, rays, different species of shark and shoals of mackerel glide past. On a journey both above and underwater, visitors are transported to the coastline of Antarctica to view the acrobatic feats of cormorants and penguins, to the temperate Pacific with its lazy sea-otters, and to the waters of the Tropics, with its explosion of colours and superb coral reefs.

Pavilhão Atlântico (former Utopia Pavilion)
This impressive arena shaped like an upturned ship with an exposed wooden internal framework has a capacity of 16 000 and is used as a venue for sports events, concerts and conferences.

Torre Vasco da Gama
This tower, situated at the far end of the park, is a belvedere with views of the Tagus and surrounds. Other facilities include the "O Nobre" panoramic restaurant.

The **Jardin da Água** Kids section of the park area is a fun and leisure area with a water-based theme. Many statues can be found among the fountains and jets of water – most enjoyable.

The attractive **Jardim Garcia da Orta** in front of the Olivais dock, alongside the Tagus, takes its name from the 16C doctor who studied and classified Asiatic plants. The vegetation contained within the gardens is from regions visited by the Portuguese during the period of the Great Discoveries. At night, concerts are held on the Praça Sony, at the Palco da Doca, in the Pavilhão Atlântico and in the park's numerous bars and restaurants.

Museu Nacional do Azulejo (Convento da Madre de Deus) ★★

Rua da Madre de Deus, 4. 🕐*Open 10am-6pm; Tues, 2-6pm.* 🚫*Closed Mon, 1 Jan, Good Fri, Easter Sun, 1 May and 25 Dec.* €3 *(no charge Sun 10am-2pm).* ☎ *218 14 77 47 - www.mnazulejos-ipmuseus.pt. See also Introduction, Azulejos.*

Despite its location in a relatively unattractive area alongside the port, this museum is well worth a visit. The history of *azulejos,* from 15C Hispano-Moorish tiles to those of today, is elegantly presented in the monastic buildings of the Convento da Madre de Deus, founded in the 16C and largely rebuilt after the earthquake. The galleries on the ground floor are arranged around the cloisters and display examples of *azulejos* imported from Seville during the 15C and 16C; these are predominantly of Italian majolica style. Particularly worthy of note is the altarpiece of Nossa Senhora da Vida (1580) depicting a nativity scene.

Leave the cloisters and enter the church through a low choir, whose walls have preserved their 16C Seville *azulejos.* The 18C **church**★★, and the Baroque altar in particular, is resplendent with gilded woodwork. The nave has a coffered vault with panels painted to illustrate scenes from the Life of the Virgin; high on the walls paintings represent the lives of St Clare and St Francis; the lower parts of the walls are covered with 18C Dutch tiles.

Before heading upstairs, pass through the delightful small **Manueline cloisters** adorned with their original 16C and 17C coloured *azulejos.* The splendour and opulence of the chapel dedicated to St Anthony, and the **chapter-house**★ in particular, is impressive. Of particular note amid this rich decoration are the panels in the ceiling with gilt frames set with 16C and 17C paintings including portraits of King João III and his queen, Catherine of Austria, attributed to Cristóvão Lopes. The walls are adorned with paintings of the Life of Christ.

In the great cloisters admire the famous **panoramic view of Lisbon** prior to the earthquake – a fine blue and white composition of 1 300 *azulejos,* 23m/75ft in length.

Museu da Água da EPAL ★

Rua do Alviela 12 🕐*Open 10am-6pm.* 🚫*Closed Sun and holidays.* €2.50 *(no charge on 22 Mar, 18 May and 1 and 5 June).* ☎ *218 10 02 15 - www.museudagua-epal.pt.*

The museum traces the history of water supply to Lisbon and more particularly of the Águas Livres (Free Water) project drawn up by the engineer Manuel de Maia. Attempts to bring water to Lisbon from springs at the foot of the Serra de Sintra had begun in 1571, but it wasn't until 1732 that the aqueduct was started (completed in 1748). The water ran into the Mão d'Água des Amoreiras reservoir and was then channelled to the town's fountains and pipes. In 1880 the third link in the chain, the Barbadinhos pumping station, was built. The combined system supplied the town with water for almost 250 years until 1967.

Museu Militar

🕐*Open 10am-5pm.* 🚫*Closed Mon and holidays.* €2.50. ☎ *218 84 24 87.*

This former 18C arsenal on the banks of the Tagus has preserved its outstanding woodwork as well as *azulejos* and interesting **ceilings**★ mainly illustrating battle scenes. Models, paintings and in particular numerous weapons from the 16C to the late 19C, some manufactured on the spot, recall Portugal's military past.

Museu Nacional de Arte Antiga★★★

Rua das Janelas Verdes. 🕐*Open 10am-6pm; Tues, 2-6pm.* 🚫*Closed Mon, 1 Jan, Good Fri, Easter Sun, 1 May and 25 Dec.* €3 *(no charge Sun before 2pm).* ☎ *213 91 28 00.*

The Museum of Ancient Art, housed in the 17C palace of the Counts of Alvor and in an annexe built in 1940, has an outstanding collection of paintings, sculptures and decorative arts from the 12C to the early 19C, reflecting the history of Portugal. The main wealth of the museum lies in the Portuguese Primitives of which the major work is the famous **polyptych**★★★ of the Adoration of St Vincent painted between

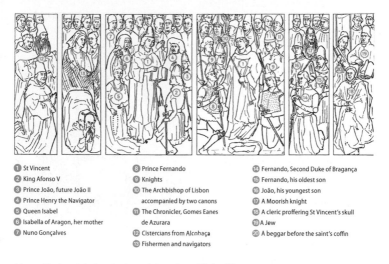

① St Vincent
② King Afonso V
③ Prince João, future João II
④ Prince Henry the Navigator
⑤ Queen Isabel
⑥ Isabella of Aragon, her mother
⑦ Nuno Gonçalves

⑧ Prince Fernando
⑨ Knights
⑩ The Archbishop of Lisbon
    accompanied by two canons
⑪ The Chronicler, Gomes Eanes
    de Azurara
⑫ Cistercians from Alcobaça
⑬ Fishermen and navigators

⑭ Fernando, Second Duke of Bragança
⑮ Fernando, his oldest son
⑯ João, his youngest son
⑰ A Moorish knight
⑱ A cleric proffering St Vincent's skull
⑲ A Jew
⑳ A beggar before the saint's coffin

Museu Nacional de Arte Antiga – Adoration of Saint Vincent

1460 and 1470 by Nuno Gonçalves. The panels of this previously unknown work were discovered in an attic in the monastery of São Vicente da Fora in 1882.

The masterly **Annunciation**★ by Frei Carlos (1523), is a remarkable example of Luso-Flemish painting. Among other Portuguese works are the *Cook Triptych* by Grão Vasco and the *Martyrdom of the Eleven Thousand Virgins* from the Igreja da Madre de Deus. It is an unsigned work showing the arrival in Portugal of the relics of Santa Auta which were given by the Holy Roman Emperor Maximilian I to his cousin Dona Leonor in 1509.

Notable among the paintings from other European schools is the extraordinary **Temptation of St Anthony**★★★ by Hieronymus Bosch. Mention should also be made of the *Virgin and Child* by Memling, *St Jerome* by Dürer, *Virgin, Child and Saints* by Hans Holbein the Elder and the **Twelve Apostles**★ by Zurbarán.

Museu Nacional de Arte Antiga – J. Pessoa/ANF-IPM

Japanese Namban screen (detail)

One of the rooms contains precious **Nambans** or **Japanese screens**★★ showing the arrival of the Portuguese on the island of Tane-ga-Shima in 1543. The Japanese called the Portuguese *Namban-jin* meaning barbarians from the south (they had approached Japan from the south) and the art that ensued came to be known as Namban.

There is also a rich collection of gold and silver plate, the finest of which is the **monstrance from the Mosteiro de Belém** (1506) attributed to Gil Vicente who, it is believed, made it from gold brought from the Indies by Vasco da Gama. The newer section of the museum houses the **chapel**★ from the former Carmelite Convent of Santa Alberto, outstanding for its gilded woodwork and its 16C-18C *azulejos*.

Panel of Polyptych of St Vincent
Museu Nacional de Arte Antiga, Lisbon

MNAA – P. Ferreira/ANF-IPM

Museu das Marionetas – Puppet Museum

Rua da Esperança, 146 (Convento das Bernardas). 🧒 ⏱*Open 10am-1pm; 2pm-6pm* ⬤*€2.50.* ☎ *213 94 28 10 - www.egeac.pt. Advance reservations are essential.*

Located in a beautiful Cistercian monastery this museum has traditional puppet shows by the São Lourenço company, as well as many older examples of puppets. The museum offers activities for children in English, French and Portuguese.

Docks

The dock area along the river was formerly occupied by warehouses and river facilities. It has recently been transformed into a fashionable district with a multitude of bars, restaurants and discos for every taste. It is a pleasant place for a stroll in the late-afternoon, or at night when activity is at its liveliest.

Cristo Rei

Leave Lisbon by ② *on the map. 3.5km/2mi from the south toll gate of the 25 de Abril suspension bridge, turn left at motorway exit 1 towards Almada. Then follow the signs and leave the car in the car park near the monument.* ⏱*Open 9.30am-8pm.* ⬤*€4 (€2 for children).* ☎ *212 75 10 00.*

The enormous statue of Christ in Majesty (28m/92ft high) was erected in 1959 to thank God for having spared Portugal during the Second World War. It is a slightly smaller replica of the statue of Christ the Redeemer in Rio de Janeiro. From the pedestal *(access by lift; plus 74 steps)* which is 85m/279ft above ground level and 113m/371ft over the Tagus, there is a **panoramic view**★★ of the Tagus estuary, the old quarters of Lisbon and the plain to the south as far as Setúbal.

Belém★★ *Allow one day.*

It was from Belém (Portuguese for Bethlehem) that sailing ships set forth to brave the ocean and discover hitherto unknown lands and continents.

▶ *Starting from Praça do Comércio, either drive alongside the Tagus or take tram number 15 to Belém.*

Mosteiro dos Jerónimos★★★

Open 10am-6pm (summer); 10am-5pm rest of year . *Closed Monday; Jan 1; Good-Friday, Easter Day, 1 May, 25 Dec.* ☎ *213 62 00 34. You are specifically asked to respect the religious services.*

In 1502, on the site of a former hermitage founded by Prince Henry the Navigator, the King, Dom Manuel, undertook to build this magnificent Hieronymite monastery, considered to be the jewel of Manueline art. This style of art glorified the great discoveries; in this case that of Vasco da Gama who, on his return from the Indies, had moored his caravels in Restelo harbour near Belém. The architects of the monastery, benefiting from the riches then pouring into Lisbon, were able to throw themselves into an ambitious, large-scale work. The Gothic style adopted by the Frenchman Boytac until his death in 1517 was modified by his successors who added ornamentation typical of the Manueline style with its diverse influences: João de Castilho, of Spanish origin, added a Plateresque form to the decoration, Nicolas Chanterene emphasised the Renaissance element, while Diogo de Torralva and Jérôme de Rouen, at the end of the 16C, brought in a Classical note.

Igreja de Santa Maria★★★

Open 10am-5pm (6.30pm in summer). No visits during religious services. Closed Mon, 1 Jan, Good Fri, Easter Sun, 1 May and 25 Dec.

The **south door**, the work of Boytac and João de Castilho, combines a mass of gables, pinnacles and niches filled with statues. Crowning all is a canopy surmounted by the Cross of the Order of the Knights of Christ.

The **west door**, sheltered beneath the 19C porch which leads to the cloisters, is by Nicolas Chanterene and is adorned with fine statues, particularly those of King Manuel and Queen Maria. Represented above the doorway are the Annunciation, the Nativity and the Adoration of the Magi.

The **interior** is outstanding for the beauty of the stonework, carved throughout in great detail but never obscuring the architectural lines, as, for instance, in the network **vaulting**★★ of equal height over the nave and aisles.

This vaulting withstood the 1755 earthquake. The decoration on the pillars and the vaulting over the transept crossing are by João de Castilho. The transepts are

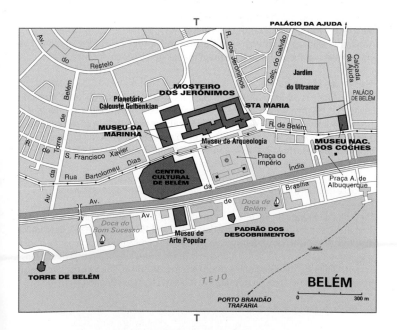

Y. Travert/ PHOTONONSTOP

Cloisters, Mosteiro dos Jerónimos

Baroque, designed by Jérôme de Rouen, and contain the tombs of several princes. In the chancel, reconstructed in the Classical period, are the tombs of Dom Manuel I and Dom João III, with their queens. Beneath the gallery of the *coro alto* at the entrance to the church are the neo-Manueline tombs of Vasco da Gama and also Camões, whose recumbent figure wears a crown of laurel leaves.

Cloisters★★★
🕑*Same opening times as the church above.* ⊜€3 (no charge Sun 10am-2pm). ☎ 213 62 00 34.
This masterpiece of Manueline art is fantastically rich in sculpture. The stone is at its most beautiful when it takes on the golden tint of the late afternoon sun. The cloisters, forming a hollow square of which each side measures 55m/170ft, are two storeys high. The ground level galleries with groined vaulting by Boytac have wide arches with tracery resting upon slender columns, and Late Gothic and Renaissance decoration carved into the massive thickness of the walls. The chapter-house contains the tomb of the writer Alexandre Herculano.
A staircase leads to the church's **coro alto** with another view of the vaulting. The graceful Renaissance stalls carved out of maple are by Diogo de Carça.

Museu da Marinha ★★
🕑*Open 1 June to 30 Sept, 10am-6pm (5pm the rest of the year).* 🕑*Closed Mon and holidays.* ⊜€3 (free Sunday before 1pm). ☎ 213 62 00 19 - www.museumarinha.pt.
This museum, containing a remarkable collection of **models**★★★ of seafaring craft over the centuries, is located on both sides of the esplanade of the **Calouste Gulbenkian planetarium** in two separate buildings: the west wing of the Mosteiro dos Jerónimos and the modern Pavilhão das Galeotas.

▶ *Once through the entrance, take the stairs in front of the door on the right.*

The Sala da Marinha de Recreio, a room dedicated to pleasure craft on the upper floor, includes a small collection of models of 18C and 19C yachts. The Sala da Marinha Mercante (Merchant Navy Room) recalls the history of merchant shipping in Portugal, with exhibits such as the *Santa Maria* and the *Infante Dom Henrique*, which transported soldiers to the ex-colonies, and the *Neiva* oil tanker. The Sala da Construção Naval at the far end takes an informative look at naval construction techniques.

▶ *Return to the main floor.*

Main building

Giant sandstone statues of historical figures (including Henry the Navigator) and ancient cannon can be seen in the entrance hall. On the ground floor there is an immense room devoted to the Discoveries and the Navy, from the 15C to the 18C, with maps and magnificent models of sailing ships, caravels and frigates, including the 18C vessel, the *Príncipe da Beira*. There are displays of figureheads and navigational instruments such as 15C astrolabes. Warships of the 19C and 20C can also be seen (small-scale models of gunboats, frigates and corvettes, and modern submarines) as well as a fishing fleet (the Henrique Seixas Collection) with models of various boats which used to fish in the estuaries or along the coast: a *muleta* from Seixal with its many sails, a *calão* from the Algarve, a *galeão* from Nazaré. Models of boats used for river navigation include frigates of the Tagus and *rabelos* of the Douro. In the last room there is a reconstruction of the royal stateroom of the yacht *Amélia* (late 19C).

Planetário Calouste Gulbenkian (Planetarium)

Praça Império, Belém – Kids ⏱*Open Sat-Sun 11am-3.30pm – Special shows for children Sun 11am.* €4. ☎ *213 62 00 02 - www.plantario.online.pt.*

A special show looking at Portugal's starry skies, an imaginary voyage through the planetary system, a trip to the moon, a journey across the polar region, various films, plus eclipses of the sun and the moon – these are just some of the audio-visual adventures on offer at the Planetarium.

Museu do Design★

⏱*Open 11am-7pm (last entrance at 6.15pm).* ⏱*Closed Christmas Day.* €3.50. ☎ *213 61 24 00.*

Housed in a wing of the cultural centre, this new museum has been created to display the collection of Francisco Capelo, who has assembled works here from the Museu de Arte Moderna in Sintra. The collection consists of works by some 230 designers of furniture and other objects representing trends in design from around the world from 1937 to the present day. The museum is divided into four main sections: Interior Design, Modernism, Pop and Cool.

Padrão dos Descobrimentos – Monument of Discoveries

⏱*Open May-Sept 10am-7pm; Oct-Apr 10am-6pm (last enry 30min before closing time).* ⏱*Closed Mon and holidays.* €4. ☎ *213 03 19 50.*

The 52m/170ft Monument to the Discoveries by the sculptor Leopoldo de Almeida, erected in 1960 beside the Tagus on the 500th anniversary of the death of Prince Henry the Navigator, represents the prow of a ship with the prince pointing the way to a crowd of important figures. Among them, on the right side, are King Dom Manuel carrying an armillary sphere, Camões holding verses from *The Lusiads* and the painter, Nuno Gonçalves.

Torre de Belém ★★★

⏱*Open 10am-5pm (6pm in summer).* ⏱*Closed Mon, 1 Jan, Good Fri, Easter Sun, 1 May and 25 Dec.* €3. ☎ *213 62 00 38.*

This elegant Manueline tower was built between 1515 and 1519 in the middle of the Tagus to defend the river mouth and the Mosteiro dos Jerónimos. Today it stands at the water's edge on the north bank, the river having altered course during the earthquake in 1755.

It is an architectural gem; the Romanesque-Gothic structure is adorned with loggias like those in venice and small domes like those in Morocco where the tower's architect, Francisco de Arruda, had travelled.

On the keep terrace, facing the sea, is a statue of Our Lady of Safe Homecoming. The tower is five storeys high ending in a terrace. On the ground floor are openings through which prisoners were thrown into the dungeons below. On the third floor paired windows with elegant balconies, a magnificent Renaissance loggia surmounted by the royal arms

Y. Tavert/PHOTONONSTOP

Torre de Belém at night

of Manuel I and two armillary spheres mellow the ganite tower's original architectural severity. It looks particularly spectacular at night when fully floodlit (👁 *see photo*).

Palácio da Ajuda★

Guided tours (1hr 30min), 10am-5pm (last entrance at 4.30pm). ○Closed Wed, 1 Jan, all of February, Easter Sun, 1 May and 25 Dec. €4 (no charge Sun and holidays 10am-2pm). ☎ 213 63 70 95.

This former royal palace (18C-19C) to the north of Belém was built after the earth-quake, yet never completed. It was the residence of the Portuguese monarchs, Dom Luís and Dona Maria Pia, from 1862 onwards. Its two floors offer a succession of rooms with painted ceilings and an interior richly filled with furniture, tapestries, statues and decorative objects from the 20C.

At the top of the Calçada da Ajuda is the **Jardim Botânico da Ajuda**, which is con-nected to the romantic **Jardim das Damas** (18C) (*○Open 9am-6pm - summer until 8pm. ○Closed Wed. €1.50)* with its waterfalls and ponds. It was here that the ladies of the Court would enjoy pleasant strolls.

Around Avenida da Liberdade *Allow half a day.*

Avenida da Liberdade★

The Avenida da Liberdade is the most majestic of Lisbon's avenues. On either side late-19C buildings and more recent constructions house hotels and offices. The pavements are covered in black and white mosaics. To the north, the Avenida leads to the **Praça do Marquês de Pombal**, Lisbon's nerve centre, where several wide avenues converge. In the centre of this circular "square" stands a monument to the Marquis of Pombal.

▸ *Take Avenida Fontes Pereira de Melo then Avenida António Augusto de Aguiar on the left.*

Parque Eduardo VII★

This formal, elegant landscaped park, crowning Avenida da Liberdade, was named after King Edward VII of England on the occasion of his visit to Lisbon in 1902. There is a magnificent **vista**★ from the upper end of the park over the Baixa district and the Tagus, dominated on either side by the castle and the Bairro Alto hills.

Estufa fria★

○Open 9am-5.30pm (4.30pm 1 Oct to 21 Mar). ○Closed 1 Jan, 25 Apr, 1 May and 25 Dec. €1.20. ☎ 213 88 22 78.

Wooden shutters in the cold greenhouse provide protection from the extremes of summer heat and winter cold. The many exotic plants displayed grow beside fishponds or cooling waterfalls near small grottoes.

Gulbenkian Foundation

Calouste Gulbenkian, an Armenian oil magnate and patron of the arts born in Istanbul in 1869, was nicknamed "Mister 5%" on account of his five per cent share in the profits of the Iraq Petroleum Company. His keenness for collecting started at an early age with the acquisition of a few old coins, and was to lead to the creation of an outstanding collection of works of art over a period of forty years. On his death in 1955 he bequeathed his immense fortune to Portugal and a year later the Calouste Gulbenkian Foundation was set up. This is a private institution which runs its museums in Lisbon as well as an orchestra, a ballet company and a choir.

The foundation's headquarters, set in beautiful gardens, consist of a complex of modern buildings which house the Gulbenkian Museum, the Modern Art Centre, four multi-purpose lecture halls, of which one is open-air, a conference centre, two large galleries for art exhibitions and a library with 152 000 books.

Museu Calouste Gulbenkian ★★★

🕐*Open 10am-6pm.* 🕐*Closed Mon and holidays.* 🕭*€5 for the two museums in the Foundation.* ☏ *217 82 30 00 or 217 82 34 57.*

The museum was especially designed for the Gulbenkian collections which consist of selected exhibits of great value and beauty. They are particularly rich in Oriental and European art. The lower floor displays contemporary art exhibitions.

Ancient art

Ancient art section is represented by works from Egypt (an alabaster bowl about 2 700 years old; a stone statuette of "Judge Bes"; a bronze sun-boat; and a silver-gilt mask for a mummy dating from the 30th Dynasty), the Graeco-Roman world (a superb 5C BC Attic crater; jewellery; the head of a woman attributed to Phidias; iridescent Roman vases; and a magnificent collection of gold and silver coins) and Mesopotamia (9C BC Assyrian stele and a Parthian urn).

Near Eastern art

The finest pieces in the vast Near Eastern art collection are the pottery and carpets. The sumptuous woollen and silk carpets, mainly Persian from the 16C and 17C and the shimmering Prusa velvets from Turkey are especially beautiful. The pottery (12C-18C), silk costumes and lamps from the mosque of Alep are as finely worked as Persian miniatures. There are also collections of poetry, Korans and Armenian manuscripts.

Far Eastern art

Far Eastern art, primarily Chinese, is represented by magnificent porcelain (a 14C Taoist bowl; a 17C vase of the hundred birds) and "rough stones" (an 18C green nephrite bowl); Japanese exhibits include prints and a selection of lacquerware from the 18C and 19C.

European art

The **European art** section begins with **medieval religious art**, some beautiful carved **ivories**, illuminated manuscripts and books of hours. A section on **15C, 16C** and **17C painting** and **sculpture** follows: The *Presentation at the Temple* by the German artist **Stephan Lochner** was one of Gulbenkian's first acquisitions. The Flemish and Dutch schools are well represented with a *St Joseph* by **Van der Weyden**, an admirable *Annunciation* by **Dirk Bouts**, a magnificent *Old Man* by **Rembrandt** and a masterly *Portrait of Helen Fourment* by **Rubens**. From the Italian school there is a delightful *Portrait of a Young Woman* attributed to **Ghirlandaio**.

The 18C French school of painting, famous for its portraits and festive scenes, is represented here by **Lancret** *(Fête Galante)*, **Hubert Robert** *(Gardens of Versailles)*, **Quentin de la Tour** *(Portrait of Mademoiselle Sallé* and *Portrait of Duval de l'Epinoy)*, and **Nicolas de Largillière** *(Portrait of M. et Mme. Thomas-Germain)*. Among the sculptures note the proud **Diana** in white marble by Houdon.

Pendant by René Lalique

18C English painting includes works by **Gainsborough** (a lovely *Portrait of Mrs. Lowndes-Stone*), **Romney** *(Portrait of Miss Constable)*, **Turner** *(Quillebœuf)* and **Thomas Lawrence**.

A gallery on **Francesco Guardi** is hung with scenes of Venice.

The 19C French school is represented by **Henri Fantin-Latour** *(La Lecture)* the Impressionists, including **Manet** *(Boy with Cherries* and *Blowing Bubbles)*, **Degas** *(Self-portrait)*, and **Renoir** *(Portrait of Mme. Claude Monet)*, a number of canvases by **Corot** *(Bridge at Mantes,Willows)*, as well as a fine collection of bronzes *(Spring)* and marble sculptures *(Benedictions)* by **Rodin**.

In the last room there is an extraordinary collection of works and jewels from the Art Nouveau period by the French decorative artist **René Lalique** (1860-1945).

Centro de Arte Moderna★

⏱*Open 10am-6pm.* 🚫*Closed Mon and bank holidays.* ✉€3 (no charge Sun). ☎ 217 82 34 74.

The centre, which was built by the British architect Sir Leslie Martin in 1983, has a roomy design in which plants have been incorporated, giving the impression of a screen of greenery. It houses modern works by Portuguese artists from 1910 to the present. Among the artists represented are Vieira da Silva, Amadeo Souza-Cardoso, Almada Negreiros and Julio Pomar. Several sculptures, including the *Reclining Woman* by **Henry Moore**, are exhibited in the gardens surrounding the centre.

Around the Gulbenkian

Igreja de Nossa Senhora de Fátima

This modern church is adorned with beautiful **stained-glass windows**★ by Almada Negreiros.

Biblioteca Municipal

The library is housed in the 16C Galveias Palace opposite the neo-Moorish **bullring** at Campo Pequeno.

Amorairas

This district is dominated by the Torres das Amoreiras and the Aqueduto das Águas Livres. The name recalls the mulberry trees which existed here to produce silkworms used in the manufacture of silk.

Torres das Amoreiras

The famous pink, grey and black post-modern towers designed by the architect Tomás Taveira were completed in 1983. They are situated close to one of the entrances to the city and can be seen from afar. They comprise three floors, and contain offices, luxury apartments, restaurants and a large shopping centre (👣 *see Address Book for Lisbon: Shopping)*.

Fundação Arpad Szenes – Vieira da Silva★

⏱Open 11am-7pm. ⊘Closed Tues and holidays. ☞€2.50 (no charge Sun). ☎ 213 88 00 44 - www.fasvs.pt.

This foundation is located on one side of the leafy Praça das Amoreiras, next to the Águas Livres aqueduct. It is a fine 18C workshop which has been remodelled in a sober, elegant manner. Maria Helena Vieira da Silva (1908-92), who lived a great part of her life in Paris with the artist Arpad Szenes, is one of Portugal's most famous 20C artists. The museum displays a small collection of exhibits by the artists, as well as works donated by collectors and institutions.

Aqueduto das Águas Livres★

⏱Open 10am-6pm. ⊘Closed Sun, Dec to Feb and holidays. Free. ☎ 218 10 02 15.

The aqueduct built between 1732 and 1748 *(see Museu da Água)* measures a total of 58km/36mi, including all its ramifications. 34 of its arches stride across the Alcântara valley. The tallest is 65m/213ft high with a span of 29m/95ft. The best view of the aqueduct is from Avenida de Ceuta, north of the N 7 motorway bridge.

Mãe d'Água das Amoreiras

⏱Open 10am-6pm. ⊘Closed Sun and holidays. ☞€2.50 (no charge on 22 Mar, 18 May and 1 and 5 June). ☎ 218 10 02 15 - www.museudaagua.epal.pt.

Water from the Águas Livres aqueduct flows into the reservoir which is housed in a building completed in 1746. Inside, you can see the water flow and the Arca d'Água or "water arch" basin which has a depth of 7m/23ft and a capacity of about 5 500m³/194 433cu ft. Beside the building is the former recording station where the levels were recorded for the water to be channelled to the city's fountains. Today, it is a centre for exhibitions, concerts and plays.

Additional Sights

Casa-Museu Anastácio Gonçalves

⏱Open 10am-6pm (Tues 2pm-6pm). ⊘Closed Mon, 1 Jan, Easter Sun, 1 May and 25 Dec. ☞€2 (free Sun until 2pm) ☎ 213 54 08 23 - www.cmag-jpmuseus.pt.

This museum is housed in two villas formerly owned by the artist José Malhoa, and more recently by Dr Anastácio Gonçalves, a great patron of the arts and a friend of Gulbenkian. The first part of the museum is used to display temporary exhibitions predominantly devoted to early-20C Portuguese artists (modernists such as Columbano, Eduardo Viana, Amadeo de Souza Cardoso, Vieira da Silva and Mário Eloy, and naturalists including Silva Porto and Sousa Pinto). The permanent collection comprises ancient Chinese porcelain, furniture, textiles and jewellery, as well as an interesting set of drawings by Almada Negreiros.

Palácio dos Marqueses de Fronteira★★

Take the metro to Sete Rios, followed by a 20min walk along Rua das Furnas and Rua São Domingo de Benfica. ⏱Guided tours (45mn), June to Sept, daily except Sun, at 10.30am, 11am, 11.30am and noon; Oct to May, daily except Sun, at 11am and noon. Gardens open Mon-Fri 2pm-6.30pm. ⊘Closed public holidays. ☞€7.50 (gardens only €3). ☎ 217 78 20 23.

The palace, to the north of the Parque de Monsanto near Benfica, was built as a hunting lodge by João Mascarenhas, the first Marquis of Fronteira, in 1670.

While a strong Italian Renaissance influence is apparent, particularly in the layout of the gardens, the palace is one of the most beautiful Portuguese creations with its **azulejos**★★ of outstanding quality and variety. Inside the palace, the *azulejos* in the Victory Room depict the main events in the War of Restoration in which the first Marquis of Fronteira distinguished himself. The dining room is adorned with 17C Delft tiles, the first to be imported into Portugal. Outside, on the terraces and in the gardens, every conceivable flat surface has been decorated with small ceramic tiles. Some depict coun-

Gardens, Palácio de Fronteira

try scenes of the seasons and work in the fields, others more stately, solemn subjects like the twelve horsemen in the Kings' Gallery which are reflected in a pool.

Jardim Zoológico★★

Metro: Sete Rios. 🧒 🕐*Open Apr-Sept 10am-8pm (6pm Oct to Mar).* €11.50 *(children €9.50).* ☎ *217 23 29 10 - www.zoo.pt.*

The park, which is both a lovely garden and a zoo as well as a great place for children to play, is laid out in the 26ha/64 acres of the Parque das Laranjeiras, which includes the rose-coloured palace of the Counts of Farrobo, to the right of the entrance. The lower part includes the rose garden, a variety of other flowers and enclosures for the 2 500 animals, many of which are exotic species.

Also make sure you see the **Museu das Crianças** (Children's Museum), established in 2006, with interactive exhibits for children from 4-13yrs. *Near the main entrance* 🧒 🕐*Open Mon-Fri 10am-5pm; Sat-Sun 10am-6pm* €2. ☎ *217 26 80 82.*

Parque Florestal de Monsanto ★

🧒 🕐*Open Mon-Fri 9.30am-5pm; Sat 9am-6pm; Sun 2pm-7pm.* €2. ☎ *217 71 09 91.*

This hilly, wooded park of 1 000 hectares is dissected by roads giving panoramic **views**★ of Lisbon, particularly from the Monsanto belvederes. The park contains several small parks that are ideal for children – the Parqu Alvito has plenty of games and two swimming pools for children 3-14yrs *(open July-Sept)*; and the Parque dos Índios, for children aged 4-12yrs, one of the most popular places in Lisbon for youngsters.

Museu da Música★

🕐*Open 10am-6pm.* 🕐*Closed Sun and Mon.* .€2. ☎ *217 71 09 91.*

The small museum, located inside the Alto dos Moinhos metro station, contains a wide variety of musical instruments and publications from the 16C-20C, including a set of Baroque harpsichords and a large collection of string and wind instruments.

Basílica da Estrela★

Tram number 28.

The white Baroque edifice was built at the end of the 18C. Inside, the transept crossing is covered by a fine **cupola** topped by a lantern tower. Note also a Christmas crib with life-size figures carved by Machado de Castro.

The **Jardim da Estrela**★ opposite the basilica is one of the most beautiful gardens in Lisbon with its varied display of exotic plants and trees.

Casa Fernando Pessoa

Rua Coelho da Rocha, 16-18. Open Mon-Fri (except holidays) 10am-6pm (8pm Thurs). Free. ☎ 213 96 81 90; www.casaf-ernandopessoa.com.

The house where the poet Pessoa spent the last 15 years of his life has been refurbished and now serves as a cultural centre specialising in Portuguese poetry as well as an exhibition centre for painting and sculpture. The works of Pessoa and his archives are also assembled here.

Brasiliera and statue of Pessoa

Museu da Cidade

Campo Grande, 345. Metro: Campo Grande. Open 10am-1pm; 2pm-6pm. Closed public holidays. €2.50 ☎ 217 51 32 00.

The municipal museum stands above Campo Grande – unfortunately near the motorway interchange – in the graceful 18C Palácio Pimenta built during Dom João V's luxurious reign. The different stages in the history of Lisbon may be traced through Roman, Visigothic, Arab and medieval remains. The emblem of the city, a caravel transporting the body of St Vincent guided by ravens, may be seen on the many coats of arms displayed. A model of Lisbon in the early 18C gives an idea of the city before the earthquake as do the *azulejos* of Terreiro do Paço square showing the Royal Palace still in place. The palace kitchens are adorned with *azulejos* of country scenes. The first floor is devoted to ceramics and engravings of Lisbon. Note the famous *Fado* canvas by Malhoa.

Museu Rafael Bordalo Pinheiro

Campo Grande, 382. Metro: Campo Grande. Open 10am-6pm. Closed Mon. €2 (no charge Sun). ☎ 217 59 08 16.

The museum, which stands across the Campo Grande from the Museu da Cidade, contains collections of drawings, caricatures and particularly **ceramics**★ by Rafael Bordalo Pinheiro (1846-1905). He was a prolific artist and together with his brother and sister had some influence on social life in Lisbon at the end of the 19C.

Museu Nacional do Traje★

Open 10.am-6pm. Closed Mon, 1 Jan, Good Fri, Easter Sun, 1 May and 25 Dec. €3, including entrance to Museu Nacional do Teatro (no charge Sun 10am-2pm). ☎ 217 59 03 18.

The graceful palace of the Marquis of Angeja now holds outstanding costume exhibitions. The beautifully presented collections bring a whole era, or a town or profession, to life, through the art of dress.

The palace of Monteiro-Mor, which was rebuilt after a fire, now houses the **Museu Nacional do Teatro** (*Open Wed-Sun 10am-6pm; Tues 2-6pm. Closed Mon, 1 Jan, Easter day, 1 May and 25 Dec. €3, (including entrance to Museu Nacional do Traje) - free Sun 10am-2pm. ☎ 217 56 74 10)*, which holds temporary exhibitions on drama-related themes.

Below the palace, the attractive botanical gardens, **Jardim Botânico do Monteiro-Mor** (*Open 10am-5.30pm (7pm Apr to Sept). Closed Mon, 1 Jan, Easter Sun, 1 May and 25 Dec. €1.50 - free Sun and holidays 10am-2pm; ☎ 217 59 03 18)*, with their pools and a rich variety of plants, lie in a wild, hilly setting.

PALÁCIO AND CONVENTO DE MAFRA★★

LISBOA

MICHELIN MAP 733 – MICHELIN ATLAS SPAIN & PORTUGAL P 58 (P 2)

Mafra monastery stands some 40km/25mi northwest of Lisbon. Its impressive size and Baroque style, in which marble proliferates, testify to the rich reign of King João V who, having no children after three years of marriage, vowed to build a monastery if God would grant him an heir. A daughter, Barbara, was born, later to become Queen of Spain. Work began in 1717 with 50,000 workers and artisans under a German architect, though the plans were drawn up by a group of Roman artists under the direction of the Marquis de Fontes, Portugal's ambassador to the Holy See. Originally planned for just 13 monks it ended up housing 300, together with the entire royal family (and their considerable staff). It has often been compared to the Escorial in Spain on account of its size, its proximity to the capital and the fact that it was built in fulfilment of a vow. At the same time it played the role of royal palace and religious centre. Its outward austerity is softened by Baroque decoration. *Av. 25 de Abril – 2640-456 – ☎ 261 81 41 04*

▶ **Orient Yourself:** 40km/25mi north-west of Lisbon: take the A8 then N116.
🍴 **Don't Miss:** The Basilica and the library in the Palace.
🕐 **Organizing Your Time:** Spend a full morning in the palace, then have lunch on the coast at Ereiceira.
👣 **Also See:** Sintra, to the south, driving through some lovely countryside.

The Mafra School

While the monastery was under construction, João V took advantage of the presence of so many foreign artists at Mafra to found a school of sculpture. The first principal was the Italian, Alessandro Giusti, and among the teachers were such men as José Almeida, Giovanni Antonio of Padua, who carved the main statues in the cathedral at Évora and, particularly, **Joaquim Machado de Castro** (1731-1822). The total number of students who attended this school is unknown but certainly their work spread far and wide and a great many works of sacred art from this renowned school can be found throughout Europe.

Visit *1hr 30min*

Basilica 🕐Open 10am-1pm; 2pm-5pm: Palace/Convent - guided tour (1hr15min) daily except Tue 10am-5pm. Last entry 1hr before closing time. 🕐Closed Sundays, Good Friday, May 1 and Dec 25. €4, free Sun and holidays 10am-2pm. ☎261 81 75 50.
The 220m/722ft long façade is flanked at either end by Germanic-style wings surmounted by bulbous domes. The basilica stands in the centre of the façade.

Basílica★★

The basilica, with its flanking wings, is built of marble, its façade breaking the monotony of the main face by its whiteness and Baroque decoration. The towers (68m/223ft tall) are joined by a double row of columns; niches high up contain Carrara marble statues of St Dominic and St Francis and below of St Clare and St Elizabeth of Hungary.
The church **interior** is strikingly elegant in its proportions and in the marble ornamentation. The rounded vaulting rests upon fluted pilasters which divide the lateral

chapels, each of which contains statues and an altarpiece in white marble with a low-relief carved by sculptors from the Mafra School. The jasper and marble altarpieces in the transept chapels and the chancel pediment are also by the Mafra School. Note especially the fine marble altarpiece of the Virgin and Child in the chapel off the north aisle and the sacristy and lavabo where marble of every description may be seen. Four delicately worked arches at the transept crossing support a magnificent rose and white marble **cupola**★ which rises to a height of 70m/230ft. The bronze candelabra and six fine organs dating from 1807 are also remarkable.

Palace and Monastery

Guided tours available by prior arrangement – ☎ *261 81 44 16.*

The tour proceeds through a museum of comparative sculpture, the monks' infirmary, the pharmacy, the kitchens and a museum of sacred art.

On the second floor, the royal apartments form a long succession of galleries, with the Queen's Pavilion at one end and the King's at the other.

The ceilings are painted and the rooms have been refurnished. The palace reached the height of its splendour at the beginning of the 19C under Dom João VI but when this king left for Brazil in 1807, he took with him some of the decorative items and furniture that had adorned Mafra.

The grandiose and harmoniously proportioned **Audience Room** (Sala da Bênção) gives onto the basilica. It was from this gallery with its columns and mouldings faced with coloured marble, that the royal family attended mass. The bust of Dom João V is by the Italian master, Alessandro Giusti.

The Trophy Room, the monks' cells and the beautiful **library**★ *(biblioteca)*, a hall 83.60m/274ft long, with magnificent rose, grey and white marble flooring are also of interest. The wooden bookshelves are Rococo in style and contain 40 000 works from the 14C to the 19C.

Library, Convento de Mafra

Additional Sight

Igreja de Santo André

⊙Visits by prior arrangement with the Casa da Cultura. ☎ 261 81 51 12. – In the old town (vila velha).

Built in the late 13C, this small church in the old town very close by presents three naves and a pentagonal apse with quadripartite vaulting.

At the entrance stand two fine Gothic sepulchres of Diego de Sousa and his wife. According to a local legend, Pedro Hispano, the future Pope John XXI (13C), was a priest here.

Compared to the Palace, the church might seem less worthy of mention, but it is worth a visit to see the changes in design and architecture that evolved between the construction of this church (13C) and the construction of the palace (18C).

Convento de Mafra

SERRA DO MARÃO★

PORTO AND VILA REAL

MICHELIN MAP 733 AND 441 – LOCAL MAP SEE VALE DO DOURO

The Serra do Marão is a block of granite and shale bounded to the east by the Corgo, to the west by the Tâmega and to the south by the Douro. The dislocations caused by the range's upheaval in the Tertiary Era are the reason for its variation of altitude; the wildness and desolation are due to intense erosion.

From Vila Real to Amarante   *70km/44mi – about 1hr 30min*
Itinerary ③ on the Vale do DOURO local map

Vila Real – 👄 *See VILA REAL.*

▶ *Leave Vila Real by the Oporto road (IP 4/E 82), heading west.*

As soon as the road reaches the slopes maize, pine and chestnut trees replace the vineyards, apple orchards and olive groves. Starting at Parada de Cunhos there are fine views of the serr'a foothills and of Vila Real far below.

▶ *After Torgueda leave the N 304, the Mondim de Basto road on your right.*

The road continues to climb and shortly, to the left the view of the summit of the **Marão**, the highest of the serra's peaks.

▶ *At the Alto do Espinho pass leave IP 4 and take the road south towards Pico do Marão. You pass the Pousada de São Gonçalo located above the pine-covered slopes. Continue for several miles then bear left.* The road rises through a mineral landscape of laminated crystaliline rocks and shale and ends on a ledge near the summit of Nossa Senhora da Serra.

Pico do Marão★★
Alt 1415m/4642ft. The summit, topped by an obelisk, commands a magnificent **panorama** of the serra's bare peaks.

▶ *Return to the road and continue westwards to Amarante via Candemil.*

Amarante ★ – 👄 *See AMARANTE.*

From Vila Real to Mondim de Basto
61km/38mi – about 1hr 30min – Itinerary ④ on the Vale do Douro local map. Leave Vila Real westwards on IP 4 described above, then bear right after Torgueda onto N 304.

The road climbs to the Alto de Velão pass from where there is a **view** to the left of the upper basin of the Olo river. You cross the western end of the beautiful **Parque Natural do Alvão** dotted with jumbled granite rock formations, then begin the **descent**★ to Mondim de Basto in the Tâmega valley.

▶ *Leave Mondim de Basto on N 312 to the north and then bear right on a forest road which climbs between rocks and pine trees.*

MARVÃO★★

PORTALEGRE

POPULATION 4 450 (159 IN VILLAGE) – MICHELIN MAP 733
LOCAL MAP SEE SERRA DE SÃO MAMEDE

Marvão is a fortified medieval village on the Serra de São Mamede near the Spanish border. This outstanding **site**★★ played a major part in the Portuguese Civil War in 1833. *Rua Dr. Matos de Magalhães – 7330-121 – ☎ 245 99 38 86*

▶ **Orient Yourself:** On the border with Spain and 22km/15mi north of Portalegre.

☺ **Don't Miss:** The castle and particularly the views from the ramparts.

○ **Organizing Your Time:** A half day is sufficient to stroll round this charming little village.

The Village ★

Igreja de Santa Maria

○*Open 9am-12.30pm and 2-5.30pm.* ☞€1. ☎ *245 90 91 32/30.*
The 13C church at the foot of the castle now houses the **Museu Municipal**, which displays megaliths, Roman stelae, old maps of Marvão and other artefacts.

Castle ★

The late-13C castle was remodelled in the 17C. It consists of a series of perimeter walls dominated by a square keep. Go through the first fortified gate and immediately to the right take the stairs which lead down to a **cistern**★. Ten wide arches are reflected in the water. A second fortified gate leads into the first courtyard where the parapet has fine **views**★ of the village stretching out below. In the second courtyard take the stairs to the right up to the parapet walk and follow it round to the keep. Impressive **views**★★ give a good idea of the various walls and particularly of the crenellated towers built on the overhanging rocks. The vast **panorama**★★ extends to the jagged mountain ranges of Spain in the east, the Castelo Branco region and Serra da Estrela in the north and the Serra de São Mamede in the southwest.

Marvão

MÉRTOLA

BEJA

POPULATION 3 347 – MICHELIN MAP 733

The town of Mértola emerges from the middle of the lonely Alentejo country-side, rising in a tiered amphitheatre up a hillside overlooking the confluence of the Guadiana and Oeiras rivers. Dominating the town are the restored keep and ruined walls of its 13C fortified castle. The former mosque, now converted into a church, testifies to Mértola's Arab past. *Largo Vasco da Gama – 7750-328 – ☎ 286 61 25 73*

▶ **Orient Yourself:** Almost in the Algarve but close to the Spanish border.
☺ **Don't Miss:** The church – which used to be a mosque.
🕓 **Organizing Your Time:** A couple of hours, plus time for a coffee, will be ideal.

Igreja-Mesquita

🕓*Open 9.30am-12.15pm and 2-5.15pm.* 🕓*Closed Mon.* ☎ *286 61 23 50.*
The square plan and forest of pillars reveal the church's origin; look at the ancient *mihrab* behind the altar, the niche from which the Imam conducted prayers, and outside at the doorway leading to the sacristy.

▶ *On leaving the church take the first street on the right.*

At Rua da República, a small **museum** displays Moorish pottery (9C-12C). *Guided tours (2hr) daily, 9am-12.30pm and 2-6pm.* 🕓*Closed 1 Jan, 25 Apr, 1 May and 25 Dec.* ☎ *286 61 25 73.*

MIRANDA DO DOURO ★

BRAGANÇA

POPULATION 8 085– MICHELIN MAP 733 OR 441

Miranda is an old town perched on a spur above the Douro valley. It has its own dialect, somewhat similar to Low Latin, known as *mirandês*. Guarding the entrance to the village from a hillock are the ruins of a medieval castle which was destroyed by an explosion in the 19C. *Largo do Menino Jesus da Cartolinha – 5210-225 ☎ 273 43 11 32*

▶ **Orient Yourself:** In the extreme north-east of the country, close to the border with Spain – only the river Douro separates them.
☺ **Don't Miss:** The upper Douro Valley from Miranda do Douro to Barca de Alva.
🕓 **Organizing Your Time:** A couple of hours for the town but a half day to see the landscapes in the Douro Valley.

Cathedral

🕓*Open Summer 10am-12.15pm; rest of year 9.30am-12.30pm; 2pm-5.30pm* 🕓*Closed Mondays all year, Jan 1Easter Day, May 1 and Dec 25. Free.*
The former cathedral *(sé)* has an austere granite façade with two quadrangular bell-towers. The three- nave interior, with its ribbed vaulting, a 16C edifice of granite,

contains a series of gilded and carved wood **altarpieces**★: the one in the chancel by the Spaniards Gregório Hernandez and Francisco Velázquez, depicts the Assumption, round which are scenes from the Life of the Virgin, the Evangelists and several bishops. The whole is crowned with a calvary. On either side of the chancel, the 18C gilded wood stalls are embellished with painted landscapes.

An amusing statuette of the Child Jesus in a top hat stands in a glass display case in the south transept. He is much loved and venerated by the people of Miranda. On the Day of the Kings (Dia dos Reis), a festival takes place, in which four boys carry the statue in a wooden frame during the procession. Opposite the cathedral, the ruins of the episcopal palace cloisters can be seen.

Museu Regional da Terra de Miranda ★

Open Mar 27-end of Oct. 9.30am-12.30pm; 2pm-6pm – Tues 2.30pm-6pm. Nov-Mar 26 9am-12.30pm; 2pm-5.30pm – Tues 2pm-5.30pm. Closed Mondays, Jan 1, May 1 and Dec 25. ☎ 273 43 11 64. €1.50.

This museum has a multitude of local items from the past, showing life through the ages and, as such, is very interesting.

MIRANDELA

BRAGANÇA
POPULATION 25 809 – MICHELIN MAP 733

Although Mirandela is Roman in origin, the town visible today was founded by Dom Afonso II. It looks down upon the Tua, which is spanned by a long Romanesque bridge, rebuilt in the 16C, which is 230m/755ft long and has 20 different arches. It is an elegant, flower-decked town with many gardens and lawns and various options for visitors, such as a boat trip on the Tua river, a journey by train along the old railway line connecting Mirandela with Carvalhais, or a visit around the city by mini-train. *Praça do Mercado – 5370-326 – ☎ 278 20 02 72*

▸ **Orient Yourself:** Halfway between Vila Real and Bragança
◉ **Don't Miss:** The Municipal Museum with its contemporary art.
◉ **Also See:** Bragança.

Sights

Palácio dos Távoras

This beautiful 18C palace, now occupied by the town hall, stands at the top of a hill. Its three-part granite façade (with the middle part the highest) is topped with curved pediments and crowned by spiral pinnacles.

A statue of Pope John Paul II sits in the middle of the square, with a more recent church to one side.

Museu Municipal Armindo Teixeira Lopes★

Open 10am-12.30pm and 2-6pm; Sat, 2.30pm-6pm. Closed Sun and holidays. No charge. ☎ 278 26 57 68.

This interesting museum, housed in the town's cultural centre, is devoted to sculpture and painting. It has been created from donations from the children of Armindo Teixeira Lopes, and contains more than 400 works by 200 predominantly Portuguese artists from the beginning of the century to the present day. These include Vieira da Silva, Tapiès, Cargaleiro, Nadir Afonso, Graça Morais, José Guimarães, Júlio Pomar and Teixeira Lopes.

Excursion

Romeu

Population 478. 12km/7mi to the northeast of Mirandela.
In the heart of the Trás-os-Montes, Romeu, together with **Vila Verdinho** and **Vale do Couço**, form a group of colourful villages bedecked with flowers, in a landscape of valleys wooded with cork oaks and chestnuts. Recent restoration work has given them a new lease of life.

Museu das Curiosidades

Open Apr to Sept, noon-6pm (4pm Oct to Mar). *Closed Mon.* €1.50. 278 93 91 34.
The museum contains the personal collection of Manuel Meneres, the benefactor of all three villages. In one room are early machines such as typewriters, sewing machines, stereoscopes and a phenakistoscope (predecessor of the cinema); in another room are objects of all kinds, including a music box, chairs, dolls and clocks. There are also some old and interesting cars and motor-bikes.

MONSANTO ★★

CASTELO BRANCO

POPULATION 4 672 – MICHELIN MAP 733

Monsanto clings to the foot of a granite hill in the middle of a plain. It is visible from afar in a chaotic mass of rocks which blends in with the rocks of its castle. The origins of the village date from prehistory, when it was linked with pagan rituals; it was subsequently occupied by the Romans, and in 1165 was handed over by Dom Afonso Henriques to Gualdim Pais, master of the Knights Templar, who built the impregnable citadel. Every year in May (*see Calendar of Events*), young girls throw pitchers of flowers from the ramparts to commemorate the defiant throwing out of a calf when the castle was once besieged and those inside wished to convince the assailants that they would never be starved into capitulation.

▶ **Orient Yourself:** In central Portugal but close to the Spanish frontier – almost straight inland from Coimbra on the map.

Don't Miss: The view from the top of the keep, and the views of Monsanto from afar.

Organizing Your Time: It's the sort of place you pass through, pausing for an hour to take in the view, but it is worth the drive to get there.

Sights

Village

Steep and rough alleys cut across the village. The façades of the houses are pierced by paired windows and, in some cases, Manueline-style doorways.

Capela de Santo António

This Manueline chapel in the village has a doorway with four ogival archivolts.

Monsanto – an impregnable site

Capela de São Miguel

This Romanesque chapel next to the castle is now in ruins, yet it has preserved its four archivolts and historiated capitals.

Castle ★

An alley and a steep path lead to the castle, where it is not unusual to find hens or rabbits in openings formed in the rocks, and the odd pig or sheep sheltering within a Roman ruin. Although it was rebuilt by Dom Dinis, countless sieges have since reduced it to a ruin. From the top of the keep, an immense **panorama**★★ spreads northwest over the wooded hills of the Serra da Estrela and southwest over the lake formed by the Idanha dam, the Ponsul valley and, in the distance, Castelo Branco.

MONSARAZ★★

ÉVORA

POPULATION 1 290 – MICHELIN MAP 733

The old fortified village of Monsaraz occupies a strategic position in an out-standing **site**★★ on a height near the Guadiana valley on the border between Portugal and Spain. When it lost its military role, Monsaraz also lost its impor-tance in favour of Reguengos de Monsaraz. As a result, the town has retained much of its historic character. *Largo D. Nuno Álvares Pereira, 5 – 7200-299 – ☎ 266 55 71 36*

▶ **Orient Yourself:** About 53km/40mi southeast of Évora.
▣ **Parking:** Just by the entry to the castle – cars are not allowed inside.
☺ **Don't Miss:** The views from the ramparts of the castle.
◔ **Organizing Your Time:** Two hours should be enough to see all you need.

Sights

Leave the car in front of the main gate.

Rua Direita★

The street retains all its original charm as it is still lined with 16C and 17C white-washed houses, many flanked by outside staircases and balconies with wrought-iron grilles. All the village monuments may be seen in this street which leads to the castle.

S. Cordier/EXPLORER

Antigo Tribunal

🕐 *Open 9am-7pm.* 💰 *€2.* ☎ *266 55 71 36.*
The former court building, on the left of Rua Direita, can be distinguished by the pointed arches above its doors and windows. Inside an interesting fresco depicts true and false Justice with, above, Christ in Majesty with arms held aloft.

Castle

The castle was rebuilt by King Dom Dinis in the 13C and given a second perimeter wall with massive bastions in the 17C. The parapet walk commands a magnificent **panorama** of the Alentejo.

MONTEMOR-O-VELHO

COIMBRA

POPULATION 25 084 – MICHELIN MAP 733 L 3 OR 441

The town of Montemor-o-Velho in the fertile Mondego Valley is dominated by the ruins of the citadel built in the 11C to defend Coimbra against the Moors.
🖪 *Praça da República (Câmara Municipal) – 3140-258 – ☎ 239 68 91 14* 🖪 *Castelo de Montemor-o-Velho – 3140-258 – ☎ 239 68 03 80*

▶ **Orient Yourself:** 25km/17mi due west of Coimbra, towards Figueira da Foz.
🫥 **Don't Miss:** The ancient castle and the views from the keep.
🕐 **Organizing Your Time:** An hour or so to see the castle.

Castle

🕐 *Open 10am-12.30pm and 2-5pm (10am-8pm in summer).* 🕐 *Closed Mon, 1 Jan, Good Fri, Easter Sun and 25 Dec. No charge.* ☎ *239 68 03 80.*
Of the original castle there remains a double perimeter wall, oval in shape, battlemented and flanked by many towers; the north corner is occupied by the church and the keep. From the top of the ramparts there is a **panorama**★ of the Mondego Valley.

MOURA

BEJA
POPULATION 8 427 – MICHELIN MAP 733

Moura, the Town of the Moorish Maiden, stands grouped round the ruins of a 13C castle. It is also a small spa, the bicarbonated calcium waters of which are used in the treatment of rheumatism. The Pisões-Moura spring, a few miles from the town, provides a table water (Água de Castelo) which is widely sold in Portugal.

▶ **Orient Yourself:** Close to the Ardila river in southern Portugal, about 40km/25mi from the Spanish frontier.

◉ **Don't Miss:** Mouraria, the Moorish part of the village and the thermal baths.

◉ **Organizing Your Time:** You will not need to spend more than an hour or so.

Sights

Igreja de São João Baptista ★
The Gothic Church of St John the Baptist is entered through an interesting Manueline **doorway** decorated with armillary spheres. Inside an elegant twisted white marble column supports the pulpit; the chancel, with network vaulting, contains a beautiful Baroque crucifixion group and the south chapel is adorned with 17C *azulejos* representing the Cardinal Virtues. Opposite the church are the **thermal baths** (Estabelecimento Termal) and a public garden.

Mouraria
This quarter recalls by its name the former Moorish occupation, which only ended in 1233 with the liberation of the town. The low houses lining the narrow streets are sometimes ornamented with panels of *azulejos* or picturesque chimneys.

NAZARÉ★

LEIRIA
POPULATION 14 324 – MICHELIN MAP 733

Nazaré lies in an exceptional **site**★★ with its long beach dominated to the north by a steep cliff. The town has three distinct quarters: **Praia**, the largest, which runs alongside the seafront, **Sítio** built on the clifftop and **Pederneira** on a hill. The name Nazaré comes from a statue of the Virgin brought back from the town of Nazareth in Palestine by a monk in the 4C.  *Av. da República – 2450-102 – ☏ 262 56 11 94*

▶ **Orient Yourself:** 100km/65ml north of Lisbon on the A8.

◉ **Don't Miss:** The Sitio quarter of the town.

◉ **Organizing Your Time:** Ideally, take a day – swim in the sea, explore Sitio and then have a glass of wine in the evening in the fishermen's area.

Kids **Especially for Kids:** The beach of São Martinho do Porto.

◔ **Also See:** The monasteries at Alcobaça; the fortified town of Óbidos.

Praia

Praia is the name of the lower town with its geometrically laid out streets giving onto the beach of fine sand. There are many hotels, restaurants and souvenir shops.

Bairro dos Pescadores
The fishermen's quarter stretches from Praça Manuel de Arriaga to Avenida Vieira Guimarães. Small whitewashed cottages line the alleys leading to the quayside.

Harbour
South of the beach a harbour shelters the fishing boats. The catch normally comprises sole, whiting, perch, coalfish, hake, skate, mackerel and especially sardines.

Sítio

The Sítio quarter may be reached by car or on foot (up a flight of steps) although most enjoyable way is by the **funicular** Funicular operates daily, 7am-midnight (2am in summer). €0.85. 262 56 11 53.

Miradouro
The belvedere, built on the edge of the cliff overlooking the sea from a height of 110m/361ft, affords a fine **view**★ of the lower town and the beach.

Ermida da Memória
Open Apr to Sept, 9am-7pm (6pm Oct to Mar). 262 56 18 78.
This tiny chapel near the belvedere commemorates the miracle which saved the life of the local lord, Fuas Roupinho. One morning in 1182 Roupinho on horseback was giving chase to a roe deer which suddenly somersaulted into the air off the top of the cliff. Just as the horse was about to do the same, Dom Fuas implored Our Lady of Nazaré for help and the horse stopped, saving the life of its rider. The façade, roof and the two floors inside the chapel are covered with *azulejos*: those of the façade on the side facing the sea evoke the knight's jump; those of the crypt, the miracle of the Marian intercession. In the staircase leading to the crypt a recess still has the footprint which the horse is said to have left on the rock face.

General view of Nazaré

G. Laurence/DIAF

Igreja de Nossa Senhora da Nazaré

This imposing 17C church is on the main square and has a façade with a forepart forming a gallery, and a Baroque doorway opening at the top of a semicircular flight of steps. The interior has a profusion of *azulejos* depicting Biblical scenes.

Lighthouse

800m/0.5mi west of the church.

The lighthouse *(farol)* is built on a small fort at the farthermost promontory of a cliff. Behind, and lower down, a path with steps and a parapet wall and then an iron staircase leads to a point *(15min Rtn)* overlooking a magnificent **seascape**★★; jagged rocks through which the sea swirls furiously. Go round the headland a little, to the left, where there is a beautiful view over the gashed rockface of the Sítio cliffs and the bay of Nazaré.

Portuguese Water Dog

The Portuguese water dog is classified by breeders as a working dog. Robust, and an adept swimmer and diver, it is a medium-sized dog with a wavy or curly coat, standing 50-56cm (20-22in) high and weighing 19-25kg (42-55lb). It has a fluffy mop of hair around its head, a long, curled tail, and resembles a cross between a standard poodle and an Irish water spaniel, both of which probably contributed to the breed. The dogs, now few in number, are black, brown, white, black and white, or brown and white. Developed along the Algarve coast by fishermen who trained them to retrieve fishing nets and tackle as well as to guard their boats, the breed is recognised by international Kennel Clubs.

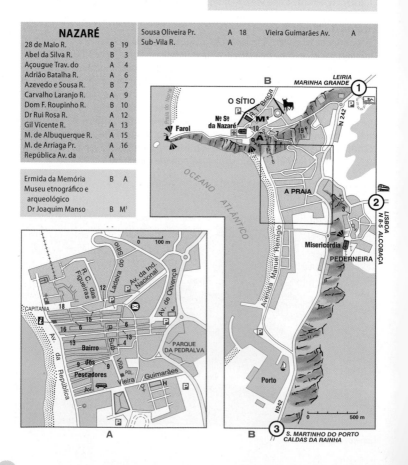

NAZARÉ

28 de Maio R.	B	19
Abel da Silva R.	B	3
Açougue Trav. do	A	4
Adrião Batalha R.	A	6
Azevedo e Sousa R.	B	7
Carvalho Laranjo R.	A	9
Dom F. Roupinho R.	B	10
Dr Rui Rosa R.	A	12
Gil Vicente R.	A	13
M. de Albuquerque R.	A	15
M. de Arriaga Pr.	A	16
República Av. da	A	

Ermida da Memória	B	A
Museu etnográfico e arqueológico Dr Joaquim Manso	B	M¹

Sousa Oliveira Pr.	A	18
Sub-Vila R.	A	

Vieira Guimarães Av.	A

Excursion

São Martinho do Porto
13km/8mi south. Leave Nazaré by the N 242.
This seaside resort lies north of a saltwater lake linked to the sea by a narrow channel edged with tall cliffs. Its sheltered location makes its **beach** one of the safest in the region for children.

ÓBIDOS★★

LEIRIA
POPULATION 10 809 – MICHELIN MAP 733

Óbidos, which commands a vast sweep of countryside consisting of green valleys and heights topped by the occasional windmill, has managed to keep its proud medieval character through the ages. The fortified city, protected by its perimeter wall, flanked by small round towers and massive square bastions, once commanded this part of the coastline. The silting-up of its bay created a lagoon (Lagoa da Óbidos) which deprived the town of its coastal position and today Óbidos stands 10km/6mi inland. *Rua Direita – 2510-060 – ☎ 262 95 92 31*

▶ **Orient Yourself:** The centre of the Province of Estremadura, about 100km/65mi north of Lisbon.
🕰 **Don't Miss:** A walking tour of the ramparts.
🕐 **Organizing Your Time:** Spend the morning here, then have lunch.
🕯 **Also See:** Alcobaça and Caldos Da Rainha. Play golf at Praia D'El Rey!

The Medieval City ★★ *1hr 30min*

Park the car outside the ramparts.

Porta da Vila
The inside walls of this double zigzag gateway are covered with 18C *azulejos*.

Óbidos and its walls

Rua Direita ★

A paved channel runs through the centre of this narrow main street bordered with white houses bright with flowers, as well as shops, restaurants and art galleries.

Praça de Santa Maria★

The church square stands below the main street and forms an attractive scene.

Igreja de Santa Maria

Open 9.30am-12.30pm and 2.30-5pm (7pm Apr to Oct). ☎ *262 95 96 33.*
It was here that the young King Afonso V married his eight-year-old cousin, Isabella, in 1444. The **interior**★ is noteworthy for its walls, entirely covered with blue 17C *azulejos*. In the chancel, in a bay on the left, a Renaissance **tomb**★ is surmounted by a *Pietà*. This outstanding work is attributed to the studio of Nicolas Chanterene. The retable at the high altar is adorned with paintings by João da Costa.

Address Book

WHERE TO STAY

🛏 **Casa do Poço** – *R. da Mouraria, 4* – ☎ *262 95 93 58* – *4 rooms* ⊡ - This charming little guest house has a terrace that looks out over the ramparts of the castle. The rooms may be a little small and dark but are comfortable and breakfast is served in an old kitchen.

🛏🛏 **Casa do Rochedo** – *R. do Jogo da Bola* ☎ *262 95 91 20* 🍴 🏊 *7 rooms* ⊡. Near the upper parts of the ramparts this lovely little hotel has excellent views of the castle, especially from the pool. The breakfast room might not be that well decorated but the overall ambience is excellent.

🛏🛏🛏 **Estalagem do Convento** – *Rua D. João d'Ornelas*– ☎ *262 95 92 16* – *estconventhotel@mail.telepac.pt* – *31 rooms* ⊡. An attractive inn set in an old convent. A rustic atmosphere, with pleasant and spacious rooms.

🛏🛏🛏🛏 **Casa das Senhoras Rainhas** – *R. Padré Nunes Tavares, 6* ☎ *262 95 53 60* - *info@senhorasrainhas.com* 📧 *10 rooms* ⊡. An old house set at the foot of the ramparts it has a simplicity but with style. There might not be a grand view, although the rooms all open onto the terrace, but it has charm.

🛏🛏🛏🛏 **Pousada do Castelo** – *Paço Real, 2510 Óbidos* – ☎ *262 95 50 80* - *recepcao.castelo@pousadas.pt* – *9 rooms* 📧 – The former palace of Óbidos today houses a comfortable *pousada* with very elegant décor. Peaceful.

EATING OUT

🍴 **Petarum Domus Bar** – *R. Direita* ☎ *262 95 96 20 12noon-2am, Closed Sun.* Old beams and stones, leather armchairs, stone tables and soft lighting go to make this wine bar a place to relax and be comfortable. *Celta*, a local speciality, will delight your taste-buds; or you can opt for a plate of cheese and charcuterie.

🍴🍴 **Alcaide** – *R. Direita* ☎ *262 95 92 20* - *www.restalcaide.com*. Its central location, beautiful views of the town and simple traditional cooking make this a very popular restaurant.

🍴🍴🍴 **A Ilustre Casa de Ramiro** – *R. Porta do Vale* – ☎ *262 95 91 94* – *Closed Thursdays and January*. Fine traditional cuisine served in an old country house outside the walls.

TRANSPORT

If you are using public transport, regular buses arrive from Nazaré, Peniche and Caldas da Rainha. They stop 50m from the Tourism Office, by the city walls.

INTERNET

Biblioteca Municipal (local library) – just to the left of the São Pedro church. Free.

Casa do Pelourinho – *R. Direita*. Free.

SPORT

Golf de Praia d'El Rey – *N114 towards Peniche*. A luxury golf and sports complex on the ocean with spectacular views, an hotel and many houses.

Museu Municipal
Open 10am-1pm and 2-6pm. Closed 1 Jan, 11 Jan (local holiday), Easter day and 25 Dec. € 1.50. 262 95 50 10.
The small municipal museum houses a statue of St Sebastian dating from the 15C or 16C and also a 17C polychrome *Pietà*. The "Josefa de Óbidos" room, in the first basement, contains various works by this artist, while exhibits in another room include mementoes of the war against Napoleon.

▶ *Go to the end of the main street to the ramparts. Follow the signs to the Pousada.*

City walls★★
The best access points are near the Porta da Vila or the Castelo.
The walls *(muralhas)* date from the Moorish occupation but were restored in the 12C, 13C and 16C. Along the north side, the highest, are the keep and the castle towers. The sentry path commands pleasant **views**★ over the fortified city and the surrounding countryside.

Castle
The castle, which is now a *pousada*, was converted into a royal palace in the 16C. Its façade has paired Manueline windows with twisted columns and a Manueline doorway surmounted by two armillary spheres.

Additional Sight

Santuário do Senhor da Pedra
Open 9.30am-12.30pm and 2.30-5pm (7pm Apr to Oct). Closed Mon. 262 95 96 33.
In a glass case above the altar is a primitive stone cross dating from the 2C. The nave contains Baroque statues of the Apostles. A coach, kept in the sanctuary, was used to transport the statue of the Virgin from the church of Santa Maria in Óbidos to the church of Nossa Senhora in Nazaré during the festival on 8 September.

OLHÃO

FARO
POPULATION 13 151 – MICHELIN MAP 733
LOCAL MAP SEE ALGARVE

Olhão is a sardine and tuna fishing port and canning centre on the Algarve coast at a point where long coastal sandbanks lying offshore have been developed into beaches, some of which (Ilha da Armona) may be reached by boat. In spite of its picturesque Moorish village appearance, Olhão's history does not go back to the Arabic occupation. It was founded in the 18C by fishermen who came to the spot by sea from the Ria de Aveiro and its architectural style came about through its commercial contacts with North Africa. *Largo da Lagoa – 8700-397 – 289 71 39 36*

▶ **Orient Yourself:** 11km/7mi east of Faro on the Algarve.
Don't Miss: The bell-tower of the parish church; the Saturday market.
Organizing Your Time: No more than an hour is necessary.

Viewpoints

The bridge over the railway at the entrance to the town affords a good view of the white houses huddled close together.

An unusual **panorama**★ of the whole town may be had from the belfry of the **parish church.** ◷*Open 9-11.30am; 3-5.30pm; Sat, 9am-11.30am.* ◷*Closed Mon.* *€1.* ☎ *289 70 51 17, standing in the main street (access through the first door on the right as you enter the church).*

OLIVEIRA DO HOSPITAL

COIMBRA
POPULATION 3 074 – MICHELIN MAP 733

Hills clad with vines, olive groves and pine trees form the setting of Oliveira do Hospital, the name of which recalls the 12C Order of the Hospitallers of St John of Jerusalem, now the Knights Templar of Malta. You will find it about 60km/40mi north-east of Coimbra along the N17. The countryside is beautiful. *(see LEÇA DO BAILIO).* 🄳 *Rua do Colégio (Casa da Cultura de Oliveira) – 3400-269 – ☎ 238 65 91 19 or 238 60 92 69.*

Visit

Parish church
◷*Open 9am-7pm.* ☎ *238 60 27 89.*

The church, originally Romanesque, was reconstructed in the Baroque period. The interior, covered by a fine ceiling painted in false relief, contains the late-13C tombs of Domingos Joanes and his wife. An equestrian **statue**★ of a 14C medieval knight has been fixed to the wall above the tombs. Also noteworthy is a beautiful 14C stone **altarpiece**★ of the Virgin.

OURÉM

SANTARÉM
POPULATION 4 498 – MICHELIN MAP 733

The fortified city of Ourém was built round the top of a hillock, the summit of which is occupied by the remains of a castle. The town lived through a period of sumptuous richness in the 15C.

▶ **Orient Yourself:** About 7km/4mi north-east of Fátima. The fortified town is 2km/1.4ml south of the new town.

 Don't Miss: The castle and the church, as detailed below.

◷ **Organizing Your Time:** Give yourself a couple of hours at most.

Sights

Castle

Two advanced towers appear on either side of the road; note the unusual brick machicolations crowning the walls all round the castle.

▸ *Go through the porch of the right tower. A path leads to a point where a former tunnel comes into view. Steps go up to a square tower commanding the entrance to an older triangular castle; in the courtyard is a Moorish underground cistern from the 9C. A path leads to the village and the collegiate church.*

Collegiate church

Enter through the south transept. A door immediately to the right opens onto a stairway down to the crypt with its six monolithic columns. The Gothic and highly ornate white limestone **tomb** of Count Dom Afonso in the crypt has a recumbent figure attributed to the sculptor Diogo Pires the Elder. Two lifting mechanisms are engraved on the tomb.

PAÇO DE SOUSA

PORTO

POPULATION 3 536 – MICHELIN MAP 733 OR 441

Paço de Sousa has retained from a former Benedictine monastery, founded early in the 11C, a vast Romanesque church (restored) in which lies the tomb of Egas Moniz, the companion in arms of Prince Afonso Henriques.

▸ **Orient Yourself:** Inland from Porto on the A4, halfway to Vila Real.
🕓 **Organizing Your Time:** It's no more than a brief stopping place along the road to or from Vila Real, but the church is worth a visit.

Visit

Igreja do Mosteiro de São Salvador

The church façade has a tiers-point doorway with recessed orders ornamented with motifs, repeated on the surround of the rose window. The tympanum is supported on the left by a bull's head and on the right by an unusual head of a man. On the tympanum on the left is a man carrying the moon, on the right one carrying the sun. Inside, the three aisles with pointed arches shelter, on the left, a naive statue of St Peter and, on the right near the entrance, the 12C tomb of Egas Moniz. Low-relief sculptures carved somewhat crudely on the tomb depict the scene at Toledo and the funeral of this loyal preceptor. A battlemented tower stands to the left.

PALMELA★

SETÚBAL
POPULATION 14 444 – MICHELIN MAP 733 – LOCAL MAP SEE SERRA DA ARRÁBIDA

This pretty white town is built in tiers on the northern slope of the Serra da Arrábida at the foot of a mound crowned by a large castle which became the seat of the Order of St James in 1423. *Castelo de Palmela – 2950-221 – ☎ 212 33 21 22*

▶ **Orient Yourself:** Just a couple of miles inland from Setúbal.

🚫 **Don't Miss:**The castle and the church, but soak up the local flavour.

🕐 **Organizing Your Time:** A couple of hours mid-morning with a coffee in the sun will be just fine.

Sights

Castle★
Follow the signs to the pousada. Leave the car in the outer yard. Open daily with the exception of one part of the castle, which opens from 9am-6pm (8pm in summer). ☎ 212 33 15 80.

The castle, now partly converted into a *pousada*, was constructed in three different periods. The western extremity is occupied by the Church and Monastery of St James, erected in the 15C by the Knights of St James, who had installed themselves in the castle in 1186.

Igreja de São Pedro
Open 10am-1pm and 2-7pm; Sun, 10am-1pm. Closed Wed and holidays. ☎ 212 35 00 25 (from 6.30-8pm only).

The church dates from the 18C. The interior is entirely lined with **azulejos**★ depicting scenes from the life of St Peter; outstanding are those in the south aisle illustrating the miraculous catch of fish, Christ walking on the waves and the crucifixion of St Peter.

PARQUE NACIONAL DA PENEDA-GERÊS★★

BRAGA, VIANA DO CASTELO AND VILA REAL
MICHELIN MAP 733

Peneda-Gerês, Portugal's only **national park**, was established in 1971 and covers 72 000ha/178 000 acres in the northern districts of Braga, Viana do Castelo and Vila Real. The valleys of the Lima, Homem and Cávado rivers divide the region into *serras* – da Peneda, do Soajo, da Amarela and do Gerês. The park is designed to protect the natural sites, archeological remains, and the outstanding flora and fauna, many of which cannot be seen elsewhere.

▶ **Orient Yourself:** Northern Portugal, on the border with Spain, with which the park shares more than 100km/65mi of common frontier.

🚫 **Don't Miss:** The wonderful journey from Mezio to Lamas de Mouro.

🕐 **Organizing Your Time:** Each circuit *(below)* has approximate times.

From Rio Cávado to Portela do Homem★★

1 Northwards from the N 103 *20km/12mi – about 3hr*

N 304 branches north from N 103 between Braga and Chaves and winds downhill through a landscape of rocks and heather. After 2km/1mi you pass the beautifully situated São Bento *pousada* with its panoramic view of the Caniçada reservoir. Two bridges cross, successively, the Cávado and its tributary, the Caldo, turned into reservoir-lakes by the Caniçada dam. The first bridge crosses over a submerged village which appears when the water level drops.

▶ *From the first bridge onto the peninsula between the two lakes, take N 308 on the right at the intersection, and then cross the second bridge. Head for Gerês.*

Gerês is a pleasant little spa at the bottom of a wooded gorge. Its waters, rich in fluorine, are used in the treatment of liver and digestive disorders. After Gerês, the road is lined first with hydrangeas, then winds up through woods of pines and oaks. Some 8km/5mi from Gerês you reach the nature reserve. The road climbs gently and crosses the Homem river, which races through a rocky course.

▶ *Turn back and take the track on the right towards Campo do Gerês. The track crosses the remains of a Roman road at two points: after 1.3km/0.8mi and 2km/1.2mi.*

Remains of the Roman Way (Geira)★

The milestones on the side of the road are the remains of the Roman Way (Via Romana) which stretched some 320km/200mi between Braga and Astorga in Spain via the Homem Pass.

The track continues, affording lovely views of, and then skirting, the **Represa de Vilarinho das Fumas**, a blue-water reservoir set in a wild, rocky landscape.

Parque Nacional da Peneda-Gerês – View of the Caniçada reservoir

Serra do Gerrês★★

② From Gerês to the Vilarinho das Furnas reservoir
15km/9mi – allow 2hr

From Gerês take N 308 to the south then turn right to **Campo do Gerês**★★
This road with tight hairpin bends offers good views of the Caniçada reservoir and
of the superb rock falls. When the road stops climbing turn right towards the **Miradouro de Junceda**★ which offers a bird's eye view of Gerês and its valley. Return
to the main road and continue on to Campo do Gerês. In the centre of a crossroads,
note an ancient Roman milestone bearing a sculpture of Christ. Continue along the
road to the right to reach the Vilarinho das Furnas reservoir.

Serra de Peneda★★

③ From Arcos de Valdevez to Melgaço
70km/44mi – allow half a day

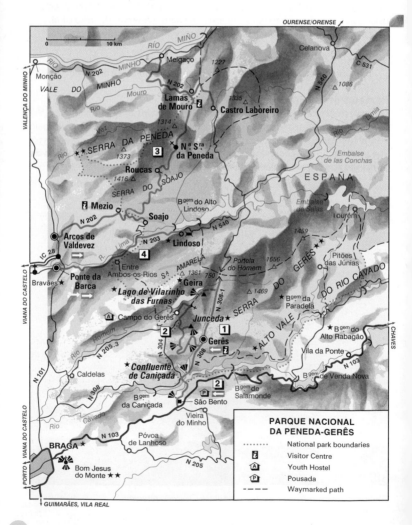

This itinerary takes you through the wildest part of the park. From **Arcos de Valde-vez**, where the towers of two churches dominate this little town on the banks of the Vez, you reach **Mezio**, a village which stands at the entrance to the national park. An information centre gives details on the park, its geology, flora and fauna.

The road to Peneda begins 2.5km/1.5mi further on, but continue towards **Soajo,** an isolated village with a wonderful group of granaries or **espigueiros**★ for drying grain (*see LINDOSO*). The granite constructions are from the 18C and 19C.

▸ *Return to the junction and take the Peneda road.*

Mosteiro de Nossa Senhora da Peneda stands in a magnificent **setting**★ preceded by 300 steps climbed by pilgrims in early September each year.

Then continue past **Castro Laboreiro** , a village which has preserved several traditional houses built of granite as well as the ruins of a castle

▸ *Return to Lamas de Mouro and take the Melgaço road.*

[4] **From Ponte da Barca to Lindoso** *31km/19mi –* *See LINDOSO*

PENICHE

LEIRIA
POPULATION 27 312 – MICHELIN MAP 733

Peniche, built to command access to the mile long promontory, is today Portugal's second most important fishing port (crayfish, sardines, tunny etc). The remains of ramparts and the citadel recall the former military role played by the city. A pleasant public garden planted with palm trees surrounds the Tourist Informa-tion Centre (Posto de Turismo) on Rua Alexandre Herculano.

▸ **Orient Yourself:** 100km/65mi north of Lisbon, on the sea.
▣ **Parking:** On the Campo da República, opposite the citadel.
🐚 **Don't Miss:** The island of Berlenga (by boat). *See Ilha da BERLENGA.*
🕐 **Organizing Your Time:** To see Berlenga you need a morning, then have lunch and wander round Peniche for a few hours.
Kids Especially for Kids: Take them cycling along the coast.
 Also See: Óbidos and Nazaré.

The revival of handmade lace
Peniche has been trying to revive its former speciality of bobbin lace. An apprentice school has been set up at the town's Industrial and Business School *(avenida 25 de Abril)*. On the first floor there is an exhibit of samples from past and present produc-tion. Lacemakers can also be seen working at the Casa de Trabalho das Filhas de Pescadores *(rua do Calvário)*, and handmade lace can still be bought in the town *(avenida do Mar)*.

Sights

Citadel
An ancient 16C fortress, converted in the 17C into a Vauban-style citadel, stands proudly with its high walls and sharp edged bastions topped with watchtowers.

Until 1974 it was a state prison, then it became an emergency city for refugees from Angola. It dominates both the harbour to the east and the sea to the south.

Harbour
The harbour is situated to the southeast of the town. The esplanade *(Largo da Ribeira)* is always the scene of a highly colourful spectacle with the **return of the fishing fleet**★, when the catch of sardines, tunny fish or crayfish is unloaded. Hundreds of squeeling seagulls hover overhead in the hope of finding some left-overs and it is a colourful scene.

Igreja de São Pedro
The 17C chancel was embellished in the 18C with gilded woodwork into which were incorporated four huge canvases from the 16C attributed to the father of Josefa de Óbidos.

PINHEL

GUARDA – POPULATION 3 237
MICHELIN MAP 733

Pinhel, an old village and former fortified outpost on a mountainous shelf near to Spain, has many houses decorated with coats of arms and beautiful wrought-iron balconies. The road approaching Pinhel from the southwest (N 221) crosses a countryside covered with olive trees and vines; towards the end, near the town, there is a large group of wine vats, with very prominent white pointed domes.

▶ **Orient Yourself:** 29km/18mi north-east of Guarda.
🕐 **Organizing Your Time:** No more than half a day.
👁 **Also See:** Almeida, a few miles to the south-east.

Sight

Museu Municipal
🕐*Open Mon-Fri 9am-12.30pm; 2pm-5.30pm. No charge.* ☎ *271 41 00 00.*
This small municipal museum contains prehistoric and Roman remains, religious works of art, weapons and Portuguese pewterware. Upstairs, there is a collection of naive folk art and other paintings.

Excursions

Serra da Marofa
20km/12mi – about 1hr 30min. Leave Pinhel on N 221 going north.
The road linking Pinhel and Figueira de Castelo Rodrigo was known locally as the **Excomungada** (Accursed Road) because of the danger presented by its countless bends when crossing the **Serra da Marofa**, after which you reach the Figueira de Castelo Rodrigo plateau which is planted with fruit trees. To the left, the *serra's* highest peak, with an altitude of 976m/3 202ft commands an interesting view of the ruins of the fortified village of **Castelo Rodrigo**, an important city since the Middle Ages,

Barca de Alva
20km/12mi to the north of Figueira.
The blossoming of the almond trees between late February and mid-May, provides a delightful spectacle with its sea of pink flowers.

Estrada de Almeida ★
25km/15.5mi to the southeast.
This route provides a picturesque link between Pinhel and Almeida.

▶ *Take N 324 southeast of Pinhel.*

The road then comes to a desolate plateau strewn with enormous blocks of granite forming a lunar **landscape**★. After Vale Verde you cross a tributary of the Côa river by a narrow old humpback bridge.

▶ *At a crossroads 2.5km/1.5mi further on, turn left onto N 340: the road then crosses a bridge over the Côa river and rejoins N 332; take the road to the left towards Almeida.*

Almeida★ – 🕭 *See GUARDA.*

POMBAL

LEIRIA

POPULATION 12 469 – MICHELIN MAP 733

The town of Pombal at the foot of its medieval castle evokes the memory of the Marquis of Pombal, who acquired a property locally and died here in 1782. He was the man responsible for the rebuilding of Lisbon after the 1755 earthquake *(see History, LISBOA).* 🔲 *Largo do Cardal – 3100-440 – ☎ 236 21 32 30.*

▶ **Orient Yourself:** About 45km/33mi south of Coimbra on the main A1 highway, on the western edge of the Serra da Lousá.
🕐 **Organizing Your Time:** Stop for an hour as you are passing through.

Castle *15min*

Take the Ansião road on the right at the corner of the Palácio de Justiça; upon reaching a cross, bear sharp right into a narrow surfaced road which rises steeply. Leave the car at the foot of the castle. 🕐*Open 8.30am-12.30pm and 2.30-5pm. No charge.* ☎ *236 21 05 00.* The castle, built originally in 1161 by Gualdim Pais, Grand Master of the Order of the Knights Templar, was modified in the 16C and restored in 1940. From the top of the ramparts, overlooked by the battlemented keep, there is a view of Pombal to the west and the foothills of the Serra da Lousá to the east.

The Marquis of Pombal

Born in Lisbon in 1699, Sebastião de Carvalho e Melo began life in the diplomatic service, in London and Vienna. In 1750 King José I called Carvalho to power. As minister, he improved Portugal's finances and oversaw Lisbon's rebuilding after the earthquake of 1755. To consolidate the monarchy's control, he expelled the powerful Jesuits and reduced the influence of the nobles. After the king was wounded in an attack, Carvalho arrested the Marquis of Távora and his family and had them killed. In 1769 the king gave Carvalho the title of Marquis of Pombal, but upon the king's death, Carvalho's enemies banished him from the Court. Retiring to his lands, he died a year later.

PONTE DE LIMA

VIANA DO CASTELO
POPULATION 4 655 – MICHELIN MAP 733

The small town between Viana do Castelo and the Parque Nacional da Peneda-Gerês has a long history. The Romans built a strategic bridge at this point, which was part of the Roman Way between Braga and Astorga in Spain. Later, in the early 12C, Queen Tareja (Teresa) came to live in Ponte de Lima and granted it local privileges. Its streets are lined with Romanesque, Gothic, Manueline, Baroque and neo-Classical constructions while its environs are particularly rich in manor houses *(solares)* and seigneurial country estates *(quintas)*. The latter are built of granite, adorned with coats-of-arms on gateways, and covered galleries, and date from the 16C, 17C and 18C. Ponte de Lima is also the centre of the *vinho verde* wine-producing region. The town's co-operative (Adega Cooperativa) offers visitors the opportunity to taste and purchase some of these famous wines.
🚩 *Praça da República – 4990-062 – ☎ 258 94 23 35/7*

▶ **Orient Yourself:** About 37km/24mi north of Braga, midway between Viana do Castelo and the Peneda-Gerês national park.
🕭 **Don't Miss:** The **Ponte Medieval**★, the bridge after which the town was named, with 16 rounded arches – five of which remain: and the Igreja-Museu dos Terceiros with its wonderful *azulejos* and woodwork.
🕓 **Organizing Your Time:** One day will be ideal.
🕭 **Also See:** Braga and the National Park of Peneda-Gerês.

PORTALEGRE

PORTALEGRE
POPULATION 24 000 – MICHELIN MAP 733
LOCAL MAP SEE SERRA DE SÃO MAMEDE

During the Middle Ages, Portalegre held a strategic position near the border. The ruins of the town's fortified castle, built by King Dinis I in 1290, are still visible. Portalegre is the starting point for the excursion in the Serra de São Mamede (🕭 *see Serra de SÃO MAMEDE)*. 🚩 *Galeria Municipal – Rossio – 7300 – ☎ 245 33 13 59*

▶ **Orient Yourself:** About 105km/69mi north-east of Évora.
🅿 **Parking:** In the Praça de República (you need to pay).
🕭 **Don't Miss:** Summer evenings in the Praça de República where there are spectacles; the Serra de São Mamede.
🕓 **Organizing Your Time:** Give yourself a good half day.
🕭 **Also See:** Marvão, Estremoz, Évira.

Museu José Régio
🗪 *Guided tours (30-45min), 9.30am-12.30pm and 2-6pm.* 🕒 *Closed Mon and holidays.* 🗪 *€2 - free on Sun morning.* ☎ *245 30 36 25.*
The collection of art assembled by the poet José Régio (1901-69) is the most interesting part of the museum, which is in the house where he lived: there are numerous 16C to 19C crucifixes and naive statuettes of St Anthony.

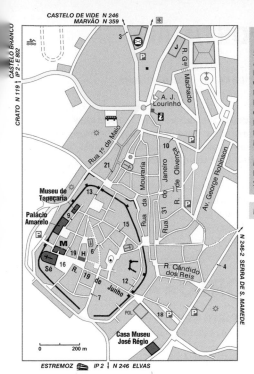

PORTALEGRE	
5 de Outubro R.	21
Alex. Herculano R.	3
Bairro Ferreira Rainho R.	4
Comércio R. do	6
Elvas R. de	7
Figueira R. da	9
G. G. Fernandes R.	10
Luís Barahona R.	12
Luís de Camões R.	13
Mouzinho de Albuquerque R.	15
Município Pr. do	16
República Pr. da	18
Sé R. da	19

Museu Municipal	M

Museu Municipal

Guided tours (30-45min), 9.30am-12.30pm and 2-6pm. Closed Mon and holidays. €2 ☎ 245 30 25 44.

Installed in the former diocesan seminary, this municipal museum contains a rich collection of sacred art: a Spanish *Pietà* in gilded wood dating from the end of the 15C, a 16C altarpiece in polychrome terracotta, a magnificent 17C tabernacle in ebony, four ivory high reliefs (18C Italian School), an 18C ivory crucifix and 16C gold and silver plate.

Cathedral (Sé)

The 18C façade has distinctive marble columns. The interior (16C) the second chapel o nthe right has a beautiful retable illustrated with the life of the Virgin. The sacristy walls are covered in azulejos.

Portugal and the Jesuits

During the period of the Great Discoveries the Jesuits played an important missionary role. Dom João III showed an interest in the followers of St Ignatius and the founding of the Society of Jesus in 1540. In 1542 St Francis Xavier, the Apostle of the Indies, started preaching in India, the Spice Islands and Japan. The Jesuits engaged in trade. These first encounters (1540s) between the Portuguese and the Japanese are amusingly depicted on the Namban screens. The lanky figures of the Jesuits in their black cloaks are easily identifiable from the colourful, gold-braided attires of the merchants. Persecution began at the beginning of the 17C and the Jesuits took refuge in Macau, the trading base on the Chinese coast. The Marquis of Pombal fought a constant battle to reduce the power and wealth of the Jesuits. He expelled them from the missions in Brazil, prohibited the Jesuits from engaging in trade, forbade them to preach or to teach and on 3 September 1759 all the members of the Society of Jesus were outlawed and expelled from Portugal.

PORTIMÃO

FARO
POPULATION 44 391 – MICHELIN MAP 733
LOCAL MAP SEE ALGARVE

Portimão is a fishing port nestled at the back of a bay. The best **view**★ is at high tide from the bridge across the Arade at the end of the bay. The town specialises in boat-building, and the canning of tunny (tuna) and sardines. The seaside resort of Praia da Rocha contains the town's famous beach.

▶ **Orient Yourself:** 34km/26mi west from Albufeira, on the coast.
◉ **Don't Miss:** The *azulejos* on benches in the Largo 1° de Dezembro.
◷ **Organizing Your Time:** A full day to see the town and nearby sights.
◔ **Also See:** Albufeira, Lagos, Silves.

PORTO★★

OPORTO – PORTO
POPULATION 302 535 – MICHELIN MAP 733

Oporto, Portugal's second largest city has a reputation for being hard-working, yet when the sun shines it comes alive with vitality and colour. Oporto (O Porto in Portuguese) occupies a magnificent **site**★★, its houses clinging to the banks of the Douro, the legendary river that ends here after its long course through Spain and Portugal. Not least among the city's claims to fame are its internationally celebrated port wines which are matured in the **Vila Nova de Gaia** wine lodges.
The best **general view**★ of Oporto is from the terrace of the former Convento de Nossa Senhora da Serra do Pilar (◔ *see below*). The historical centre of the city was declared a World Heritage site by UNESCO in 1996. ⓘ *Rua Clube dos Fenianos 25 – 4000-172 – ☏ 222 05 27 40 or 223 39 34 72*

▶ **Orient Yourself:** Second largest city in Portugal, Porto is in the north, along the Atlantic coast. Lisbon is 220km/136ml to the south.
🅿 **Parking:** Difficult to find. There are several large underground car-parks and these are recommended over parking on the streets.
◉ **Don't Miss:** Go over the D. Luís bridge (on metro or foot); try to see a match at the FC Porto stadium;
◷ **Organizing Your Time:** Give yourself three days to get to know the city.
🄺🄸🄳🅂 **Especially for Kids:** See the bridges; play in the park by the Crystal Palace; and there's always the beach
◔ **Also See:** Braga, the Douro Valley in particular.

The City
The city centre spreads across a network of shopping streets around Praça da Liberdade and São Bento station. This is very lively during the day with its crowds of people, its old-fashioned shop fronts in Rua Santa Catarina, Formosa, Sá da Bandeira and Fernandes Tomás, and its numerous cake shops and tearooms.
The working districts of **Ribeira** and **Miragaia** near the Douro have been restored and renovated over the last few years. Oporto's nightlife is now centred in Ribeira with its many fashionable restaurants. The quarter also provides a good selection of

moderately priced restaurants and bars and is the best place to look for two of the local dishes, tripe or *tripas à modo do Porto* and cod or *bacalhau à Gomes de Sá*. Oporto's business centre has been moving gradually westwards around **Avenida da Boavista** between Oporto and Foz. Major banks, businesses and shopping centres are springing up in modern tower blocks.

The Bridges

The river banks are linked by several technically outstanding bridges.

The **Ponte Ferroviária Maria**★, a railway bridge which is the furthest upstream and the most graceful, was designed by the French engineer Eiffel in 1877.

The **Ponte Rodoviária D. Luís I** ★★ is the most spectacular of Oporto's bridges with two superimposed road tracks, serving both upper and lower levels of the town on both banks. It is the symbol of Oporto and is a World Heritage site. It has a span of 172m/564ft and was built in 1886.

The **Ponte Rodoviária Arrábida**, opened in 1963 and used by the IC 1 road which runs through Oporto, is a particularly bold structure. It crosses the Douro in a single reinforced concrete span of nearly 270m/886ft.

The **Ponte do Freixo**, which is used by the IP 1, is situated to the east of Oporto, providing motorists with an alternative route avoiding the city centre.

A Bit of History

Portucale

In Roman times, the Douro was a considerable obstacle between north and south Lusitania. Two cities faced each other across the river, controlling the estuary: Portus (the harbour) on the north bank, Cale on the south. In the 8C the Moors invaded Lusitania but Christian resistance prevented them from settling permanently in the region between the Minho and the Douro. Later, this region was to be one of the mainsprings for the **Reconquest**, and so gave its name to the whole country.

Oporto and the D. Luís I bridge

Address Book

USEFUL INFORMATION

Pass Porto – Tourist pass valid for one day (€7.50) or three days (€15.50) with free or reduced entry to 18 museums and monuments; free travel on all public transport; rebates in 28 shops, on cruises, visits to wine cellars or bus tours. Available at ticket machines on the metro or at Tourist Information Centres.

Pass Transport – Two passes that give free public transport in the city. One-day €4; three-day €9. On sale at the three Tourist Information Centres.

TRANSPORT

Airport – The Dr Francisco Sá Carneiro airport, recently rebuilt, is on the EN107 about 14km/10mi north-west of the town. A metro line runs direct into the city centre. There are also regular buses to Av. dos Aliados from 6.45am-7.15pm.

Railways – Two main stations:

Campanhá, *R. da Estação* ☎ 808 20 82 08 or 225 19 13 74 - both national and international services;

São Bento – *Praça Almeida Garret* ☎ 808 20 82 08 or 225 05 17 14 – serves the north of Portugal and local destinations.

Metro – There are four lines serving the entire city and its outskirts. For more information obtain maps from any metro station or Tourist Information Centres or visit *www.metro-porto.pt*

Buses (STCP) – Porto has 78 different lines covering the entire city with an efficient service. Single tickets are available for €0.85; day tickets for €1.55 cover the city centre. If you're a night-owl there are 13 lines that run all night. *www.stcp.pt*

TOURS

Porto Tours – A good way to get the know the city quickly is by bus. ☎ 222 00 00 73 - www.portotours.com

Wine Cellar visits – To visit some of the 18 wine cellars producing Port, contact the wine-producers' association – Associação das Empresas de Vinho do Porto *(R. Dr António Granjo, 207, Vila Nova de Gaia* ☎ 223 74 55 20).

River Cruises – A dozen or more companies operate river cruises on the Douro, each taking about one hour. Departures are from the Quai Ribeira or Quai Amarelo every day from 10am. €10.

Helicopter Tours – Helitours. If you really feel flush, see Porto from the air. Minimum 4 persons €50 pp. Lasts about 10min. ☎ 225 43 24 64 - www.douroazul.com

WHERE TO STAY

Residencial Vera Cruz – *R. Ramalho Ortigão, 14*– ☎ 222 32 33 96 – www.residencialveracruz.com – 29 rooms. Very nice little hotel with beautifully styled bedrooms and, from the 8th floor, where breakfast is served, a lovely view over the city. A very central location, ideal for touring the city.

Castelo Santa Catarina – *R. de Santa Catarina 1347, (metro: Marquês, line D)* – ☎ 225 09 55 99 - www.castelosantacatarina.com.pt – 26 rooms. This astonishing fairy-tale villa complete with a crenellated tower, extensive terraced gardens and massive reproduction furniture provides reasonably priced, comfortable accommodation close to Oporto's centre.

Da Bolsa – *R. Ferreira Borges, 101* - www.hoteldabolsa.com – ☎ 222 02 67 68 – 36 rooms. An interesting address in the lively Ribeira district. Beautiful 19C façade, although the interior has been completely refurbished in a rather dull modern style. The top-floor rooms are more expensive but offer wonderful views of the port.

América - *R. Santa Catarina, 1018* ☎ 223 39 29 30 - www.hotel-america.net - 30 rooms. On the same road as the Santa Catarina, this budget hotel has wood floors and lovely furniture. The staff members extend a warm welcome.

Grande Hotel do Porto – *R. de Santa Catarina 197* – ☎ 222 07 66 90 - www.grandhotelporto.com – 100 rooms. Although this landmark hotel has lost much of its former splendour, its public areas still retain an old fashioned charm. The rooms are appointed in a basic modern style. Its location on a bustling pedestrian shop-

B.Barbier

Typical Oporto houses

ping street in the centre is a plus for those visiting the city on foot.

Infante de Sagres – *Praça D. Filipa de Lencastre 62 – ☎ 222 39 85 00 – www.hotelinfantasagres.pt -* 72 rooms . The centrally-located Infante de Sagres, close to the Praça da Liberdade, is the most prestigious hotel in Oporto with a charm all of its own. Its interior contains wood-panelling, period furniture and stained glass.

EATING OUT

Filha da Mãe Preta – *R. Cais da Ribeira, 40 – ☎ 222 05 5 15 - filhad-amaepreta@clix.pt – closed Sundays.* One of the numerous cafés, bars and restaurants in Ribeira overlooking the port, serving fine cuisine at reasonable prices. Fish dominates the menu but also traditional local fare such as tripe or kidneys. You won't find a more congenial atmosphere anywhere else.

Cometa – *R. Tomaz Gonzaga, 87 – ☎ 222 00 87 74 – Closed Sundays - reservations recommended on Fri/Sat.* Close to the S. João Novo church in the Miragaia district this little restaurant has a wonderful 1950s feel to it. The hearty food served here might remind you of the type of dishes your grand-mother would have prepared.

D. Luis – *Av. Ramos Pinto 264-266 ☎ 223 75 12 51 - closed Mon.* Beautiful décor makes this little restaurant in Vila Nova de Gaia a cosy place to spend the evening, with room for only 20 guests. Fish playsa big part on the menu. The is atmosphere tranquil and calming, compared to the rush and bustle outside. Reservations essential at weekends.

O Chanquinhas – *R. de Santana 243 – ☎ 229 95 18 84 –* Closed *Sundays.* An ancient family mansion has been converted into an elegant family restaurant whose quality of cuisine matches the surroundings.

A Mesa Com Bacchus – *R. de Miragaia, 127 (tram no. 1, Alfândega stop) 222 00 08 96, closed Sun, reservations essential for evenings* . At the heart of the old town and not far from the river, this is a restaurant not to miss if you enjoy fine food and great service. As you might iimagine from the name it is a wine-lover's paradise with wines chosen by the *patron*, with a different suggestion for every dish. You will enjoy excellent food in an intimate and friendly atmosphere.

The Centre

Praça da Liberdade and Praça do General Humberto Delgado

These two squares in the city centre form a vast open space dominated by the Town Hall. Nearby is the pedestrian **Rua de Santa Catarina**, with the city's smartest shops and the famous Café Majestic. The **Mercado Muncipal de Bolhão**, the municipal market, located between Rua de Fernandes and Rua Formosa, is colourful.

Igreja dos Clérigos

A Baroque church built by the architect Nasoni between 1735-48. The oval plan of the nave bears out the Italian influence. Dominating the church is the 75.60m/248ft high **Torre dos Clérigos**★ (◷*Tower and belfry open 9.30am-12.30pm; 2.30pm-6.30pm;* ◉*€2. ☏ 222 00 17 29)*, Oporto's most characteristic monument, which in the past served as a seamark to ships. The extensive **panorama**★ from the top takes in the city, the cathedral, the Douro valley and the wine lodges.

Igreja do Carmo and Igreja das Carmelitas

The two Baroque churches stand side by side. The Igreja do Carmo is decorated on the outside with a large panel of *azulejos* showing Carmelites taking the veil.

Museu Nacional Soares dos Reis

◷*Open 10am-6pm; Tues 2pm-6pm only.* ◷*Closed Mon, 1 Jan, Easter Sun, 25 Apr, 1 May and 25 Dec.*◉*€3. ☏ 223 39 37 70 or 225 09 56 25.*

The museum, housed in the 18C Palácio dos Carrancos, exhibits permanent collections of Portuguese paintings and sculpture from the 17C to 20C. Most interesting among the sculptures are those by **Soares dos Reis** (1847-89). Portuguese painting between 1850 and 1950 is represented by canvases by Silva Porto, Henrique Pousão, who was influenced by the Impressionists and Symbolists, José Malhoa, João Vaz and Columbano.

Older paintings on display include Portuguese works by Frei Carlos, Gaspar Vaz, Vasco Fernandes and Cristóvão de Figueiredo, and foreign works by Francis Clouet (portraits of *Marguerite de Valois* and *Henri II of France*), Quillard, Pillement, Teniers, Troni and Simpson. The museum also contains a collection of old ceramics, gold articles and sacred art. Particularly worthy of note are two 17C Namban screens illustrating the arrival of the Portuguese in Japan.

OPORTO SIGHTS INDEX		
Biblioteca Almeida Garrett	BV	M⁷
Bom Jesus	AU	
Carmo e Carmelitas	EY	
Casa do Infante	EZ	
Casa Tait	BV	D
Castelo da Foz	AV	
Castelo do Queijo	AU	
Caves	EZ	
Cedofeita	DX	
Centro Português de Fotografia	EY	F
Estação de São Bento	EY	
Fundação António de Almeida	BU	M¹
Fundação de Serralves (Museu de Arte Contemporânea)	AU	
Galeria do Palácio	BV	M⁷
Hospital Santo António	DY	
Igreja da Imaculada Conceição	BU	F
Igreja de Santa Clara	EZ	R
Igreja de São Francisco	EZ	
Igreja de São Lourenço dos Grilos	EZ	S
Jardim do Palácio de Cristal	DY	
Mercado Ferreira Borges	EZ	
Mercado municipal do Bolhão	FY	K
Museu Guerra Junqueiro	EZ	M⁵
Museu Nacional de Soares dos Reis	DY	
Museu Romântico	BV	M⁶
Nossa Senhora da Serra do Pilar	EFZ	
Palácio da Bolsa	EZ	
Ponte D. Luis I	EZ	
Ponte da Arrábida	BV	
Ponte Maria Pia	FZ	
Porto de Leixões	AU	
Santa Casa da Misericórdia	EZ	P
Sé	EZ	
Torre dos Clérigos	EY	

OPORTO
STREET INDEX

24 de Agosto Campo	FY	
31 de Janeiro R. de	EY	126
5 de Outubro R. de	BU	125
Alberto Aires Gouveia R. de	DY	3
Albuquerque R. Af. de	DYZ	4
Alegria R. da FXY	CU	
Alexandre Herculano R. de	FYZ	
Alfândega L. da	DYZ	
Alferes Malheiro R. do	EXY	6
Aliados Av. dos	EY	
Almada R. do	EXY	
Almeida Garrett Pr. de	EY	7
Álvares Cabral R. de	DEX	
Amiral R. do	BU	
Aníbal Cunha R. de	DX	
Antero de Quental R.de	BU,EX	10
Augusto Rosa R. de	FZ	12
Azevedo de Magalhães R.	BCV	13
Barão de Forrester R. do	DX	
Barão do Corvo R.	BV	14
Batalha Pr. da	FY	
Belchior Robles R.	AU	15
Bélgica R. da	BV	
Belomonte R. de	EZ	16
Boa Hora R. da	DXY	18
Boa Nova R.	DY	
Boavista Av. da	DEX AU	
Bonfim R. do	CV FY	
Bonjardim R. do	FX,EXY	19
Bragas R. dos	EX	
Brasil Av. do	AUV	
Breyner R. do	DY	
Brito Capelo R. de	AU	
Brito Capelo R. de	AU	
Cabo Simão R.	FZ	
Camões R. de	EX	
Campo Alegre R. do	BV	22
Cândido dos Reis R.	BV	24
Carlos Alberto Pr. de	EY	
Carlos Malheiro Dias R. de	CU	25
Carmelitas R. das	EY	27
Carmo R. do	DEY	28
Carvalhido R. do	BU	30
Cedofeita R. de	DYE	
Cimo da Vila R. de	EY	31
Circunvalação Estrada da	ABU	
Clérigos R. dos	EY	33
Coelho Neto R. de	FY	34
Combatentes da Granda Guerra Av. dos	AU	35
Conc. Fernandes R.	CV	
Conceição R. da	EY	36
Conselheiro Veloso da Cruz R. do	BV	37
Constituição R. da	BCU	
Coronel Helder Ribeiro R.	AU	38
Coronel Pacheco Pr. do	EY	
Coronel Raul Peres R. do	AV	39
Costa Cabral R. de	CU	
Dinis R. de Julio	DXY	
Dinis R. de S.	BU	
Diogo Botelho R. de	AV	
Diogo Leite Av.	EZ	
Diu R. de	AV	40
Dom Afonso Henriques R. de	CU	
Dom Afonso Henriques Av.	EYZ	46
Dom Afonso Henriques Av. de	AU	
Dom Carlos Av. de	AV	48
Dom João I Pr.	EY	
Dom João IV R. de	FXY	
Dom Manuel II R.	DY	
Dona Filipa de Lencastre Pr. de	EY	49
Dr A. Guimarães R.	AU	
Dr António Emilio de Magalhães R. de	EY	42
Dr Antunes Guimarães Av. do	AU	
Dr E. Torres R.	AU	
Dr F. Aroso Av.	AU	
Dr Magalhães Lemos R. do	EY	43
Dr R. Frias R.	CU	
Dr Tiogo de Almeida R. do	DY	45
Dr. A. Guimarães R.	AU	
Duque de Loulé R. do	FY7	
Duque de Saldanha R. do	FYZ	
Engenheiro Duarte Pacheco R. do	AU	51
Entreparedes R. de	FY	52
Entre-Quintas R. de	AU	53
Falcão R. de	EY	
Faria Guimarães R. de	BU,EX	54
Fernandes Tomás R. de	EFY	
Fernão de Magalhães Av. de	CUV	
Firmeza R. da	FY	
Flores R. das	EYZ	
Fonseca Cardoso R. de	EX	57
Fontainhas Passeio das	FZ	
Fontainhas Alam. das	FZ	
Formosa R.	EFY	
França Av. de	BU	58
Freixo R. do	CU	60
Gaia Cais de	DZ	
Gen. H. Delgado Pr.	EY	
Gomes Teixeira Pr. de	EY	61
Gonçalo Cristóvão R. de	EFX	
Gonzales Zarco Pr. de	AU	63
Guedes de Azevedo R. de	FXY	64
Gustavo Eiffel Av.	FZ	
Heróis de Franca R.	AU	65
Heróis e Mártires de Angola R. dos	EY	66
Heroísmo R. do	CV	67
Império Pr. do	AV	
Infante D. Henrique Ponte	FZ	
Infante Dom Henrique Pr. e R. do	EZ	69
Infante Dom Henrique Av.	BV	
João das Regras R. de	EX	70
Lapa R. da	EX	
Lapa L. de	EX	
Latino Coelho R. de	FX	
Liberdade Pr. da	EY	
Liberdade Av. de la	AU	
Lisboa Pr. de	EY	72
Loureiro R. do	EY	73
Marechal Carmona Via	AU	
Marechal Gomes da Costa Av.	AU	
Marechal Saldanha R.	AUV	
Marquês de Pombal Pr. do	BCU	75
Mártires da Liberda de R. dos	EY	
Mártires da Pátria Campo dos	DEY	76
Maternidade R. da	DY	78
Miguel Bombarda R. de	DY	
Monchique R. de	DY	
Monte dos Búrgos R. do	BU	79
Montevideu Av. de	AU	
Moreira R. do	FX	
Morgado Mateus R. de	FY	
Mouzinho da Silveira R.	YZE	
Mouzinho de Albuquerque Pr.	BU	81
Norte Via	BU	
Norton de Matos Av.	AU	
Nova de Alfândega R.	DZ	
Nova de São Crispim R.	FX	82
Nova do Seixo R.	BU	
Nuno Álvares Pereira Av. de	AU	84
Oliveira Monteiro R. de	DX	
Oliveiras R. das	EY	85
Ouro R. de	ABV	
Paraíso R. do	EFX	87
Passos Manuel R. de	FY	88
Pedro Hispano R.	BU	
Pedro Nunes Pr. de	DX	
Pedro V R. de	BV	89
Piedade R. da	DX	90
Pinto Bessa R. de	CV	91
Prov. Vincente José de Carvalho R. do	DY	93
Raimundo de Carvalho R.	CV	
Rainha D. Amélia Pr. da	FX	
Rei Ramiro R. do	DZ	
República Pr. da	EX	
República Av. da	BCV	
República Av. da	AU	94
República Av. da	EFZ	
Restauração R. da	DY	
Ribeira Pr. da	EZ	96
Ribeira Cais da	EZ	
Rio de Janeiro Espl. de	AU	97
Rodrigues de Freitas Av. de	FY	
Rodrigues de Freitas R.	FZ	
Rosário R. do	DY	
S. Roque da Lameira R. de	CU	
Sá da Bandeira R.	FXY	
Sacadura Cabral R.	DX	99
Santa Catarina R. de	FXY	
Santo Ildefonso R. de	FY	
Santos Pousada R. de	FXY	
São Domingos L. de	EZ	100
São Gens R. de	BU	
São João R. de	EZ	102
São João Novo Pr. de	DZ	103
São Lázaro Passeio de	FY	105
São Vítor R. de	FYZ	
Saraiva de Carvalho R. de	EZ	106
Sé Terreiro da	EZ	108
Sendim R.	AU	
Senhora da Luz R. da	AV	109
Serpa Pinto R. de	BV	113
Serralves R. de	AU	
Sidónio Pais Av.	BU	114
Soares dos Reis L. de	FY	115
Soares dos Reis R.	BV	117
Sobreiras R. de	AV	118
Sol Poente R. do	AU	119
Taipas R. das	DEZ	
Torrinha R. da	DX	
Trindade R. da	EY	120
Trindade Pr. da	EY	
Vasco da Gama Av.	CV	
Veloso Salgado R. de	AU	121
Villagarcia de Arosa Av.	AU	122
Vimara Peres Av.	EZ	123
Vitória R. da	EYZ	124

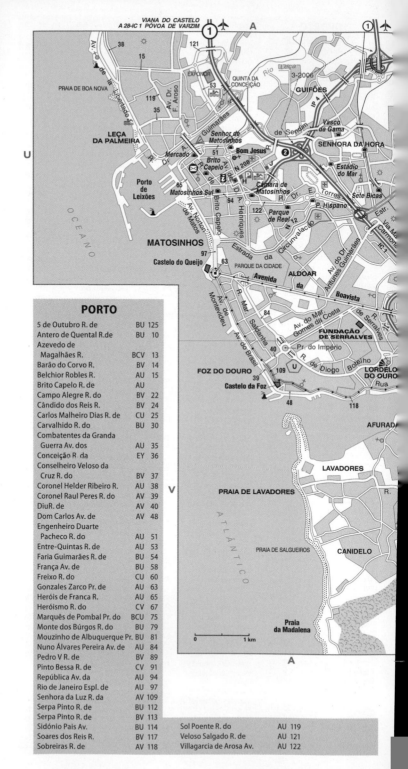

PORTO

5 de Outubro R. de	BU	125
Antero de Quental R.de	BU	10
Azevedo de		
Magalhães R.	BCV	13
Barão do Corvo R.	BV	14
Belchior Robles R.	AU	15
Brito Capelo R. de	AU	
Campo Alegre R. do	BV	22
Cândido dos Reis R.	BV	24
Carlos Malheiro Dias R. de	CU	25
Carvalhido R. do	BU	30
Combatentes da Granda		
Guerra Av. dos	AU	35
Conceição R. da	EY	36
Conselheiro Veloso da		
Cruz R. do	BV	37
Coronel Helder Ribeiro R.	AU	38
Coronel Raul Peres R. do	AV	39
DiuR. de	AV	40
Dom Carlos Av. de	AV	48
Engenheiro Duarte		
Pacheco R. do	AU	51
Entre-Quintas R. de	AU	53
Faria Guimarães R. de	BU	54
França Av. de	BU	58
Freixo R. do	CU	60
Gonzales Zarco Pr. de	AU	63
Heróis de Franca R.	AU	65
Heróismo R. do	CV	67
Marquês de Pombal Pr. do	BCU	75
Monte dos Búrgos R. do	BU	79
Mouzinho de Albuquerque Pr.	BU	81
Nuno Álvares Pereira Av. de	AU	84
Pedro V R. de	BV	89
Pinto Bessa R. de	CV	91
República Av. da	AU	94
Rio de Janeiro Espl. de	AU	97
Senhora da Luz R. da	AV	109
Serpa Pinto R. de	BU	112
Serpa Pinto R. de	BV	113
Sidónio Pais Av.	BU	114
Soares dos Reis R.	BV	117
Sobreiras R. de	AV	118
Sol Poente R. do	AU	119
Veloso Salgado R. de	AU	121
Villagarcia de Arosa Av.	AU	122

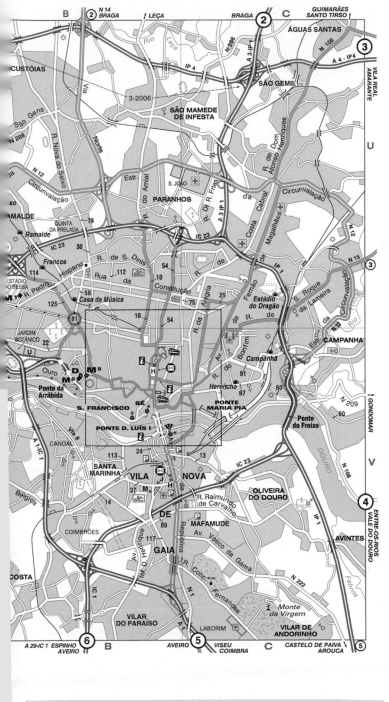

Biblioteca Almeida Garrett	BV	M⁷	Galería do Palácio	BV	M⁷
Casa Tait	BV	D	Igreja da Imaculada Conceição	BU	F
Fundação António de Almeida	BU	M¹	Museu Romântico	BV	M⁶

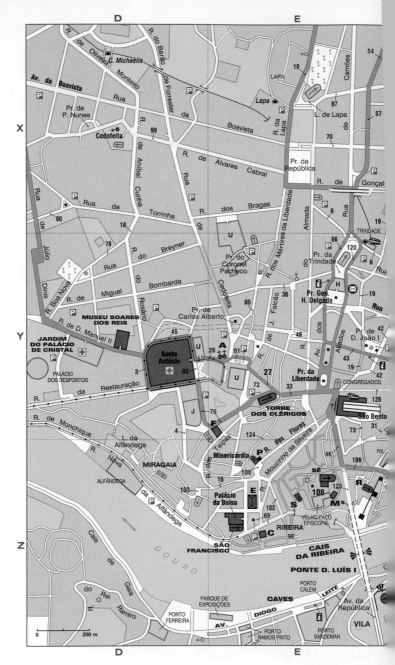

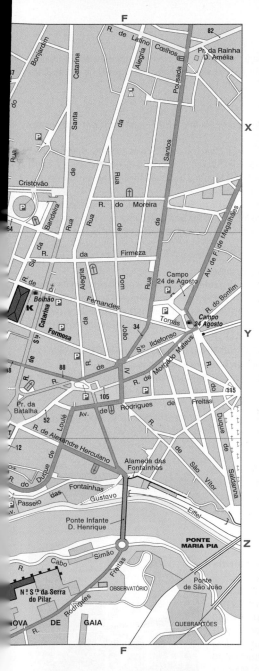

PORTO

31 de Janeiro R. de	EY	126
Alberto Aires Gouveia R. de	DY	3
Albuquerque R. Af. de	DYZ	4
Alferes Malheiro R. do	EXY	6
Almada R. do	EXY	
Almeida Garrett Pr. de	EY	7
Antero de Quental R.de	EX	10
Augusto Rosa R. de	FZ	12
Belomonte R. de	EZ	16
Boa Hora R. da	DXY	18
Bonjardim R. do	EXY	19
Carmelitas R. das	EY	27
Carmo R. do	DEY	28
Cimo da Vila R. de	EY	31
Clérigos R. dos	EY	33
Coelho Neto R. de	FY	34
Dom Afonso Henriques Av.	EYZ	46
Dona Filipa de Lencastre Pr. de	EY	49
Dr António Emílio de Magalhães R. do	EY	42
Dr Magalhães Lemos R. do	EY	43
Dr Tiogo de Almeida R. do	DY	45
Entreparedes R. de	FY	52
Faria Guimarães R. de	EX	54
Fernandes Tomás R. de	EFY	
Flores R. das	EYZ	
Fonseca Cardoso R. de	EX	57
Formosa R.	EFY	
Gomes Teixeira Pr. de	EY	61
Guedes de Azevedo R. de	FXY	64
Heróis e Mártires de Angola R. dos	EY	66
Infante Dom Henrique Pr. e R. do	EZ	69
João das Regras R. de	EX	70
Lisboa Pr. de	EY	72
Loureiro R. do	EY	73
Mártires da Pátria Campo dos	DEY	76
Maternidade R. da	DY	78
Nova de São Crispim R.	FX	82
Oliveiras R. das	EY	85
Paraíso R. do	EFX	87
Passos Manuel R. de	FY	88
Piedade R. da	DX	90
Prov. Vicente José de Carvalho R. do	DY	93
Ribeira Pr. da	EZ	96
Sá da Bandeira R. de	FXY	
Sacadura Cabral R.	DX	99
Santa Catarina R. de	FXY	
São Domingos L. de	EZ	100
São João R. de	EZ	102
São João Novo Pr. de	DZ	103
São Lázaro Passeio de	FY	105
Saraiva de Carvalho R. de	EZ	106
Sé Terreiro da	EZ	108
Soares dos Reis L. de	FY	115
Trindade R. da	EY	120
Vimara Peres Av.	EZ	123
Vitória R. da	EYZ	124

Carmo e Carmelitas	EY	A	Igreja de São Lourenço		
Casa do Infante	EZ	C	dos Grilos	EZ	S
Centro Português			Mercado Ferreira Borges	EZ	E
de Fotografia	EY	F	Mercado municipal do Bolhão	FY	K
Igreja de Santa Clara	EZ	R	Museu Guerra Junqueiro	EZ	M³
			Santa Casa da Misericórdia	EZ	P

Old Oporto★★

Terreiro da Sé

In the middle of the vast esplanade overlooking the old town stands a neo-Pombaline pillory. The square is bordered by the massive cathedral, the former episcopal palace dating from the 18C and a 14C granite tower.

Cathedral★

⊙Open Apr-Oct 8.45am-12.30pm and 2.30-7pm - rest of year until 6pm. Entrance to cloisters: ⊗€2. ☎ 222 05 90 28.

The cathedral *(sé)*, begun as a fortress-church in the 12C, was considerably modified in the 17C and 18C. The main façade, flanked by two square, domed towers, has a 13C Romanesque rose window and a Baroque doorway. Inside, the narrow central nave is flanked by aisles on a lower level.

The transept and chancel were modified in the Baroque period. The Chapel of the Holy Sacrament, which opens off the left arm of the transept, contains a very fine **altar**★ with a chased silver altarpiece worked by Portuguese silversmiths in the 17C.

Cloisters

Access through the right arm of the transept.

The 14C cloisters are decorated with **azulejos**★ panels, illustrating the Life of the Virgin, and Ovid's *Metamorphoses*, made by Valentim de Almeida between 1729 and 1731. The original Romanesque cloisters containing several sarcophagi can be seen from these cloisters. A fine granite staircase leads to the chapter-house which has a coffered ceiling painted by Pachini in 1737.

Behind the cathedral is the delightful **Museu Guerra Junqueiro** (♿ *see below*). The Mannerist-style **Igreja de São Lourenço dos Grilos**, built by the Jesuits in the 17C, is now the headquarters of the Grand Seminary. The church also houses a **museum of sacred art** (*⊙Open 10am-noon and 2-5pm. ⊗€1*).

▶ *On reaching Rua Mouzinho da Silveira, cross over to Largo de São Domingos. Leading off from it is the picturesque Rua das Flores.*

Rua das Flores

This narrow street leading to São Bento railway station is bordered by traditional shops and 18C houses with coats-of-arms adorning the façades. It was once the main street for jewellers as well as gold and silversmiths.

The **Santa Casa da Misericórdia** (*⊙Open 10am-noon and 2.30pm-5.30pm. ⊙Closed Mon and during Aug. ⊙Museum open Mon-Fri 9.30am-noon; 2pm-5.30pm. ⊙Closed Sat/Sun and holidays ⊗€1.50 ☎ 222 07 47 10*). Beside the Baroque Igreja da Misericórdia, contains an outstanding painting from the Flemish School called **Fons Vitae**★ or the Fountain of Mercy. It has been attributed to different people including Holbein, Van der Weyden and Van Orley: maybe it was the work of a Portuguese artist who drew his inspiration from Flemish painters.

Igreja de São Francisco

▶ *Return to Largo de São Domingos and then take Rua Belomonte.*

Igreja de São Francisco ★★
🕐*Open 9am-6pm (5pm Oct to Apr).* ≋*€2.* ☎ *222 00 84 41.*
The Gothic church has kept its fine rose window and 17C doorway. The original restraint of the edifice was in keeping with the Franciscan order's ideal of poverty. However, in the 17C the order became extremely powerful with the result that privileges and material possessions were bestowed upon it. This is borne out by the triumph of **Baroque decoration**★★ inside: altars, walls and vaulting disappear beneath a forest of 17C and 18C carved and gilded woodwork. The **Tree of Jesse**★ in the second chapel on the left is particularly noteworthy, as is the high altar. Beneath the gallery, to the right on entering the church, is a polychrome granite statue of St Francis dating from the 13C.

Casa dos Terceiros de São Francisco (House of the Third Order of St Francis)
The building houses a permanent collection of sacred art with objects from the 16C-20C. The crypt contains the sarcophagi of Franciscan friars and nobles. An ossuary is also visible in the basement through an iron railing.

Casa do Infante
Rua da Alfândega. This is where Prince Henry the Navigator is believed to have been born. It was the city's Customs House from the 14C to 19C.

Cais da Ribeira★
The quayside dominated by the tall outline of the D. Luís I bridge is the most picturesque spot in Oporto. Ancient houses look down from a great height on the waterfront with its fish and vegetable market and lively night-life. Several old boats lie moored at the water's edge. This section of the old city is a World Heritage site and has undergone major restoration work over the past few years. Cross the Douro by the D. Luís I bridge to reach the wine lodges *(5min on foot – ⚓ see Wine Lodges below).*

Solar do Vinho do Porto
Below the Museu Romântico. 🕐*Open 2pm-midnight.* 🕐*Closed Sun and holidays. No charge.* ☎ *226 09 77 93 or 226 09 47 49.*
This is the headquarters of the Port Wine Institute. Hundreds of different types of port may be tasted in very pleasant surroundings.

Port wine lodge

Ribeiro district, Oporto

Wine Lodges★

The city's wine lodges cover several acres on the south bank of the Douro in the lower quarter of **Vila Nova da Gaia**. More than 58 port companies are established in the area. In bygone days, boats known as *barcos rebelos* would transport the wines of the Upper Douro some 150km/90mi along the river to the lodges where they would be transformed into port. Approximately twenty wine lodges may be toured including those of Cálem, Sandeman, Ramos Pinto and Ferreira.

Additional Sights

Igreja de Santa Clara★
Open 9.30-11.30am and 3-6pm. Closed Sat-Sun. ☎ 222 01 48 37.
The church, which dates from the Renaissance, has kept its original granite doorway with figures in medallions. The rather austere exterior contrasts with the profuse decoration of 17C **carved and gilded woodwork**★ inside. The ceiling is Mudéjar in style.

Jardim do Palácio de Cristal
Kids *Open 8am-7pm (Oct-Mar); 8am-9pm (Apr-Sept).*
This garden provides a haven of peace in its tree-lined paths, its beautiful flowers, lagoons, grottos and fountains. Animals roam freely and it is the ideal place for a picnic whilst watching the children play. There are some spots with lovely views over Vila Nova da Gaia, the Douro and the coast. A crystal palace was built here similar to that used for the great Exhibition of 1865 in London, but it has since been demolished and replaced by a rather uninspiring sports pavilion, to the chagrin of many locals. At one part of the garden you will find the Galeria do Palácio, which has regular exhibitions and also houses the biblioteca Almeida Garrett.

Fundação Eng° António de Almeida
Guided tours (30min), 2.30- 5.30pm. Closed Sun, holidays and in Aug. ⊚€2. ☎ 226 06 74 18 - www.feaa.pt.
Throughout his lifetime the rich industrialist António de Almeida put together a fine **collection of gold coins**★ (Greek, Roman, Byzantine, French and Portuguese) which is exhibited in the house where he lived.
The interior decoration includes antique furniture and porcelain.

Fundação de Serralves (Museu de Arte Contemporânea)★

Open Apr-Sept 10am-7pm (8pm Sat-Sun and school holidays, until 10pm for the museum Fri/Sat); Oct-Mar 10am-7pm. Closed Mon. ☎ 226 15 65 00; www.serralves.pt Museum and park €5; museum Fri, Sat after 7pm €3; park only €2.50; free Sun 10am-2pm.

The Casa de Serralves complex, which stands in a magnificent 18ha/44 acre **park**★, is an outstanding example of 1930s architecture with Art Nouveau interior decoration. Inside, note the architecture, decoration, graceful **forged iron grilles**★ designed by Lalique and the luxurious inlaid parquet floors on the first floor.

Igreja da Cedofeita

Open 10am-12.30pm; 3pm-7pm. ☎ 222 00 56 20.

This is the city's oldest church and dates from the 12C. It is a fine example of early Romanesque architecture although it has been transformed over the centuries, particularly in the 17C. The original Romanesque portal adorned with a Lamb of God and the barrel vaulting in the nave are intact.

Antigo Convento de Nossa Senhora da Serra do Pilar

Across Luís I bridge in Vila Nova de Gaia.

The old convent above the city affords one of the finest views of Oporto including the remains of the 14C walls to the right of D. Luís I bridge. It is a curious building erected in the 16C and 17C in the form of a rotunda which is said to have been designed by Filippo Terzi.

PÓVOA DE VARZIM

PORTO
POPULATION 23 846 – MICHELIN MAP 733

Póvoa de Varzim is an old fishing port and also an elegant seaside resort. It is also the birthplace of the great novelist Eça de Queirós (1845-1900).

- ▶ **Orient Yourself:** About 35km/25ml north of Porto, on the coast.
- **Don't Miss:** The Fishermen's quarter, south of the main beach.
- **Organizing Your Time:** Soak up some sun but see the two churches nearby.

Excursion

Romanesque Churches of Rio Mau and Rates – *15km/9mi – about 1hr.*

- ▶ *Leave Póvoa de Varzim by the Oporto road (N 13) going south; after 2km/1mi turn left onto the N 206 towards Guimarães.*

Rio Mau

Turn right opposite the post office onto an unsurfaced road.

The small Romanesque **Igreja de São Cristóvão** is built of granite; the rough decoration of the capitals contrast with the more detailed ornamentation on the **capitals**★ in the triumphal arch and in the chancel which is later in date.

- ▶ *2km/1mi beyond Rio Mau, take a turning to the left to Rates (1km/0.5mi).*

Rates

The granite Igreja de São Pedro was built in the 12C and 13C by Benedictine monks from Cluny. The façade is pierced by a rose window and a door with five arches, and capitals decorated with animals; on the tympanum a low-relief sculpture presents a Transfiguration.

PALÁCIO NACIONAL DE QUELUZ★★

LISBOA
MICHELIN MAP 733 – MICHELIN ATLAS SPAIN & PORTUGAL P 58 (P 2)

The **Royal Palace of Queluz**, just a few miles west of Lisbon, takes the visitor right back into the heart of the 18C. In the formal gardens adorned with pools and statues, overlooked by pastel-coloured Rococo façades with their many windows, one almost expects to come upon a romantic scene from a painting by Watteau. Although Inspired by Versailles, the Queluz Palace is smaller in proportion, making it more intimate. ⓘ *Av. Dr. Miguel Bombarda (Estação C.P.) – 2745-616 –* ☎ *219 23 11 57 or 219 24 17 00*

A Bit of History

At the end of the 16C, the land belonged to the Marquis of Castelo Rodrigo, who had a hunting lodge here. After the restoration of the monarchy and Dom João IV's accession to the throne, the property was confiscated and several years later, in 1654, became the residence of the *Infantes*. Dom Pedro (1717-86), son of Dom João V and the future Dom Pedro III, was the first *infante* to show a real interest in the estate and decided to build a palace. From 1747 to 1758, the Portuguese architect Mateus Vicente de Oliveira built the main façade as well as the wing that would later contain the Throne Room. While the overall style of the palace is Rococo, architectural differences between the three periods are apparent.

Visit

ⓘ*Open 10am-5pm.* ⓘ*Closed Tues, 1 Jan, Good Friday, Easter Sun, 1 May, 29 June and 25 Dec.* ⓘ*Palace and gardens: €4 (gardens only: €1.50).* ☎ *214 34 38 60.*

A Victim of the Revolution

This palace, built as a place of celebration, was also the setting for the dramatic life of **Maria I.** Maria was pious almost to the point of superstition and considered the death of her uncle and husband Pedro III in 1786 to be a warning of the misfortune that was to afflict her family and people. The loss in 1788 of two of her children, Crown Prince Josef, who died at the age of 27, and the Infanta Maria-Anna, who was married to the son of the Spanish king, in less than two months, merely confirmed her premonitions. Her feelings of melancholy were increased by the death of her confessor soon after. She became so disturbed by the outbreak of the French Revolution that by 1791 she was already showing the first signs of dementia. Her second son, João, governed in her name and took the title of Regent in 1799. When French troops invaded Portugal, João took his mother to Brazil, where she died, still Portugal's reigning sovereign, in 1816.

Palácio Nacional de Queluz

The sumptuous **Sala do Trono**★ (Throne Room), recalls the Hall of Mirrors in Versailles. Magnificent Venetian crystal chandeliers hang from the ceiling decorated with allegorical illustrations and supported on caryatids.

The Sala dos Azulejos is so called on account of the wonderful multi-coloured 18C *azulejos* depicting landscapes of China and Brazil. The Sala da Guarda Real (Royal Guard Room) contains a fine 18C Arraiolos carpet. The **Sala dos Embaixadores** (Ambassadors' Hall), decorated with marble and mirrors, has a painted ceiling of a concert at the court of King Dom José and diverse mythological motifs.

Beyond the Queen's Boudoir, French Rococo in style, lies the **Sala Don Quixote** where eight columns support a circular ceiling, and where paintings of Cervantes's hero decorate the walls. In the Sala das Merendas (Tea Room), embellished with gilded woodwork, are several 18C paintings of royal picnics.

Gardens

The sumptuous gardens were designed by the French architect JB Robillon in the style of the 17C French landscape gardener, Le Nôtre. Individual attractions include the Amphitrite basin. The walls of the **Grand Canal** are covered in 18C *azulejos* of between which flows the Jamor river. In the past the royal family went boating along the canal. Note the façade of the Robillon wing, fronted by a magnificent **Lion Staircase**★ (Escadaria dos Leões) which is extended by a beautiful colonnade.

PONTA DE **SAGRES**
AND CABO DE **SÃO VICENTE**★★★

FARO
MICHELIN MAP 733
LOCAL MAP SEE ALGARVE

The windswept headland falling steeply to the sea is the southwest extremity of mainland Europe. It was here, facing the Atlantic Ocean, the great unknown, that Prince Henry the Navigator retired in the 15C to found the Sagres School of Navigation, which would prepare the way for the Great Discoveries.

The Sagres School

In 1415, Prince Henry the Navigator retired to Sagres where he founded a School of Navigation, using the best Arab and other cartographers he could find. Theories were tested and put to practical use in expeditions which set out on several voyages (👁 *see LAGOS).* Improvements in the astrolabe and the sextant and increased knowledge in their use, enabling calculations to be made far out to sea, led to the prince's introduction of navigation by the stars: mariners who had been used to a chart and compass as guides and had only estimated their position, learned to calculate their latitude from the height of the stars above the horizon and chart their positions with greater accuracy.

The demands of the voyages also compelled the Portuguese to design a new type of ship which revolutionised navigation – the **caravel**. 👁 *See Sidebar.*

Cabo de São Vicente

The Caravel

One of Portugal's most significant contributions to maritime history is the **caravel**. This type of light sailing ship, developed by Portuguese fishermen, was widely used in the 15C-17C in Europe, particularly for exploring uncharted seas. Caravels were rigged with lanteen (triangular) sails, which enabled them to sail to windward (taking advantage of a wind from the side of the ship). These elegant craft, which superseded the oared galley, generally measured about 23m/75ft in length, with two or three masts (later versions added a fourth with square rigging for running before the wind). The caravel was capable of remarkable speed, and was well-adapted to long voyages. Two of the three ships under the command of Christopher Columbus in 1492, the *Niña* and the *Pinta*, were caravels.

Sights

Ponta de Sagres★★★

The headland Is partially occupied by the remains of a 16C **fortress** (◷Open 10am-8.30pm (6.30pm Nov to Apr). ◷Closed 1 May and 25 Dec. ⊜€3. ☎ 282 62 01 40). The entrance tunnel leads into a vast courtyard with an immense wind compass.

Cabo de São Vicente★★★

Cape St Vincent, the most southwesterly point of continental Europe, towers above the ocean at a height of 75m/246ft. The Romans called it *Promontorium Sacrum*. Its present name derives from a legend recounting how the vessel containing the body of St Vincent after he had suffered martyrdom in Valencia in the 4C ran aground at the cape. The ship, guarded by two ravens, remained here for centuries before continuing its way to Lisbon which it reached in 1173.

SANTA MARIA DA FEIRA

AVEIRO

POPULATION 4 877 – MICHELIN MAP 733

The castle of Santa Maria da Feira stands on a wooded height facing the town which lies scattered over the opposite hillside. ⬛ Rua dos Descobrimentos – 4520-201 – ☎ 256 37 20 32 ⬛ Praça da República – 4520-201 – ☎ 256 37 08 00.

▶ **Orient Yourself:** 30km/20mi south of Porto, just off the main A1 highway.
◷ **Organizing Your Time:** A "passing-through" town – no more than an hour.

Visit

Castle★

◷Open 9am-noon and 2-6pm. ◷Closed Mon ⊜€2. ☎ 256 37 22 48.
The 11C castle was reconstructed in the 15C. A keep flanked by four tall towers with pepperpot roofs overlooks a fortified perimeter wall whose entrance is defended on its eastern side by a barbican. Follow the wall walk; latrines can still be seen. Stairs lead to the first floor of the keep where there is a vast Gothic hall; the upper platform (60 steps) affords a panorama of the castle's fortifications, the town, the surrounding wooded hills and the coastline, where one can make out the Ria de Aveiro in the distance.

Igreja da Misericórdia
The chancel, under a coffered ceiling, has a lovely gilded altarpiece. In a south chapel there are some unusual statues, one of which is a Saint Christopher, 3m/10ft high.

SANTARÉM

SANTARÉM
POPULATION 63 418 – MICHELIN MAP 733

Irene, a young nun in a convent near Tomar, was murdered by a monk whose advances she refused. Her body was thrown in the Tagus and washed up in the former Roman town of Scalabis. The town was renamed Saint Irene – Santarém – in her honour. On a hill on the north bank of the Tagus, it overlooks the vast Ribatejo plain. It was recaptured from the Moors in 1147 by Alfonso I and later became a royal residence. From this rich past, Santarém retains several monuments, mostly Gothic, dotted about the town's attractive old quarter. ⊞ *Rua Capelo e Ivens, 63 – 2000-039 – ☎ 243 39 15 12* ⊞ *Campo Infante da Câmara (Casa do Campino) – 2000-014 – ☎ 243 33 03 30*

- ▶ **Orient Yourself:** About 80km/50ml north-east of Lisbon, on the Tagus.
- ⊙ **Organizing Your Time:** An afternoon is best to enjoy the atmosphere.
- ⊘ **Also See:** Abrantes, Fátima, Óbidos and Tomar.

Old Town

The historical centre, with its alleyways and steps, is a pleasant area for a stroll.

Igreja do Seminário
The late-18C Baroque façade of this former Jesuit college has as its main feature the superimposition of several storeys outlined by cornices and pierced by windows and niches, which gives the church more the appearance of a palace than a church.
The **interior** remains austere in spite of the marble incrustations decorating the altar and the pilasters. The single nave is covered with a ceiling painted to represent the Immaculate Conception and Jesuit evangelical activities overseas.

Igreja de Marvila
This church was founded in the 12C by King Afonso Henriques following the reconquest of Santarém from the Moors in 1147. 16C additions included the graceful Manueline doorway. The interior is lined with *azulejos*, the most interesting being those known as carpet or *tapete azulejos*, painted in many colours with plant motifs, which date from 1620 and 1635. Note the Manueline features in the three chapels and the Baroque gilded wood altar.

Igreja do Santíssimo Milagre
Built in the 14C and subsequently modified on several occasions. The sacristy contains the host that is said to have been transformed into the blood of Christ in 1247.

Igreja da Misericórdia
This 16C church had a Baroque façade added following the earthquake of 1755. The interior is noteworthy for its elegant ribbed vault supported by Tuscan columns.

Igreja de São João de Alporão (Museu Arqueológico) ★
*Open Tue-Wed 9.30am-12.30pm;2-5.30pm; Thu-Sun 10am-12.30pm; 2-5.30pm.
Closed Mon and holidays.* €1. ☎ 243 39 15 17.

To the left of the entrance of this Romanesque and Gothic church is the **cenotaph** of Duarte de Meneses, Count of Viana, which was erected by his wife in the 15C to contain a tooth, the only remains of her husband who had been killed by the Moors in North Africa. The stone balcony was carved by Mateus Fernandes.

Torre das Cabaças
Open 9am-12.30pm and 2-5.30pm. Closed Mon. €2. ☎ 243 30 44 41.

There is a good overall **view** of Santarém from the top of Calabash Tower, a vestige of the old medieval wall, which faces the church of São João de Alporão.

Igreja da Graça ★
Open 9am-12.30pm and 2-5.30pm. Closed holidays. ☎ 243 32 55 52.

This Gothic church of 1380 has a fine Flamboyant façade with a lovely rose window carved from a single block of stone. The **nave** has been restored to its original lines. The church contains several tombs including, in the south transept, that of Dom

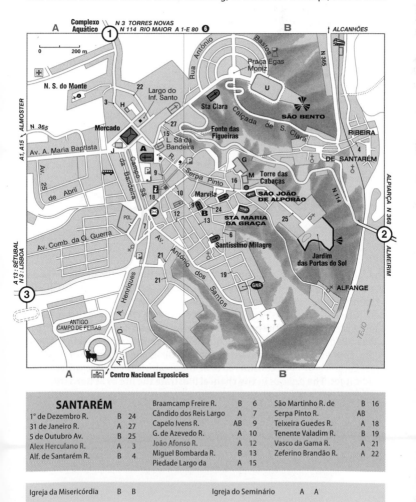

SANTARÉM								
1° de Dezembro R.	B	24	Braamcamp Freire R.	B	6	São Martinho R. de	B	16
31 de Janeiro R.	A	27	Cândido dos Reis Largo	A	7	Serpa Pinto R.	AB	
5 de Outubro Av.	B	25	Capelo Ivens R.	AB	9	Teixeira Guedes R.	A	18
Alex Herculano R.	A	3	G. de Azevedo R.	A	10	Tenente Valadim R.	B	19
Alf. de Santarém R.	B	4	João Afonso R.	A	12	Vasco da Gama R.	A	21
			Miguel Bombarda R.	B	13	Zeferino Brandão R.	A	22
			Piedade Largo da	A	15			

Igreja da Misericórdia	B	B		Igreja do Seminário	A	A

Pedro de Meneses, first Governor of Ceuta. The 15C tomb, resting on eight lions, is carved with leaf motifs and coats of arms. On the pavement of the south apsidal chapel can be seen the funerary stone of the navigator Pedro Álvares Cabral who discovered Brazil in 1500.

Additional Sights

Igreja de Santa Clara
Open 9am-12.30pm and 2-5.30pm. Closed Mon and holidays. ☎ 243 32 55 52.
This vast Gothic church was once part of a 13C convent. The lack of a doorway on the façade intensifies the bare appearance of the church's exterior.
Inside, the narrow nave ends with a beautiful rose window above the 17C tomb of Dona Leonor, founder of the convent. The church also contains the original 14C tomb of Dona Leonor. On either side of it are Franciscan monks and Poor Clares, at the foot St Francis receiving the stigmata, and at the head the Annunciation.

Miradouro de São Bento★
The belvedere affords a vast **panorama**★ of the Tagus plain and Santarém where the main buildings can easily be distinguished.

Fonte das Figueiras
This 13C fountain, against a wall, is covered by a porch roof crowned with pyramid shaped merlons.

Capela de Nossa Senhora do Monte
The 16C chapel stands in the middle of a horseshoe-shaped square. The façade is bordered on both sides by an arcaded gallery with capitals adorned with leaf motifs and heads of cherubim. At the east end stands 16C statue of Our Lady.

SÃO JOÃO DE TAROUCA

VISEU
POPULATION 1 054 – MICHELIN MAP 733

The former monastery of Tarouca, overlooked by the heights of the Serra de Leomil, lies squat in a hollow in the fertile Barossa valley. The church (*Open 10am-noon and 2-5pm. Closed Mon.* ☎ 254 67 98 49 *(Senhor Caetano)*) erected in the 12C by Cistercian monks, was remodelled in the 17C. The side chapel contains paintings attributed to Gaspar Vaz: a picture of St Peter (third chapel, south) is outstanding. The monumental 14C granite tomb contains the remains of Dom Pedro, Count of Barcelos, bastard son of King Dimis and also the author of the Great Chronicle of 1344, considered to be the greatest Portuguese writer of the Middle Ages. The *azulejos* in the chancel illustrate the life of St Bernard.

SERRA DE SÃO MAMEDE★

PORTALEGRE

MICHELIN MAP 733

The Serra de São Mamede is a small island of greenery in an arid and stony region; its altitude (highest point: 1 025m/3 363ft) and the impermeable soil combine to provide sufficient humidity for a dense and varied vegetation. The triangular-shaped massif is composed of hard rock that has resisted erosion.

Excursion   73km/45mi – about 2hr 30min

▷ *Leave Portalegre to the east; then turn northwards.*

The road rises through woods, with views of Portalegre.

▷ *Go to São Mamede.*

São Mamede

From the top there is a vast **panorama**★, extending south over the Alentejo, west and north over the Serra de São Mamede and east over the Spanish *sierras*.

▷ *Return to the main road and on to Marvão.*

Marvão ★★ – 🚗 *See MARVÃO.*

Castelo de Vide; Monte da Penha
– 🚗 *See CASTELO DE VIDE.*

▷ *Return to Portalegre on the Carreiras corniche* **road**★.

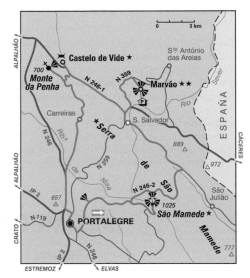

SERNANCELHE

VISEU

POPULATION 1 060 – MICHELIN MAP 733

The old town of Sernancelhe, off the beaten track about 50km/30ml north-east of Viseu, occupies a rocky height in the Beira Alta. It was once a commandery of the Order of Malta which built the castle, which is now in ruins.

Church

The façade of this Romanesque church, flanked by a squat square belfry, is pierced by a beautiful rounded doorway in which one of the arches is adorned with an unusual frieze of archangels. The tympanum is carved with plant motifs. Two niches on either side of the door shelter six granite statues of the Evangelists St Peter and St Paul.

Solar dos Carvalhos

This elegant Baroque manor house (18C) with a façade flanked by pilasters, belongs to the Marquis of Pombal's family.

SERPA

BEJA

POPULATION 9 200 – MICHELIN MAP 733

Serpa, a market town in the Lower Alentejo east of the Guadiana river, crowns a hilltop overlooking vast plains of wheat fields interspersed with rows of olive trees. The town has kept its ramparts which partially surmount an **aqueduct**.

 Largo D. Jorge de Melo, 2 – 7830-382 – ☎ 284 54 47 27

Visit *1hr 30min*

The fortified gate, the **Porta de Beja**, leads through the ramparts into the white-washed town. The main square, the **Largo dos Santos Próculo e Hilarião**, with its olive and cypress trees, is dominated by the façade of the Igreja de Santa Maria. A street on the right leads to the **castle**. The entrance looks like a romantic 19C engraving with its crumbling tower which now forms a porch.

Capela de Guadalupe

1.5km/1mi. Follow signs to the Pousada.
The bare, white Moorish building with domes overlooks the valley, affording wonderful views of the surrounding countryside.

SESIMBRA

SETÚBAL

POPULATION 25 138 – MICHELIN MAP 733
LOCAL MAP SEE SERRA DA ARRÁBIDA

Sesimbra occupies a pleasant site in an inlet at the foot of the southern slope of the Serra da Arrábida. Its beach is popular with Lisbonites.
Sesimbra is a centre for harpooning as well as deep-sea fishing for swordfish. These sports provide a counterpoint to the more traditional fishing activities which remain the town's main industry.

▶ **Orient Yourself:** Cross the 25 de Abril bridge along the A2 and turn onto the N378 and just keep going. It's on the coast.

▣ **Parking:** No major problems apart from the tiny village centre at night.

☺ **Don't Miss:** The old town on a warm evening with the smell of fish cooking.

◔ **Organizing Your Time:** Midafternoon is the time to arrive and stay for dinner in one of the restaurants along the seashore.

◔ **Also See:** Drive along the coast road to Setúbal – there are some lovely bays and a couple of restaurants on the beach.

Fishing boats, Sesimbra

Visit

The small fishing harbour has grown into an important seaside resort but has none-theless preserved its atmosphere, seen best in its steep streets leading down to the sea. Along these picturesque alleyways you'll see washing hanging out to dry. The many restaurants along the shore serve grilled fish and seafood. The **beach** is alive with holidaymakers at weekends and in summer. The rest of the time it reverts to fishermen who may be seen mending their lines and nets on either side of **Fortim de Santiago** (fort). The fishing boats bring in sardines, eel, bream and shellfish every morning and evening. The **castle**, on the crest of a bare ridge, occupies a first-class defensive position which the first King of Portugal, Afonso Henriques, captured from the Moors in 1165. From its crenellated walls surrounding the cemetery there are fine **views**★ of Sesimbra and its harbour.

SETÚBAL★

SETÚBAL
POPULATION 97 762 – MICHELIN MAP 733
LOCAL MAP SEE SERRA DA ARRÁBIDA

Setúbal, situated in the foothills of the Serra da Arrábida on the north bank of the wide Sado estuary, is an industrial town, port and tourist centre. It has an old quarter with narrow alleys which contrast sharply with the wide avenues of the modern town. The town's moscatel wine and orange marmalade are popular.
🛈 *Tv. Frei Gaspar, 10 – 2900-388 – ☎ 265 52 42 84* 🛈 *Rua do Porto Santo – 2900-334 – ☎ 265 53 42 22*

▶ **Orient Yourself:** Cross the Vasco da Gamal bridge from Lisbon and keep going south. It will take almost an hour from central Lisbon.
🅿 **Parking:** No major problems although you'll hunt for parking in the centre from time to time.

- 🕙 **Don't Miss:** The Church of Jesus, the São Filipe castle (ideal for an evening glass of wine) and the paintings in the museum. Go to the market one morning.
- 🕙 **Organizing Your Time:** Pretty much a whole day, with an afternoon trip to Troia.
- 🕙 **Also See:** Take the ancient ferry across the Sado to Troia.

A busy port

The town has a variety of commercial activities; salt marshes; car and truck assembly; chemicals; fish canning and agriculture. Shipbuilding is a major industry here. Setúbal is Portugal's third port after Lisbon and Oporto. It consists of a fishing port (sardines) with a fleet of about 2 000 boats, a marina and a commercial port.

Casteloda São Filipe★

▶ *Take Avenida Luísa Todi to the west then follow the signs to the Pousada.*

The fortress overlooking the town has been partially converted into one of Portugal's most beautiful *pousadas*. It was built in 1590 on the orders of King Philip II of Spain to prevent the English from establishing themselves in Tróia. Cross a covered passage to a chapel with 18C *azulejos* attributed to Policarpo de Oliveira Bernardes which illustrate the life of St Philip. There is a wide **panorama**★ from the top of the ramparts.

Old Quarter (Bairro Antigo)

Between Avenida Luísa Todi, Praça Almirante de Reis and the Igreja de Santa Maria lies the picturesque old quarter with its narrow streets and interesting monuments.

Igreja de Jesus ★
🕙*Open 9am-noon; 1.30pm-5.30pm.* 🕙*Closed Sun-Mon.* ☎ 265 53 78 90. Free.
This church, constructed of Arrábida marble in 1491, was designed by the architect Boytac and is the first example of a building with Manueline decoration. It is a late-Gothic building, judging by its Flamboyant doorway – twin doors with bracketed arches framed in ringed columns – and its three lines of vaulting of equal height which make it into a hall-church.

Museu de Jesus
🕙*Open 9am-noon; 1.30pm-5.30pm.* 🕙*Closed Sun-Mon.* ☎ 265 53 78 90.
The museum is in the Gothic cloisters of the Igreja de Jesus. The upper galleries house a large collection of 15C and 16C Portuguese Primitives. All these **paintings**★ are said to be by the anonymous artist known as the Master of the Setúbal Altarpiece. The lower galleries contain 15C-18C *azulejos*.

Igreja de Jesus, Setúbal

Igreja de São Julião
The trefoil door in the north face of the church is Manueline. Two columns, twisted like cables, frame the door and rise above it in a moulding before ending in pinnacles. Inside, beautiful 18C *azulejos* depict the life of St Julian.

Museu Regional de Arqueologia e Etnografia

🕒 *Open 9.30am-6pm.* 🚫 *Closed Sun, Mon, holidays and Sat in Aug.* ☎ *265 23 93 65.*
The museum contains prehistoric objects, Luso-Roman coins, collections of folk art and crafts, costumes and small scale models of boats.

Península de Tróia

The Tróia peninsula, an immense strip of fine sand barring the Sado estuary, lined with dunes and pine trees, has been developed for tourism along the north and west coasts: hotels, residential villas and high-rise blocks already make it a kind of city, facing the Serra da Arrábida.

▶ *Cross the Sado by the ancient ferry (10mn – departures every 30mn, and just continue along the 4km/2.5mi from the pier, 2.5km/1.5mi along a sandy though the road off N 253-1.)*

You reach the **Roman ruins at Cetóbriga**. Some of the remains of an important Roman town destroyed by the sea in the early 5C have been excavated in a pleasant site beside the Sado lagoon. They include an installation for salting fish, a sepulchral vault, the remains of a temple decorated with frescoes, and some baths.

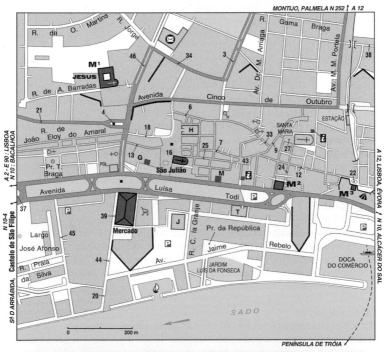

SETÚBAL		Augusto Cardoso R. de	13	Exército Pr. do	27
22 de Dezembro Av.	46	Bocage R. do	18	Major Afonso Pala R. do	33
Alexandre Herculano		Bocage Pr. do	16	Mariano de Carvalho Av.	34
Av. de	3	Clube Naval R.	20	Marquês de Pombal Pr.	37
Almirante Reis Pr. do	4	Combatentes da Grande		Mirante R. do	38
Almocreves R. dos	6	Guerra Av. dos	21	Ocidental do Mercado R.	39
Álvaro Castelões R.	7	Defensores da		Santo António Largo de	43
António Girão R.	9	República Largo dos	22	Tenente Valadim R.	44
Arronches Junqueiro R.	12	Dr António J. Granjo R.	24	Trabalhadores do	
		Dr Paula Borba R.	25	Mar R. dos	45

Galería de pintura quinhentista	M¹	Museu Regional de Arqueologia e Etnografia	M²
Museu do Trabalho	M³		

SILVES★

FARO

POPULATION 9 845 – MICHELIN MAP 733
LOCAL MAP SEE ALGARVE

Of the ancient city of Xelb with its many mosques, the Moorish capital of the Algarve, the magnificence of which was said to eclipse even that of Lisbon, there remain the red sandstone walls of a castle standing above the white-walled town which rises in tiers up the hillside. Thanks to its protected position inland, in the foothills of the Serra de Monchique, Silves has managed to preserve its character with its steep, cobbled streets. *Rua 25 de Abril – 8300-184 – ☎ 282 44 22 55*

▸ **Orient Yourself:** Inland from the coast road midway between Albufeira and Lagos.
☺ **Don't Miss:** The cathedral and the castle.
○ **Organizing Your Time:** To see it all you need almost a full day, including time for lunch.
Kids Especially for Kids: Fabrica do Inglés
☝ **Also See:** Albufeira, Lagos and Portimão.

Visit

Castle★

Leave the car in the town and walk up - no parking by the castle. ○Open 9am-8pm, summer, 5pm the rest of the year). ☞€1.25. ☎ 282 44 56 24.
The sentry path around the magnificently restored crenellated ramparts affords good **views** of the town and surrounding countryside: northwest to the irrigated Arade valley, cork factories, and behind, the Serra de Monchique; south to peach and almond orchards and, in the far distance, the coast. Inside the fortress with its gardens of oleanders are two large underground water cisterns.

Cathedral★

○Open 9am-8pm.
The cathedral was built on the site of a former mosque. The 13C Gothic nave and aisles have a beautiful and striking simplicity; the chancel and transept are of the later Flamboyant Gothic style. The numerous tombs are said to be of the Crusaders who helped to capture the town in 1242. Note the **Manueline door** opposite the cathedral's entrance.

Fábrica do Ingles

Kids R. Gregório Mascarenhas. ☎ 282 44 04 80 - www.fabrca-do-ingles.pt.
This old factory (acquired by English investors - hence the name) has been transformed into a vast pleasure park. Games for youngsters, boutiques, cafés, several restaurants. In the summer there are evening performances including the highly-acclaimed Aquavision and street theatre.

Museu Arqueológico

○Open 9am-6pm. ○Closed Sun, Jan 1 and Dec 25. ☞€1.50. ☎ 282 44 08 38.
The archeological museum is housed in a modern building beside the town walls, built around a large 12C-13C cistern. The collections retrace the history of the region beginning with the Palaeolithic Age. Note the menhirs and the funerary stelae from the Iron Age. The Moorish period with its ceramics and architectural displays is particularly well presented.

Cruz de Portugal (The Portuguese Cross)
At the eastern exit of the town, N 124, the São Bartolomeu de Messines road.
On one side of this 16C Calvary is Christ crucified, on the other, a *Pietà*.

SINTRA★★★

LISBOA

POPULATION 363 556 – MICHELIN MAP 733
PLAN IN THE MICHELIN GUIDE SPAIN & PORTUGAL

Less than an hour from Lisbon, Sintra, up against the north slope of the *serra*, is a haven of peace and greenery. For six centuries the town was the favourite summer residence of the kings of Portugal. In the 19C several English Romantic poets, including Lord Byron, stayed here.

Three different areas make up the town of Sintra: the old town (Vila Velha), grouped round the royal palace, the modern town (Estefânia), and the former village of São Pedro, famous for its market of secondhand goods held on the second and fourth Sundays of each month.

Sintra's popularity, particularly during weekends, is reflected in the old town's many antique and craft shops, smart boutiques, restaurants and tea-rooms where one may sample the local gastronomic speciality: delicious small tarts known as *queijadas*. *Praça da República (Edifício do Turismo) – 2710-616 – ☎ 219 23 11 57 or 219 23 39 19*

▶ **Orient Yourself:** 25km/17mi north-east from Lisbon.
🅿 **Parking:** Difficult in the centre, especially weekends - use alternate parking.
🎴 **Don't Miss:** The royal palace.
🕐 **Organizing Your Time:** Ideally a couple of days to explore the region.
Kids Especially for Kids: The toy museum (Museu do Brinquedo).
🕸 **Also See:** The Palace at Mafra, Cabo da Roca, the western edge of Europe.

Palácio Real, Sintra

Y. Travert /DIAF

The Convention of Sintra

Wellington's victory at Vimeiro in August 1808 was followed by an armistice and subsequently an agreement, known as the Convention of Sintra (30 August 1808). Under this pact the British made some material gains and the French were granted a passage home on board British ships with their arms and baggage. The terms distressed the Portuguese, who renamed the Dutch Ambassador's residence, where the Convention was signed, the **Seteais** or House of the Seven Sighs. This residence is now a luxury hotel, the Palácio de Seteais (& *see Address Book*).

Palácio Real★★

Open 10am-5.30pm. Closed Wed, days of official ceremonies, 1 Jan, Good Fri, Easter Sun, 1 May, 29 July and 25 Dec. €4 (no charge Sun 10am-2pm). 219 10 68 40.
The royal palace's irregular structure is due to the additions made during different periods; the central edifice was erected by Dom João I at the end of the 14C and the wings by Dom Manuel I early in the 16C. Apart from the two tall conical chimneys, the paired Moorish-style *(ajimeces)* and Manueline windows are the most striking features of the exterior.
The interior is interesting for its remarkable decoration of 16C and 17C **azulejos★★**. The finest embellish the dining room or Arabic Hall (Sala dos Árabes), the chapel and the Sirens' Hall (Sala das Sereias). The **Sala dos Brasões** (Armoury), which is square, is covered with a **ceiling★★** in the form of a dome on squinches, the dome itself consisting of coffers painted with the coats of arms of Portuguese nobles

Address Book

GETTING THERE

The easiest, fastest and most environmentally-friendly way of getting to Sintra is by train from Lisbon (Rossio). From Sintra station there is a bus to the centre of the old town. Trains run every 10-15min and the journey takes 35min.

WHERE TO STAY

⊝⊜⊜⊜ **Pensão Residencial Sintra** – *Traversa dos Avelares, 12 219 23 07 38 pensao.residencial.sintra@clix.pt* 🛁🅿 *15 rooms* ⌑. This 19C building in the centre of town has a certain elegance. Large bathrooms and a beautiful garden for breakfast on summer mornings.

⊝⊜⊜⊜ **Quinta da Capela** – *On the Colares road, 4.5km/3mi from Sintra* – *219 29 01 70 - quintadacapela@hotmail.com (open Mar 1-Nov 15)* 🛁🅿7 *rooms* ⌑ . This former homestead, superbly situated in the heart of the Serra de Sintra, offers guests a level of comfort and charm in keeping with its setting. A delightful garden (with a small pool) and fine views over the surrounding area.

⊝⊜⊜⊜ **Palácio de Seteais** – *R. Barbosa do Bocage 8, 2710-517 Sintra* – *219 23 32 00 - htpseteais@tivolihotels.com* – 🛁🅿 *29 rooms* ⌑. This elegant 18C palace was the site where the Convention of Sintra was signed in 1808. Nowadays the hotel, with its magnificent park, is considered one of Portugal's finest luxury hotels.

TEA-ROOMS

Casa de Chá Raposa – *Ruu Conde Ferreira, 29* – 219 24 44 82. This timeless residence is both a tea-room and a shop. Enjoy a pot of tea in these cosy surroundings, decorated with old furniture, tea sets, silverware, paintings and plants. There is also a reading area for moments of quiet contemplation. Tea is served with toast, scones and home-made jams.

Fábrica das Queijadas da Sapa – *Volta do Duche, 12* – 219 23 04 93. Queijadas are the traditional pastries from Sintra made with eggs, *fromage frais* and cinnamon. This particular pastry company, founded in 1786, has a small tea-room with a fine view overlooking the royal palace where these famous local delicacies can be enjoyed accompanied by a pot of tea.

of the early 16C – the missing blazon is that of the Coelho family who conspired against Dom João II.

The **Sala das Pegas** (Magpie or Reading Room) has a ceiling painted in the 17C with magpies holding in their beaks a rose inscribed with the words: *por bem* – for good – words pronounced by Dom João I when his queen caught him about to kiss one of her ladies-in-waiting. To put an end to the gossip the king had as many magpies painted on the ceiling as there were ladies at court.

A fine Venetian chandelier adorns the queen's audience chamber.

Museu do Brinquedo★ (Toy Museum)

Kids *R. Visconde de Monserrate.* ○*Open 10am-6pm.* ○*Closed Mon, May 1 and Dec 25.* €*3.* ☎ *219 24 21 71; www.museu-do-brinquedo.pt.*

This toy museum is the result of the enthusiasm of a single collector, João Arbués Moreira. He has brought together a vast collection of toys from around the world, ranging from small, 3 000-year-old bronze figures to modern robots. The wooden horses, miniature trains, lead soldiers and typical Portuguese toys from the past are just some of the exhibits which will provide visitors with nostalgic memories of their childhood years.

Museu de Arte Moderna (Colecção Berardo)★

○*Open 10am-6pm.* ○*Closed Mon.* €*3, free Sun 10am-2pm.* ☎ *219 24 81 70.*

This museum, housed in the town's former casino, was opened in 1997 to exhibit the valuable private collection of the benefactor, J Berardo. It features works from the second half of the 20C, and represents the avant-garde artistic trends which developed after 1945. The exhibits, which are shown on a rotating basis, include works by Dubuffet (the oldest on display), Gilbert & George, David Hockney, Jeff Koons, Joan Mitchele, Richter, Rosenquist, Stella, Tom Wesselmann and Andy Warhol.

The museum also contains a cafeteria, a bookshop and a gift shop.

Quinta da Regaleira ★★

R. Barbosa da Bocage - on the road to Steais, 800m from the village centre. ○*Open Jun-Sep 10am-6pm; Mar-May and Oct-Nov 10am-4pm; Dec-Feb 11am-3.30pm.* ○*Closed Jan 1, Dec 25.* €*5.* *Guided tours: general €10; themed €15; specialised €25.* ☎ *219 10 66 50.*

On the site of a 17C quinta *(farmhouse)* Carvalho Monteiro (1848-1920), a successful businessman and freemason, adopted an esoteric lifestyle and built, on his land, an eclectic mix of buildings, notably in Gothic, Manueline or Renaissance style.

There are beautiful gardens here full of unexpected treasures – various styles of monument, chapels, statues (many of which have religious or mytholgical overtones, or refer to freemasonry). Notable are the **gruta de Leda** (grotto of Leda), the **Capela da Santíssima Trinidade** and the **tour da Realeira**. There is a restaurant as well as a terrace café.

SERRA DE SINTRA★★

LISBOA
MICHELIN MAP 733

The Serra de Sintra is a granite block forming a mountain barrier with the Cruz Alta with an altitude of 529m/1 736ft as its highest point. Rain from the Atlantic falls upon the impermeable rock giving rise to the dense vegetation which covers the whole massif and largely masks the granite spikes left exposed by the erosion of other rocks. The flora is varied with oaks, cedars, tropical and subtropical trees, bracken and camellias.

Parque da Pena★★

🕐 *Open mid-Jun-end Oct, 9.30am-7pm; Nov-Apr 9.30am-6pm; May-mid Jun 9am-7pm.*
🕐 *Closed Jan 1 and Dec 25.-* *€3.50* ☎ *219 23 73 00. Minibus service inside the park.*

From Sintra to Cruz Alta *5km/3mi – about 2hr*

South of Sintra the beautiful **Parque da Pena**★★ covers 200ha/500 acres on the granite slopes of the Serra de Sintra; the park is planted with rare species of trees, and there are a great number of lakes and fountains. It is best visited on foot to fully appreciate its great charm, but the motorist in a hurry can simply drive along the small roads which cross it, or at least go to the top of the two culminating points; the Palácio da Pena stands on one, and the Cruz Alta (High Cross) on the other.

▶   *Leave Sintra to the south,on the road to Pena.*

After skirting on the right the Estalagem dos Cavaleiros, where Lord Byron planned *Childe Harold*, the road rises in a series of hairpin bends.

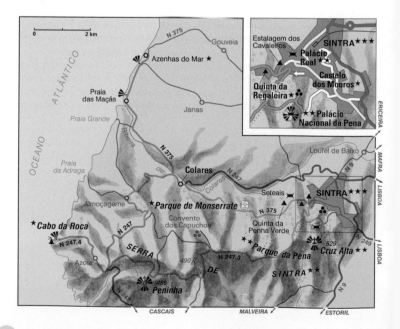

The Artist King

Prince **Ferdinand of Saxe-Coburg-Gotha** (1816-85), n
king, Léopold I, married Queen Maria II, widow of Duke Au
Leuchtenberg, the grandson of the Empress Josephine, in
of Crown Prince Pedro in 1837, he received the honorary ti
Portugal. Intelligent and diplomatic, modern and liberal, Fe
of Portugal from 1853 to 1855 and was offered the Spanish thr   ...e was
a highly cultured man, gifted with a rare artistic sensitivity, who devoted himself
to etching, ceramics and watercolours. President of the Royal Academy of Science
and Fine Arts and a patron of Coimbra University, he purchased the ruined monastery of Nossa Senhora da Pena in 1838 and built around it a palace which was
in keeping with his philosophical tastes. Ferdinand was also a Grand Master of
the Order of the Rosy Cross and his château is rich in alchemical symbols. Here,
Ferdinand and his second wife, Elisa Hensler, a singer of Swiss origin, received the
greatest artists of the day. Richard Strauss said of the palace, where he stayed and
which prefigured the castles of Ludwig II of Bavaria: "The gardens...are the gardens of Klingsor, and above them is the castle of the Holy Grail".

▶ *At the crossroads with the N 247-3, turn left to Pena.*

Castelo dos Mouros★

30min round trip on foot from the car park. ◷*Open 10am-5pm (6pm in summer). No
charge.* ☎ *219 24 72 00.*
The Moors' Castle, built in the 8C or 9C, still has a battlemented perimeter wall
guarded by four towers and a ruined Romanesque chapel. From the tower, which
is climbed by a series of staircases, there is a commanding **view**★ of Sintra and its
palace, the Atlantic coast and the Castelo da Pena.

▶ *Go through the wrought-iron gate at the entrance to the Parque da Pena and leave
the car in the car park.*

Palácio Nacional da Pena★★

◷*Open July-mid Sept, 10am-7pm; mid-Sept-Jun 30, 10am-5.30pm.* ◷*Closed Mon, Jan
1, Good Fri, Easter Sun, May 1, Jun 29 and 25 Dec.* ☜€*6 (no charge on Sun and holidays
until 2pm).* ☎ *219 10 53 40.*
The palace, perched on one of the highest peaks of the range, was built in the middle
of the 19C around a former Hieronymite monastery dating from the 16C. Its eccen-
tric architecture evokes some of Ludwig II of Bavaria's castles although it predates
them by 30 years. It is a pastiche in which several styles merge with varying degrees
of success: Moorish, Gothic, Manueline, Renaissance and Baroque. A drawbridge
leads through a Moorish doorway to the palace courtyard where the remains of
the monastery, the Manueline cloisters and the chapel – with an alabaster altar by
Nicolas Chanterene – are decorated with *azulejos*. From the terraces there are fine
views★★ over the Atlantic coast to the Tagus.

Round Tour of the Serra★   *30km/19mi – about 3hr*

▶ *Leave Sintra on the road towards Pena then turn onto the N 247-3 towards Cabo da
Roca.*

After several kilometres a 16C **Capuchin monastery** appears amid a striking landscape of jumbled rocks. The monks' cells were cut out of the living rock and the
walls lined with cork, the best insulator at the time.

...ards Peninha along the narrow road opposite the one leading to the ...tery. This road passes through a landscape dotted with enormous rocks.

...ninha
The panoramic **view**★★ from the chapel terrace includes the vast Praia do Guincho in the foreground.

▶ *You can go directly to Cabo da Roca by heading towards Azóia.*

Cabo da Roca★
The Serra da Sintra ends in a sheer cliff, the Cabo da Roca or Cape Rock, nearly 140m/459ft above the sea. This cliff is continental Europe's most westerly point.

▶ *Return to the N 247 and continue to Colares.*

Colares
Colares is an attractive town known for its red and white table wines.
From here continue northwards to **Azenhas do Mar**★ *(6km/4mi)* via the resort of **Praia das Maçãs**. The approach to Azenhas do Mar gives a good general view of the town's **setting**★, with its houses rising in tiers up a jagged cliff above the Atlantic.

▶ *From Colares return to Sintra on the N 375. This narrow road offers some superb views of the surrounding hills as it winds its way through the lush landscape.*

Parque de Monserrate★
🕐*Open mid-Jun-mid-Sept, 9am-8pm; mid-Sept-end Oct, 9am-7pm; Nov-Apr 9.30am-7pm.* 🕐*Closed 1 Jan, 1 May and 25 Dec.* ⬡€3.50 (⬡ guided tour €7 (90min)). ☎ 219 23 73 00.
The landscape **park**★ surrounding the neo-Oriental palace built by Sir Francis Cook in the 19C contains many different species of trees and plants including cedars, arbutus, bamboos and bracken, which stand beside pools and waterfalls.

TAVIRA★

FARO
POPULATION 24 317 – MICHELIN MAP 733
LOCAL MAP SEE ALGARVE

Tavira is a charming town with whitewashed houses and numerous churches, pleasantly situated on an estuary of the Gilão river at the foot of a hill girded by the remains of ramparts built by King Dinis. The Roman bridge and Moorish walls testify to the town's long history.
The earthquake in 1755 demolished most of Tavira's buildings and silted up the harbour, thus cutting the town off from the coast. In the past Tavira was an important centre for tuna and today fishing is still important.

▶ **Orient Yourself:** Near the Spanish frontier in the south, 30km/21ml east of Faro.
🔎 **Don't Miss:** The old town and especially the Roman bridge.
🕐 **Organizing Your Time:** Try to spend best part of a day here and in the surrounding area.

Sights

Park in the town centre near Praça da República.
The well-preserved centre of Tavira is attractive with its narrow streets, river banks lined with gardens, and a lively covered market. From Praça da República you can see the **Roman bridge**. To visit the old quarter go through the Arco da Misericórdia, where you will see the Renaissance doorway of the **Igreja da Misericórdia**. The inside of the church is covered with 18C *azulejos* representing the works of the Misericord. Turning left as you exit the church you will come to the Moorish castle, **Castelo dos Mouros**, which has some fine gardens within its crenellated walls. Higher up the hill is the **Igreja de Santa Maria do Castelo**, built over an old mosque, which has preserved its Gothic façade. The choir still contains the tomb of seven knights from the Order of St James. Their murder by the Moors triggered the reconquest of Tavira. The church stands facing the Largo de Graça, an attractive sloping square with flowers and shade. From here, return to Praça da República and cross the bridge. Head up Rua 5 de Outubro as far as Praça Dr. Padinha to the right, where you will discover the 17C **Igreja de São Paulo**. The inside of the church contains seven chapels with impressive Baroque gilded wood decoration dating from the 18C. On leaving the church, follow Rua de São Brás to the 18C Baroque-style **Igreja do Carmo** in the Largo do Carmo with its fine gilded wood altarpiece.

TOMAR★★

SANTARÉM
POPULATION 14 821 – MICHELIN MAP 733

Tomar stretches along the banks of the Nabão at the foot of a wooded hill crowned by a fortified castle built in 1160 by Gualdim Pais, Grand Master of the Order of the Knights Templars. Within the castle grounds stands the Convento de Cristo. ▯ *Av. Doutor Cândido Madureira – 2300-531 – ☎ 249 32 26 01 or 249 32 24 27*

- ▶ **Orient Yourself:** Take the A1, IP6 and N110, 133km/90mi north of Lisbon.
- ⊚ **Don't Miss:** The Convent of Christ.
- ⊙ **Organizing Your Time:** Visit the convent early before the groups of tourists, then have lunch in Tomar.
- ⚘ **Also See:** The monastery at Batalha; Fátima, Leiria and Santarém.

From Knights Templars to Knights of Christ
In the early 12C, at the height of the **Reconquest**, the border between Christian and Moorish territories passed through Tomar. The Order of the Knights Templars, founded in Jerusalem in 1119, built a convent-fortress in Tomar in 1160 which became the headquarters for the Order in Portugal. In 1314 Pope Clement V ordered the suppression of the Templars. A new Order, the Knights of Christ, was founded by King Dinis in Portugal in 1320. It took over the possessions of the Knights Templars and moved to Tomar in 1356. The golden period of the Knights of Christ was at the beginning of the 15C when Prince Henry the Navigator was Grand Master (1418-60). The Order's vast fortune enabled him to finance expeditions for the Great Discoveries.

Convento de Cristo★★

⊙*Open 9am-5.30pm (6.30pm June to Sept).* ⊙*Closed on public holidays.* ⊛€4.50. ☎ *249 31 34 81.*

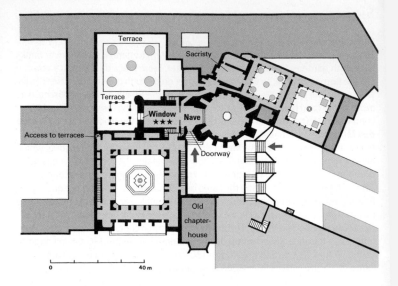

The 12C walls crowning the summit of the hillock dominating the town enclose the **Convent of Christ** which was begun in the 12C and only completed in the 17C. The result is a museum of different Portuguese architectural styles.

▶ *Once inside, cross the garden of clipped box trees that precedes the convent.*

The **church**★ doorway is by the Spanish architect Juan de Castilla, successor of Diogo de Arruda. To the former church of the Templars, which now forms the east end of this church, King Manuel added a nave. The **Charola dos Templários**★★ (The Templar's Rotunda) was built in the 12C , modelled on the Holy Sepulchre in Jerusalem. The two-storey octagonal construction is supported by eight pillars. An ambulatory with a ring vault divides the central octagon from the exterior polygon which has sixteen sides. The paintings decorating the octagon are by 16C Portuguese artists and the polychrome wooden statues date from the same period.

The **Claustro Principal (Cloisters)** were built between 1557 and 1566. They are Renaissance in style with two storeys, the ground level gallery having Tuscan columns, the upper, Ionic. The most outstanding features of the decoration are on three windows of which only two are visible. The first may be seen to the right on entering the cloisters but the second, the most famous, is below, in the Claustro de Santa Bárbara (Santa Barbara cloisters).

Window★★★
👁 *See photo in Art and Culture, Introduction.*

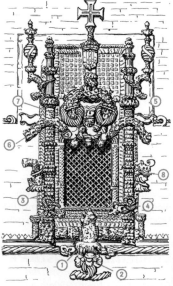

The Manueline window at Tomar

Convento de Cristo

This window *(janela)* is the most amazing example of Manueline-style ornament in Portugal. It was designed by the architect Diogo de Arruda and sculpted between 1510 and 1513. The decoration which rises from the roots ① of a cork oak, supported on the bust of a sea captain ②, climbs two convoluted masts. Among the profusion of plant and marine motifs can be seen coral ③, ropes ④, cork for use in the construction of ships ⑤, seaweed ⑥, cables ⑦ and anchor chains ⑧. The whole is crowned with the royal emblems of Manuel I – a blazon and armillary spheres – and the cross of the Order of Christ, which recurs as a motif on the balustrades surrounding the nave. The window is "moored" by cables to two turrets that bear the same decorative stamp. These are encircled, one by a chain, representing the Order of the Golden Fleece, and the other by a ribbon, the Order of the Garter.

PARQUE ARQUEOLÓGICO DO
VALE DO CÔA★★

GUARDA
MICHELIN MAP 733

The **Parque Arqueológico do Vale do Côa** is situated in the northeast of the country on the border between Trás-os-Montes and Beira Alta in an isolated and majestic natural setting. The archeological park was created to preserve one of the world's most important open-air sites for Paleolithic rock art alongside the Côa river, close to its confluence with the Douro. *Visits must be organised at least two months in advance during the high season.*

A Bit of History

The landscape has hardly changed since the age when Cro-Magnon people made rock engravings of animals living in nature. As a result of the area's isolation, the rock art in the Côa valley has been preserved to the present day; one could even say that it has been perpetuated over the course of history with every age leaving its mark engraved in stone as travellers passed through the region.

In 1992, during the construction of a dam at Canada do Inferno, rocks with engravings from the Paleolithic period (between 30 000 and 10 000 years ago) were discovered. Work on the dam was suspended and, to date, about 150 rocks with engravings have been found, of which 18 can be visited. Other sites containing ornamented rocks have also been discovered (some of which are under water); as a result, the park is in a state of continual flux as more discoveries are being made by current excavations.

Paleolithic rock art

The Paleolithic Age was the oldest, and longest (2.5 million years), era in the history of humanity and corresponds to the Stone Age. The oldest engravings in the Vale do Côa, identifiable by the species of animals represented, come from the Upper Paleolithic, or Solutrean, Age and are 20 000 years old. Rock engravings can also be seen at Siega Verde in the Duero (Douro) valley in Spain, just 60km/37mi from the Vale do Côa site, although discoveries on this site date from a later era.

Engraving techniques used in the Côa valley (where paintings may have been made as well) are of three main types: **abrasion**, which consisted of creating a deep groove through the repeated use of an instrument (a fragment of stone) along a marking; **pecking**, a succession of points hammered into the rock using a stone, occasionally finished off using the abrasion technique; and **fine line incision**, which resulted in finer markings that are more difficult to distinguish. The animals most frequently represented were the horse, aurochs and mountain goat. In general, the same rock was used to depict various animals, with one drawing added on top of another.

View of Ribeira de Piscos site

P. Martins/MICHELIN

What is particularly special about art in the Côa valley is the exceptional beauty of the engravings, the representation of the shape and movement of the animals through the simple, firm lines.

Visit

Penascosa
Visit: 1hr 40min, including 40min round trip by jeep.
The Reception Centre at **Castelo Melhor** (👆 *see GUARDA*) is located in an old schist house which is typical of the region. The jeep ride provides beautiful views of the surrounding hills planted with vines used for Port, particularly the famous Quinta da Ervamoira. Penascosa is the most accessible of the three sites and contains engraving which are the most legible in the park. It is located alongside the river, which has created a beach in this part of its course, and jeeps can park just a few metres from the rocks. The site is best visited in the afternoon, when the light is at its best for viewing the engravings. The movement of animals has been reproduced to an extraordinary degree here, particularly in a mating scene, in which a mare is mounted by a horse with three heads to interpret the downward movement of its neck. Seven rocks can be visited here at present.

Ribeira de Piscos
Visit: 2hr 30min, including 1hr round trip by jeep and 40min return on foot.
The visit in itself is an extremely pleasant stroll along the river bank. The engravings, particularly fine line incisions, are dispersed over the hills and are not easily

---

😊 A Bit of Advice 😊

ACCESS
The easiest way of getting to the Vale do Côa is by car.
From Lisbon: 387km/242mi via Albergaria-a-Velha, allow 5hr.
From Oporto: 214km/134mi via Mirandela, allow 3hr 30min.

ORGANISING YOUR VISIT
Visits must be reserved at least a week (more in summer) in advance by calling the **Tourism Office** for the Park - *Avenida Gago Coutinho, 19-2° –* ☏ *279 76 82 60/61 - www.ipa.min-cultura.pt/parc.* The Reception Centre for **Castelo Melhor** is on ☏ *279 71 33 44.* The Reception centre for **Muxagata** is on ☏ *279 76 42 98.* Transport to the sites is by 8-seater **jeep.** *Closed Mon, 1 Jan, 1 May and 25 Dec. Admission fee:* ☜€5 per visit (children are counted as an adult in the vehicles). Visits are led by specially trained young guides from the region and last two hours. The Park reserves the right to temporarily cancel visits during bad weather. Exact times for visits will be advised when reservations are made.
Two days should be allowed for those wishing to see all three sites. If you only have time to visit one site we would suggest that Penascosa is the one to choose. The park can also organise walks and mountain-bike excursions (bikes not provided) for groups of up to 15 people.
The visit to the Ribeira de Piscos site can also be arranged in conjunction with a Port tasting or lunch at the Quinta da Ervamoira, ☏ *279 75 93 13 or 935 26 34 90* where there is a museum devoted to the environment of the Côa valley.

DON'T FORGET...
Suitable footwear, boots in winter, a hat in summer, a bottle of water; keep your hands free (use a backpack) to make walking easier, particularly in Canada do Inferno and Ribeira de Piscos, where the uneven terrain and slopes mean you might need both hands to cling onto something. Visitors who are sensitive to heat should avoid the summer months, when temperatures can reach 40°C (104°F).

discernible. The grace and purity of the engraving are moving in their beauty. Five engraved panels are currently on display.

Canada do Inferno

Visit: 1hr 40min, including 20min round trip journey by jeep and 20min return on foot. Jeeps depart from the **park head-quarters** *(sede do parque)* in **Vila Nova de Foz Côa**. This site is situated in the steepest part of the valley, where a can-yon has formed, 130m/426ft deep, mak-ing access a little more difficult. From here the suspended work on the dam 400m/0.25mi downstream can be seen. The best time of day to see the engrav-ings, the majority of which are fine line incisions, is in the morning. Although Canado do Inferno is the most interest-ing of the three sites, many rocks are under water, and only six are currently visible.

Paleolithic rock art, Penascosa

P. Martins/MICHELIN

VALENÇA DO MINHO★

VIANA DO CASTELO
POPULATION 14 044 – MICHELIN MAP 733

Valença, on a hillock overlooking the south bank of the Minho, has stood guard for centuries over Portugal's northern border. The town is situated on the main highway linking Santiago de Compostela with Oporto, as well as on the northerly and westerly pilgrims' route to the shrine of St James. The road crosses the river by a metal **bridge** built by Gustave Eiffel in 1884. The old town is an unusual double city, consisting of two fortresses and a single bridge spanning a wide ditch and continuing through a long vaulted passage.

▶ **Orient Yourself:** 54km/37mi north-east of Viana do Castelo.
😊 **Don't Miss:** The fortified town and the Minho Valley.
🕐 **Organizing Your Time:** Two hours or so.
👍 **Also See:** Caminha, Ponte de Lima.

Fortified Town (Vila Fortificada) ★

Access by car from the south on a shaded road off N 13.
Each of the two fortresses in this double town, unchanged since the 17C, is in the shape of an irregular polygon with six bastions with double redans and watchtow-ers, in front of which are the defensive outworks and two monumental doorways emblazoned with the arms of the kingdom and the governor. Old cannon are still in position on the battlements. From the north side of the ramparts there is a fine **view**★ over the Minho valley, Tui and the Galician mountains. Each stronghold is a self-sufficient quarter with its own churches and narrow cobbled streets, fountains, shops, and houses.

Excursions

Monte do Faro★★
7km/4mi. – Leave Valença on N 101 going towards Monção; bear right towards Cerdal and shortly afterwards left to Monte do Faro.
Leave the car at the last roundabout and walk up the path to the summit 565m/1854ft which lies to the left of the road. From the summit, the **panorama**★★ is extensive: to the north and west lies the Minho valley, scattered with white houses grouped in villages, and dominated in the distance by the Galician mountains; to the east is the Serra do Soajo and southwest the wooded hills of the coastal area and the Atlantic.

Vale do Minho
From Valença to São Gregório 52km/32mi; leave Valença on N 101, to the east. – The Portuguese bank of the Minho on the east side of Valença is the most interesting. The river, which at the beginning is majestically spread out, becomes hemmed in until it is practically invisible between the steep green slopes. The road is cobbled and winding, thickly bordered with trees (pines, eucalyptus and even palm trees) and climbing vines which make the well-known *vinho verde*. It passes through large wine-making villages.

Monção
This attractive little town overlooking the Minho is also a spa whose waters are used in the treatment of rheumatism. The **parish church**, which has preserved some of its Romanesque features, the **belvedere**★ over the Minho and surrounding countryside, and the well-known local Alvarinho wine all make Monção a pleasant place to stop for a couple of hours.
3km/1.8mi south on the road towards Arcos de Valdevez, the early-19C **Palácio da Brejoeira** can be seen. Below the road vines, fields of maize and pumpkins grow on terraces facing the verdant slopes of the Spanish side, dotted with villages.
After Melgaço, the N 301 climbs to offer wonderful **views** of the Minho, still hemmed in at this point, before reaching the border post at São Gregório.

VIANA DO ALENTEJO

ÉVORA
POPULATION 12 674– MICHELIN MAP 733

This agricultural town in the vast Alentejo plain, away from the main roads, hides an interesting church behind its castle walls. The castle's ramparts present fortified walls flanked at each corner by a tower with a pepperpot roof surrounding the pentagonal edifice. The entrance porch is adorned with worn capitals decorated with animals, including tortoises and lions.

The church façade has a fine Manueline doorway: a slender twisted column serves as the supporting pier for twin arches framed by two candlestick shaped pilasters; it also supports the tympanum which is decorated with stylised flowers and the cross of the Order of Christ in a medallion surmounted by the Portuguese coat of arms: a gable formed by a twisted cable ends in a type of pinnacle flanked by two armillary spheres. The interior, which is Romanesque is outstanding for its size. The walls are decorated at their base with 17C azulejos. A particularly fine Crucifix can also be seen in the chancel. ⛶ *Câmara Municipal – 7090-909 – ☎ 266 95 31 06*

VIANA DO CASTELO★★

VIANA DO CASTELO
POPULATION 88 409 – MICHELIN MAP 733

Viana do Castelo, lying on the north bank of the Lima estuary at the foot of the sunny hillside slope of Santa Luzia, is a pleasant holiday resort.

Until the 16C Viana was a humble fishermen's village but it attained prosperity when, following the Great Discoveries, its fishermen set sail to fish for cod off Newfoundland and to trade with the Hanseatic Cities. It was during this period that the Manueline and Renaissance houses were built which today make the old town so attractive. *Rua do Hospital Velho – 4900 540 – ☏ 258 82 26 20 or 258 82 49 71*

- ▶ **Orient Yourself:** Midway between Porto (80km/50ml) and the northern border of Portugal, on the coast.
- 😊 **Don't Miss:** The old quarter and the views from Santa Luzia.
- 🕐 **Organizing Your Time:** A half day is plenty, unless you're here for the *Festa*.
- 🧒 **Especially for Kids:** Take them to the beach at Cabadelo, south of the town.
- 👣 **Also See:** Braga, Caminha and Ponte de Lima.

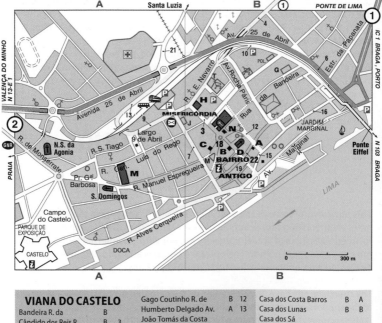

VIANA DO CASTELO		Gago Coutinho R. de	B	12	Casa dos Costa Barros	B	A
Bandeira R. da	B	Humberto Delgado Av.	A	13	Casa dos Lunas	B	B
Cândido dos Reis R.	B 3	João Tomás da Costa			Casa dos Sá		
Capitão Gaspar de		Largo	B	15	Sottomayores	B	C
Castro R.	B 4	Luís de Camões Av.	B	16	Igreja Matriz	B	D
Carmo R. do	B 6	República Pr. da	B	18	Museu Municipal	A	M
Combatentes da		Sacadura Cabral R.	B	19	Paços do Concelho	B	N
Grande Guerra Av. dos	AB 7	Santa Luzia Estrada	A	21	Palácio de Carreira	B	H
Conde da Carreira Av. da	A 9	São Pedro R. de	B	22			
Dom Afonso III Av.	B 10						

Pinheira/DIAF

Festival of Our Lady in Sorrow

Festa de Nossa Senhora da Agonia

The festival dedicated to Our Lady in Sorrow, which is held in August *(see Calendar of Events)*, is one of the most famous in the Minho region. It includes a procession, bull-running, fireworks on the Lima, a parade of carnival giants and dwarfs, illuminations and traditional folklore events. A festival of regional dancing and singing is also held, and on the last day a procession in regional costumes winds its way through the streets of the town.

Miradouro de Santa Luzia★★

4km/2.5mi on the road from Santa Luzia, or 7min by the funicular.
This belvedere is on the hill of Santa Luzia, north of the town and topped by a modern basilica which has developed into a place of pilgrimage. By car the approach is via a cobbled road with a series of hairpin bends which climbs through pines, eucalyptus and mimosas.

The Old Quarter★ (Bairro Antigo)

Praça da República ★

The 16C buildings, including **Casa dos Sá Sottomayores**, surrounding the vast square, make up a graceful, picturesque ensemble. There is a **Fountain** built by João Lopes the Elder in 1554, crowning its several basins with sculptured decoration supporting an armillary sphere and a cross of the Order of Christ.
Only the façade of the former **town hall** has retained its original 16C appearance. It bristles with merlons above, has pointed arches at ground level, and on the first storey has windows crowned with the coat of arms of Dom João III, the armillary sphere or emblem of Dom Manuel I and the town's coat of arms which features a caravel, as many sailors from Viana do Castelo took part in the Great Discoveries.

Hospital da Misericórdia★

This 1589 Renaissance hospice, with Venetian and Flemish influence in its style, was designed by João Lopes the Younger. Its noble façade, to the left of the monumental doorway, rises from a massive colonnade with Ionic capitals as two tiers of loggias supported on atlantes and caryatids. The adjoining **Igreja da Misericórdia** (*Open 10am-4pm (guided tours July, Aug and Sept). ☎ 258 82 23 50*) was rebuilt in 1714. It is decorated with *azulejos* and gilded woodwork dating from the same period.

Rua Cândido dos Reis

Some of the houses fronting the street have Manueline façades. Particularly noteworthy is **Palácio de Carreira** which houses the present Town Hall. Its beautiful Manueline front is strikingly symmetrical. The **Casa das Lunas**, Italian Renaissance in style, also has some Manueline features.

Parish church

The church dates from the 14C and 15C, but the two crenellated towers flanking the façade are Romanesque. The Gothic doorway has a series of three historiated archivolts which rest on statue columns of St Andrew, St Peter and the Evangelists; the outer archivolt shows Christ surrounded by cherubim holding the emblems of the Passion. In the baptistry, a carved polychrome wooden panel (17C) represents the Baptism of the Infant Jesus.

Museu Municipal ★

Open Jun-Sept 10am-1pm; 3pm-7pm; Oct-May 10am-1pm; 3pm-6pm. Closed Mon and holidays. €2. 258 82 03 77.

The museum is housed in a former 18C palace. The interior walls are covered with lovely **azulejos**★★ depicting distant continents, hunting and fishing scenes and receptions painted by Policarpo de Oliveira Bernardes in 1721. These *azulejos* together with some fine wooden ceilings decorate the rooms on the first floor which contain an outstanding collection of **Portuguese glazed earthenware**★ said to be the largest in Portugal.

The rooms on the ground floor, with coffered ceilings of varnished wood, contain some fine pieces of 17C Indo-Portuguese furniture, carved or inlaid, including a sumptuous cabinet made of ivory and tortoiseshell, ceramics, antique Portuguese, Italian and Dutch earthenware, and a small Virgin and Child in ivory.

Address Book

WHERE TO STAY

Casa da Torre das Neves – *Lugar de Neves, Vile de Punhe (10km/6ml south-east of Viana do Castelo)* 258 77 13 00 - www.casatorre-dasneves.com - 5 rooms. In a 16C family mansion this comfortable hotel reflects the Minho region perfectly with its charm.

Estalagem Casa Melo Alvim – *Ac Conde da Carreira,* 28 258 80 82 00 - www.meloalvimhouse.com - 17 rooms. An old country mansion house has been converted into a beautiful hotel with contrasting and artistic styles. The rooms have every comfort and particularly beautiful bathrooms.

EATING OUT

Cozinha das Malheiras – *Rua Gago Coutinho, 19* – 258 82 36 80 – *Closed Tuesdays and Dec 22-28.* This restaurant has been created inside a former chapel. The menu focuses on local dishes, as well as fish and seafood specialities.

Os 3 Potes – *Beco dos Fornos (near the Praça da República)* – 258 82 99 28. A typical restaurant with live music and *fado* on summer Saturdays.

Casa d'Armas – *Largo 5 de Outubro, 30* – 268 82 49 99 –casadamas@hotmail.com – *Closed Wednesdays.* The Casa d'Armas serves tasty, regional cuisine within the walls of an old mansion. House specialities include fish, seafood and grilled meats.

RIVER CRUISES

A river cruise is particularly good here and can be taken from the beach at Cabedelo. 258 84 22 90.

INTERNET ACCESS

The municipal library is the best place – it's free. *9.30am-12.30pm; 2pm-7pm; Sat 9.30am-12.30pm. Closed Sunday.*

VILA DO CONDE

PORTO

POPULATION 20 245 – MICHELIN MAP 733

Vila do Conde at the mouth of the Ave, birthplace of the poet José Régio, is a seaside resort, fishing harbour and industrial centre (shipbuilding, textiles and chocolate). The town is also well known for its pillow-lace and for its festivals. The Feast of St John *(see Calendar of Events)* is the occasion for picturesque processions by the *mordomas* adorned with magnificent gold jewellery and by the *rendilheras*, the town's lacemakers in regional costumes. *Rua 25 de Abril, 103 – 4480-722 – ☎ 252 24 84 73/22*

▶ **Orient Yourself:** Just about 25km/17mi north of Porto, on the coast.
◉ **Don't Miss:** The lace museum.
◷ **Organizing Your Time:** On a normal day a couple of hours to stroll around and buy some lace; but if arriving at festival time, plan to spend longer.

Sights

Museu-Escola das Rendas de Bilros
◷*Open 9am-noon and 2-6pm; Sat-Sun, 2.30-6pm. ☎ 252 24 80 70.*
Pilllow-lace has been manufactured in Vila do Conde since the 16C. This **lace museum-school** has been created to revitalise this manual activity, which requires great skill on the part of the lace-makers who use a cylindrical cushion to produce the designs for the models. Onto these they then insert pins, between which they pass the spindles containing the threads of cotton, linen or silk. The museum provides visitors with an introduction to the different aspects of this activity through an exhibition of old and modern lace, photos, and the presence of the lace-makers.

Convento de Santa Clara★
Guided tours 9am-12.30pm and 2.30-6pm. ☎ 252 63 10 16.
The monumental edifice rises above the Ave river. Behind the 18C façade are 14C buildings. Today the convent is a reformatory and only the church and cloisters are open to the public.
The **church**, founded in 1318 and designed as a fortress, has retained its original Gothic style. In the west face is a beautiful rose window. The interior, with a single aisle, has a coffered ceiling carved in the 18C. The Capelada Conceição *(first chapel on the left)*, built in the 16C, contains the Renaissance **tombs**★ of the founders and their children. The low-relief sculptures on the sides of the tomb of **Dom Afonso Sanches** represent scenes from the Life of Christ. The reclining figure on the tomb of **Dona Teresa Martins** is dressed in the habit of a nun of the Franciscan Tertiaries. Scenes of the Passion are depicted on the sides and St Francis receiving the stigmata is shown at the head. The children's tombs have the Doctors of the Church *(left tomb)* and the Evangelists *(right tomb)* carved upon them. A fine grille divides the nave from the nun's chancel. The arches of the 18C cloisters can still be seen to the south of the church; the fountain in the centre of the close is the terminal for the 18C aqueduct from Póvoa de Varzim.

VILA FRANCA DE XIRA

LISBOA

POPULATION 19 823 – MICHELIN MAP 733

This industrial town on the west bank of the Tagus. inland from Lisbon, is known for its festivals and bullfights. The city comes alive, particularly in July *(see Calendar of Events)*, at the time of the Festival of the **Colete Encarnado**, the *campinos'* "red waistcoat" festival, with its picturesque processions of *campinos* and bulls running loose through the streets. Folk dancing, bullfights, open-air feasts and the occasional regatta on the Tagus complete the festivities. 🛈 *Rua Almirante Cândido dos Reis 147-149 – 2600-055 – ☎ 263 27 60 53*

▶ **Orient Yourself:** Follow the Tagus (and A1) inland from Lisbon until it narrows about 35km/25mi north-east.

🔎 **Don't Miss:** The belvedere at Monte.

🕐 **Organizing Your Time:** No more than half a day will allow you to see all you need.

♿ **Also See:** The aviation museum, the convent at Mafra.

Museu Etnográfico

South side of town on Lisbon Rd (N 10). ⟶ *Guided tours, 10am-12.30pm and 2-6pm.* 🕐*Closed Mon and holidays. No charge.* ☎ *263 27 30 57.*

This small museum, housed in the bullring, displays paintings, sketches, photos and sculptures relating to the region and its traditions. Aspects covered include bullfighting, fishing on the Tagus, 19C traditional costumes (fishermen, peasants, cattle breeders) and 18C and 19C *campinos*.

Miradouro de Monte Gordo

3km/2mi to the north on the Rua António Lucio Baptista, passing under the motorway, and then onto a surfaced road which climbs steeply. – From the belvedere between two windmills at the top of the hill there is a **panoramic view** to the west and north

---

Address Book

EQUESTRIAN CENTRES

Centro Equestre da Lezíria Grande – *3km/2mi from the centre of Vila Franca on the N 1 towards Carregado –* ☎ *263 28 51 60 – Restaurant – Function rooms available for receptions and special events – Closed Mondays.* The centre, which is situated in a rural setting, is devoted to the native Lusitanian horse. It was established by the great equestrian master Luís Valença, who taught Portuguese equestrian art to riders from around the world. The names of the centre's most famous horses are engraved on *azulejos* above their individual stables.

A high level of horsemanship is required to be taught here, although ordinary visitors to the centre can eat at the pleasant restaurant *(open lunchtime)*, from where they can enjoy the centre's special atmosphere.

Centro Equestre do Morgado Lusitano – *Quinta de Santo António de Bolonha. From the bullring, follow the N 10 towards Lisbon – 2665 Póvoa de Santa Iria –* ☎ *263 56 35 43/ 219 53 54 00 – Function rooms available for receptions and special events – Shop selling riding equipment – Closed Mondays.* This centre breeds Lusitanian horses and trains experienced riders. It also presents a magnificent show of Portuguese equestrian art using 18C traditional costumes and harnesses.

The Lusitanian horse and Portuguese equestrian art

The Lusitanian thoroughbred was already known to humans during the Upper Paleolithic period, as shown by engravings on rocks in the Côa valley. It has been ridden for almost 5 000 years and is the world's oldest saddle horse. Its spirited, yet docile temperament, its agility, strength and courage have made this particular breed the battle horse par excellence. Since the Middle Ages in Portugal, the nobility used the Lusitanian horse during times of war, preparing it for battle by pitting it against Iberian bulls. Although the Portuguese School of Equestrian Art was created in the 18C, Portuguese riders of today still wear the same ceremonial dress and the horses the same equipment as in the past. These features combine to create an equestrian show of rare beauty, in which the rider and horse execute highly complex manoeuvres in perfect harmony, with a lightness and agility that do justice to the "son of the wind" nickname which has been given to this magnificent breed.

over the other hills covered with woods, vineyards and *quintas*; to the east over the Ribatejo plain which stretches to the Ponte de Vila Franca crossing the Tagus; to the south over the first two islands in the river's estuary.

Excursion

Alverca do Ribatejo

8km/5mi southwest on N 1, then follow signs to the Museu do Ar. A hangar at the military aerodrome has been converted into an aviation museum, the **Museu do Ar** (◷*Open 10am-5pm (6pm July to Sept).*◷*Closed Mon, 1 Jan, Easter Sun and 24-25 Dec.* €1.50 *(no charge Sun 10am-12.30pm).* ☎ *219 58 27 82 - www.emfa.pt).*
The history of Portuguese aviation is retraced through a collection of photographs, archives and, in particular, genuine old planes and replicas such as the Blériot XI, the 1908 Demoiselle XX, which was piloted by the Brazilian Santos-Dumont, and the 1920 Santa Cruz flying boat which was the first to cross the South Atlantic.

VILA REAL

VILA REAL
POPULATION 22 000 – MICHELIN MAP 733
LOCAL MAP SEE VALE DO DOURO

Vila Real is a lively small town enhanced by numerous houses dating from the 16C and 18C. It stands on a plateau among vineyards and orchards at the foot of the Serra do Marão. Fine black pottery is made in the surrounding countryside and can be bought in the town, particularly on 28-29 June at St Peter's Fair *(Feira de São Pedro).* Vila Real is also known for its car racing circuit. *Av. Carvalho Araújo 94 – 5000-657 – ☎ 259 32 28 19*

▶ **Orient Yourself:** 120km/80mi east of Porto along the A4.
☺ **Don't Miss:** The Manor-house at Mateus - and taste the wine!
◷ **Organizing Your Time:** A morning in the Mateus mansion and park, lunch in the town.
⚘ **Also See:** The towns in the Douro Valley; Amarante.

Walking Tour

The main sights are to be found in the vicinity of Avenida Carvalho Araújo.

▶ *From the central crossroads by the cathedral, walk down the avenue on the right.*

Cathedral
The cathedral, a former conventual church built at the end of the Gothic period, has preserved certain Romanesque details. These details are particularly noticeable in the treatment of the capitals in the nave.

Casa de Diogo Cão
At no 19 (door-plate).
So-called because, according to tradition, the well-known navigator, Diogo Cão, was born here. The façade was remodelled in the 16C in Italian Renaissance style.

Town Hall
Built early in the 19C, the town hall has a lantern pillory in front, and a remarkable monumental stone staircase with balusters in the Italian Renaissance style.

▶ *Continue along towards the cemetery which you skirt round on the right.*

Esplanada do Cemitério
This shaded walk along the cemetery esplanade, on the site of the old castle, over-looks the junction of the Corgo and Cabril rivers. In direct line with the cemetery and behind it there is a **view** looking steeply down into the Gorges of the Corgo and its tributary. Farther to the left, there is an extensive view over the Corgo ravine and the houses which overhang it.

▶ *Return to Avenida Carvalho Araújo, turn right and climb upwards.*

Tourist Information Centre
At no 94. The Tourist Information Centre *(Poste de Turismo)* occupies a 16C house which has a lovely Manueline façade.

▶ *From here take the first road on the right (by the law courts) to the Igreja de São Pedro.*

Igreja de São Pedro
St Peter's Church is decorated in the chancel with 17C multicoloured *azulejos* and a fine coffered **ceiling**★ of carved and gilded wood.

Excursion

Mateus
3.5km/2mi to the east on N 322 towards Sabrosa.
Chestnut trees, vines and orchards herald the approach to the village of Mateus, famous for the manor belonging to the Counts of Vila Real and the renowned rosé wine made on the estate.

Solar de Mateus★★
Guided tours (30min), Jun-Sept, 9am-7.30pm; Oct and Mar-May, 9am-1pm; 2-6pm; Nov-Feb 10am-1pm; 2pm-5pm. Closed 25 Dec. €6.25 (gardens only €3.25)
☎ 259 32 31 21.

Solar de Mateus

Dating from the first half of the 18C, this manor by Nicolau Nasoni is a perfect example of Portuguese Baroque architecture. Behind lawns planted with cedars, followed by a garden laid out with clumps of boxwood and a tree-covered walk, appears the **façade**★★ of the manor, preceded by a mirror of water. The central section of the manor is set back, and has a beautiful balustraded stairway and a high emblazoned pediment, surrounded by allegorical statues. The main courtyard is protected by an ornamental stone balustrade. The windows upstairs are topped with moulded gables. Beautiful pinnacles top the roof cornices. To the left of the façade there is a tall elegant Baroque chapel built in 1750, also by Nasoni.

Inside the palace there are magnificent carved wooden ceilings in the main hall and the salon, a rich library, furniture from Portugal, Spane, China and 18C France, and in two rooms which have been made into a museum **copperplate engravings** by Fragonard and Baron Gerard, precious fans, liturgical objects and vestments, a 17C altar and religious sculptures, one of which is a 16C ivory crucifix.

VILA REAL DE SANTO ANTÓNIO

FARO
POPULATION 13 379 – MICHELIN MAP 733
LOCAL MAP SEE ALGARVE

The border town was founded by the Marquis of Pombal in 1774 as a counterpoint to the Andalusian city of Ayamonte on the opposite bank of the Guadiana. The new town, which was built in five months, is a fine example of the town planning of the day with its grid plan streets and whitewashed houses with distinctive roofs. Vila Real de Santa António has become one of the largest fishing and commercial ports on the Algarve and is also a considerable fish canning centre. Yachts for export are also built here. Vila Real de Santo António is very popular with the Spanish who cross the border to buy cotton goods (table linen, sheets, towels etc).

▶ **Orient Yourself:** Right on the Spanish border in the far south-east of Portugal.
🐾 **Don't Miss:** The bustling port area, full of life and colour.
🕓 **Organizing Your Time:** A half day is enough; have lunch and then head for the beach in the afternoon.

Sight

Praça do Marquês de Pombal
This is the main square in the centre of the Pombaline quarter, surrounded by orange trees and paved with a black and white mosaics. The pedestrianised streets around the square are lined with shops selling cotton goods.

VILA VIÇOSA ★

ÉVORA
POPULATION 4 282 – MICHELIN MAP 733

Vila Viçosa, on a hillside where orange and lemon groves abound, is a town of shade *(viçosa)* and bright flowers. Vale Viçosa, as this village was first called, was granted a charter in 1270 by Alfonso III under its new name, Vila Viçosa (the charter was renewed in 1512). It was at one time the seat of the Dukes of Bragança and also the residence of several kings of Portugal.

Nowadays Vila Viçosa is a quiet little town making a living from various crafts such as pottery and wrought iron as well as the marble quarries nearby. While the centre around Praça da República is fairly lively, the atmosphere in the town near the ducal palace and the old quarter is more like that of a museum-city, evoking the sumptuous past of the Bragança family.

North of the town is a huge park of 2 000ha/4 950 acres which was formerly the Bragança hunt. Just a few miles away, on 17 June 1665, the Battle of Montes Claros was fought, which confirmed Portugal's independence from Spain. 🏛 *Câmara Municipal – 7160-260 – ☎ 268 98 03 05.*

▶ **Orient Yourself:** Vila Viçosa lies east of Évora, almost on the border with Spain, and 20km/12ml south-east of Estremoz.

- **Don't Miss:** The old town and the Ducal Palace.
- **Organizing Your Time:** Give yourself half a day here, and have lunch too.
- **Especially for Kids:** The Museu dos Coches (old coaches and carriages).
- **Also See:** Évora, Monsaraz and Elvas.

A Bit of History

The ducal court
It was as early as the 15C that the second Duke of Bragança, Dom Fernando, chose Vila Viçosa as the residence of his court. The execution of the third duke, Dom Fernando *(see below)*, however, annihilated the ducal power, and it was only in the following century that court life became really sumptuous. In the palace, built by Duke Jaime, great seignorial festivals followed one after the other, as did gargantuan banquets and theatrical performances, with bullfights in the grounds outside..

This golden age ended in 1640 when the eighth Duke of Bragança acceded to the throne of Portugal as Dom João IV.

The execution of the Duke of Bragança
On his succession to the throne in 1481, King João II instituted stern measures to abolish the privileges granted by his father, King Alfonso V, to the nobles who had taken part in the Reconquest. The first to be brought low was the Duke of Brangança, brother-in-law of the king, the richest and most powerful nobleman in the land, and a man already guilty of plotting against the monarchy. After a summary trial, the duke was executed in Évora in 1483.

Terreiro Do Paço★

Paço Ducal★
Guided tours (1hr), Apr-Sept: Tue 2pm-5.30pm; Wed-Fri 10am-1pm; 2.30pm-5.30pm; Sat-Sun 9.30am-1pm; 2.30pm-6pm; Oct-Mar; Tue 2pm-5pm; Wed-Sun 9.30am-1pm; 2pm-5pm. ○*Closed Mon, Tue morning and holidays.* ⊙€5. ☎ 268 98 06 59.

The **Ducal Palace** overlooks the Terreiro do Paço, in the centre of which is a bronze statue of Dom João IV. Tired of the discomfort of the old castle which dated from the time of King Dom Dinis, the fourth duke, Dom Jaime I, began the construction of the present palace in 1501.

The interior is now a museum. The well of the staircase to the first floor is adorned with wall paintings depicting the 15C Battle of Ceuta and the 16C Siege of Azamor.

The Main wing is decorated with 17C *azulejos*, Brussels and Aubusson tapestries and Arraiolos carpets.

The rooms are embellished with finely painted ceilings representing a variety of subjects including David and Goliath, the adventures of Perseus and the Seven Virtues. There are also portraits of the Braganças by the late 19C Portuguese painters Columbano, Malhoa and Sousa Pinto, and paintings by the 18C French artist Quillard in the Sala dos Tudescos (Teutonic Hall). The west face looks over a boxwood topiary. **The Transverse**

Porta dos Nós

wing comprises the apartments of King Carlos I (1863-1908), who was a talented painter and draughtsman, and Queen Amelia. In the chapel there is an interesting 16C triptych, attributed to Cristóvão de Figueiredo, illustrating scenes from the Calvary. The 16C Manueline style cloisters are beautifully cool.

Museu dos Coches ★ [Kids]

🕐 *Open same hours as the Ducal Palace (see above) except that it opens 10am Wed Oct-Mar; 10am Apr-Sept; closes Tue 5pm and opens Sat-Sun 9am.* €1.50.

More than 70 coaches, four-wheelers and carriages dating from the 18C to the 20C are displayed in four buildings including the **Royal Stables★**, built at the request of King José I in 1752. The stables, with room for hundreds of horses, are 70m/230ft long with a vaulted roof resting on marble pillars.

Among the carriages, note number 29, the landau in which Dom Carlos I and his son were assassinated on 1 February 1908. The condition and the variety of exhibits are outstanding; there are mail coaches, charabancs, phaetons, landaus, four-wheelers and state carriages.

On leaving the museum the "Knot Gate" (👓 *see below*) stands beside the Lisbon road.

Porta dos Nós★

The so-called Knot Gate is one of the last remains of the 16C perimeter wall. The House of Bragança, whose motto was *Despois vós, nós* (After you, us), chose knots as emblems on account of the two meanings of the word *nós* (us or we and knots).

▶ *Return to the Terreiro do Paço.*

Convento dos Agostinhos

The **church**, rebuilt in the 17C by the future Dom João IV, stands at the east end of the Terreiro do Paço and is now the mausoleum of the Dukes of Bragança. Bays in the chancel and the transept contain the veined white marble ducal tombs.

Antigo Convento das Chagas

The building on the south side of the Terreiro do Paço was founded by Joana de Mendonça, the second wife of Duke Dom Jaime I. The walls of the church, which serves as the mausoleum for the Duchesses of Bragança, are covered in *azulejos* dating from 1626.

Old Town (Vila Velha)
Leave the car outside the ramparts.

The castle and ramparts built at the end of the 13C on the order of King Dinis were reinforced with bastions in the 17C. The crenellated walls flanked with towers still gird the old town. Enter through a gateway cut into the ramparts. The alleys are lined with whitewashed houses, their lower sections painted with bright colours. A narrow street leads to the western glacis on which stand the **Igreja da Conceição** and a 16C **pillory** (pelourinho).

Castle

👓 *Guided tour (1hr 30min) Apr-Sept; Tue 2pm-5.30pm; Wed-Fri 10am-1pm; 2.30pm-5.30pm; Sat-Sun 9am-1pm; 2.30pm-6pm; Oct-Mar 9.30am-1pm; 2pm-5pm (except Wed, from 10am).* 🕐*Closed Mon, Tues morning and holidays.* €3.

The castle, which has been modified since the earliest parts were built in the 13C, is surrounded by a deep moat. The tour includes the original building's dungeons.

An archeological museum, **Museu Arqueológico** 🕐*Same opening times as Paço Ducal.* €3. ☎ 268 98 01 28, on the first floor, displays a collection of Greek vases. The sentry path affords views of the old town.

VILAMOURA

FARO
MICHELIN MAP 733
LOCAL MAP SEE ALGARVE

The resort of Vilamoura and its southeast neighbour **Quarteira** are modern tourist resorts, with Vilamoura being one of the best golf destinations on the Algarve. Quarteira's high-rise blocks line a wide avenue beside Vilamoura's holiday villages, hotels, casino, seven golf courses and a vast marina which can accommodate several hundred yachts. The ruins of a Roman city come as a surprise among all these modern constructions.

▸ **Orient Yourself:** On the Algarve coast, 30 minutes west from Faro airport.

▣ **Parking:** No problems other than around the marina at night-time.

☺ **Don't Miss:** The Marina at night with its lively atmosphere. Any of the golf courses if you ar a golfer.

🕐 **Organizing Your Time:** The sort of place you might want to be based in for a few days.

Kids **Especially for Kids:** The beach !

☝ **Also See:** Faro, Albufeira and, for a change, Vila Rreal de S. António.

Visit

Museu e Estação Arqueológica do Cerro da Vila
On the northeast corner of the marina. 🕐*Open May-Oct, 10am-1pm; 3-8pm; Nov-Apr 9.30am-12.30pm; 2-6pm.* 🕐*Closed 1 Jan, Easter and 25 Dec.* ⊛€2. ☎ *289 31 21 53 - www.vilamoura.net.*
The excavations undertaken here since 1964 have revealed a Roman city underneath Moorish and Visigothic remains. Apart from a patrician villa dating from the 1C with private baths and a cellar, there are wells, a crematorium, silos, stables, a wine press and the ruins of 3C public baths. These baths once stood near the harbour before the sea retreated. Beautiful panels and fragments of mosaics, some polychrome, others black and white, still adorn the floors and pools (the latter have subsequently been converted into salting vats and fishtanks).

Address Book

NIGHTLIFE

Along with Albufeira, Vilamoura has some of the Algarve's liveliest night-life. The promenade along the **marina** has a huge number of bars and restaurants to get your evening underway. Another possibility is the dinner-show at the **casino** in Vilamoura *(dinner: 8.30pm; show: 10.30pm – ☎ 289 30 29 99)*. The **Black Jack** disco in the same building is also one of the Algarve's most popular clubs *(open 11pm to 6am)*. If the Black Jack is too crowded, you might want to try its twin, the **Black Jack Beach Club**, just a few kilometres down the road in Vale do Lobo, with its pool, three dance floors and views overlooking the ocean. The **Kadok**, on the old road between Vilamoura and Albufeira, is one of the biggest and liveliest clubs on the Algarve with three dance floors and music for all tastes (house, pop/rock and techno), seven bars and spacious outdoor areas *(closes around 6am)*. In Quinta do Lago, the same venue is home to both the **T Clube** (popular with the Portuguese jet set) and the **Trigonometria** on the first floor (for their children), both of which attract a mix of party-goers and styles.

The museum contains an interesting reconstruction of this large villa as it would have appeared during Roman times, as well as items from various periods discovered on the site, including coins and ceramics.

VISEU★

VISEU

POPULATION 93 259– MICHELIN MAP 733

The town of Viseu has developed in the region of the famous Dão vineyards in a wooded and somewhat hilly area on the south bank of the Pavia, a tributary of the Mondego. It is an important centre of agriculture (rye, maize, cattle and fruit) and crafts (lace, carpets, basketmaking and black clay pottery). Its egg sweetmeats *(bolos de amor, papos de anjo, travesseiros de ovos moles, castanhas de ovos)* are a speciality. *Av. Gulbenkian – 3150-055 – ☎ 232 42 20 14 or 232 42 09 50*

▶ **Orient Yourself:** North-east of Coimbra; south-east of Porto, almost midway.

Don't Miss: The Grão Vasco museum with its wonderful paintings; the Serra Caramulo.

Organizing Your Time: Between two and four hours will be enough.

Also See: Aveiro, Coimbra. Guarda.

Viseu School of Painting

Viseu had a flourishing school of painting in the 16C, led by two masters, Vasco Fernandes and Gaspar Vaz who, in their turn, were greatly influenced by Flemish artists such as Van Eyck and Quentin Metsys.

VISEU	
Alexandre Herculano R. de	3
Alexandre Lobo R.	4
Andrades R. dos	5
Árvore R. da	6
Augusto Hilário R.	7
Casimiros R. dos	8
Chão do Mestre R.	9
Comércio R. do	10
Conselheiro Sousa Mercado R.	12
Direita R.	13
Dom Duarte R.	15
Dr M. de Aragão R.	16
Emídio Navarro Av.	18
Escura R.	19
Formosa R.	21
G. Barreiros R.	24
Gen. Humberto Delgado Largo	25
Hospital R. do	27
Infante D. Henrique Av.	28
Maj. Leop. da Silva R.	30
Nunes de Carvalho R.	31
República Pr. da	33
São Lázaro R.	34
Sé Adro da	36
Senhora da Piedade R. da	37
Vigia Calçada da	39
Vitória R.	40

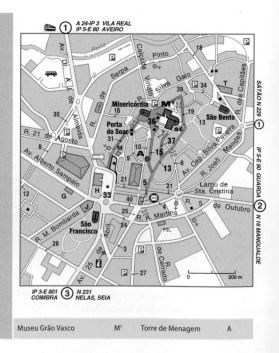

Museu Grão Vasco	M¹	Torre de Menagem	A

Gaspar Vaz, who died about 1568, developed his style at the Lisbon School. He was gifted with a brilliant imagination and could give great intensity of expression to forms and draped figures. The landscapes he painted kept their regional flavour. His principal works, still showing considerable Gothic influence, hang in the Igreja de São João de Tarouca.

The early works of **Vasco Fernandes** (1480-c 1543), to whom legend has given the name of Grão Vasco (Great Vasco), reveal Flemish influence (altarpieces at Lamego in the regional museum and at Freixo de Espada-à-Cinta). His later work showed more originality, a distinct sense of the dramatic and of composition, a richness of colour and a violent realism inspired by popular and local subjects particularly in his portraits and landscapes. His principal works are in the Viseu museum.

The two masters probably collaborated in the creation of the polyptych in Viseu cathedral, which would explain its hybrid character.

Old Town★ (Cidade Velha) *2hr*

Old Viseu is an ancient town with narrow alleys paved with granite sets and Renaissance and classical corbelled houses emblazoned with coats of arms.

▶ *Follow the route marked on the plan starting at Praça da República.*

Praça da República (or Rossio)
Facing the town hall, this pleasant tree-planted square is the town's lively centre.

Porta do Soar
Go through this gate built in the town wall by King Dom Afonso in the 15C to enter the old town.

Adro da Sé ★
The peaceful cathedral square in the heart of the old town is lined with noble granite buildings: the Museu de Grão Vasco, the cathedral and the Igreja da Misericórdia.

Museu Grão Vasco★★
🕐*Open Tues 2pm-6pm; Weds-Sun 10am-6pm.* 🚫*Closed Mon, 1 Jan, Good Fri, Easter Sun, 1 May and 25 Dec.* €3 *(no charge Sun until 2pm).* ☎ *232 42 20 49.*

St Peter by Grão Vasco

Museu Nacional Grão Vasco – J. Pessoa/ANF-IPM -

The museum is the former Palácio dos Três Escalões, which was built in the 16C and remodelled in the 18C. The ground floor is devoted to 13C-18C sculpture. Outstanding are the 14C **Throne of Grace**★, of which only a representation of God the Father remains, and the 13C *Pietà*; some 16C Spanish-Arabic *azulejos* and Portuguese porcelain (17C and 18C) are also interesting.

On the **First floor** are several works by Portuguese painters of the 19C and early 20C.The **Second floor** , with the exception of one room which contains paintings by **Columbano** (1857-1929) including a self-portrait, the second floor is devoted to the **Primitives**★★ of the Viseu School. Particularly noteworthy is the painting of **St Peter on his Throne**, one of Vasco Fernandes's masterpieces. While it is a copy of the one in São João de Tarouca attributed to Gaspar Vaz, it shows great originality. Another major work by Grão Vasco is the **Calvary**, in which the figures are depicted with forceful violence. The fourteen paintings, which comprise the altarpiece which stood formerly in the cathedral, are by a group of artists from the Viseu School: the *Descent from the Cross* and the *Kiss of Judas* are among the best. In the *Adoration of the Magi*, the Black King has been replaced by an Indian from Brazil, as the country had just been discovered by Pedro Álvares Cabral in 1500. Also from the Viseu School are *The Last Supper* and *Christ in the House of Martha*.

Cathedral ★

This Romanesque cathedral was considerably remodelled between the 16C and 18C. The façade was rebuilt in the 17C, the central statue among the six which ornament the façade is of São Teotónio, patron saint of Viseu.

The roof, which rests on Gothic pillars, is supported by twisted **liernes**★ which form knots at regular intervals; the keystones are decorated with the arms of the founder bishop and the royal mottos of Afonso V and João II (the latter's symbol is a pelican). The chancel is 17C; the barrel vaulting shelters a monumental Baroque **altarpiece**★ of gilded wood; above the high altar is a 14C Virgin carved in Ançã stone. The north chapel is decorated with *azulejos* dating from the 18C.

Stairs lead from the north transept to the gallery *(coro alto)* where there is a wooden lectern brought from Brazil in the 16C. Go to the first floor of the cloisters where the chapter-house contains a **treasury of sacred art** ○*Open 9am-noon and 2-5pm; Sat-Sun and holidays 2pm-5pm.* ○*Closed Monday.* ☞€2.50. ☎ *232 42 88 18. (Tesouro de Arte Sacra)* including two 13C Limoges enamel reliquary caskets, a 12C Gospel in a 14C binding and a crib by Machado de Castro.

The **cloisters** are Renaissance. The ground level gallery, where the arches rest on Ionic columns, is decorated with 18C *azulejos*. In the Chapel of Our Lady of Mercy there is a fine 16C low relief of the Descent from the Cross which is said to be by the Coimbra School. A beautiful doorway in the transitional Gothic style leads from the cloisters back into the cathedral.

Igreja da Misericórdia

This Baroque building has an attractive rhythmic façade in contrast to its white walls and grey granite pilasters. The central section, focused beneath an elegant pediment, is pierced by a pretty Baroque doorway surmounted by a balcony.

Casas Antigas

The following old houses are worthly of note: in the **Rua Dom Duarte** a keep *(Torre de Menagem)*, embellished with a lovely Manueline window; in the picturesque narrow, bustling **Rua Direita**, 18C houses with balconies supported on wrought-iron brackets; in the **Rua dos Andrades** (south of the Rua Direita), corbelled houses; and in the **Rua da Senhora da Piedade**, houses built in the 16C.

▶ *Take the Rua Direita before returning to Praça da Sé via Rua Escura.*

For the best little places, follow the leader.

Looking for the latest news on today's best hotels and restaurants? Pick up the Michelin Guide and look for the Bib Gourmand and Bib Hotel symbols. With 45,000 addresses in Europe, in every category and price range, the perfect place to dine or stay is never far away.

Madeira landscape: Paúl do Mar

MADEIRA AND THE AZORES

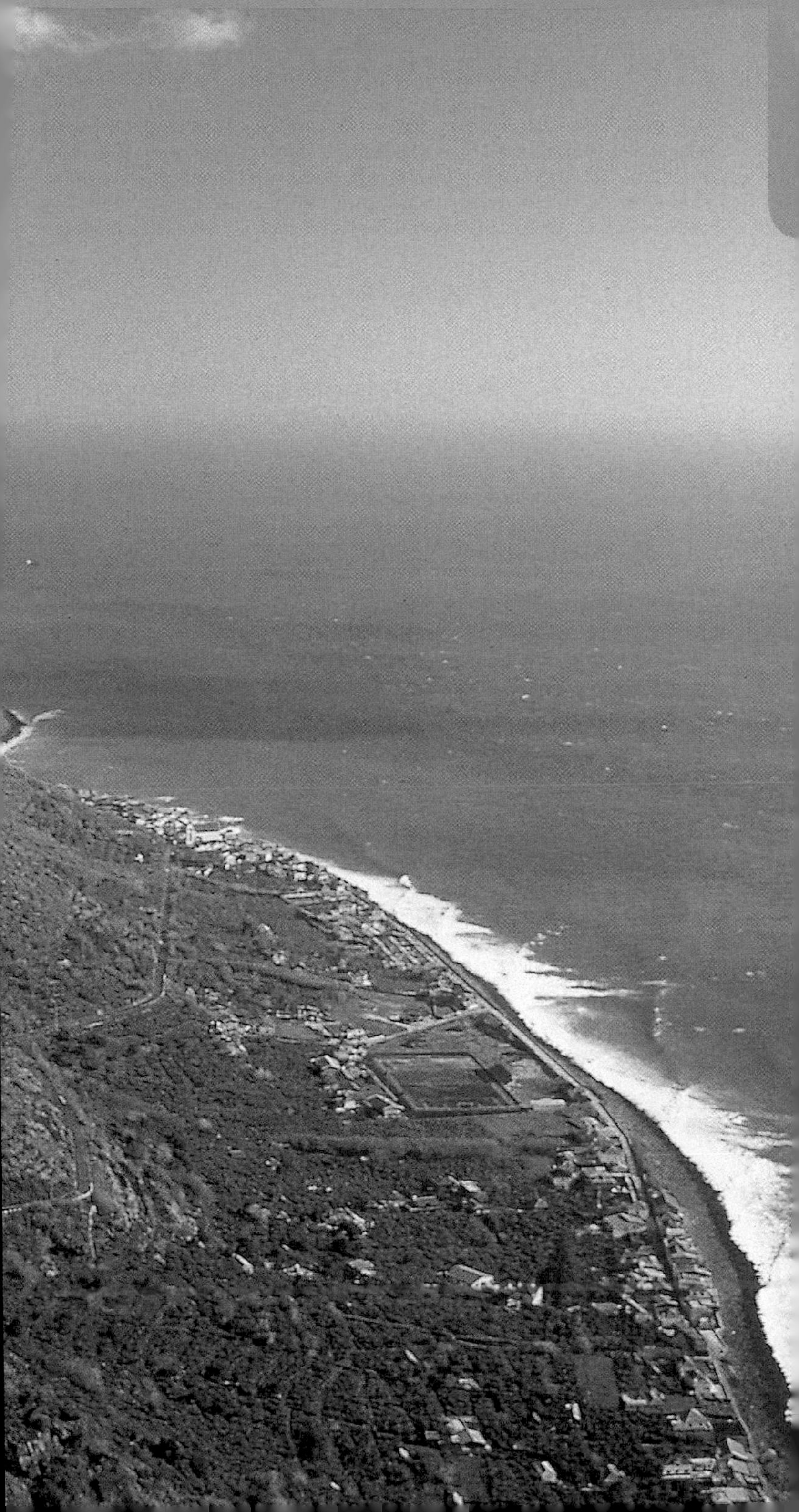

THE MADEIRA ARCHIPELAGO

The Madeira Archipelago consists of the main island which has the greatest area (740km²/286sq mi) and the largest population (254 880), the island of Porto Santo (42km²/16sq mi), lying 40km/25mi to the northeast, and two groups of uninhabited islands, the Ilhas Desertas or Empty Isles, 20km/12mi from Funchal and the Ihlas Selvagens or Wild Isles, situated near the Canaries, 240km/150mi away.

😄 A Bit of Advice 😄

ACCESS BY AIR
There are regular direct flights from the UK and daily flights from Lisbon (👜 see Planning Your Trip for connections between the UK and Lisbon and the USA and Lisbon) to Funchal Airport, Madeira.

WHEN TO GO
The temperature is mild throughout the year with an average of 16°C/61°F in January and 22°C/72°F in July. Rain falls in March, April and October.
To choose a hotel or restaurant in Madeira, consult the *Michelin Guide Spain & Portugal*. Funchal has most of Madeira's hotels, although the island of Porto Santo, beautiful and calm, has on-site accommodation.

MADEIRA BY CAR
Madeira has spectacular landscapes that may be explored from the places to stay mentioned above by following the routes described hereafter. Taxis may be used for short distances and cars hired for longer ones. There are also many regular **bus services** 🕐 *For information on bus itineraries (there are a number of options at varying prices), ask at the Direcção Regional de Turismo, Avenida Arriaga, 18 – 9004-519 Funchal. ☎ 291 22 90 57.*

MADEIRA ON FOOT
Madeira offers a wide choice of walks. Some paths follow the *levada* network, while others take mountain routes around Pico Ruivo. The paths are rated according to difficulty. The Direcção Regional de Turismo runs several mountain huts, but they are not open all year and must be booked in advance. Some of the walks including Pico Ruivo, Balcões, Levada do Norte to Estreito do Lobos, and Rabaçal are described in this guide.

BEACHES
Madeira island itself has practically no beaches. The island of Porto Santo, however, has Portugal's most beautiful beach –8km/5mi of white sand, with an ideal temperature for most of the year.

OTHER SPORTS
Sports here include golf at Serra da Santo and Palheiro, angling and deep-sea fishing.

MADEIRA★★★

FUNCHAL

POPULATION 253 427 – MICHELIN MAP 733 FOLD 43

Madeira rises from the Atlantic Ocean, a volcanic island mass climbing high above the ocean swell. The "pearl of the Atlantic", 900km/559mi from Lisbon, offers visitors a climate which is mild as well as vegetation which is subtropical and transforms the island into a blossoming garden all year round. The landscape, beautiful and varied, opens out into vast panoramas.

- ▶ **Orient Yourself:** 900km/559mi south-west from Lisbon, on the same latitude as Casablanca.
- 🅿 **Parking:** Parking in Funchal can be a problem, but elsewhere in the island you will encounter no major difficulties.
- 🕒 **Don't Miss:** The Botanical Gardens; Funchal itself for it s great atmosphere
- 🕐 **Organizing Your Time:** Stay a week to really enjoy Madeira; be sure to take a few day trips, including one to Porto Santo.
- **Kids Especially for Kids:** The Aquarium at the Museu Municipal and swimming at the beach on Porto Santo.
- 🖢 **Also See:** Porto Santo if you have the chance – if not, go out on a cruise from Funchal.

J.P.Garcin/DIAF

Terrace farming

y and colonisation

In 1419, **João Gonçalves Zarco** and Tristão Vaz Teixeira, leaders of an expedition dispatched by Prince Henry the Navigator, landed first on the island of Porto Santo, and later on Madeira itself. The island appeared to be uninhabited and entirely covered in woodland and they therefore named it the wooded island, *a ilha da madeira*.

The navigators reported their discovery to Prince Henry, who commanded them to return the following year and divided the territory into three *captaincies*: Zarco received the land centred on Funchal and extending south of an imaginary line drawn from Ponta do Oliveira to Ponta do Tristão; Tristão Vaz Teixeira received Machico and all the rest of the island, and **Bartolomeu Perestrelo** the island of Porto Santo.

The islands are volcanic having been thrust up from the Atlantic during a period of volcanic eruption in the Tertiary Era, and climb to over 1 200m/3 936ft culminating in high peaks such as Pico Ruivo (1 862m/6 107ft).

Madeira, which is almost at the same latitude as Casablanca, enjoys a temperate climate. Mild and with no extremes, the mean temperature only varies from 16° to 21°C/61° to 70° F from winter to summer.

Flowers

The whole island of Madeira is a mass of flowers; every hillside, every garden and roadside verge is covered with hydrangeas, geraniums, hibiscus, agapanthus, bougainvilleas, fuchsias and euphorbias. Certain species such as orchids, anthuriums and strelitzias (or Birds of Paradise) are grown in large quantities for export. There are also several species of flowering trees – mimosas, magnolias, sumaumás and jacarandas. Bananas are the island's major export crop.

Madeira wine

Vines were introduced to Madeira in the 15C from Crete and planted in the rich and sunny volcanic soil along the south coast. In 1660 a commercial treaty between England and Portugal encouraged the export of the wine and increased production. Overseas buyers, for the most part English (Blandy, Leacock and Cossart Gordon), were drawn to Madeira by the prosperous trade which reached its height in the 18C and 19C.

There are three principal wines. **Sercial**, made from grapes whose vines originally came from the Rhine valley, is a dry wine with a good bouquet; it is amber in colour and is served chilled and drunk as an aperitif. **Boal** originates from Burgundy; the rich, full-bodied flavour of this red-brown wine makes it primarily a dessert wine. **Malmsey**, the most famous, is rare today; again a dessert wine, honeyed in flavour with a deep-red, almost purple colour. A medium sweet all-purpose wine, **Verdelho**, a Muscatel and *Tinto* or red wine are also produced.

At one time, barrels of Madeira were used as ballast in ships making the long journey to India or America; the trip there and back gave the wine ample time to heat.

Vintage Madeira made from the best wines in exceptionally good years may be consumed up to and over 150 years later.

Madeira embroidery

Embroidery is one of the mainstays of the island's economy. Madeira embroidery owes its origin to an Englishwoman. In 1856 **Miss Phelps**, the daughter of a wine importer, started a workroom where women embroidered designs after the manner of *broderie anglaise*. The work was sold for charity. Samples of the embroidery reached London and were received with such enthusiasm that Miss Phelps decided to sell the work abroad. In less than a century, embroidery became one of Madeira's major resources; today 30 000 women are employed. The embroidery on linen, lawn or organdie is very fine and varied in design.

Agapanthus

Mimosa

Orchid

Strelitzia

Hibiscus

Magnolia

Anthurium

Funchal★★

🅸 *Av. Arriaga 18 – 9004-519 –* ☎ *291 21 19 00 or 291 21 56 58.*
The island's capital rises in tiers up the slopes of a vast amphitheatre around the bay.
When the early settlers arrived they found the heights covered in wild fennel, hence
the name Funchal, meaning fennel garden. The luxuriant vegetation, the *quintas*,
hotels, night-life and sports facilities combine to form a popular city resort, attracting
visitors from many countries year round. The harbour faces central Funchal. East of
this stretch the alleyways of the old town.

The Centre
Follow the itinerary indicated on the town plan.

Avenida das Comunidades Madeirenses or Avenida do Mar
This wide promenade bordered with flowers runs parallel to the marina. Along the
quayside are restaurants and cafés, one of which is on a boat that belonged to the
Beatles. There is a fine **view**★ of the town from the end of the jetty.

Avenida Arriaga
This is Funchal's main street. The jacaranda trees along it are covered in purple
flowers throughout the spring. The **Jardim Público de São Francisco** is an interesting botanical garden with a wide variety of plants. Between the garden and the
tourist information centre (Turismo) are the cellars, **Adegas de São Francisco**★
(🖝*Guided tours (approx 1hr 30min including wine-tasting), 9am-7pm (until 1pm Sat).*
🚫*Closed Sun and hols.* ☎ *291 74 01 00 or 291 22 80 58).* They are housed in a former
16C Franciscan monastery. Opposite the cellars is **Forte de São Lourenço**, which
still serves as residence to the Commandant of Madeira.

Cathedral (Sé) ★
Enter by the main altar or at the back of the church. 🚫*Open Mon-Fri 10am-noon, 1-5pm;
Sat 10am-noon.* 🚫*Closed Sun and public hols.* ☎ *291 22 81 55.*

View of Funchal port

xxx Pic Photographer xxx

The first Portuguese cathedral to be constructed overseas. The apse, decor[...]
openwork balustrades and twisted pinnacles, is flanked by a crenellated
belfry, the roof of which is tiled with *azulejos*. In the nave, slender columns su[...]
arcades of painted lava rock while above, and also over the transept, extend[...]
remarkable *artesonado* **ceiling**★ in which ivory inlays in the cedar have been use[...]
to emphasise the stylistic motifs.

Praça do Município
The square is bordered to the south by the former episcopal palace, now the Museu
de Arte Sacra (Sacred Art Museum) and to the east by the town hall.

Town Hall
The town hall, formerly the 18C palace of Count Carvalhal, is surmounted by a tower
that dominates the area. The inner courtyard is decorated with *azulejos*.

Museu de Arte Sacra
🕐 *Open Tue-Fri, 10am-noon, 2-5.30pm; Sat-Sun 2-5.30pm.* 🕐*Closed Mon and public
hols.* ⊜€2. ☎ 291 22 89 00.
The Museum of Sacred Art is housed in the former episcopal palace which has a
beautiful arcaded gallery overlooking the square. It contains fine religious items
and liturgical ornaments but its main interest lies in a collection of **paintings**★ on
wood from the 15C and 16C Portuguese and Flemish Schools. From the Portuguese
School, note the triptych depicting *St James and St Philip*. From the Flemish School
are a *Descent from the Cross* attributed to Gérard David; a full-length portrait of *St
James the Less*; a triptych attributed to Quentin Metys of *St Peter*; an *Annunciation*, a
portrait of *Bishop St Nicholas*, a *Meeting between St Anne and St Joachim*, a *Crucifixion*,
and an *Adoration of the Magi*.

Igreja do Colégio
Same hours as the Museu de Arte Sacra. ☎ 291 723 35 34.
The Church of St John the Evangelist was built early in the 17C in the Jesuit style.
The austere white façade has also been hollowed out to form four statuary niches.
These contain marble figures on the upper level of St Ignatius and St Francis Xavier,
and on the lower of St Francis Borgia and St Stanislas.

Museu Municipal
Kids 🕐 *Open 10am-6pm; Sat-Sun and hols, noon-6pm.* 🕐*Closed Mon, 1 Jan, Easter Sun
and 25 Dec.* ⊜€3 (no charge Sun). ☎ 291 22 97 61.
The former mansion of Count Carvalhal now houses an aquarium and a natural history museum. The aquarium contains various sea creatures from the waters around
Madeira, including red scorpion fish, mantis shrimps and morays. Among many
stuffed and mounted animals are sharks, horned rays and white-bellied seals.

Museu Frederico de Freitas ★
🕐 *Open 10am-12.30pm and 2pm-5.30pm.* 🕐*Closed Sun afternoon, Mon and hols.*
⊜€2 (no charge Sun). ☎ 291 22 05 78.
The former mansion of Dr Frederico de Freitas contains engravings, drawings and
water-colours illustrating Madeira through the centuries. The more intimate first
floor shows the interior of a 19C middle-class home. Its English furniture has been
preserved as have its 'sugar chest' cupboards, musical instruments and cabinets
adorned with ivory and whalebone.

Convento de Santa Clara
🡒 *Guided tours (20min), 10am-noon and 3-5pm.* 🕐*Closed Sundays and hols.* ⊜€2.
☎ 291 74 26 02.

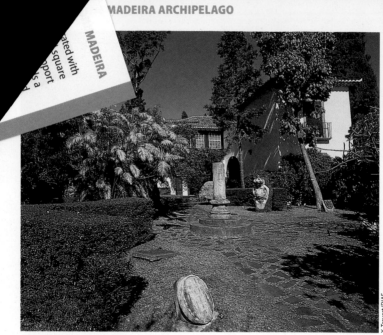

Y. Travert/DIAF

Quinta das Cruzes, Funchal

The convent was built in the 17C on the site of a church founded in the 15C by Zarco. His Gothic tomb, supported by lions, is at the far end, and his two granddaughters who founded the original convent of the Order of St Clare are buried here.

Quinta das Cruzes★★

🕐 *Open 10am-12.30pm and 2-5.30pm; Sun, 10am-1pm.* 🕐*Closed Mon and hols.* ⊛€2.
☎ *291 74 13 82/84/88.*

Zarco's former mansion has been converted into a museum of decorative arts (Museu de Artes Decorativas). The ground floor contains 16C Portuguese furniture. There are many 17C cabinets and chests known as *caixa de açucar* or sugar chests made with wood taken from boxes in which Brazilian sugar was transported. At the back of one room stands a 15C Flemish altarpiece of the Nativity. The rooms on the first floor contain a rich collection of 18C and 19C English furniture in the Hepplewhite and Chippendale style.

Additional Sights

Mercado dos Lavradores

This worker's market, which is now housed in a modern building, is particularly lively in the morning when you can buy all types of fresh fish, fruit and vegetables. At the entrance are the brightly-attired flower sellers.

Vila Velha (Old Town)

This is the site where the original town was founded in the 15C. Today, the narrow streets are a multitude of boutiques, taverns, bars and restaurants.

Madeira Story Centre

Rua D Carlos 1. 27/29. 🕐 *Open 9am-8pm.* ⊛€10. ☎ *291 00 07 70; www.storycentre. com.*

Opened in 2005 this well laid-out centre explains the details and history of Madeira from its volcanic origins to the present day.

Mercado dos Lavradores

Forte de São Tiago
🕘Open 10am-12.30pm; 2pm-5.30pm. 🚫Closed Sunday. ☚Guided tour (30min). ✦€2. ☎ 291 21 33 40.
The fort was built in 1614. Its yellow walls rise above the shore where fishing boats lie moored beside small blue and white striped huts.

Instituto do Bordado
🕘 Open 10am-12.30pm and 2.pm-5.30pm. 🚫Closed Sat-Sun and hols.✦€2. ☎ 291 22 31 41.
Several rooms in the embroidery institute have been converted into a museum where magnificent examples of Madeiran workmanship are displayed.

Instituto do Vinho de Madeira
🕘 Open 9am-noon and 2-5pm. 🚫Closed Sat-Sun and hols. ☎ 291 20 46 00.
Founded to promote Madeira wine, this institute offers free wine-tastings.

Western Funchal

Jardins do Casino
Funchal casino was built in 1979 by the Brazilian architect Óscar Niemeyer, and stands in a park of beautiful exotic trees.

Botanical Gardens★
🕘 Open 9am-6pm. 🚫Closed 25 Dec. ✦€3. ☎ 291 21 12 00. Accesible by bus, no. 29, 30 or 31.
Many outstanding examples of Madeiran flora can be viewed. The elegant white house with green shutters contains a small old-style museum with wooden display cases showing botanical, geological and zoological collections; note the vulcanised wood.
From the topmost belvedere, there is a **view**★ of Funchal harbour.

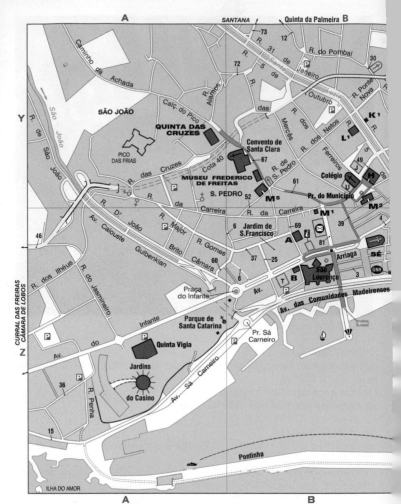

FUNCHAL

31 de Janeiro R.	BY	Carvalho Araújo R.	AZ 15	Hortas R. das	BY
5 de Outubro R.	BY	Casa da Luz R.	CZ 16	Hospital Velho R. do	CYZ 34
Acciauoli R.	DYZ	Chafariz Largo do	CZ 19	Ilhéus R. dos	AZ
Achada Caminho da	AY	Comunidades		Imperatriz D. Amélia	
Alamos R.	AY	Madeirenses Av. das	BZ	R. da	AZ 36
Alf. V. Pestana R.	CY	Conceição R. da	CY 22	Infante Av. do	AZ
Alfândega R. da	BZ 3	Conde Carvalhal R. do	DY	Infante Pr. do	AZ
Aljube R. do	BZ 4	Conselheiro Aires		Ivens R.	BZ 37
Aranhas R. dos	ABZ 6	Ornelas R.	CY 24	Jasmineiro R. do	AZ
Arriaga Av.	BZ	Conselheiro José		João de Deus R.	CY
Autonomia Pr. da	CZ 7	Silvestre Ribeiro R.	BZ 25	João Tavira R.	BZ 39
Bela de São Tiago R.	DZ	Corpo Santo Largo do	DZ	Latino Ceolho R.	CZ 40
Bettencourt R. do	CY 9	Cota 40	ACY	Lazareto Caminho do	DZ 42
Bom Jesus R.	BY	Cruzes R. das	AY	Major R.	AZ
Bompal R. do	BY	Dom Carlos I R.	CZ	Maravilhas R. das	AZ 46
Brigadeiro Oudinot R.	CY 10	Dr Fernão de Ornelas R.	CZ 28	Marquês do Funchal R.	BY 49
Calouste Gulbenkian Av.	AZ	Dr João Brito Câmara R.	AYZ	Mercês R. das	BY
Carmo R. do	CY	Dr Manuel Pestana R.	CDY	Miguel Carvalho R.	CY 51
Carmo Pr. do	CY 20	Elias Garcia R.	BCY	Mouraria R. da	BY 52
Carne Azeda R. da	BY 12	Encarnação Calç	BY 30	Municipio Pr. do	BY
Carreira R. da	ABZ	Ferreiros R. dos	BY	Netos R. dos	BY
		Gomes R.	AZ	Nova de Alegria R.	DYZ

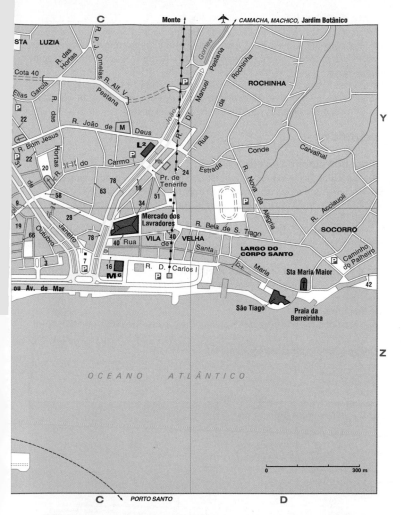

Palheiro Caminho do	DZ	Rochinha R. da	CDY	Saúde Calç.	BY	72
Pedro José de Ornejas R.	CY	Sá Carneiro Pr.	BZ	Tenerife Pr. de	CY
Penha R.	AZ	Sá Carneiro Av.	AZ	Til R. do	BY	73
Phelps Largo do	CY 58	Sabão R. do	CZ 66	Visconde do Anadia R.	CYZ	78
Pico Calç. do	AY	Santa Clara Calç.	BY 67	Zarco Av.	BZ	81
Ponte de S. Lázaro R.	AZ 60	Santa Maria R. de	CDZ		
Ponte Nova R.	BY	São Francisco R. de	BZ 69		
Pretas R. das	BY 61	São João R.	AY		
Ribeirinho R.	CY 63	São Pedro R. de	BY		

Adegas de São Francisco	BZ	A	Museu Cristóvão			Praia da Barreirinha	DZ	
Câmara Municipal	BY	H	Colombo	BZ	M⁴	Quinta da Palmeira	B	
Casa Borges	BY	K¹	Museu da Fotografia			Quinta das Cruzes	AY	
Convento de Santa Clara	BY		"Vicentes"	BZ	M¹	Quinta Vigia	AZ	
Igreja do Colégio	BY		Museu de Arte Sacra	BY	M²	Santa Maria Maior	DZ	
Instituto do Bordado	CY	L²	Museu de Electricidade	CZ	M⁶	São Lourenço	BZ	
Instituto do Vinho			Museu Frederico de			São Tiago	DZ	
da Madeira	BY	L¹	Freitas	ABY		Sé	B	
Jardim Botânico	D		Museu Municipal	BY	M⁵	Toyota	BZ	B
Jardim de São Francisco	BZ		Parque de Santa				
Jardins do Casino	AZ		Catarina	AZ			
Mercado dos Lavradores	CZ		Pontinha	BZ			

Quinta da Palmeira

Take Rua da Carne Azeda north. Bear left on Rua da Levada de Santa Luzia. The Quinta entrance is just before a left bend; its name is in white shingle inlaid in the roadway. Although it is private property, visitors may walk in the gardens Leave the car near the entrance gate.

The terraces of this well-kept park overlook Funchal. There are fine *azulejo* benches and a Gothic stone window. This window was formerly in the house in which, it is said, Christopher Columbus stayed when he lived in Funchal.

Excursions

Quinta do Palheiro Ferreiro★★

Leave Funchal on Rua Dr Manuel Pestana towards the airport. Take the first road towards Camacha. After several bends, turn right on a narrow cobbled road signposted Quinta do Palheiro Ferreiro. ◷ *Open 9.30am-4pm.* ◷*Closed Sat-Sun and hols.* ✆€8.50. ☎ 291 79 30 40.

The vast mansion is set in a well-maintained **park** approached by paths lined with camellias. Over 3 000 plant species include exotic trees and rare flowers.

Eira do Serrado and Curral das Freiras ★★

Round trip of 34km/21mi, 2hr. Leave Funchal on Avenida do Infante.

São Martinho

In São Martinho the parish church stands at the top of a "peak" 259m/850ft high.

▷ *As you come to the cemetery, turn right.*

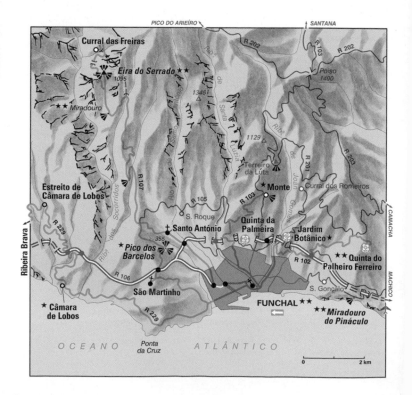

Pico dos Barcelos★★

The viewpoint (alt 355m/1 164ft) gives a panorama of Fur
the mountain ranges, the ragged outlines of which can be
António sits snugly in its valley clustered round its villa
Martinho, the church of which is silhouetted against the sea

▶ *Continue along the road towards Eira do Serrado.*

Several kilometres farther on, beyond a wood of eucalyptus trees, the road nears the Ribeira dos Socorridos (River of Survivors) named after the survivors who took refuge in its course when the island was set on fire. There is an impressive **sight**★ of the deep defile caused by a volcanic fracture through which the stream flows. There is a magnificent **view**★★ of the defile.

▶ *A right fork takes you to Eira do Serrado where you leave the car.*

Eira do Serrado ★★★

A path *(10min round trip on foot)* goes round the Pico do Serrado (1 095m/3 591ft) on the right to a viewpoint. The panorama is outstanding: the white houses of the village of Curral das Freiras lie scattered around mountain ravines.

▶ *Take the road down to Curral das Freiras.*

Curral das Freiras

Curral das Freiras lies in an enclosed **setting**★ at the foot of a grandiose cirque of extinct volcanoes. It belonged to the sisters of the Convent of St Clare who took shelter here when French pirates pillaged Funchal in 1566. The event was commemorated in the name of the village, which in Portuguese means the "nuns' shelter".
As you return uphill pause on leaving the village at a paved terrace on your left, to get an interesting **view**★ of the circle of mountain peaks.

▶ *Leave the Pico dos Barcelos road on your right as you enter Funchal.*

Santo António

This is Funchal's smart residential quarter. It has an 18C Baroque church.

▶ *Return to Funchal by Caminho de Santo António which drops rapidly into the town centre.*

Monte★

7km/4mi. About 1hr.
Monte, at an altitude of 600m/1 970ft, is a country resort much appreciated for its cool climate and rich vegetation. The Quinta do Monte, which lies below the former Belmonte Hotel, became the house of the last Emperor of Austria when he was exiled to the island in 1921. Karl I died in the house the following year. You can reach Monte by cable-car from the old town of Funchal *(10min trip. ⊙ Open 9am-6pm. ⊘Closed 25 Dec. ⊜€9.50 one-way; €14.50 round trip).* There is also a Tropical Garden which is well worth seeing if you adore beautiful flowers and plants. ⊙ *Open 9.30am-6pm ⊜€10. ☎ 291 74 26 50; www.montepalace.com.*

Igreja de Nossa Senhora do Monte

The church was built on the site of a chapel erected in 1470 by Adam Gonçalves Ferreira. He and his twin sister Eva were the first children to be born on the island. The Baroque façade is highly decorative. In a chapel to the left of the nave is the iron tomb of Emperor Karl I of Austria. A tabernacle worked in silver above the high altar shelters a small cloaked statue of Our Lady of the Mountain, the patron saint of

. The figure, discovered in the 15C at Terreiro da Luta at the spot where the
appeared to a young shepherdess, is the goal of a popular pilgrimage held
4 and 15 August each year. At the foot of the church stairway is the departure
int for the traditional cane sledges or *carros de cesto* which are driven at great
peed down Caminho do Monte.

▶ *Walk down Largo dos Barbosas to the left of the staircase.*

Largo dos Barbosas leads to a small square shaded by plane trees and overlooked by
the **Capela de Nossa Senhora da Conceição**, built in Baroque style in 1906. From
the square there is a view across the wooded valley of the Ribeira de João Gomes.

Terreiro da Luta
15km/9mi from Funchal and 2km/1mi from Monte.
When the bombardment of Funchal by German submarines in 1917 ceased, the
Bishop of Funchal made a vow to erect a monument to the Virgin, provided peace
followed quickly. The monument to Our Lady of Peace, (1927) stands where Our
Lady of the Mountain is said to have appeared. Encircling the monument are anchor
chains from the torpedoed ships.

From Funchal to Ribeira Brava via Cabo Girão ★
30km/19mi west. About 1hr. Leave Funchal on Avenida do Infante.

Câmara de Lobos ★
Câmara de Lobos (Seals' House) was named on after the great number of seals (*lobos
marinhos* in Portuguese) on the shores when Zarco first arrived. The picturesque town
is built round a harbour protected by two cliffs of volcanic rock. Along the harbour
you have a view of the town **setting** ★. The white houses stand scattered on terraces
among banana-trees. Below, on the beach, fishing boats lie drawn up in the shade
of palm trees with their bizarre black nets suspended on willow frames to dry.

Câmara de Lobos

▶ *Continue along the road.*

Banana plantations give way to vineyards, the only crop in the region of Estreito de Câmara do Lobos. Malmsey and Verdelho are made from the white grape; Tinto from the black. Above 500m/1 640ft in the Jardim da Serra region vines are grown on espaliers, their grapes producing the well-known Sercial.

Estreito de Câmara do Lobos
This small bustling village is dominated by its white parish church. A narrow road beside the church leads to the upper village and the Levada do Norte.

Walk along the Levada do Norte ★
2hr round trip.
The *levada* leads to the valley of the Ribeira de Caixa. As you walk among the flowers, only the sound of the water breaks the silence.

▶ *Return to R 101 and continue westwards.*

The approaches to Cabo Girão are clad with pinewoods and eucalyptus groves.

▶ *Bear left towards Cabo Girão.*

Cabo Girão★
From the belvedere there is an extensive view of the coastal plain as far as Funchal, the sea 580m/1 900ft below. The road continues through terraced land and banana plantations before descending abruptly to Ribeira Brava.

Ribeira Brava – 👤 *See Southwest Coast.*

East Coast ★ *Itinerary* 1 *on the map of the island.*

This itinerary is along one of the sunniest of Madeira's coasts. Rivers flowing from the mountains have formed ravines and inlets along which villages have grown. The often desolate countryside bears traces of terraces that were once cultivated.

1 Round trip starting from Funchal *90km/56mi – about 4hr.*

▶ *Leave Funchal on Rua de Conde Carvalhal towards the airport.*

Miradouro do Pináculo ★★
2km/1mi beyond São Gonçalo.
A belvedere on a rocky promontory *(pináculo)* gives a wonderful view of Funchal, lying spread out at the end of its beautiful bay. Cabo Girão stands out on the horizon. The Desertas can be seen far out to sea.

Caniço
Caniço is a small town whose inhabitants live from fishing and the cultivation of bananas and sugar cane. On Ponta do Garajou stands a tall statue of **Christ in Majesty** raised by a Madeiran family.

Santa Cruz
Santa Cruz, a fishing village, possesses several Manueline monuments. The **Igreja São Salvador** ★ borders the main square. Built in 1533 it is the oldest on the island. The interior, divided into three aisles, is covered with a painted ceiling. The chancel contains a metal memorial plaque to João de Freitas. The tomb of the Spínolas is in

the north aisle. The former **Domus Municipalis**, with beautiful Manueline windows, stands on the other side of the church square. The small street on the east side of the square leads to the present **town hall** *(Câmara Municipal)*, a fine 16C building.

Miradouro Francisco Álvares Nóbrega★

A road to the left leads to this belvedere named after a Portuguese poet, known also as the Lesser Camões (1772-1806), who sang Madeira's praises. From the belvedere there is a view of Machico and the Ponta de São Lourenço.

Machico

The town of Machico, situated at the mouth of the Ribeira de Machico valley, is divided by a river: the fishermen's quarter, the Banda d'Além, lies on the east side, the old town on the west. It was at Machico that Zarco and his companions landed.

Parish church

The 15C Manueline parish church stands in a square shaded by plane trees. The façade is pierced by a lovely rose window and a doorway adorned with capitals carved with the heads of animals. The side doorway, a gift from King Manuel I, consists of paired arches supported on white marble columns. A Manueline arch in the north wall leads to the Capela de São João Baptista.

Capela dos Milagres

As ruler, Tristão Vaz Teixeira had a chapel constructed in 1420 on the east bank of the river. This Chapel of Miracles was destroyed by floods in 1803. The original Manueline doorway was reinstalled when it was rebuilt.

▶ *Take the Caniçal road.*

There are views, as the road rises, of the valley of Machico dominated by mountain summits. The road leaves the valley through a tunnel under Monte Facho.

Caniçal

After losing its role as a station for whaling when this was banned in 1981, Caniçal stagnated for a few years before regaining its status as a major Portuguese port, this time for tunny fishing which has become an important activity as the port facilities and canning factory testify.

▶ *Continue to Ponta de São Lourenço.*

Ponta de São Lourenço ★

The headland of red, black and ochre-coloured volcanic rocks stretches far out into the sea and is the only place on the island with a sand beach, **Praínha**. This lies sheltered at the foot of a hillock upon which stands the hermitage of **Nossa Senhora da Piedade**. The road continues to a parking area near Abra bay. A footpath leads to

---

The Lovers of Machico

There is a legend that in 1346 an English ship sank in a tempest at the mouth of the river. Robert Machim and Ana d'Arfet, who had fled from Bristol to get married in spite of their parents' opposition, survived the shipwreck but died a few days later. Their companions took to sea again on a raft, were captured by Arab pirates and taken to Morocco. The story of their adventure was told by a Castilian to the King of Portugal who thereon decided to equip an expedition to find the island. When Zarco landed at Machico he found the lovers' tomb at the base of a cedar tree and named the village after the young Englishman, Machim.

a viewpoint overlooking some extraordinary rocks. There are impressive **views**★★ from here of the sheer cliffs on the island's northern coast, in particular from the **Miradouro Ponta do Resto** viewpoint *(narrow road to the left before the chapel)*.

▶ *Return to Machico and take the road to Portela.*

As you climb, the banana and cane sugar plantations of the valley floor give way to pine and eucalyptus trees.

Boca da Portela
At the Portela Pass (alt 662m/2 172ft) crossroads, go up to look at the view from the belvedere overlooking the green Machico valley.

Santo da Serra
Santo da Serra, built on a forest-covered plateau (pines and eucalyptus) at an altitude of 800m/2 500ft, has become popular with the residents of Funchal as a country resort with a cool climate in a restful setting. The golf course is well-known to enthusiasts. From the main square by the church, go into the Quinta da Junta park, formerly the property of the Blandy family. At the end of the main drive lined with azaleas, magnolias and camellias, a belvedere provides a view of the Machico valley; in the distance can be seen the Ponta de São Lourenço and, in clear weather, Porto Santo.

Camacha
Camacha is a village set in the woods at an altitude of 700m/2 296ft. It is famous for its basketwork and for its group of folk dancers and musicians. The dances are accompanied by chords from a *braguinha*, a four string guitar, while the rhythm is accentuated by an amusing looking stick caparisoned with a pyramid of dolls and castanets, known as a *brinquinho*.

▶ *Follow the signs back to Funchal.*

Tour of the Island ★★
Itineraries 2 , 3 *and* 4 *on the Island map. Starting from Funchal – 220km/137mi. Allow two days.*

The following tour of the island covers Madeira's main sights. It can be done in a day but if you wish to go on some of the walks we advise you to allow at least two days with a stopover in Santana, for instance.

2 From Funchal to Santana via Pico do Arieiro

This section of the itinerary describes the journey north from Funchal up to the island's highest peaks and then the descent to the north coast.

▶ *Leave Funchal by Rua do Til.*

Beyond Terreiro da Luta the road, lined with flowering hedges, rises in hairpin bends through pine and acacia woods becoming more barren.

▶ *At the Poiso Pass (Boca do Poiso), take the road on the left to the Pico Aceiro.*

The road follows the crest line of the mountains in the centre of the island providing good views of both Funchal, and the southern and northern coasts. Flocks of sheep graze on desolate moorlands. The road ends near the Pousada do Pico do Arieiro.

Around the Pico do Arieiro

Miradouro do Pico do Arieiro ★★

There is a magnificent panorama of the mountains in the central part of the island from the Arieiro belvedere on the very summit of the mountain at 1 818m/5 965ft. The landmarks include the Curral das Freiras crater, the distinctive outline of the crest of the Pico das Torrinhas (turrets) and, standing one before the other, the Pico das Torres and Pico Ruivo. To the northeast are the Ribeira da Metade, the Penha d'Águia (Eagle's Rock) and the Ponta de São Lourenço.

▶ *A path has been constructed from Pico do Arieiro to Pico Ruivo.*

Miradouro do Juncal★

A path goes round the summit of Pico do Juncal – 1 800m/5906ft – to the belvedere *(15min round trip on foot)* from which there is an attractive view along the full length of the Ribeira da Metade valley to the sea below Faial near a curious rock spike, the Penha d'Águia.

▶ *Return to Poiso and take the road on the left going to Faial. The road descends in a series of hairpin bends through pines and tree laurels.*

Ribeiro Frio★

Near a little bridge over the Ribeiro Frio (meaning cold river) stands a restaurant, settled in a pleasant site amid the greenery at an altitude of 860m/2 822ft.
The **Levada do Furado**, which irrigates these slopes as far as Porto da Cruz and Machico, passes through Ribeiro Frio. It is possible to walk along it eastwards to the Portela Pass *(3hr 30min)* or westwards as far as Balcões.

Balcões★★

40min round trip on foot. Take the path to the left of the bend below Ribeiro Frio.
The path runs alongside the Levada do Furado through passages hewn out of the basalt rock to the Balcões belvedere. This viewpoint stands in the Metade valley on a hillside surrounded by the last of the high mountains. The view extends from the

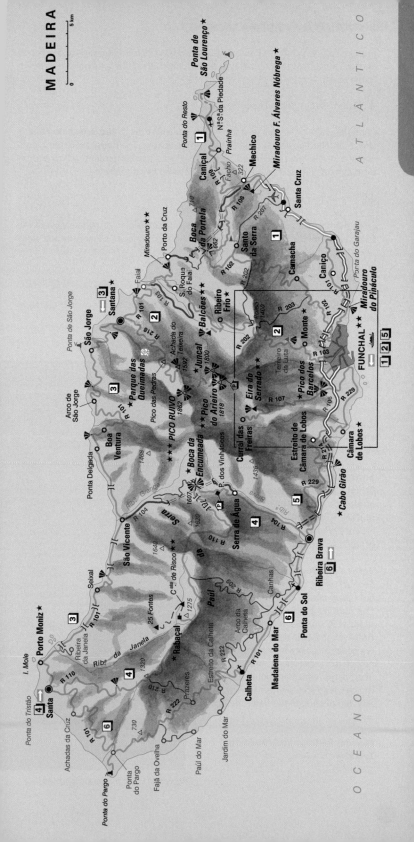

upper valley, which begins among jagged peaks (Pico do Arieiro, Pico das Torres and Pico Ruivo), to the open valley with its richly cultivated slopes which runs down to the coast.

▶ *Return to the road and head for Faial.*

Continuing along the course of the valley you will come to **São Roque do Faial**, a village perched on a long crest between two valleys. The houses with tiled roofs covered in vines are surrounded by small, terraced market gardens, willow plantations and orchards scattered with straw-thatched byres *(palheiros).*

▶ *Turn right towards Portela.*

From the bridge over the Ribeira de São Roque there is an attractive view of the Faial valley and the village perched on the clifftop. Bananas, sugar cane and vines are grown on the sunniest slopes.

▶ *Head for Porto da Cruz.*

A belvedere built on the left of the road has one of the island's most interesting **views**★★, that of Porto da Cruz, a village nestled at the foot of a cliff.

▶ *At Porto da Cruz turn round and make for Faial.*

4km/2.5mi from Faial, two belvederes on the right provide an overall **view**★ of Faial, the Penha d'Águia, the village of São Roque at the confluence of the Metade and São Roque valleys and, on the horizon, the Ponta de São Lourenço.

Santana★
Santana, situated on a coastal plateau at an altitude of 436m/1 430ft, is one of the prettiest villages on the island. The villagers once lived in attractive cottages made of wood with pointed thatched roofs.

Parque das Queimadas
Bear left off the main road onto Caminho das Queimadas.
The road leads to some thatched cottages, at 883m/2 897ft. In a peaceful **setting**★ at the foot of the Pico Ruivo slopes is a beautiful park where the trees stand reflected in a small pool. Some rather difficult paths, which are not advisable in the wet, lead off from here to Pico Ruivo and the Caldeirão Verde crater *(1hr 30min walk).*

Pico das Pedras and Achada do Teixeira
10km/6mi.

Waterfall along the Porto Moniz road

The road from Santana runs to Pico das Pedras and then continues to Achada do Teixeira. A path leads from here to Pico Ruivo. A short distance along this path there is a fine **view**★★ of the Pico Ruivo massif. From the viewpoint near the car park you can see Faial and, in the foreground, a basalt formation known as **Homem em Pé** (the Man Standing).

③ **From Santana to Santa** *70km/44mi*

As you leave Santana there is a splendid panorama to your left of the mountains. The road, lined with hydrangeas, arum and cana lilies, crosses coastal valleys where a variety of crops are grown.

São Jorge

São Jorge's 17C **church** is rich in its Baroque ornament. This abundance in a country parish church recalls the sumptuous period of King João V. The decoration includes a ceiling painted in false relief, *azulejos*, a gilded wooden altarpiece, paintings, twisted columns and, in the sacristy, an elegant vestment cupboard. Before beginning the descent to **Arco de São Jorge**, a belvedere to the right of the road affords a wide **vista**★ of the coast as it curves to form São Vicente bay. Many vines grow on trellises on the more sheltered slopes, for this is a region which produces Sercial wine.

G. Durand/PHOTONONSTOP

Boa Ventura

This small village lies scattered among vineyards in a pretty setting on a hill dividing two valleys *(lombos)*. 3km/2mi on there is a beautiful **view**★ to the right over the harsh coastline which, beyond the nearby Moinhos river, sweeps away in a series of headlands and inlets. To the left is **Ponta Delgada** with its white church. Beyond Ponta Delgada, the coast becomes even more rugged.

São Vicente

São Vicente stands in a protected site at the mouth of the river of the same name, grouped in a cliff hollow a little way from the sea. It makes a pleasant stop with its recently renovated houses huddled around the church. At the point where the river flows into the sea, a rock has been hollowed out to form the Capela de São Vicente.

The road from São Vicente to Porto Moniz★★

The falls which drain the Paúl da Serra can be seen cascading down the slopes. 3km/2mi from Seixal the road passes
through a long tunnel over which a waterfall cascades. A belvedere at the far end provides a good **viewpoint**★.

Seixal

This village occupies a pleasant **setting**★ surrounded by vineyards on a promontory which ends in a series of reefs. Three small islands *(ilhéus)* rise out of the sea at the mouth of the Ribeira da Janela. The largest is pierced by a sort of window *(janela)* which has given its name to the river and the village. At a distance from the bridge the unusual formation of this rock islet can be clearly seen.

Porto Moniz★

Porto Moniz provides the only sheltered harbour along the north coast. North of the village the coast is strewn with a mass of pointed **reefs**★ On leaving Porto Moniz the road climbs in hairpin bends up the cliff which dominates the village. Two successive belvederes afford **views**★ of Porto Moniz, its houses and church.

Santa

At Santa, short for Santa Maria Madalena, a curious belfry resembling a minaret flanks the white church.

▷ *Beyond Santa bear left onto the 204 towards Paúl da Serra and Encumeada, or take itinerary* ⑥ *to follow the coast in the opposite direction.*

④ From Santa to Ribeira Brava via Paúl da Serra
55km/34m

The 204 road, which is very pleasant and a good deal faster than the coast road, links the west of the island, near Santa, to the Boca da Encumeada. It crosses the high plateau pastures, the only flat surface on the island, where cattle can be seen grazing. Between Santa and Rabaçal the road follows the mountain crests affording fine views of both sides of the island and particularly of the **Ribeira da Janela**.

Rabaçal★

A narrow road *(4km/2.5mi)* twists and turns through the shrubs to the Rabaçal mountain huts (Casas de Rabaçal) set in a wild and remote spot.

Cascata de Risco★★
50min walk round trip from the hut.

A path alongside the Levada de Risco leads to a magnificent waterfall which drops about 101m/330ft into a pool in the Ribeira da Janela valley. Another path, which branches off the Risco, leads to the **25 springs** along the Levada das 25 Fontes *(allow at least 2hr round trip on foot)*.

Paúl da Serra

This vast plain, atypical of Madeira in its unending flatness and aridity, is grazed in summer by flocks of sheep. In winter it becomes a marshland *(paúl)*. Some parts of the road between Paúl da Serra and Encumeada overlook the south side of the island with fine views of the mountains dominating the coast and its banana plantations.

Boca da Encumeada★

A belvedere in the Encumeada Pass at an altitude of 1 007m/3 304ft looks down over both sides of the island. There is a general view of Madeira's two central valleys which occupy a volcanic fault area between the Paúl da Serra plateau and the mountain ranges near Pico Ruivo. The **Levada do Norte**, which passes beneath the road and descends to Serra de Água before irrigating the region between Ribeira Brava and Câmara do Lobos, is 60km/38mi long.

Serra de Água

The village of Serra de Água is in a pretty **setting**★ halfway up a slope in the Riveira Brava valley surrounded by abundant crops. The river flows through a narrow valley with rich plant life, mostly willows and black poplars along the water's edge.

From Ribeira Brava to Funchal *35km/22mi.*

Drive described in itinerary 5 *going in opposite direction (* ☁ *see FUNCHAL, Excursions).*

Southwest Coast ★
Tour of 145km/90mi – allow one day – Itineraries 5 *and* 6 *on the map of the island.*

Southwest Madeira has a much sunnier climate than the northern coast and its slopes are thick with banana trees and all sorts of flowers.

5 From Funchal to Ribeira Brava via Cabo Girão

☁ *See FUNCHAL, Excursions.*

6 From Ribeira Brava to Santa *– 70km/44mi*

Ribeira Brava

The small town of Ribeira Brava (Wild River) was built at the mouth of the river which bears the same name. In the centre of the town on a square where the cobbles have been laid to form a mosaic, stands a 16C **church** flanked by a belfry with a decorative blue and white tiled roof. The church still retains the original pulpit and an interesting Manueline font.
Leave Ribeira Brava on the road that runs west alongside the shoreline. The lie of the land has necessitated numerous tunnels.

The west coast of Madeira is more isolated. The road, banked on either side by a profusion of flowers, crosses a green countryside where occasional cultivated terraces can be seen scattered amid the laurel woods, briar trees, eucalyptus and pines.

The road passes near the headland, **Ponta do Pargo**, the westernmost tip of Madeira and so called because sailors from Zarco's ship caught a huge type of gilt-head (*pargo*) offshore at this spot. The lighthouse is half hidden by a hill.

▶ *Continue along the west coast to the junction with the 204. Return to Funchal via Paúl da Serra – the itinerary* ④ *is described above.*

Pico Ruivo★★★

Pico Ruivo, Madeira's highest point, stands at 1 862m/6 109ft. Its slopes are covered in giant heathers and from the summit there is an incomparable panorama. The peak can only be reached on foot. There are spectacular views from the top, over pretty much the entire island.

Access from Pico do Arieiro
8km/5mi on foot, about 4hr round trip. This is the best-known approach and a most rewarding hill walk. ☺ *However, the walk is hazardous, particularly for people who suffer from vertigo.*
The path begins by following a rock crest line which, on the left, overlooks the Curral das Freiras valley and, on the right, that of the Ribeira da Metade.
After the tunnel through the Cabo de Gato peak, a second tunnel avoids the climb up to the Pico das Torres. On leaving the tunnel you see a vast circle of mountains, the source of the upper tributaries of the Ribeira Seca. The remains of a remarkable volcanic chimney lie not far from the path.

Access from Achada do Teixeira
This is a much easier, faster route. 1hr on foot along on a paved pathway to the refuge at Pico Ruivo. From here there is a 15min walk to the Ruivo summit.
A good plan, if one can arrange local means of transport, is to set out from Pico do Arieiro, continue to Achada do Teixeira and beyond to Queimadas and Santana. From Pico do Arieiro to Achada do Teixeira allow 3hr 30min; 6hr for the whole trip.

Pico Ruivo

T. Perrin/HOA QUI

PORTO SANTO ★

FUNCHAL
POPULATION 4 441 – MICHELIN MAP 733 FOLD 43

The island of Porto Santo, though only 40km/27mi to the north-east of Madeira, could not be more different. With an area of 42km2/16sq mi, it is less densely inhabited – 241 inhabitants to the square mile – and geographically consists of a large plain edged to the northeast and southeast by a few so-called "peaks", of which the highest, the Facho, has an altitude of only 517m/1 696ft.

Av. Henrique Vieira e Castro – 9400-165 – ☎ 291 98 23 61 (ext 203)

▶ **Orient Yourself:** Just north-east of Madeira.
⊗ **Don't Miss:** The beach, but touring the island is easy, fun and very peaceful.
◷ **Organizing Your Time:** If you plan to relax, spend a couple of days – though a tour of the island can be achieved on a day trip from Funchal.
Kids **Especially for Kids:** the glorious beach!

Sights

Vila Baleira

Vila Baleira is a fitting capital for the island. At the centre of the town is the **Largo do Pelourinho**★, an attractive square shaded by palm trees. Around it stand some fine white buildings including the church and an emblazoned edifice which houses the town hall. An alleyway to the right of the church leads to the house of Christopher Columbus, the **Casa de Cristóvão Colombo** (◷ *Open Jul-Sep, Tue-Sat 10am-12.30pm; 2pm-7pm; Sun 10am-1pm. Oct-Jun, Tue-Sat 10qm-12.30pm; 2pm-5.30pm. Sun 10am-1pm.* ◷*Closed Sun and hols.* ☞€1. ☎ 291 98 34 05). You can see two rooms where

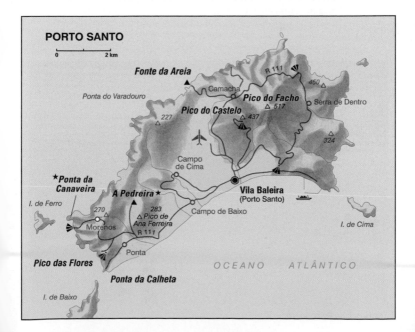

☺ A Bit of Advice ☺

ACCESS

By plane: TAP (☎ *291 98 21 46 - www.flytap.com*) operates several daily flights both ways between Madeira and Porto Santo. The flight takes about 15min and a one-way ticket costs from ☜€44.

By ferry: By Porto Santo Line (☎ *291 98 29 38 - www.portosantoline.pt*). Sailing time between Funchal and Porto Santo is 2hr 45min. A ferry leaves Funchal at 8am and sets out on the return journey from Porto Santo at 6pm (except Tues); the frequency of service may be increased at busy times of year. Day return (round trip) ticket ☜€49.50 to 57.90 - one-way from €25 to €29.50 according to season.

TOUR OF THE ISLAND

As a complete tour takes 3-4hr it is possible to make a day trip to Porto Santo from Madeira. One can tour the island by taxi, hired car or by bicycle. If you plan on spending several days on Porto Santo, why not visit the island on foot? The island's main interest is its beautiful sandy **beach** which attracts tourists and Madeirans alike. During summer it can be crowded so it is best to book a hotel ahead of time.

he lived with his wife and, in an annexe, engravings and maps recalling events from his life including his various voyages.

To tour the island and take in all the main sights is easy. Take the road from Vila Baleira round **Pico do Facho.** There are good views over the entire island and shepherds looking after sheep and cattle. **Pico do Castelo** is reached next before you come to the **Fonte da Areia**. This fountain in the sands flows near cliffs that overlook a wild and rocky coast, worn into strange shapes by erosion.

A Pedreira★

Take the road parallel to the beach towards the headland, Ponta da Calheta. Beyond the Porto Santo Hotel, bear right onto a track which after 2km/1.2mi leads to a quarry.
A Pedreira, which stands on the slope to **Pico de Ana Ferreira**, is a spectacular basalt rock formation of organ pipes soaring skywards. You reach **Pico das Flores** and then **Ponta da Canaveira** with wonderful views and a lighthouse.

The beach on Porto Santo

J. Ducange/TOP

THE AZORES ARCHIPELAGO

For many people the Azores are still a *terra incognita*. They are often confused with the Canaries or Madeira. In fact, the nine islands, which share the same latitude as Lisbon and are two hours by plane from Portugal, are more like Ireland, albeit volcanic. As for the beaches, the few there are black sand. The Azores are scattered over an area of 600km/373mi. In spite of their remoteness, the islands form part of the European continent and, as part of Portugal, are members of the European Union.

Goshawks

The first Portuguese to discover the islands were struck by the presence of birds which reminded them of a type of sparrow-hawk, the goshawk (*açor* in Portuguese). The birds were in fact buzzards, but the name remained.

Geography

Layout of the archipelago – There are three distinct groups of islands between latitudes 36°55N and 39°43 N. The eastern group consists of São Miguel and Santa Maria, the central one of Terceira, Graciosa, São Jorge, Faial and Pico, and the western group of Flores and Corvo. The total surface area is 2 335km²/902sq mi, less than a third of that of Corsica. Santa Maria, the easternmost island, is 1 300km/808mi from Portugal, and Flores, the westernmost, is 3 750km/2 330mi from North America.

Formation – The geological origins of the Azores have been difficult to date. Like other islands belonging to archipelagos in the Atlantic, they are volcanic. Their formation dates from the Quaternary Era with the exception of Santa Maria where Tertiary soil from the Miocene period has been found. The islands, which emerged from ocean depths of over 6 000m/19 700ft, are among the youngest in the world. The archipelago originated from a weak zone where the Atlantic rift meets the fault line which separates the African and Eurasian continental blocks. Apart from Corvo and Flores, which belong to the American plate and have a North-South relief line, the Azores form part of the Eurasian plate with an East-West relief line.

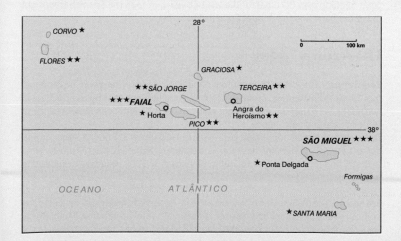

Ever since the islands were settled in the 15C they have been subject to intense seismic and volcanic activity including the upheaval of the Sete Cidades caldera in 1440, eruptions in the Lagoa do Fogo crater in 1563, lava flows known as *misterios* on Pico (in 1562, 1718 and 1720) and Faial (in 1672), as well as eruptions on São Jorge (1808). Volcanic activity continues (fumaroles, geysers, hot springs) and, from time to time, a volcano erupts (Capelinhos on Faial in 1957) or an earthquake strikes (Terceira in 1980).

A great many eruptions have also been noted beneath the sea. Their presence is marked by a bubbling of the water, emissions of gas and clouds of steam. The most spectacular of these occurred in 1811 when an islet 90m/295ft high, with a perimeter of 2 000m/6 562ft, appeared off the coast of São Miguel.

Physical appearance – Volcanic activity on the islands has given rise to large amounts of ash and the formation of **caldeiras** or vast craters formed either by explosion or, in larger cases, collapse. Further explosions inside and around these calderas have formed small cones. Unusual examples of lava flows resulting from effusive types of eruptions, can be seen on the islands of Pico and Faial where they are known as **misterios**. As for the island's coastlines, most consist of black cliffs dropping sheer to the sea. One of the most characteristic features of isea-erosion is the **fajã**, a collapsed cliff face which forms a platform, the most striking of which can be seen at São Jorge. There are also basalt organ pipe formations resulting from the crystallisation of volcanic rocks.

A Bit of History

In the 14C, the islands were mentioned in several accounts of voyages and appeared in portolanos (navigation manuals). By the time Prince Henry the Navigator had founded the School of Navigation at Sagres in the early 15C, he had heard reports about these "sea islands" and decided to send out an expedition to investigate. Santa Maria was discovered in 1427.

By 1452 all the islands had been discovered but not all were settled immediately: Terceira in 1450, Pico and Faial in 1466, Graciosa and São Jorge in 1480 and Flores and Corvo only a century later.

In the 16C the Azores were involved in the succession to the throne after King Sebastião's death. One of the pretenders to the crown, **Dom António, Prior of Crato**, had taken refuge in Terceira where he obtained such support from the islanders that he was proclaimed king in 1582 in spite of the fact that Philip II of Spain had been reigning over Portugal for the last two years. In 1583 the Spanish troops got the upper hand and the Prior of Crato fled to France.

The Azores Today

Population – The Azores have a mixed population. Early settlers were heterogeneous: landless Portuguese, Moorish captives, and Flemings sent by the Duchess of Burgundy, the daughter of King Dom João I. In the 19C, American families came to settle in Faial and São Miguel.

Today the estimated population is 237 795; in 1960 it was 327 000. A large proportion of each new generation has tended to emigrate. In the 17C people mostly went to Brazil, and later to the United States. More than 130 000 islanders emigrated to North America between 1955 and 1974.

Economy – The main source of livelihood in the Azores is **farming**, particularly dairy farming which accounts for a quarter of Portugal's total production. Dutch cattle are a common sight throughout the islands. São Miguel has also specialised in the large-scale cultivation of tea, tobacco, beet, and especially pineapples which are grown under glass. Crops are grown according to the altitude: potatoes, bananas and vines up to 150m/500ft; maize and fodder crops between 150-400m/500-1 300ft, and pastures above 400m/1 300ft.

Although **fishing** has diminished since whaling was banned, it is still an important activity. Almost 90% of Portuguese tunny is fished in these waters.

São Miguel and Terceira, the archipelago's two most densely populated islands are the centres for most of the administrative and economic bodies.

Climate and Vegetation

The French geographer Elisée Reclus predicted in the mid-19C that the cable "which will link the Azores with European observatories will be of immense importance to meteorologists." In 1893 Reclus's prediction was realised: an underwater cable was laid between Faial and the European continent to transmit information from the weather stations in Faial, Flores, São Miguel, Terceira and Santa Maria to the Paris observatory.

Slopes of the Pico volcano

J.P.Garcin/DIAF

Th. Vogel/EXPLORER

Scrimshaws

The Azores anticyclone arises because the Azores archipelago lies in the contact zone between cold currents from the North Atlantic and warm ones from the tropical Atlantic. It is at this point that the two high atmospheric pressures merge – the warm, subtropical ones on the one hand and the Arctic intensified ones on the other.

The weather changes extremely quickly in the Azores; it is commonly said that each of the four seasons can be experienced in a single day. Clouds tend to settle thickly over highland regions, leaving the coast in full sunshine. The climate is mild and very humid throughout the year, with a humidity rate that can reach 80% and average temperatures of 14°C/57°F in winter and 23°C/73°F in summer.

Vegetation on the Azores is very dense and varied on account of the humidity, latitude and volcanic soil. Tropical species thrive beside European plants giving a surprising combination of sequoias, dragon trees, tulip trees, jacarandas, pines, beeches, monkey-puzzle trees, palms and cedars. The most characteristic tree is the Japanese cryptomeria.

The variety of flora is even more striking in the case of flowers. The most emblematic of the Azores is the **hydrangea,** which is either white or blue depending on the season. It grows wild alongside tropical species like the canna.

Whaling

From the 17C onwards, whaling was carried out in the ocean around the Azores, organised first by the English and then by the Americans. In 1870 when oil was discovered and replaced whale blubber as fuel, American whalers became scarce and the Azoreans decided to hunt from their own shores.

Whaling continued until 1981 and many Azoreans still look back nostalgically to the dangerous days of hunting. It was an important source of income for the islanders and while it has been partly replaced by tunny fishing, the gap it has left in the economy has caused many of the young to emigrate.

Address Book

Information such as entry formalities, accommodation, post and telecommunications, currency, changing money that is also relevant for the rest of Portugal, is contained in the Planning Your Trip section at the front of this guide.

TIME DIFFERENCE

There is a time difference of 2hr between continental Portugal and the Azores: when it is 8am in Lisbon it is 6am in the Azores.

TELEPHONE

To call the Azores from the United Kingdom, dial 00 (Ireland 16) + 351 + 96 for São Miguel and Santa Maria, 95 for Terceira, Graciosa and São Jorge, and 92 for Faial, Pico, Flores and Corvo. To make an international call from the Azores, dial 00 then the country code (44 for the United Kingdom, 353 for Ireland, 1 for the United States and Canada), the area code (excluding the first zero, where applicable) and the number.

TOURIST INFORMATION

REGIONAL TOURISM DIRECTORATE:
Casa do Relógio, Colónia Alemã, 9900-014 Horta, Faial. ☎ (092) 29 38 01 /2/3.

DELEGAÇÃO DE TURISMO:
São Miguel:
   Avenida Infante Dom Henrique, 9500-150 Ponta Delgada.
   ☎ (096) 28 57 43 or 28 51 52.
Terceira:
   Rua Recreio dos Artistas, 35, 9700-160 Angra do Heroísmo.
   ☎ (095) 21 61 09 or 21 33 93.
Faial:
   Rua Vasco da Gama, 9900-014 Horta.
   ☎ (092) 29 22 37 or 29 38 01/2/3.

INFORMATION CENTRES:
Santa Maria:
   Aeroporto de Santa Maria,
   9580 Vila do Porto. ☎ (096) 88 63 55.
Graciosa:
   Praça Fontes Pereira de Melo, 9880 Santa Cruz. ☎ (095) 71 25 09.
Pico:
   Rua Conselheiro Terra Pinheiro, 9950 Madalena. ☎ (092) 62 35 24.

São Jorge: *Rua Conselheiro Dr. José Pereira, 9800. Velas ☎ (095) 41 24 40.*
Flores:
   9970 – Santa Cruz das Flores.
   ☎ (092) 5 23 73.
Corvo:
   please enquire at Faial as the island does not have a tourist information centre.

WHEN TO GO

The most pleasant season to visit the Azores is between May and September when there is less rain. The temperatures are mild and the hydrangeas are in full bloom. In October there can be thick fog and the rest of the year the weather is often dull although winters can sometimes be fine.

WHAT CLOTHES TO TAKE

Whatever the season it is best to take a raincoat, good walking shoes and a pullover. Warm clothes are required in winter. It is never cold in summer except at high altitudes; light trousers and dresses are ideal.

HOW TO GET THERE

By air, with TAP Air Portugal (www.flytap.com) or SATA (www.sata.pt) which has flights to Ponta Delgada (São Miguel), Lajes (Terceira) and Horta (Faial). There are some seasonal flights to these three islands from Boston, Toronto, Montreal and London in the summer season.

LANGUAGE

The Portuguese spoken in the Azores is slightly different from that on the continent on account of various archaisms. However, staff in all tourist information centres, hotels, restaurants and car rental firms generally speak English, French and German.

BANKS

Banks can be found on all the islands except Corvo.

Walking is a popular activity in th Azores

TRANSPORT BETWEEN THE ISLANDS

SATA *(Av. Infante D. Henrique, 55 – Ponta Delgada – ☎ (096) 28 22 55 - www.sata.pt)*, the local airline, has flights to all the islands. Some are only once or twice a week so take this into account when organising your trip if you wish to visit several islands.

In the summer there are boat connections between the islands in the central group several times a week. Crossings can be long: 4 hr between Terceira and Graciosa, 3hr 30min between Terceira and São Jorge and 1hr 15min between São Jorge and Pico.

There are boat links between Faial and Pico several times a day *(30min crossing)* and between Flores and Corvo daily in the summer *(2hr both ways)*.

The Portuguese Tourist Office provides boat timetables.

TRANSPORT ON THE ISLANDS

Taxis: Each of the islands has a good many beige taxis which generally run excursions for a fixed sum.

Car rental: There are car rental firms on all the islands. Cars on some of the smaller islands, such as Graciosa and Flores, are not always in good condition and it is advisable to check the brakes.

Buses: The main islands have a regular bus service.

ROADS

On the whole, the roads are in fairly good condition, though minimally signposted.

ACCOMMODATION

- Tourist accommodation varies depending on the island. São Miguel (Ponta Delgada and Furnas), Terceira (Angra do Heroísmo and Praia da Vitória) and Faial (Horta) are well equipped while the smaller islands often only have two or three hotels. There are no hotels on Corvo.

- It is best to book ahead of time in the tourist season.

- Prices are comparable to those on the Portuguese mainland. The cheapest accommodation is with local families whose addresses may be obtained from tourist offices.

- Camp sites are being developed on some of the islands.

RESTAURANTS, FOOD AND DRINK

There are a good many reasonably priced restaurants in the Azores. Grilled fish served with chilled *vinho verde* is delicious as are local specialities such as the *furnas cozido*, a kind of hotpot stewed in underground ovens hollowed out of the hot volcanic earth.

SPORTS AND LEISURE

WALKING
This is one of the most popular pastimes in the Azores. The most pleasant islands to walk on are Pico for the climb up the volcano, São Jorge with its wonderful coastal rambles, Flores and Corvo for their caldera and São Miguel, which has a wide choice of walks.

SWIMMING
There are not many beaches in the Azores apart from those on São Miguel (long ones on the south coast), Santa Maria (São Lourenço bay and Praia Formosa), Faial (Porto Pim, Praia do Almoxarife and Praia do Norte) and Terceira (Praia da Vitória). Swimming is possible on the other islands in natural swimming-pools that have been hewn out of the lava. Local children swim in the harbours.

DIVING
The coastal waters around the Azores are very beautiful and a number of diving clubs have been set up in São Miguel, Terceira and Faial.

SAILING
The main pleasure boat harbours are at Horta, Angra do Heroísmo and Ponta Delgada.

GOLF
There are three main golf courses on the Azores – one on Terceira near Lajes and two on São Miguel, at Furnas and near Ribeira Grande.

SPAS
Several spas have been developed to take advantage of the therapeutic waters from hot springs. There are baths at Furnas on São Miguel, Veradouro on Faial and Carapacho on Graciosa.

CALENDAR OF EVENTS

Festivals for village patron saints are held throughout the year. All the islands also celebrate the well-known feast of the **Holy Ghost**, when a gift-bearing emperor is elected. Brightly coloured buildings known as Empires of the Holy Ghost are used to house objects for the festival.

Empire of the Holy Ghost

J.P.Garcin – Ag. : DIAF

The following is a selection of the main festivals:

5TH SUNDAY AFTER EASTER
São Miguel — Santo Cristo Festival at Ponta Delgada.

29 JUNE
São Miguel — São Pedro Cavalcade at Ribeira Grande.

LAST WEEK IN JUNE
Terceira — Midsummer's Day (St John) Festival with processions and bullfights.

22 JULY
Pico — Madalena Festival.

WEEK OF 1ST TO 2ND SUNDAY IN AUGUST
Faial — Sea Festival at Horta harbour with boats.

15 AUGUST
Santa Maria — Island Festival. Election of Holy Ghost emperor.

SÃO MIGUEL★★★

PONTA DELGADA
POPULATION 135 875
MICHELIN ATLAS SPAIN & PORTUGAL P 96

São Miguel, the largest of the Azorean islands with more than half of the total population, forms the eastern group of islands with Santa Maria. It is known as the green island or *ilha verde*. In spite of a certain amount of modernity for which neighbouring islanders nickname it Japan, one can still see traditional scenes such as milk churns being transported on horse-drawn carts.

🔲 *Av. Infante D. Henrique – 9500-769 – ☎ 296 28 57 43 or 296 28 51 52*

▶ **Orient Yourself:** The largest island to the east of the main group, 1300km/800mi from the mainland.

🅿 **Parking:** Difficult in Ponta Delgada but no problems anywhere else.

🐨 **Don't Miss:** Sete Cidades, Lagoa do Fogo and Furnas.

🕐 **Organizing Your Time:** It's a good idea to spend a few days on the island with several day trips.

Geography

São Miguel consists of two volcanic mountain massifs divided by a depression which is covered in lava from recent volcanic eruptions between Ponta Delgada and Ribeira Grande. The oldest massif, in the east, is dominated by **Pico da Vara** at 1 103m/3 619ft. The island's most impressive features are its craters which contain lakes: Sete Cidades, Lagoa do Fogo and Furnas. Volcanic activity is still abundantly apparent today in the form of geysers and bubbling mud springs *(solfatares)* at Furnas, Ribeira Grande and Mosteiros. The jagged coastline, particularly in the north and east, consists of sheer cliffs at the foot of which are sometimes narrow beaches of black sand. The gentler, southern coast has wider beaches at Pópulo, Água de Alto, Ribeira Chã, Vila Franca do Campo and Ribeira Quente.

Ponta Delgada★

Ponta Delgada is the main town and home to the Regional Government and the University for all the islands in the Azores. It became capital of the island in 1546 and fortifications were built in the 16C and 17C to protect the town from pirates.

The **historical quarter** of Ponta Delgada is set back from **Avenida do Infante Dom Henrique**, a wide boulevard that runs alongside the harbour. The quarter is a tight network of streets along which stand fine 17C and 18C mansions. Open spaces are provided by squares and public gardens shaded by monkey-puzzle trees.

Praça Gonçalo Velho Cabral

On the square stand the statue of Gonçalo Velho, who discovered the island, and the 18C **Town Gates** which consist of three archways set in basalt. Extending from the square is the **Largo da Matriz**, dominated by the tall façade of the 16C church of São Sebastião and the 17C Baroque **Town Hall** *(Paços do Conselho)*.

> 🐨 **A Bit of Advice** 🐨
>
> **Access:** There are direct flights daily to and from Lisbon, Madeira, North America (seasonal) and the other islands in the Azores archipelago.
>
> **Length of stay:** If you are short of time, it is possible to see Ponta Delgada, Sete Cidades and Furnas in two days. However, you should allow a minimum of four days for a thorough visit.

Igreja Matriz de São Sebastião

The 16C parish church, built on the site of a former chapel, is famous for its graceful **Manueline doorway**★ in white limestone. The stone was brought from Portugal. The interior is noteworthy for the vaulting in the chancel and the gilded Baroque statues of the Evangelists on the high altar. The sacristy to the left of the chancel is decorated with *azulejos* and has some beautiful 17C furniture made of jacaranda. The **treasury** to the right of the chancel contains gold and silver plate as well as some extremely precious 14C vestments from Exeter Cathedral in England.

Forte de São Brás

This fort was first built in the 16C and remodelled in the 19C. The vast **Praça 5 de Outubro** (also known as Largo de São Francisco) with a bandstand and a huge tree stretches out before the fort. Two large churches give onto the square: the Igreja de São José, which was part of a former Franciscan convent, and the Igreja de Nossa Senhora de Esperança.

Convento de Nossa Senhora da Esperança★

The convent houses the statue of **Cristo dos Milagres** (Christ of Miracles), believed to have been given by Pope Paul III to nuns who petitioned in Rome for the setting up of their convent near Ponta Delgada in the 16C. Inside, the long narrow church is divided by a wrought-iron grille, behind which are the church treasures including the statue of Santo Cristo, gold and silver plate and polychrome *azulejos* by António de Oliveira Bernardes.

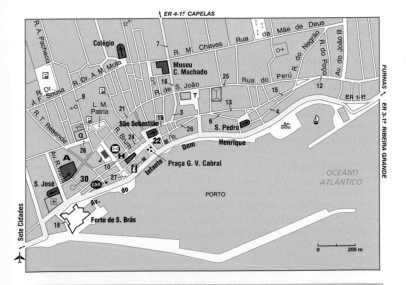

PONTA DELGADA

2 de Março Largo	28	Cor. Silva Leal R.	9	L. V. Bens R.	19
5 de Outubro Pr.	30	Dr L. M. Camara R.	10	Machado dos Santos R.	21
Ant. J. N. Silva R.	3	Eng. José Cordeiro R.	12	Matriz Largo da	22
Calhau R. do	4	Ernesto do Canto R.	13	Melo R. do	24
Clérigos R. dos	6	João de Melo Abreu R.	15	Mercado R. do	25
Contador R. do	7	João Moreira R.	16	Mercadores R. dos	26
		Kopke Av.	18	Vasco da Gama Pr.	27

Convento de Nossa Senhora da Esperança	A	Paços do Concelho	H

Outside the church, beneath an anchor carved in the wall and inscribed with the word *Esperança*, is the spot where the Azorean poet **Antero de Quental** (1842-91) committed suicide.

Igreja de São José

The church belonged to a 17C Franciscan monastery which is now a hospital. Inside, the vast nave is covered in wooden vaulting painted in false relief. The late-18C chapel of Nossa Senhora das Dores has a Baroque façade.

Igreja de São Pedro

This 17C and 18C church overlooks the port and faces the **São Pedro Hotel**. Behind the church's graceful façade is a rich Baroque interior with gilded altarpieces and ceilings painted in false relief. The chapel to the right of the chancel contains the 18C **statue of Our Lady of Sighs**★, one of the most beautiful statues in the Azores.

Museu Carlos Machado

o━*Temporarily closed for repairs.* ☎ 296 28 38 14.
The museum, housed in the 17C-18C Santo Andres Monastery, has a collection of early 16C paintings and two delightful **panels**★ in the style of the Master of Sardoal (early 16C), one of St Catherine and St Barbara and the other of St Margaret and St Apollonia.

Igreja do Colégio

The church of the former Jesuit College is behind the museum. Its unusual Baroque façade, more like that of a palace than a church, was added in the 18C.

1 Sete Cidades and the West of the Island ★★★
80km/50mi – allow half a day.

▶ *Take the airport road from Ponta Delgada and then the fork marked Sete Cidades.*

Pico do Carvão★

A lookout point at this spot dominates a large area of the island affording views of the centre, the northern coast and Ponta Delgada. The road runs past a moss-covered aqueduct and then some small lakes including **Lagoa do Canário** which is surrounded by botanical gardens.

Sete Cidades★★★

Sete Cidades, the natural wonder of the Azores, is a caldera with a circumference of 12km/7mi. It is best seen from the **Vista do Rei**★★★ belvedere south of the crater. The view takes in the twin lakes, one green, the other blue, and the village of Sete Cidades at the bottom of the crater. The caldera is believed to have been formed in 1440 when an eruption completely changed the lie of the land in this part of the island.

▶ *A road (marked Cumeeiras) leads from Vista do Rei along the edge of the crater (allow 2hr to walk). There are views of both sides of the crater, inside and out. The road crosses another one leading down to Sete Cidades. Beyond that are the lakes.*

The road runs across a bridge built between the two lakes. On the other side of the bridge a path to the left leads to a picnic area beside the blue lake, Lagoa Azul. The route back to Ponta Delgada depends upon the amount of time you have:

Sete Cidades, São Miguel

🏛 if you have about 1hr, take the road round **Lagoa de Santiago**, and back up to Vista do Rei, then the road which begins near Monte Palace. This descends between banks of hydrangeas to join the road to Ponta Delgada.

🏛 if you have at least 3hr, head northwest to **Miradouro do Escalvado**★ on the coast which has a fine view of Mosteiros and its rocks, then continue along a winding road to Capelas where you head south to Ponta Delgada via Fajã de Cima.

Achada das Furnas ★★

The **Achada valley** is an idyllic site set in a crown of hills and mountains. The best views of it are from the Pico do Ferro and Salto do Cavalo belvederes *(see below)*. The name Furnas meaning caves derives from the hollows in the ground from which spurt hot springs and sulphurous, bubbling mud geysers which can be identified from a distance by their jets of steam. The vegetation surrounding the charming, whitewashed town of Furnas is exceptionally luxuriant thanks to the area's warm, moist soil and the humidity.

Furnas
Furnas is very popular for its waters which are used in the treatment of respiratory ailments, rheumatism and depression.

Caldeiras★★

The extraordinary sulphurous waters in the area with their volcanic emanations and vapours boil at temperatures of around 100°C/212°F. Known as *caldeiras*, the geysers punctuate the landscape with their boiling water from deep in the earth.

Parque Terra Nostra★★

🕐 *Open 9am-5.30pm.* ⊜€4. ☎ *296 58 47 06.*
The park contains a diverse range of plant species with hibiscus, azaleas, hydrangeas and tropical plants and flowers thriving in the shade beneath Japanese larches. The avenues are bordered by magnificent royal palms.

Lagoa das Furnas

3.5km/2mi along the Ponta Delgada road.
Clouds of steam rising up from the northwest shores of the lake at the foot of steep slopes mark the presence of geysers. The warm earth has been hollowed out and cemented to form underground ovens with large wooden lids. The local speciality, *cozido*, is cooked inside the ovens.

Excursion

Ribeira Quente

8km/5mi from Furnas.
The road between Furnas and Ribeira Quente is one of the most attractive on the island. At a point between two tunnels an impressive waterfall cascades down to the right. The village of Ribeira Quente (Hot River) is mainly known for its beach warmed by the hot springs after which the place is named.

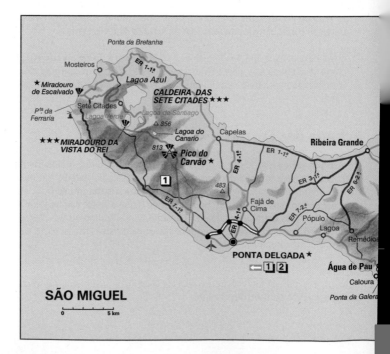

The Centre of the Island★★

2 From Ponta Delgada to Furnas *71km/44mi – 4hr*

▶ *Take the Lagoa road east of Ponta Delgada. Beyond Lagoa head north towards Remédios and Pico Barrosa.*

Lagoa do Fogo★★

An eruption in the 16C formed a crater lake which was given the name Fire Lake. Today this is a peaceful, beautiful spot with the clear water of the lake covering the crater floor. A white sand beach borders the lake on one side, a sheer cliff face on the other. The road continues downhill towards Ribeira Grande.

Ribeira Grande

Ribeira Grande, the second largest town on the island, has some fine 16C-18C mansions including **Solar de São Vicente** which houses the arts centre.

The vast garden square in the middle of town, alongside which flows the Ribeira Grande, is surrounded by interesting buildings including the 16C **Town Hall** with its double staircase and square tower, and the **Igreja do Espírito Santo** with its elaborate Baroque façade. The church is also known as the Dos Passos Church as it contains the statue of Christ (Senhor dos Passos) which is carried in traditional processions. The large 18C **Igreja de Nossa Senhora da Estrela** stands at the top of a wide flight of steps. Inside, the walls and ceilings are painted and, as elsewhere on the island, the gilt altarpieces are richly decorated.

▶ *Head south from Ribeira Grande following signs to Caldeiras.*

Caldeiras

This is an active volcanic area heralded by a group of small fumaroles. There is a thermal establishment and some springs that produce a well-known mineral water.

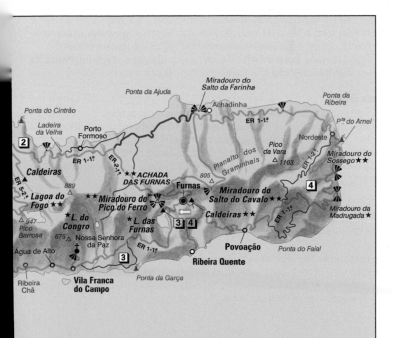

▶ *Return to the coast road and head east.*

The coast is a series of capes and bays within which nestle small beaches like that of **Porto Formoso**.

▶ *Take the Furnas road.*

Miradouro de Pico do Ferro★★
The view stretches across the whole Furnas valley, taking in the village, Terra Nostra park and the lake.

Furnas – ♿ *See above.*

③ From Furnas to Ponta Delgada *52km/32mi – 3hr*

▶ *Leave Furnas on the Ponta Delgada road. After 16km/10mi turn right and 3km/1.8mi farther on turn left. After 330yd you reach a fork; turn right and continue for another 550yd.*

Lagoa do Congro ★
To reach Lagoa do Congro, an emerald green lake at the bottom of a crater, you leave the pastureland with its hydrangea hedges and follow a footpath *(40min round trip)* which leads rapidly down the crater slopes through thick vegetation and magnificent trees.

Vila Franca do Campo
The town, the island's early capital, was partly destroyed by an earthquake in 1522. Facing the town is a volcanic **islet** which appeared when a crater subsided. In the town centre is a beautiful square with a public garden dominated by the Gothic **Igreja de São Miguel**.
Standing on a rise above Vila Franca is the **Capela de Nossa Senhora da Paz**, a chapel which is approached by a flight of steps rather like a small-scale version of that of Bom Jesus at Braga on mainland Portugal. There is a fine **view**★ of the coast, Vila Franca and the sea of white hothouses in which pineapples are ripened.
Once past the long **Água do Alto beach** turn south to the headland, **Ponta da Galera**, with the delightful little harbour of Caloura and attractive holiday homes.

Água de Pau
Follow the signs to Ermita and Miradouro (20min round trip on foot).
The lookout point gives an interesting **view**★, to one side, Ponta da Caloura and a volcanic cone covered right to the top in a patchwork of fields, and to the other, the hermitage which stands out against a mountain background. The road continues along the coast past a series of beaches including those of Lagoa and Pópulo to Ponta Delgada.

④ The East of the Island from Furnas
85km/53mi – about 4hr

The road climbs from Furnas eastwards onto the Graminhais plateau. There is a beautiful view of the Furnas valley from **Miradouro de Salto do Cavalo**★★. The road continues to the coast where the **Salto da Farinha** belvedere beyond Salga affords a good view of the north coast.

The East Coast ★★

The eastern part of the island has a strikingly beautiful coastline. The most spectacular views are from belvederes south of the village of Nordeste: **Miradouro do Sossego**★★ and **Miradouro da Madrugada**★. Cliffs drop sheer to the sea. Beyond Miradouro da Madrugada a narrow winding road 2km/1.2mi long leads to the beach at Lombo Gordo. This coast is dominated by **Pico da Vara**, where, in 1949, the French violinist Ginette Neveu and the boxer Marcel Cerdan were killed in a plane crash.

Povoação

This is the first place on the island to have been settled (*povoação* means population). The village stands at the mouth of a picturesque valley under intense cultivation.

SANTA MARIA★

PONTA DELGADA

POPULATION 6 922
MICHELIN ATLAS SPAIN & PORTUGAL P 96

Santa Maria is one of the least visited islands of the Azores and yet it is one of the most pleasant with its warm climate, its **beaches** and its delightful countryside dotted with white houses. These have tall cylindrical chimneys and are painted with brightly coloured borders to outline the façades. The landscape one first sees on arrival in Santa Maria is somewhat unexpected: a dry plateau of yellow grass that looks more like Texas than the Azores. Several kilometres beyond the airport the landscape changes to the green countryside typical of the Azores.

▶ **Orient Yourself:** The southernmost island in the Azores.
☺ **Don't Miss:** The view from Pico Alto; also Baía do São Lourenço.
🕐 **Organizing Your Time:** Spend as much of one day if you can, depending upon how long transportation takes.

An Island of Dyes

The original wealth of the island came from the cultivation of woad and the gathering of orchil. Woad was exported for use in the dyeing industries in Flanders and Spain until it was superseded by indigo blue from Brazil, while orchil, a type of lichen that gives a brown dye and grows on rocks beside the sea, was collected in perilous conditions from the coast and exported until the mid-19C.

☺ A Bit of Advice ☺

Access: There are regular flights between Santa Maria and the neighbouring island of São Miguel.

Length of stay: Allow a whole day for an unhurried tour of the island.

Sights

Vila do Porto

The town is in the south of the island between Cabo Marvão and Cabo Força. It stretches along a strip of basalt plateau between two ravines which join to form a creek. Among the buildings dating from the 16C and 17C are the **Convento de Santo António**, now the public library and the Franciscan monastery, now the **Town Hall**. The **Igreja de Nossa Senhora da Assunção**, which was originally founded in the 15C and rebuilt in the 19C, has preserved Gothic and Manueline features in its doorways and windows.

House on Santa Maria

Almagreira

Below the village lies **Praia Formosa**, literally "beautiful beach". The beach is one of the finest in the Azores.

Pico Alto (view) ★★

Take the road to the left and drive for 2km/1.2mi.

The view from the top of Pico Alto (590m/1 936ft) takes in the whole island. It is one place you must visit.

Santo Espírito

In the village is the **Igreja de Nossa Senhora da Purificação** with a white façade. Beyond Santo Espírito the road descends to **Ponta do Castelo** through a dry landscape dotted with aloes and cacti, in the middle of which stands a lighthouse. Lower still is **Maia**, a former whaling station.

Return to Santo Espírito and head towards Baía do São Lourenço. Make a right turn just before you get there and go to the **Miradouro do Espigão**★★ which has a most beautiful view of the bay.

Baía do São Lourenço★★

The bay, once a crater that has since been invaded by the sea, is an outstanding site with concave slopes covered in terraced vineyards. Bordering the narrow beaches around the turquoise water are houses occupied only in the summer season.

Santa Bárbara

Houses are scattered over the hills and along the steep coastline bordering Tagareite bay. The **church** was rebuilt in 1661 and is a fine example of popular architecture.

Anjos

The small fishing harbour is mainly known for its history.

Baía de São Lourenço, Santa Maria

A statue of **Christopher Columbus** recalls that the Genoese explorer is believed to have stopped here on his return from his first voyage and to have attended Mass in the **Capela da Nossa Senhora dos Anjos**. The chapel altar, consisting of a triptych of the Holy Family with St Cosmas and St Damian, is believed to have come from the caravel that brought Gonçalo Velho to the island.

TERCEIRA★★

ANGRA DO HEROÍSMO
POPULATION 75 706
MICHELIN ATLAS SPAIN & PORTUGAL P 96

Terceira, the Portuguese word for third, was the third island in the archipelago to be discovered. It is also the third largest island, after São Miguel and Pico. While its landscape is less striking than those of the other islands, Terceira is more interesting in terms of architecture, traditions and festivals.

Terceira is a tableland overlooked in the east by the Serra do Cume, the remains of Cinco Picos, the island's oldest volcano. The central area is demarcated by a vast crater known as Caldeira de Guilherme Moniz which is surrounded by other volcanic formations. To the west is the Serra da Santa Bárbara, the island's most recent and highest (1 021m/3 350ft) volcanic cone with a wide crater. The islanders live essentially from farming, cultivating maize and vines, as well as stock rearing. Terceira is the granary of the Azores. ▯ *Rua Direita, 74 – 9700-066 – ☎ 295 21 61 09*

▸ **Orient Yourself:** The eastern-most of the five islands grouped together in the Azores – about 100mi/160km north-west of São Miguel

▯ **Parking:** Not too bad, even in the main town.

⊘ **Don't Miss:** Make a special effort to seek out some of the "Impérios" - the little chapels dedicated to the Holy Spirit. You'll find them in every village.

◑ **Organizing Your Time:** You'll find it beneficial to stay here a couple of nights to enjoy all this lovely island has to offer.

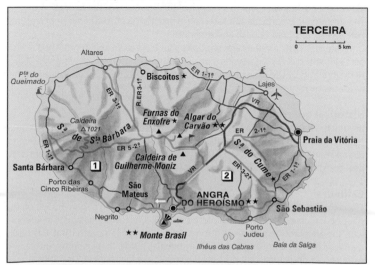

A Bit of History

Impérios

The Azorean tradition of the worship of the Holy Ghost is particularly strong in Terceira. Every quarter in each village has its little chapel known as an *império* or "empire" of the Holy Ghost. The chapels look like salons, their picture windows adorned with net curtains; they are maintained by brotherhoods whose chief task is to organise festivals. The festivals follow a ritual that dates back to the early days of colonisation when the islanders would call upon the Holy Ghost in times of natural disaster. They were originally intended to be charitable events and one of their main functions was to provide meals for the poor.

During today's festival an "emperor" is still elected by the people. He is presented with a sceptre and crown on a silver platter and is crowned by a priest. He is then accompanied to the *Império do Santo Espírito* where he receives the gifts to be distributed to the poor and then invites the whole village to take part in the feast which is followed by a traditional *tourada da corda* (👣 *see below*).

> ### 😊 A Bit of Advice 😊
>
> **Access:** There are regular flights between Terceira and Lisbon, some cities in North America (seasonal) and the other islands in the archipelago.
>
> In summer, the boat connecting the central group of islands calls at Terceira several times a week.
>
> **Length of stay:** Allow two days to tour the island and spend some time in Angra do Heroísmo.

The Island of Bulls

Terceira is famous for its **touradas à corda** which take place during village festivals. A bull with a long rope about its neck and its horns adorned with baubles is held by four men in white coats and grey trousers. The animal is allowed to rush at crowds of men who speed away leaving the bravest to taunt the bull by opening a large black umbrella beneath its muzzle.

Angra de Heroísmo★★

The town, set in the curve of a wide bay or *angra* and dominated by Monte Brasil, is without doubt the most beautiful haven in the archipelago and is home to the Minister of the Republic and to a branch of the University of the Azores.

The architecture is particularly interesting in that it is a synthesis of different features: Portuguese, Brazilian, English and American.

On 1 January, 1980, a violent **earthquake** shook the town and demolished a large part of it without taking any lives. In 1983 Angra do Heroísmo was given World Heritage status by UNESCO and the outstanding work carried out has since restored its former beauty.

Historical quarter

Beyond the Bahía de Angra lies the geometric street plan that follows the original layout. The houses within the square of streets bordered by the harbour, Rua Direita, Rua da Sé and Rua Gonçalo Velho, are adorned with wrought-iron balconies and window and door frames made of stone that set off the pastel colours of the façades.

Cathedral

The cathedral *(Sé)* is the Episcopal See of the Azores. Building began in 1570 on the site of a 15C church and was completed in 1618. The austere design is in keeping with the architecture prevalent during Philip II's reign. The cathedral was badly damaged both by a fire and the 1980 earthquake. Inside, there is some fine carved wooden vaulting and a beautiful silver altarpiece in the chancel. The collection of

17C sculptures by Masters of the Cathedral of Angra show a Spanish and Oriental influence, a sure sign of the voyages undertaken by the Portuguese.

Palácio dos Bettencourt

Open Jul-Sept, Mon-Fri 9am-5pm; Oct-Jun, Mon-Sat 9am-7pm (noon Sat). Closed Sun and public hols. No charge. 295 21 26 90/7.
The 17C mansion in the Baroque style houses the public library and the city archives. *Azulejos* inside illustrate episodes from the history of Terceira.

Igreja da Misericórdia

The late-18C church overlooks the bay.

Praça da Restauração or Praça Velha

The 19C **Town Hall** or Paços do Concelho looks onto the square.

Igreja do Colégio

The collegiate church was built by the Jesuits in the middle of the 17C. Of particular interest are the carved cedarwood ceiling, the delft earthenware in the sacristy and the many altarpieces and Indo-Portuguese ivory statues.

Palácio dos Capitães-Generais

The former Jesuit college was converted into the Palace of the Captain-Generals after the expulsion of the Society of Jesus by the Marquis of Pombal. The palace was largely rebuilt in 1980 and painted white and yellow. Today it houses the offices of the Regional Government of the Azores. It was in this palace that President Pompidou of France held a meeting with President Nixon in 1971.

Jardim Público Duque da Terceira

The gardens stand in the former grounds of the Monastery of São Francisco.

Convento de São Francisco: Museu de Angra

Open Tue-Fri, 9.30am-noon, 2-5pm; Sat-Sun 2-5pm. Closed Mon and public hols. €2 (no charge on Sun or for children under 14). 295 21 31 47/8.
The museum houses collections of weapons, musical instruments, ceramics, porcelain, furniture and paintings, including some 16C panels of St Catherine.

Igreja de Nossa Senhora de Guia

This vast church with painted pillars forms part of the São Francisco Monastery. It was built in the 18C on the site of a chapel where Vasco da Gama buried his brother Paulo who died on his return from a voyage to the Indies.

Igreja de São Gonçalo

The 17C church adorned with *azulejos* has interesting cloisters.

Alto da Memória

The obelisk was erected on the site of the castle to honour Dom Pedro IV.

Castelo de São João Baptista

The fortress stands at the foot of Monte Brasil and commands the entrance to the harbour. Built during the Spanish domination of Portugal, it was first called the St Philip Fortress and is one of the largest examples of military architecture from 16C and 17C Europe. The Igreja de São Baptista inside the fortress was built by the Portuguese to celebrate the departure of the Spanish.

Monte Brasil★★

To benefit fully from the site you must climb to the Pico das Cruzinhas, passing the fortress of São João Baptista. There is a view of the Monte Brasil crater and an outstanding **panorama**★★ of Angra from the commemorative monument or *padrão*.

Fortaleza de São Sebastião

This was built during the reign of King Sebastião and dominates Pipas harbour.

1 Tour of the Island

From Angra do Heroísmo – *85km/53mi – Allow one day*

The coast road between Angra do Heroísmo and the village of São Mateus is lined by country estates with fine houses *(quintas)*. There is a beautiful view of São Mateus.

São Mateus

The picturesque fishing village is dominated by its church, the tallest on the island. The west of the island is dotted with charming little villages such as the summer resorts of **Porto Negrito** and **Cinco Ribeiras**. There are also views of the islands of Graciosa, São Jorge and Pico.

Santa Bárbara

The 15C village **church** contains a statue of St Barbara in Ançã stone (which comes from mainland Portugal).

ANGRA DO HEROÍSMO		Conceição R.	10	Jacome de Bruges Av.	21
		Cons. José Silvestre		M. Terras R. das	22
		Ribeiro R.	12	Miragaia R. da	24
Alfândega Pátio da	3	Covas Alto das	13	Oliveira R. da	25
Barreiro Can. do	4	Dr Anibal Bettencourt R.	15	Palácio R. do	27
Canos Verdes R. dos	6	Faleiro R. do	16	San Francisco Ladeira de	29
Carreira dos Cavalos R.	7	Gançalo Velho Cabral R.	19	Santo Espírito R. do	30
Ciprião Figueiredo R.	9	Gaspar Corte Real Estrada	18	Velha Pr.	32

Museu de Angra	M	Palácio dos Bettencourts	P¹
Paços do Concelho	H	Palácio dos Capitães-Generais	P²

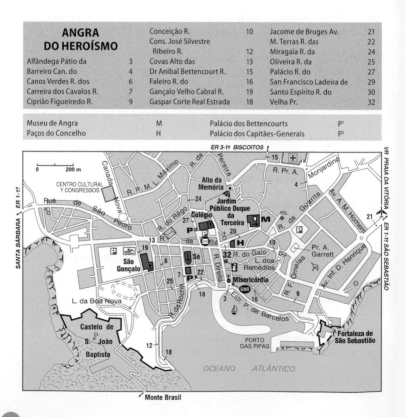

Angra do Heroísmo

Serra da Santa Bárbara road
Head towards Esplanada then bear left onto a forest road which climbs to the summit.

The road affords wonderful panoramas of the island. From the top there is a view of the vast crater of the **Caldeira de Santa Bárbara.**

▶ *Return to the road, bear left, continue to the junction with the road between Angra do Heroísmo and Altares. Turn left.*

Biscoitos ★
The name *biscoitos* has been given to the strangely shaped layers of lava which flowed up from the earth during volcanic eruptions and formed a lunar landscape.

Biscoitos is famous for its vines or *curraletas*, protected by stone walls beneath which they grow. A wine museum, **Museu do Vinho** (🕐*Open Tue-Fri 10am-noon, 1.30-5.30pm (4pm Oct-Mar).* 🕐*Closed Sun, Mon and third week of Sept. No charge.* ☎ *295 90 84 04),* displays the equipment in which generations of wine-growers have made *verdelho*, a sweet aperitif wine. Dry and sweet *verdelho*, which is produced exclusively from verdelho stock, is produced and bottled by the museum itself.

▶ *Take the Angra road from Biscoitos and bear left towards Lajes.*

The terrain in the centre of the island has suffered from volcanic upheaval which has left craters like the vast Caldeira de Guilherme Moniz.

▶ *Follow signs to Furnas do Enxofre.*

Furnas do Enxofre★
Follow the path to the left (after taking the Estrada do Cabrito at the Pico da Bragacina crossroads) until you reach a small car park. 10min round trip on foot.

You soon reach a wild landscape where fumaroles rise up from sulphur wells in the ground. The air is hot and smelly. The sulphur crystallises into beautiful bright yellow flowers; in some places a red colour dominates, spreading over the ground and rocks.

Caldeira de Guilherme Moniz
As the road descends between Furnas do Enxofre and Algar do Carvão you catch glimpses of the immense crater with its 15km/9mi perimeter.

Algar do Carvão★★
🕐 *Open Apr, May and Oct: 3pm-5.30pm; June and Sept: 2.30pm-5.45pm; July-Aug: 2pm-6pm.* ✎*€3.50. Contact "Os Montanheiros", Rua da Rocha 6/8 – 9700-169 Angra do Heroísmo.* ☎ *295 21 29 92.*
A tunnel some fifty yards long leads to the base of a volcanic chimney, a sort of moss-covered well of light 45m/148ft high. You continue down into an enormous cave which was formed by escaping gases when the lava cooled. Above is a series of majestic overlapping arches of different colours: beige, obsidian black and ochre. Several siliceous concretions have formed milky white umbrella shapes on the cave walls. The arches can be seen reflected in a pool.

▶ *The road connects with the Via Rápida which leads back to Angra do Heroísmo. One can also follow itinerary* 2 *in the opposite direction to return to Angra.*

2 From Angra do Heroísmo to Praia da Vitória
35km/22mi – 2hr

The strange rocks, Ilhéus Cabras, a short distance beyond Angra, look as though they have been sawn through the middle.

São Sebastião
The village was the first site to be settled on the island and has preserved some old monuments.

Igreja de São Sebastião ★
The Gothic church built in 1455 has a graceful doorway and chapels with Manueline and Renaissance vaulting. The nave has some interesting 16C frescoes, illustrating on the left, the Last Judgement, and on the right, St Martin, St Mary Magdalene and St Sebastian set in a medieval castle.
Opposite the church is the **Império do Espírito Santo** decorated with romantic paintings. A commemorative monument or *padrão* stands in the neighbouring square.

The tourada à corda in São Sebastião

B. Brillion/MICHELIN

▶ *Beyond São Sebastião take ER 3.2 left to Serra do Cume, then a road right which climbs to the top.*

Serra do Cume★
The gentle slopes of this eroded volcano form a patchwork of fields divided by low stone walls where Dutch cows can be seen grazing. At certain times of the day, particularly in the evening, the countryside takes on a lush bucolic air.

Praia da Vitória

The "Praia" in the name derives from the beautiful white sand **beach** which stretches the full length of the bay, and the "da Vitória" commemorates the battle in 1829 between Liberals and supporters of Dom Miguel. A harbour sheltered by a breakwater some 1 400m/1 500yd long serves as a dock for ships, while the Lajes air base nearby, which was established by the British in 1943 and enlarged by the Americans in 1944, is still used by the United States Air Force.

Praia da Vitória is a lively place when the weather is fine and the beach and surrounding cafés fill with people. The old town centre has been preserved and has a 16C **Town Hall** and an old parish church.

Parish church

This large church was founded by Jacomo de Bruges, the island's first donee-captain. Its main doorway, a gift from the King, Dom Manuel, is Gothic in style, while another portal, a side entrance, is Manueline. The rich interior decoration includes *azulejos* and gilt altarpieces.

GRACIOSA★

ANGRA DO HEROÍSMO

POPULATION 7 759 – MICHELIN ATLAS SPAIN & PORTUGAL P 96

Graciosa is the second smallest island after Corvo and has the lowest altitude (the highest point, Pico Timão, rises to just 398m/1 306ft). The whole of the eastern part of the island is occupied by a vast crater.Graciosa or "gracious" island owes its name to its attractive main town, Santa Cruz, its countryside of well-tended vineyards and fields of maize, and its villages bright with flowers set at the foot of gently rolling hills dotted with windmills. These Dutch-style windmills with their pointed, onion-shaped tops that pivot in the direction of the wind are a rather surprising feature of the island's landscape. There are not so many as there once were but they are still an interesting feature and would make a good painting.

🛈 *Praça Fontes Pereira de Melo – 9880-377 – Santa Cruz –* ☎ *295 71 25 09*

▶ **Orient Yourself:** A small island just north of São Jorge and Pico.
⊙ **Don't Miss:** The caves at Furna de Enxofre.
🕓 **Organizing Your Time:** Being such a small island a day tour will suffice.

😊 A Bit of Advice 😊

Access: There are regular flights between Terceira and Graciosa and boat connections between the two islands several times a week.

Length of stay: One can tour the island in a few hours although it is pleasant to spend time strolling through Santa Cruz or driving along narrow country roads.

Santan Cruz da Graciosa★ *Population 2 000*

Santa Cruz is a delightful small town with its bright white house façades set off by volcanic stone and several older fishermen's cottages.

Parish church
Built in the 16C and reconstructed two centuries later. Some **panels**★ at the high altar illustrate the Holy Cross. A chapel has Flemish statues of St Peter and St Anthony.

Museu Etnográfico
Guided tours, summer: Tue-Fri 9.30am-12.30pm, 2-5pm; winter: Tue-Fri 10am-noon, 2-5.30pm. €1 *(no charge for senior citizens or students).* ☏ *295 71 24 29.*
The collections housed in a former mansion show traditional island life through various displays including tools, clothes and pottery.

Ermidas do Monte da Ajuda
The three hermitages devoted to São João, São Salvador and **Nossa Senhora da Ajuda** dominate the town. There is a beautiful **view**★ of Santa Cruz.

Excursions

Farol da Ponta da Barca★
4.5km/3mi west of Santa Cruz.
There is a view from the lighthouse of the headland of red rocks plunging to a bright blue sea.

Praia
The old village stretches along its harbour and the beach after which it is named.

Furna do Enxofre ★★
Guided tours, 11am-4pm. ⊘*Closed Mon.* €0.50. ☏ *295 71 21 25 or 295 73 00 40. The best time to visit is from 11am to 2pm when the sun shines into the cave.*
Furna de Enxofre is in the middle of a vast caldeira or crater. A tunnel has been dug through one of the sides of the crater giving access by car. Once inside the crater the road zigzags down to the entrance of the chasm. From here a path and then a spiral staircase lead down to the chasm. The cave itself is immense and contains a lake of hot sulphurous water.

Furna Maria Encantada
Leave the caldeira. Once through the tunnel take the first road left. About 100yd further on there is a sign on the right to Furna de Maria Encantada. A path reinforced by logs leads up to a rock above the road (5min).
A natural tunnel in the rock about ten yards long opens onto the crater with a good overall view.
The road continues around the crater. There are views over Graciosa island with Terceira in the distance.

Carapacho
Carapacho is a small spa as well as a seaside resort. The hot springs that rise from the sea-bed are used for therapeutic purposes, particularly in the treatment of rheumatism.

FAIAL★★★

HORTA

POPULATION 14 920

MICHELIN ATLAS SPAIN & PORTUGAL P 96

The blue island, as Faial is also known, owes its name to the mass of hydrangeas that flower there in season. There is a magnificent view from Faial of Pico's volcano, while Faial itself has some interesting volcanic features such as the Caldeira crater and the Capelinhos volcano. The island's particular charm derives from Horta, the main town and harbour, its attractive villages, windmills and beaches (Porto Pim, Praia do Almoxarife and Praia do Fajã). *Casa do Relógio, Colónia Alemã – 9230-053 – ☎ 292 29 38 01*

▶ **Orient Yourself:** Just west of Pico, on the edge of the main group of islands.
☺ **Don't Miss:** The volcano – it's spectacular!
🕐 **Organizing Your Time:** Stay a night and get to know this peaceful island.

Capelinhos, the birth of a volcano

The headland on the west of the island is covered in ashes from Capelinhos, the volcano that rose up from the depths of the ocean in 1957. On 27 September, there was a huge eruption under the sea accompanied by gaseous emissions and clouds of steam that reached a height of 4 000m/13 000ft. A first islet surfaced only to disappear a short time afterwards. Then a second islet-volcano formed and was joined to Faial by an isthmus of lava and ash. For thirteen months, until 24 October 1958, volcanic activity continued in the form of underwater explosions, lava flows, eruptions

> ### ☺ A Bit of Advice ☺
>
> **Access:** There are direct flights from Lisbon to Horta and regular flights between Faial and the other islands. Boats connect Faial and the port of Madalena on Pico island (30min) several times a day, and Faial, São Jorge and Terceira several times a week in summer.
>
> **Length of stay:** Allow at least two days to explore Horta and tour the island.

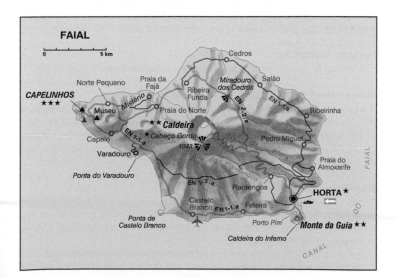

and showers of ash that covered the village of Capelo and the lighthouse. As Capelinhos volcano rose, so the water level of the lake inside Faial's crater or caldeira, fell. By the end of the eruption the volcano had increased the size of Faial by 2.4km²/0.9sq mi, although marine erosion has since reduced this to 1km²/0.38sq mi.

Horta★

Horta stretches out alongside a bay which forms one of the rare sheltered anchorages in the archipelago. Anglo-Saxon influence is apparent in Horta's architecture. This heritage comes down from the **Dabneys**, a family of wealthy American traders in the 19C. When they left, American presence in Faial continued through transatlantic cable companies. In the 1930s, Faial was a port of call and a refuelling station for seaplanes and it was not uncommon to see one or more of these in Horta harbour.

Marina da Horta★
The marina is where yachtsmen on their journeys across the Atlantic congregate. It has become a kind of open-air art gallery since each crew leaves a visual trace of its stay, otherwise, as the superstition goes, some mishap will befall it.

Historical quarter
The quarter is dominated by the imposing façades of its churches which face the sea. It comprises the area around **Rua Conselheiro Medeiros**, **Rua W. Bensaúde** and **Rua Serpa Pinto** which are lined with 18C and 19C shops and houses surmounted by unusual wooden upper storeys. This main thoroughfare leads to **Praça da República**, a charming square. The striking façade of the **Sociedade Amor da Pátria** building, dating from 1930 and decorated with a frieze of blue hydrangeas, can be seen in the northeast corner of the square on Rua Ernesto Rebelo.

Igreja Matriz de São Salvador
This vast 18C church, which formerly belonged to the Jesuit College, has some fine *azulejos* and interesting Baroque furniture.

Museu da Horta
Guided tours 10am-12.30pm, 2-5.30pm. €2. ☎ 292 29 33 48.
The museum housed in the former Jesuit College, traces the history of the town, in particular the laying of the underwater cables. There is also a collection of **miniatures made of fig-tree pith**★ carved by Euclíades Rosa between 1940 and 1960.

Forte de Santa Cruz
The fort was begun in the 16C, enlarged at a later date and now houses an inn.

"Chez Peter" Café
The café, a popular meeting place for sailors, contains the **Museu do Scrimshaw** (*Guided tours, 9am-noon, 2-5pm. ⓄClosed 1 Jan and 25 Dec. €1.50. ☎ 292 29 23 27*). Among the items on display are sperm-whale teeth engraved by whalers and newer portraits of well-known yachtsmen such as Sir Francis Chichester and the Frenchman Eric Tabarly.

Monte da Guia
A road leads up to the summit of Monte da Guia.
Horta bay is sheltered by two volcanoes linked to the mainland by isthmuses. The first volcano, Monte Queimado, dominates the harbour and is linked by an isthmus to the second, Monte da Guia.
From the top of Monte da Guia, beside the **Ermida de Nossa Senhora da Guia**, there is a view of **Caldeira do Inferno**, a former crater that has been filled in by the sea.

As you return to Horta there is a good **view**★ of the town and the beach at Porto Pim. Porto Pim inlet was originally protected by fortifications.

Tour of the Island *80km/50mi from Horta – allow 5hr.*

▶ *Take the airport road from Horta and drive along the southwest coast.*

The road leads past **Castelo Branco** headland, named on account of its white cliffs, and continues to **Varadouro**, a small spa.

▶ *Follow signs to Capelinhos.*

Cross Capelo village with the ruins of houses destroyed by Capelinhos in 1957.

Capelinhos★★★
The best way to explore the volcano is to see it on foot. Park below the lighthouse and then allow for a walk of at least 1hr.
The landscape of the volcano, so recent it is still devoid of vegetation, is fascinating. The volcano's structure, with its ash, bombs (solidified lava) and scoria, is gradually being eroded by the sea, and the different mineral colours of ochre, red and black stand out.

Capelinhos volcano

Before reaching the lighthouse, you arrive at a house that has been rebuilt and now contains a **museum** (🕐 *Open in summer, 10am-12.30pm and 2.30-5.30pm; in winter, 10am-noon and 2-5pm.* 🕐*Closed Mon, and mornings on Sat, Sun and public hols. No charge.* ☎ *292 94 51 65*) which traces the different phases of the eruption from 1957 to 1958.

Between Capelinhos and Praia do Norte the road passes through Norte Pequeno with houses are still buried in ash, then crosses a *mistério* or lava flow covered in thick vegetation: hydrangeas, cedars and mango trees. The coast beyond Praia do Norte becomes steep with a succession of lookout points.

▶ *Beyond Ribeira Funda go right onto the road for Horta and Caldeira.*

There is a fine view from the **Miradouro dos Cedros**. After entering the **Ribeiro dos Flamingos** you join up with a road that rises in zigzags through hydrangeas, roses and cryptomerias to Caldeira and its crater.

Caldeira★★
Walk through a short tunnel into the crater.
Caldeira's vast crater is 400m/1 312ft deep with a diameter of 1 450m/4 757ft. It is a nature reserve covered in cedars, ferns, junipers and moss. The floor of the crater is flat and the contours of the former lake which emptied during the eruption of Capelinhos can be clearly seen.

▶ *A path leading round the crater takes about 2hr. A second path, which is for experienced walkers leads down into the crater (allow at least 5hr round trip).*

Beside the crater is **Cabeço Gordo**★ *(45min round trip walk from Caldeira car park)*, a lookout point at an altitude of 1 043m/3 422ft, with wonderful views of the islands of Pico and São Jorge and, in clear weather, of Graciosa.

▶ *Return to Horta through Ribeira dos Flamengos.*

PICO★★

HORTA

MICHELIN ATLAS SPAIN & PORTUGAL P 96

Pico is a long island only 7km/4mi east of Faial. It is the second largest island in the archipelago after São Miguel and is dominated by the volcano after which it is named. The small population is spread between the different coastal villages.
🛈 *Rua Conselheiro Terra Pinheiro – 9950-329 – Madalena – ☎ 292 62 35 24*

▶ **Orient Yourself:** The southern-most of the main group of islands.
🚫 **Don't Miss:** The volcano – it is the island!
🕐 **Organizing Your Time:** A day trip is possible but more time is needed if you intend to climb the volcano.

A Bit of History

Volcanic activity
The island is a volcano. At 2 351m/7 713ft, it is the highest point in the whole of Portugal. Recent volcanic activity is visible in the form of **mistérios** or "mysteries". These are lava flows which occurred during eruptions after the island had been settled and

so destroyed various cultivated areas. The most striking *mistérios* are those of **Praínha** (1572), **Santa Luzia** (1718) and **São João** (1720).

Pico Wines

The vines grown on lava produced a wine known as **verdelho** which was particularly appreciated in England, America and Russia. Then the vines were attacked by vine-mildew in the middle of the 19C. The wine trade is slowly being built up again on the island today.

🙂 A Bit of Advice 🙂

Access: There is a boat shuttle service between Horta on Faial and Madalena on Pico several times a day. In summer, boats call in at Cais do Pico from Terceira and São Jorge several times a week.

There are also flights to Pico.

Length of stay: It is possible to tour Pico island in a day from Faial. However, if you wish to climb the volcano, allow at least one night on the island.

Pico Volcano★★★

Crater: 🕐*open daily 2.30-5.30pm.* ⬤*€3.*
Pico's greatest attraction is the ascension of its volcano. The volcano is a perfect cone, sometimes snow-capped in winter but more often than not hidden by clouds that gather on the top or ring the volcano like a scarf. No matter the weather, Pico is rarely completely cloud-free.

▶ *Allow at least 7hr for the walk (3hr to climb to the crater, 30min to walk round it, 1hr to climb up to and down from Pico Pequeno and 2hr 30min to come right down again). The walk is fairly difficult and tiring on account of the difference in altitude and the volcanic rocks one has to walk over. Strong climbing shoes are an absolute must. It is a good idea to take at least 1l of drinking water per person or 1.5l if the weather is hot. Most walkers like to climb at night to be able to reach the summit as the sun rises. In this case it is best to have a guide (enquire at the Tourist Office or at your hotel). Otherwise, during the day and when the weather is fine, the path is easy to follow.*

B. Brillon/MICHELIN

Pico volcano

Access: *Taxis from Madalena can drive you to the beginning of the path. If you have a car, take the central road and turn right after 13km/8mi. A narrow road climbs for 5km/3mi up to the path.*

After a 3hr climb you reach the crater which is 30m/98ft deep. It is impressive – a bare landscape forming a circle with a 700m/2 297ft perimeter. **Pico Pequeno** (70m/230ft) rises at the far end to form the mountain summit. The fumaroles and smell of sulphur at the top act as a reminder that a volcano is never completely dormant. On a clear day the **panorama**★★★ takes in São Jorge island and Faial island with its volcano, Capelinhos. In the far distance are Graciosa and Terceira.

On the way back to Madalena, the cave at **Furnas de Frei Matias** *(a 5min walk)* is a series of long underground galleries stretching out between mossy wells of light.

Tour of the Island

1 **From Madalena to São Roque** 28km/17mi – 2hr

Madalena
The harbour is protected by two rocks, Em Pé (meaning upright) and Deitado (meaning recumbent), which are home to colonies of sea birds. Madalena is a pleasant little town centred around the **Igreja de Santa Maria Madalena**.

Cachorro★
After Bandeiras bear left off the main road and follow the signs. The small village built of lava stretches out behind the airport landing strips beside black rocks and cliffs. These have been eroded into caves into which the sea rushes and roars.
The road continues through the villages of **Santa Luzia** and **Santo António**, where the plain-looking church contains a naïve Baroque altarpiece.

Convento and Igreja de São Pedro de Alcântara
The Baroque building has an interesting façade and, inside, the chancel is adorned with *azulejos* and an abundantly decorated altarpiece.

Igreja de São Roque
The church is a large 18C building decorated inside with statues, jacaranda wood furniture inlaid with ivory, and a silver lamp donated by Dom João V.

From São Roque to Lajes do Pico

There are two possible itineraries:

2 **Via the Coast** 50km/31mi, allow 2hr 30min.
This itinerary is for those who have the time and who don't mind winding roads.

The villages along this route include **Prainha**, which is well-known for its

mistério, **Santo Amaro** with its shipbuilding yard, and **Piedade** and the attractive countryside at the end of the island. The itinerary continues along the southeast coast and the fishing villages of **Calheta de Nesquim** and **Ribeiras**.

③ Via the Centre of the Island

32km/20mi including an excursion to Lagoa do Caiado – allow 1hr.

▷ *Take the Lajes road which soon rises to cross the centre of the island. After 10km/6mi take the road left marked Lagoa do Caiado and continue for 5km/3mi.*

The centre of the island, at an altitude of 800-1 000m/2 625-3 280ft, is often covered in cloud. There are a good many small crater lakes and the vegetation consists of strange low plants, some of which are indigenous species.

▷ *A road crosses the island from east to west affording good views of beautiful countryside (if one is lucky enough to be travelling on a clear day). After visiting Lagoa do Caiado, return to the main road and continue towards Lajes.*

Lajes do Pico

This was the first settlement on the island. The main activity from the 19C, up until 1981, was whaling. Lajes, a small, quiet, white town in the middle of maize fields, extends into a lava plateau known as a Fajã (👆 *see SÃO JORGE*).

Museu dos Baleeiros ★

🕐 *Open Tue-Fri 9.30am-12.30pm, 2-5.30pm (5pm Oct-Apr), Sat-Sun 2-5.30pm (5pm Oct-Apr).* ⊘*Closed Mon and public hols.* ☎ *292 67 22 76.*
The whaling museum is housed in a former boat shelter in the harbour. The fine **scrimshaw collection** contains engraved sperm-whale teeth and ivory walrus tusks.

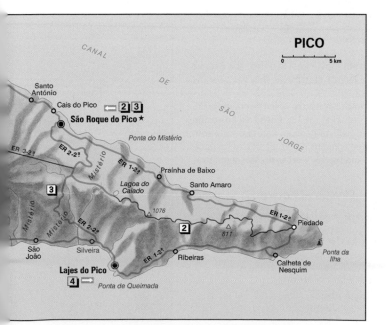

Ermida de São Pedro

By continuing along the quayside you arrive at a white chapel, the oldest on the island with an attractive altarpiece. Beside the chapel stands the **Padrão** monument, which commemorates the five-hundredth anniversary of the settlement of the island.

④ From Lajes to Madalena – Mistérios and vineyards ★★ –35km/22mi – allow 1hr 30min.

The road crosses the *misterios* on either side of **São João** which date from an eruption in 1718.

São Mateus

The village is dominated by its impressive church.
The road passes through vineyards closed off by low lava walls. The countryside is striking with the black of the lava walls contrasting sharply with the soft green of the abandoned vines and the deep blue of the sea beyond.
The road passes through **Candelaria** and **Criação Velha**, the village in which *verdelho* wine originated, before reaching Madalena.

SÃO JORGE

HORTA

POPULATION 10 219 – MICHELIN ATLAS SPAIN & PORTUGAL P 96

The cigar-shaped island stretches out parallel to Pico. Its wild, grandiose landscapes make a splendid environment for walking. *Rua Conselheiro Dr. José Pereira – 9800-530 Velas – ☎ 295 41 24 40*

▶ **Orient Yourself:** Almost at the centre of the main group of islands.
🕐 **Organizing Your Time:** One day is fine to see everything.

Velas

Velas has grown on a fajã near the Baía de Entre-Morros, literallly the "bay between the hillocks".
The small town has preserved several old buildings including the 18C **Paços do Concelho** (Town Hall), of Azorean Baroque style with twisted columns on either side of its doorway, and the 18C **Portas do Mar**, a gateway

😊 A Bit of Advice 😊

Access: There are flights between São Jorge and the other islands throughout the year. In summer, the boat that serves the islands in the central group of the archipelago calls at São Jorge several times a week.

Length of stay: Allow a full day to tour the island by car.

remaining from the old ramparts. The 16C church of São Jorge has an interesting façade.

From Velas to Ponta dos Rosais
14km/9mi west. The road runs alongside Baía de Entre-Morros, crosses the village of Rosais and continues to **Sete Fontes**, an attractive forest. You can continue to Ponta da Rosais by car although it is better to walk *(2hr 30min round trip)*. There are fine views of both sides of the island. At the headland there is a lighthouse and an islet.

Tour of the Island ★★
83km/52mi – 4hr

The North Coast

▶ *Take the Santo António road out of Velas.*

Fajã do Ouvidor★★
The *fajã* with its hamlet is the largest on the north coast with a bird's eye view of a flat stretch of land covered in cultivated fields and houses, dominated by a sheer cliff.

Miradouro da Fajã dos Cubres★★
The landscape viewed from this lookout point, on the road beyond Norte Pequeno, is highly characteristic of São Jorge. The most impressive, **Fajã da Caldeira do Santo Cristo**, is occupied by

View from the Miradouro da Fajã dos Cubres

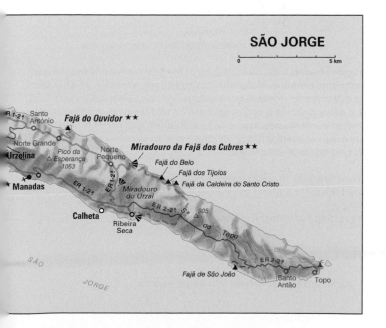

a lagoon that has been made into a nature reserve to protect its clams, a particular type of scallop-shell only found here.

The road from the north coast to the village of Ribeira Seca on the south coast crosses beautiful woodland criss-crossed by hedges of hydrangeas. The **view**★★ is particularly fine from the **Miradouro de Urzal**.

The South Coast

The itinerary suggested here begins at **Ribeira Seca** and includes **Serra do Topo** and **Fajã de São Jorge**.

Calheta
This fishing village has preserved some old houses.

Manadas
The picturesque hamlet is mainly known for its **Igreja de Santa Bárbara**★ (*Guided tours, 9am-12.30pm and 2-5pm (Mon-Fri only). For visits, contact Senhora Albertina (Junta de Freguesia).* ☎ 295 41 40 12). It dates from the 18C and is one of the prettiest churches in the Azores. The very rich interior decoration was directed by an Italian artist. The finely worked **cedarwood ceiling**★ is adorned with naive sculptures including St George slaying the dragon. The *azulejos* relate the story of St Barbara.

Urzelina
The village, rebuilt after the volcanic eruption in 1808, was named after the island's brown lichen or orchil *(urzela)*. A tower emerges out of the lava beneath which the church lies buried. Small windmills still functioning beside the shore stand out against Pico island in the background.

FLORES★★

HORTA
POPULATION 4 329 – MICHELIN ATLAS SPAIN & PORTUGAL P 96

The island of flowers is the most westerly of the Azorean islands and the westernmost point in Europe. Along with its sister Corvo, Flores lies at quite some distance from the other islands in the archipelago. It is 236km/147mi from Faial. Flores is thinly populated, very rugged and its wild landscapes are among the most majestic in the Azores. Its luxuriant vegetation is explained by the very high rainfall; it rains on average nearly 300 days a year. *Câmara Municipal – 9970-909 – Santa Cruz das Flores –* ☎ 292 59 23 73

▶ **Orient Yourself:** This really is the western-most tip of Europe.
⊛ **Don't Miss:** The Convent and the Church of Christ (Igreja do Senhor Santo Cristo).
🕐 **Organizing Your Time:** This island can be seen in one day.

Santa Cruz das Flores

Santa Cruz is a quiet, pleasant town with a small harbour.

Museu Etnográfico
🕐 Open 9am-noon and 2-5pm. 🚫Closed Sat-Sun and hols. Call for admission prices.
☎ 292 59 21 59.
The museum, set up in an old house, displays several reconstituted interiors of traditional homes as well as a collection of items illustrating the inhabitants' way of life on the island. This was centred around fishing and whaling – there are some scrimshaw pieces – and work in the fields.

Convento de São Boaventura
The 17C building, once a Franciscan monastery, has been restored to house part of the museum. The Baroque chancel in the church shows a Hispano-Mexican influence.

Tour of the Island ★★ 68km/42mi – about 4hr

▶ *Take the Lajes road out of Santa Cruz.*

The road twists and turns with the relief, dipping into deep ravines and running alongside mountain ridges with superb views above the banks of bright red and yellow cannas and blue hydrangeas that line it.

Fazenda das Lajes
The **Igreja do Senhor Santo Cristo**, with its *azulejo* decoration on the façade, is one of the most representative examples of Azorean religious architecture.

Lajes
The island's second largest town thrives on its harbour activities and a major radio station.

▶ *Once past Lajes, take the road south. Turn right towards Lagoa Funda.*

Lagoa Funda★★
Lagoa Funda, meaning deep lake, is a crater lake that stretches for several kilometres below the road. After 3km/1.8mi you reach an area where, to the right, and at

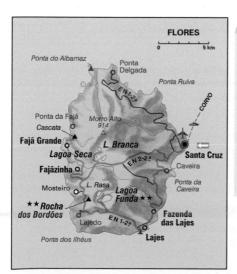

😊 A Bit of Advice 😊

Access: Flores is only accessible by air from the other islands.

Length of stay: It is possible to tour the island in a day although it is well worth taking the time to explore Flores on foot. An extra day is required for an excursion to the island of Corvo.

Fajãzinha, Flores, Azores

a great depth, you can see the end of Lagoa Funda and, to the left, at road level, **Lagoa Rasa**.

▶ *Return to the road; 600m/660yd beyond the 25km marker, look up to admire the Rocha dos Bordões rock formation.*

Rocha dos Bordões★★

Masses of flowers can be seen bursting from basalt organ pipes. These high, vertical stria were formed when the basalt solidified.

▶ *Take the Mosteiro road.*

The road passes **Mosteiro**, set in enchanting countryside with the sea in the background.

▶ *A little farther on, take the road to Fajãzinha and Fajã Grande.*

Fajãzinha

As the road approaches Fajãzinha there is a beautiful **view**★★ of the village. The **Igreja de Nossa Senhora dos Remédios** dates from the 18C. The 300m/984ft Ribeira Grande waterfall is in the vicinity.

Waterfall

Turn right towards Ponta da Fajã. Continue for 400m/440yd and stop at the first bridge. Take the track on the left of the bridge as you stand looking towards the cliff. 20min round trip on foot.
The track follows the stream and passes three water-mills. The waterfall plunges from the top of the cliff onto a ledge where it divides into a multitude of smaller cascades.

▶ *Return to the main road and head for Santa Cruz. Turn left towards the lakes.*

CORVO ★

HORTA

POPULATION 393 – MICHELIN ATLAS SPAIN & PORTUGAL P 96

A large, black, sea-battered rock rises out of the water 15 nautical miles north-east of Flores. This is Crow Island, the visible part of Monte Gordo (718m/2 356ft), a marine volcano. As there is no protected bay, access is difficult. In 1452, Corvo was the last of the islands in the archipelago to display the Portuguese flag and settlement began only in the middle of the 16C. A remote community of farmers and herders began to develop. In winter, for weeks on end, it was impossible for boats to moor so communication with Flores was made through lighting fires on a hillock. *Rua Jogo da Bola (Câmara Municipal) – 9970-024 – ☎ 292 59 61 15*

▶ **Orient Yourself:** The most north-westerly island, just above Flores.
⊙ **Don't Miss:** The Caldeirão.
⊙ **Organizing Your Time:** Plan no more than half a day to see the Caldeirão.

Sights

Vila Nova do Corvo
The **Igreja de Nossa Senhora dos Milagres** has preserved a 16C Flemish statue.
Vila Nova do Corvo may well be the smallest and least populated district in Portugal, yet it possesses an airport. Walk alongside the landing strip and you reach some disused windmills and a restaurant.

Caldeirão ★
6km/3.7mi from Vila Nova. The volcanic crater may be visited any time, free of charge.
The local restaurant runs **jeep excursions** (⊙ *Ascent by jeep: 1 000$.* ☎ *292 59 61 15*) to the caldeira *(45min round trip)*, which is also accessible on foot along the road. *(3hr round trip).* There is a difference in altitude of 550m/1 804ft. Bring warm clothes as the uplands are often covered in cloud and can be cool. The road crosses beautiful countryside brightened by hedges of hydrangeas. The crater has a perimeter of 3.4km/2mi and is 300m/984ft deep, in the bottom of which are two blue lakes with two islets at the bottom. Tradition has it that these islets have the same layout as the islands in the Azores (without Flores and Corvo). The slopes of the crater were once cultivated.

Caldeira do Corvo

B. Maltaverne/EXPLORER

A

Abrantes (Santarém) 86
Accessibility 16
Achada das Furnas
    (São Miguel, Azores) 349
Achada do Teixeira (Madeira) 332
Afonso, João 59
Afonso, Jorge 61
Afonso Henriques 42, 172
Água de Pau (São Miguel, Azores) 352
Airlines 17
Albufeira (Faro) 87
Alcobaça (Leiria) 88
Algar do Carvão (Terceira, Azores) 360
Algar Seco (Faro) 125
Algarve 90
Alicatados technique 64
Aljezur (Faro) 94
Aljubarrota, Battle of 42
Almada Negreiros, Josè de 64
Almagreira (Santa Maria, Azores) 354
Almansil (Faro) 95
Almeida (Guarda) 170
Almourol, Castelo de (Santarém) 96
Alte (Faro) 93
Alto, Pico (Santa Maria, Azores) 354
Alto Rabagão,
    Barragem do (Vila Real) 131
Alturas do Barroso (Vila Real) 132
Alvados, Grutas de (Leiria) 168
Alvão, Parque Natural do (Vila Real) 233
Álvares, Afonso 61
Álvares, Baltazar 61
Álvares Pereira, Nuno 108
Alverca do Ribatejo (Lisboa) 301
Alvoco da Serra (Guarda) 153
Amado, Jorge 68
Amarante (Porto) 97
Andrade, Eugènio de 68
Angra do Heroísmo
    (Terceira, Azores) 356
Anjos (Santa Maria, Azores) 354
António (Dom), Prior of Crato 340
António, Lauro 69
Antunes, Bartolomeu 66
Antunes, João 62
Arcos de Valdevez
    (Viana do Castelo) 251
Arieiro, Pico do (Madeira) 330
Arouca (Aveiro) 97
Arrábida, Serra da (Setúbal) 98
Arraiolos (Évora) 100
Arrifana (Faro) 94
Arruda, Diogo de 60
Arruda, Francisco de 60
Arruda, Miguel de 61
Aveiro (Aveiro) 100
Avis (Portalegre) 105
Avis dynasty 42
Azenhas do Mar (Lisboa) 288
Azores Archipelago 339
Azulejos 64

B

Bacalhoa, Quinta da (Setúbal) 105
Balcıes (Madeira) 330
Barca de Alva Guarda 252
Barcelos (Braga) 106
Barcelos, Pico dos (Madeira) 325
Barriga (Faro) 94
Barró (Viseu) 147
Barroso, Serra do (Vila Real) 132
Basic Information 32
Batalha, Mosteiro da (Leiria) 108
Beaches 22
Beja (Beja) 111
Belmonte (Castelo Branco) 112
Berlenga, Ilha da (Leiria) 113
Bessa Luís, Agustina 68
Bico (Aveiro) 104
Bird-watching 24
Biscoitos (Terceira, Azores) 359
Boal Wine 316
Boa Ventura (Madeira) 334
Boa Vista, Miradouro da (Viseu) 147
Boca do Inferno (Lisboa) 126
Bocage, Manuel MB do 67
Bom Jesus do Monte (Braga) 118
Books 28
Bordalo Pinheiro, Columbano 63
Botelho, João 69
Boticas (Vila Real) 131
Boytac, Diogo de 59
Braga (Braga) 113
Bragança (Bragança) 118
Bragança dynasty 43
Brasil, Monte (Terceira, Azores) 358
Bravães (Viana do Castelo) 120
Buçaco, Mata do (Aveiro) 120
Bullfighting 77
Bullfights 24
Burgau (Faro) 94
Burgundy, Henry of 41
Business Hours 32

C

Cabeço da Neve (Viseu) 125
Cabo da Roca (Lisboa) 288
Cabral, Pedro Álvares 43, 48
Cacela Velha (Faro) 90
Cachorro (Pico, Azores) 368
Caldas de Manteigas (Guarda) 152
Caldeira (Faial, Azores) 366
Caldeirão (Corvo, Azores) 375
Caldeirão, Serra do (Faro) 90
Caldeiras 340
Calendar of Events 24
Calheta (São Jorge, Azores) 372

INDEX

Câmara de Lobos (Madeira) 326
Camıes, Luís de 67
Caminha (Viana do Castelo) 123
Camping 20
Campo do Gerês (Braga) 250
Candelaria (Pico, Azores) 370
Caniçada, Represa de (Braga) 130
Caniçal (Madeira) 328
Caniço (Madeira) 327
Cão, Diogo 47
Capelinhos (Faial, Azores) 365
Caramulinho (Viseu) 124
Caramulo (Viseu) 124
Caramulo, Serra do (Viseu) 124
Carapacho (Graciosa, Azores) 362
Caravels 273
Cardoso Pires, José 68
Carlos I 44
Carnation Revolution 46, 184
Carrapateira (Faro) 94
Carvalhelhos (Vila Real) 132
Carvão, Pico do (São Miguel, Azores) 348
Carvoeiro (Faro) 125
Cascais (Lisboa) 125
Castelejo (Faro) 94
Castelo Branco (Castelo Branco) 126
Castelo Branco (Faial, Azores) 365
Castelo Branco, Camilo 67
Casteloda São Filipe (Setúbal) 280
Castelo de Vide (Portalegre) 129
Castelo Melhor (Guarda) 170, 293
Castelo Mendo (Guarda) 170
Castelo Rodrigo (Guarda) 252
Castilho, António F de 67
Castilho, Diogo de 60
Castilho, João de 60
Castro Laboreiro (Viana do Castelo) 251
Castro Marim (Faro) 129
Cávado, Alto Vale do Rio
    (Braga/Vila Real) 130
Celorico da Beira (Guarda) 170
Centum Cellas (Castelo Branco) 112
Cerro da Vila (Faro) 307
Cetóbriga (Setúbal) 281
Chafes, Rui 64
Chantarene, Nicolas 61
Chaves (Vila Real) 132
Chaves, Caldas de (Vila Real) 133
Children, Activities for 24
Cinfães (Viseu) 146
Co-operatives 39, 81, 89

COIMBRA (COIMBRA)   134

Botanical Gardens 140
Casa Museu Bissaya-Barreto 139
Convento de Santa Clara-a-Nova 141
Jardim da Sereia 140
Miradouro do Vale do Inferno 141
Mosteiro de Santa Cruz 140
Parque de Santa Cruz 140
Porta de Almedina 135

Portugal dos Pequeninos 141
Quinta das L-grimas 141
Sé Nova 136
Sé Velha 135
Universidade Velha 137
Colares (Lisboa) 288
Columbus, Christopher 47
Congro, Lagoa do
    (São Miguel, Azores) 352
Conímbriga (Coimbra) 142
Consulates 15
Convento de Cristo (Santarém) 289
Convento de Santa Clara (Porto) 299
Corda seca technique 64
Cordoama (Faro) 94
Correia, Natália 68
Corte Real, Gaspar 48
Corvo (Azores) 375
Costa, Pedro 69
Costa da Caparica (Setúbal) 144
Covilhã (Castelo Branco) 153
Crato (Portalegre) 144
Criação Velha (Pico, Azores) 370
Croft, João Pedro 64
Cruz Amarante, Carlos da 63
Cume, Serra do (Terceira, Azores) 360
Curral das Freiras (Madeira) 325
Cutileiro, João 64

D, E

Days of the Week 26
Deus, João de 67
Dias, Bartolomeu 47
Driving in Portugal 18
Dunas de São Jacinto,
    Reserva Natural (Aveiro) 104
Eanes, Gil 47
Eça de Queirós 67
Eira do Serrado (Madeira) 325
Electricity 32
Elvas (Portalegre) 148
Embassies 15
Empedrados 73
Encumeada, Boca da (Madeira) 335
Ericeira (Lisboa) 149
Espichel, Cabo (Setúbal) 149
Espigão, Miradouro
    do Santa Maria (Azores) 354
Estalagems 20
Estói, Palácio de Faro 91
Estoril (Lisboa) 150
Estrela, Serra da
    (Guarda/Castelo Branco) 150
Estremoz (Évora) 153

ÉVORA (ÉVORA)   155

Capela dos Ossos 160
Casa de Garcia de Resende 160
Casa dos Condes de Portalegre 160
Casa Soure 160
Cathedral 158

Convento dos Lóios 159
Fortifications 161
Igreja de São Francisco 160
Jardim Público 161
Largo da Porta de Moura 160
Paço dos Condes de Basto 160
Paço dos Duques de Cadaval 159
Praça do Giraldo 158
Rua 5 de Outubro 158
Templo Romano 159
Universidade de Évora 161
Évoramente (Évora) 162
Expo'98 46

F

Facho, Pico do
 (Porto Santo, Madeira) 338
Fado 75
Faial (Azores) 363
Fajã 340
Fajã da Caldeira do Santo Cristo
 (São Jorge, Azores) 371
Fajã do Ouvidor (São Jorge, Azores) 371
Fajã dos Cubres, Miradouro de
 (São Jorge, Azores) 371
Fajãzinha (Flores, Azores) 374
Faria, Almeida 68
Faro (Faro) 163
Faro, Monte do (Viana do Castelo) 295
Fátima (Santarém) 166
Ferdinand of Saxe-Coburg-Gotha 287
Fernandes, Garcia 61
Fernandes, Mateus 59
Fernandes, Vasco 61, 309
Ferreira, António 62, 67
Ferreira, Virgîlio 68
Ferreira de Castro 68
Ferro, Pico do (São Miguel, Azores) 352
Ferry Services 17
Figueira da Foz (Coimbra) 168
Figueiredo, Cristóvão de 61
Fishing 23
Flor da Rosa, Mosteiro de
 (Portalegre) 144
Flores (Azores) 372
Flores, Mosteiro (Azores) 374
Fogo, Lagoa do (São Miguel, Azores) 351
Fonseca e Costa, José 69
Fonte da Areia
 (Porto Santo, Madeira) 338
Football 23
Francisco Álvares
 Nóbrega Miradouro (Madeira) 328
Franco, Francisco 64
Frei, Carlos 60
Freitas, Nicolau de 66
Funchal (Madeira) 318
Furna do Enxofre (Graciosa, Azores) 362
Furna Maria Encantada
 (Graciosa, Azores) 362
Furnas (São Miguel, Azores) 349

Furnas, Lagoa das
 (São Miguel, Azores) 350
Furnas do Enxofre (Terceira, Azores) 359

G

Gama, Vasco da 43, 48
Gand, Olivier de 60
Garrett, Almeida 67
Geira (Braga) 249
Gerês (Braga) 249
Gerês, Serra do (Braga) 250
Girão, Cabo (Madeira) 327
Giusti 62
Golf 23
Gonçalves, Nuno 60
Gouveia (Guarda) 151
Graciosa (Azores) 361
Grilo, João Mário 69
Guarda (Guarda) 168
Guilherme Moniz,
 Caldeira de (Terceira, Azores) 360
Guimarães (Braga) 171
Guimarães, José de 64
Gulbenkian, Calouste 225

H, I, J, K

Handicrafts 73
Health 16
Henriques, Francisco 60
Herculano, Alexandre 67
Holidays 32
Holy Queen Festival 140
Horta (Faial, Azores) 364
Hostels, Youth 21
Hotels 20
Houdart 61
Huguet, Master 59
Idanha-a-Velha (Castelo Branco) 128
Ílhavo (Aveiro) 104
International Visitors 15
Isabel of Aragon, Queen Saint 154
Jesuits 255
João I 42
João V 43
Jorge, Lidia 68
José I 43
Juncal, Miradouro do (Madeira) 330
Junceda, Miradouro de (Braga) 250
Junqueiro, Guerra 67
Knights of Christ 289
Knights Templar 289

L

Lagoa Funda (Flores, Azores) 373
Lagos (Faro) 175
Lajes (Flores, Azores) 373
Lajes, Fazenda das (Flores, Azores) 373
Lajes do Pico (Pico, Azores) 369
Lamego (Viseu) 178

INDEX

Laprade 62
Leça do Bailio (Porto) 179
Leiria (Leiria) 179
Lindoso (Viana do Castelo) 180
Linhares (Guarda) 171
Lino, Raúl 63

LISBOA (LISBOA) 182

Alfama 210
Alto de Santa Catarina 209
Amoreiras 226
Aqueduto das Águas Livres 227
Avenida da Liberdade 224
Bairro Alto 209
Baixa 206
Basílica da Estrela 228
Beco das Cruzes 212
Beco do Carneiro 212
Belém 220
Biblioteca Nacional 226
Boat trips 216
Campo de Santa Clara 213
Casa-Museu Anastácio Gonçalves 227
Casa do Alentejo 206
Casa dos Bicos 216
Casa Fernando Pessoa 229
Castelo de São Jorge 212
Cathedral 210
Centro Cultural de Belém 196
Centro de Arte Moderna 226
Comuna 196
Convento da Madre de Deus 218
Convento da Nossa Senhora da Graça 213
Cristo Rei 220
Docks 220
Éden Teatro 206
Elevador de Santa Justa 207
Escadinhas de Santo Estêvão 212
Estação do Oriente 217
Estação do Rossio 206
Estação do Sul e Sueste 207
Expo'98 site 216
Fundação Arpad Szenes-Vieira da Silva 227
Fundação Ricardo Espírito
   Santo da Silva 211
Graça 213
Igreja da Conceição Velha 213
Igreja da Nossa Senhora da Graça 213
Igreja de Nossa Senhora de Fátima 226
Igreja de Santa Engrácia 213
Igreja de Santa Maria 221
Igreja de Santo António da Sé 211
Igreja de São Miguel 211
Igreja de São Roque 209
Igreja de São Vicente de Fora 213
Igreja do Carmo 208
Jardim Botânico da Ajuda 224
Jardim Boto Machado 213
Jardim das Damas 224
Jardim Garcia da Orta 217
Jardim Zoológico 228
Largo das Portas do Sol 211
Largo de São Rafael 211
Lisbon Players 196
Mãe d'Água das Amoreiras 227
Miradouro da Senhora do Monte 213
Miradouro de Santa Luzia 211

Miradouro de São Pedro de Alcântara 210
Mosteiro dos Jerónimos 221
Museu Antoniano 211
Museu Calouste Gulbenkian 225
Museu da Água da EPAL 218
Museu da Cidade 229
Museu da Marinha 222
Museu da Música 228
Museu das Marionetas 220
Museu de Arte Sacra de São Roque 209
Museu de Artes Decorativas 211
Museu do Design 223
Museu Militar 218
Museu Nacional de Arte Antiga 218
Museu Nacional do Azulejo 218
Museu Nacional do Chiado 208
Museu Nacional do Teatro 229
Museu Nacional do Traje 229
Museu Rafael Bordalo Pinheiro 229
Oceanário de Lisboa 217
Paço Real 212
Padrão dos Descobrimentos 223
Palácio da Ajuda 224
Palácio dos Marqueses de Fronteira 227
Palácio Foz 206
Palácio Lavradio 213
Parque das Nações 216
Parque Eduardo VII 224
Parque Florestal de Monsanto 228
Pavilhão Atlântico 217
Ponte Vasco da Gama 216
Port 216
Praça da Figueira 207
Praça de Touros (Bullring) 196
Praça do Comércio 207
Praça do Marquês de Pombal 224
Praça dos Restauradores 206
Praça Luís de Camies 209
Rossio 206
Rua Augusta 207
Rua da Atalaia 209
Rua da Judiaria 212
Rua da Misericórdia 209
Rua de São Pedro 212
Rua do Carmo 208
Rua do Diário de Notícias 209
Rua do Ouro 207
Rua dos Remédios 212
Rua Garrett 208
Rua Norberto de Araújo 211
Rua Portas de Santo Antão 206
Teatro Maria Vitória 195
Teatro Municipal Maria Matos 196
Teatro Nacional de São Carlos 209
Teatro Nacional São Luís 195
Terreiro do Paço 207
Torre de Belém 223
Torres das Amoreiras 226
Torre Vasco da Gama 217
Lisbon - See Lisboa 182
Lisbon School 61
Lobo Antunes, António 68
Lopes, Fernando 69
Lopes, Fernão 66
Lopes, Gregório 61
Lopes, Teixeira 63
Loriga (Guarda) 153

Loulé (Faro) 93
Lourenço, Eduardo 68
Ludwig, Friedrich 62
Luís I 44
Lusiads 48
Luso (Aveiro) 120
Luz de Tavira (Faro) 90

M

Macedo, António de 69
Machado de Castro, Joaquim 62, 230
Machico (Madeira) 328
Madalena (Pico, Azores) 368
Madeira (Funchal) 315
Madeira, Monte 325
Madeira Archipelago 314
Madeira Embroidery 316
Madeira Wine 316
Madrugada, Miradouro da
    (São Miguel, Azores) 353
Mafra, Convento de (Lisboa) 230
Mafra School 230
Magalhães, Fernão de 49
Magellan 43, 49
Maia (Santa Maria, Azores) 354
Mail 32
Majolica technique 65
Malhoa 63
Malmsey Wine 316
Manadas (São Jorge, Azores) 372
Manteigas (Guarda) 152
Manuel I 43
Manuel II 44
Marão, Pico do (Vila Real) 233
Marão, Serra do (Porto/Vila Real) 233
Mardel 62
Maria I 270
Maria II 44
Marialva (Guarda) 171
Marofa, Serra da (Guarda) 252
Martim Moniz 212
Martins, Oliveira 67
Marvão (Portalegre) 234
Mateus (Vila Real) 302
Maximilian of Austria 207
Measurement 33
Melo Breyner, Sofia de 68
Mendes Pinto, Fernão 67
Mértola (Beja) 235
Methuen Treaty 79
Mezio (Viana do Castelo) 251
Milreu (Faro) 91
Minho, Vale do (Viana do Castelo) 295
Mira de Aire, Grutas de (Leiria) 167
Miradouro de Santa Luzia
    (Viana do Castelo) 297
Miranda do Douro (Bragança) 235
Mirandela (Bragança) 236
Moliceiros 104
Monção (Viana do Castelo) 295

Money 32
Monsanto (Castelo Branco) 237
Monsaraz (Évora) 238
Monserrate, Parque de (Lisboa) 288
Montalegre (Vila Real) 131
Monteiro, João César 69
Montemor-o-Velho (Coimbra) 239
Moura (Beja) 240
Mouranitos (Faro) 94
Mouros, Castelo dos (Lisboa) 287
Museu-Escola das
    Rendas de Bilros (Porto) 299
Museu de Arte Moderna (Lisboa) 285
Museu do Brinquedo (Lisboa) 285
Museu Grão Vasco (Viseu) 309
Museu Nacional
    Soares dos Reis (Porto) 260

N

Namora, Fernando 68
Nasoni, Nicolau 62
Nazaré (Leiria) 240
Nemésio, Vitorino 68
Newspapers 33

NIGHTLIFE
Albufeira 87
Coimbra 141
Lisboa
    A Brasileira 194
    Bar das Imagens/Costa Do Castelo 194
    Café Nicola 194
    Frágil 194
    Ginginha do Rossio 194
    Hot Clube 194
    Kapital 194
    Lux 195
    Pavilhão Chinês 194
Vilamoura 307
Nossa Senhora da Peneda,
    Mosteiro de (Viana do Castelo) 251

O

Óbidos (Leiria) 243
Óbidos, Josefa de 61
Odeceixe (Faro) 94
Olhão (Faro) 245
Oliveira, Carlos de 68
Oliveira, Manoel de 69
Oliveira, Marquês de 63
Oliveira Bernardes, António de 66
Oliveira Bernardes, Policarpo de 66
Oliveira do Hospital (Coimbra) 246
Oranges, War of the 44
Ourém (Santarém) 246
Outdoor Fun 22

P

Paço de Sousa (Porto) 247
Paço Ducal (Évora) 305
Padrão 47

Padrões 73
Palheiro Ferreiro,
    Quinta do (Madeira) 324
Palmela (Setúbal) 248
Paradela, Represa da (Vila Real) 131
Paúl da Serra (Madeira) 335
Pedras, Pico das (Madeira) 332
Pedras de El Rei (Faro) 90
Pedreira (Porto Santo, Madeira) 338
Pedro II 43
Pedro IV 207
Pedro V 44
Pena, Palácio Nacional da (Lisboa) 287
Pena, Parque da (Lisboa) 286
Penamacor (Castelo Branco) 128
Peneda, Serra da (Viana do Castelo) 250
Peneda-Gerês,
    Parque Nacional da (Braga) 248
Penedono (Viseu) 171
Penhas da Saúde (Castelo Branco) 150
Peniche (Leiria) 251
Peninha (Lisboa) 288
Pensões 20
Pereira, António 66
Perestrelo, Bartolomeu 316
Pero, Master 59
Pessoa, Fernando 67
Pets 16
Philip II of Spain 43
Pico (Azores) 366
Pico Volcano (Pico, Azores) 367
Pináculo, Miradouro do (Madeira) 327
Pinhão (Vila Real) 147
Pinhel (Guarda) 252
Pinoucas (Viseu) 124
Pinto, Sousa 63
Pires the Elder, Diogo 59
Pires the Younger, Diogo 60
Pitões das Júnias (Vila Real) 131
Poço do Inferno (Guarda) 152
Pomar, Júlio 64
Pombal (Leiria) 253
Pombal, Marquis of 43, 184, 253
Ponta Delgada (São Miguel, Azores) 346
Ponte da Barca (Viana do Castelo) 181
Ponte de Lima (Viana do Castelo) 254
Portalegre (Portalegre) 254
Portela, Boca da (Madeira) 329
Portimão (Faro) 256
Portinho da Arrábida (Setúbal) 99

PORTO (PORTO)   **256**

    Cais da Ribeira 267
    Casa do Infante 267
    Cathedral 266
    Convento de Nossa Senhora
        da Serra do Pilar 269
    Fundação António de Almeida 268
    Fundação de Serralves 269
    Igreja da Cedofeita 269
    Igreja das Carmelitas 260

    Igreja de Santa Clara 268
    Igreja de São Francisco 267
    Igreja de São Lourenço dos Grilos 266
    Igreja do Carmo 260
    Igreja dos Clérigos 260
    Mercado Municipal de Bolhão 260
    Museu Guerra Junqueiro 268
    Museu Nacional Soares dos Reis 260
    Praça da Liberdade 260
    Praça do General Humberto Delgado 260
    Rua das Flores 266
    Santa Casa da Misericórdia 266
    Solar do Vinho do (Porto) 267
    Terreiro da Sé 266
    Torre dos Clérigos 260
    Wine Lodges 268
Porto, Silva 63
Porto Moniz (Madeira) 334
Porto Santo (Madeira) 337
Portucale, County of 257
Portuguese Water Dog 242
Port Wine 79
Pousadas 20
Pousão, Henrique 63
Povoação (São Miguel, Azores) 353
Póvoa de Varzim (Porto) 269
Praia (Graciosa, Azores) 362
Praia das Maçãs (Lisboa) 288
Praia da Vitória (Terceira, Azores) 361
Praia do Guincho (Lisboa) 126
Prainha (Pico, Azores) 368

Q, R

Queimadas, Parque das (Madeira) 332
Queluz, Palácio Nacional de (Lisboa) 270
Quental, Antero de 67, 348
Querença (Faro) 92
Quinta da Regaleira (Lisboa) 285
Quinta do Lago (Faro) 94
Rabaçal (Madeira) 334
Rail Services 17
Rates (Porto) 270
Real República Corsário das Ilhas 135
Reconquest 41, 59, 257, 289
Régio, José 68
Rego, Paulo 64
Reis, António 69
República dos Kágados 135
Resende (Viseu) 147
Residencias 20
Resto, Ponta do (Madeira) 329
Ria Formosa, Parque natural (Faro) 90
Ribeira Brava (Madeira) 335
Ribeira da Janela (Madeira) 334
Ribeira Grande (São Miguel, Azores) 351
Ribeira Quente (São Miguel, Azores) 350
Ribeiro, Bernardim 66
Ribeiro Frio (Madeira) 330
Rio Mau (Porto) 269
Risco, Cascata do (Madeira) 334
Rocha, Paulo 69
Rocha dos Bordões (Flores, Azores) 374

Rodriguez, Amália 76
Romarias 76
Romeu (Bragança) 237
Rouen, Jean de 61
Ruivo, Pico (Madeira) 336

S

Sabrosa (Vila Real) 147
Sabugal (Guarda) 171
Sá Carneiro, Mario de 68
Sá de Miranda, Francisco 66
Sagres, Ponta de (Faro) 272
Sagres School 272
Sailing 22
Salazar 44
Salema (Faro) 94
Salir (Faro) 92
Salto da Farinha
    (São Miguel, Azores) 352
Salto do Cavalo, Miradouro de
    (São Miguel, Azores) 352
Sanches, Rui 64
Santa (Madeira) 334
Santa Bárbara (Santa Maria, Azores) 354
Santa Bárbara (Terceira, Azores) 358
Santa Cruz (Madeira) 327
Santa Cruz da Graciosa
    (Graciosa, Azores) 362
Santa Cruz das Flores
    (Flores, Azores) 372
Santa Espírito (Santa Maria, Azores) 354
Santa Luzia, Miradouro de
    (Viana do Castelo) 297
Santa Maria (Azores) 353
Santa Maria da Feira (Aveiro) 273
Santa Maria de Crquere,
    Priorado de (Viseu) 146
Santana (Madeira) 332
Santarém (Santarém) 274
Santa Rita 64
Santo António, Grutas de (Leiria) 168
Santo da Serra (Madeira) 329
Santos, Carlos Eugénio dos 63
Santos, Manuel dos 66
São Brás de Alportel (Faro) 91
São Jacinto (Aveiro) 104
São João da Pesqueira (Viseu) 148
São João de Tarouca (Viseu) 276
São Jorge (Azores) 370
São Jorge (Madeira) 333
São Lourenço, Baía de
    (Santa Maria, Azores) 353
São Lourenço, Ponta de (Madeira) 328
São Mamede, Grutas de (Leiria) 167
São Mamede, Serra de (Portalegre) 277
São Martinho (Madeira) 324
São Mateus (Pico, Azores) 370
São Mateus (Terceira, Azores) 358
São Miguel (Azores) 346
São Roque do Faial (Madeira) 332

São Sebastião (Terceira, Azores) 360
São Vicente (Madeira) 334
São Vicente, Cabo de (Faro) 272
Sapiãos (Vila Real) 131
Saramago, José 68
Sardoal, Master of 60
Scrimshaws 369
Scuba diving 22
Sebastião I 42
Seia (Guarda) 151
Seixal (Madeira) 334
Senhora do Desterro (Guarda) 153
Sequeira, Domingos António de 63
Sercial Wine 316
Sernancelhe (Viseu) 277
Serpa (Beja) 278
Serra de Água (Madeira) 335
Sesimbra (Setúbal) 278
Sete Cidades (São Miguel, Azores) 348
Sete Fontes (São Jorge, Azores) 371
Setúbal (Setúbal) 279
Severa, Maria 75
Shopping 27
Sightseeing 27
Silves (Faro) 282
Sintra (Lisboa) 283
Sintra, Convention of 284
Sintra, Serra de (Lisboa) 286
Siza, Álvaro 64
Soajo (Viana do Castelo) 251
Soares dos Reis 63, 260
Solar de Mateus (Villa Real) 302
Sortelha (Guarda) 171
Sossego, Miradouro do (São Miguel,
    Azores) 353
Souza Cardoso, Amadeo de 64
Spas 24

T

Taveira, Tomás 64
Tavira (Faro) 288
Távora, Fernando 64
Taxes 33
Teixeira, Manuel 62
Telephone 33
Temperature 33
Terceira (Azores) 355
Terra Nostra, Parque
    (São Miguel, Azores) 350
Terreiro da Luta (Madeira) 326
Terzi, Filippo 61
Time 33
Tinoco, João Nunes 62
Tipping 33
Tomar (Santarém) 289
Tordesillas, Treaty of 43, 48
Torga, Miguel 68
Torralva, Diogo de 61
Torre, Monte da (Castelo Branco) 151
Torre de Aspa (Faro) 94

Torreira (Aveiro) 104
Tourist Offices 15
Train Services 17
Tróia, Península de (Setúbal) 281
Turiano, João 62

U

UNESCO 26
Unhais da Serra (Castelo Branco) 153
Urzal, Miradouro de
    (São Jorge, Azores) 372
Urzelina (São Jorge, Azores) 372
Useful Words & Phrases 30

V

Vale do Côa,
    Parque Arqueológico do (Guarda) 291
Vale do Couço (Bragança) 237
Vale do Douro 145
Vale do Lobo (Faro) 94
Valença do Minho
    (Viana do Castelo) 294
Vara, Pico da
    (São Miguel, Azores) 346, 353
Varadouro (Faial, Azores) 365
Vasconcelos, António Pedro de 69
Vaz, Gaspar 61, 309
Velas (São Jorge, Azores) 370
Venda Nova, Represa de (Vila Real) 131
Verdelho Wine 316
Viana do Alentejo (Évora) 295
Viana do Castelo (Viana do Castelo) 296
Vicente, Gil 67, 172
Vicente, Mateus 63
Vieira, António 67
Vieira, Domingos 61
Vieira, Jacinto 62
Vieira da Silva, Maria Helena 64

Vieira Lusitano 63
Vila Baleira (Porto Santo, Madeira) 337
Vila da Ponte (Vila Real) 131
Vila do Bispo (Faro) 94
Vila do Conde (Porto) 299
Vila do Porto (Santa Maria, Azores) 354
Vila Franca de Xira (Lisboa) 300
Vila Franca do Campo
    (São Miguel, Azores) 352
Vilamoura (Faro) 307
Vila Nogueira de Azeitão (Setúbal) 99
Vila Nova da Gaia (Porto) 268
Vila Nova do Corvo (Corvo, Azores) 375
Vila Real (Vila Real) 301
Vila Real de Santo António (Faro) 304
Vilarinho das Furnas (Braga) 249
Vilarinho Seco (Vila Real) 132
Vila Verdinho (Bragança) 237
Vila Viçosa (Évora) 304
Vinho Verde 81
Viseu (Viseu) 308
Viseu School 61
Vista Alegre (Aveiro) 105

W, Y, Z

Waterparks 22
Web Sites 15
Wellington Plate 217
What to Do and See 22
When to Go 14
Where to Eat 21
Where to Stay 20
Windsurfing 22
World Heritage List 26
Ypres, Jean d' 60
Zarco, João Gonçalves 316
Zêzere, Vale glaciário do (Guarda) 152

ACCOMMODATIONS

Braga
Albergaria Bracara Augusta 115
Hotel Residencial Dona Sofia 115
Coimbra
Astória 136
Pensão Santa Cruz 136
Residencial Coimbra 136
Residencial Domus 136
Residencial Vitória 136
Évora
Albergaria Solar de Monfalim 155
Casa de São Tiago 155
Hotel da Cartuxa 155
Pousada dos Lóios 155
Residencial Policarpo 155
Faro
Faro 163
Pensão Residencial Adelaide 163
Pensão Residencial Central 163
Pensão Residencial Oceano 163
Guimarães
Paço de São Cipriano 173
Pousada de Nossa Senhora da Oliveira 173
Residencial das Trinas 173
Residencial Mestre d'Avis 173
Lisboa
Albergaria Senhora do Monte 189
As Janelas Verdes 190
Bairro Alto Hotel 189
Britânia 190
Casa de S. Mamede 189
Lisboa Regency Chiado 189
Lisboa Tejo 188
Metropole 189
NH Liberdade 190
Palácio Belmonte 189
Pensão Estrela do Mondego 188
Pensão Imperial 188
Pensão Londres 189
Pensão Ninho das Aguias 189
Pensão Pérola da Baixa 188
Pensão Residencial Setubalense 190
Portugal 188
Residencial Alegria 189
Residencial Iris 189
Residência Roma 189
York House 190
Óbidos
Casa das Senhoras Rainhas 244
Casa do Poço 244
Casa do Rochedo 244
Estalagem do Convento 244
Pousada do Castelo 244
Porto
América 258
Castelo Santa Catarina 258
Da Bolsa 258
Grande Hotel do Porto 258
Infante de Sagres 259
Residencial Vera Cruz 258
Sintra
Palácio de Seteais 284
Pensão Residencial Sintra 284
Quinta da Capela 284
Viana do Castelo
Casa da Torre das Neves 298
Estalagem Casa Melo Alvim 298

RESTAURANTS

Aveiro
Salpoente 102
Braga
Anjou Verde 115
Inácio 115
Coimbra
Adega Paço do Conde 136
Feb 136
Shmoo Café 136
Snack-Bar Daniel Sun 136
Faro
Camané 163
Chalavar 163
Mesa dos Mouros 163
O Aldeão 163
Pontinha 163
Lisboa
Adega das Cegonhas 191
Alcântara Café 192
Antiga Confeitaria de Belém 193
Bota Alta 191
Café Malaca 192
Café Taborda 192
Casa da Comida 193
Caseiro 192
Chapitô/Restô 191
Comida de Santo 192
Confeitaria Nacional 193
Divina Comida 192
Doce Real 191
Heróis- Café Lounge 191
Mesa de Frades 191
O Funil 192
Os Tibetanos 192
Panificação Reunida de S. Roque 193
Pão de Canela 192
Pap'Açorda 191
Pastelaria Suiça 193
Pateo 13 191
Picanha 192
Ponto Final 193
Porco Preto 192
Santo António de Alfama 191
Tavares 191
Viagem de Sabores 191
Via Graça 192
Óbidos
A Ilustre Casa de Ramiro 244
Alcaide 244
Petarum Domus Bar 244
Porto
A Mesa Com Bacchus 259
Cometa 259
D. Luis 259
Filha da Mãe Preta 259
O Chanquinhas 259
Viana do Castelo
Casa d'Armas 298
Cozinha das Malheiras 298
Os 3 Potes 298

MAPS AND PLANS

LIST OF MAPS

THEMATIC MAPS

Map of principal sights 8
Map of touring programmes..........10
Map of places to stay 11
Relief map 36
Principal Portuguese expeditions 48
Provinces and districts................70
Wines and regional specialities 80

AREA MAPS

Algarve 92
Serra da Arrábida 99
Vale do Douro........................ 146
Serra da Estrela 151
Eastern fortified towns
    (around Guarda) 170
Parque Nacional da Peneda-Gerês .. 250
Serra de São Mamede 277
Serra de Sintra 286
The Madeira Archipelago 314
Outskirts of Funchal 324
Madeira............................331
Porto Santo 337
The Azores Archipelago 339
São Miguel......................... 350
Santa Maria 353
Terceira............................ 355
Graciosa 361
Faial 363
Pico 368
São Jorge 371
Flores.............................. 377

TOWN/CITY PLANS

Aveiro 101
Braga................................114
Coimbra 138
Évora 156
Faro 164
Guimarães 172
Lagos...............................176
Lisbon 202, 204
Nazaré..............................242
Ponta Delgada 347
Portalegre 255
Oporto 262, 264
Santarém 275
Setúbal 281
Viana do Castelo 296
Viseu 308
Funchal............................ 322
São Miguel: Ponta Delgada 347
Angra do Heroísmo................ 358

PLANS OF MONUMENTS AND ARCHEOLOGICAL SITES

Alcobaça: Mosteiro de Santa Maria....89
Mosteiro da Batalha 108
Braga: Cathedral 116
Mata do Buçaco......................122
Conímbriga 143
Lisbon: Alfama 214
Lisbon: Belém...................... 221
Tomar: Convento de Cristo.......... 290

COMPANION PUBLICATIONS

MAP OF PORTUGAL NO 733

- a 1:400 000 scale map of Portugal showing the Portuguese road network, the sites and monuments described in this guide, in addition to a detailed index of place names

MAP OF NORTH WEST SPAIN NO 571 (GALICIA, ASTURIAS-LEÓN)

- a 1:400 000 scale map of northwest Spain and the northern half of Portugal

SPAIN/PORTUGAL ROAD ATLAS

- a useful 1:400 000 scale, spiral-bound atlas with a full index of place names and numerous town plans

SPAIN/PORTUGAL MAP NO 734

- a 1:1 000 000 scale map of the Iberian Peninsula

WWW.VIAMICHELIN.COM

- Michelin offers motorists a complete route planning service (fastest, shortest etc) on its comprehensive web site

Legend

Selected monuments and sights

◉ ⇒		Tour - Departure point
🏠 ⚲		Catholic church
🏠 ✝		Protestant church, other temple
✡ ▣ 🕌		Synagogue - Mosque
▬▬		Building
■		Statue, small building
✝		Calvary, wayside cross
◎		Fountain
●■►		Rampart - Tower - Gate
⋈		Château, castle, historic house
∴		Ruins
⌣		Dam
✿		Factory, power plant
✩		Fort
∩		Cave
▣		Troglodyte dwelling
⚇		Prehistoric site
▼		Viewing table
⋎		Viewpoint
▲		Other place of interest

Special symbols

GNR	Portuguese National Police (Guarda Nacional Republicana)
Ⓟ	Pousada (Hotel managed by the State)

Sports and recreation

🐎		Racecourse
⛸		Skating rink
≋ ≋		Outdoor, indoor swimming pool
🎥		Multiplex Cinema
⛵		Marina, sailing centre
⌂		Trail refuge hut
□■■■□		Cable cars, gondolas
□++++□		Funicular, rack railway
🚂		Tourist train
◆		Recreation area, park
🎭		Theme, amusement park
⚥		Wildlife park, zoo
❀		Gardens, park, arboretum
🐦		Bird sanctuary, aviary
🚶		Walking tour, footpath
🎃		Of special interest to children

Abbreviations

G	District government office (Governo civil)
H	Town Hall (Câmara municipal)
J	Law courts (Palácio de justiça)
M	Museum (Museu)
POL.	Police (Polícia)
T	Theatre (Teatro)
U	University (Universidade)

	Sight	Seaside resort	Winter sports resort	Spa
Highly recommended ★★★	★★★	☆☆☆	✳✳✳	♯♯♯
Recommended ★★	★★	☆☆	✳✳	♯♯
Interesting	★	☆	✳	♯

Additional symbols

🛈	Tourist information
═══ ═══	Motorway or other primary route
❶ ❶	Junction: complete, limited
⊨══ ═══	Pedestrian street
ɪ════ɪ	Unsuitable for traffic, street subject to restrictions
⊡⊡⊡⊡ ‑‑‑‑	Steps – Footpath
🚂 🚃	Train station – Auto-train station
🚌 S.N.C.F.	Coach (bus) station
⊶⊶	Tram
Ⓜ	Metro, underground
ᴘ ʀ	Park-and-Ride
♿	Access for the disabled
✉	Post office
☏	Telephone
▭	Covered market
⚔	Barracks
△	Drawbridge
⋃	Quarry
✗	Mine
Ⓑ Ⓕ	Car ferry (river or lake)
🛥	Ferry service: cars and passengers
🛶	Foot passengers only
③	Access route number common to Michelin maps and town plans
Bert (R.)...	Main shopping street
AZ B	Map co-ordinates

Hotels and restaurants

Hotels- price categories:

	Provinces	Large cities
🛏	<40 €	<60 €
🛏🛏	40 to 65 €	60 to 90 €
🛏🛏🛏	65 to 100 €	90 to 130 €
🛏🛏🛏🛏	>100 €	>130 €

Restaurants- price categories:

	Provinces	Large cities
🍽	<14 €	<16 €
🍽🍽	14 to 25 €	16 to 30 €
🍽🍽🍽	25 to 40 €	30 to 50 €
🍽🍽🍽🍽	>40 €	>50 €

20 rooms : €48/72	Number of rooms price for one person/ double room (In the high season)
⊐ €4	Price of breakfast (If not included in the price of the room)
€13/22	Restaurant : mini/maxi price for a complete meal (beverages not included)
rest. €15/22	Lodging where meals are served mini/maxi price
⊘	No credit cards accepted
ᴘ	Reserved parking for hotel patrons
⊿	Swimming Pool
▤	Air conditioning
♿	Rooms accessible to persons of reduced mobility

The prices correspond to the higher rates of the tourist season

MICHELIN

Michelin Maps and Guides
One Parkway South – Greenville, SC 29615 USA
☎ 800-423-0485
www.MichelinTravel.com
michelin.guides@us.michelin.com

Manufacture française des pneumatiques Michelin

Société en commandite par actions au capital de 304 000 000 EUR
Place des Carmes-Déchaux – 63000 Clermont-Ferrand (France)
R.C.S. Clermont-Fd B 855 200 507

Although the information in this guide was believed by the authors and publisher to be accurate and current at the time of publication, they cannot accept responsibility for any inconvenience, loss, or injury sustained by any person relying on information or advice contained in this guide. Things change over time and travellers should take steps to verify and confirm information, especially time-sensitive information related to prices, hours of operation, and availability.